VEGETABLE CROP DISEASES

Vegetable Crop Diseases

G. R. Dixon
Head of Horticulture Division,
School of Agriculture, Aberdeen, UK

AVI PUBLISHING COMPANY, INC.
Westport, Connecticut

AMERICAN EDITION
1981
THE AVI PUBLISHING COMPANY, INC.
Westport, Connecticut

© *Copyright 1981; G.R. Dixon*

ISBN 0 87055-390-9

Printed in Hong Kong

Contents

xii Contents

Preface

In writing this book a general objective has been to present the reader with a study of the more important and interesting pathogens which affect vegetable crops world-wide and to set these into context with recent developments in plant pathology as a whole. Thus the first four chapters cover the broad concepts of symptomatology; invasion, colonisation and symptom development; epidemiology; and pathogen control. These are followed by eight chapters dealing with pathogens of individual crop families. No attempt is made to review every known pathogen of each crop, nor indeed all vegetable crops: to do so would require a work of several volumes. Those crops and pathogens which have world significance are discussed in depth, covering host symptoms, characteristics of the pathogenic organism, conditions favouring infection, host—parasite physiology and control. The literature has been reviewed in detail for the last 10 years and I have aimed to provide sufficient reference sources so as to give a lead into the subject in greater depth by use of the bibliographies placed at the end of each chapter. Where a recent monograph is available few additional references are provided and the reader is directed to use this work for further details.

Stress is laid on the characteristics of the disease syndrome and pathogenic organism. In few cases is it possible to find these two brought together with physiological and epidemiological information, and yet all these are needed by the practising pathologist. In the sections dealing with control, emphasis is given to the use of resistance and husbandry techniques. Many problems have been associated with the use of resistance, especially where specific monogenic resistances have been utilised in back-crossing programmes in an attempt to control air-borne pathogens. It is hoped that sufficient examples of these problems are cited in this book so that plant breeders will consider carefully whether such methods can be safely employed against further vegetable pathogens. Nonetheless, the hazards of chemical control together with the high cost of developing, registering and manufacturing crop protective chemicals will result in fewer chemicals being available for vegetable crops in the future. Consequently, control by resistance will become even more important, as will the as yet little understood forms of husbandry control. Within each chapter the pathogens are arranged in the following order: bacterial, aerial fungal, soil-borne and root fungal, and viral. Pathogens which affect a range of crops are treated in a specific section, with reference and discussion given to hosts in other Angiosperm families. Thus, for example, *Thanetophorus cucumeris* (damping off) is considered in chapter 5 as a crucifer pathogen together with details of its effects on legume, cucurbit and solanaceous crops.

It is intended that this book will be of value and interest to all those concerned with vegetable production in its diverse forms. In particular, it is directed towards plant pathologists, horticulturalists, agriculturalists, plant breeders and those concerned with diagnosis and control of vegetable crop diseases. But it is hoped that a wider audience, such as the general botanist who needs a broad appreciation of plant pathogens affecting a range of crops, will find much of use in this book.

Many people have given invaluable help in the preparation of this work. In particular I acknowledge the steadfast support of my wife, Kathy, and my family; editorial work by Professor L. Broadbent, Bath University; the secretarial assistance of Mrs J. Stevenson, Mrs M. Sinclair and Miss S. Cruickshank and the librarianship of Mrs A. Park and Mrs M. Forbes. Permission to use various figures is acknowledged at appropriate points in the text.

March, 1980   G.R.D.

Abbreviations

a.i.	active ingredient
°C	degrees Celsius
cm	centimetre
DNA	deoxyribose nucleic acid
g	gram
h	hour
K	potassium
K_2O	potassium oxide
km	kilometre
min	minute
mm	millimetre
N	nitrogen
nm	nanometre
P	probability level (statistical context)
P	phosphorus (chemical context)
P_2O_5	phosphorus pentoxide
iP	inorganic phosphate
p.p.m.	parts per million
RH	relative humidity
RNA	ribose nucleic acid
s	second
S.D.	Significant Difference
S.E.	Standard Error
UK	United Kingdom
USA	United States of America
USSR	Union of Soviet Socialist Republics
μm	micrometre
μg	microgram

1
Pathogens and Host Symptoms

Pathology has been described by Wood (1967) as 'a science rooted in the practice of learning about diseases of economically important plants in order to reduce losses of crops caused by them'. Hence it is important for the pathologist to understand the relative significance of the crops whose pathogens he investigates. The following data highlight the value of vegetable crops, albeit they refer solely to the UK, but similar trends are found elsewhere, while in underdeveloped countries the very dietary importance of vegetables gives them even greater value. The 1975 farm-gate value of vegetables was £384 million, compared to £807 million for cereals and £100 million for fruit. In that year Britain spent £14 000 million on food of which £1500 million went on vegetables. This is equal to twice the expenditure on fruit, three times that on fish, equal to the outlay on bread and half that spent on meat, which is the largest cost in the food budget. In general terms the housewife spent 18 per cent of her money on fruit and vegetables. In this area of crop production the UK is very largely self-sufficient which, in terms of import savings, is an important factor. The UK is well suited climatically for vegetable production, and in general crops are produced on large scale, highly mechanised farms with a high level of efficiency. Land area needed for vegetable production is small, 185 000 ha in the UK, of which 109 000 ha are processing vegetables and of this 54 000 ha are vining peas; this compares to 3 713 000 ha needed for cereal production. In terms of cash return per unit land area, vegetables are 10 times more profitable than cereals. Concomitantly, a 10 per cent loss in a vegetable crop due to a plant pathogen is financially far more damaging to the producer than a similar loss in a cereal crop. In value of output terms the brassicas form over one-third of all field vegetables, roots 30 per cent, legumes 14 per cent and lettuce 11 per cent.

Three factors complicate the study of vegetable crop pathogens: the differing characteristics of the crops which are vulnerable to pathogen invasion; the wide variety of form which crop loss can take; and the wide range of botanical types embraced by the term 'vegetable' and equally wide range of pathogens which cause disease. The student of vegetable pathology must be aware of the influence of environment, production method and range of eventual uses for vegetables in order to elucidate the importance of the patterns of pathogen and disease development.

1.1 TERMINOLOGY

First, various terms used in pathology must be defined. These are drawn from *A Guide to the Use of Terms in Plant Pathology*, published by the Federation of British Plant Pathologists (1973).

Aetiology The science of the causes of disease; the study of the causal factor, its nature and its relations with the host. In the American literature aetiology is taken to cover the effects of mineral deficiencies and pollution damage in addition to the effects of pathogenic organisms. In Europe the term is taken to cover only the latter group, and in this work the European definition will be used.

Causal organism An organism causing disease.

Compatible Of a relation between host and pathogen in which disease can develop.

Disease Harmful deviation from the normal functioning of physiological processes.

Epidemic A widespread temporary increase in the incidence of an infectious disease.

Epidemiology The study of the factors affecting the outbreak of disease and spread of infectious pathogens.

Host An organism harbouring a parasite.

Immunity Freedom from disease due to lack of qualities permitting, or to possession or acquirement of qualities preventing, the operation of the pathogenic factor.

Parasite An organism or virus existing in intimate association with a living organism from which it derives an essential part of the material for its existence while conferring no benefit in return.

Pathogen An organism or virus able to cause disease in a particular host or range of hosts.

Resistance The ability of an organism to withstand or oppose the operation of, or to lessen or overcome the effects of, an injurious or pathogenic factor.

Susceptible Non-immune, that is subject to infection. Similarly, susceptibility is the inability of an organism to oppose the operation or overcome the effects of an injurious or pathogenic factor.

Symptom A visible or otherwise detectable abnormality arising from infection.

Tolerant Able to endure infection by a particular pathogen without showing severe disease.

Further terms will be introduced throughout the text and defined in context.

1.2 CAUSAL ORGANISMS – PATHOGENS

1.2.1 Fungi

The largest group of plant pathogens is the fungi, which abound in most environments. Since they lack chlorophyll the fungi must be either parasites –

gaining energy from other living organisms – or saprophytes – gaining energy
from dead organic material. Several classifications of the fungi have been erected;
that used by Hawker (1966) is perhaps the simplest:

(1) *Lower Fungi (Phycomycetes)* These are either unicellular fungi or lack
septa in the actively growing hyphae (figure 1.1). Alternatively, if septate they
have life cycles resembling those of particular aseptate species.

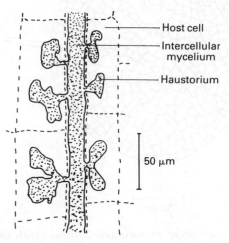

Figure 1.1   Coenocytic mycelium of a Phycomycete fungus – *Peronospora
parasitica* (downy mildew) – from a cabbage leaf.

(2) *Higher Fungi* These include all but a few of the regularly septate
fungi. The yeasts, which are mainly unicellular, are included because their life
cycle is similar to that of certain septate hyphal species. The higher fungi are
further subdivided into the following groups:
   (a) *Ascomycetes*   In this group the characteristic spores (ascospores) are
   formed inside asci (figure 1.2).
   (b) *Basidiomycetes*   The characteristic spores are basidiospores borne
   externally on basidia (figure 1.3).
   (c) *Fungi Imperfecti*   So called because they lack an identified sexual or
   perfect stage and produce only asexually formed spores.
   (d) *Mycelia Sterilia*   These fungi produce no spores at all.

Most Fungi Imperfecti can be identified by analogy with members of the
Ascomycetes, while the remainder are probably Basidiomycetes. For this reason,
Hawker (1966) groups them as a form class of the Deuteromycetes. More
recently, Webster (1970) used a classification based on the scheme proposed by
Ainsworth (1966); in this the slime moulds, which have a vegetative phase
consisting of a plasmodium (a multinucleate mass of protoplasm lacking a cell
wall) or a pseudoplasmodium (an aggregate of separate amoeboid cells) are

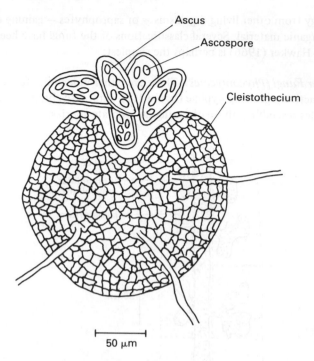

Figure 1.2   Cleistothecium of an Ascomycete fungus with asci and ascospores
– *Erysiphe* spp. (powdery mildew).

termed Myxomycota. This division contains only one pathogen of significance
to the present work – *Plasmodiophora brassicae*, the causal agent of clubroot of
Cruciferae. All other fungi are placed in the division Eumycota, the members of
which have a vegetative phase consisting of either a single cell, as in the yeasts, or,
more commonly, as branched filaments (hyphae) forming a composite mycelium.
Different forms of spore are produced either sexually, involving nuclear fusion
and meiosis at some point in the life cycle, or asexually, where only mitosis
is involved. The latter process does not mean that fungi such as the Fungi
Imperfecti, which lack a sexual stage, are composed solely of clones. Nuclear
fusion and parasexual processes lead to enormous variation in such organisms
(Fincham and Day, 1965).

Sexually formed spores in the Phycomycetes result from one of the following
processes:

(1) The fusion of motile gametes.
(2) The fusion of sexually differentiated hyphal branches (gametangia). The
male branch is known as an antheridium and the female as an oogonium. The
oogonium contains one to several eggs (oospheres) which become thick walled
oospores after fertilization.

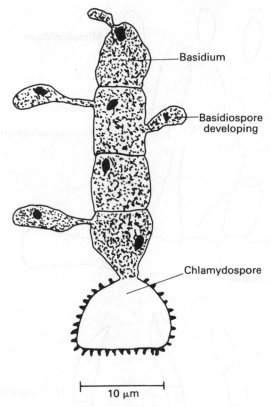

Figure 1.3   Basidiospores produced from a basidium by a Basidiomycete
fungus – *Ustilago maydis* (maize smut).

(3) Fusion between morphologically indistinguishable gametangia to form
a thick walled zygospore.

In the Ascomycetes and Basidiomycetes there may be no morphologically
differentiated sexual organs or sexual fusion may start with the transfer of a
non-motile spermatium or microconidium to a receptive hypha (figure 1.4).
Meiosis and mitosis in the Ascomycetes lead to the formation of haploid nuclei
contained in an ascus or sac (figure 1.5). From this the ascospores may be
violently ejected. The basidium is the corresponding result of nuclear fusion in
the Basidiomycetes (figure 1.6), from which four outgrowths develop and into
each of these a nucleus is passed to form a single spore (basidiospore). These are
then released violently from the basidium.

1.2.2 Bacteria

There tend to be fewer bacterial plant diseases in comparison with the fungi and

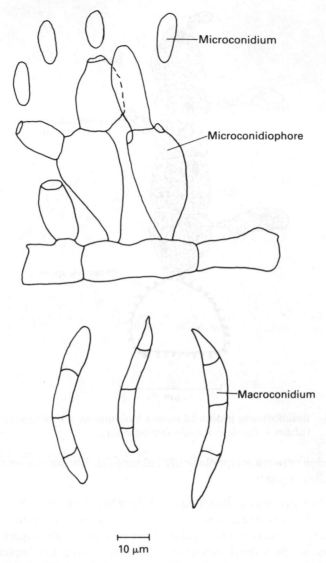

Figure 1.4   Microconidia and macroconidia of *Fusarium oxysporum*.

viruses and several reasons have been advanced for this — *see* Tarr (1972). Bacteria are too small for much of their structure to be resolved by conventional light microscopy. They are single-celled organisms either with a thick outer capsule or a thinner outer wall and possessing flagella. Bacterial identification is based on morphological and biochemical criteria such as the presence or absence, number and position of flagella, production of pigments in culture, reaction to histochemical stains, serological tests and, more recently, bacteriophage typing. The standard reviews of plant pathogenic bacteria were made by Dawson (1957)

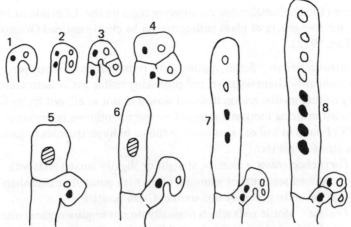

Figure 1.5   Diagrammatic representation of ascus formation in a Discomycete Ascomycete. Plus nuclei are shown as closed circles; minus nuclei are shown as open circles; diploid nuclei are cross-hatched.

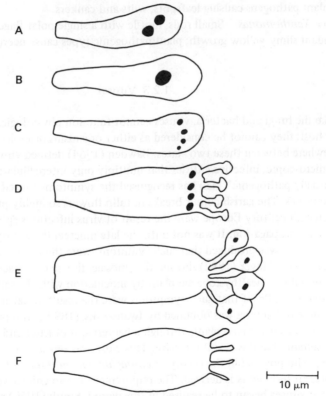

Figure 1.6   Basidium and basidiospore development in a Basidiomycete – *Agaricus* spp. Meiosis occurs between stages B and C.

and Stapp (1961). Considerable controversy rages on the definition of bacterial species, but five genera of plant pathogens can be clearly defined (Wescott, 1967; Tarr, 1972).

(1) *Agrobacterium* Small, motile, short rods with one to four peritrichous flagella, ordinarily Gram-negative, not producing visible gas or detectable acid in ordinary culture media; gelatin liquified slowly or not at all; not fixing free nitrogen but utilizing inorganic forms of nitrogen; optimum temperature 25–30°C. Found in soil or plant roots in soil or in hypertrophies or galls on roots or stems of plants

(2) *Corynebacterium* Slender, straight or slightly curved rods with irregularly stained segments or granules, often with pointed or club-shaped swellings at the ends; generally non-motile; Gram positive.

(3) *Erwinia* Motile rods which normally do not require organic nitrogen for growth; producing acids and without visible gas from a variety of sugars and invading plant tissues to produce dry necroses, galls, wilts and soft rots.

(4) *Pseudomonas* Motile straight rods with polar flagella; Gram negative; many species produce a greenish water-soluble pigment. Found in soil and water, the plant pathogens causing leafspots, wilts and cankers.

(5) *Xanthomonas* Small rods, motile with a single polar flagellum; form abundant slimy yellow growth; plant pathogenic types cause necroses.

1.2.3 Viruses

Unlike the fungi and bacteria, viruses cannot function physiologically outside their host; they cannot be considered as either organisms or molecules but exist somewhere between these two states. Bawden (1964) defined viruses as 'submicroscopic, infective entities that multiply only intercellularly and are potentially pathogenic'. Man has recognised the symptoms caused by viruses for centuries. The garish colour breaks in tulip flowers so highly prized in seventeenth century Europe were the result of virus infections spread during vegetative propagation. It was not until the late nineteenth century, however, that evidence was produced that such symptoms were the result of the presence of a pathogen. Mayer (1882) showed that mosaic disease of tobacco could be transmitted to a healthy tobacco plant by inoculation with the sap of an infected plant. Proof that such symptoms were the result of particles smaller than those of bacteria was obtained by Iwanowsky (1892), who passed sap from mosaic-infected tobacco plants through a bacteria-proof filter and found that the resultant eluant was still infective. This work was repeated by Beijerinck (1898), who postulated the theory of *contagium vivum fluidum* from which the present term *virus* is derived. The requirement for an animal vector to transmit viruses began to be realised in this period. Smith (1960) reported that the first experimental proof was by Hashimoto in 1894, working in Japan, with dwarf disease of rice and the leaf hopper *Nephotettix apicalis* var. *cincticeps*. In the USA it was shown that a single leaf hopper (*Circulifer tenellus*) taken from a sugar beet plant infected with curly top and placed on a healthy beet plant for 5 min would transmit the disease (Smith and Boncquet, 1915). Isolation and identification of viruses began with the work of Stanley using Tobacco Mosaic Virus in 1935 and that of Bawden and Pirie in England.

A wide range of vectors is now associated with the spread of viruses, particularly insects and nematodes; these may be biting insects – beetles, grasshoppers and earwigs – or sucking insects – aphids, whiteflies, thrips and mealy bugs – together with free-living and cyst-forming nematodes. Undoubtedly aphids are the most widespread vectors of viruses. Some insects will transmit only a single virus while others, especially aphids, can spread several.

Transmission can be classified as follows:

(1) *Non-persistent*   Here the virus is only viable in the vector for an hour or so; it is quickly picked up (acquired) by the vector on its mouth parts, probably in less than 1 min. The non-persistence may be due to some inhibitory substance present in the insect mouth parts which gradually reduces the virus stability.

(2) *Persistent*   The vector remains infective for a long period, perhaps even for life. It is often necessary for the insect to feed for an hour or more before the virus is acquired.

(3) *Semi-persistent*.

Once inside the vector viruses can be grouped in two forms:

(1) *Circulative*   These viruses pass from the gut of the insect to its circulatory system and thence to the salivary glands. When this has been accomplished the insect becomes infective. Thus there is a delay or latent period between acquisition of the virus and the ability of the vector to transmit it.

(2) *Propagative*   Viruses which multiply within the vector, for instance Potato Leaf Roll Virus, are known as propagative. Much of the early work on these viruses was done with leaf hopper-transmitted pathogens which are now known to be mycoplasmas and are dealt with in section 1.2.4.

Other vectors include the following:

(a) *Eriophyid mites*   These are responsible for the transmission of Reversion Disease in currants (*Ribes* spp.) and Ryegrass Mosaic Virus.

(b) *Nematodes*   Nematodes of the genera *Xiphinema*, *Longidorus* and *Trichodorus* transmit several viruses of economic importance, for instance in strawberries, raspberries and *Narcissus* (Harrison, 1964; Cadman, 1963).

(c) *Fungi*   Big Vein Virus of lettuce is transmitted by the soil-borne fungus *Olpidium brassicae*.

Means of transmission other than by animals include:

(1) *Seed transmission*   Here the virus is capable of passing across the

placenta and into the developing embryo (for instance, Lettuce Mosaic Virus).

(2) *Propagative transmission*   This occurs during grafting, budding and other vegetative means of reproduction. This is especially important in perennial fruit and in crops grown from tubers, such as potatoes.

(3) *Mechanical transmission*   Contact between infected and healthy plants can lead to the spread of some viruses, as can the subterranean union of roots of healthy and infected plants. Man may transmit a few viruses on his clothing or tools.

Until recently virus identification has rested largely on the description of the host—parasite relationship rather than on the description of the characteristics of the virus particle itself. Thus ranges of indicator plants giving characteristic reactions to known viruses have been used to classify the pathogens. It is now realised that viruses are composed of two parts, an outer protein case or capsid containing within it a single or double strand of nucleic acid. Most plant viruses contain ribonucleic acid (RNA), although cauliflower mosaic has been shown to contain deoxyribonucleic acid (DNA) (Shepherd *et al.*, 1968). Under electron microscopy virus particles appear as flexuous or rigid rods or as polyhedral structures. The means of transmission of a virus is another tool used in its identification, as are serological tests whereby sap from infected plants is brought into contact with sera obtained from the blood of mammals (usually rabbits) which have been injected with authenticated viruses. The resultant agglutination reaction will indicate whether the diseased plant is infected with the same virus as that used to inject the mammal. Thermal inactivation point and dilution end-point are other properties used to describe a virus.

It has been suggested that viruses should be coded by a crytogram (Gibbs *et al.*, 1966) consisting of pairs of symbols for (a) type of nucleic acid and degree of strandedness; (b) molecular weight of nucleic acid (in millions of daltons) and percentage of nucleic acid in the infective particles; (c) outline of the particle and outline of the nuclear capsid; (d) kinds of host infected and kinds of vector. Two additional symbols are used: * = property of the virus unknown; ( ) = enclosed information is doubtful or unconfirmed.

1.2.4 Mycoplasmas

Since 1967 it has been realised that certain diseases previously attributed to viruses may in fact be caused by *Mycoplasma* species. This is particularly so for 'yellows' pathogens spread by leaf hoppers. Mycoplasmas are the smallest known forms of independent life, with a size range of 150—200 nm. They are just visible to the light microscope and occur as spheres, irregular shapes, chains and filaments. Both DNA and RNA are present, but mycoplasmas have a limited enzyme content; consequently, preformed substances such as protein are necessary for growth. Growth conditions tend to be exacting, therefore they live close to the host cells. Mycoplasmas are resistant to penicillin but have close similarity to L-form bacteria which are produced by the lysis of the bacterial coat. The two can be differentiated by growing on solid media and studying colony morphology. Mycoplasmas produce colonies up to 0.25 mm in diameter with a characteristic humped dome form, from the base of which a pointed plug protrudes into the nutrient medium; no such plug is produced by colonies of L-form bacteria. Mycoplasma cells are Gram negative, stain with Geisher's stain, and are resistant to thallium acetate but sensitive to tetracycline; the cell is bounded by a triple-layered membrane.

1.3 HOST SYMPTOMS

A wide range of symptoms develop in and on the host plant as a result of infection by fungi, bacteria, viruses and mycoplasmas. The following descriptions are of symptoms pertinent to vegetable crops. They are based on those provided by the Federation of British Plant Pathologists (1973) glossary and have been amplifed where appropriate and examples drawn from vegetable crops such that they provide information additional to that given in chapters 5—12.

Blotch   An expanding area of macerated tissue usually on a fruit but sometimes on a leaf; for instance in purple blotch of onions caused by *Alternaria porri* the initial symptom is a small white speck on the leaf surface which develops into a brown water-soaked tissue with a reddish-purple margin; the centre of the blotch will become covered with black conidiophores in moist weather (*see* section 10.2.4).

Canker   Sunken necrotic lesions on roots, stems or branches, arising from the destruction of the epidermal and cortical tissues, for example canker of pumpkin and radish caused by *Sclerotinia sclerotiorum*, which under dry conditions produces a brown canker which girdles the host stem, causing it to collapse (*see* section 6.4.5).

Chlorosis   A general term to describe the yellowing of foliage consequent upon the loss of chlorophyll or chloroplasts, for example Pea Leaf Roll Virus induces a general chlorosis of pea leaflets.

Damping-off   Collapse and shrivelling of plants, usually at the seedling stage, resulting from infection and lesion formation at the base of the plant. Usually the lesion causes the base of the host to have a pinched appearance and the area around it is brown and water soaked. In the USA *Alternaria solani* is a principal cause of damping-off in tomatoes at the seed bed stage (*see* section 12.2.3(a)).

Dieback   Death of a shoot, starting at the apex and progressing towards the main stem, for example dieback of cucurbits caused by *Venturia cucumerina*; small pink to pale brown lesions develop on the shoots and unite into long streaks leading to the collapse of the shoot.

Dwarfing   Reduction in size with the retention of proportionality between the various plant organs, for example growth reduction in French bean (*Phaseolus vulgaris*) caused by Bean Yellow Mosaic Virus (*see* section 6.5.7).

Enation   An outgrowth from the surface of an organ such as a stem or leaf, as with the effects of Pea Enation Virus in broad bean causing the development of swellings generally on the leaf undersurface (*see* section 6.2.2)

Fasciation   Proliferation of a shoot with incomplete separation of the vascular elements, for example the effects of clover phyllody mycoplasma on carrot seedlings, which induces the formation of large numbers of leaves and can cause premature flower development.

Gall   A localised proliferation of plant tissue often having characteristic shape but unlike the organ of a normal plant, for example *Agrobacterium tumefasciens* (crown gall), which attacks a wide range of vegetables causing the proliferation of vascular, cortical and epidermal tissue which erupts on the plant surface as a cankerous gall (*see* section 9.1.1).

Gummosis   Production of gum from a tissue or organ either internally or externally. Internal gummosis occurs in Pierce's virus disease of grapevine in which gums are produced in the xylem leading to its occlusion. External gummosis is illustrated by the sticky excretions associated with the infection of cucurbits by *Cladosporium cucumerinum* and which are described in detail in section 11.2.3.

Hyperplasia   A condition in which tissue is enlarged as a result of excessive production of cells, as described above for *A. tumefasciens* (crown gall) and in section 9.1.1.

Hypertrophy   Excessive growth due to an enlargement of individual cells as in the galling of crucifers infected with *Plasmodiophora brassicae* (clubroot) and described in detail in section 5.1.8. Similarly, tomatoes infected with Stolbur or tomato big bud mycoplasma, where the caylx enlarges considerably even before flowering, leading to the big (flower) bud symptom.

Hypoplasia   Underdevelopment of a tissue or organ resulting from reduced cell division.

Leaf curl   Distortion resulting from the unequal growth or expansion of leaf tissue. *Pyrenopeziza brassicae* (light leaf spot) (figure 1.7) will induce this symptom in cauliflowers, when the lesions are confined to one side of the leaf lamina.

Leaf roll   Curving of the lamina generally towards and parallel with the mid rib, for example the upward curling of potato leaves in plants infected with Leaf Roll Virus (*see* section 12.3.16).

Leaf scorch   Browning and desiccation of the leaf lamina, usually beginning at the outer edges of the leaf. Under severe infection this symptom is common in marrows infected with *Erysiphe cichoracearum* (powdery mildew) (*see* section 7.1.2).

Mosaic   A leaf symptom in which numerous small areas of discoloration stand out against a background of a different tint, tending to have a clearly defined boundary delineated by the veins. A pattern of green angular areas against a

Figure 1.7   Symptoms caused by *Pyrenopeziza brassicae* (light leaf spot) on
a Brussels sprout leaf. (Copyright © North of Scotland College of
Agriculture, Aberdeen. Reproduced by permission.)

predominantly yellow background may result; alternatively, the areas bounded
by the veins may be chlorotic, giving a yellow-on-green mosaic. If discrete areas
of colour later coalesce a mottle symptom may result. These symptoms occur
typically in virus-infected leaves; a spectacular example is given by Reid and
Matthews (1966) of Turnip Yellow Mosaic Virus infecting Chinese cabbage.
Mosaic patterns may occur mainly between the larger veins; interveinal mosaic is
typified by the effects of some strains of Cauliflower Mosaic Virus on lettuce.

Mottle   A leaf symptom in which small but numerous areas of discoloration, commonly chlorotic, irregularly shaped and without sharply defined boundaries, stand out against a background of a different tint, the pattern being unrelated to the vein network. As with mosaic symptoms, mottles are usually associated with virus infection, for example Potato Mottle Virus, which is now regarded as a synonym of Potato Virus X.

Necrosis   Death of part of a plant or tissue; usually the affected organ turns black or dark brown. Necrosis is usually rapid with a clear borderline between dead and live tissue, especially where dark melanin-like substances occur in the dead cells. Where such discoloration is absent death may be accompanied by rapid desiccation. Necrotic spotting and speckling are common in brassicas, particularly those grown for storage, for example the necrotic stipple of Dutch White (Langedijk) cabbage, which may be virus- or physiologically induced.

Ooze   Extrusion of viscous fluid, usually associated with bacterial diseases; as an example, *Erwinia stewartii* produces copious yellow ooze from the kernels of infected sweet-corn, particularly if the cob is cut lengthways and stood in water (*see* section 10.1.2)

Phyllody   Replacement of the floral parts by leaf-like structures, usually as a result of mycoplasma infection. All floral organs may be changed in this manner; the effect on tomatoes infected with Stolbur is referred to above. Changes of the ovules to leaf-like organs at the edge of the open carpel is described for two tropical crops – Sunn hemp (*Crotalaria juncea*) (Bose and Misra, 1938) and phyllody of *Sesamum indicum* (Pal and Nath, 1935), both in India.

Pustule   A blister-like spot on a leaf or other organ from which erupts a fungal fruiting structure; in this context pustules are usually associated with the rust fungi, for example rust of broad bean caused by *Uromyces fabae* (*see* section 6.4.1).

Ringspot   A spot, often on leaves surrounded by concentric rings which are chlorotic, necrotic or abnormally dark green. Chupp and Sherf (1960) describe a virus ringspot which affects a wide range of vegetable crops in North America and probably elsewhere. Hosts cited include bean, beet, cowpea, cucumber, pea, rhubarb, squash and tomato.

Rosetting   Severe reduction of internode growth in a vertical axis without comparable reduction in the size of leaves, for example Ground Nut Rosette Virus, which reduces the host plant to little more than a close tuft of small leaves forming a cushion a few centimetres in diameter; alternatively the branches may be of some length but bear terminal tufts of small leaves.

Rot   Disintegration of tissue as a result of enzymic action by invading pathogens. The condition is qualified by a series of adjectives:

(1) *Collar rot*   Rotting of the stem or main axis at or about the level of the soil surface, for example *Sclerotinia sclerotiorum* in lettuce, where the plants rot at soil level leaving a dark lesion filled with sclerotia and white mycelium (*see* section 6.4.5).

(2) *Dry rot*   Rotting which proceeds at a rate that allows drying of the lesion to keep pace with lysis, for example storage rot of carrots caused by *Fusarium roseum*, where the root takes on a dry shrivelled appearance sometimes covered with sparse white mycelium.

(3) *Foot rot*   (a) Rotting of the axis from immediately above the seed in seedlings with hypogeal cotyledons, similar to damping-off caused by *Thanetophorus cucumeris* (*see* section 5.1.6). (b) More generally, rotting involving the lower part of the stem—root axis but not the distal part of the root, for example *Fusarium solani* f. *pisi* (foot rot of pea). On infected plants, chocolate-brown or purplish streaks develop at the stem base (*see* section 6.1.5).

(4) *Neck rot*   Rotting of the neck of a bulb or swollen hypocotyl region in root crops such as swedes, turnips, beet and mangolds. As an example, onion neck rot caused by *Botrytis allii, B. byssoidea* and *B. squamosa*; lesions first appear as sunken dry areas about the neck, the tissue is soft and brownish in colour with grey mycelium and small black sclerotia (resting bodies) (*see* section 10.2.5)

(5) *Root rot*   Rotting of any part of the root system, for example *Phytophthora megasperma*, which attacks a wide host range (crucifers, carrot, potato, spinach and beet) in many parts of the world. The host root system is completely destroyed and as a result the aerial organs collapse.

(6) *Soft rot*   Rotting of tissue by the action of the pathogen on the middle lamella of the cell walls; cells are separated but retain their identity for a period. This condition is particularly associated with bacterial diseases, for example *Erwinia* spp., which have a large host range all developing similar symptoms; the initial lesion is a small water-soaked area which grows rapidly wider and deeper while the tissue becomes soft and mushy. The fruit, root or tuber collapses within a few days.

(7) *Wet rot*   The tissue rapidly and completely disintegrates with the release of free water from the lysed cells. This condition probably differs from soft rot only in the rate at which cells lose their capacity to retain water. As an example, wet rot of cucurbits and peppers caused by *Choanephora cucurbitarum* which attacks squash, pumpkin, pepper, peas, cowpeas and okra. The invaded part of the blossom, fruit or pod resembles a pin-cushion covered with minute black-headed pins (fruiting bodies). The host tissue beneath this layer is water-soaked with a soft moist rot.

(8) *White rot*   Rotting which results from a white mycelial growth on the host, for example white rot of onion caused by *Sclerotium cepivorum*, which is characterised by a basal rot in which the tissue is covered with a white weft of hyphae (*see* section 10.2.6).

Scab   A discrete superficial lesion involving localised severe roughening or pitting, for example *Streptomyces scabies* which has a wide host range: beet, cabbage, carrot, egg plant, salsify, spinach, mangel, onion, parsnip, potato, radish, swede and turnip. Lesions begin as small brown specks at the lenticel, coalesce with other specks and eventually form a continuous scabby area.

Scald   Lesions which appear mainly bleached and possibly translucent but not chlorotic. These symptoms may be produced by *Phytophthora porri*, white tip of leek which under certain conditions causes large scalded areas on the length of the leaf lamina (*see* section 10.2.3).

Shot hole   Necrotic lesions of limited size which fall out of the lamina leaving roughly circular holes, for example *Marssonina panattoniana* on lettuce causes lesions which as they enlarge become yellow or brown, generally circular but angular when near to a vein or elongated if on the mid rib. The affected tissue shrinks, forming a depression on the vein, or breaks away leaving a hole in the leaf.

Spot   A discrete lesion, usually more or less circular, differing in tint from the surrounding tissues, for example spinach, which is attacked by at least seven leaf spotting fungi in various parts of the world: *Alternaria spinaciae, Ascochyta spinaciae, Cercospora bertrandii, Cladosporium macrocarpum, Heterosporium variable, Phyllosticta chenopodii,* and *Ramularia spinaciae.*

Streak   Elongated lesions or areas of tissue discoloration on leaves or stems, for example Tobacco Streak Virus, which has a host range of 87 species (Fulton, 1948). Symptoms are most evident in tobacco, where the lesions tend to spread along the veins with parallel necrotic lines appearing in the surrounding tissue and sometimes causing the collapse of the mid rib and petiole.

Tiger stripe   A leaf symptom in which clear yellow areas separate as marginal and interveinal areas of dark necrotic tissue from persistently green areas along and adjacent to the main veins, giving a striped yellow and black effect. This term was originally applied to symptoms induced by *Verticillium albo-atrum* in hop but now is used for other diseases.

Tylosis   Tyloses are swellings of xylem parenchyma or medullary ray cells which protrude into the xylem vessels. Some workers have thought of them as resistance mechanisms for vascular wilt diseases, but it is more likely that they result from weakening of the xylem vessel walls due to enzymic action by the pathogen and hence indicate host susceptibility. Diseases caused by *Verticillium* spp., *Fusarium* spp. and certain viruses are characterised by the presence of tyloses in the host (*see* section 12.2.6).

Vein banding   A change of colour in a narrow zone of leaf tissue alongside the main veins, for example Gooseberry Vein Banding Virus, where the bands are cleared and semi-transparent, so that they appear brighter by transmitted rather than reflected light. The banding starts from the veins without any interposed green tissues. Frequently the banding is restricted to a part of the leaf which is then distorted by the reduced growth of the affected side.

Vein clearing   An increased translucency of the veinal system in a leaf, making the pattern more pronounced, light against dark, by transmitted light. This symptom is easily confused with vein banding and some authorities use the terms synonymously. It is a condition typical of virus diseases where the pathogen reaches the veins of systemically infected leaves and symptoms begin in or close to invaded veins with vein clearing, chlorosis and yellowing. If the young veins are highly sensitive, vein necrosis will result; this is typical of French beans (*Phaseolus vulgaris*) infected with Black Root Virus where vascular necrosis in root, stem, leaves and pods is a general symptom.

Wilt   Symptoms are initially similar to physiological water stress, with loss of turgor and collapse of the leaves. Progressively the condition becomes irreversible by application of water. Indeed, the soil around infected plants is often waterlogged. *Verticillium* spp., *Fusarium* spp. and some bacteria and viruses cause wilt diseases in a wide range of crops, particularly of the families Cruciferae, Leguminosae, Solanaceae and Cucurbitaceae (*see* sections 10.1.2, 11.1.2, 12.1.1 and 12.2.6).

Yellows   Diseases where the most conspicuous symptom is deep yellowing of the foliage associated mainly with virus- and mycoplasma-caused diseases. Yellows disease of sugar beet is widespread throughout the temperate zones and is caused by Beet Yellows Virus and Beet Mild Yellowing Virus (*see* sections 9.3.12 and 9.3.3). These symptoms are also found in cabbage plants infected with *Fusarium oxysporum* f. *conglutinans*, as described in section 5.1.7)

REFERENCES

Ainsworth, G. C. (1966). *A General Purpose Classification of Fungi.* Bibliography of Systematic Mycology, Vols 1–4. Commonwealth Mycological Institute, Kew.

Bawden, F. C. (1964). *Plant Viruses and Virus Diseases.* Ronald Press, New York.

Beijerinck, M. W. (1898). *Verhandel K. Akad. Wet.* 6, 1–22.

Bose, R. D. and Misra, S. D. (1938). *Indian J. agric. Sci.* 8, 417–23.

Cadman, C. H. (1963). *A. Rev. Phytopath.* 1, 143–72.

Chupp, C. and Sherf, A. F. (1966). *Vegetable Diseases and Their Control.* Ronald Press, New York.

Dawson, W. J. (1957). *Plant Diseases Due to Bacteria.* Cambridge University Press, London.

Federation of British Plant Pathologists (1973). *A Guide to the Use of Terms in Plant Pathology.* Phytopathological Papers no. 17. Commonwealth Mycological Institute, Kew.

Fincham, J. R. S. and Day, P. R. (1965). *Fungal Genetics.* Blackwell Scientific Publications, Oxford.

Fulton, R. W. (1948). *Phytopathology* 38, 421–8.

Gibbs, A. J., Harrison, B. D., Watson, D. H. and Wildy, P. (1966). *Nature, Lond.* 209, 450–4.

Harrison, B. D. (1964). In *Plant Virology* (M. K. Corbett and H. D. Sisler, eds). Florida University Press, Gainesville, Fla, pp. 118–47.

Hawker, L. E. (1966). *Fungi.* Hutchinson, London.

Iwanowsky, D. (1892). *St Petersb. Acad. imp. Sci. Bull.* 35, 67–70.

Mayer, A. E. (1882). *Voorloopie Meded. Landbou. Tijdschr.* 359—64.
Pal, B. P. and Nath, P. (1935). *Indian J. agric. Sci.* 5, 517—22.
Reid, M. S. and Matthews, R. E. F. (1966). *Virology* 28, 563—70.
Shepherd, R. J., Wakeman, R. J. and Ramanko, R. R. (1968). *Virology* 36, 150—2.
Smith, K. M. (1960). *Plant Viruses.* Methuen, London.
Smith, R. E. and Boncquet, P. A. (1915). *Phytopathology* 5, 103—7.
Stapp, C. (1961). *Bacterial Plant Pathogens.* Oxford University Press, London.
Tarr, S. A. J. (1972). *The Principles of Plant Pathology.* Macmillan, London.
Webster, J. (1970). *Introduction to Fungi.* Cambridge University Press, London.
Westcott, C. (1967). *Plant Disease Handbook.* Van Nostrand, Princeton, N. J.
Wood, R. K. S. (1967) *Physiological Plant Pathology.* Blackwell Scientific Publications, Oxford.

FURTHER READING

Bos, L. (1970). *Symptoms of Virus Diseases in Plants.* PUDOC, Wageningen.
Ogilvie, L. (1969). *Diseases of Vegetables.* Ministry of Agriculture, Fisheries and Food Bulletin No. 123. HMSO, London.
Smith , K. M. (1977). *Plant Viruses*, 6th edn. Science Paperbacks, London.
Stapp, C. (1961). *Bacterial Plant Pathogens.* Oxford University Press, London.
Walker, J. C. (1952). *Diseases of Vegetable Crops.* McGraw-Hill, New York.
Wheeler, B. E. J. (1976). *Diseases in Crops.* Institute of Biology Studies in Biology no. 64. Edward Arnold, London.

2

Invasion, Colonisation and Symptom Development

This chapter describes how pathogens infect and colonise a host and the metabolic changes which take place in the diseased plant leading to the visual expression of symptoms. Infection can be said to start as soon as the host and pathogen are in contact and interact with each other. This may occur at any place on the host: roots, stems, leaves or flowers. Most studies of infection have been made using host leaves for the reason that this is the simplest system to study, lending itself easily to *in vitro* work with detached leaves under controlled conditions; various levels of inoculum can be applied easily and the effects on photosynthetic activity can be measured, thereby giving an indication of the likely yield reduction caused by the pathogen. Colonisation commences when the pathogen has established itself in close association with host cells and has begun to obtain energy for growth from the host. The third stage of host symptom expression may quickly follow colonisation, as in bacterial infections, or take days or weeks, as in infection by *Plasmodiophora brassicae* (clubroot) of crucifers. It is usually at this stage that the pathogen forms reproductive structures whereby passage to a new and uninfected host may be achieved as the energy resources of the present host are depleted.

2.1 INVASION

Contact between host and pathogen is largely a random process, although physical and chemical stimuli may aid attraction, especially with soil-borne pathogens, for example the reaction of *Fusarium oxysporum* f. sp. *pisi* (wilt) spores to exudates from pea roots. Penetration, and thereby infection, starts as soon as the two organisms are sufficiently intimate for their metabolic activities to affect each other. The penetration process may occur (a) mechanically, (b) enzymically, or (c) passively.

2.1.1 Mechanical penetration

One of the clearest studies of mechanical penetration has been made by Williams *et al.* (1973) working with primary zoospores of *Plasmodiophora brassicae* (clubroot) and seedlings of Jersey Queen cabbage. Roots of cabbage seedlings were dipped in a suspension of primary zoospores for 30–60 min and then returned to a pathogen-free nutrient solution. Zoospores collided with the root hairs several times before eventually becoming attached. The point at which the zoospore became attached was not random but was on the side of the spore opposite to the flagellar insertion. There followed a quiescent period during which a thick cell wall formed around the zoospore (encystment). Inside the spore, penetration apparatus formed. Fifteen minutes prior to penetration, a vacuole within the cyst enlarged to fill half the cyst volume with lipid bodies closely adpressed to the vacuole. At the start of penetration a sock-like structure (rohr) evaginated from the spore to become pressed against the outer wall of the host. This formed a bulb-shaped adhesorium. Within the rohr, a needle-shaped structure (stachel) passed down the rohr, through the adhesorium and was forced through the root hair wall. Immediately a stream of cytoplasm was transferred from the pathogen spore to the host cell (*see* figure 2.1).

2.1.2 Enzymic penetration

Enzymic penetration may be illustrated by the relationship between *Bremia lactucae*, the cause of downy mildew, and lettuce leaves (*see* figure 2.2). Here, even prior to penetration, nutrients are absorbed by the pathogen from the leaf surface. The sequence of events may be summarised as follows:

Time after release of spores from inhibition (h)	Stage of development of the fungus
0	Spores placed on surface of cotyledon in a droplet of water
1–2	Spore germination
2–3	Elaboration of the germ tube and appressorium
3–4	Penetration and enlargement of the primary vesicle in an epidermal cell
4–13	Enlargement of the secondary vesicle; commencement of nuclear division
13 onwards	Continued enlargement of secondary vesicle; the first appearance of divided nuclei; invasion of adjacent cells and tissues by haustoria and intercellular hyphae

(after Sargent *et al.*, 1973). This represents the time course of infection of the lower epidermal cells of detached cotyledons of the lettuce cultivar Trocadero Improved by *B. lactucae* race W5 at 15 °C.

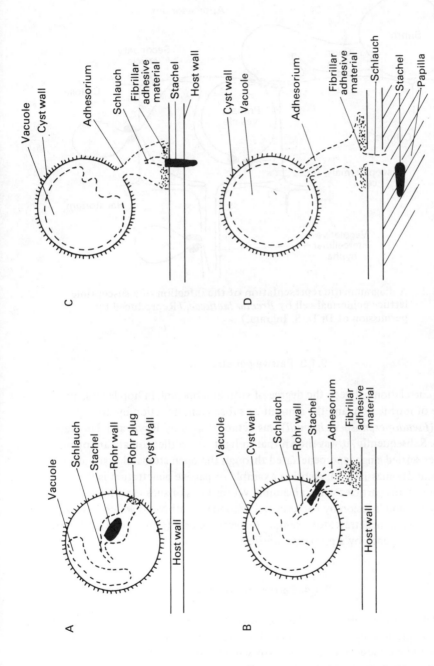

Figure 2.1   Diagrammatic summary of penetration by *Plasmodiophora brassicae* (clubroot). A, Cyst vacuole not enlarged; B, vacuole enlarges and small adhesorium appears; C, stachel punctures host wall; D, penetration has occurred and host protoplasm has deposited a papilla at the penetration site. (Reproduced by permission of Professor P. H. Williams.)

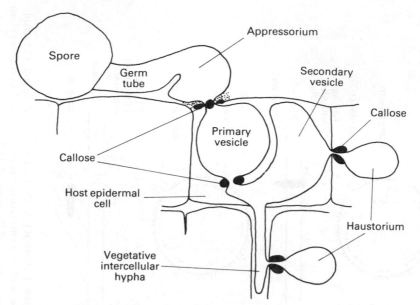

Figure 2.2   A diagrammatic representation of the infection of a susceptible
lettuce epidermal cell by *Bremia lactucae*. (Reproduced by
permission of Dr D. S. Ingram.)

2.1.3 Passive penetration

Positive correlation between the degree of stomatal opening in hop leaves, at
the time of inoculation, and the amount of subsequent infection by downy
mildew (*Pseudoperonospora humuli*) was demonstrated by Royle and Thomas
(1971*a*). Subsequently, it was shown that in light, when the stomata are open,
zoospores settled singly and penetrated through the open stomatal vestibule
(Royle and Thomas 1971*b*). Another example of passive penetration is the
injection of virus particles when an animal vector bites or sucks at a host organ.
Similarly, wound invasion by bacteria and secondary pathogens which have a
weak capacity to penetrate, for example *Botrytis cinerea* (grey mould), follows a
route already opened by a primary parasite.

2.1.4 Barriers to invasion

The structural characteristics of the host surface may present the first barrier to
invasion by influencing the retention of inoculum once it has been deposited.
Waxiness and hairiness may contribute to whether or not an infection is
successful. Waxless mutant Brussels sprouts are more heavily infected with
Albugo candida (white blister) than normal types. The roles played by the cuticle

and the epidermal layer in preventing invasion need to be differentiated. In many studies this has not been done, but Martin (1964) and Martin and Juniper (1970) concluded that the cuticle provides no serious barrier to penetration, and its contribution to resistance either through physical or chemical properties is not great. Generally, pathogens tend to penetrate younger tender parts of the host more easily than the older thickened regions. Attempts have been made to correlate the ease with which penetration can take place with the thickness of the plant cuticle. A correlation between age, resistance of the skin of tomato fruits to puncture, and infection by *Macrosporium tomato* (table 2.1) was demonstrated by Rosenbaum and Sando (1920).

Table 2.1   Relation between age, resistance to puncture, and infection of tomato fruits by *Macrosporium tomato* (Rosenbaum and Sando, 1920).

Age (days)	Pressure (g) needed to puncture skin of the fruit	Percentage of fruit infected
7	0.97	100
14	2.99	100
21	4.21	85
28	4.90	49
35	5.08	23
41	5.96	0
48	6.74	0
55	5.56	0

The dangers of interpreting a correlation between cell wall thickness and infection under only a single set of environmental conditions as an explanation for resistance is illustrated by Weinhold and English (1964) with *Sphaerotheca pannosa* (powdery mildew) of peach. Young leaves are susceptible, but they become resistant as they mature. The combined thickness of cuticle and epidermal cell wall correlated well with leaf age but showed no differences in leaves of comparable age between two cultivars (table 2.2). Mature leaf resistance, however, could not be explained by the thickness of the cuticularised cell wall, first because mature resistant leaves became susceptible when plants were transferred to darkness even though the wall remained unchanged and second because rudimentary haustoria were observed in epidermal cells of resistant leaves.

Invasion of potato tubers by *Oospora pustulans* (skin spot) has been shown to be influenced by periderm thickness, number of cell rows in the periderm, thickness of the suberin layer and content of crude fibre (cellulose, hemicellulose and lignin) in the skin cell walls (Nagdy and Boyd, 1965). Resistance to invasion could be influenced by numbers, arrangement, structure or functioning of

Table 2.2   Average combined thickness (in micrometres) of the outer epidermal cell wall and cuticle and susceptibility to *Sphaerotheca pannosa* of leaves of two peach cultivars and of various ages as represented by leaf position (Weinhold and English, 1964).

Leaf position	Susceptible cultivar		Resistant cultivar	
	Cuticularised wall thickness	Mildew susceptibility	Cuticularised wall thickness	Mildew susceptibility
Apex	3.4[a]	+ +	3.0[a]	+ (weak)
Node 1	3.5	+ +	3.3	+ (weak)
Node 2	4.1	+	3.6	–
Node 3	4.5	–	4.0	–
Node 4	4.0	–	3.9	–
Node 5	4.4	–	–	–

[a] Mean of 20 measurements with confidence limits ±0.2–0.4 ($P = 0.05$).

stomata. The subject has been little researched despite its obvious implications for resistance breeding.

Stomatal density has been suggested as a reason for resistance by several workers but refuted by others, so that the situation is confused. There is better evidence for differences in stomatal structure and function acting as a resistance mechanism. Studies of citrus susceptible and resistant to *Pseudomonas citri* (bacterial canker) showed that in susceptible species the stomatal entrance was widely distended while in resistant ones it was closed due to occlusion by cuticular ridges (Maclean, 1921). The opening and closing of stomata by diurnal rhythm will also influence invasion. The work on this aspect by Royle and Thomas (1971a,b) using hop and *S. humuli* has been referred to above. Other evidence comes from Diachun (1940), who found that infection of tobacco leaves by *Bacterium tabacum* was less when stomata were closed than when open, and Allington and Feaster (1946) showed that soybeans were infected most severely when inoculum of *Xanthomonas phaseoli* var. *sojae* was applied to leaves between the hours of 08.00 and 14.00, the period when stomata were open.

Differences in the rate at which stomata open could influence invasion. Early workers with *Puccinia graminis* (wheat stem rust) suggested that in resistant cultivars the stomata opened more slowly, thereby preventing entry of germ tubes stimulated to grow by the presence of dew on the leaf. In susceptible cultivars the stomata were open earlier in the day and successful penetration took place. Cytological work by Allen (1923a,b) suggested that the resistant cultivar

Kanred had narrower stomatal pores than susceptible ones. The concentration of carbon dioxide in the stomata may also influence invasion since penetration of *P. graminis* is suppressed by high carbon dioxide levels; cultivars with slowly opening stomata utilise the carbon dioxide evolved by respiration in the dark and can effectively suppress invasion by *P. graminis* (Yirgou and Caldwell, 1963).

Darling (1937) showed that *Streptomyces scabies*, the cause of common scab in potatoes, used lenticels as a main portal of entry. Infection of a tuber, however can probably occur only during a brief 'susceptible' phase when the guard cells are lost from the raised stoma to expose the underlying tissue of the young lenticel (Adams, 1975). Soil moisture status then governs the success of infection, which can proceed only in dry soil and before suberisation (which is encouraged by dry conditions) has sealed up the lenticel.

2.2 COLONISATION

Following invasion the pathogen either establishes a compatible or a non-compatible association with the host. In the compatible reaction the diseased state ensues with the development of metabolic changes and symptom expression (section 2.3 onwards). The incompatible state occurs when host defence mechanisms are successful and further development of the pathogen is prevented. Such defence mechanisms may be physical or chemical.

2.2.1 Physical defence

(a) Lignitubers and suberisation
When the roots of resistant flax are attacked by *Fusarium oxysporum* f. *lini*, a corky layer is deposited in the cortical cells (Tisdale, 1917; Boyle, 1934). A similar report was made by Anderson and Walker (1935) that gum-like substances were deposited between cortical cells of cabbages resistant to *Fusarium oxysporum* f. sp. *conglutinans* (yellows) which prevented further invasion by the fungus. The term lignituber was first used by Fellows (1928) to describe thickenings formed on the walls of wheat cells opposite penetrating hyphae of *Gaeumanomyces graminis*. Buckley (1958) discussed these structures in relation to invasion of tomatoes by *Verticillium albo-atrum*, and considered they were a product of an active host cell stimulated by a growing hypha. One lignituber was associated with each infecting hypha. Isaac and Griffiths (1962) showed that while *V. albo-atrum* and *V. tricorpus* rapidly penetrated tomato roots without inciting lignituber formation, hyphae of *V. dahliae* were often arrested from colonising by lignituber formation. *V. albo-atrum* and *V. tricorpus* were more virulent than *V. dahliae*. Chemical composition of lignitubers was shown by Griffiths and Lim (1964) to be an inner region of cellulose deposited round the advancing hyphae encased in an outer layer of lignin. Deposition of suberin in the

endodermis may serve to exclude *V. albo-atrum* from the pericycle of hop
(Talboys, 1958).

(b) Tyloses
Tyloses are expansions of medullary ray parenchyma cells through the pit
apertures of xylem vessels. They have a two-layered structure, the outer layer of
randomly orientated microfibrils being covered with amorphous granular
material and the inner layer being of multilamellate microfibrils. The function of
tyloses is disputed. They may be important in symptom formation as suggested
by Struckmeyer, Kuntz and Riker (1958) working with *Ceratocystis fagacearum*
(oak wilt). Others consider they act in sealing off areas of plants infected by
vascular pathogens (Suchorukov, 1957). Talboys (1958) proposed a general
hypothesis that high tylosis development is associated with sparse mycelial
colonisation and resistance; conversely, with intense mycelial colonisation,
production of tyloses is limited. This was based on work with *V. albo-atrum*,
causing hop wilt. Studies of the pathogen in tomato showed that tyloses were
not a resistance mechanism but occurred with a range of compatible and
incompatible host—parasite combinations.

2.2.2 Chemical defence

Essentially, chemical defence involves the hypersensitive response to invasion.
The host reacts to the presence of a pathogen by the localised death of cells
which have been invaded, thereby sealing off the parasite in an area of dead
cells. The term hypersensitivity was coined by Stakman (1915) in discussing the
resistance of cereals to *Puccinia graminis*. It is probable that the host cell dies
before the pathogen because there are numerous reports of the pathogen
continuing to grow, albeit slowly, inside dead cells for several hours. Intimately
bound in with the concept of hypersensitivity is that of phytoalexin production.
Müller and Borger (1941) envisaged that cells of potato expressing hypersensitivity
to avirulent races of *Phytophthora infestans* (potato blight) did so through the
formation of substances termed phytoalexins. These were produced by the host
in response to invasion and were toxic to the host cells, leading to the
hypersensitive response. The definition now accepted is broader, in that they are
antibiotics produced in plant—parasite interactions or as a response to injury or
other physiological stimuli (Kuć, 1976). Most chemicals classed as phytoalexins
can be detected in small quantities in healthy non-stimulated plants. There is
little distinction, therefore, between phytoalexins and what have been termed
phytonicides — substances preformed in the healthy cell which cause the death of
a parasite. The implication of phytoalexins in hypersensitivity has been
summarised by Deverall (1977) as follows:

(1) Death of a host cell may cause synthesis of phytoalexins in neighbouring
cells.

(2) Molecules diffusing from a pathogen may induce phytoalexin formation and cell death, perhaps at increasing doses.

(3) Phytoalexin accumulation may cause death of host cells, as speculated by Mansfield *et al.* (1974).

Phytoalexins were first described chemically following work by Müller (1958), who showed that if droplets containing *Monilinia fructigena* were placed on the inside cavities of bean pods a hypersensitive response followed and the droplets were increasingly fungistatic. The active material was extracted but not identified until later by Perrin and Bottomley (1962), who obtained similar reactions with pea pods inoculated with *M. fructigena*. The material was shown to be a complex aromatic compound of the pterocarpan family and named pisatin. Since then basic structures have been identified which have phytoalexin properties: pterocarpan, isoflavan and isoflavone. Additionally, the aliphatic materials wyerone and wyerone acid were detected by Fawcett *et al.* (1971) in bean (*Vicia faba*) as antifungal compounds produced in response to infection by *Botrytis* spp. A wide range of host families has been shown to produce phytoalexin materials, for example:

Leguminosae:	medicarpin, pisatin, phaseollin, glyceollin (pterocarpans), vestitol, sativan, phaseollin-isoflavan (isoflavans), kievitone (isoflavanone), wyerone, wyerone acid (acetylenic ketofuranoid)
Solanaceae:	rishitin, phytotuberin, capsidol, glutinosone (terpenoids)
Malvaceae:	vergosin, hemigossypol
Umbelliferae:	xanthotoxin
Convolvulaceae:	ipomeamarone
Compositae:	safynol, dehydroxysafynol
Orchidaceae:	orchinol, hircinol

The mechanism of phytoalexin formation is still far from clear, but the hypothesis has been advanced that a substance of parasitic origin acts to induce the formation of phytoalexins by live host cells (Deverall, 1977). Caution needs to be used in accepting this idea since, in *Vicia* beans infected with *Botrytis* (Mansfield and Deverall, 1974), *Phaseolus* beans infected with *Colletotrichum lindemuthianum* (Bailey and Deverall, 1971; Rahe, 1973) and *Phaseolus* beans infected with *Uromyces appendiculatus* (Bailey and Ingham, 1971), phytoalexins began to accumulate at about the time that necrosis was first visible. This leads to the suggestion that phytoalexin formation is induced as a consequence of cellular death in those specific host—parasite combinations. This could still be consistent with the hypothesis that phytoalexins are active defence mechanisms, and evidence for this has been supplied by Mansfield and Deverall (1974) working with *Botrytis cinerea* and *B. fabae* as pathogens of *V. fabae*. *Botrytis cinerea* is a weak pathogen of this host, causing very limited lesions, while *B. fabae* is very aggressive. These workers showed that the spread of *B. cinerea* lesions is inhibited by the production of wyerone acid in the cells at the periphery of the lesion. *Botrytis fabae*, however, was able to reduce wyerone acid to a less active phytoalexin which then allowed the lesions to spread out on the bean leaf. This and other studies of the abilities of fungi to metabolise phytoalexins would suggest that, for the establishment of some compatible host—parasite relations with subsequent extensive colonisation of the host, an ability to degrade phytoalexins is a prerequisite for the pathogen.

Colonisation leads to a wide range of metabolic changes in the host, resulting in visual symptom expression. For convenience, these changes are discussed under individual headings, but it should be borne in mind that several are likely to take place at any one time in specific host—parasite combinations.

2.3 SYMPTOM DEVELOPMENT

2.3.1 Photosynthetic changes

Loss of yield in terms of dry weight is one of the commonest symptoms of most host—parasite complexes, and this is indicative of reduced photosynthetic activity. The most obvious sign of this is the development of chlorotic symptoms, resulting from a loss of chlorophyll in the leaves of plants invaded by foliar pathogens. Prior to symptom expression, however, there may be large accumulations of sucrose and to a lesser extent glucose and fructose in heavily infected leaves. It has also been shown with bean leaves infected with *Uromyces* spp. (rust) (Daly, 1967) that while leaves which showed symptoms have very reduced rates of carbon assimilation those elsewhere on the plant have rates increased 1.5—2.0-fold. In many plants infected with foliar pathogens, starch accumulation at first declines and then rises rapidly, especially at the leaf margins, only to decline again subsequently. The process of fixation of carbon dioxide in the dark often increases in diseased leaves, especially where the leaves are invaded by a rust or powdery mildew pathogen, at the point of sporulation in the immediate vicinity of the lesion. It may be that the fungus can fix carbon dioxide because both bean and cereal rust uredospores contain the malic enzymes necessary to catalyse the reaction

$$\text{pyruvate} + CO_2 \rightleftharpoons \text{malate},$$

which Mirocha and Rick (1967) showed was responsible for carbon dioxide fixation in the dark in diseased leaves. The process may also occur in diseased leaves if the pathogen has been killed. The activity of toxins may be involved here since it is postulated that increased permeability of vacuole membranes allows cations to be released which enhance carbon dioxide fixation via phosphoenol-pyruvate to oxalacetate, which is converted to malic acid. This, in turn, buffers the excess release of cations.

Increased dark fixation of carbon dioxide is a feature of pathogenesis in plants which do not use the normal Calvin cycle. Thus maize, a highly efficient plant photosynthetically, uses the C_4 dicarboxylic acid pathway for carbon assimilation. Mirocha (1972) showed that when maize was infected with *Helminthosporium carbonus* carbon assimilation in the dark was increased. A common feature of the Calvin and C_4 dicarboxylic acid pathways is the synthesis of ribulose-5-phosphate and ribulose-1,5-phosphate; pathogens may act on carbon dioxide fixation by raising the turnover of these sugar phosphates.

2.3.2 Respiratory changes

A characteristic of most disease syndromes, except possibly those caused by systemic viruses, is a rise in respiration rate. This begins to increase at or just before the onset of visible symptoms, continuing until a two- to fourfold increase has taken place compared to uninfected tissue. Respiratory increases are maintained if the pathogen is removed, indicating that the rise is due to increased host metabolism. Two hypotheses have been advanced to account for increased host respiration during pathogenesis.

(a) Uncoupling hypothesis
The uncoupling hypothesis postulates that uncoupling of phosphorylation from electron transport is responsible for respiratory rises. Experiments by Sempio (1950) showed that the ratio of anaerobic to aerobic carbon dioxide production was lower (about 0.3) in diseased compared to healthy tissue (0.5—0.6). Allen (1953) interpreted this effect as due to a diffusable toxin which increased the availability of adenosine diphosphate (ADP), thereby removing the normal control on respiratory rate. Results produced by various workers who have tried to test this hypothesis mostly suggest that uncoupling cannot be responsible for respiratory rate increases early in pathogenesis, although it may be a feature when disease has reached an advanced stage. This is especially so because increased synthetic activities take place in diseases caused by biotrophic fungi. The accumulation of organic and inorganic materials around lesions is energy dependent, and hypocotyls of rust-infected plants elongate and increase in dry weight (Daly, 1967). These effects could not be expected if energy were being dissipated by uncoupling.

(b) Pentose phosphate (PP) pathway hypothesis
The usual respiratory pathway in higher plants is the tricarboxylic acid (TCA) cycle; the PP pathway hypothesis suggests a shift towards a direct oxidative mechanism known as the hexose monophosphate shunt. This requires nicotinamide adenine dinucleotide phosphate (NADP)-dependent oxidation of glucose-6-phosphate followed by decarboxylation at the first carbon (C1) of the sugar phosphate. The involvement of the PP pathway in respiration can be

investigated using glucose labelled with ^{14}C at different carbons on its chain. Usually the labels are placed at C6 to give [6-^{14}C] glucose and C1 to give [1-^{14}C] glucose. In the TCA cycle the ratio of respired radioactive carbon dioxide ($^{14}CO_2$) from [6-^{14}C] glucose to [1-^{14}C] glucose (the C6/C1 ratio) should be unity. If, however, the PP cycle operates, the C6/C1 ratio starts nearer to zero and then gradually rises. A drop in C6/C1 ratio in a host—parasite complex indicates a shift from the TCA cycle to the PP pathway. The situation is complicated since most fungi tend to have low C6/C1 ratios. Working with *Puccinia carthami* on safflower, Daly (1967) found that respiratory increases took place 24 h before the C6/C1 ratio declined, and that such falls then coincided with sporulation of the pathogen. Much of the increased respiratory activity and increased participation of the PP pathway may be due to the production of metabolites by the fungus. The situation with most viruses which produce local lesions is simplified because the area adjacent to the lesion is free from pathogen and metabolites. Increased respiratory rates accompanied by falls in C6/C1 ratios in virus-infected tissues have led Bell (1964) and Dwurazna and Weintraub (1969) to conclude that the PP pathway is responsible for increased respiratory rates. Workers have tried to track the fate of the missing C6 atom during pathogenesis. It is likely that it is incorporated into cell wall materials such as hemicellulose and lignin. The shikimic acid pathway provides phenolic precursors of lignin in higher plants (Neish, 1964). Initially this involves condensation of phosphoenolpyruvate and erythrose-4-phosphate. The latter is derived from the PP pathway and will carry a radioactive label if derived from [6-^{14}C] glucose but not if derived from [1-^{14}C] glucose in tracer experiments. Results indicate that incorporation of phenolic components in the cell wall is geared to the respiratory rate. It appears that both the TCA cycle and PP pathway contribute to increased respiration during pathogenesis. Energy consumed in increased synthesis of cell wall components would raise the supply of ADP. The decrease in C6/C1 ratio and increase in cell wall precursor substances are consistent with greater activity by the PP pathway and utilisation of C6 to build up cell wall components.

2.3.3 Water relations

(a) Changes in cell permeability

Alterations in cell permeability are associated with the primary stages of pathogenesis. Cells become leaky, releasing electrolytes and losing the ability to accumulate salts. The water-soaked condition associated with some foliar diseases such as potato blight, caused by *Phytophthora infestans*, is probably symptomatic of this loss of water. In those host—parasite combinations where a necrotic ring develops, the cells surrounding the ring are less permeable and accumulate substances to a higher degree than healthy cells. The hypothesis has been advanced, therefore, that changes in permeability may regulate the

availability of substrates for the growth of the parasite. The basic nature of
changes in cell permeability has been illustrated by experiments using enzymes
which cause cell death and maceration. The latter effects occur subsequent to an
increase in permeability in infected cells. Toxins produced by pathogens may act
similarly to such enzymes and have been implicated in changes in permeability.
By definition, toxins cause cellular damage and must affect cell permeability.
Disagreement exists, however, as to whether such changes are the cause of
cell disruption or the effects of other events in pathogenesis. Probably the most
extensive studies which have been made on this aspect have used the toxin
victorin produced by *Helminthosporium victoriae*, the cause of leaf stripe of
oats. When applied to cells of susceptible cultivars, victorin is associated with
increased permeability; very much greater concentrations are required to cause
comparable effects in the tissues of resistant cultivars. The effects on cell
permeability are virtually instantaneous, whereas other pathological changes,
such as increases in respiration, take at least 30 min to occur. In the salts lost by
leaky cells are large amounts of potassium, which would have come from the
cell vacuoles and indicate disruption of the tonoplast membrane. Similar
concentrations of potassium when applied exogenously give rise to increased
respiration and the release of phenolic compounds which may prelude the
development of other pathogenic symptoms. Victorin has an effect within 5 min
of application on the cell walls of susceptible oat coleoptiles, leading to
increased elongation. This is a far more rapid response than can be induced even
by application of hormones such as auxins.

(b) Changes in water relations

There are three areas of water relations which may be affected by pathogenesis:
(1) the ability to absorb water; (2) changes in water transport; (3) effects on
stomatal function.

The ability of roots to absorb water is largely governed by the water flow
across the cortex and endodermis. Measurements to compare water flow in
infected and healthy roots have usually been made by creating a pressure
difference across excised roots either by applying suction to the stump or by
exerting pressure on the root solution and observing changes in the rate of flow.
In this way it was shown that tobacco roots infected with *Phytophthora parasitica*
var. *nicotiana* (black shank) had a higher resistance to water flow than healthy
roots (Schramm and Wolf, 1954). Mechanisms for such effects have been
demonstrated in Tabasco pepper (*Capsicum fructescens*) infected with Tobacco
Etch Virus. In diseased plants a ring of dead phloem and cambial cells forms
around the xylem, inhibiting the movement of water into the root.

The main effects of vascular pathogens are to disrupt the passage of water
through the stem. This may be attributed to the physical presence of the
pathogen mycelium, development of tyloses which block the xylem, and
gummosis within the vessels. These mechanisms are argued to lead to failure on

the part of the xylem vessels to transport an adequate supply of water to the other aerial organs. On the other hand, it has been suggested that tyloses and gums are resistance mechanisms whereby the host limits spread of the pathogen and that wilting is caused by dysfunction in cell permeability caused by toxins. Certainly, the presence of parasites like *Verticillium* and *Fusarium* in the vessels causes a four- to 60-fold increase in the resistance of the stem to water flow. Further xylem occlusion comes from high molecular weight polysaccharides produced by the pathogen or cleaved from the xylem walls by hydrolytic enzymes. These block the pit membranes, reducing lateral water flow and occluding the small vessels in petioles and leaves. Proponents of the wilt toxin theory base their case on the isolation and characterisation of toxic metabolites by *Fusarium* spp. in culture which, when applied to tomatoes, increased leaf cell permeability. Some metabolites, such as fusaric acid and marticin, have been isolated from diseased plants, but others like lycomarasmin are only found *in vitro*. Symptoms caused by the toxins alone are atypical of the normal pathogen-induced wilt syndrome. Possibly these substances have a secondary role in vascular diseases, although in tomatoes infected by *Fusarium*, as resistance to water flow increased, symptoms formed. The pathogen does not, however, alter the water content of leaf discs; the resistance to water movement is most likely to be associated with changes in the xylem rather than with the layers of living cells in the leaf, as would be suggested by the toxin theory.

Changes in stomatal transpiration during pathogenesis have been studied in detail using bean plants infected with *Uromyces fabae* (rust). In the early stages of infection transpiration rate decreases by the partial inhibition of stomatal opening in the light. By contrast, when the uredosori mature, the epidermis and cuticle are damaged and transpiration rate increases. Increased stomatal opening is induced by some pathogens, for example *Rhynchosporium secalis* on barley reduces the back pressure of epidermal cells on the guard cells, thus stimulating stomatal opening. *Phytophthora infestans* causes stomata of potato leaves to open before the sporangiophores emerge through them, and they then remain open longer than normal stomata if excised and allowed to dry. In vascular diseases transpirational effects may not be important in contributing to wilting since transpiration of leaves from potatoes infected with *V. albo-atrum* was similar to that from healthy plants when plotted as functions of relative water content (figure 2.3). Figure 2.3 relates the water content in tissues at fresh weight, fully turgid weight and oven dry weight.

Necrosis of the phloem and gummosis that occur with viral infections lead to abnormal patterns of translocation of organic and inorganic materials. There is interference with the long-range transport of photosynthetic products from leaves to storage organs. Starch accumulation takes place in the older leaves — often before symptoms become visible. Infection by rust and powdery mildew pathogens leads to the accumulation of starch in mesophyll cells around the lesions. In the later stages of pathogenesis this accumulation disappears in bean leaves

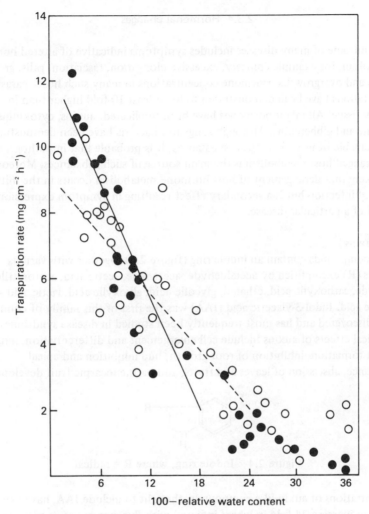

Figure 2.3   Relation between (100 − relative water content) and transpiration rate in detached leaves of potato plants cv. King Edward infected with *Verticillium albo-atrum* (●——●, infected; ○——○, controls). (Reproduced by permission of the late Professor Ivor Isaac.)

infected by *U. fabae*. Other organic and inorganic materials accumulate around lesions, and there is evidence for the transport of these materials from healthy parts of the plant to infected areas. Areas of such accumulation around lesions frequently remain green after the rest of the leaf has turned chlorotic, indicating that these cells are benefitting from the inflow of nutrient, which exceeds that required by the pathogen for growth.

2.3.4 Hormonal changes

The syndrome of many diseases includes symptoms indicative of altered hormone metabolism, for example epinasty, excessive elongation, fasciation, galls, green islands and overgrowths. Hormone concentrations in many such host—parasite combinations have been demonstrated to be at least 10-fold higher than in healthy tissue. All major hormones have been implicated: auxins, cytokinins, ethylene and gibberellins. Although fungi and bacteria have been demonstrated to be capable of producing these substances, it is probable that in pathogenesis the deranged host metabolism is the main source of such substances. Moreover, it is unlikely that derangement of host hormone metabolism occurs in the initial stages of infection but is a secondary effect resulting in symptom expression typical of a particular disease.

(a) Auxins

These compounds contain an indole ring (figure 2.4) together with various radicals (R) exemplified by acetaldehyde, acetamide, acetic acid, acetonitrile, aldehyde, carboxylic acid, ethanol, glycolic acid, glyoxylic acid, lactic acid and pyruvic acid. Indol-3-ylacetic acid (IAA) was the first of this family of compounds to be discovered and has most frequently been studied in disease syndromes. The biological effects of auxins include cell enlargement and differentiation, initiation of root formation, inhibition of root growth, bud inhibition and apical dominance, abscission of leaves and fruits, and parthenocarpic fruit development.

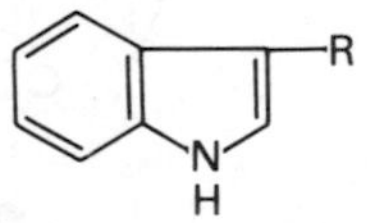

Figure 2.4   Indole ring, where R = radical.

Concentrations of auxin-like compounds, thought to include IAA, have been shown to increase 24-fold in wheat infected with *Puccinia graminis tritici* (black rust); only fivefold increases could be detected in barley infected with *Erysiphe graminis* (powdery mildew). Direct evidence for the involvement of auxins in pathogenesis has come from the study of vascular pathogens. Exogenously applied IAA leads to the development of tyloses in tomato shoots, and substantially greater quantities of IAA have been extracted from tomatoes and cotton infected with *Verticillium albo-atrum* than from healthy tissues. Diseases showing hypertrophy such as blister rust caused by *Albugo candida* are obvious candidates to investigate for increased auxin levels. Artificially applied IAA has been shown to cause similar symptoms on shepherd's purse (*Capsella bursa-pastoris*), but specific auxins have not been satisfactorily re-isolated from diseased tissue. In bacterial diseases there is evidence for both increased IAA and stimulation of the host metabolism for its formation. Auxin precursors such as tryptophan, phenylalanine, tyrosine and dihydroxyphenylalanine have been detected in large quantities in tobacco inoculated with *Pseudomonas solanacearum.*

(b) Gibberellins

Work in Japan first associated these compounds with disease syndromes. Exaggerated growth of rice plants infected with *Gibberella fujikuroi* (*Fusarium moliniforme*) was shown to be associated with the presence of large quantities of gibberellins in the host. These substances have a complex ring structure and are chemically identified as cyclic diterpenes possessing a gibbane skeleton. The biological effects of gibberellins include stimulation of internode growth, flower induction, sub-apical cell division, induction of parthenocarpy and stimulation of α-amylase synthesis. Gibberellins have been identified in culture filtrates of *G. fujikuroi* and in the tissues of a wide range of Angiosperms; gibberellin-like substances have been extracted from several Basidiomycetes. *Azotobacter chrococcum* and *Pseudomonas* spp. from the rhizospheres of tomato and cucumber plants have the capacity to produce gibberellin-like substances *in vitro.* Direct evidence for involvement in specific host—parasite combinations is very sparse, resting on studies of *G. fujikuroi* on rice, the presence of gibberellin A_1 or A_2 in thistles (*Circium arvense*) infected with *Puccinia obtegens* (rust) and greatly increased levels of gibberellin-like substances in legume roots inoculated with *Rhizobium* spp.

(c) Cytokinins

Micro-organisms, plant tissues and animal tissues have been shown to contain N^6-substituted purines which affect growth. These occur as the free purine base, free nucleoside, free nucleotide and as transfer RNA (tRNA). The general structure is shown in figure 2.5, where R_1 and R_2 are side chains. Most commonly

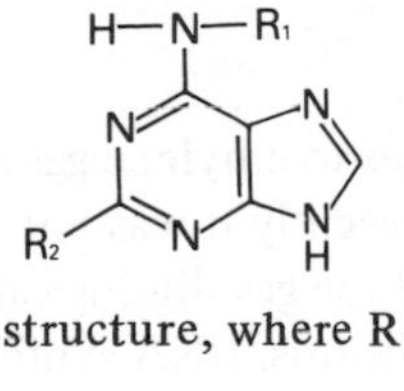

Figure 2.5   Cytokinin structure, where R_1 and R_2 are radicals.

encountered cytokinins are zeatin, 6-benzylaminopurine (BA) and 6-furfurylaminopurine (kinetin). Biological effects include stimulation of cell division and cell enlargement, retardation of senescence and induction of metabolite mobilisation.

There is a resemblance between the effects of cytokinins in delaying senescence in leaves and the stimulation of green island formation typical of several host—parasite combinations. Bean leaves infected with *Uromyces fabae* (rust) have been shown to contain enhanced cytokinin levels. Fasciation of pea seedlings caused by *Corynebacterium fascians*, in which the number of lateral shoots increases and they are swollen and misshapen, can be duplicated by exogenous application of kinetin or benzyladenine. Also, a cytokinin has been extracted from culture filtrates of *C. fascians*. The syndrome known as crown gall caused by *Agrobacterium tumefascians* is thought to be initiated by an hypothetical tumour-inducing principle which causes normal healthy cells to switch to tumour cells, and once this switch has occurred further proliferation of tumour cells could be independent of the presence of the pathogen. It has been shown that tumourous cells are capable of auxin and cytokinin synthesis whereas healthy cells are not. But it is unlikely that either auxins or cytokinins initiate the switch from healthy to tumourous tissue. Compounds with cytokinin-like activity have been isolated from cells of *Vinca rosae* infected with crown gall bacteria. Crucifer roots and hypocotyls infected with *Plasmodiophora brassicae* (clubroot) exhibit enhanced cell division and enlargement. Both cells containing the pathogen and uninvaded neighbouring cells are stimulated to divide, which is indicative of enhanced hormone activity. Turnip roots infected with *P. brassicae* have been shown to contain 0.1–1 mg zeatin equivalent per 100 kg of fresh clubroots, whereas healthy roots contained 10- to 100-fold less. Infected callus tissue explants are independent for cytokinins and auxins necessary for growth, whereas callus of healthy turnip tissue requires supplies of these hormones for continued growth.

Experiments with *Cronartium* rust have indicated that cytokinin activity is associated with the gall formation typical of this pathogen. Galled stem wood from loblolly pines (*Pinus taeda*) infected with *C. fusiforme* contained 10-fold greater amounts of cytokinin-like substances than uninfected tissue. Some syndromes may be associated with reduced cytokinin activity, particularly host–parasite combinations where senescence is accelerated. It has been demonstrated that root exudates from cotton and tomato contain lower quantities of cytokinins when the host is infected with *Verticillium* spp.

(d) Ethylene

In plants, hormone-like responses to ethylene gas have been known since the mid-nineteenth century. Until recently it was not possible to measure the effects of low concentrations of the gas. Biological properties ascribed to ethylene include inhibition of meiosis, DNA synthesis, cell wall expansion, polar and lateral auxin transport; induction of abscission of leaves, flowers and fruits, epinasty of leaves, fruit ripening, enzyme synthesis and phytoalexin production; stimulation of cell expansion. Synthesis of ethylene is thought to take place from methionine either via transamination to 4-methylmercapto-2-oxobutyric acid and peroxidation, or in light mediated by flavomononucleotide to methional and peroxidation to ethylene.

As with other hormone-related effects in the disease syndrome, it is generally held that the gas is of host origin, although some pathogens have been demonstrated to be capable of producing the gas *in vitro*. Increased concentrations of ethylene in the host tissue have been associated with enhanced enzyme synthesis, particularly of peroxidases. Similar stimulation has been reported for sweet-potatoes infected by *Ceratocystis fimbriata* (black rot) and cowpeas infected with Mosaic Virus. Wheat infected with *Puccinia graminis tritici* showed increased ethylene content and enhanced peroxidase activity compared to uninfected plants. Ethylene may also affect RNA and protein synthesis, polyphenoloxidase and polysaccharide hydrolase activity. Symptoms typically induced by ethylene include leaf and organ abscission, chlorosis, epinasty and adventitious root development. These are closely similar to the syndrome associated with vascular pathogens. Tomatoes and cotton infected with *Fusarium oxysporum* f. sp. *lycopersici* and *Verticillium albo-atrum* have been demonstrated to contain excessive quantities of ethylene. In hops, exogenous application of 2-chloroethylphosphonic acid (ethrel), which releases ethylene in the tissues, produced foliar chlorosis and stomatal dysfunction similar to that produced in plants infected with *V. albo-atrum*. Leaf abscission in roses infected with *Diplocarpon rosae* (black spot) has been associated with raised levels of ethylene.

Some workers suggest that ethylene could be implicated in resistance reactions through (1) induction of necrotic reactions by the liberation of peroxidase enzymes, which oxidise wall-bound glucose and amino acids; (2) the stimulated production of polyphenoloxidase, which oxidises phenolic compounds to produce antifungal quinones; (3) induction of phytoalexins, for example stimulation of phenylalanine ammonia lyase activity in pea tissue has been linked to the formation of pisatin.

2.3.5 Nitrogen and protein changes

(a) Amino acids

Early work with fungal pathogens showed that nitrogen metabolism is severely disrupted by infection. It is, however, often difficult to decide whether the nitrogen discussed is soluble or protein nitrogen. Changes in host amino acid composition as part of a disease syndrome were first reported for potatoes infected with *Synchytrium endobioticum*. Extracts from infected shoots when applied to healthy ones led to the degradation of healthy shoot proteins to amino acids. Similarly, extracts from tomatoes susceptible to *Fusarium oxysporum* f. sp. *lycopersici* after inoculation contained increased concentrations of asparagine, glutamine, leucine, isoleucine, methionine, phenylalanine, valine, cystine and serine. Extensive studies of nitrogen metabolism in wheat susceptible to *Puccinia graminis tritici* after inoculation showed striking increases in total nitrogen per gram fresh weight and in the ratio of soluble to insoluble nitrogen. There were fourfold increases in non-protein and twofold increases in protein amino acids. Detailed studies of the effects of *Verticillium albo-atrum* on the amino acid metabolism of tomato cultivars showed that in compatible combinations free amino acid concentrations within the host stem rose rapidly

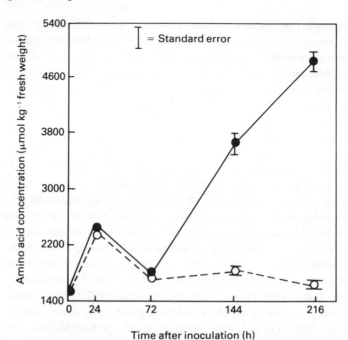

Figure 2.6   Concentration of amino acids in tomato (cv. Potentate) stems
infected with a compatible strain of *Verticillium albo-atrum*.
(After Dixon, 1969.)

72 h after inoculation (figure 2.6). These continued in the stems, petioles and
leaflets until 216 h after inoculation, meanwhile concentrations in the roots had
begun to decline. Similarly, there were increased concentrations of free amino
acids in the xylem sap of infected plants, but analysis of culture filtrates
showed them to contain little free amino nitrogen, indicating that stimulation
of amino acid content was a host-mediated effect. Similar reactions have been
demonstrated for bacterial and viral host—parasite combinations. An
accumulation of methionine in the halo region of beans (*Phaseolus vulgaris*)
infected with *Pseudomonas phaseolicola* is thought to be evidence that the
failure to incorporate this sulphur amino acid into protein is an initial step in the
development of chlorosis and necrosis. Increases of other amino acids have also
been linked to symptom development; stimulation of basic and aromatic amino
acids in tobacco leaves infected with *Pseudomonas solanacearum*, including
3,4-dihydroxyphenylalanine, tyrosine, phenylalanine and tryptophan, which are
precursors of phenolics and indole auxins, led to the suggestion that these are
primary precursors in the development of melaninisation and hyperauxiny which
are typical of the vascular wilt syndrome.

Initially in virus infections a depression of free amino acid content has been
noted and ascribed to utilisation for the synthesis of viral coat protein. Later in

pathogenesis, however, the whole spectrum of amino acids in tomatoes inoculated with Tomato Spotted Wilt Virus has been shown to increase.

Sources for abnormally high levels of amino nitrogen during pathogenesis are likely to be as follows:

(1) Increased synthesis from nitrates absorbed from the soil. This would be indicated by increased levels of glutamic and aspartic acids from which other amino acids are formed by transamination.

(2) Proteolysis as pathogenesis continues. Accumulation of protein amino acids in the cell could result in their transamination to non-protein amino acids such as ornithine, β-alanine or other nitrogen-containing compounds such as pipecolic acid. The latter has been shown to be associated with Multiplier virus disease of strawberries. Excessive formation of phenolic and auxin-like compounds will occur when their amino acid precursors accumulate in the cell, leading to symptom expression.

(b) Proteins

Enzymes

Implicit in previous sections has been the notion that in a compatible host— parasite combination there will be stimulation of host enzyme synthesis. This results in increased products of photosynthesis, respiration and conversion of inorganic to organic nitrogen, which provides substrates for growth of the parasite. It is possible that oxidative enzymes such as peroxidases, cytochrome oxidases, ascorbic acid oxidases, glycolic acid oxidases and dehydrogenases may be implicated in resistance reactions, but evidence for this is extremely conflicting. Most probably this is caused by the activation of oxidative enzymes after infection as a result of cellular injury caused by the invading organism, not as a consequence of specific defence reactions of the infected plant.

Cell walls

Although cell walls are largely composed of α-cellulose, hemicellulsoe, pectin and lignin, the primary wall has a protein component — glycoprotein rich in hydroxyproline. The carbohydrate components of this protein are primarily galactose and arabinose. The latter is glycosidically linked to the hydroxyl of the proline moiety, whereas galactose is covalently linked to serine. Cell wall proteins have properties similar to phytoagglutins and are capable of binding with and serving as potent inhibitors of certain polygalacturonases. Recently, attention has focused on the possible significance of this group of inhibitors in the enzymic decomposition of plant cell walls. Polygalacturonase is an enzyme produced by some pathogens which degrades host cell walls leading to tissue maceration. Work *in vitro* with tomato cell walls protected by the polygalactu- ronase inhibitor prevented cell degradation by *Fusarium oxysporum* f. sp. *lycopersici.* As yet there is no evidence of the importance of cell wall proteins *in vivo.* In order to degrade the protein constituent of cell walls, proteolytic enzymes must be produced by the pathogen. These have been demonstrated as present in many micro-organisms and are often found in diseased tissue, where they could be of host origin. So far an ability to degrade cell wall protein has not been satisfactorily demonstrated *in vivo* for any pathogen.

2.3.6 Nuclear changes

Knowledge of changes at the nuclear level following penetration could indicate how the initial interchange of information takes place in pathogenesis. This might show how the host's metabolism is altered to favour activities directed to the parasite's advantage. So far understanding at this level is scant and fragmentary. Early workers reported that in brassicas infected by *Plasmodiophora brassicae* and wheat by *Puccinia graminis tritici*, host cell hypertrophy was accompanied by increased nuclear size. More recently, such changes have been shown to be associated with a higher content of RNA. Time course studies of nuclear size in resistant and susceptible cultivars of wheat infected by *P. graminis tritici* showed that RNA content increased more quickly in mesophyll cells of the resistant cultivar, but failed to reach the magnitude of the increase found in susceptible cells, which persisted longer. The DNA content per host nucleus in resistant leaves was only slightly reduced on the fourth and sixth day after inoculation and up to 46 per cent by the 12th day. In susceptible leaves a 25 per cent loss of DNA in the nuclei was recorded 12 days after inoculation. It would seem that changes in RNA and nuclear size are less pronounced but occur more rapidly in the incompatible host—parasite combination. In susceptible cultivars a considerable increase in nucleolar size, RNA content and protein content was observed.

In the root hairs of cabbage seedlings inoculated with primary zoospores of *P. brassicae*, an increased size in the host nucleolus was detected within 4 h and continued until 18—24 h after penetration by the zoospore. Accompanying this were increases in quantities of nuclear RNA and non-histone protein. The amount of nuclear histone, particularly the lysine-rich fraction, decreased at the same time, but was not accompanied by increased DNA, which may reflect the inability of the root hair to support this stage of the pathogen life cycle for any prolonged period. In the secondary stage of the life cycle, the cortical cells contain enlarged nucleoli, the sizes of which are proportional to the number of *P. brassicae* nuclei. Nuclear DNA is increased by doubling and may reach $32n$ in infected cells.

At the same time there were increases in nucleic acids, particularly nuclear histones. The cabbage cell response to infection seems to be an increase in protein synthesis apparatus in the cytoplasm, nucleus and nucleolus, leading to stimulation of DNA and RNA synthesis with attendant increases in the production of lipids, amino acids, sugars and starch prior to sporogenesis by *P. brassicae*. The effects of a pathogen on host nucleic acid metabolism depends on the stage of organ development. In fully grown leaves such as the primary leaves of cereals, senescence may be retarded following infection by *Puccinia* spp. or *Erysiphe graminis* with a concomitant stimulation of RNA synthesis. In expanding leaves, competition by the parasite can lead to diminished overall RNA synthesis. On a single leaf, both increases and decreases in RNA synthesis may be observed. The 'green island' phenomenon illustrates the higher RNA content in non-infected areas compared to the infection sites. In host—parasite combinations where hyperplasia and hypertrophy are not part of the syndrome, alterations of DNA amount are usually small, except in very late stages of pathogenesis. At this point DNA content decreases due to degeneration of the nuclei.

From studies of *Puccinia coronata* (crown rust) on oats it is concluded that increased ribosomal RNA originates mostly from the fungus in susceptible leaves but from the host in resistant leaves. Differentiation between cytoplasmic and chloroplast RNA has been made in barley leaves infected with *Erysiphe graminis* (powdery mildew). Within 5 days after inoculation chloroplast ribosomal RNA (rRNA) had been degraded into smaller fragments. Four days later no chloroplast rRNA species were detected in infected leaves. By contrast, 9 days after inoculation twice as many cytoplasmic ribosomes existed in inoculated as non-inoculated leaves, on a fresh weight basis. Thus total ribosome content at this stage was 20 per cent higher in infected than control leaves. Decreases in chloroplast rRNA apparent 5 and 9 days after inoculation reflects the non-specific degradation of chloroplasts in this foliar disease. At very early stages of infection the molar ratio of cytoplasmic to chloroplast RNA was two or three times higher in infected compared to healthy leaves due to decreases in chloroplast RNA. In contrast, this ratio in resistant leaves was only slightly altered by inoculation. Since *E. graminis* is an ectoparasite, development of haustoria takes place only in epidermal cells. Influence on the chloroplast RNA in the mesophyll cells may result from diffusible products of the fungus, and the differences between resistant and susceptible hosts reflect different cell permeabilities to such products. Investigations of soluble RNA (sRNA) have shown changes similar to those with rRNA. It would seem there is a general stimulation of RNA synthesis during pathogenseis.

An exchange of nucleic acids and possibly messenger RNA (mRNA) might occur between host and parasite. As yet there is only very limited information of an increase in mRNA synthesis in infected leaves. Also it has been shown that nucleic acid degrading enzymes such as ribonucleases and deoxyribonucleases increase during pathogenesis. Such increases have so far only been measured some days after inoculation, when general cell disruption is already in progress.

REFERENCES

Adams, M. J. (1975). *Ann. appl. Biol.* **79**, 265—73.
Allen, R. F. (1923*a*). *J. agric. Res.* **23**, 131—51.

Allen, R. F. (1923*b*). *J. agric. Res.* **52**, 917–32.
Allen, P. J. (1953). *Phytopathology* **43**, 221–9.
Allington, W. B. and Feaster, C. V. (1946). *Phytopathology* **36**, 385–6.
Anderson, M. E. and Walker, J. C. (1935). *J. agric. Res.* **50**, 823–36.
Bailey, J. A. and Deverall, B. J. (1971). *Physiol. Pl. Path.* **1**, 435–49.
Bailey, J. A. and Ingham, J. L. (1971). *Physiol. Pl. Path.* **1**, 451–6.
Bell, A. A. (1964). *Phytopathology* **54**, 914–22.
Boyle, L. W. (1934). Technical Bulletin no. 458. United States Department of
    Agriculture, Washington D.C. (Abstract in *Rev. appl. Mycol.* **14**, 362 (1935).)
Buckley, W. R. (1958). A study of some factors influencing the early stages of
    infection of tomato roots by *Verticillium albo-atrum*. M.Sc. thesis, University
    of London.
Daly, J. M. (1967). Some metabolic consequences of infection by obligate
    parasites. In *The Dynamic Role of Molecular Constituents in Plant Parasite
    Interaction* (C. J. Mirocha and I. Uritani, eds). American Phytopathological
    Society, St. Paul, Minn.
Darling, H. M. (1937). *J. agric. Res.* **54**, 305–17.
Deverall, B. J. (1977). *Defence Mechanisms of Plants.* Cambridge University
    Press, London.
Diachun, S. (1940). *Phytopathology* **30**, 268–72.
Dixon, G. R. (1969). Studies on the physiology and resistance of tomato
    cultivars in relation to infection by strains of *Verticillium albo-atrum*. Ph.D.
    thesis, University of London.
Dwurazna, M. M. and Weintraub, M. (1969). *Can. J. Bot.* **47**, 731–6.
Fawcett, C. H., Firn, R. D. and Spencer, D. M. (1971). *Physiol. Pl. Path.* **1**, 163–6.
Fellows, H. (1928). *J. agric. Res.* **37**, 647–61.
Griffiths, D. A. and Lim, W. C. (1964). *Mycopath. Mycol. appl.* **24**, 103–12.
Harrison, J. A. C. (1971). *Ann. appl. Biol.* **68**, 159–68.
Ingram, D. S., Sargent, J. A. and Tommerup, I. C. (1976). Structural aspects of
    infection by biotrophic fungi. In *Biochemical Aspects of Plant–Parasite
    Relationships* (J. Friend and D. R. Threlfall, eds). Academic Press, London.
Isaac, I. and Griffiths, D. A. (1962). *Proc. 16th int. hort. Congr.* **2**, 333–42.
Kuć, J. (1976). Terpenoid phytoalexins. In *Biochemical Aspects of Plant–
    Parasite Relationships* (J. Friend and D. R. Threlfall, eds). Academic Press,
    London.
McLean, F. T. (1921). *Bull. Torrey bot. Club* **48**, 101–6.
Mansfield, J. W. and Deverall, B. J. (1974). *Ann. appl. Biol.* **77**, 227–35.
Mansfield, J. W., Hargreaves, J. A. and Boyle, F. C. (1974). *Nature, Lond.* **252**,
    316–7.
Martin, J. T. (1964). *A. Rev. Phytopath.* **2**, 81–100.
Martin, J. T. and Juniper, B. E. (1970). *The Cuticles of Plants.* Edward Arnold,
    London.
Mirocha, C. J. (1972). Phytotoxins and metabolism. *Phytotoxins in Plant*

Diseases (R. K. S. Wood, A Ballio and A. Graniti, eds). Academic Press, London.

Mirocha, C. J. and Rick, P. D. (1967). Carbon dioxide fixation in the dark as a nutritional factor in parasitism. In *The Dynamic Role of Molecular Constituents in Plant—Parasite Interaction* (C. J. Mirocha and I. Uritani, eds). American Phytopathological Society, St. Paul, Minn.

Müller, K. O. (1958). *Aust. J. biol. Sci.* **11**, 275–300.

Müller, K. O. and Borger, H. (1941). *Arb. biol. Anst. ReichsAnst., Berlin* **23**, 189–231.

Nagdy, G. A. and Boyd, A. E. W. (1965). *Eur. Potato J.* **8**, 200–14.

Neish, A. C. (1964). Major pathways of biosynthesis of phenols. In *Biochemistry of Phenolic Compounds* (J. B. Harbone, ed.). Academic Press, London.

Perrin, D. R. and Bottomley, W. (1962). *J. Am. chem. Soc.* **84**, 1919–22.

Rahe, J. E. (1973). *Can. J. Bot.* **51**, 2423–30.

Rosenbaum, J. and Sando, C. E. (1920). *Am. J. Bot.* **7**, 78–82.

Royle, D. J. and Thomas, G. G. (1971a). *Physiol. Pl. Path.* **1**, 329–43.

Royle, D. J. and Thomas, G. G. (1971b). *Physiol. Pl. Path.* **1**, 345–9.

Sargent, J. A., Tommerup, I. C. and Ingram, D. S. (1973). *Physiol. Pl. Path.* **3**, 231–9.

Schramm, R. J. and Wolf, E. T. (1954). *J. Elisha Mitchell scient. Soc.* **70**, 255–61.

Sempio, C. (1950). *Phytopathology* **40**, 799–819.

Stakman, E. C. (1915). *J. agric. Res.* **4**, 193–9.

Struckmeyer, B. E., Kuntz, J. E. and Riker, A. J. (1958). *Phytopathology* **48**, 556–61.

Suchorukov, K. T. (1957). The physiology of immunity of some agricultural plants. In *Plant Protection Conference.* Butterworth, London.

Talboys, P. W. (1958). *Trans. Br. mycol. Soc.* **40**, 415–27.

Tisdale, W. H. (1917). *J. agric. Res.* **11**, 573–605.

Weinhold, A. R. and English, H. (1964). *Phytopathology* **54**, 1409–14.

Williams, P. H., Aist, J. R. and Bhattacharya, P. K. (1973). Host—parasite relations in cabbage clubroot. In *Fungal Pathogenicity and the Plant's Response* (R. J. W. Byrde, and C. V. Cutting, eds). Academic Press, London.

Yirgou, D. and Caldwell, R. M. (1963). *Science, N.Y.* **141**, 272–3.

FURTHER READING

Byrde, R. J. W. and Cutting, C. V. (eds) (1973). *Fungal Pathogenicity and the Plant's Response.* Academic Press, London.

Deverall, B. J. (1977). *Defence Mechanisms of Plants.* Cambridge University Press, London.

Friend, J. and Threlfall, D. R. (eds) (1976). *Biochemical Aspects of Plant Parasite Relationships.* Academic Press, London.

Harbone, J. B. (ed.) (1964). *Biochemistry of Phenolic Compounds.* Academic Press, London.

Heitefuss, R. and Williams, P. H. (eds) (1976). *Physiological Plant Pathology.* Springer-Verlag, Berlin.

Mirocha, C. J. and Uritani, I. (eds) (1967). *The Dynamic Role of Molecular Constituents in Plant—Parasite Interaction.* American Phytopathological Society, St. Paul, Minn.

Wheeler, H. (1975). *Plant Pathogenesis.* Springer-Verlag, Berlin.

Wood, R. K. S., Ballio, A. and Graniti, A. (eds) (1972). *Phytotoxins in Plant Diseases.* Academic Press, London.

Rubin, B. A. and Artsikhovskaya, Ye. V. (1969). *Biochemistry and Physiology of Plant Immunity.* Pergammon Press, London.

3
Epidemic Development and the Measurement of Disease Levels and Crop Losses

Epidemiology has been the subject of much recent experimentation and thought by pathologists. Basically, this is an attempt to quantify in scientific terms the reasons why epidemics develop in particular ways and to differentiate between different forms of epidemic. From this work has developed a set of equations describing disease incidence and relating this to the likely success of control techniques, especially the use of various forms of host resistance. The topic has evolved a mathematical basis, and hence prediction of epidemics has changed from an art to a science. In order to control plant pathogens by host resistance, by husbandry methods or by chemicals, it is essential to understand that host—parasite interactions differ in the manner of their development and their interrelation with the environmental conditions. Techniques of disease measurement and prediction need to become objective so that they may be applied on the widest possible basis. Hence disease assessment keys need to be internationally standardised, allowing uniform and unbiased evaluation of disease amount. Epidemiological studies now permit advance calculation of the likely life expectancy of novel forms of host resistance in relation to the capacity of the pathogen population to develop compatible virulences at high frequency levels. Such work is now becoming integrated with studies of population genetics of host and pathogen. Notice is also being taken of the need to quantify losses due to pathogens. This means that eventually it should be possible to quantify what pathogens cost in terms of lost production and weigh this against the costs of developing control measures and the likely efficacy of these controls. Such data is of major significance in the ordering of research and development priorities.

3.1 THEORY OF EPIDEMICS

Whenever a host—parasite complex is studied, whether it be under controlled conditions or in the field, assessments of disease severity are likely to be made at several points over a period of time. Essentially, this forms an analysis of the spread of a pathogen within a plant population or of disease symptoms on individual plants. From the information obtained, the rate (r) of spread can be calculated. If on day 0 no disease is seen, on day 1 50 per cent of the plants are affected, and on day 2 100 per cent are diseased, then the rate of spread is 50 per cent per day: in other words

$$r = 50 \text{ per cent per day}$$

or, less clumsily,

$$r = 0.5 \text{ per day.}$$

If information like this were illustrated graphically, a straight line would be obtained (figure 3.1).

An infection rate of $r = 0.5$ is extremely high and would indicate that the pathogen was very aggressive, the host cultivar extremely susceptible and the environment very favourable to growth of the pathogen. Generally the rate will be less than this, producing a curve rather than a straight line. This has been compared by van der Plank (1963) to the increase in money under different interest systems and can be illustrated by three well-known systems.

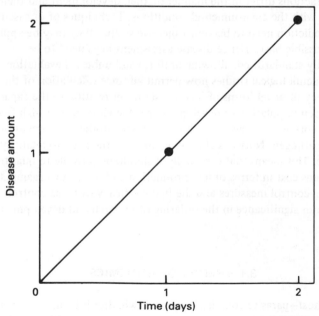

Figure 3.1   Diagrammatic illustration of rate of increase of disease.

(1) *Simple interest*   In financial terms the interest is paid solely on the original sum of money (principal). Thus, if £100 is invested at 20 per cent, at the end of the first year principal plus interest totals £120, at the end of the second year a further £20 interest is accumulated making a total of £140, but no interest is paid on the extra £20 invested between year 1 and year 2.

(2) *Discontinuous compound interest*   With this system the reinvested interest earns further interest, so that, from the example in (1), at the end of year 1 £120 would still be accumulated; but at the end of year 2 interest would amount to £20 on the initial principal plus £4 interest on the reinvested interest between year 1 and year 2, making a total of £144. In the simplest terms, the interest as it is paid becomes incorporated into the principal.

(3) *Continuous compound interest*   This enables interest to be added and exert its earning power to gain further interest over periods of time smaller than a year. Many banks pay compound interest on deposit accounts at 6-monthly intervals, while credit card companies levy interest at monthly intervals, and in large financial transactions interest is levied on a daily basis.

These systems are illustrated in figure 3.2.

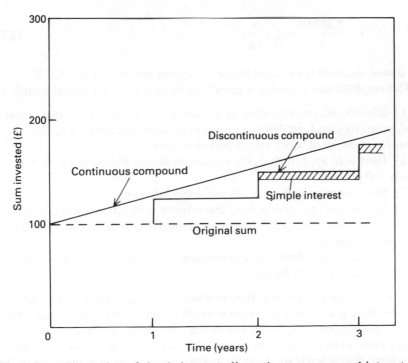

Figure 3.2   Illustration of simple interest, discontinuous compound interest and continuous compound interest rates (shaded area is the margin between simple and discontinuous compound interest).

It is continuous compound interest which is of most importance in relation to the study of disease and which has been most often analogised to the proliferation of pathogen populations. The factor by which the original principal increases and is added to is given the symbol 'e'. An equation can be obtained to give the total level of disease at any point in time:

$$x = x_0 e^{rt} \tag{3.1}$$

where x is the total disease level, x_0 is the original disease level, e is the factor by which the disease level increases, r is the rate of disease increase, t is the time. The rate of increase is logarithmic, meaning that the rate of increase of disease from any initial disease level is proportional to that disease level. A logarithmic expression may be derived from equation (3.1),

$$\log_e x = \log_e x_0 + rt \tag{3.2}$$

to obtain log $_e$, which is called a natural logarithm. The natural logarithm is equal to the common logarithm multiplied by 2.302 59.

Rearranging equation (3.2) to find r, we obtain

$$r = \frac{2.302\ 59}{t} \log_{10} \frac{x}{x_0}. \tag{3.3}$$

For disease studies it is sufficient to use the approximation $2.3 \cong 2.302\ 59$.

This simplification of pathogen spread can be challenged on several fronts:

(1) Infection occurs intermittently and not continuously, thus a spore must grow, penetrate a host, establish an infection site and then produce further spores to spread, all of which takes a period of time.

(2) There is an upper limit to the amount of disease which can develop, namely 100 per cent.

(3) Newly infected tissue is not immediately infectious.

(4) Diseases tend to occur in foci, that is heavy concentrations of diseased plants amongst less severely infected or uninfected ones. Within a focus, spread is less than logarithmic.

(5) Not all diseases develop in a continuous compound manner; some may be termed simple interest diseases.

For the general purposes of the study of disease epidemiology, however, the equations hold good. There is one point which should be clarified; money interest can increase without limit, disease can increase only so far as there is still healthy tissue to be colonised. In most disease studies the importance centres on times when disease levels are at low or moderate intensities. It is the study of the conditions conducive to slight to moderate infections which is essential in order to evaluate new forms of resistance or other types of control. Once a disease is rampant there is very little that can be done except to let it 'burn out'. (This policy has been adopted with the epidemic caused by *Ceratocystis ulmi* (Dutch elm disease) in the UK.) Consequently, time course studies of infection generally deal with the establishment of periods when diseases are initiated and begin to cause detectable yield losses. When disease is far advanced its effects can be judged by simple inspection as complete crop failure. Thus r can now be termed the apparent infection rate and it is usually given the subscript 'l' to denote logarithmic increase. To study the course of infection in a crop the equation used is

$$r_1 = \frac{2.3}{t_2 - t_1} \log_{10} \frac{x_2}{x_1}, \tag{3.4}$$

where x_1 and x_2 are the proportions (for example percentage leaf area infected) of disease at dates t_1 and t_2. To allow for the loss of healthy tissue as the infection increases, equation (3.4) can be rewritten as

$$r = \frac{2.3}{t_2 - t_1} \log_{10} \frac{x_2 (1 - x_1)}{x_1 (1 - x_2)}. \tag{3.5}$$

or, more conveniently,

$$r = \frac{2.3}{t_2 - t_1} \left(\log_{10} \frac{x_2}{1 - x_2} - \log_{10} \frac{x_1}{1 - x_1} \right). \tag{3.6}$$

3.1.1 Displaying data

If the limited definition of an epidemic as being an increase in disease against time is accepted, one of the parameters in displaying data will always be time. Data can be displayed simply as a table with time recorded either vertically or horizontally; but tables are often complex and difficult to digest. An alternative is to use a graphical display with the axes as percentage disease amount against time on an arithmetic scale (figure 3.3). Usually this gives a sigmoid curve showing the log phase (a) when the pathogen is becoming established, the exponential phase (b) when the disease increases rapidly, and finally a plateau (c) where no new host tissue is available for colonisation and the pathogen goes into a quiescent or a sexually reproductive state.

To record a wider range of data other techniques can be employed, such as use of probits, probability paper, logarithms and logits.

Depending on the type of disease, either $\log [x/(1 - x)]$ or $\log [1/(1 - x)]$ are recorded against time.

Compound interest diseases which increase logarithmically against time, for

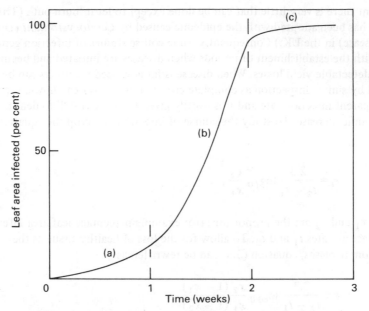

Figure 3.3   Diagrammatic illustration of a sigmoid curve of disease
development. (a), (b) and (c) are defined in the text.

example foliar diseases such as powdery mildew caused by *Erysiphe* spp., are
plotted as log $[x/(1-x)]$. This indicates that the disease multiplies through
several successive generations in the course of an epidemic. Simple interest
diseases which do not multiply at this rate are plotted as log $[1/(1-x)]$
against time. Initial inoculum remains constant, more plants become infected
only because they contact the source of infection rather than the infection
spreading to them. An example would be the infection of glasshouse tomatoes
by the soil-borne pathogen *Verticillium albo-atrum* from a point source. More
plants become infected as the season advances because the roots grow into the
infected zone of soil.

    In both equations the correction factor $(1-x)$ is used to stop points being
crowded together on the curve. Its use implies that conditions remain uniform
throughout the course of the experiment. In practice this is unlikely to happen.
Under these conditions the correction factor will under-correct, particularly
where the proportion of disease is high.

3.2 PREDICTION

Attempts may be made to forecast disease epidemics using data on environmental
conditions. Such data come from meteorological observations which, when

correlated with the known conditions under which pathogens are at an advantage, can be used to warn growers of the possibility of an epidemic. Decisions can then be made as to whether or not chemical control measures are required and the optimal dates on which to apply them.

For forecasting to be of practical value, four basic requirements need to be fulfilled:

(1) The disease causes economically significant damage in terms of yield quantity or quality in the area concerned.

(2) There is seasonal variation in the impact of the disease, that is time of onset, speed of build-up and ultimate level. Also an appreciable part of this variation can be attributed to environmental factors acting directly or indirectly.

(3) Control measures, whether curative or preventative, are available at an economic cost.

(4) Information is available from field and laboratory investigations on the nature of the weather dependence of the disease.

The course of a plant disease may be considered as the interplay of three factors arranged in a triangle (figure 3.4). Environment, in terms of forecasting or prediction, is the microclimate in which the pathogen develops and the host is attacked. For the triangle to be completely symmetrical would demand that the host and pathogen each influence the environment to equivalent degrees — this is an unlikely event.

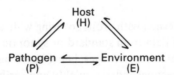

Figure 3.4   Hypothetical triangle of host, pathogen and environment interaction.

Aspects of host, pathogen and environment likely to be important in this relationship are as follows:

(1)   *Host*
(a) The level of resistance to the particular pathogen: this can vary with the age of the host; juvenile foliage may be more susceptible than the adult and vice versa.
(b) Density and distribution of the crop: those grown on limited acreages and in scattered locations are less likely to be infected than large areas of monoculture.
(c) The physiological condition of the host: lush soft growth encouraged by excessive nitrogen fertilisation may be more easily penetrated than tissues with a more balanced nutrition.

(2)   *Pathogen*
(a) The initial level of inoculum: often this is an unknown factor and most warning systems presuppose that infections begin from the same base level each season.
(b) Conditions favourable and adverse to the growth of the pathogen: warning systems generally take into account only those conditions favourable to the pathogen; recent work with *Phytophthora* spp. on lima bean shows that it is equally important to consider conditions which prevent successful infection.
(c) Competition with other micro-organisms: the environmental conditions most conducive to an epidemic are likely to be those which give a competitive advantage to the pathogen rather than those which give optimal growth in sterile cultures.
(3)   *Environment*   Three types of climate need to be considered:
(a) that within the crop,
(b) the local climate,
(c) general regional macroclimate.

Differences between (3)(a) and (3)(b) depend on the canopy density and the level of soil moisture. Calm sunny days give rise to the biggest differences while cloudy wet ones minimise them. The latter, incidentally, are the periods most favourable to many fungal pathogens. Gross variations between (3)(b) and (3)(c) are likely to be due to factors such as elevation and proximity to large water masses. Under stable weather conditions variations are small but very large in unstable conditions.

For forecasting concerned with crops covering wide areas there is no real alternative to the use of data from standard or synoptic weather observations. These have very considerable advantages, being based on large volumes of data collected by trained personnel and are quickly and easily available. As the weather satellite system is expanded, together with attendant computerisation of data handling, the reliability of such data increases many-fold.

3.2.1 Forecasting models

The original systems of forecasting were derived from direct comparison of disease incidence and meteorological data collected over a number of seasons. For example, the Beaumont and Staniland (1933) system for forecasting the incidence of *Phytophthora infestans* (potato blight) was based on the following events:

(1) dew either at night or in the morning;
(2) minimum temperature not below 10 °C;
(3) sunshine of less than 5 h;
(4) rainfall of at least 0.2 mm;

(5) relative humidity at 15.00 of not less than 75 per cent;

(6) if warm dry weather succeeded such a day, no blight outbreak would follow.

This system worked well for England, especially for the South-West (Devon and Cornwall). In the Netherlands, van Everdingen (1926) produced a parallel system:

(1) night temperature below the dew point for a least 4 h;

(2) minimum temperature above 10 °C;

(3) minimum degree of cloudiness on the following day of 0.8 or above;

(4) rainfall at least 0.1 mm in the next 24 h.

In Ireland the Beaumont system produced likely periods for blight incidence too frequently to provide a satisfactory warning system and was modified by Bourke (1955) to

(1) 12 h relative humidity of not less than 90 per cent

(2) followed by 4 h when the potato foliage remained wet, and

(3) minimum temperature of 10 °C.

Similar systems were developed for *Venturia inaequalis* (apple scab) and *Plasmopara viticola* (vine downy mildew) in Europe. Few attempts have been made to predict disease outbreaks for pathogens other than those which are air-borne and invade foliage. A correlation was, however, obtained by Grainger (1969) between the amount of rainfall in September and the severity of *Plasmodiophora brassicae* (clubroot) in turnip crops grown in western Scotland. A warning system has also been devised to combat virus yellows in sugar beet based on environmental factors favourable to the spread of the aphid vectors.

More recent modelling has utilised data obtained under controlled conditions on the growth of pathogens. Models usually require information on moisture, air humidity and air temperature. The latter, with some exceptions, plays a minor role. Moisture, usually as rainfall totalled over a period of days, and rainfall duration give an indication of the period over which free moisture covers the plant. In the case of splash-transmitted diseases, rainfall intensity is important. The empirical models above indicate that humidity is of over-riding importance due to its influence on pathogen life cycles. At its most simple, relative humidity parameters specify that the air moisture should not drop below a particular percentage. This is generally around 90 per cent.

Simple models often neglect some factors which operate in the development of an epidemic. Thus total rainfall figures can obscure the fact that all the rain fell as a single heavy shower over a short period, whereas a similar quantity of rain occurring as slow steady drizzle is more likely to encourage certain pathogens. Dew can have an important effect in keeping foliage moisture films intact, but is often not part of simple models. Temperature is often treated as maximum and minimum values above and below which the pathogen is inoperative; however, the most usual response to temperature is asymmetric growth about an optimal figure. A method of overcoming this is to assign greater weight to temperature units close to the optimum.

Early forecasters identified single periods of weather which related to the seasonal appearance of plant diseases. This obscured the fact that disease build-up is a gradual process often resulting in premature forecasts of widespread epidemics. The concept of 'zero date' reduced this risk by erecting a barrier preventing forecasts of disease in periods when for physiological or husbandry reasons no disease was likely to develop. Prediction now tries to relate a sequence of weather events to epidemic development, identifying recurrent meteorological situations from weather charts.

Potato blight forecasts in western Europe rely heavily on studies of the movement of maritime tropical air from the Gulf Stream. Warm moist air masses originating in the tropical Atlantic Ocean which cool as they approach Europe give ideal conditions of temperature, air humidity and rainfall for several Phycomycete pathogens. Similarly, in the United States, basidiospore production and the infection of pines with fusiform rust is favoured when a surface high pressure system is centred off the south-eastern coast of the USA, causing persistent broad currents of maritime tropical air to move towards the Gulf states. Prevalence and persistence of the same air mass has been related to outbreaks of *Phytophthora* spp. (downy mildew) on lima bean in New Jersey. This type of forecasting does not require the precise day-to-day timing of expected events, thereby avoiding some of the pitfalls of earlier forecasting.

One of the most sophisticated forecasting systems is the West German 'Phytoprog' for potato blight. This takes into account four different stages in the life cycle of the fungus related to different types of weather:

(1) sporulation, requiring moist conditions over 10 h;
(2) germination and infection, requiring moist conditions over 4 h;
(3) mycelial growth, depending on temperature but independent of moisture;
(4) suppression of disease extension in dry periods.

Moist hours are defined as those during which either the relative humidity is at least 90 per cent or measurable precipitation occurs. Dry periods are those with relative humidities below 70 per cent. Weather sequences are weighted by multiplying with parameters in accordance with air temperature. Current total weather ratings are reckoned each week by adding weekly values starting from a known average date for the emergence of early potato crops. The date on which the total weather rating reaches 150 is called the first critical date before which no appreciable disease is to be expected. First symptoms are generally seen 10–40 days after the first critical date, and this is used to alert growers to keep crops under scrutiny for primary symptoms. The date on which total weather ratings reach 270 is the second critical date and a call is issued for immediate control measures since disease lesions will be found 15 days before or after the date on which this rating is reached.

3.3 CYCLES OF DISEASE

Outbreaks of many diseases occur on a cyclic basis — some years are 'bad disease' years, with considerable crop devastation, while others are 'good disease' years when a pathogen is virtually absent. This, as indicated in section 3.2, can be due to the effects of environment: some weather conditions are more conducive than others to outbreaks of disease. But levels of host resistance can also influence the frequency of epidemics. This has been chiefly demonstrated for air-borne foliar pathogens of cereal crops and given the title 'boom and bust cycle' (Priestley, 1978) (figure 3.5). Studies have been chiefly reported for *Puccinia striiformis* (yellow rust) on winter wheat. The theory supposes that as the area devoted to a new cultivar possessing a distinctive combination of resistance genes increases, so the pathogen population will react by an increase in virulences capable of attacking the new resistance combination. Initially the new cultivar exhibits markedly superior resistance to that possessed by existing cultivars. This stimulates growers to use it, which in turn provides an ever increasing crop area for the multiplication of pathogen populations containing compatible virulences until the host resistance apparently collapses, with attendant considerable yield losses. The area of the cultivar then declines rapidly and the virulences capable of attacking it fall to low frequency in the pathogen population. Such spectacular increases and declines in crop area have occurred in the UK with the wheat cultivars Rothwell Perdix, Maris Beacon and Maris Templar.

An equivalent horticultural example of this phenomenon has been seen in lettuce cultivars grown in the Westland region of Holland and attacked by *Bremia lactucae* (lettuce downy mildew). Here, since 1970, the Dutch authorities have

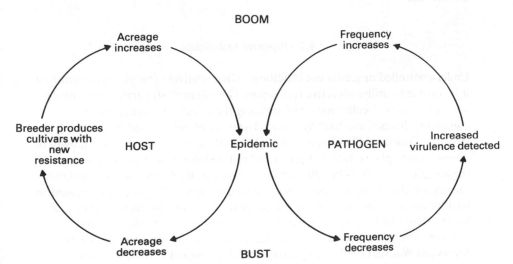

Figure 3.5   'Boom and bust cycle' of host resistance and pathogen virulence. (Reproduced by permission of Dr R. Priestley.)

identified an increasing number of *B. lactucae* races (labelled NL1–NL7). The response by plant breeders has been to produce a series of lettuce cultivars incorporating resistance to each new race (virulence combination) as it arose. Unfortunately the basic genetic material from which new resistant cultivars have been selected is extremely limited. In very short periods of time, often less than a year, new races of *B. lactucae* have segregated and multiplied which are compatible with the new resistant cultivar.

These rapid cycles appear to be associated with air-borne foliar pathogens, being characterised by very rapid spread and multiplication under favourable environmental conditions which presumably allow quicker recombination of virulences within the pathogen population. More detailed discussion of this topic is given in chapter 4, sections 4.1 and 4.3.

3.4 DISEASE ASSESSMENT

Crop diseases are monitored to establish

(1) which are the most significant pathogens,
(2) those cultivars most vulnerable to a specific disease,
(3) a body of data in order to predict the conditions under which epidemics are likely to develop and warning systems may be devised,
(4) alterations in pathogen virulence such that growers may be advised which cultivars are likely to remain resistant and breeding programmes initiated of modified to combat changed virulence spectrums in the pathogen population. population.

3.4.1 Objective techniques

Under controlled or glasshouse conditions when relatively few plants are involved it is feasible to utilise objective techniques. Growth analysis parameters provide one of the most effective means of assessing the effects of a pathogen or comparing diseased and healthy plants. The work of Selman and Pegg (1957) elegantly illustrated the effects of wilt (*Verticillium albo-atrum*) on the growth of young tomato plants. Infected plants had reduced dry weight and leaf area (figures 3.6 and 3.7) within 30 days of inoculation. By 60 days after inoculation the dry weight of infected plants was reduced by almost 70 per cent compared to healthy controls, and leaf area by 80 per cent. Infection also reduced (but to a lesser extent) the length and breath of leaves and stem height (figure 3.8).

Clear differences between healthy and diseased tissue were established by Myers and Watson (1969) using pyrolysis and gas–liquid chromatography. Large peaks occurred with oat leaves infected by Barley Yellow Dwarf Virus but not with healthy material even when at an advanced stage of senescence.

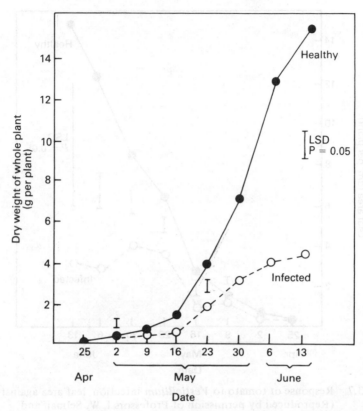

Figure 3.6   Response of tomato to *Verticillium* infection, dry weight against
time. (Reproduced by permission of Professors I. W. Selman and
G. F. Pegg.)

Similar results where obtained with wheat leaves separately infected with *Puccinia striiformis* (rust) and *Erysiphe graminis* (powdery mildew) when compared to controls. This technique offers a rapid means of assessing the distribution of fungal tissue in the host and measuring degrees of infection in the laboratory.

3.4.2 Subjective techniques

In field trials large numbers of plants and plots are involved, probably grown at several sites over a number of seasons. Simply from the logistic point of view, subjective techniques are the only ones likely to be used in the foreseeable future. One is likely to measure either disease incidence, that is the number of plants infected, or disease severity and amount when an estimate of the percentage area of the plant or crop infected by a pathogen is established. Visual assessment keys

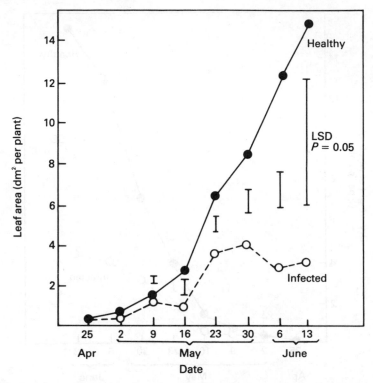

Figure 3.7   Response of tomato to *Verticillium* infection, leaf area against time. (Reproduced by permission of Professors I. W. Selman and G. F. Pegg.)

are used for the latter and these can be classified into three groups:

(1) those dealing with a plot or part of a crop, for example the assessment key for assessing *Sclerotinia trifoliorum* (clover rot) in red and white clover (Dixon, 1974*a*) (figure 3.9);

(2) those dealing with whole plants, for example the key for assessing the percentage basal area of lettuce plants infected with *Bremia lactucae* (downy mildew) (Dixon *et al.*, 1973) (figure 3.10);

(3) those dealing with individual leaves or other organs.

In general, keys in group (3) are found to be the most satisfactory keys since very precise instructions can be given for their use to different personnel. It is generally accepted that these keys will be constructed on a standard seven point model with illustrations of five of these points, namely 0, 5, 10, 25, 50, 75 and 100 percentage area infection. This is illustrated by the key for *Erysiphe cruciferarum* (powdery mildew) on Brussels sprout leaves (Dixon, 1974*b*) (figure 3.11).

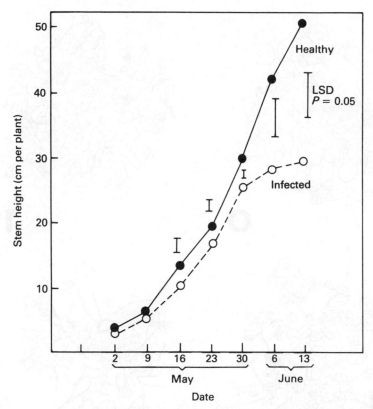

Figure 3.8   Response of tomato to *Verticillium* infection, stem height against time. (Reproduced by permission of Professors I. W. Selman and G. F. Pegg.)

3.4.3 Preparation of assessment keys

Direct and indirect means of measuring areas of disease on plant organs have been developed. Direct methods involve the use of photoelectric scanner techniques whereby recordings are made of areas of infected and uninfected tissue. Indirect means necessitate the establishment of a measured image on which is overlaid the appropriate infected area; this is done by one of the three following methods:

(1) drawing on squared paper, the areas of which can be determined by counting the numbers of squares or by use of a wheel planimeter;

(2) photographic processes using diazo paper which, when exposed to strong light and then treated chemically, will reproduce the image of a leaf the area of which can be established as in (1);

(3) air flow planimetry, whereby the area of an organ is established by

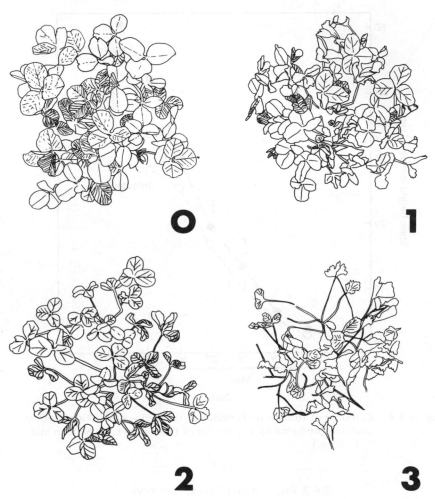

Figure 3.9   Disease assessment key for clover rot caused by *Sclerotinia trifoliorum*, an arbitary key for assessing areas of experimental plots infected by this pathogen. (From Dixon (1974a). Reproduced by permission of National Institute of Agricultural Botany, Cambridge.)

causing it to impede the air flow into a vessel and measuring the impedance manometrically.

3.4.4 Growth stage keys

All assessments of disease levels should take account of the growth stage of the host at which the assessments are made. Such keys describe the various phases

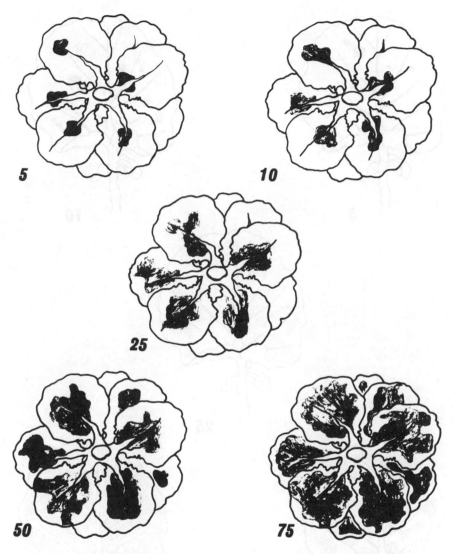

Figure 3.10   Disease assessment key for lettuce downy mildew caused by
Bremia lactucae, a key for assessing the percentage infected area
of the underside of individual plants. (From Dixon *et al.* (1973).
Reproduced by permission of National Institute of Agricultural
Botany, Cambridge.)

through which a crop passes from emergence to maturity. Their construction and
use is relatively straightforward for determinate annual crops such as cereals, and
the most often cited growth stage key applies to these (Feekes, 1941). Vegetable
crops, however, are often indeterminate and biennial, making the construction of

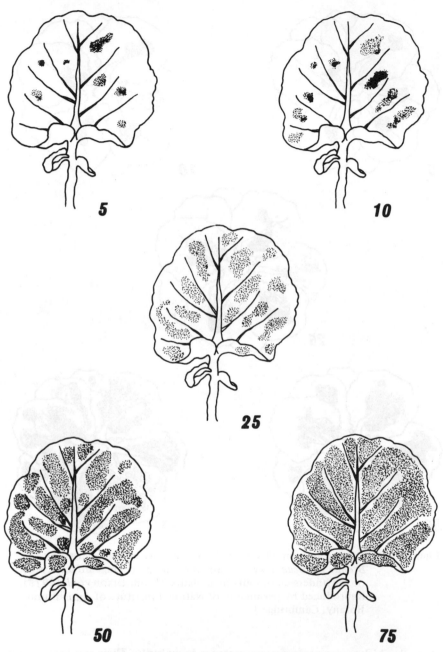

Figure 3.11   Disease assessment key for sprout powdery mildew caused by
Erysiphe cruciferarum, a key for assessing the percentage infected
area of single leaves. (From Dixon (1974*b*). Reproduced by
permission of National Institute of Agricultural Botany, Cambridge.)

a key more arbitary, for example that for peas:

Growth stage	Description
1	First leaf present
2	Vegetative stage
	2.1 = 2nd true leaf
	2.2 = 3rd true leaf
	2.3 = 4th true leaf
	$2.n$ = nth true leaf
3	Bud development
4	Open flower stage
5	Pod emergence
6	Flat pod development
7	Harvest stage

T. Webster and J. D. C. Bowring, personal communication.

Harvest stage with peas is especially difficult to define since harvesting date will depend on the use to which the crop is put, that is young immature seeds for quick freezing, a somewhat more mature stage for canning, or totally mature and dried for seed or animal feed.

3.5 CROP LOSS

In addition to the objectives of disease assessment outlined in section 3.4, a prime consideration will be to establish the amount of crop loss associated with particular levels of infection by a pathogen. This had been done with considerable precision with some cereal crops when Large and Doling (1962) established that the square root of the percentage leaf area infected with powdery mildew due to *Erysiphe graminis* is related to the loss in grain yield in tonnes per hectare. Vegetable crops, however, have a combination of yield characters which make such direct estimations difficult.

3.5.1 High value

Land areas devoted to individual vegetable crops are relatively small and often widely dispersed around the country. This tends to confound the agricultural yardstick of area statistics for assessing the importance of crops. The cash value of individual plants, however, is extremely high; thus with glasshouse tomatoes a 1 per cent reduction in plants due to disease with plants grown at 25 000 plants/ha and each plant worth £5.00 would represent a loss of £1250/ha to the grower.

For some crops such *pro rata* calculations may not operate. A 10 per cent infection by *Erysiphe cruciferarum* (powdery mildew) of bud area of Brussels sprouts which are valued at £7500/ha, could mean the whole crop is rejected for processing, meaning total crop failure, or the produce is downgraded in the open market.

3.5.2 Quality

Blemishes can diminish the value of a crop by affecting its visual acceptability. These may even be the result of resistance reactions, for example ghost spotting of tomatoes caused by single spores of *Botrytis cinerea* (grey mould) germinating on the fruit surface but being unable to penetrate and establish a lesion. This has no effect on the eating quality of the fruit but makes it unacceptable to the supermarket buyer because of loss of visual quality. Blemished material has to be removed manually in the processing of vegetables, which is an expensive operation. Processing companies freely admit that with green beans they would be prepared to accept a reduction in yield in exchange for resistance to *B. cinerea.*

3.5.3 Intensity and continuity of production

This heading covers intensity of time scale whereby several crops are grown in one season on the same land. There are very precise requirements for the crops to mature on specific dates. Pathogens can wreck this type of scheduling, for example *Peronospora viciae* (downy mildew) causes the pea crop to ripen unevenly, making harvesting difficult. This usually results in the whole crop being rejected for freezing because it gets out of synchrony with the previously agreed production schedule and is fit only for use as seed or dried peas.

3.5.4 Forms of vegetable crop loss

There are various forms which crop loss may take with vegetable crops.

(a) Direct yield loss
This is a measurable reduction in tonnes per hectare or crates per hectare and can be illustrated by the survey results (table 3.1) on the advantage of control of *Plasmodiophora brassicae* (clubroot) in cauliflowers.

(b) Rejection
Either the whole crop may be rejected or perhaps only part of it, and this can be influenced by a range of market factors. Buyers for the supermarket chains may reject lettuces with only single lesions of *Bremia lactucae* (downy mildew) in

Table 3.1   Advantage of clubroot control in cauliflowers

---

1. Average net return per hectare in the absence of clubroot
   (1635 crates at 40p) = £654.00

2. Average net return per hectare if clubroot is present
   and not controlled (832 crates at 40p) = £332.95

3. Average net return per hectare if clubroot is present
   and controlled (cost of control = £46.48/ha)
   (1180 crates at 40p) = £472.00

Source: D. J. Harrison (1973), unpublished data. Agricultural Development and Advisory Service, Lincolnshire, UK.

glut periods, but in times of scarcity 5 per cent leaf area infection could be accepted. Factors which influence this decion will be: time of year, weather (is there a demand for salads?) and the availability of alternatives such as cress or celery.

(c) Change of grade
Otherwise sound produce can be downgraded by the Market Inspectorate because it has been blemished by a pathogen. Disease criteria form part of Common Market grading schemes for carrots, cucumbers, sprouts and tomatoes.

(d) Shifts in harvest period
Abortion of early trusses of tomato fruit caused by infection with Tomato Mosaic Virus leads to later yields when prices are falling.

(e) Alteration of crop rotation
Entry of P. brassicae (clubroot) on land used for intensive brassica production means that areas of a holding have to be isolated to prevent further spread of the pathogen. This complicates the planning of rotations and reduces the value of the holding for brassica vegetable production.

REFERENCES

Beaumont, A. and Staniland, L. N. (1933). A. Rep. Seale Hayne agric. College 1932

Bourke, P. M. A. (1955). The Forecasting from Weather Data of Potato Blight

and Other Plant Diseases and Pests, Technical Note No. 10. World
Meteorological Organisation, 42, 3—48.

Bourke, P. M. A. (1970). A. Rev. Phytopath. 8, 345—70.

Dixon, G. R. (1974a) Euphytica 23, 671—9.

Dixon, G. R. (1974b). Pl. Path. 25, 105—9.

Dixon, G. R., Tonkin, M. H. and Doodson, J. K. (1973). Ann. appl. Biol. 74,
307—13.

van Everdingen, E. (1926). Tijdschr. PlZiekt. 32, 129—39.

Feekes, W. (1941). Vers XVII tech. Tarive Commissie, Groningen, 560—1.

Grainger, J. (1969). The Reduction of Crop Disease Losses in West Scotland,
Research Bulletin No. 43. West of Scotland Agricultural College, Ayr.

Large, E. C. and Doling, D. A. (1962). Pl. Path. 11, 47—57.

Myers, A. and Watson, L. (1969). Nature, Lond. 223, 964—5.

van der Plank, J. E. (1963). Plant Diseases: Epidemics and Control. Academic
Press, London.

Priestley, R. H. (1978). Detection of increased virulence in populations of wheat
yellow rust. In Plant Disease Epidemiology (P. R. Scott and A. Bainbridge,
eds). Blackwell Scientific Publications, Oxford.

Selman, I. W. and Pegg, G. F. (1957). Ann. appl. Biol. 45, 674—81.

FURTHER READING

Anon. (1971). Crop Loss Assessment Methods: Food and Agriculture Organisation
Manual on the Evaluation and Prevention of Losses by Pests, Disease and
Weeds (L. Chiarappa, ed.). Commonwealth Agricultural Bureau, Farnham Royal.

Anon. (1976). Manual of Plant Growth Stages and Disease Assessment Keys.
Ministry of Agriculture, Fisheries and Food, London.

Kranz, J. (ed.) (1974). Epidemics of Plant Diseases: Mathematical Analysis and
Modelling. Springer-Verlag, Berlin.

Large, E. C. (1952). Pl. Path. 1, 109—17.

Large, E. C. (1955). Ann. appl. Biol., 42, 344—54.

van der Plank, J. E. (1968). Disease Resistance in Plants. Academic Press, London.

van der Plank, J. E. (1975). Principles of Plant Infection. Academic Press, London.

Scott, P. R. and Bainbridge, A. (1978). Plant Disease Epidemiology. Blackwell
Scientific Publications, Oxford.

4
Pathogen Control

The most convenient method of controlling plant pathogens is through the use
of resistant cultivars. Only when this avenue is absent or unsatisfactory are other
techniques required. Husbandry methods are those most likely to be under the
control of the grower and often these are practised in advance of a full
scientific explanation for their effectiveness. Indeed the higher the standard of
crop husbandry the lower is the likelihood that disease will be a problem in the
crop. To rely solely on husbandry methods may, however, prevent the grower
from maximising yield by, for example, shortening the growing season or
requiring very extended rotations. Chemical control should be sought only
when disease is apparent or occurs with such seasonal regularity that prior
application of fungicidal materials may be used in the knowledge that without
them there would be considerable crop losses.

4.1 RESISTANCE

4.1.1 Transmission of resistance

It is not the intention of this work to provide an explanation of the genetics of
either the host or the parasite; this has been done far more effectively elsewhere
(*see* Further Reading at the end of this chapter). As with other attributes, disease
resistance is mainly inherited according to Mendel's laws. This was first
demonstrated by Biffen (1905, 1912), who showed that the resistance of the
wheat cultivar Rivet to *Puccinia striiformis* (yellow rust) was determined by
a single recessive gene. Subsequently, this has been realised to be an atypical
situation since where resistance is controlled by one or a few genes whose affects
are readily demonstrable they are usually dominant. This has been termed major
gene or oligogenic resistance. Such resistance is often highly specific against a
portion of the total pathogen population and operative at both the seedling and
mature plant stages.

4.1.2 Expression of Resistance

Linking resistance genes and their expression in physiological or biochemical
terms takes a long time. It has been termed 'genetic dissection' by Levine (1968)

and has been used in a preliminary way to identify the infection processes
of *Erysiphe graminis* (powdery mildew) in relation to resistance expressed by
wheat and barley (Ellingboe, 1972). No host genes were found which blocked
spore germination, appressorial maturation or the formation of infection pegs.
In several different incompatible reactions, however, the percentage of infection
pegs which produced rudimentary haustoria was reduced. Also, with some
interactions, genetic blocks were identified at the later stages of the infection
process whereby haustorial maturation and the formation of secondary hyphae
were prevented.

In earlier literature an explanation for the resistance of red- or yellow-skinned
onions to *Colletotrichum circinans* (smudge) stands out as almost achieving a
direct correlation between the biochemical attributes of the host and resistance
to a pathogen. Pigmentation in the outer scale of the onion is developed under
the influence of three genes each having two alleles. The dominant allele *C* is
essential if pigmentation is to develop while the two alleles *R* and *r* at the
second locus interact with the incompletely dominant inhibitor allele *I* present
at the third locus to produce red, pink, yellow or cream-coloured outer scales.
The range of phenotypes is as follows:

Genotype	Colour of outer scales	Resistance to *C. circinans*
cc (all)	White	Susceptible
II (all)	White	Susceptible
RR or *Rr*, *CC* or *Cc, ii*	Red	Highly resistant
rr, CC or *Cc, ii*	Yellow	Highly resistant
RR or *Rr, CC* or *Cc, Ii*	Pink	Fairly resistant
rr, CC or *Cc, Ii*	Cream	Fairly resistant

Inheritance of colour in the outer scales is apparently identical with the
inheritance of resistance to *C. circinans*. It has been concluded, therefore, that
one genetic system governs both phenotypic expressions and that the chemical
basis of resistance is related to the substances involved in pigment synthesis. The
presence of two phenolic compounds, catechol and protocatechuic acid, in the
outer scales of pigmented onions and their toxicity to spores of *C. circinans* was
demonstrated by Angel *et al.* (1930) and Link and Walker (1933). Both
chemicals are water soluble and diffuse on the outer surface of moistened onion
scales, killing fungal spores before the infection process begins.

4.1.3 Gene-for-gene theory

This theory provides a basis for correlating major gene resistance in the host with virulence in the pathogen. It is especially useful in the consideration of air-borne foliar invading pathogens where many apparently unrelated races are segregated as a result of the use of monogenic resistance in a series of host cultivars. In general terms the theory can be stated as follows: *the ability of a pathogen to grow and produce disease symptoms on a host carrying major genes for resistance is determined by alleles governing virulence at corresponding loci in the pathogen.* Thus for each gene in the host capable of mutating to give resistance there exists a gene in the pathogen capable of mutating to overcome that resistance (Fincham and Day, 1965). The theory was originated by Flor (1955) as a menas of understanding the resistance relationship between flax cultivars (*Linum ultissimum*) and isolates of the rust fungus *Melampsora lini.* Genes for reaction to rust infection in the host were identified by the pathogenicity of specific races of the parasite and conversely genes for pathogenicity in the parasite were identified by the reaction of specific cultivars of the host. Cultivars with the same reaction to all races were considered to possess identical genes for rust reaction. Races having the same pathogenicity on a cultivar were considered to possess identical genes for pathogenicity on that cultivar.

There are four possible interactions among a pair of alleles governing resistance in a plant and a corresponding pair controlling virulence in the pathogen (Loegering and Powers, 1962). This may be illustrated by what is termed the quadratic check:

Plant genotypes

		R	r
Pathogen	A	Resistant	Susceptible
genotypes	a	Susceptible	Susceptible

(Note that capital and lower case letters differentiate alleles only and do not imply dominance or recessiveness.)

In the quadratic check it is assumed that the difference between a resistant and a susceptible reaction will be clearly defined since resistance is associated with the complete absence of symptoms or fungal reproductive structures. This situation can be satisfied to an extent for foliar pathogens in that lesion types may be arbitrarily classified as belonging to either a resistant or a susceptible category. For other types of host—parasite relationship, such as the vascular wilts, especially where the host is of an out-breeding type giving rise to a high level of innate variation in the host population, the line between resistance and susceptibility is far more difficult to establish. A great deal of effort has been put into the understanding of rust fungi, especially those infecting cereal crops. Gene-for-gene relationships have been suggested for the following vegetable crops:

	Host	Pathogen	Reference
Fungi	Tomato	*Fulvia fulvum*	Day (1956)
	Lettuce	*Bremia lactucae*	Crute and Johnson (1976)
Bacteria	Legumes	*Rhizobium* spp.	Nutman (1969)
Viruses	Tomato	Tobacco Mosaic Virus	Pelham (1966)
	Tomato	Spotted Wilt Virus	Day (1960)

Taking one example, the presence of up to 10 genes for resistance to *B. lactucae* (lettuce downy mildew) has been postulated by Crute and Johnson (1976). Although some subsequent modifications were required to this original scheme because at least two genes were shown to be a complementary pair of dominant genes (*dm 7/1* and *dm 7/2*) the theory allowed the identification of sources of disease resistance in lettuce progenitors and the systematic classification of pathogen isolates which were previously named in random and arbitrary manners (table 4.1).

Table 4.1 Sources of resistance to *Bremia lactucae* in lettuce breeding material.

Postulated resistance gene to *B. lactucae*	Source	Lettuce type
1	Blondine	No information of origin, spring butterhead
2	Meikoningen	Winter forcing butterhead 1902
3, 4	Gotte à forcer types	French, winter forcing
5	*L. serriola* PI 167150	Wild collection from Turkey
6	Grand Rapids	Oak Leaf
7	Romaine blonde lente à monter	French 'Romaine'
8	*L. serriola* PI 91532	Wild collection from USSR
9	Bourguignonne grosse blonde d'hiver	French winter forcing butterhead
10	Sucrine	Cos, 1880

After Crute and Johnson (1976).

4.1.4 Nomenclature of physiological races

Physiological races can by definition only be distinguished from each other by differential reactions on a range of host genotypes. These are usually commercial cultivars, although some workers have developed specialised groups of isogenic lines for this purpose. The latter have similar genotypes and differ solely in reaction to physiological races. Resulting from the use of commercial cultivars is usually a lengthening list of equivalent races numbered or lettered in an arbitrary sequence with no indication of any relationship between them:

Cultivar	Races			
	1	2	3	4
1	−	+	+	+
2	−	−	+	+
3	−	−	−	+
4	−	−	−	−

−, resistant; +, susceptible.

Extra cultivars are introduced to the list as new races develop. Examples of host—parasite combinations where this has happened are as follows:

(1) *Fusarium oxysporum* f. sp. *pisi* (pea wilt): up to 12 races.
(2) *Colletotrichum lindemuthianum* (anthracnose): races α–ι.
(3) *Plasmodiophora brassicae* (club root): 30+ races.
(4) *Bremia lactucae* (lettuce downy mildew): 15+ races.
(5) *Pseudomonas phaseolicola:* up to 5 races.

The differential series used often varies from one worker to another, making correlations difficult. Commercial cultivars go out of use rapidly, leading to problems with the extension of such lists after a few years.

   The first scheme to break away from arbitrarily assigned names or letters was that of Black *et al.* (1953) for *Phytophthora infestans* (potato blight). Postulated genes for resistance in the host were identified as *R1–R11* and physiological races numbered to indicate their virulence towards them. Race 0 was *avirulent* on all resistant cultivars whereas race 1, 2, 3, for example, was avirulent on any combination of genes *R1, R2* and *R3*. It is now customary to term the pathogen virulences as V1, V2, V3 and so on. A similar system was proposed for *Fulvia fulvum* (tomato leaf mould) by Day (1956). For such systems to be established, some knowledge of the numbers of host resistance genes is essential so that pathogen virulence factors may be correlated with them.

   Where such data are absent the binary notation system proposed by Habgood (1970) may be of value. Such a system has been employed internationally for

Plasmodiophora brassicae (clubroot) by Buczacki *et al.* (1975). Using an agreed list of host differentials, each assigned a unique binary number, formulae can be derived for the reaction of any *P. brassicae* population. This is achieved by the summation of the denary numbers (table 4.2) of those cultivars showing a susceptible reaction to a particular *P. brassicae* population. Since *P. brassicae* is

Table 4.2   European clubroot differential set (ECD): host species with their binary and denary values.

Differential number	Differential host (species classification according to genome analysis by U (1935))	Binary number series	Denary number series
	20.chromosome group (*Brassica campestris* L. *sensu lato*)		
01	ssp. *rapifera* line aaBBCC	2^0	1
02	ssp. *rapifera* line AAbbCC	2^1	2
03	ssp. *rapifera* line AABBcc	2^2	4
04	ssp. *rapifera* line AABBCC	2^3	8
05	ssp. *pekinensis* cv. Granaat	2^4	16
	38 chromosome group (*Brassica napus* L.)		
06	var. *napus* line Dc 101	2^0	1
07	var. *napus* line Dc 119	2^1	2
08	var. *napus* line Dc 128	2^2	4
09	var. *napus* line Dc 129	2^3	8
10	var. *napus* line Dc 130	2^4	16
	18 chromosome group (*Brassica oleracea* L.)		
11	var. *capitata* cv. Badger Shipper	2^0	1
12	var. *capitata* cv. Bindsachsener	2^1	2
13	var. *capitata* cv. Jersey Queen	2^2	4
14	var. *capitata* cv. Septa	2^3	8
15	var. *acephala* subvar. *lacinata* cv. Verheul	2^4	16

pathogenic to all *Brassica* species, but workers may be interested in only in individual species, the differentials are arranged in three groups: *B. campestris,* *B. napus* and *B. oleracea.* Thus all or only part of the differential series can be used, depending on the requirements of a particular worker.

4.1.5 Vertical resistance

Vertical resistance is generally equated with the gene-for-gene theory. It usually involves resistance mechanisms whose inheritance is governed by single genes, and consequently it is easy to manipulate in a breeding programme. For this reason it is often preferred to other forms of resistance which usually involve mechanisms whose inheritance is governed by polygenes and which are difficult to manipulate genetically. While vertical resistance can provide a complete control of disease, it is also liable to 'break down' when the pathogen population evolves segregants capable of overcoming the major gene resistance. The rate at which segregation occurs varies widely with different host—parasite combinations. Examples of cases where simply inherited resistance has been successful for periods greater than 10 years are shown in table 4.3. The use of vertical resistance was summarised into 14 points by Robinson (1971):

(1) Perennial crops and those difficult to breed cannot be replaced with sufficient speed for vertical resistance to be of value.

(2) Pathogen segregants with a new virulence combination spread only slowly if they are of the simple interest type but rapidly if of the compound interest type. Consequently, vertical resistance is more likely to be valuable against the former than the latter.

(3) Where a pathogen can produce a new virulence segregant quickly, this means it is highly mutable and vertical resistance should be avoided.

(4) Crops which are grown as extensive monocultures, are genetically uniform, or have large areas of the same cultivar exert a selection pressure on the pathogen which encourages segregation of new virulence combinations capable of attacking the crop.

(5) If stabilising pressure through the use of a 'strong' gene for vertical resistance can be exploited, such resistance is likely to be of greater value. The strength of resistance genes is measured against the rate of decay or disappearance of the equivalent virulence genes in the pathogen population (van der Plank, 1968). It is thought that with 'strong' resistance genes this rate of decay is faster than with 'weak' resistance genes. Stabilising pressure is the antithesis of selection pressure. Thus selection pressure from a particular form of host vertical resistance leads to an increase in the equivalent pathogen virulence. Withdrawal of a particular vertical resistance leads to a stabilising pressure on the pathogen population such that a specific virulence frequency may decrease possibly to extinction.

(6) If the pathogen is an obligate, at least two 'strong' genes are required to exploit stabilising pressure. This is because stabilisation can only occur in the parasitic phase of growth where the parasite is growing on a host which lacks the complementary resistance gene. It is postulated that to exploit stabilising pressure in this way cultivars with different vertical resistance combinations must be grown in controlled patterns and for this at least two 'strong' genes for vertical

Table 4.3 Host—parasite combinations where major gene resistance has lasted for more than 10 years (after Eenink, 1976).

Host—parasite	Genetics of resistance	Duration of resistance
Bean—*Colletotrichum lindemuthianum*	1 gene	~ 15 years
Cabbage—*Fusarium oxysporum*	1 gene	> 60 years
Cucumber—*Cladosporium cucumerinum*	1 gene	> 12 years
Cucumber—*Corynespora casiicola*	1 gene	> 15 years
Cucumber—Cucumber Mosaic Virus	3 genes	> 17 years
Lettuce—Lettuce Mosaic Virus	1 gene	> 10 years
Pea—*Fusarium oxysporum*	1 gene	> 15 years
Pea—Pea Early Browning Virus	1 gene	> 10 years
Spinach—*Peronospora spinaciae*	2 genes	~ 25 years
Spinach—Cucumber Mosaic Virus	1 gene	> 20 years

resistance must be known. If the pathogen is a facultative parasite, stabilising pressure can also occur during its saprophytic growth and from this Robinson (1971) infers that only one 'strong' gene is required.

(7) It is thought that using mixtures of cultivars within a single season will prevent the build-up and spread of new pathogen virulence combinations. This avenue of control is most likely to be effective against compound interest diseases.

(8) Where various combinations of host resistances are used in different seasons this is more likely to be effective against simple interest diseases.

(9) Where the pathogen is transmitted with propagating material, for example

the seed, vertical resistance is likely to have little value. It requires only a single infection focus in the crop to come from an infected seed or tuber for the disease to spread rapidly outwards, especially if the disease is of the compound interest type.

(10) A vertical resistance mechanism may confer either complete or incomplete protection against non-matching virulences. If the protection is incomplete, the pathogen can grow on the host and this increases the changes of segregation of virulences capable of overcoming the vertical resistance completely.

(11) The value of vertical resistance is increased where, for climatic or cultural reasons, there is a complete break between the end of one crop and sowing the next.

(12) If legislation can be used to prevent the use of specific cultivars or crops this will enhance the life expectancy of vertical resistance.

(13) Incorporation of horizontal resistance with vertical resistance is likely to provide more satisfactory control of a particular pathogen than vertical resistance alone. If a cultivar possesses only vertical resistance, which is overcome by a pathogen, the resultant plants will be extremely susceptible and crop losses very high.

(14) It is speculated that a host with complex vertical resistance, that is containing several major genes, will suffer less disease when the resistance is overcome by the pathogen than a host with a single or few major genes for resistance.

4.1.6 Quantification of virulence frequency

The systematic classification of pathogen virulence factors by application of the gene-for-gene theory makes possible their study in a quantitative form. Thus the relative importance of separate virulences, their geographical distribution, and any evolutionary changes in the pathogen population in responses to pressures exerted by changed host cultivars can be identified. This type of work, however, requires a complex sampling organisation covering a wide geographical area and capable of functioning for several years backed up by a centralised laboratory for analysing the samples. Even then the results will be influenced by the relative enthusiasm of individual samplers for collecting isolates. A survey of this type was undertaken for *B. lactucae* (lettuce downy mildew) in the UK (Dixon and Wright, 1978; Dixon, 1978) utilising the Agricultural Development and Advisory Service (ADAS) to collect samples and the National Institute of Agricultural Botany (NIAB) to do the analyses over the 5 year period 1973–77. The flow of samples can be illustrated as follows:

Diseased lettuce sample collected
|
Post
↓
Central laboratory pathogen isolate made and inoculated
on to a specified differential series of hosts with known
resistance genes
|
Incubation under standard conditions
↓
Resultant sporulation on differential hosts used to postulate
the virulence factors present in the original diseased sample
From these data predictions of the most usefully resistant
cultivars can be made
|
Predictions tested under conditions of natural infection
in the field.

High or low frequencies were defined in an isolate of *B. lactucae* if more or less, respectively, than 50 per cent of cotyledons of a differential cultivar showed sporulation following inoculation. The overall occurrence of virulence factors on a national basis is shown in Table 4.4.

Since 1973 virulence factors V2, V3, V4 and V7 have been present at high frequency. This result reflected the use of the equivalent resistance genes in the

Table 4.4 Occurrence of virulence factors in *Bremia lactucae* samples 1973–77.

Year	Virulence factors								
	1	2	3	4	5	7	8	9	10
1973	—	92	50	62	—	36	50	—	—
1974	—	76	86	88	—	58	51	—	—
1975	100	65	66	70	65	72	60	41	51
1976	100	71	79	79	62	85	49	64	63
1977	100	85	94	100	52	92	39	44	37
Mean	100	78	75	80	60	69	50	50	50

—, not tested.

Data are the percentage of samples containing each virulence at high frequency.

predominant commercial lettuce cultivars. Virulence factors V5, V8, V9 and V10 were less common, this might have been expected for V5, V9 and V10 because few lettuce cultivars possess the equivalent resistance genes. The effect of low levels of V8 in the pathogen population was that cultivars with resistance gene 8 were uninfected by *B. lactucae*. Thus cultivars such as Avondefiance, Avoncrisp, Diana and Tina were usefully resistant during this period. It is essential to test predictions made from the results of such surveys by field trials under conditions of natural infection. This might be compared to the use of Koch's postulate in that isolates are made from diseased samples, grown on specified test plants under controlled conditions and from the results predictions of usefully resistant cultivars are made. These predictions must then be verified in the field.

From this particular survey it was also clear that no combination of resistance genes was available in commercial lettuce cultivars which would be completely effective against the whole *B. lactucae* population in Britain. There were no general geographical patterns of virulence factor frequency although considerable locality. This survey radically changed the strategy for lettuce breeding in the UK.

4.1.7 Other forms of resistance

(a) Tolerance and horizontal resistance
Tolerance has been defined by Caldwell *et al.* (1958) as the ability of plants to endure pathogen infection without severe losses in yield or quality. Tolerance can only be expressed where the level of crop loss is less than that found for related cultivars affected by a specified amount of disease. This infers that in a tolerant interaction there must be good growth of both host and parasite. The various possible interactions could be

		Host growth	
		Good	Poor
Parasite	Good	Tolerant	Susceptible
growth	Poor	Resistant	Intolerant

This highlights the difference between tolerance and resistance; in the later case host growth is good and that of the pathogen poor. Resistance is considered to be of two types, 'vertical' and 'horizontal'. Vertical resistance (*see* sections 4.1.5) is very specific and governed by one or few genes such that the resistance of cultivar x operates solely against a small portion y of the total host population. If cultivar x were horizontally resistant it would have some measure of protection against the whole pathogen population. Previously, this has also been interpreted as a form of tolerance, and there is considerable confusion in the literature concerning these terms to the extent that some authorities have suggested that the concept of tolerance should be abandoned. The confusion has arisen mainly in host–parasite combinations where parasite growth is reduced, for example by reduction of numbers of leaf lesions or the sporulation within the lesions or the amount of mycelium colonising the vascular bundles is smaller in comparison with other combinations. These would now be classed as manifestations of horizontal resistance. Tolerance would be defined as the capacity of a cultivar to produce a higher yield or superior quality when parasitised to the same extent as other cultivars. As Schafer (1971) states, 'tolerance is not likely to provide a high level of disease protection and should be used in combination with other measures'. Horizontal resistance is frequently equated with 'minor gene resistance' and its suggested mechanism is through the interactive effects of several to many genes which individually are of small effect. They operate collectively to give a cultivar a comparative measure of resistance. Distinction between vertical and horizontal resistance is drawn by Robinson (1973) on the thesis that the former may be rendered ineffective due to changes in the pathogen population, that is by an increased frequency of specific virulences in the host population, whereas horizontal resistance is unaffected by the capacity for change inherent in the pathogen population. If this definition is accepted, then it is possible that horizontal resistance may result from the effects of a few genes, and oligogenic horizontal resistance may exist. This would be qualitative in expression, whereas horizontal resistance due to many genes is quantitative.

Robinson (1973) suggests that horizontal resistance is unaffected by change in the pathogen, but this may not be rigidly so, for the counterpart to race-specific vertical resistance is virulence in the pathogen (vertical pathogenicity), while the counterpart of non-race-specific horizontal resistance is aggressiveness (horizontal pathogenicity). Hence, by definition, increased aggressiveness in the pathogen would result in corresponding decreases in the resistance of cultivars with horizontal resistance (Johnson and Taylor, 1976). Changes in pathogen aggressiveness may only affect the host resistance if this is developed by screening for resistance using a pathogen population with less than maximal horizontal pathogenicity. For completely effective horizontal resistance a pathogen with the highest possible level of aggressiveness is required; the practical difficulties of obtaining such a population are self-evident. It must also be accepted that because horizontal resistance is polygenically inherited its levels may differ in degrees from one genetic background to another and only rarely will it provide complete protection against a pathogen. Indeed the usefulness of attempting to breed for horizontal resistance in horticultural and particularly glasshouse crops may be questionable. This is especially the case where the pathogen affects the organ (root, leaf, flower or fruit) which is eaten. With horticultural crops, quality is of paramount importance. The loss of quality attendant on the use of horizontal resistance may be such as to make the product unacceptable to the consumer. It is possible, however, that with sufficient understanding of the mechanisms of horizontal resistance it may prove possible to combine it with high yields and quality.

In other crops, use of high density planting, alone, would be sufficient to negate the usefulness of horizontal resistance, because under these conditions the pathogen is put at a highly favourable ecological advantage vis-à-vis the host, preventing horizontal resistance from acting as an effective control. Changes in cultivation systems, such as the concentration of rotations, can permit the pathogen an advantage over the horizontally resistant host. Horizontal resistance can probably be exploited most successfully with vegetatively propagated perennial crops. Nonetheless, vertical resistance has been proved to have so many attendant difficulties, and requires such expensive continuous breeding programmes, that horizontal resistance should be tested to see if it can be more successfully exploited.

Proof that a particular resistance is of a horizontal nature is very difficult to achieve, and evidence is usually highly circumstantial. Most convincing proof comes from the constant ranking of cultivars when tested against a range of pathogen isolates. If the relative levels of resistance remain the same under all conditions, then it is probable that resistance is horizontal. It is difficult to test any cultivar with a sufficiently representative range of pathogen isolates; also there are wide variations in the magnitude of differential interactions – and problems of statistical interpretation – making it difficult to confirm experimentally that any cultivar possesses resistance which can be described as non-race-specific or horizontal in Robinson's (1973) strict sense. Equally, it is difficult to separate aggressiveness from virulence in the pathogen. It is well recognised, however, that some resistances have been maintained over considerable time periods and in the face of highly virulent new strains of a pathogen. Such resistance has been termed 'durable'. This term can be employed without any knowledge of its mechanism, that is whether the genetic control is race-specific or not, thereby implying no necessity for knowledge of the racial composition of the pathogen population.

(b) Immunity and disease escape

There is general agreement that the state of plant immunity to a pathogen is absolute. It describes the situation where no disease occurs at all because the pathogen is not able to enter the host under any circumstances whatsoever. Thus tomatoes are immune to the brassica pathogen *Plasmodiophora brassicae* (clubroot) and brassicas are immune to the tomato leaf mould (*Fulvia fulvum*). Disease escape implies that for some reason plants which are otherwise susceptible to a pathogen are unaffected. This may be due to a husbandry reason, whereby the plants are grown too early or too late for infection; or the plants may possess an attribute which does not permit invasion to take place. An example of such an escape mechanism is the ability of barley cultivars which have closed flowers to escape infection by chlamydospores of *Ustilago nuda hordei* (loose smut) (Macer,

1960). If these cultivars are artificially infected with chlamydospores they are as completely susceptible as those with open flowers.

4.1.8 Resistance — the predominant response?

Resistance and susceptibility form parts of a continuous series of responses between a host and potential pathogens. Most higher plants are resistant to the majority of pathogenic organisms. Simple cultivar testing soon reveals that within a range of cultivars, if they posses no specific race-cultivar response, there will be a gradient from those which are highly resistant through moderate resistance to moderate susceptibility to highly susceptible. Even highly susceptible cultivars can be made more resistant by changes in environmental conditions; hence there is no such state as absolute susceptibility. It would appear, therefore, that resistance, that is an incompatible reaction between host and pathogen, is the most usual response, whereas a compatible response is unusual. There is, however, controversy between pathologists over these interpretations. If resistance is more common some revision of Flor's hypothesis is required because this implies that only a quarter of responses result in resistance — where a resistant host and an avirulent parasite are combined. It has been suggested that avirulent races of pathogens differ from genetically related virulent races only in their inability to produce a specific molecule which can interact with the host metabolism. Instead, variant molecules are produced which do not fit the host receptor sites but which nonetheless may impose a stress on the host metabolism. This stress response in the host metabolism could account for hypersensitivity which characterises the resistance reaction between some hosts and avirulent parasites (Ward and Stoessl, 1976).

4.1.9 Techniques used in breeding for disease resistance

(a) Mass selection
This is the simplest breeding method. At its most basic, susceptible plants are removed from a seed crop and the rest bulked up either for sale or to be put through another cycle of selection. Generally, this approach involves using areas where natural infection is known to occur regularly. A more positive approach is to save seed only from the most highly resistant plants in the field. The disadvantage of mass selection is that resistance is increased only slowly and there are too few controls in the system. In a cross-pollinated crop there is no control of pollen source, and since the process is likely to be done at only one site differences due to interactions between environment and the pathogen may be greater than differences due to heredity and the pathogen.

(b) Pedigree selection
By this technique individual plants and their progenies are separated for breeding. Selection is based on the comparative resistance, under conditions of either

natural or artificial infection, of the different pedigree lines. This approach
enables the breeder to control and define the genetic properties of the material
and thereby environmental interactions are minimised. Pedigree selection can be
practised very sucessfully with self-pollinated crops. This effectively isolates pure
lines which can be repeatedly tested to determine if they are more resistant
than existing cultivars. In some cases such differences may be very small, and
statistical techniques such as multiple regression analysis are needed to determine
if they are valid. Where this technique is applied to cross-pollinated crops,
artificially controlled self-pollination is necessary for each pedigree line. This may
not be easy since cross-pollinated species have often evolved mechanisms to
prevent self-pollination. In *Brassica oleracea*, for example, bud pollination
techniques are needed to achieve self-pollination in order to circumvent the
self-sterility mechanisms which develop as the flower opens.

(c) Back-crossing

Resistance to a pathogen may be identified in a wild relative of a cultivated crop.
One of the simplest ways of transferring resistance into standard cultivars is to
cross them with the wild relative and then back-cross through several generations
to the standard cultivar. This stabilises the resistance in the genetic background of
the standard cultivar:

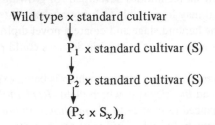

This process is known as recurrent selection and has been used, for example, to
transfer male sterility into a range of crops.

(d) F_1 hybrids

By this technique two separate lines are selfed until they show genetical
homozygosity and are then crossed:

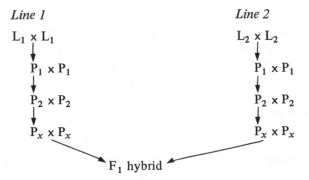

This exploits the phenomenon of heterosis; the F_1 hybrid is heterozygous for the majority of alleles, and in some (but not all) crops this gives rise to greatly enhanced attributes such as resistance to disease. Resistance may be introduced through one or both of the parent lines. Seed from the F_1 hybrid is unlikely to retain the levels of resistance of the original hybrid. New F_1 hybrid seed must be produced each year, this gives the plant breeder great control over the use of the new cultivar. The process has been exploited for several crops: Brussels sprouts, cabbage, carrots, cucumbers, onions and tomatoes.

(e) Interchange between species and genera

Where desirable resistance exists in a closely allied species which interbreeds easily with the crop species, back-crossing can be employed. Crosses between the wild type *Lactuca serriola* and *L. sativa* have been used to introduce resistance to *Bremia lactucae* (downy mildew) into lettuce cultivars. Where interbreeding barriers exist, techniques are beginning to be developed for the transfer of resistance. One such is the use of haploid material developed from pollen grains. The process has been exploited successfully for potatoes, where subsequent diploidisation of haploid individuals gave completely homozygous diploid lines, thereby providing a short-cut to the production of maximally homozygous stocks. Following from techniques developed for growing naked protoplasts in nutrient culture, it may be possible to bring nuclear material from unlike individuals together in the haploid stage and create a novel diploid. Such methods are as yet only in their infancy, but in coming decades could provide a powerful plant breeding tool.

Crosses between genera are rare in nature, but one which is being exploited is that between *Raphanus* spp. and *Brassica* spp. which yields *Raphanobrassica* hybrids. These have greatly enhanced resistance to *Plasmodiophora brassicae* (clubroot) and *Erysiphe cruciferarum* (powdery mildew) compared to *Brassica* spp. Artificial crosses of this type have been achieved between wheat and rye in the hopes of transferring the immunity of rye to *E. graminis* (powdery mildew) into wheat. Unfortunately the progeny, *Triticale*, was not entirely immune to *E. graminis*, suggesting that the reaction to the pathogen was conditioned by several interacting alleles in both the rye and wheat genomes.

(f) Mutations and polyploids

Mutations of single genes, of whole chromosomes and of whole genomes occur in nature and increase disease resistance in some instances. It is possible to induce these changes artificially by the use of chemicals such as colchicine and by radiation (ultraviolet light or atomic radiation).

Types of change in chromosome complement which occur are divided into *euploids* and *aneuploids.*

Euploids

These exhibit changes in the *total* chromosome number, where A, B, C and D

are non-homologous chromosomes:

Monoploid	n	$(ABCD)$
Diploid	$2n$	$(ABCD)(ABCD)$
Triploid	$3n$	$(ABCD)(ABCD)(ABCD)$
Autotetraploid	$4n$	$(ABCD)(ABCD)(ABCD)(ABCD)$
Allotetraploid	$4n$	$(ABCD)(ABCD)(A'B'C'D')(A'B'C'D')$

Aneuploids

These exhibit changes in *part* of the chromosome number:

Monosomic	$2n - 1$	$(ABCD)(ABC)$
Trisomic	$2n + 1$	$(ABCD)(ABCD)(A)$
Tetrasomic	$2n + 2$	$(ABCD)(ABCD)(A)(A)$
Double trisomic	$2n + 1 + 1$	$(ABCD)(ABCD)(AB)$

Definitions

Euploid   The chromosome number is an exact multiple of the haploid number (x).

Aneuploid   The chromosome number differs from an exact multiple of the haploid number, since an aneuploid possesses either more chromosomes than the euploid state below it or less chromosomes than the euploid state above it.

Monoploid   This is the true haploid state, where a single or basic complete set of chromosomes only is present, haploid and monoploid may be treated as synonymous terms.

Diploid   Possessing two sets of chromosomes $(2x)$ capable of complete pairing at meiosis.

Triploid   Possessing three similar and complete basic chromosome sets $(3x)$.

Autotetraploid   Possessing four similar and complete basic chromosome sets $(4x)$.

Allotetraploid   Possessing four basic chromosome sets which compose two diploid pairs. Some degree of homology may exist between the chromosomes of the two different pairs and this can lead to multivalent formation at meiosis.

Monosomic   Possessing the diploid chromosome number less one $(2x - 1)$; thus one chromosome is represented only singly.

Trisomic   Possessing the diploid chromosome number plus one $(2x + 1)$; thus one chromosome is represented three times.

Tetrasomic   Possessing the diploid chromosome number plus two $(2x + 2)$; thus one chromosome is represented four times.

Double trisomic   Possessing the diploid chromosome number plus two additional chromosomes of different types; thus two chromosomes are represented three times but both belong to the same genome.

4.2 HUSBANDRY CONTROL

In this sphere, control of plant pathogens is directly in the hands of the grower. Careful manipulation of plant environment by husbandry techniques can prevent or ameliorate pathogen effects. Methods used for protected and field crops are treated separately, but it should be borne in mind that husbandry methods often evolve from one sphere of cultivation to another.

4.2.1 Protected cultivation

(a) Soil-borne diseases
Under glasshouse conditions the soil environment presents the most intractable source of pathogenic problems. Because of the very high costs of installing glasshouses, growers use them for the monoculture of crops such as tomatoes, cucumbers or lettuce which pay high returns. This limits the scope for crop rotation on any extended scale, leading inevitably to problems with soil-borne diseases. In situations where labour costs are low, this can be overcome to some extent by changing the topsoil within the glasshouse each year. With the development of steam boilers, soil removal was superseded by soil sterilisation. This was accomplished by

(1) introducing steam through perforated pipes placed up to 50 cm deep in the soil;
(2) pulling a steam plough consisting of a series of perforated pipes through the top 20–30 cm of cultivated soil;
(3) surface sterilization achieved by introducing steam beneath polythene sheeting laid on the soil.

The costs of these methods are now prohibitive in terms of labour and fuel and alternatives have been sought, such as chemical sterilisation, which are described further on in this chapter.

A number of other methods are used in conditions of protected cultivation:

(1) *Resistant rootstocks in tomato and cucumber crops*   Here use is made of the pathogen resistance present in wild species of *Cucurbita* and *Lycopersicon* without transferring it into commercially acceptable cultivars. The wild species is used as a rootstock and the otherwise disease-susceptible commercial cultivar as the scion. Seedlings of both the rootstock and scion are raised in the normal way and when the plants are of sufficient size to handle the scion is bench-grafted on to the rootstock. When the graft union is complete the scion cultivar can be severed from its own root system and grown throughout its cropping period on the roots of the stock. The scion is thus protected from soil-borne pathogens by the resistance properties of the rootstock. For cucumbers, *C. ficifolia* is used as a rootstock having resistance to *Fusarium oxysporum* f. sp.

niveum (wilt), while for tomatoes a range of rootstocks with resistance to different pathogens is available. In the Netherlands, F_1 hybrids produced by *L. exculentum* x *L. hirsutum* crosses had the added bonus of increasing yields, probably due to the marked heterosis associated with the F_1 hybrid rootstock (Bravenboer and Pet, 1962). Rootstocks with resistance to *Pyrenochaeta lycopersici* (corky root). *Didymella lycopersici* (canker), *Fusarium oxysporum* f. sp. *lycopersici, Verticillium albo-atrum* (wilts) and *Meloidogyne* spp. (root knot nematode) are available for grafting on to tomato scions (Maxon-Smith and Proctor, 1965).

(2) *Cross-protection*   There are many reports that inoculation with an avirulent strain of a pathogen or a non-pathogen prior to inoculation with a virulent pathogen will prevent development of disease symptoms. For example, incubated droplets containing spores of an avirulent race of *Colletotrichum lindemuthianum* (anthracnose) produced diffusates which would prevent growth of a virulent race (Berard *et al.*, 1972). The protection factor was also effective on different host cultivars provided they possessed the same genes for resistance as the donor cultivar. A cultivar bearing genes for resistance to two different races of *C. lindemuthianum* produced two protection factors which could be distinguished by their effects on cultivars carrying the genes separately (Berard *et al.*, 1973).

This concept has been used commercially to control Tomato Mosaic Virus (TMV). Deliberate inoculation of tomato seedlings as a cultural method to minimise losses in yield and fruit quality by TMV was suggested by Broadbent (1964). Rast (1972) isolated a TMV mutant, M-II-16, which protected plants against infection by the distorting and yellow strains of TMV. This has become a particularly useful commercial technique for treatment of tomato cultivars which are susceptible to TMV but capable of producing very high yields if protected from the disease.

(3) *Soil-less systems*   Under this general heading are systems which avoid use of glasshouse border soil. An early attempt in this direction was the use of straw bales. These were placed in the glasshouse, saturated with water, and as decomposition began a layer of sterilised compost was placed on top into which the crop plants were inserted. One major problem with this method was to obtain cereal straw free from residues of selective herbicides. From this has followed the development of peat bolsters. These consist of bags of peat containing nutrient additives, the crop plants being placed in holes in the top of the bag. Careful husbandry is a prerequisite with this technique in order to maintain the correct nutrient, salt and moisture balances for plants which are grown for many months in an environment where the roots are restricted to a very small volume of growing medium. Complete freedom from soil and solid substitutes has been achieved with the nutrient film technique. Here plants are grown in polyethylene or concrete troughs through which a steady trickle of nutrient solution is passed which forms a film around the roots but still permits aeration. In the hands of a skilled grower this method can produce very high

yields but requires exceedingly careful control since all the buffering effects of a solid rooting medium are absent. In avoiding traditional soil-borne disease problems this technique may produce new ones such as sudden root death and foliar scorching, which may be of pathological origin or due to nutrient imbalance or fluctuations in salt concentrations. Also, if any of the young plants are produced in an infected growing medium the pathogen may spread very rapidly throughout the crop, for example, Lettuce Big Vein Virus transmitted by zoospores of *Olpidium brassicae.*

(b) Air-borne diseases

Husbandry techniques have an important role in the control of air-borne pathogens, especially if resistance is difficult to achieve and chemical control is of limited efficiency. Maintenance of a buoyant atmosphere through skilful use of heating systems and ventilation will prevent many air-borne pathogens from becoming a problem. This is increasingly difficult to achieve as fuel costs rise because the grower is tempted to keep the ventilators closed and pipe temperature low to conserve fuel. It is now becoming common practice to install polyethylene thermal screens which prevent heat loss to the apex of the glasshouse where no crop is grown. These lead to very high humidity and dew formation when the screens are withdrawn, giving rise to considerable problems with *Botrytis cinerea* (grey mould). Work in the Netherlands has shown that there is significant correlation between the points where water condenses on the foliage and fruit of tomatoes and subsequent incidence of *B. cinerea* infection (Strijbosch, 1976). Additionally, shading effects from thermal screens, even when drawn back, reduce yield.

4.2.2 Field cultivation

Empirical observations by growers showed that cultural techniques could be associated with disease control long before the development of a scientific rationale for crop protection. Reasons for the usefulness of such techniques are still being sought and the picture is far from clear since the study of cultivation methods is a long-term process involving the resolution of a multitude of interrelated factors. Nonetheless, it is possible to identify certain areas for study, most of which are related to climatology and soil science, where there are indications that cultural practice might be manipulated to help control plant pathogens.

(a) Rotation

A prime reason which is always advanced for the use of rotations rather than a monocropping system is to control plant pathogens. Direct evidence for a positive correlation between rotation and disease control is, however, highly tenuous, and the arguments in favour of either system are well balanced (Shipton, 1977). The classic case advanced for rotational control is that of *Plasmodiophora brassicae* (clubroot). It must be borne in mind, however, that the resting spores are extremely long-lived and that there is increasing evidence that at least part of the life cycle can be accomplished on non-cruciferous hosts. Under these conditions, the soil-borne inoculum of *P. brassicae* could be unaffected by the absence of cruciferous hosts for a period of years. Reductions in the soil population might be achieved by the use of deep cultivation (Colhoun, 1958) or by other techniques. In South Wales, frequent soil movement by rotavation causing the top soil layer to dry out is claimed to result in dessication of resting spores of *P. brassicae* and allows frequent cropping with cauliflowers (H. Davies, personal communication). There may also be antifungal effects from crops within a rotation. Peppermint was reported by Ellis (1950) to reduce or eliminate *P. brassicae*. Control of soil pH has also been associated with control of this pathogen. K. G. Proudfoot (personal communication) reports that in Newfoundland up to 40 tonne/ha of lime is applied to raise soil pH and thereby permit brassica production on land heavily infested with *P. brassicae*.

(b) Fertilisers

Use of high levels of nitrogen fertilisation has been observed to increase disease severity, but the form of nitrogen used may be at least as important as the rate of application (Huber and Watson, 1974). In general, ammonium nitrogen appears to increase disease severity more than nitrate nitrogen, but this is not always the case. Thus damping-off of lettuce caused by *Thanetophorus cucumeris* increased with the use of ammonium nitrate (Das and Western, 1959), but varying the rate of nitrate nitrogen had no effect (Shephard and Wood, 1963). This has been correlated with increases of the amides, glutamine and asparagine, in ammonium nitrate-fertilised plants. *Aphanomyces euteiches* (root rot) in peas was suppressed by nitrate nitrogen and increased by ammonium nitrogen in non-sterile soil (Carley, 1969). Vascular wilt of tomato (*Verticillium albo-atrum*) increased with raised levels of nitrate nitrogen (Walker *et al.*, 1954), but cabbage yellows (*Fusarium oxysporum* f. sp. *conglutinans*), tomato wilt (*F. oxysporum* f. sp. *lycopersici*) and pea wilt (*F. oxysporum* f. sp. *pisi*) decreased as the concentration of nitrate nitrogen increased (Gallegly and Walker, 1949; Walker, 1946). Although fusarial wilt pathogens are primarily xylem invaders and can use nitrate nitrogen, increasing its levels tends to reduce disease severity. Bacterial wilt and canker of tomato (*Pseudomonas solanacearum* and *Corynebacterium michiganense*) increased in severity concomitantly with increased nitrate nitrogen.

There is a similarly confused picture with foliar pathogens. Rusts and powdery mildews generally increase with nitrate nitrogen and are reduced by ammonium nitrogen (Daly, 1949; Last, 1953). Other pathogens such as *Botytis fabae* on broad bean reacts in the opposite manner (Blakeman, 1971; Sol, 1967).

High potassium levels are believed to reduce infection by most wilt diseases, such as *Fusarium* wilt of tomato (Walker and Foster, 1946), but was without effect on *Verticillium* and bacterial wilts of tomato (Walker *et al.*, 1954; Gallegly and Walker, 1949). For foot and root rots the influence of potassium is rarely noticed, but high potassium — especially if associated with high nitrogen — reduced *Fusarium culmorum* on wheat (Onuorah, 1969). The reaction with *Gibberella zeae* (stalk rot) on maize is more complex and depends on nitrogen level; an increase in potassium reduced stalk rot when nitrogen was low, had no effect at medium nitrogen, and increased it at high nitrogen; with low potassium, nitrogen level had no effect (Thayer and Williams, 1960). Root rots are generally reduced by high phosphate nutrition; in Canada the reappearance of browning root rot of cereals due to *Pythium* spp. was attributed to insufficient use of phosphate fertilisers (Vanterpool, 1962). The relationship of calcium to disease severity is even more tantalising since there are various side effects — for instance the action on pH, causing in turn imbalances of trace elements. Also related to calcium is the influence of sodium. Increased sodium in the nutrient solution increased the susceptibility of tomato to wilt (*Fusarium oxysporum* f. sp. *lycopersici*). This may be connected with the lowering of calcium induced by sodium. Hubbeling (1969) showed clearly that high calcium was related to reduced disease severity in tomatoes infected with *Verticillium albo-atrum*.

(c) Irrigation
High levels of soil moisture are often associated with increased disease severity. This may be due to the provision of moisture films through which motile spores can move. Also, water-logged soil or compost will weaken and asphyxiate root systems, thereby giving portals for the entry of pathogenic organisms. For foliar diseases the manner in which water is applied can be important. Tomato plots irrigated by overhead sprinkling were more severely infected by *Stemphyllium botryosum* f. sp. *lycopersici* and *Xanthomonas vesicatoria* than furrow-irrigated plots (Rotem and Cohen, 1966). The reverse was true for *Oidiopsis taurica* (powdery mildew). Furrow irrigation did not affect the prevailing microclimate, but sprinkler irrigation was associated with increased relative humidity and reduced air temperature. The period during which the altered microclimate persisted after conclusion of irrigation, as well as the time required for evaporation of water deposited on sprinkled plants, increased with lower temperatures and higher relative humidity; wind velocity and cloudiness also influenced the duration of these periods. The reverse effect on *O. taurica* is attributed to its requirement for dry periods in which to spread.

(d) Sowing/planting date
Disease may be avoided by early or late sowing or planting so that the crop and its pathogen are out of phase with each other and an epidemic cannot build up. A traditional method for reducing *Erysiphe cruciferarum* (powdery mildew) infection on brassicas is to sow late (Searle, 1920) so that the foliage is immature and cannot support the pathogen during the main period when the crop is at risk. A heavy price is paid, however, in terms of reduced yield (Doling and Willey,

1969). Cabbage and other cole crops which are grown in the colder seasons traditionally suffer less from *Plasmodiophora brassicae* since the pathogen is less active; summer cabbage and cauliflower are at high risk from the disease. Mid and late season Brussels sprouts in Bedfordshire and the Vale of Evesham are less badly attacked by *E. cruciferarum*, perhaps because the environmental conditions are such that the pathogen is at a disadvantage compared with early season crops.

(e) Cleaning crops

Use of non-economic crops to stimulate the germination and growth of soil-borne organisms which are then killed has long been sought with little real effect. In Germany, where a high value is set on the maintenance of good soil conditions (H. Toxopeus, personal communication), considerable use is made of green manuring crops such as mustard and radish. These may have antifungal properties due to their mustard oil content which reduce the populations of soil-borne pathogens, but detailed proof is lacking.

4.3 CHEMICAL CONTROL

This section deals principally with fungicides because the chemical control of fungi has been outstandingly more successful than the control of bacteria and viruses. For a fungicide to be successful it must fulfil the following criteria:

(1) The fungicide must provide adequate and consistent disease control.

(2) Interactions with climate, soil or crop cultivars should be as limited as possible.

(3) There must be no phytotoxic effects at the dose rates used to provide protection.

(4) Harmful effects on environment, toxicity to livestock and plant species must be non-existent.

(5) The active ingredient must be capable of formulation into a suitable physical form which is easy and cheap to store, transport and apply.

(6) Application must yield an adequate economic return for a given effort so that the financial improvement from use exceeds the total cost of control. This has been summarised by the formula of Headley (1973):

$$\frac{B}{C} \geqslant 1$$

where B is the expected benefit from treatment and C is the total cost of application.

This oversimplification of the situation neglects the biological problems associated with the assessment of disease levels and their attendant levels of yield loss and economic problems such as the varying elasticities of crops and their products.

4.3.1 Eradicant and protective fungicides

Eradicants are substances which inhibit growth of a pathogen after infection has taken place, to be effective they must be applied when the first signs of infection are seen. Protectants are applied in advance of infection, adhering to the outside of the host and preventing the establishment of the pathogen. Their disadvantage is that only foliage present at the time of application is protected and therefore frequent sprays are needed.

(a) Copper

The discovery of Bordeaux mixture for control of *Plasmopara viticola* (downy mildew) of vines by Millardet in 1885 may be described as the beginning of modern crop protective chemistry. Bordeaux mixture is made from copper sulphate and lime in aqueous solution. Reaction of copper sulphate with other alkalis gave rise to Burgundy mixture (sodium carbonate), Azurin (ammonium hydroxide) and Chesthunt compound (ammonium carbonate). The most efficient form for Bordeaux mixture is to add concentrated lime paste to dilute copper sulphate solution. These materials have two disadvantages:

(1) the need for two separate containers, one of which must withstand the corrosive effects of copper sulphate;

(2) application is at very high volume, so that large volumes of water are needed to apply the active ingredient at low concentrations.

Nonetheless, Bordeaux mixture remained in widescale use until the 1930s when it was replaced by mixtures using fixed coppers based on insoluble basic salts such as chlorides, sulphates, phosphates and silicates of copper or cuprous oxide, which were formulated as wettable powders. These had the advantage of being less corrosive, dispensing with the need for special containers, and could be applied at higher concentrations, thereby reducing the volume of spray which needed to be applied. These materials were universally accepted for control of downy mildews and other foliar pathogens. For specific purposes other copper compounds have been utilised: copper napthenate, copper oximate (copper 8-hydroxyquinoline) and copper—zinc chromate complexes.

(b) Sulphur

Sulphur fungicides are based on either elemental sulphur or polysulphide derivatives. They are applied either as dusts, where fungitoxicity is associated with particle size, or as wettable powders, slurries or paste formulations. These often contain wetting and dispersing agents to maintain suspendability in storage and while being applied. Calcium polysulphide spray was prepared by boiling lime and elemental sulphur in water; the supernatant was decanted and then diluted for application. Other preparations include sodium, potassium, ammonium and polyethylene polysulphide. Sulphur-based fungicides are specifically effective against the Ascomycetes, particularly members of the Erysiphales.

(c) Mercury

Both organic and inorganic formulations of mercury have been used. Most widely used are mercurous chloride (calomel) and mercuric chloride (corrosive sublimate). The latter is utilised as a weak aqueous solution to disinfect bulbs, corms and seed for the control of bacterial pathogens. Calomel slurry has remained the most widely used material for control of *Plasmodiophora brassicae* (clubroot) on transplanting material and to combat a range of turf pathogens. It is now being replaced by the systemic material benomyl because of the hazards involved in handling mercury-based materials. Extreme phytotoxicity limited the widespread use of inorganic mercury compounds. This was reduced by preparing organic formulations of the type $R - Hg - X$, where R is an aryl or alkyl radical and X an organic or inorganic acid group. Most frequently used were phenyl mercury acetate, phenyl mercury chloride, ethyl mercury chloride, ethyl mercuric chloride, ethyl mercury phosphate and ethoxy derivatives. Extreme mammalian toxicity has led to the rapid replacement of these materials by safer compounds.

(d) Dithiocarbamates

Derived from dithiocarbamic acid ($NH_2 CS_2 H$), these materials have had widespread acceptance because of their efficacy and low mammlian toxicity. Three main groups form the basis of the fungicides used (figure 4.1).

The tetramethyl derivative of thiuramdisulphide known as thiram (TMTD) is used widely for control of some downy mildews, powdery mildews, *Botrytis* and as a seed dressing. The thiram soak technique developed by Maude (1966) gave control of a large number of seed-borne diseases of vegetable and other crops. Metal dithiocarbamate derivatives with iron (ferbam) and zinc (ziram) were introduced as broad spectrum fungicides for vegetables. Unfortunately, ferbam leaves an undesirable black deposit while ziram can induce dermatitis in the user. Another metal derivative, metham-sodium (sodium-*N*-methyl dithiocarbamate) is used as a soil fumigant; being unstable it forms the active material methyl isothiocyanate. A cyclic dithiocarbamate, dazomet (tetrahydro-3,5-dimethyl-1,3,5-thiadiazine-2-thione) has similar uses.

The most successful of this group of compounds are the ethylene *bis* derivatives, which are highly active fungicides and non-phytotoxic. Most widely used are nabam, zineb and maneb: these are disodium, zinc and manganese salts of ethylene-*bis*-dithiocarbamate. Nabam forms a solution while zineb and maneb are insoluble and are used as wettable powders. Nabam is especially useful for making tank-mixed zineb by reaction with zinc sulphate. Zineb and maneb have

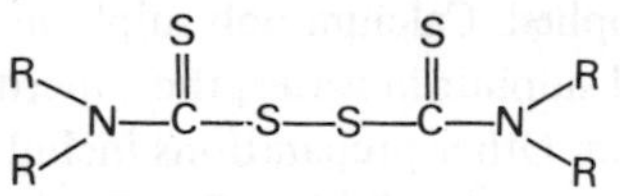

S
‖
R   S   S   R
 \   ‖   ‖   /
  N—C—-S—S—C—N
 /   \
R   Thiuramdisulphides   R

Thiuramdisulphides

S
‖
R
 \
  N—C—S—Metal
 /
R

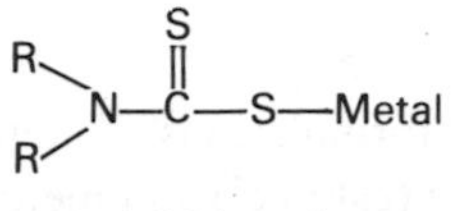

Dimethyldithiocarbamates

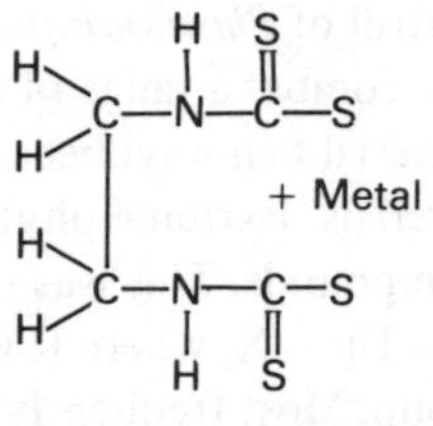

H   S
| ‖
H   C—N—C—S
 \   /
  C
 /   \
H
                    + Metal
H
 \
  C—N—C—S
 / | ‖
H   H   S

Ethylene-*bis*-dithiocarbamate

Figure 4.1   Structural formulae of the dithiocarbamates. R = radical.

been the predominant fungicides for vegetable crops, controlling a wide spectrum of pathogens for many years and have the bonus of improving the appearance of foliage of many field crops. Recently a complex, mancozeb, was produced to control *Phytophthora infestans* (potato blight).

(e) Quinones
These materials are unstable in light and are therefore unsatisfactory foliage protectants, but tetrachloro-*p*-benzoquinone (chloranil) and 2,3-dichloro-1,4-naphthaquinone (dichlone) are used as seed dressings for brassicas and legumes.

(f) Dinitro compounds
The activity of dinitrophenols as herbicides and insecticides was recognised as early as 1925. The compound 2-methyl-4,6-dinitrophenol (DNOC) has limited uses as a fungicide for hardwood subjects in dormant periods but has the disadvantage of high mammalian toxicity. Derivatives such as dinocap (2-(1-methyl-*n*-heptyl)-4,6-dinitrophenyl crotonate) and binapacryl (2-(1-methyl-*n*-propyl)-4,6-dinitrophenyl-2-methyl crotanate), which have lower toxicity, are widely used for control of *Erysiphe* spp. on vegetable crops.

(g) Chlorinated nitrobenzenes
Pentachloro and tetrachloro derivatives of nitrobenzene — quintozene (PCNB)

and tecnazene (TCNB) — were introduced in the late 1930s and 1940s
respectively. Quintozene has useful properties for the control of soil-borne
pathogens, particularly those which cause damping-off diseases, for example
Thanetophorus cucumeris, and as such is often added to composts or worked
into seed beds. It is practically insoluble in water, of low volatility and stable
in soil, and therefore has long persistance combined with low mammalian
toxicity. Tomatoes and cucumbers are sensitive to it and should not be planted
in treated soil. Tecnazene has similar fungicidal properties but is more volatile
and hence has lower persistence. It was often used to control *Botrytis cinerea*
(grey mould) on tomatoes as a smoke or dust preparation.

(h) Cyclohexene dicarboximides
Various derivatives of these compounds are active by the addition of a
chlorinated sulphur radicale $-SSCl_3$. Captan (*N*-(trichloromethylthio)-cyclohex-
4-ene-1,2-dicarboximide) is used to control many seed- and soil-borne diseases
either alone or in combination with other fungicides, but is ineffective against
Erysiphe spp. (powdery mildews).

(i) Dodine acetate
Chemically, this material has some of the properties of a cationic wetting agent,
making it difficult to combine with other materials. It is a long-chained aliphatic
material containing both acidic and basic radicals,

$$C_{12}H_{25} NHCNH_2 CH_3 COOH$$
$$\overset{\parallel}{NH}$$

correctly known as dodecylguanidine acetate. Mammalian toxicity is low but
the concentrate can give rise to skin irritations.

(j) Organotin compounds
Two materials of this type have been marketed: triphenyl tin acetate and
hydroxide (fentin acetate and hydroxide). They are especially useful for control
of *Cercospora beticola* (leaf spot) on beet.

(k) Nickel compounds
Organic and inorganic derivatives of nickel were some of the initial systemic
compounds used to control rust pathogens.

(l) Miscellaneous materials
Dichlofluanid (*N*-dichlorofluoromethanesulphenyl-*N'*,*N'*-dimethyl-*N*-phenyl-
sulphamide) was introduced in 1966 as a wide-spectrum fungicide for control of
Erysiphe spp. (powdery mildew) and *Botrytis cinerea* (grey mould) on soft fruit,
vegetable crops and ornamentals. Dicloran (2,6-dichloro-4-nitroaniline) has been
successfully used to control *B. cinerea* (grey mould), particularly on lettuce. Its

mode of action differs from most protective fungicides in that it has little effect on spore germination but appears to intervene in cell division.

Lead arsenate (diplumbic hydrogen arsenate) was introduced in 1892 and is now of only historic interest, its toxic qualities are such that it has been totally discarded. In the UK it is illegal to sell, deliver or import food containing arsenic in amounts by weight exceeding 1 p.p.m. expressed as elementary arsenic or lead in amounts exceeding 2 p.p.m.

Quinomethionate (6-methyl-2-oxo-1, 3-dithiolo-[4,5-b]-quinoxaline) was developed for control of powdery mildews and is still one of the few compounds recognised for use against *E. cichoracearum* on marrow crops.

(m) Mineral oils
Initially used as carriers for other compounds, these were soon shown to have fungicidal properties. Their action is to arrest the early stages of infection. They suffer from being of variable quality and often induce phytotoxicity which is attributed to the physical and chemical properties of the oil and its method of application, particularly the droplet size.

4.3.2 Systemic fungicides

Systemic materials are absorbed into the plant metabolism rendering the tissues fungicidal. This prolongs the period of protection by giving new tissue these properties as it develops. Since the mid 1950s large numbers of systemic materials have been tested, many have been discarded very quickly due to toxicity or formulation problems. The types described below illustrate the range of compounds developed, but are limited to those which have activity against vegetable pathogens and for which approval has been given in the United Kingdom under the Agricultural Chemicals Approval Scheme, thereby ruling out those with highly undesirable toxic characteristics.

(a) Heterocyclic compounds
Benzimidazoles
Systemic fungicidal activity was discovered in several substituted 2-amino-benzimidazoles, including methyl-(1-butylcarbamoyl)-benzimidazol-2-yl carbamate (benomyl) (figure 4.2), which possesses outstanding systemic properties and is used against a wide range of fungal pathogens, although it has no effect against Phycomycetes. Within the plant it is rapidly hydrolysed to

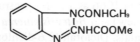

Figure 4.2   Structural formula of benomyl. Me = methyl radical.

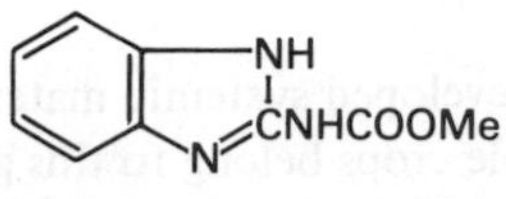

Figure 4.3   Structural formula of carbendazim. Me = methyl radical.

methylbenzimidazol-2-yl carbamate (carbendazim) (figure 4.3), also referred to as MBC. The rapidity of this change was illustrated in beans by Peterson and Edington (1969), who found that benomyl was totally transformed to carbendazin in 5 days. Its mode of action is thought to involve changes in the pathogen DNA synthesis or closely related processes such as nuclear or cell division (Clemons and Sisler, 1971).

A similar compound, 2-(thiazol-4-yl)-benzimidazole (thiabendazole) (figure 4.4) is an effective broad-spectrum systemic fungicide used for a range of vegetable crops and especially for control of post-harvest infections by dipping.

Long alkyl substituents of triazinobenzimidazole, particularly the dodecyl analogue, are effective against the Phycomycetes *Peronospora* and *Phytophthora*. This may be due to release of dodecylamine, which increases the permeability of plasma membranes.

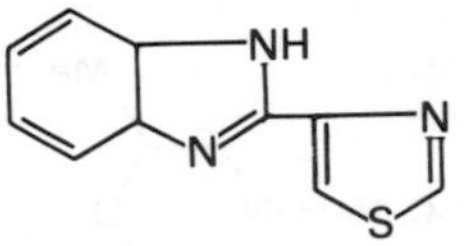

Figure 4.4   Structural formula of thiabendazole.

Hydroxypyrimidines

This group provided the first efficient means of control of powdery mildew on glasshouse cucurbit crops in the form of 5-*n*-butyl-2-dimethylamino-4-hydroxy-6-methylpyrimidine (dimethirimol) (figure 4.5).

Mostly used as a soil drench, the material is translocated in the xylem and metabolised in the plant by dealkylation to the desmethyl derivative, which is fungicidal, and the amine, which is less active. The fungicide and its metabolites are further reacted to form water-soluble conjugates, possibly involving glucose, which are also fungicidal, so that the antifungal properties are likely to be a combined effect.

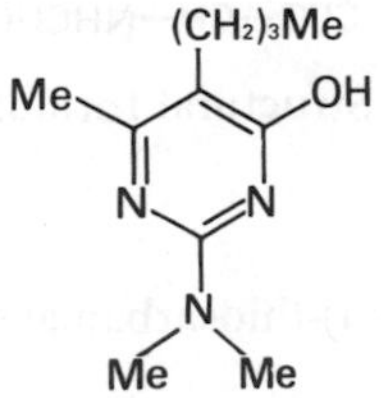

Figure 4.5   Structural formula of dimethirimol. Me = methyl radical.

1,2,4-Triazoles

Some of the most recently developed systemic materials for the control of powdery mildews on vegetable crops belong to this group. Of special interest is 1-(4-chlorophenoxyl)-3,3-dimethyl-1-(1,2,4-triazol-l-yl)-butan-2-one (triadimefon) (figure 4.6). This has the remarkable property of being translocated both upwards and downwards in cucurbits under glass (Kaspars *et al.*, 1975).

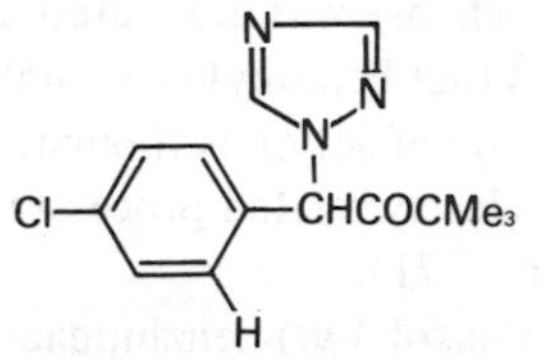

Figure 4.6   Structural formula of tridemorph. Me = methyl radical.

N-substituted tetrahydro-1,4-oxazines

This group of chemicals is based on morpholine, for example 2,6-dimethyl-4-tridecylmorpholine (tridemorph) (figure 4.7). The fungicidal activity increases with the length of the side chain up to a maximum of 13 carbon atoms, but phytotoxicity also increases.

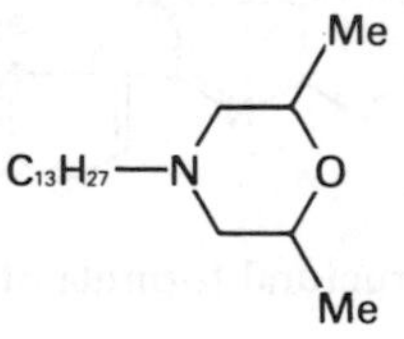

Figure 4.7   Structural formula of triadimefon. Me = methyl radical.

Azepines

Piperazine (1,4-di-(2,2,2-trichloro-1-formamidoethyl)-piperazine), given the common name triforine (figure 4.8), is very active against powdery mildews.

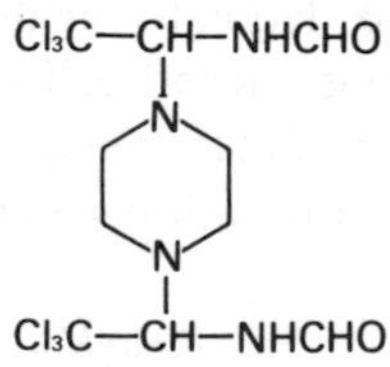

Figure 4.8   Structural formula of triforine.

(b) Aliphatic compounds

Ethyl N-(3-dimethylaminopropyl)-thiocarbamate hydrochloride (Prothiocarb),

$$Me_2NCH_2CH_2CH_2NHCOSEt.HCl,$$

(Et = ethyl radical) is a soil-applied systemic compound with activity against Phycomycetes, especially *Pythium, Phytophthora* and *Peronospora* spp. Its mode of action is highly dependent on soil pH.

(c) Aromatic compounds

Thiourea-based fungicides

This group, formed from thiourea and an aromatic nucleus, may depend on conversion to the benzimidazole nucleus for activity. Two are of importance: 1,2-di(3-ethoxycarbonyl-2-thioureido)benzene (thiophanate) (figure 4.9) and the methyl form (figure 4.10). These are converted to ethyl- and methylbenzimidazol-2-yl carbamates, respectively, in aqueous solution, but analogues which cannot cyclise in this way have no fungicidal properties. Both compounds are extremely active via root absorption against *Erysiphe* spp. (powdery mildews).

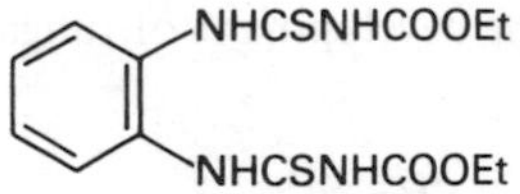

Figure 4.9   Structural formula of thiophanate. Et = ethyl radical.

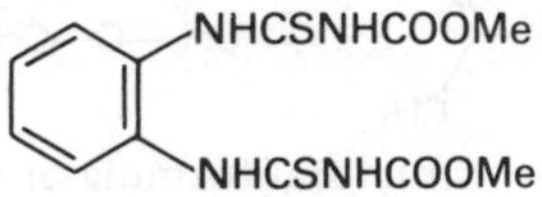

Figure 4.10   Structural formula of thiophanate-methyl. Me = methyl radical.

Phenols and their derivatives

These are of particular historical interest since phenols were amongst the earliest chemicals to be used as fungicides. Now materials such as 1,4-dichloro-2,5-dimethoxybenzene (chloroneb) (figure 4.11) have been shown to be taken up by root absorption and concentrated in both the roots and lower stem. So far only used experimentally, they are active when used as a soil treatment, at planting, against seedling diseases of beans, for example *Thanetophorus cucumeris* and *Pythium*. Substituted nitrophenols are active against powdery mildews, but since nitrophenols act as inhibitors of oxidative phosphorylation those analogues which can penetrate the leaf surface will interfere with energy production in the plant

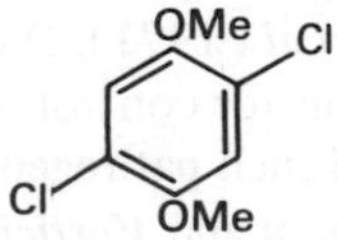

Figure 4.11   Structural formula of chloroneb. Me = methyl radical.

leading to phytotoxic effects. This correlates with the suggestion of Sijpesteijn (1969) that successful systemic fungicides act by inhibition of biosynthetic pathways rather than inhibition of energy production.

Acylalanines

A new class of systemic fungicides has been discovered recently. They have activity against Phycomycetes, particularly the order Peronosporales. Previously, no systemic materials were capable of combating this group of pathogens. Among the first such materials to be marketed is methyl-*N*-(2,6-dimethylphenyl)-*N*-(2-methoxyacetyl)-alaninate (metalaxyl) (figure 4.12). This compound is absorbed by leaves, taken up by stems of annuals, green shoots of perennials and by roots, from which it is translocated acropetally (Urecht *et al.*, 1977). The last-mentioned property means that in addition to spray application, the material could be mixed with blocking composts for crops such as brassicas and lettuce to control *Peronospora parasitica* and *Bremia lactucae*, respectively. It has been withdrawn from use due to the development of fungal strains resistant to its action.

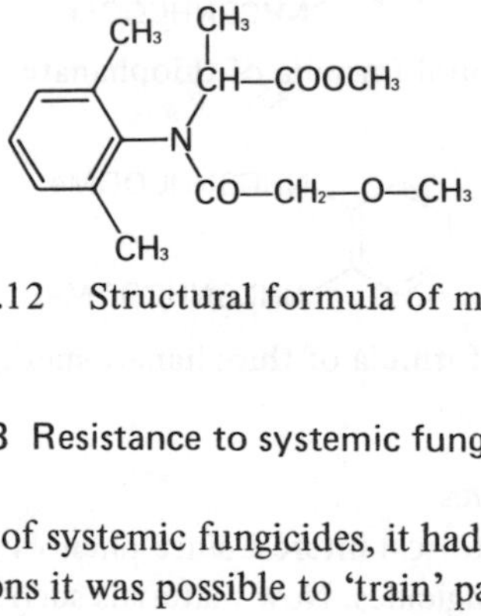

Figure 4.12   Structural formula of metalaxyl.

4.3.3 Resistance to systemic fungicides

Prior to the development of systemic fungicides, it had been demonstrated that under laboratory conditions it was possible to 'train' pathogens to resist increased doses of fungicides, but this phenomenon was of little practical significance. The widespread use of systemic materials has, however, been accompanied by dramatic examples of the development of tolerance to fungicides. One of the first such incidents occurred with *Sphaerotheca fuliginea* (powdery mildew) of cucumber and the pyrimidine derivative dimethirimol. This material was introduced into the Netherlands in 1968 and used on a large scale for powdery mildew control. A suspension of dimethirimol applied to the base of cucumber plants provided protection for 5–6 weeks. By 1970 reports of the loss of efficacy were beginning to emerge and it was shown that dimethirimol-tolerant strains of *S. fuliginea* had emerged (Bent *et al.*, 1971). Dimethirimol has now been virtually abandoned as a commercial means for control of cucumber powdery mildew. Subsequently, tolerant strains of such pathogens as *Botrytis*, *Cercospora*, *Colletotrichum*, *Erysiphe*, *Fusarium* and *Verticillium* have appeared in vegetable crops where benomyl, thiabendazole and thiophanate-methyl have been used for disease control (Dekker, 1977). Mechanisms for such loss of efficacy are as follows:

(1) *Decreased permeability*   Resistance in pathogens to the antibiotics blasticidin-S and polyoxin D have been attributed to a decreased permeability of the fungal protoplast membranes to these antibiotics.

(2) *Increase of detoxication*   This may occur by a modification of the fungicide molecule or by binding to cell constituents with a concomitant loss of activity after entry into the fungal cell.

(3) *Decrease of conversion into fungitoxic compound*   Some fungicides operate through lethal synthesis in which the fungus converts an inactive compound into a fungicide. In resistant strains, such synthesis may diminish, as appeared to be the case with a 6-azauracil (AzU)- resistant strain of *Cladosporium cucumerinum* (gummosis or scab of curcubits), obtained after exposing conidia to ultraviolet light. For antifungal activity AzU is first converted to 6-azauridine-5′-phosphate (AzUMP) via 6-azauridine (AzUMP):

$$\text{AzU} \rightleftharpoons \underset{\substack{\text{Uridine} \\ \text{phosphorylase}}}{} \text{AzUR} \rightleftharpoons \underset{\substack{\text{Uridine} \\ \text{kinase}}}{} \text{AzUMP}$$

The final product inhibits one of the fungal enzymes of pyrimidine biosynthesis; the resistant strain was incapable of converting AzU to AzUR so that the toxic material AzUMP was not formed. This resistance was due to a loss of activity of the enzyme uridine phosphorylase, since if the fungus was fed AzUR or AzUMP no resistance was observed (Dekker, 1967).

(4) *Decreased affinity at the action site*   When a fungicide reaches the site of action without being detoxified, tolerance of the fungus may be due to lack of affinity for the inhibitor at the reactive site. This form of tolerance has occurred with systemic materials such as benomyl and thiophanate-methyl which form MBC or carbendazim within the host plant. For susceptible fungal strains this is toxic through inhibition of chromosome separation at mitosis (Hammerschlag and Sisler, 1973; Davidse, 1973), which occurs through binding to the protein subunits of the spindle microtubules, preventing assembly of the spindle. Resistance has been ascribed to a slight change in the protein subunits of the spindle due to a mutation resulting in decreased affinity for carbendazim (Davidse 1973, 1975*a,b*).

(5) *Circumvention*   Where a fungicide blocks a reaction at one site in the fungal metabolism, the fungus may adapt by shifting its metabolism in such a way that the blocked site is bypassed. The antibiotic actimomycin A acts upon electron transport in the respiratory chain between cytochromes *b* and *c*. Tolerance of *Ustilago maydis* (maize smut) to this fungicide was attributed to a shift in electron transport at a site preceding cytochrome *b* to an alternative terminal oxidase (Georgopoulos and Sisler, 1970).

(6) *Compensation*   When a particular enzyme is the primary site of attack by
a fungicide, increased tolerance may be the result of the ability of the organism
to compensate for the effect of inhibition. Some strains of *Cladosporium
cucumerinum* become resistant to 6-azauracil (*see* (3) above) simply by producing
more enzyme for pyrimidine synthesis (Dekker, 1971).

4.3.4 Soil sterilants

Chemical sterilisation on a field scale has been practised for the last 20 years
in California, USA, to control pathogens such as *Verticillium* spp. on areas
monocropped with strawberries and tomatoes (Wilhelm, 1971). In Europe,
however, crop rotation is still the principal means of controlling soil-borne
pathogens on a field scale, but with the intensification of crop production and
higher values of land and crops, chemical sterilisation of arable land is becoming
economically feasible. For protected cropping, soil sterilisation has been a
standard practice to control pathogenic fungi such as *Phytophthora, Pythium*
and *Thanetophorus* spp.

To achieve successful sterilisation the land must be thoroughly worked
before treatment and should be evenly moist but not wet. Soils with a high
organic matter content absorb chemicals more strongly than lighter sandy soils
and retain the materials longer, thus greater intervals are required between
treatment and planting. Adequate distribution of chemical sterilants in the soil
is essential; soils which cannot be broken down to a reasonable tilth are unsuitable
for treatment since lumps are not penetrated by the chemical. Most sterilants
are either highly volatile or decompose to volatile compounds, and it is necessary
to seal the soil surface for a few days by compaction or flooding to a depth of
1–2 cm. Alternatively, materials such as methyl bromide, which is a gas at
temperatures above 5 °C, are allowed to diffuse into the soil when released from
cylinders under plastic sheeting, the edges of which are buried in the soil to a
depth of 10 cm to prevent the gas from escaping to the atmosphere. The rate
at which sterilisation is completed and the speed of elimination of the sterilant
from the soil are greater at higher temperatures, consequently it is inadvisable
to treat with chemicals during the late autumn and winter.

Before using soil which has been treated, its freedom from phytotoxic residues
should be established by ensuring that cress seed will germinate normally on the
moistened surface of a 1 kg soil sample in a gas-tight container.

A variety of chemicals is now available for soil sterilisation.

(a) Chloropicrin
Chloropicrin (trichloronitromethane, CCl_3NO_2) is a most unpleasant and
dangerous material. Originally developed for the explosives industry, it is
becoming out-moded for use under protected cultivation but does have potential
in the arable situation. It is injected into the soil at a rate of 600 kg/ha to a

depth of 15 cm every 30 cm and the soil surface is sealed either with plastic
sheets or by flooding.

(b) Dazomet

Dazomet (tetrahydro-3,5-dimethyl-1,3,5-thiadiazone-2-thione) (figure 4.13) is
an aromatic dithiocarbamate which is becoming widely used in both field and
protected situations. Application is in a granular form at the rate of 50 kg/ha, which
which is then immediately worked into the soil by rotary cultivation. Dazomet is
advocated is for field-scale control of *Plasmodiophora brassicae* (clubroot) as well
as for the control of a range of other fungal pathogens.

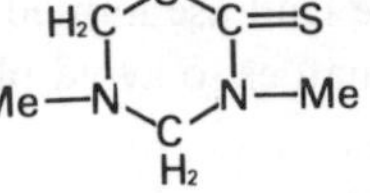

Figure 4.13   Structural formula of dazomet. Me = methyl radical.

(c) 'D-D' mixture

'D-D' mixture (dichloropropane + dichloropropene, $(CH_2)_3Cl_2 + (CH_2)_2CHCl_2$) is
used in a similar way to chloropicrin, at a rate of 500 kg/ha. Some formulations
have proved successful for field-scale control of soil pathogens as well as under
protection. Regular use on heavy soils is inadvisable since some crops have been
tainted following use of the mixture.

(d) Formaldehyde

Formaldehyde (HCHO) was one of the original chemical sterilants used to replace
steam sterilisation, but is now tending to decline in use, particularly in view of
its carcinogenic properties. It is generally used as a solution containing 0.8 per
cent active ingredient at 2500 litres/ha.

(e) Metham-sodium

As with dazomet, metham-sodium (sodium N-methyldithiocarbamate,
MeNHCSSNa) can be used to sterilise small quantities of soil for potting
composts in addition to application to greater volumes either in the field or
under cover. Both materials produce phytotoxic fumes which should be tested
for before using the soil. Metham-sodium can be mixed into the soil with a rotary
cultivator, the soil surface then being sealed, or injected as with chloropicrin.
Formulations vary greatly in concentration, but the usual dose rate is 35 litres
a.i./ha.

(f) Methyl bromide

Methyl bromide (MeBr) is becoming widely used as a seed surface decontaminant
particularly for eradication of bacterial pathogens as well as for soil sterilisation
purposes. Methyl bromide has the advantage of rapid diffusion into and away from
the soil, consequently the interval between treatment and planting is short. But

the material is highly toxic to mammals and special equipment is required to use it, including impermeable sheeting to retain it in the soil. In the UK only specialist contractors are licensed to apply it (Anon, 1980). Application is usually at the rate of 50 kg/ha.

(g) Methyl isothiocyanate

In combination with 'D-D' mixture, methyl isothiocyanate (MeSCN) has been used successfully on the Continent and in the Channel Islands for control of pathogens such as *Phytophthora, Pythium, Thanetophorus, Fusarium* and *Verticillium* under glass. Injected at a rate of 170 kg/ha, results are comparable with those obtained with metham-sodium. It is, however, very unpleasant to use and there are limitations on the land use immediately after application. The first crop can only be lettuce or tomatoes to avoid phytotoxic effects.

4.3.5 Bactericides

There has been no development of bactericides comparable to the discoveries of chemicals for the control of fungi. Except for a limited number of medical antibiotics, the materials used to control bacterial plant pathogens have remained the same for the last 50 years. All plant pathogenic bacteria are seed-borne, or potentially so, and many perennate on vegetative propagating material. Secondary spread is by insect vectors or by mechanical transmission. The most satisfactory methods of control are, therefore, either through seed certification schemes to maintain freedom from pathogens in the initial planting material, or by breeding resistant cultivars. The latter is at best a long-term solution, but may be impossible for some pathogens where resistance appears to be absent in the host. For example, of 8700 rice cultivars tested in the Phillipines none was satisfactorily resistant to *Xanthomonas oryzae* (bacterial blight).

The main avenues for chemical control are via seed treatment and field sprays.

(a) Seed treatment

Materials used include copper, mercury and quaternary ammonium compounds, sodium hypochlorite, malachite green, phenacridane chloride, sulphuric acid and antibiotics. Particular uses in vegetable crops have been organomercury for control of *Corynebacterium betae* (leaf spot). It was later shown that soaking the seed in 400 p.p.m. streptomycin (Keyworth and Howell, 1961) for 18 h was a superior treatment. Control of *Pseudomonas phaseolicola* (halo blight) has been achieved by Taylor *et al.* (1975) using slurries of streptomycin or kasugamycin. The mean number of primary infections per 1000 plants fell from 8.31 with untreated seed to 0.11 for kasugamycin-treated seed and 0.06 for streptomycin-treated seed. Brassica seed, however, could not be freed from *Xanthomonas campestris* (black rot) without the use of phytotoxic concentrations. Elimination of *Corynebacterium michiganense* (bacterial canker) from tomato seed has been achieved by fermenting the fruit pulp for 4 days at 20 °C and then treating the extracted seed with 0.8 per cent acetic acid for 24 h (Blood, 1942). Hot water treatment has also been successful as a control for this pathogen.

(b) Field sprays
In several bean-growing regions, control of halo blight has been achieved by field spraying. Four sprays of Bordeaux mixture (Reid and Taylor, 1945) successfully reduced the disease in New Zealand and the material was found to be more successful than streptomycin in the USA (Afansiev and Sharp, 1958) *Xanthomonas phaseoli* (common blight) and *Pseudomonas syringae* (brown spot) of bean were controlled with sprays of tribasic copper sulphate and basic copper hydroxide, with yield increases of over 40 per cent (Hagedorn *et al.*, 1969; Saettler and Potter, 1967). Mixtures of streptomycin and tribasic copper sulphate (Cox and Hayslip, 1957) gave the best control of bacterial leaf spot of field peppers and tomatoes caused by *X. vesicatoria*. The efficacy of streptomycin, however, has declined as strains of the bacterium resistant to the antibiotic have developed (Thayer and Stall, 1961; Stall and Thayer, 1962). The use of drugs such as streptomycin to control bacterial plant pathogens is viewed with apprehension by the medical profession since it may lead to a lessening of the effectiveness of these materials for the control of bacteria pathogenic to humans. Drug resistance can be transmitted from one cell to another by extracellular DNA (transformation), by bacteriophages (transduction) and by direct contact between bacterial cells (conjugation). In some Gram-negative bacteria resistance has been shown to be controlled by extrachromosomal DNA (episomes) and to be transferred with episomal replicates from resistant to sensitive bacteria during conjugation.

4.3.6 Virus control

There are no direct methods for the control of viruses, consequently they are treated separately from fungi and bacteria. Control techniques mostly involve evasive measures designed to reduce sources of infection inside and outside the crop and limit the spread of vectors, thereby minimising the effect of infection on yield. In a few cases a satisfactory source of resistance to a specific virus has been introduced into horticulturally acceptable cultivars. As with other pathogens, correct diagnosis of the virus is essential for effective control, but disease symptoms alone cannot be relied on and techniques such as serology and electron microscopy must be used. The complexity of viral diagnosis can be seen from the observation by Cock (1968) that there are 14 viruses affecting lettuce, variously spread by aphids, thrips, nematodes and fungi.

(a) Removal of sources of infection
Primarily, this entails removal of alternative hosts, which include weeds, perennial

ornamental plants (many of which can harbour infection in a mild form), unrelated crops which are infected by the same virus, volunteer plants of the same species remaining from a previous crop, and seed crops (which with many vegetables mature at about the time the ware crop is emerging). Plant residues, particularly of glasshouse crops, are a very dangerous reservoir for the transmission of viruses from one crop to another. With very stable viruses such as Tobacco Mosaic Virus (TMV) complete eradication of crop residues can be difficult (Broadbent *et al.*, 1965). Crop roguing, to remove isolated foci of infection, can be worthwhile if the virus is one which spreads slowly (simple interest type – *see* section 3.1) and infection comes mainly from within the crop. But where virus spread is rapid (compound interest type – *see* section 3.1), and mostly from outside sources, then roguing has little effect.

(b) Virus-free seed

Viruses which are seed-transmissible introduce disease into the crops from the earliest stage of its growth. Therefore, if seed infection is the major source of infection and seed crops can be produced in reasonable isolation, use of virus-free seed may provide an effective control technique. Control of Lettuce Mosaic Virus (LMV) can be obtained in this way, but even a small proportion of infected seed can give rise to very heavy infections in the crop, particularly if the vector is highly active (Zink *et al.*, 1956). Very strict limits on the permissible levels of infection in virus-free seed must therefore be maintained.

(c) Virus-free vegetative stocks

Where crops are vegetatively propagated the basic stocks can often be a major source of virus infection. To obtain disease-free planting material a nucleus stock must first be freed from infection and then bulked up under conditions where reinfection is excluded. The initial mother stocks are selected from material with the lowest possible virus titre. Identification of this material involves mechanical inoculation on indicator hosts, serological tests and for hardwood species grafting on indicator plants. This process is known as indexing. Sometimes naturally occurring plant tissue may be virus free; this is particularly the case with rapidly growing shoot tips. Tissue may be freed from virus particles by heat treatment. The material is subjected to several weeks at elevated temperatures (usually 37 °C) using either hot water or hot air. Subsequently, small cuttings are made from the shoot tips and then grown on. Even more refined is culture from meristematic tips, which has proved an extremely effective means of obtaining virus-free material. The technique has been defined as the 'aseptic culture of the apical dome plus the first pair of leaf primordia' (Hollings, 1965). Media used to culture meristem cuttings include mineral salts, sucrose, indoleacetic acid, and gibberellic acid, sometimes formulated in agar, but better results are often obtained when the tips are grown on filter paper dipping into sterile nutrient solution.

(d) Cultural techniques

Infection may often be prevented by breaking the cycle of virus transmission by having a period when no crop is available for the vector to feed on. In California, USA, Sevrerin and Freitag (1938) reported that interruption of a previously continuous cycle of celery production by a 3—5 month break was sufficient to reduce the build-up of virus infection which was having a catastrophic effect on yields. In New Zealand an eradication programme whereby all *Allium* spp. were removed eliminated Onion Yellow Dwarf Virus (OYDV) altogether (Chamberlain and Baylis, 1948). Changes in planting or sowing date to avoid the migration dates for air-borne vectors may also prevent infection, but this requires a monitoring service to sample the vector populations at regular intervals and inform growers when it is safe to plant. Increased plant populations have been shown to reduce the overall level of virus infection (A'Brook, 1964, 1968). Destruction of haulm from previous crops before a certain date will also help to avoid the spread of viruses.

(e) Vector control

Before control is achieved the vector must be accurately identified. Insecticides are very effective controls against viruses which are circulative and aphid-borne since they reduce spread within the crop, but if the virus is stylet-borne the incoming aphid rapidly loses infectivity and killing it will make little difference to infection of the crop emanating from outside. Granular formulations of systemic insecticides now permit placement at planting time, thereby reducing the handling of very toxic chemicals and the damage which was previously done to standing crops by spraying machinery.

In the glasshouse, Loebensteijn *et al.* (1964) showed that 1 per cent emulsion of oil in water plus detergent was effective in preventing *Aphis gossypii* from infecting cucumbers with Cucumber Mosaic Virus (CMV). Oils with molecules containing less than 16 carbon atoms were ineffective due to volatility. The spread of about 10 per cent of stylet-borne viruses has been shown to be inhibited by oil sprays (Matthews, 1970). Their major advantage over insecticides is a lack of mammalian toxicity.

Barrier crops can be used to prevent some virus infections. Surrounding cauliflower seed beds with narrow strips of barely reduced virus incidence in seedlings by about 80 per cent (Broadbent, 1957). A straw mulch has been used effectively in the Middle East to control the white fly vector of Bottle Gourd Mosaic Virus (BGMV) in cucurbits. In mulched plots, development of infection was delayed and substantial increases in yield obtained due to delayed infection (Nitzany *et al.*, 1964). This was attributed to the vector landing on the straw mulch being unable to feed and flying off. Variable results have been obtained with the use of aluminium strips laid alongside crops; reflection of ultraviolet light is thought to act as an aphid repellant.

Predators are now being used to control various insect pests such as white fly and mites under glass, and this may be one means of biological control of viruses. Control of nematode-transmitted viruses should be possible through the use of nematicides. Movement and dispersal of nematodes is slow, which should permit a single treatment to remain effective for a considerable time. On the other hand, nematodes tend to penetrate deeply into soil where the nematicides do not reach, so that total control does not take place. A single fumigation of dichloropropane+dichloropropene (D-D) or pentachloronitrobenzene (PCNB) fully protected strawberries against Tomato Black Ring Virus (TBRV) and Raspbery Ringspot Virus (RRV) transmitted by *Longidorus elongatus* (Murrant and Taylor, 1965). Under glass, Lettuce Big Vein Virus (LBVV) transmitted by the soil-borne fungus *Olpidium brassicae* can be controlled by fumigation with chloropicrin or D-D (Grogan *et al.*, 1958). Mechanical spread of viruses on pruning knives can be controlled with 3 per cent trisodium orthophosphate (Broadbent, 1963).

(f) Resistant cultivars
Resistance to virus diseases can be achieved as follows:

(1) By breeding cultivars which are unattractive to the vector so that no infection takes place.

(2) By breeding cultivars which have suppressed symptom development; such cultivars are dangerous since they act as unseen reservoirs of infection for more susceptible hosts; if used for vegetative propagation large numbers of virus-infected plants come into cultivation; also there has been an attendant increase in susceptibility to other pathogens in such cultivars.

(3) By breeding truly resistant cultivars, because virus replication does not occur in the host cell. Considerable success has been achieved in the production of tomato cultivars resistant to Tomato Mosaic Virus (TMV) utilising up to three genes for resistance. Unfortunately breeders have used varying numbers of resistance genes, resulting in variation in the level of resistance between cultivars. This has given rise to the evolution of TMV strains capable of overcoming at least some of the resistances.

(g) Antiviral chemicals
Compounds such as 2-thiouracil (Holmes, 1955) and 8-azaguanine (Matthews, 1953) have been shown to control or reduce viral symptoms under experimental conditions, but have not proved successful for commercial application. More recently, Tomlinson *et al.* (1977) have shown that carbendazim when used as a root drench treatment is effective in the suppression of symptoms of Beet Western Yellow Virus (BWYV) in lettuce and TMV in tobacco plants.

(h) Quarantine measures
These are worthwhile for viruses which are transmitted through seed or dormant vegetative organs. The operation of quarantine schemes requires considerable international co-operation and is often the subject of political factors which dilute their efficacy. It is often difficult to assess how successful schemes are,

especially in the short term. Strict regulations were established in New Zealand in 1952, since when a number of new viruses have been identified; these may have been present before the regulations, and it will take several more decades before the effectiveness or otherwise of the measures is proved. For further details readers are referred to Ebbels and King (1979) who give an up to date account of the use of legislation to control fungal, bacterial and viral pathogens.

REFERENCES

A'Brook, J. (1964). *Ann. ₐppl. Biol.* **54**, 199–208.

A'Brook, J. (1968). *Ann. appl. Biol.* **61**, 289–94.

Afansiev, M. M. and Sharp, E. L. (1958). *Pl. Dis. Reptr* **42**, 1071–3.

Angel, H. R., Walker, J. C. and Link, K. P. (1930). *Phytopathology* **20**, 431.

Anon (1980). *Agricultural Chemicals Approval Scheme: List of Approved Products and their Uses for Farmers and Growers.* Ministry of Agriculture, Fisheries and Food, London.

Bent, K. J., Cole, A. M., Turner, J. A. W. and Woolner, M. (1971). *Proc. 6th Br. Insectic. Fungic. Conf.* **1**, 274–82.

Berard, D. F., Kuć, J. and Williams, E. B. (1972). *Physiol. Pl. Path.* **2**, 123–7.

Berard, D. F., Kuć, J. and Williams, E. B. (1973). *Physiol. Pl. Path.* **3**, 51–6.

Biffen, R. H. (1905). *J. agric. Sci.* **1**, 4–8.

Biffen, R. H. (1912). *J. agric. Sci.* **4**, 421–9.

Black, W., Mastenbroek, C., Mills, W. R. and Peterson, L. C. (1953). *Euphytica* **2**, 183–9.

Blakeman, J. P. (1971). The chemical environment of the leaf surface in relation to growth of pathogenic fungi. In *Ecology of Leaf Surface Micro-organisms* (T. F. Preece and C. H. Dickinson, eds). Academic Press, London.

Blood, H. L. (1942). *Can. Agric.* **23**, 221–3.

Bravenboer, L. and Pet, G. (1962). *Proc. 16th int. hort. Congr.* **2**, 317–24.

Broadbent, L. (1957). *Investigations of Virus Diseases of Brassica Crops*, Agricultural Research Council Report Series No. 14. Cambridge University Press, London.

Broadbent, L. (1963). *Ann. appl. Biol.* **52**, 225–32.

Broadbent, L. (1964). *Ann. appl. Biol.* **54**, 209–24.

Broadbent, L., Read, W. H. and Last, F. J. (1965). *Ann. appl. Biol.* **55**, 471–83.

Buczacki, S. T., Toxopeus, H., Mattusch, P., Johnston, T. D., Dixon, G. R. and Hobolth, L. A. (1975). *Trans. Br. mycol. Soc.* **65**, 295–303.

Caldwell, R. M., Schafer, J. F., Compton, L. E. and Patterson, F. L. (1958). *Science, N.Y.* **128**, 714–5.

Carley, H. E. (1969). Factors affecting the epidemiology of pea (*Pisum sativum* L.): Root rot caused by *Aphanomyces euteiches* Dresch. Ph.D. thesis, University of Minnesota, St. Paul, Minn.

Chamberlain, E. E. and Baylis, G. T. S. (1948). *N.Z. J. Sci. Technol. A* **29**, 300—301.

Clemons, G. P and Sisler, H. D. (1971). *Pesticide Biochem. Physiol.* **1**, 32—43.

Cock, L. J. (1968). *N.A.A.S. Quart. Rev.* **79**, 126—38.

Colhoun, J. (1958). *Clubroot Disease of Crucifers Caused by* Plasmodiophora brassicae *Woron*. Phytopathological Paper no. 3. Commonwealth Mycological Institute, Kew.

Cox, R. S. and Hayslip, N. C. (1957). *Pl. Dis. Reptr* **41**, 878—83.

Crute, I. R. and Johnson, A. G. (1976). *Ann. appl. Biol.* **83**, 125—37.

Daly, J. M. (1949). *Phytopathology* **39**, 386—94.

Das, A. C. and Western, J. H. (1959). *Ann. appl. Biol.* **47**, 37—48.

Davidse, L. C. (1973). *Pesticide Biochem. Physiol.* **3**, 317—25.

Davidse, L. C. (1975*a*). Mode of action by methyl benzimidazole-2-yl carbamate (MBC) and some biochemical aspects of acquired resistance against this fungicide in *Aspergillus nidulans*. In *System Fungizide* (H. Lyr and C. Potter, eds). Akademie-Verlag, Berlin.

Davidse, L. C. (1975*b*). Antimitotic activity of methyl benzimidazole-2-yl carbamate in fungi and its binding to cellular protein. In *Microtubules and Microtubule Inhibitors* (M. Borgers and M. Brabander, eds). North Holland, Amsterdam.

Day, P. R. (1956). *Tomato Genet. Co-op. Rep.* **6**, 13—14.

Day, P. R. (1960). *A. Rev. Microbiol.* **14**, 1—16.

Dekker, J. (1967). Conversion of 6-azauracil in sensitive and resistant strains of *Cladosporium cucumerinum*. In *Mechanisms of Action of Fungicides and Antibiotics* (W. Girbardt, ed.). Akademie-Verlag, Berlin.

Dekker, J. (1971). *Proc. 6th Br. Insectic. Fungic. Conf.* **3**, 715—23.

Dekker, J. (1977). Resistance. In *Systemic Fungicides* (R. W. Marsh, ed.). Longman, London.

Dixon, G. R. (1978). Monitoring vegetable diseases. In *Plant Disease Epidemiology* (P. R. Scott and A. Bainbridge, eds). Blackwells Scientific Publications, Oxford.

Dixon, G. R. and Wright, I. R. (1978). *Ann. appl. Biol.* **88**, 287—94.

Doling, D. A. and Willey, L. A. (1969). *Expl Husb.* **18**, 87—90.

Eenink, A. H. (1976). *Neth. J. Pl. Path.* **82**, 133—45.

Ellingboe, A. H. (1972). *Phytopathology* **62**, 401—6.

Ellis, N. K. (1950). The effect of growing peppermint on the persistence of clubroot in muck soil. Dissertation, Michigan State College (Publication No. 1737).

Ebbels, D. L. and King, J. E. (1979). *Plant Health*. Blackwell Scientific Publications, Oxford.

Fincham, J. R. S. and Day, P. R. (1965). *Fungal Genetics*. Blackwell Scientific Publications, Oxford.

Flor, H. H. (1955). *Phytopathology* **45**, 680—5.

Gallegly, M. E. and Walker, J. C. (1949). *Am. J. Bot.* **36**, 613—23.

Georgopoulos, S. G. and Sisler, H. D. (1970). *J. Bact.* **103**, 745–50.
Grogan, R. G., Zink, F. W., Hewitt, W. B. and Kimble, K. A. (1958).
Phytopathology **48**, 292–7.
Habgood, R. M. (1970). *Nature, Lond.* **227**, 1268–9.
Hagedorn, D. J., Wade, E. K. and Weiss, G. (1969). *Pl. Dis. Reptr* **53**, 178–81.
Hammerschlag, R. S. and Sisler, H. D. (1973). *Pesticide Biochem. Physiol.* **3**,
42–54.
Headley, J. C. (1973). *Environmental Quality and the Economics of Agricultural
Pest Control.* European and Mediterranean Plant Protection Organisation,
Conference of Plant Protection Economy, Brussels.
Hollings, M (1965). *A. Rev. Phytopath.* **3**, 367–96.
Holmes, F. O. (1955). *Virology* **1**, 1–9.
Hubbeling, N. (1969). *Meded. Rijksfakulteit Landbouwweetenschappen Gent*
34, 937–43.
Huber, D. M. and Watson, R. D. (1974). *A. Rev. Phytopath.* **12**, 139–65.
Johnson, R. and Taylor, A. J. (1976). *A. Rev. Phytopath.* **14**, 97–119.
Kaspars, H., Greive, F., Brandes, W., Scheinflug, H. and Büchel, K. A. (1975). *Proc.
8th int Pl. Protect. Congr.* **3**, 398–401.
Keyworth, W. G. and Howell, S. J. (1961). *Ann. appl. Biol.* **49**, 173–94.
Last, R. T. (1953). *Ann. appl. Biol.* **40**, 312–22.
Levine, R. P. (1968). *Science, N.Y.* **162**, 768–71.
Link, K. P. and Walker, J. C. (1933). *J. biol. Chem.* **100**, 379–83.
Loebensteijn, G., Alper, M. and Deutsch, M. (1964). *Phytopathology* **54**,
960–2.
Loegering, W. Q. and Powers, H. R. (1962). *Phytopathology* **52**, 547–54.
Macer, R. F. (1960). *Nature, Lond.* **186**, 857.
Matthews, R. E. F. (1953). *J. gen. Microbiol.* **8**, 277–88.
Matthews, R. E. F. (1970). *Plant Virology.* Academic Press, New York.
Maude, R. B. (1966). *Rep. natn. Veg. Res. Stn* **1966**, 73.
Maxon-Smith, J. W. and Proctor, P. (1965). *Expl Hort.* **12**, 6–20.
Murrant, A. F. and Taylor, C. E. (1965). *Ann. appl. Biol.* **55**, 227–37.
Nitzany, F. E., Geisenberg, H. and Koch, H. (1964). *Phytopathology* **54**,
1059–61.
Nutman, P. S. (1969). *Proc. R. Soc. B* **172**, 417–37.
Onuorah, P. E. (1969). *Pl. Soil* **30**, 99–104.
Pelham, J. (1966). *Euphytica* **15**, 258–67.
Petersen, C. A. and Edington, I. V. (1969). *Phytopathology* **59**, 1044.
van der Plank, J. E. (1968). *Disease Resistance in Plants.* Academic Press, London.
Rast, A.Th. B. (1972). *Neth. J. Pl. Path.* **78**, 110–2.
Reid, W. D. and Taylor, G. G. (1945). *N.Z. J. Sci. Technol. A* **27**, 90–3.
Robinson, R. A. (1971). *Rev. Pl. Path.* **50**, 233–39.
Robinson, R. A. (1973). *Rev. Pl. Path.* **52**, 483–501.
Rotem, J. and Cohen, Y. (1966). *Pl. Dis. Reptr* **50**, 635–9.
Saettler, A. W. and Potter, H. S. (1967). *Pl. Dis. Reptr* **51**, 622–5.

Schafer, J. F. (1971). *A. Rev. Phytopath.* **9**, 235–52.
Searle, G. D. (1920). *Trans. Br. mycol. Soc.* **6**, 274–94.
Sevrerin, H. P. and Freitag, H. J. (1938). *Hilgardia* **11**, 495–558.
Shephard, M. C. and Wood, R. K. S. (1963). *Ann. appl. Biol.* **51**, 389–402.
Shipton, P. J. (1977). *A. Rev. Phytopath.* **15**, 387–407.
Sijpesteijn, K. H. (1969). *Wld Rev. Pest Control* **8**, 138–145.
Sol, H. H. (1967). *Meded. Landbouwhogesch. Opzoekingssta. Staat. Gent* **32**, 768–75.
Stall, R. E. and Thayer, P. L. (1962). *Pl. Dis. Reptr* **46**, 389–92.
Strijbosch, Th. (1976). *A. Rep. Glasshouse Crops Res. Exp. Stn, Naaldwijk* **1973 and 1974**, 79–80.
Taylor, J. D., Dudley, C. L. and Gray, L. (1975). *Rep. natn. Veg. Res. Stn* **1974**, 115–6.
Thayer, P. L. and Stall, R. E. (1961). *Phytopathology* **51**, 568–71.
Thayer, P. L. and Williams, L. E. (1960). *Phytopathology* **50**, 212–14.
Tomlinson, J. A., Ward, C. M., Webb, M. J. W. and Faithfull, E. M. (1977). *A. Rep. natn. Veg. Res. Stn* **1976**, 105–6.
Urecht, P. A., Schwinn, F. and Staub, T. (1977). *Proc. 9th Br. Insectic. Fungic. Conf.* 623–31.
U, N. (1935). *Jap. J. Bot.* **7**, 389–452.
Vanterpool, T. C. (1962). *Can. Pl. Dis. Surv.* **42**, 214–5.
Walker, J. C. (1946). *Soil Sci.* **61**, 47–54.
Walker, J. C. and Foster, R. E. (1946). *Am. J. Bot.* **33**, 259–64.
Walker, J. C., Gallegly, M. E., Bloom, J. R. and Shepherd, R. D. (1954). *Am. J. Bot.* **41**, 760–2.
Ward, E. W. B. and Stoessl, A. (1976). *Phytopathology* **66**, 940–1.
Wilhelm, S. (1971). Principles and practice of Verticillium wilt control in strawberries in California by preplant soil fumigation with chloropicrin–methyl bromide mixtures. Paper presented at the International Verticillium Symposium, Wye College, University of London, Wye.
Zink, F. W., Grogan, R. G. and Welsh, J. E. (1956). *Phytopathology* **46**, 622–4.

FURTHER READING

Anon (1959). *Soil Sterilization.* Bulletin No. 22. Ministry of Agriculture, Fisheries and Food, London.
Baker, K. F. and Snyder, W. C. (eds) (1965). *Ecology of Soil Borne Plant Pathogens.* John Murray, London.
British Crop Protection Council (1976). *Insecticide and Fungicide Handbook for Crop Protection* (H. Martin, ed.), Blackwell Scientific Publications, Oxford.
Crosse, J. E. (1971). *Proc. 6th Br. Insectic. Fungic. Conf.* **3**, 694–705.
Day, P. R. (1974). *Genetics of Host Parasite Interaction.* Freeman, San Francisco.

Deverall, B. J. (1977). *Defence Mechanisms in Plants.* Cambridge University Press, London.

Evans, E. (1968). *Plant Diseases and their Chemical Control.* Blackwell Scientific Publications, Oxford.

Marsh, R. W. (ed.) (1977). *Systemic Fungicides.* Longman, London.

North, C. (1979). *Plant Breeding and Genetics in Horticulture.* Macmillan, London.

Smith, K. M. (1974). *Plant Viruses.* Chapman and Hall, London.

Srb, A. M. and Owen, R. D. (1952). *General Genetics.* Freeman, San Francisco.

Stakman, E. C. and Harrar, J. G. (1957). *Principles of Plant Pathology*, Ronald Press, New York.

Watts, L. (1980). *Flower and Vegetable Plant Breeding.* Grower Books, London.

Wheeler, H. (1975). *Plant Pathogenesis.* Springer-Verlag, Berlin.

Williams, W. (1964). *Genetical Principles and Plant Breeding.* Blackwell Scientific Publications, Oxford.

5
Pathogens of Crucifer Crops

This is the first chapter dealing with pathogens of a particular crop family, in this case the Cruciferae. Within this family the Brassicae are an example of a major and ancient horticultural crop with a wide diversity of morphological form. The edible parts range from swollen hypocotyls as in swede (*Brassica napus*) and turnip (*B. campestris*), through the swollen axillary buds of Brussels sprout (*B. oleracea* var. *gemmifera*) and swollen apical buds of the various cabbage types (*B. oleracea* var. *capitata*) to the inflorescences of cauliflower (*B. oleracea* var. *botrytis*). A similar range of pathogens affects all these crops, but the relative importance varies from crop to crop. Thus *Plasmodiophora brassicae* (clubroot) is of most significance on those with a summer production phase and less so on the winter brassicas while, for example, *Alternaria* spp. cause greatest damage to seed crops. Pathogens such as *Peronospora parasitica* (downy mildew) and *Thanetophorus cucumeris* (damping-off) are of world-wide importance at the seedling growth stage. *Mycosphaerella brassicicola* (ringspot) is usually restricted to crops produced in warm maritime climates. Cauliflower Mosaic Virus is a good example of a widespread plant virus which has been investigated in depth not only because of its agronomic importance but also for intrinsic biological reasons. More than one virus may be present within crop plants causing a complex disease syndrome and this aspect is discussed at the end of this chapter.

5.1 FUNGAL PATHOGENS
5.1.1 *Peronospora parasitica* (downy mildew)

Most members of the Cruciferae are hosts of this pathogen. Various specific names have been applied to the fungus, for example, *P. brassicae*, but these are now regarded as applying to a single species, *P. parasitica* (Yerkes and Shaw, 1959). The host range of individual isolates of *P. parasitica* is highly variable and unrelated to the taxonomy of the original host (Dickinson and Greenhalgh, 1977). This variability is also reflected in callus culture studies made by Ingram (1969). In such culture *P. parasitica* is found to be an aggressive parasite which contrasts with its growth habit in intact *Brassica* cotyledons. Additionally, the susceptibility of *Brassica* callus clones and root organ cultures to *P. parasitica* is not constant and is frequently at variance with results obtained using intact plants.

Symptoms first become apparent as discrete areas of chlorotic-yellow cells on the upper surfaces of host leaves. Opposite these lesions on the leaf undersurface

are areas of diffuse white sporangiophores. As the severity of infection increases
the lesions expand, but are generally limited by major veins (figure 5.1). In very
heavy infections, or under favourable environmental conditions, sporulation
may appear on both leaf surfaces. This is especially so with young seedlings
where the cotyledons exhibit profuse sporulation, then become senescent and
eventually desiccated. These dead, dry cotyledons may abscise or remain attached
to the weakened young plant. At this stage *P. parasitica* is capable of becoming
systemic and quiescent (Lebeau, 1945). As the host matures *P. parasitica* can
again become evident, particularly in cauliflower and calabrese (*B. oleracea* var.
botrytis and *italica*) where the curds and spears are invaded, leading to
discoloration and rotting during storage. Symptoms at this stage include
development of pale brown lesions on the inflorescence surface with blackened
zones and streaks along the stalks often penetrating to the central medulla.
Abundant sporulation is found, encouraged by the moist microclimate of the
curd interior, and generalised rotting caused by secondary soft rot bacteria takes
place in store or in the market place. Infection of mature Brussels sprouts (*B.
oleracea* var. *gemmifera*) leads to sporulation on the buttons as well as on the

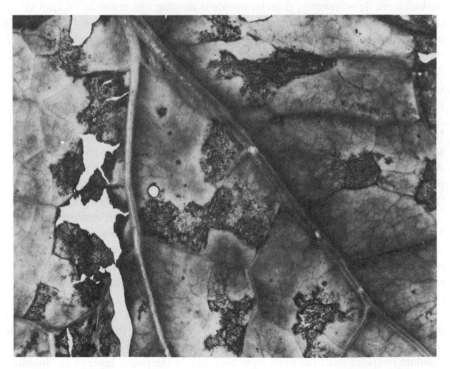

Figure 5.1   Lesions on swede leaves caused by *Peronospora parasitica* (downy
mildew). (Reproduced by permission of National Institute of
Agricultural Botany, Cambridge.)

foliage. As with cauliflower, rotting frequently follows infection, reducing the buttons to a slimy mass. A technique for measuring levels of infection by *P. parasitica* quantitatively is reported by McMeekin (1971).

Peronospora parasitica is a Phycomycete fungus, class Oomycetes. A coenocytic intercellular mycelium forms within the host from which intracellular haustoria are produced. Usually these occur in leaves and are spherical with two or three lobes, 8–11 µm in size. The haustoria do not actually penetrate the host protoplast (Fraymouth, 1956). At the point of penetration into each cell the haustorium is surrounded by a sheath of host wall material. It becomes enclosed along its length by a further sheath, the zone of apposition, which may be derived from host material. Around it are concentrated large numbers of host-produced secretory bodies and ribosomes. The haustorium acts as a metabolic sink for transport of nutrients from host to pathogen. Asexual sporangiophores form from the internal mycelium through the host stomata; which are hyaline and dichotomously branched. They bear hyaline, elliptical sporangia, 16–20 µm x 20–22 µm in size, which germinate by means of a germ tube. Sexual oogonia and antheridia form as the host nutrient reserves are depleted. The oogonia are hyaline spheres and are fertilized by a single antheridium. Subsequently, globular oospores develop which are 26–43 µm in size. Physiological races of *P. parasitica* are reported, some apparently being capable of forming oospores more abundantly than others. Some races appear to be restricted pathogenically to invasion of hypocotyl tissue alone. Heterothallism has been reported for *P. parasitica* but not confirmed. Sansome and Sansome (1974) suggest that the sexual cycle of *P. parasitica* can only be completed in the presence of *Albugo candida*, the cause of white rust of Cruciferae.

Cool, moist conditions favour *P. parasitica* and sporangia are liberated due to changes in RH around the leaf. Optimum temperatures for sporangia formation are 8–10 °C, for germination 8–12 °C, and for host penetration 16 °C. Appressoria and germ tubes have smooth surfaces and penetration usually takes place through the cuticle, although entry through the stomata is often seen (Shiraishi *et al.*, 1975). Following penetration, haustoria form most rapidly at 20–24 °C while lesions expand most quickly at 20 °C. But temperatures of 10–15 °C are the most favourable for epidemic development since this range favours sporulation, germination and reinfection. Under field conditions *P. parasitica* is found to be most severe in areas where rainfall exceeds 750–1000 mm per annum and at times of year when day-length is in the range 14–15 h (Vladimirskaya *et al.*, 1975).

Studies of host–parasite relations using Japanese radish (*R. sativus* var. *hortensis*), in which the swelling hypocotyl is invaded by *P. parasitica*, show that lignification of the parenchyma cell walls is induced by infection. This is initiated first in the cellulose microfibrils of the inner layer and then in the pectic layer of the middle lamella (Asada and Kugoh, 1971). This probably involves a change in the biosynthetic pathway for lignin in the infected host since healthy vessel walls are composed of syringlylpropane units while the lignin found in parenchyma cell

walls of diseased plants is composed of guaiacylpropane units (Asada and
Matsumoto, 1971, 1972). In the neighbourhood of infected cells peroxidase
activity increases up to 11 days after infection. Such increases are in the basic
fractions while activity of neutral and acidic fractions decreases (Ohguchi *et al.*,
1974). Enhanced enzyme activity in diseased tissues is responsible for the
accumulation of lignins and the enzyme, or enzymes, involved participate in
dehydrogenation polymerisation of *p*-hydroxycinnamyl alcohols (Ohguchi and
Asada, 1975). Dioxane lignins are isolated from both healthy and infected root
tissue. But L-phenylalanine ammonia lyase (PAL) activity increases only in
diseased roots. Consequently, the presence of lignification-inducing substances
exhibiting *de novo* synthesis of PAL is found only in homogenates of diseased
tissue (Asada, 1974). Studies with cabbage (*B. oleracea* var. *capitata* cv.
Primo) infected by *P. parasitica* show that respiration rate rises sharply immediately
after inoculation, reaching a maximum of almost twice that of uninfected
controls at the time when sporulation is initiated. But the chlorophyll content
of healthy and infected tissues is similar. Since no polyhydric alcohols can be
detected in diseased leaves or fungal sporangia, Thornton and Cooke (1974)
suggest that, unlike the biochemical changes which accompany rust (*Puccinia*
spp.) or powdery mildew (*Erysiphe* spp.) infection, in this host–parasite
complex there is no shift to the pentose phosphate respiratory pathway (*see*
section 2.3.2).

Attempts to control *P. parasitica* by use of resistance so far appear to have
been limited to the use of a highly specific major gene, and this (as might be
anticipated) has had little practical value (Natti *et al.*, 1967). Several studies
suggest, however, that more generalised resistance is available which could be
exploited. Following artificial inoculation of cauliflower (*B. oleracea* var.
botrytis cv. Veitche's Autumn Giant) Greenhalgh and Dickinson (1975) found
it to be totally susceptible whereas cabbage (*B. oleracea* var. *capitata* cv.
January King) and wallflower (*Cheirianthus cheiri* cv. Covent Garden Blood
Red) have greater resistance. The surface and epidermal reactions do not
appear responsible for resistance, which is expressed as necrosis of the
cotyledonary mesophyll cells and inhibition of hyphal growth within the host
tissue. Cotyledons were found to be more susceptible than hypocotyls. Further
studies using populations of wild cabbage (*B. oleracea*) suggest that resistance
may be associated with high levels of flavour volatiles, particularly allyl
isothiocyanate (Greenhalgh and Dickinson, 1976; Greenhalgh and Mitchell, 1976).
The latter has been selected against in order to improve palatability in
commercial cultivars. There are noticeable differences in susceptibility of
Brussels sprout (*B. oleracea* var. *gemmifera*) and calabrese (*B. oleracea* var.
italica) cultivars to *P. parasitica* (G. R. Dixon, unpublished observations) which
breeders might exploit.

This pathogen may be controlled chemically by use of 0.2 per cent a.i.
dichlofluanid, particularly with seedling brassicas. Addition of 0.1 per cent
non-ionic wetter greatly improves the efficacy of this compound, especially

when infection spreads to the true leaves. Repeated use, however, may lead to phytotoxic damage (Channon and Turner, 1970). More recently, prothiocarb (Ryan, 1977) at a rate of eight application each using l g a.i. per 10 m² has been shown to give control of *P. parasitica* in early summer cauliflower (*B. oleracea* var. *botrytis*) seedlings. This material may also be used as an additive to blocking composts used to raise *Brassica* transplants (Baines, 1975). Prothiocarb has, however, toxic side effects and has not been cleared for use in the UK. The acylalanine systemic materials (*see* section 4.3) may well prove to be an efficient alternative.

Traditionally, *P. parasitica* is thought of as an aerially and aqueously disseminated pathogen, but there are some suggestions that it may also be seed-borne. Heat treatment of seed for 20 min at 48–50 °C is reported to reduce disease incidence from 42.5 to 2.5 per cent (Klinkovskaya, 1976). Seed infections of 50–60 per cent in cabbage (*B. oleracea* var. *capitata*) are reported to reduce yields by 16–20 per cent (Vasileva, 1976).

Good husbandry is of major importance in control of downy mildew; excessive overhead irrigation will encourage pathogen spread. Every effort should be made to keep seedlings as dry as possible by use of abundant ventilation and prevention of water from remaining on plants for prolonged periods. Where sprays are applied, use should be made of ultra-low volume techniques or dust formulations to prevent accumulation of moisture on the foliage. Plant density should be regulated to prevent overcrowding within the seed bed. The deliberate check to growth often given to seedlings to prevent them becoming too large before planting out is often associated with *P. parasitica* attack. With direct drilled crops, wider spacings should be employed where downy mildew is known to be a hazard. Growth stimulation by fertiliser application can be used to enable seedlings to outgrow infections. Crop debris must be removed from seed beds since this fungus can perennate as oospores in old foliage (D'Ercole, 1975). Where crops are grown intensively for leaf production, as with turnips (*B. campestris*) in California, USA, *P. parasitica* is a major disease problem (Sumner *et al.*, 1978).

5.1.2 *Erysiphe cruciferarum* (powdery mildew)

All *Brassica* crops appear to be susceptible to this air-borne fungal pathogen and disease reports indicate that crops in most countries are at risk (Dixon, 1978).

Symptoms begin as star-shaped white lesions on the upper surface of the foliage. These develop from single conidia which have established points of entry into the host epidermis. The mycelium remains as a superficial parasite, forming haustoria in the epidermal cells with only limited intercellular hyphal growth. The superficial mycelium gradually coalesces from the points of infection until the entire leaf surface is covered in an off-white mealy stroma (figure 5.2). On Brussels sprout (*B. oleracea* var. *gemmifera*) the pathogen progresses on to the

Figure 5.2   *Erysiphe cruciferarum* (powdery mildew) on sprout leaves,
comparison of infected (left-hand) and healthy (right-hand) leaves.
(Reproduced by permission of National Institute of Agricultural
Botany, Cambridge.)

stems, where typical mycelial symptoms develop together with a purplish
discoloration of the host tissue. Sprout buds (buttons) can become heavily
infected on both the outer wing leaves and on the more tightly wrapped inner
foliage (Dixon, 1974). Greatest economic damage is caused by *E. cruciferarum*
infecting the buds, which are then unacceptable for processing or for the fresh
and supermarket trades. In periods of low temperatures the mycelium turns
black, making infected buds even less attractive. Two forms of infection have been
identified on cabbage and cauliflower (*B. oleracea* var. *capitata* and *B. oleracea*
var. *botrytis*, respectively): first, necrosis of the outer leaves with obvious
powdery mildew lesions accompanied by much reduced curd or head size, and
second, disease lesions on the outer leaves and necrosis of the inner wrapper
leaves starting at the tips and progressing towards the curd, which at the same
time begins to rot due to invasion by soft rot bacteria. Swede (*B. napus*) and
turnip (*B. campestris*) are regularly defoliated by *E. cruciferarum* in the UK.
Infected foliage rapidly turns chlorotic and is abscissed.

   Erysiphe cruciferarum is an Ascomycete (class Plectomycetes), but the
sexual cleistothecial stage has not been reported on *B. oleracea* and only rarely

has been found on other hosts. Asexual barrel-shaped conidia, 30–52.5 μm x 11.0–17.5 μm in size, develop from the mycelium on the host foliage, hence the mealy appearance of the host. The nomenclature of powdery mildew on *Brassicae* was clarified by Junell (1967), who erected the name *E. cruciferarum* to embrace the pathogen on this group of crops. Previously, the causal organism was named as part of *E. polygoni* (Salmon, 1900) and *E. communis* (Blumer, 1967). There may be subspecific variants within *E. cruciferarum* since it is difficult to transmit isolates of the fungus from Brussels sprout to turnip and vice versa (G. R. Dixon, unpublished data).

Considerable efforts are being made to control *E. cruciferarum* by use of resistant cultivars. Resistance in cabbage is attributed to a single dominant gene which is influenced by numbers of minor genes, since in parental generations resistance is incompletely dominant (Walker and Williams, 1965). Thus, under conditions of heavy inoculum, a heterozygotic host may support limited fungal growth. Powdery mildew is found in semi-arid and humid areas of the USA, especially following protracted drought. It is of especial importance on kraut cabbage, causing disfigurement and irregular development; the latter interferes with mechanical harvesting and processing. Symptoms range from the whole plant becoming covered in mycelium to a fine necrotic flecking which may indicate limited disease resistance. Multiple disease-resistant cabbages were produced by Williams *et al.* (1968): thus Hybelle (Badger Inbred 12 x Globelle) and Sannibell (Badger Inbred 13 x Globelle) were aimed at quality sauerkraut production in the northern USA and at the fresh market trade in Florida during the winter. Globelle was derived from Resistant Glory, which in turn was selected from the European cultivar Glory of Enkhuizen. Badger Inbreds 12 and 13 came from Wisconsin All Seasons and Bugner, respectively. Globelle has been shown to be homozygous for resistance to powdery mildew (Walker and Williams, 1973).

In the UK, powdery mildew on Brussels sprouts, in particular, is of increasing importance. This can be attributed to intensification of production and the use of very susceptible F_1 hybrid cultivars which mature rapidly and are aimed at supplying the processing industry. Originally, *E. cruciferarum* was found sporadically in Bedfordshire and in the Vale of Evesham, but over the last decade it has spread and become very severe on crops in Lincolnshire, Norfolk and Yorkshire, where most processing crops are grown. Open pollinated cultivars maintained by growers in Bedfordshire and the Vale of Evesham have considerable field resistance to *E. cruciferarum*. Breeders are now producing more resistant F_1 hybrid cultivars using some of the older Bedfordshire and Evesham types as progenitors. But these tend to be of the mid season and late maturing types, whereas early types, especially those bred in the Netherlands, where only limited incidence of *E. cruciferarum* is reported and consequently selection pressure for resistance is low, tend to be highly susceptible.

Eradicant fungicides based on sulphur compounds such as dinocap give some control of *E. cruciferarum*. Early systemic materials of the benomyl type have little effect against this pathogen since translocation in autumn and winter crops of a highly lignified nature is low. Some newer materials, for example fluotrimazole, are more effective, providing considerable control, and are now regularly incorporated with aphicidal sprays applied in August and early September when the primary lesions become visible. The husbandry control technique of late sowing to avoid the worst epidemics of *E. cruciferarum* has been practised for many years with swede and turnip crops. Although this is moderately successful in avoiding infection there is a very considerable penalty in that yield is reduced concomitantly with the shortening of the growing season. The need for such measures is now reduced by use of fungicides and availability of resistant swede cultivars.

Few data are available on epidemiological aspects of *E. cruciferarum*. Traditionally, epidemics are associated with low RH and water stress within the host. But there is a requirement for free moisture at the time of spore germination.

5.1.3 *Alternaria* spp. (dark leaf and pod spot)

Considerable damage is caused to cruciferous seed crops by air- and seed-borne *Alternaria* spp. on a world-wide scale. These fungal pathogens are apparently less damaging to crops intended for direct human or animal consumption, although *A. brassicicola* has recently been recognised as an important cause of deterioration of white cabbage (*B. oleracea* var. *capitata* – Langedijk types) in cold storage (Kear *et al.*, 1977). Infection is, however, usually confined to the lower mature leaves, inflorescence and seed pods. Two species, *A. brassicae* and *A. brassicicola*, infect a wide range of *B. campestris*, *B. oleracea* and *B. napus* crops, while *A. raphani* attacks radish (*Raphanus* spp.).

Symptoms consist of circular foliar lesions 0.5–2.5 cm in diameter, having distinct margins with a sunken centre surrounded by a bright yellow chlorotic halo; generally with a ragged margin. *Alternaria brassicae* produces conidia 75–350 μm long, while those of *A. brassicicola* are 18–130 μm long. Sporulation is profuse, giving a sooty black appearance to the lesion, while *A. brassicae* has light brown-orange sporulation with stubble-like conidiophores. Host tissue at the centre of each lesion is reduced to a thin, dry, papery texture which may fall out to give a shot-holed appearance. Coalescence of the lesions leads to irregular areas of necrotic tissue on the leaves, which abscise prematurely. Trails of secondary lesions run in dark streaks from the site of primary infection. Lesions are not usually found on juvenile foliage. Elongated lesions are found on stems and petioles, while on leaves they spread across veins, indicating that this pathogen produces pectic enzymes capable of dissolving the thickened tissue of vein collenchyma. Severe infection may cause lodging or complete collapse of the host. Infection of Brussels sprout (*B. oleracea* var. *gemmifera*) buds leads to development of small dark brown or black infection spots when *A. brassicicola* is the causal agent and similar lesions, but with dark green margins, where *A. brassicae* is involved. The lesions extend through several leaf layers within the sprout bud. Both *A. brassicicola* and *A. brassicae* are implicated in 'brown rot' of cauliflower (*B. oleracea* var. *botrytis*) curds. This syndrome begins as small brown spots which gradually darken and eventually cover the entire curd surface. Greyish aerial mycelium bearing copious conidia grow from the rotten curd. Root rotting of turnip (*B. campestris*) crops, reportedly due to *Alternaria* spp., is found in the USA (Chupp, 1935).

The major damage caused by these pathogens is to the inflorescence of seed crops. Dark necrotic lesions form on the inflorescence branches which sporulate freely. Irregular necrotic streaks are found on infected sepals and calyces, while on pods small dark spots form which eventually coalesce, producing large numbers of conidia. Seedlings developing from diseased seed are covered in tiny necrotic lesions, the cotyledons being stunted and withered, with black streaks on the hypocotyl. *Alternaria brassicae* has also been associated with damping-off of cabbage (*B. oleracea* var. *capitata*) seedlings, causing 80–100 per cent losses (Govshkov, 1976).

Alternaria spp. are Fungi Imperfecti (order Moniliales); no perfect stages have been identified but it is likely that they would be Ascomycetes (class Pyrenomycetes) and belong to the genera *Leptosphaeria, Pleospora* or *Sporodesmium* (Roscoe, 1967). Mycelium of *A. brassicae* is branched, septate, hyaline and 4–8 μm thick, bearing conidiophores in groups of 10 or more which emerge through the host stomata from intercellular hyphae. The conidiophores are simple, more or less cylindrical, often with a slightly swollen base, septate, mid-pale greyish-olive in colour, up to 170 μm long and 6–11 μm thick. The conidia are usually solitary or sometimes in chains of up to four in number, club-shaped with 16–19 transverse septa and 0–8 longitudinal or oblique septa; they are pale or very pale olive or greyish-olive in colour, carrying a beak which is up to half as long as the entire conidium and 5–9 μm thick. Characteristics of *A. brassicicola* are similar but the conidiophores are shorter, being 70 μm long and 5–8 μm thick. Conidia are borne in chains of 20 or more, having 1–11 transverse septa and six longitudinal ones and a beak one-sixth the length of the entire conidium. Each conidium develops from a bud produced on the apical surface of the preceeding conidium and takes about 150 min to reach maximum size (Campbell, 1972). *Alternaria raphani* closely resembles *A. brassicae* except that it forms chlamydospores and the conidial beak is shorter.

The temperature growth optimum of *A. brassicicola* is at 25–27 °C, but growth continues to the extremes of 6 °C and 37 °C. *Alternaria brassicae* has more demanding growth requirements, with a distinct optimal growth peak at 22.5 °C. Conidial germination of *A. brassicicola* is optimal at 30 °C and of *A. brassicae* at 17–19 °C. Conidia will germinate in both light and dark conditions. But maximum growth and sporulation by *A. brassicae* occurred with alternating light and darkness; continuous light completely inhibits sporulation (Gupta *et al.*, 1972). Both fungi have simple nutritional requirements and are able to utilize a wide range of carbon and nitrogen sources as is typical of relatively unspecialised parasites (Roscoe, 1967). Conidia of *A. brassicicola* are remarkably resistant to phytoalexins such as phaseollin, phaseollidin, phaseollinisoflavan, kievitone, medicarpin and pisatin (Skipp and Bailey, 1977). *Alternaria* spp. are destructive as opposed to balanced parasites, and in this respect may be considered as weak pathogens essentially deriving nutrition from necrotic host tissue. Degradation of host tissues is by cellulase enzymes (Nehemiah and Deshpande, 1977). The unspecialised nature of *Alternaria* spp. is reflected in the absence of haustoria as a means of obtaining nutrient supplies. Various toxins, for example alternaric acid, have been implicated in this disease syndrome (Wood, 1967).

Greatest invasion occurs when liquid water is present on the host surface, for which dew is probably the commonest source. This will be present for 5–8 h, which is sufficient for the infection process of both *A. brassicicola* and *A. brassicae* to be accomplished. Cuticular penetration is most frequent with *A. brassicicola*, but stomatal penetration occurs to a lesser extent. Penetration is preceeded by formation of appressoria, which are unicellular swellings formed from the tip of germ tubes and are either sperical or club-shaped and 3–8 μm in diameter. Stomatal penetration is more common with *A. brassicae*. Once within the host the epidermal cells are fully invaded, mycelium then ramifies through and between the cells, into the mesophyll and palisade tissue, until the entire leaf is parasitised. Early in the post-penetration phase the invaded epidermal cells become necrotic, and ahead of the advancing hyphal front is a region of collapsing parenchyma tissue.

Infected seed is the main avenue of transmission of all three *Alternaria* spp. This can take place both externally as conidia adhering to the testa or as internal mycelium present within the seed tissues. The latter may lead to complete destruction of the embryo. Infected seeds have a shrivelled appearance, impaired germination and low vigour. Four phases of seed transmission can be distinguished:

(1) Transmission from seed to developing seedlings.

(2) Transmission from seed to adjacent seed.

(3) Transmission from adult plant to seed by fungal growth through the green siliqua coat into the moist atmosphere within the seed pod. As the pods mature and desiccate sporulation may take place.

(4) Transmission from adult plant to adult plant.

Seed-borne *Alternaria* are capable of surviving as viable conidia and/or as internal mycelium for periods long enough for the seed to be harvested, stored, transported and finally sown. The proportions of *Brassica* seed carrying *Alternaria* spp. are high; Richardson (1970) found 40 and 10 per cent, respectively, of *Brassica* seed infected with *A. brassicicola* and *A. brassicae*, the latter being more pathogenic than the former. Infection levels up to 50 per cent were found on *B. oleracea* var. *capitata* cv. Houston Evergreen and up to 90 per cent on turnip rape (*B. campestris*) in Canada (Petrie, 1974*a,b*). Infected seed pods shed their contents more quickly than healthy ones and seeds from infected pods are lighter (Maude and Humpherson-Jones, 1977).

Resting stages are unknown for *A. brassicae* and *A. brassicicola*, thus reservoirs of infection come from the infected host and saprophytic stages outside the host. Conidia are thought of as 'dry conidia' which are wind dispersed, maximum release taking place in mid-afternoon. There is not thought to be a numerical threshold for infection, consequently lesions can be initiated from a single germinating conidium.

A few studies have been made of the potential for using resistance as a control for these pathogens. Variations in resistance in rape (*B. napus*) and field mustard (*B. campestris*) have attributed differences to changes in the thickness of epicuticular waxes (Skoropad and Tewari, 1977). Surveys of cauliflower (*B. oleracea* var. *botrytis*) introductions by Braverman (1971) showed that PIs 231208, 231209, 217934 and 267725 have resistance. Similarly, Brussels sprout (*B. oleracea* var. *gemmifera*) PIs 343669, 365156 and 343671 are resistant (Braverman, 1977).

Fungicidal control may be achieved to a limited extent by use of Bordeaux mixture, sulphur dust and dithiocarbamates. The latter give particularly good control on cauliflower (*B. oleracea* var. *botyrtis*) (Jouan *et al.*, 1972). More recently, iprodione has offered much greater degree of control, being used both as a spray and seed dressing (Maude and Humpherson-Jones, 1978). Hot water treatment of seed at 50 °C for 25 min is the traditional technique for decontaminating infected seed.

Isolation of seed crops, especially of high value horticultural crops, from farm oil seed rape crops is essential in order to avoid infection during harvesting. Maude and Humpherson-Jones (1977) found that marrowstem kale (*B. oleracea* var. *acephala*) liberated 50 spores per cubic metre of air just prior to harvesting. 190 spores per cubic metre of air at cutting and 3200 spores per cubic metre of air when windrowed crops were harvested, and spores could be carried up to 1000 m downwind during harvesting.

Biological control may be of value in the future; saprophytic phylloplane fungi such as *Aureobasidium pullulans* and *Epicoccum nigrum* are pathogenic to *A. brassicicola* (Pace and Campbell, 1974). Parasitism of *A. brassicae* by the *Verticillium* state of *Nectria inventa* occurs either by penetration or contact without penetration. Parasitic hyphae induce abnormal responses in host cells upon contact. A reaction tube consisting largely of electron-dense transparent matrix and dispersed tubule-like electron-dense material develops between the cell wall and invaginated plasma membrane. The tubule-like elements subsequently aggregate to form electron-dense deposits below the cell wall. The affected cell forms a septal plug, accumulates membranes and finally degenerates. Hyphae of *N. inventa* penetrate the conidial cells of *A. brassicae* mainly by a process which appears primarily enzymic in nature. The cytoplasm of the penetrated cell becomes progressively less dense and the cell eventually appears empty (Tsundea *et al.*, 1976). Penetration of *A. brassicae* hyphae causes separation of the cells; penetration of conidia occurs most frequently at the septum or at the basal pore in juvenile conidia (Tsuneda and Skoropaid, 1977).

5.1.4 *Leptosphaeria maculans* (stem and leaf canker)

Previously named *Phoma lingam*, this fungus is the causal agent of blackleg disease. It is seed-borne and of major significance on a wide range of agricultural and horticultural cruciferous crops. Those crops at greatest risk from *L. maculans* are grown in temperate regions and at high altitudes in the tropics.

Symptoms are initially found on the juvenile foliage as brown papery lesions which become desiccated and dotted with black asexual spore bodies or pycnidia. Plants killed by *L. maculans* at this stage have withered cotyledons still attached and are covered in pycnidia. Those not killed show a very inconspicuous bluish lesion around the cotyledonary scar. Under moist conditions the lesions become surrounded by a halo of white fluffy mycelium. Alternatively, infection may first be recognised as a stem decay developing as a dry rot at or near ground level. Plants wilt and die due to destruction of the stem and root system (figure 5.3). Affected plants lodge easily, the stem tissues becoming ashy grey and covered with black pycnidia. Diseased plants are usually noticeable by virtue of their reduced size and glaucous blue foliage. When cabbages (*B. oleracea* var. *capitata*) are infected near to maturity the heads may be apparently healthy at harvest but develop sunken black lesions in store (Sherf, 1968). When root crops such as swede (*B. napus*) and turnip (*B. campestris*) are infected, the swollen hypocotyl often cracks open, leading to destruction of the cortical tissues and rotting due to secondary bacterial action. Along the edges of such cracks ashy grey mycelium and black pycnidia are found.

Herbicide damage may exacerbate blackleg symptoms. Such plants form proliferations of tissue beneath the epidermis and cortex, frequently extending several centimetres upwards from ground level. Splitting and sloughing-off of the cortex covering such proliferations is common and pycnidia form on the loosened tissues (Petrie, 1973). Growth, particularly of infected turnips (*B. campestris*), is inhibited by a toxin produced by *L. maculans* related to epipolythiodicetopiperazine compounds (Bousquet *et al.*, 1977).

Leptosphaeria maculans is an Ascomycete, class Loculoascomycetes. The sexual fruiting body is a pseudothecium (*see* section 5.1.5), initially immersed within the host tissue but erupting above the epidermis at maturity. It is globular, black and possesses a protruding ostiole and is 300–350 μm in diameter. Inside are cylindrical to club-shaped asci which may be directly attached to the pseudothecial wall or borne on short stalks. Each ascus has two distinct walls and contains eight ascospores, it is 80–125 μm x 15–22 μm in size. The ascospores

Figure 5.3   Root system of a cabbage destroyed by *Leptosphaeria maculans* (canker). (Reproduced by permission of National Institute of Agricultural Botany, Cambridge.)

are cylindrical to elliptical, usually with rounded ends, yellow-brown in colour and measure 35–70 μm x 5–8 μm. Numerous needle-shaped, hyaline, segmented pseudoparaphyses are found amongst the asci. Asexual pycnidia of two types are produced:

(1) *The sclerotioid form*   These are initially immersed in host tissue but

eventually erupt. They are of variable shape with narrow ostioles, having a wall composed of several layers of thick walled sclerenchymatous cells and 200–500 μm in diameter.

(2) *The globular form.*   These are again black with walls composed of several cell layers, but the cells are thickened on the outer layer only.

Conidia produced within both types of pycnidia are hyaline, cylindrical, and usually straight, but a few may be curved; they are single celled and 3–5 μm x 1.5–2 μm in size.

Information concerning physiological specialization of *L. maculans* is conflicting. For instance, Thurling and Venn (1977), found that some oil rape (*B. napus* and *B. campestris*) cultivars were substantially more resistant than others to infection by ascospores from specific sources. Whereas Barbetti (1978), using isolates of *L. maculans* from oil rape (*B. napus*), wild radish (*R. raphanistrum*) and wild turnip (*B. tournefortii*), could find no evidence of host specificity.

Epidemiological studies suggest that for oil rape (*B. napus* and *B. campestris*) crops infection via diseased seed is of only minor significance. The potential amount of ascospore inoculum on crop residues is far more closely related to severity of infection in the field (Lacoste *et al.*, 1969; McGee, 1977). Rainfall greater than 1.0 mm is required for large ascospore discharges, but smaller ones occur in light rain or dew. Symptom development is most severe at 18–24 °C (Barbetti, 1975). But with horticultural crops seed is a significant source of infection in that in areas such as the UK, where strict seed sanitation has been observed for many years, *L. maculans* is rarely seen. The upsurge of rapeseed production with the attendant risk of infection spreading from rape stubble has placed horticultural crops at risk from a new avenue of infection. This danger is highlighted by the recent epidemic of *L. maculans* in the UK. Initially, diseased rape seed was imported and rapid infection took place within crops by means of pycnospores. Carriage being by rain-splash and encouraged by a succession of mild wet winters, gradually *L. maculans* was established on rapeseed stems which then lodged just prior to harvest in July–August. This permitted the pathogen to invade developing seed pods and thereby infect the next seed generation. Additionally, after harvest, pseudothecia formed on residual stubble, producing ascospores which were wind transported to infect newly emergent new sown rapeseed crops in September. Ascospores can be transported by this means up to 2 km. Poor crop husbandry aggravated the epidemic since one oil rape crop was scarcely harvested before the next was drilled and farmers would often retain volunteer crops which grew from seed left in the field after harvest. In general there has been inadequate appreciation of the need for spatial and time separations in rotations containing rapeseed crops. Once land has grown an infected rapeseed crop the resultant debris will carry the imperfect stage of *L. maculans* in a viable state for up to 3 years.

Hot water treatment can be used to free seed of *L. maculans*, by soaking for

25 min at 50 °C for cabbage and Brussels sprouts (*B. oleracea* vars *capitata* and *gemmifera*) and 20 min for cauliflower and broccoli (*B. oleracea* vars *botrytis* and *italica*). But the technique is unreliable, often impairing subsequent germination. Slurry treatments with thiabendazole at 1.0 g a.i. per kilogram of seed, or seed soaked for 24 h at 30 °C using 0.2 per cent thiabendazole or thiram, have been shown to be effective in disinfesting artificially infected cabbage (*B. oleracea* var. *capitata*) seed (Maude *et al.*, 1973). Similarly, Jacobsen and Williams (1971), who found *L. maculans* mycelium present in the seed coat tissues of *B. oleracea* varieties and within the embryo, found that soaking for 24 h in 0.2 per cent benomyl would eradicate the pathogen. Continuation of this work by Gabrielson *et al.* (1977) shows that seed lots with 0.6 per cent seed-borne *L. maculans* did not develop infection at the seedling stage, whereas lots with 1.5 per cent or more contamination did give rise to diseased seedlings. Application of zineb to soil at 5 g per square metre 3 days prior to sowing cabbage (*B. oleracea* var. *capitata*) reduces infection from 25 per cent in untreated control plots to 2.5 per cent in treated ones (Klinkovskaya, 1976).

Studies by Sherf (1968) show that crucifers can be ranked for resistance to *L. maculans:*

(1) *Very susceptible*: red and green cabbage, Savoy cabbage, Chinese cabbage, Brussels sprouts, some radish varieties, some swede varieties, white mustard and kohlrabi.

(2) *Medium susceptible*: cauliflower, broccoli, rape, kale, collards, some turnip varieties, wild radish, black mustard.

(3) *Mildly susceptible*: some turnip and swede varieties, Chinese mustard, garden cress and many strains of mustard.

(4) *Very resistant*: horseradish, penny cress, ball mustard, yellow rocket, shepherd's purse and pepper cress.

Swede cultivars appear to be a mixture of susceptible and resistant populations, but the Wilhelmsburger types contain a high proportion of resistant material (Cruickshank and Palmer, 1954).

Husbandry controls include use of a rotation which ensures breaks of 4–5 years between *Brassica* crops, with lucerne (*M. sativa*) or clover (*Trifolium* spp.) being particularly good break crops. Provision of adequate soil drainage and manipulation of plant stand density to ensure air movement are essential, thereby discouraging the build-up of a moist microclimate within the crop. Ploughing should be done deeply in the autumn to hasten destruction of infected debris.

5.1.5 *Mycosphaerella brassicicola* (ringspot)

Outbreaks caused by this pathogen are widespread on *Brassica* crops grown in cool moist regions of the world. It is a particular problem to crops produced in north-western Europe, southern England, parts of the USSR, the western coastal valleys of California, USA, and in New Zealand. The majority of *Brassica* spp. have been recorded as hosts of *M. brassicicola*.

Symptoms are found on all aerial plant organs from the cotyledons to the seed pods, but usually mature foliage is most heavily affected and defoliation is a frequent result. Lesions commence as small dark spots, visible on both leaf surfaces which expand up to 2–3 cm in diameter. Concentric zones of growth are conspicuous, hence the name 'ringspot', with grey-yellow and brown tints. Each lesion usually has a definite edge bounded by a narrow water-soaked area a and chlorotic zone; where lesions are numerous the entire leaf becomes yellowish, showing curled, cracked and ragged edges. The ring-like appearance of lesions is enhanced by the development of reproductive structures, pseudothecia, 3–4 weeks after infection. These form in a typically zonate manner, often being extremely numerous and giving the lesion a black colour. On leaf midribs, stems and siliquas lesions may be rectangular or oval-shaped. Where Brussels sprout (*B. oleracea* var. *gemmifera*) buds are infected they rapidly become covered in characteristic ringspot lesions which are often subsequently invaded by soft rotting bacteria. Studies by Geeson and Robinson (1975) show that *M. brassicicola* is a serious storage pathogen of cabbage (*B. oleracea* var. *capitata*). Dark brown to black lesions develop on stored cabbage which eventually becomes shrivelled and leathery. Lesions are often more restricted than those due to *Botrytis cinerea* (grey mould) (*see* section 6.4.3); they can penetrate the cabbage head more deeply, necessitating extensive trimming before sale.

Mycosphaerella brassicicola is an Ascomycete fungus, class Loculoascomycetes. Sexual pseudothecia form as locules developed by dissolution of hyphae from around the ascal initials. They are mostly found on leaves, but sometimes on stems and seed pods, as globular dark brown structures with apical papillate ostioles 100–130 μm in diameter. Within are several bitunicate eight-spored asci, 30–45 μm x 12–18 μm in size. Ascospores are hyaline, cylindrical, bicellular with rounded ends and no constriction at the septum, 18–23 μm x 3–5 μm in dimension. Pycnidia-like bodies also develop which are thought by some to contain spermatia, which are small non-infective spores whose function is to act as male gametes. Others suggest that these spores are infective pycnospores which are formed in profusion and aid in rapid colonisation of the host. The pycnidia-like bodies are found either singly or in groups as globular dark brown structures with papillate ostioles 100–200 μm in size, each having a pseudoparenchymatous wall of several cell layers. The spores, or spermatial cells, are hyaline, cylindrical and 3–5 μm x 1 μm in size. No physiological specialisation has been reported for *M. brassicicola*, and it is thought to be homothallic. Transmission is largely attributed to air-borne ascospores, although Vanterpool (1969) reports the production of *Cercospora*-like conidia in spring. Invasion takes place through the stomata and the hyphae become established between and within host cells throughout the leaf, giving rise to the appearance of lesions on both leaf surfaces. Optimal temperatures for invasion are between

16 and 20 °C. Largest numbers of viable ascospores develop at 20 °C, while lesions do not form mature pseudothecia where there is less than 100 per cent RH for four consecutive days. Penetration of the testa is reported, but the importance of seed-borne infection has not been determined. The chief source of infection appears to be diseased crop debris from which ascospores are released or from mature infected crops growing near to younger ones. Proximity to agricultural *Brassica* crops can be a hazard for the high value horticultural *Brassica* crops since Vanterpool (1968) showed that *M. brassicicola* may survive in winter on rape (*B. napus*) as dark, thick-walled mycelium.

Cultural measures are of paramount importance for control of *M. brassicicola*. Seed beds should be sited well away from existing crops and be free of infected debris. Infection leads to premature leaf abscission, particularly in Anger-type cauliflowers (*B. oleracea* var. *botrytis*); growers encourage rapid production of new foliage in spring by application of nitrogenous fertilisers. Additionally, heavy dressings with potassium fertilisers (400 kg/ha) are considered as a means of avoiding infection. Hot water treatment may be used to eradicate seed-borne infection by steeping the seed for 20 min at 45 °C.

Chemical control can be achieved by use of high volume sprays of maneb or mancozeb, applied every 14 days with between four and six times the recommended rate of wetter (Rogers and Wicks, 1970). The systemic fungicide benomyl has given very good control of *M. brassicicola* in trials in California, USA, and New Zealand (Welch *et al.*, 1969; Wilson, 1971).

Resistance to *M. brassicicola* is claimed to exist in Roscoff-type cauliflowers (*B. oleracea* var. *botrytis*) which have been selected for centuries against this pathogen in Brittany, France. Similar selection of Brussels sprout (*B. oleracea* var. *gemmifera*) in south-western England is reputed to have produced cultivars, for example Moases, which have ringspot resistance.

5.1.6 *Thanetophorus cucumeris* (damping-off and other diseases)

The preferred name for this pathogen is *T. cucumeris*, which is the basidial stage of the Imperfect sterile mycelial fungus *Rhizoctonia solani*. Other synonyms include *Corticium solani*, *Hypochnus cucumeris*, *H. solani* and *Pellicularia filamentosa*. A very wide range of hosts are attacked by *T. cucumeris*, causing an equally wide range of disease syndromes: seed decay, damping-off, stem cankering, root rots, fruit decay and foliar diseases. These are discussed below:

(1) *Seed decay*   The pathogen invades the seed while it is within the fruit, causing either rotting of the capsule or becoming quiescent only to resume pathogenesis once the seed starts to germinate. Infected seeds are a potential threat to uninfected ones since after germination the fungus invades neighbouring seeds. Transmission via the seed is reported in 38 crop species.

(2) *Damping-off*   This may be divided into two categories. (a) *Pre-emergence phase*, where seedlings are killed due to seed infection or due to adverse environmental conditions such as the soil temperature being too low, too high or the soil over-moist or saline, thereby delaying germination and permitting invasion from the soil. Plants with hypogeal germination, for example pea (*Pisum* spp.), may remain in a soil zone of high infection risk for a longer period than those with epigeal germination, for example bean (*Vicia* or *Phaseolus* spp.), and require chemical protection against cotyledon decay.
(b) *Post-emergence phase*, in which symptoms develop at any point after emergence until the host is past the juvenile stage. Susceptibility declines with maturity and consequent lignification of host tissues. This may be due to the conversion of pectin to calcium pectate, rendering the host tissues resistant to the polygalacturonase enzyme of the fungus. Damping-off is a term used to refer to the decay of the stem at about soil level, causing the seedlings to collapse. The name is derived either from the moist conditions under which disease develops or to the moist nature of the rot produced. It is possible to differentiate between post-emergence damping-off due to *T. cucumeris* and that caused by *Pythium* spp. (section 6.1.4); the former produces stem decay near to soil level and may later advance downwards into the roots. *Pythium* spp. generally infect at the tips of small roots or root hairs and advance upwards through the plant to the soil surface. Small pieces of soil or organic matter adhere to the coarse, tough mycelium of *T. cucumeris* attached to infected seedlings when removed from the soil; this is not found with *Pythium* spp. The coarse hyaline to brown mycelium of *T. cucumeris* can be distinguished with a hand lens from the fine mycelium of *Pythium* spp. This pathogen tends to form in circular or irregular patches, representing the foci of survival or introduction of the pathogen. Attempts to suppress *T. cucumeris* in infected transplanting material usually leads to outbreaks at later stages, especially with *Brassica* spp. and pepper (*C. annuum*) crops. Use of infected transplants will also lead to transmission of the pathogen to previously uninfected land.

(3) *Wirestem and sore-shin*   Some crops can be invaded by *T. cucumeris* beyond the juvenile stage. Brassicas, for instance, may be invaded when up to 10–15 cm high. If the environment becomes dry after infection, the host cortex decays in sharply defined areas encircling the stem and the cells collapse; the stele, however, provides sufficient support, so that the plants remain upright. Yield losses amongst slightly infected brassicas are estimated as 12 per cent loss of heads and 10 per cent loss in crop weight, whereas under severe infection losses increase to 36 per cent fewer heads and 30 per cent lower yield. Pepper (*C. annuum*) and tomato (*L. esculentum*) plants may also be infected in this manner. In tomatoes the lesions have alternating bands of light and dark tissue.

(4) *Root rot*   The term *Rhizoctonia*, which in literal translation means 'root killer', was coined by de Candolle for a sterile mycelium causing root rot of lucerne (*Medicago sativa*). The pathogen causes dark circular to oblong sunken cankers having brown margins which develop from points of invasion on

secondary roots. In root crops such as beet (*B. vulgaris*), carrot (*D. carota*) and turnip (*B. campestris*), lesions up to 2.5 cm in diameter form on the side of the swelling root from early in the season onwards. Sclerotia will grow on infected roots at such lesion sites if the roots are stored.

(5) *Hypocotyl and stem cankers*   Cankers develop on field-grown tomatoes (*L. esculentum*) at the bases of stem branches, infection taking place via leaves in contact with the soil and spreading through the cortex and stele. When grown under glass, infected tomatoes exhibit foot rot symptoms. The petioles and leaves of celery (*A. graveolens*) develop a crater spotting symptom as a result of invasion by *T. cucumeris* from infected soil particles being splashed by rain or irrigation water on to these organs. Spread of the fungus by this means in bean (*Ph. vulgaris*) leads to brown cortical stem cankering.

(6) *Bottom rot and head rot*   Cabbage (*B. oleracea* var. *capitata*) and lettuce (*L. sativa*) crops develop this syndrome when infection occurs after head formation. Leaves in contact with infected soil are invaded and the fungus spreads to the stem and leaves above, on which a fruiting white fungal hymenium forms on the stem and leaves. Initially, lesions are sharply defined and brown in colour. The pathogen spreads upwards within the head, causing mummification in less than 10 days; sclerotia are usually abundant in the infected head, while under some conditions the leaves may be shed, leaving a naked stalk capped by a small head.

(7) *Crown and bud rot*   Invasion of seedling beet (*B. vulgaris*) leaves and petioles leads to decay of the crown leaves, which may be replaced by laterals; but eventually the crown is killed and the fungus grows into the top of the fleshy root, causing a dry brown rot.

(8) *Aerial blights*   In the Tropics, during warm, humid cycles, *T. cucumeris* spreads to foliage and may become independent of a soil phase. Strains of *T. cucumeris* capable of this activity are characterised by rapid growth rate, in order to utilise any short climatic periods favourable to infection, carbon dioxide sensitivity, since the general environment is constantly low in this gas, and are capable of abundant sclerotial formation as a means of survival in unfavourable conditions. An aerial strain of *T. cucumeris* is found on beans (*Phaseolus* spp.) in Costa Rica and similar humid tropical areas which causes small brown necrotic foliar lesions resulting from basidiospore infections. These spots coalesce and from them mycelium spreads to other leaves and plants.

(9) *Rots of host organs in contact with soil*   Any aerial organs which contact soil infected with *T. cucumeris* may be invaded. Fruits are a common example; tomatoes (*L. esculentum*), either green or ripe, develop small firm brown spots on the areas in contact with the soil. Such lesions enlarge, often with concentric zones of fungal growth, while sclerotia may form on the fruit surface. A white basidial hymenium may also develop on the fruit surface in contact with the soil. Less frequently, infections have been reported following heavy rain or overhead irrigation from soil splashed on to fruits 35—45 cm above the ground. The fungal invasion path is through the intact fruit epidermis or via

wounds. The range of crops which may be affected by fruit lesions includes bean (*Phaseolus* spp.), cucumber (*C. sativus*), eggplant (*S. melongena*), pea (*Pisum* spp.) and pepper (*C. annuum*). Where infection takes place near to harvest, full symptom expression may not occur until after storage.

(10) *Storage rots and blemishes*   The best documented disease syndrome associated with *T. cucumeris* is the appearance of black sclerotia on potato (*S. tuberosum*) tubers. These are disfiguring but otherwise of little significance. Names for this disease include black scurf, black speck, scurf, black scab and black speck scab. Rots of other root crops in store are refered to in (4) above.

Thanetophorus cucumeris is a Basidiomycete classed as a Hymenomycete. Sclerotia develop as a crust radiating out from the infection site or as separate entities. Hyphal cells are up to 12 μm wide and 250 μm long; branches develop from near to the distal end of the cell, with a constriction at the point of origin and septa forming above it. Conspicuously, the septa are of the dolipore type. Older mycelia show great variation in hyphal size, some hyphae are differentiated into swollen monilioid cells up to 30 μm in width. The sexual hymenium consists of a thin sheet composed of barrel-shaped or subcylindrical basidia 10–25 μm x 6–19 μm, from which between four and seven sterigmata develop which are 5.5–36.5 μm long with occasional septa. Borne on the sterigmata are basidiospores which are hyaline, oblong to broad ellipsoid and unilaterally flattened. They are smooth and thin walled, 6–14 μm x 4–8 μm in size. There are such wide variations in morphology, pathogenicity and physiology of *T. cucumeris* strains that only broad characteristics can be used to describe them. Those characteristics which are consistently present include multinucleate cells in the young vegetative hyphae, prominent septal pore apparatus, branching near the distal septum of cells in young vegetative hyphae, constriction of the mycelial branches and formation of septa near to the point of origin, some shade of brown in culture. Characters which are usually present but one or more of which may be occasionally lacking in individual isolates include monilioid cells, sclerotia undifferentiated into rind and medulla (compare to sclerotia of Ascomycete fungi), hyphae greater than 5 μm in diameter and rapid growth rate.

Fungi grouped as *T. cucumeris* types occur in all parts of the world and are probably indigenous to uncultivated areas. Variants of *T. cucumeris* are not easily introduced into new soils and basidiospores do not seem to serve as a ready means of disseminating strains. Numerous variants have apparently adapted to the range of climatic, soil and vegetational regimes of the world, and these are isolated by their ecologies. Particular strains of *T. cucumeris* can exist naturally as saprophytes, symbionts and pathogens, with a high degree of adaptability to environmental conditions. Strains differ in host range affected; aggressiveness of attack (ranging from non-pathogenic to highly pathogenic); temperature at which invasion will occur; the ability to grow in the lower soil levels, the soil surface or in an aerial habitat; ability to tolerate carbon dioxide;

and ability to form sclerotia. Some strains cause only pre-emergence damage while others only post-emergence damage. From these at least three groupings can be drawn: true aerial types, strains active only in or near the soil surface, and subterranean strains.

Penetration by *T. cucumeris* takes place either through the intact cuticle and epidermis or through natural openings such as stomata and via wounds. Entry is from complexly organised infection structures, although some strains are capable of penetrating an host without them. The most frequent infection structure is a dome-shaped cushion formed from branched hyphae producing short swollen cells which aggregate into spongy microsclerotia. These develop in various ways – aggregation of stubby side branches from adjacent hyphae or aggregation of such branches from one hypha only or by terminal branching. Infection cushions vary in size on different hosts, those on brassicas are 300 μm in diameter and 150–179 μm high. Aggregation into infection cushions may be due to attraction between neighbouring hyphae. Penetration from the cushion into the host takes place through the simultaneous formation of infection pegs by the hyphal cells at the base of the cushion. Some strains can penetrate from the cushion without prior formation of infection pegs. Where pegs form they penetrate the cuticle, enlarge, and then grow into or between cells. Alternatively, lobate appressoria may form on fungal hyphae outside the host, which grow along the lines of junction of the underlying host epidermal cells to form short swollen side branches. These then swell at the tip, each branch becoming an appressorium from which penetration takes place. As with infection cushions, each appressorium is capable of multiple penetration of the plant surface.

Entry through natural openings such as stomata on stems, leaves and cotyledons requires no appressorium formation. Hyphae of *T. cucumeris* simply grow through the opening and into the substomatal cavity. Wound invasion is a secondary route for strains which normally use other means of penetration; examples include entry through cracks in the testa of bean seeds which result from the growth of the radicle and plumule. Roots are invaded at the point where laterals form and the exodermis is ruptured by the emerging root tip. The ability of an isolate to establish infection is determined at the stage of infection cushion formation and penetration. On susceptible hosts the process is successful, whereas on resistant hosts it is halted at some point. Probably there is interaction between exudates from a susceptible host and the pathogen which allows successful completion of the invasion process in compatible combinations. Host age may have a role in the development of resistance, especially with the 'damping-off' syndrome. Complete loss of bean seeds may take place if seeds are sown in infected compost but relatively small losses take place if more mature plants are transplanted into such compost. Bean seeds exude large amounts of chemicals capable of stimulating fungal growth whereas the hypocotyls produce relatively little. Additionally, it has been noted that the number of infection cushions formed by *T. cucumeris* decreases with the age of the host. Possibly development of complex infection structures has evolved in

T. cucumeris because of its inability to produce spores readily. Multiple penetration from a single complex structure may achieve successful colonisation for *T. cucumeris*, whereas fungi which can sporulate freely achieve similar results by the action of large numbers of spores. Successful penetration is followed by browning of the host cell walls succeeded by intracellular colonisation and tissue collapse. The latter is characteristic of *Thanetophorus* diseases and is associated with extensive intracellular growth by the pathogen and its possession of enzymes capable of rapid degradation of cell walls.

Sclerotia usually form following death of the host cells and are limited to areas of most extensive fungal growth. This includes the cortex, vascular bundles and central medulla. Sclerotia originate from barrel-shaped cells which aggregate together; they are devoid of organisation into rind and medulla which are found in the sclerotia formed by Ascomycete fungi. A wide variety of enzymes have been associated with *T. cucumeris*. Studies of these have usually been made *in vitro* and their effects *in vivo* are not well elucidated. These enzymes include polygalacturonase and pectin esterase, which aid the rapid degradation of host cell walls. Additionally, it is claimed that *T. cucumeris* forms toxins, some with phenolic and glycosidic properties; other toxins implicated with this pathogen are phenylacetic acid and its *p*- and *m*-hydroxy derivatives. Such properties would be associated with an organism such as *T. cucumeris* which rapidly destroys the host.

Control of *T. cucumeris* can be grouped into four categories:

(1) *Modification of cultural practices*   This involves avoiding transmission of the pathogen with propagating material, for example bean seeds from pods which have been in contact with the soil or those damaged in harvesting and cleaning operations should be discarded. Alteration of sowing date will reduce the risk of infection from soil-borne inoculum for crops where the seed requires high temperatures for germination. Shallow seeding to encourage rapid emergence is also important where there is a risk of *T. cucumeris* infection. Movement of soil around the hypocotyls of emerging seedlings should be avoided, this usually occurs during irrigation. Crop sequence can influence the extent of *T. cucumeris* infection by increasing or reducing the inoculum levels in soils. Growing lucerne (*M. sativa*) or clover (*Trifolium* spp.) increased the level of infection in subsequent beet (*Beta vulgaris*) crops, whereas beans (*Phaseolus* spp.) had no such effect.

(2) *Resistant cultivars*   It is difficult to obtain resistance to such a highly variable pathogen; however, there have been reports of tolerance in some cultivars of bean (*Phaseolus* spp.) and lettuce (*L. sativa*). While the cabbage cultivar 3654R (*B. oleracea* var. *capitata*) from Wisconsin University, USA, is reported to possess monogenic dominant resistance.

(3) *Biological control*   Cropping with cereals reduced the *T. cucumeris* population in infected soil, as did incorporation of cereal straw into the soil. This effect was thought to be due to increased soil carbon dioxide, reduced nitrogen levels in the soil solution (*T. cucumeris* growth is favoured by high soil

nitrogen), and stimulation of antagonistic soil organisms. *Trichoderma lignorum*, for instance, produces a toxin which destroys *T. cucumeris.*

(4) *Eradication*   Treatment of composts at 60 °C for 30 min is reputedly sufficient to sterilise soil of *T. cucumeris*, while incorporation of pentachloronitrobenzene (PCNB) dust will also eradicate this organism. The chemical may be dusted on to soil around lettuce plants to prevent infection. Some chemical sterilants such as nabam will control *T. cucumeris* and prevent attacks on crops such as peas (*Pisum* spp.) and beans (*Phaseolus* spp.).

5.1.7 *Fusarium oxysporum* f. sp. *conglutinans* (yellows)

This soil-borne fungal pathogen causes a destructive disease of a wide range of Cruciferae throughout the world. It was first recognised by E. F. Smith in 1899 on cabbage (*B. oleracea* var. *capitata*) grown in the Hudson Valley area of the USA.

Symptoms will develop on plants at any growth stage. Since symptom development is temperature dependent, infected plants may grow until early summer before disease becomes apparent. Initially the foliage turns to a dull yellow-green colour; all or only part of individual leaves may be affected. Where only part of a leaf exhibits symptoms the lamina may curl up due to uneven growth effects. Where lower leaves are affected first the syndrome gradually progresses upwards towards the plant apex. Usually leaves die prematurely and abscission takes place. As the chlorotic tissue ages it becomes brown, dead and brittle. Typically the vascular system becomes dark brown or yellow. In some respects symptoms are similar to those caused by the bacterium *Xanthomonas campestris* (black rot). These organisms may be distinguished by symptoms since *X. campestris* causes the veins to turn black rather than brown, as with *F. oxysporum* f. sp. *conglutinans*, and the smaller veins of diseased leaves are more generally discoloured. Invasion by *F. oxysporum* f. sp. *conglutinans* is through the root system, passing across the cortex to the vascular strands where growth and sporulation take place. Conidia are transported upwards in the host xylem vessels by the transpiration stream. Most frequent hosts are varieties of *B. oleracea*, but considerable damage is caused to radish (*R. sativus*) crops in the USA. Symptoms are similar to those on cabbage, but the plants tend to yellow and die more rapidly. Those plants which are not killed become stunted, with unilateral yellowing of leaves and extensive vascular discolouration in the fleshy hypocotyls.

Fusarium oxysporum f. sp. *conglutinans* is a member of the Fungi Imperfecti, order Moniliales; *see* section 6.1.5 for mycological details of *F. oxysporum* and also sections 11.2.7 and 12.2.6. This fungus produces abundant single-celled, hyaline, oval to ellipitical microconidia, 2.5–4 μm x 6–15 μm in size; macroconidia form only rarely, they are needle-shaped, hyaline, divided by two or three septa and measure 3.5–5.5 μm x 25–33 μm. Four physiological races have been distinguished by Armstrong and Armstrong (1952):

(1) Race 1 infects cabbage, kale, Brussels sprouts, cauliflower, broccoli, kohlrabi, rutabaga, turnip, mustard, rape, Chinese cabbage, garden cress, stock and radish.

(2) Race 2 is usually found on radish but also attacks the hosts of race 1 with the exception of cabbage, Brussels sprouts and cauliflower.

(3) Race 3 is found on stocks in California, USA.

(4) Race 4 is found on stocks in New York, USA.

More recently, *Crambe* sp. has been shown to be resistant to race 1 from cabbage and susceptible to race 2 from radish, whereas *Brassica carinata* is susceptible to race 1 and resistant to race 2 (Armstrong and Armstrong, 1974). This classification is disputed by Gordon (1965) who recognises three distinct *formae speciales*: *F. oxysporum* f. sp. *conglutinans, F. oxysporum* f. sp. *raphani* and *F. oxysporum* f. sp. *mathioli.*

Transmission is by soil particles on implements, wind-borne soil, surface drainage water and water-borne soil. Carriage over long distances is in soil adhering to the roots of transplants and vegetative organs such as seed potato tubers. Soil temperature is a limiting factor to disease expression, with greatest severity at 17—35 °C, although with very susceptible cultivars signs of the disease are seen at 12 °C. In the southern Ukraine, where summer temperatures are 17—35 °C, this pathogen is of considerable significance (Vladimirskaya *et al.*, 1975). In addition to symptom expression, invasion is more rapid at higher temperatures (Reyes, 1970). Under cooler conditions, such as winter, the mycelium in vessels of the infected plant develops chlamydospores as a means of survival (Anisimov, 1969).

Soil moisture content has a relatively minor influence on disease development. But soil nutrient status can critically affect symptom expression; potassium deficiency will lead to a much intensified syndrome. Fusaric acid toxin has been implicated in this host—parasite complex but has not been conclusively found *in vivo*. Pectolytic enzymes such as pectin methyl esterase are produced by *F. oxysporum* f. sp. *conglutinans* and are likely to be implicated in the syndrome. Infection of cabbage (*B. oleracea* var. *capitata*) by *F. oxysporum* f. sp. *conglutinans* leads to very drastic changes in host protein metabolism. Although total protein content of infected plants declines there is a change to the formation of new protein complexes (Heitefuss *et al.*, 1960). Studies by Beckman (1967) show that in resistant radish (*R. sativus*) there is an initial rise in respiration rate after inoculation, but this then falls back to a level similar to that of uninfected plants. In susceptible cultivars respiration rises more slowly but continues to increase. The same author advances the following hypotheses:

(1) The sealing-off process, gelation and hyperplasia, which follows most vascular infections, is a normal response by vascular plants which enables them to resist invasion by a range of potential parasites.

(2) These responses are possibly dependent on respiration.

(3) Pathogenesis can be elicited only by a few organisms which disrupt normal responses, thereby gaining progressive and extensive distribution within the vascular system.

Control of *F. oxysporum* f. sp. *conglutinans* is largely by use of resistant cultivars and may be considered as a classic example of the success of this technique, which has remained effective for decades. Although the pathogen is an extremely variable organism so far as its growth characteristics *in vitro* are concerned, it is apparently very stable in its pathogenicity towards its hosts. Most work to produce resistant cabbage (*B. oleracea* var. *capitata*) cultivars has been done over the last 70 years at Wisconsin University, USA. Initially this was accomplished by field selection for resistant plants within diseased crops. This method resulted in the release, in 1916, of Wisconsin Hollander. Subsequently, this cultivar was found to have incomplete resistance. At high temperatures, when pathogen growth is most vigorous, some yellowing would develop. Further work, using inbred lines produced from selfing plants by bud pollinations, led to the development of cultivars possessing resistance which is unaffected by temperatures below 26 °C. Most recently released are the cultivars Hybelle and Sanibel (Williams *et al.*, 1968). Two forms of resistance to yellows have been identified: a quantitatively inherited polygenic resistance (Type B), as found in Wisconsin Hollander, which is sensitive to relatively small increases in temperature, and a monogenic qualitatively inherited (Type A) resistance, which is only rendered inoperative at very high temperatures (Walker, 1959). Type A resistance prevents penetration by *F. oxysporum* f. sp. *conglutinans* into the spiral vessels of the vascular system and host potassium nutrition does not affect disease development. On the other hand, Type B resistance is rendered inoperative as temperature rises and the vascular system is penetrated by *F. oxysporum* f. sp. *conglutinans* and potassium deficiency increases symptom severity.

Some chemicals are effective in the control of *F. oxysporum* f. sp. *conglutinans*. Dipping the roots of transplants in 1 per cent of an 80 per cent solution of zinc dimethyldithiocarbamate is effective in controlling this pathogen (Gangopadhyny and Kapoor, 1976). Husbandry controls obviously include use of high levels of potassium fertilisers. Greatest control is reported by Anisimov and Kovalchuk (1969), where 100 kg/ha of potassium was applied. Cruciferous weed hosts might be expected to be a serious reservoir of infection, but this was shown not to be the case by Kaszonyi (1974). Simultaneous infection of Chinese cabbage (*B. campestris* var. *chinensis*) with *F. oxysporum* f. sp. *conglutinans* and Turnip Mosaic Virus (*see* section 5.2.5) leads to increased severity of yellows symptoms and greater stunting. The interaction is most severe at 28 °C (Reyes and Chadha, 1972). Forms of biological control may be available in the future since cross-protection against *F. oxysporum* f. sp. *conglutinans* may be achieved by prior inoculation with other *formae speciales* of *F. oxysporum* (Davis, 1967).

5.1.8 *Plasmodiophora brassicae* (clubroot)

Since Woronin (1878) described *P. brassicae* as the causal agent of clubroot, it has become recognised on world-wide basis as the most devastating pathogen of cruciferous crops. The pathogen probably originated in southern Europe and the western Mediterranean and spread in the wake of turnip (*B. campestris*) production (Watson and Baker, 1969). Although clubbing symptoms are restricted to members of the Cruciferae, *P. brassicae* is capable of infecting the root hairs of non-cruciferous hosts such as *Agrostis alba* var. *stolonifera, Dactylis glomerata, Holcus lanatus, Lolium perenne, Fragaria* spp., *Papaver rhoeas* and *Rumex* spp. (Colhoun, 1958).

Typical symptoms caused by *P. brassicae* are galling and contusion of the host root and hypocotyl; the extent of galling varies with the age, size and type of roots (figure 5.4). Galls on swollen hypocotyls of crops such as swede (*B. napus*) and turnip (*B. campestris*) may partially or completely cover the surface of the swollen 'root'. Fibrous rooted crops such as cabbage (*B. oleracea*) become covered in coralloid galls. Prior to obvious gall symptoms the host foliage becomes flaccid and blue-green, indicating that host water metabolism is seriously impeded. Growth is retarded, leading to stunted and unthrifty plants. Infection of cabbage (*B. oleracea* var. *capitata*) alters the distribution of dry matter within the host (MacFarlane and Last, 1959). After the clubs become visible, increases in root growth rate are almost entirely attributable to growth by the galls, while growth by the foliage is diminished. Diseased plants tend to form fewer and smaller leaves which expand more slowly than those of uninfected plants. The extent of galling is dependent mainly on the period of time over which the plant is subject to infection rather than its age at first infection.

Plasmodiophora brassicae is a relatively simple fungus forming no mycelium, the vegetative phase consists of a multinucleate mass of protoplasm lacking a cell wall (plasmodium). Taxonomically it is placed in the division Myxomycota and class Plasmodiophoromycetes. Studies of the life history of *P. brassicae* have continued for over a century; even so, many aspects remain to be resolved. The fungus is present in soils as a thick-walled, hyaline, resting spore up to 4 μm in diameter and possessing a crenellated surface. Resting spores can apparently remain viable in a dormant state for decades. In the presence of a suitable host they germinate to form thin-walled, biflagellate, amoeboid primary zoospores. Reports of the size of zoospores vary widely from 0.5 to 6.0 μm, in view of which it is suggested that growth may take place after emergence from the resting spore. Penetration of the host root hairs is elegantly described by Samuel and Garrett (1945) and Aist and Williams (1971) (*see* section 2.1.1). Once inside the root hair a small uninucleate stage develops. Mitotic division follows giving rise to a plasmodium containing 30–100 nuclei; thereafter the plasmodial cytoplasm cleaves to form multinucleate zoosporangia, 6.0–6.5 μm in size. Invasion of the root hair leads to host nucleolar enlargement; the parasitised cells become stunted

Figure 5.4   Galls on the root system of Brussels sprout caused by *Plasmodiophora brassicae*. (Copyright © North of Scotland College of Agriculture, Aberdeen. Reproduced by permission.)

and often enlarged at the tips (Williams *et al.*, 1971). Secondary zoospores, 1.5 μm long, are liberated from the zoosporangia. Opinion is divided as to whether these zoospores are liberated from the root hair back into the soil environment or whether they penetrate immediately into the host cortical and vascular tissue. In either event, once inside these tissues the secondary zoospores fuse to form binucleate plasmodia which then become multinucleate. Nuclear fusion follows, giving rise to diploid multinucleate secondary plasmodia. Two size ranges of plasmodia are reported by Dekhiujzen (1975): irregular shaped ones 7–90 μm in diameter and smaller spherically shaped ones, 5–30 μm in diameter. Meiosis and cleavage of the plasmodial cytoplasm ensue giving rise to haploid resting spores. These are released back into the soil as the gall tissue decays (Tommerup and Ingram, 1971).

Environmental factors could be expected to influence the severity of club root symptoms, and although there are many empirical references to such effects little durable evidence is available. Disease severity will increase where soil moisture content rises from 50 per cent of maximum water holding capacity up to saturation. Studies by Buczacki et al. (1978) show that temperature influences the percentage of plants showing symptoms, complete infection only occurring where mean daily temperature is not less than 19.5 °C. Increases above this to about 26 °C will influence symptom severity. Soil acidity is perhaps the most vexed parameter connected wtih clubroot infection. Although the disease is primarily associated with acid soils, it is now apparent that in alkaline soils club development will take place provided soil moisture content, temperature and spore load are sufficiently high (Colhoun, 1953, 1961). Although infection is not inhibited by alkaline soil, the range of conditions suitable for infection is more limited compared to those for acid soils. Light intensity 14–21 days after infection influences the severity of symptoms, maximum severity being found at 600 W h m^{-2} day^{-1} (Buczacki et al., 1978). Spore concentration will influence infection, but only limited investigations have been made which show that soils containing less than 1000 spores per gram are unlikely to cause heavy clubbing. Work with nitrogen fertilisation is conflicting; some reports suggest that additional nitrogen will increase clubroot whereas others suggest the reverse. Potassium fertilisers might have a greater effect by affecting the calcium: potassium ratio in soil.

Dissemination of P. brassicae on a local scale is by drainage water, farm implements, wind-borne infected soil, manure from animals fed on infected roots, and diseased transplanting material. It is unlikely that P. brassicae is seed-borne, so that transplant material is the only means of long-range spread. The pathogen is thought to have been carried from Europe on infected turnips, which were a favourite fodder for cattle carried by colonists to America, Africa and Australia.

The gall symptoms associated with infection by P. brassicae have provoked considerable interest in the biochemistry of this host–parasite relationship. High levels of auxin-like hormones are found in clubbed roots of Brassica spp. (Katsura et al., 1966), which may indicate that such growth substances are synthesised by P. brassicae or by the host tissues in response to the pathogen at or close to the infection site, and could be responsible for host cell hypertrophy in infected roots and hypocotyls. Indeed Ingram (1969) found that tissue explants from clubbed roots of B. oleracea var. capitata and B. napus cv.

Balmoral were able to form callus on a culture medium devoid of such growth substances, whereas uninfected explants required the addition of auxins for callus growth. Precursors of such auxins may originate from glucobrassicin and neoglucobrassicin found in the roots of susceptible brassicas. In the presence of glucosinolase these glucosinolates are degraded to 3-indoleacetonitrile (IAN), which may be converted to indoleacetic acid by nitralase. Furthermore, the level of IAN is found to be highest in infected plants during the early stages of club development followed by high levels of indole auxin activity during the most active period of growth by secondary plasmodia (Butcher *et al.*, 1974). The effect of *P. brassicae* on host cell division leading to the formation of large numbers of new cells in infected roots may be attributed to increased levels of cytokinins such as zeatin and its nucleoside, zeatin riboside, found in clubbed roots of *B. campestris* cv. Gelria by Dekhiujzen and Overeem (1971). Considerable studies of other biochemical changes during pathogenesis by *P. brassicae* have been made by Williams and his co-workers. In the first 30 days after planting *B. oleracea* var. *capitata* seedlings into infected soil the parasite grows vegetatively and there is rapid gall development with attendant increases in protein, DNA, RNA, amino acids, sugars, starch and lipids found in infected roots. Starch accumulation has been related to the relatively high activities of starch synthetic enzymes, uridine diphosphate glucose (UDPG), pyrophosphorylase, adenine diphosphate glucose (ADPG) and starch transglucosylase. These increases are reflected in the enrichment of infected host cell cytoplasm in ribosomes, mitochondria, dictyosomes and starch grains (Williams and McNabola, 1967; Williams and Yukawa, 1967) and in increased rates of sugar transportation to the roots. This period could be termed as a synthetic or commensal phase of parasitism (Keen *et al.*, 1968; Williams *et al.*, 1968). After 30 days, however, when the plasmodia sporulate a degradative phase ensues during which sugars, RNA and starch levels decrease but protein, amino acids, DNA and lipids remain high. At this stage, high specific activities of α-amylase were found in isolated plasmodia of *P. brassicae* (Keen and Williams, 1969). During sporogenesis the cytoplasm of infected cells within the gall loses its integrity (Williams, 1966); concomitantly the tops of infected plants become chlorotic and stunted. Cytoplasmic changes are restricted to those cells which contain plasmodia.

    Useful genes for resistance to *P. brassicae* are infrequent in the germ plasm of cultivated crucifers, and the pathogen would appear to possess considerable undefined variation which allows it to overcome resistance. These factors have made the successful use of resistance as a control for *P. brassicae* difficult. Studies of the virulence composition of *P. brassicae* isolates and attempts to erect racial classifications have been made in various parts of the world (Colhoun, 1958; Karling, 1968), but their value is confounded by the unco-ordinated use of a wide variety of unrelated differential hosts from several *Brassica* spp. The situation is further complicated by the confused taxonomy of *Brassica* spp. themselves. In an attempt to produce virulence

studies which could be universally understood the European Clubroot
Differential (ECD) series has been developed (Buczacki *et al.*, 1975).

Sources of resistance in the Cruciferae are reviewed by Colhoun (1958), Karling
(1968) and Crute *et al.* (1980). The nature of resistance is, however, little
understood. But it is generally suggested that resistance in *B. campestris* (turnip)
and *B. napus* (swede) is controlled by monogenic dominant systems, whereas
that in *B. oleracea* (cole crops) is of a polygenic recessive nature. Resistance was
demonstrated in swede and rape (*B. napus*) by Lammerink (1967), where two
separate and non-allelic dominant genes in swede cultivars Wye and Wilhelmsburger controlled resistance to New Zealand race C of *P. brassicae*. In both hosts
there were also indications of recessive genes operating. Resistant swedes tend to
be derived from either green-skinned Wilhelmsburger or bronze-skinned Bangholm
types. Similarly, Sterling (1951), working with swedes of the Danish and Ditmars
type, found a number of 'factors' operating to control resistance. York swede was
found by Ayers and Lelacheur (1966) to possess one dominant gene for resistance
to each of the Canadian races 2 and 3 of *P. brassicae*, while Wilhelmsburger swede
had one gene for resistance to race 3 and two genes for resistance to race 2. A range
of turnips (*B. campestris*) have been developed in the Netherlands with
considerable resistance to *P. brassicae* (Tjallingii, 1965) from turnip land races
found in Belgium and southern Holland. Resistance in this crop was identified
by Wit (1966) as the combined action of three dominant genes, A, B and C. The
first resistant cabbage (*B. oleracea* var. *capitata* cv. Badger Shipper) was developed
by Walker and Larson (1960) from a chance cross of cabbage with kale (*B.
oleracea* var. *acephala*). Attempts have also been made to transfer resistance to
Brussels sprout (Rick and Perkins, 1955) and cauliflower and broccoli
(Gallegly, 1956; Luzny, 1965; Sciaroni and Welch, 1969; Weisaeth, 1967).
Resistance in *B. oleracea* cvs Red Acre and Golden Acre was controlled by two
recessive genes and only expressed in the homozygous recessive $pb_1 pb_1 pb_2$
(Chiang and Crete, 1970). The Chinese cabbage (*B. campestris* var. *pekinensis* cv.
Michihili) possesses one dominant gene for clubroot resistance (Strandberg and
Williams, 1967). Attempts are being made to transfer resistance from *B. napus* to
B. oleracea var. *capitata* in order to insert dominant resistance into the cabbage
genome (Chiang *et al.*, 1977). Similarly, use might be made of the clubroot
resistance found in some *Raphanobrassica* hybrids (McNaughton, 1973).
Additionally, some resistance is indicated in culinary radish cultivars since
Tjallingii (1965) reports that inoculated seedlings are only sporadically infected.
A major problem with the use of clubroot resistance is the development of
predominant virulences within the pathogen population which can overcome
them. Surprisingly for a soil-borne pathogen, it would seem that relatively rapid
changes can occur in virulence frequency, and this is influenced by the *Brassica*
spp. grown in particular pieces of land (Dixon, 1977).

Chemical control of *P. brassicae* for transplanted brassicas has long been
practiced by use of 4 per cent calomel (mercurous chloride) slurry into which the
roots are dipped just prior to planting. This will protect the treated roots from

infection but gives no protection to those produced subsequently. Benomyl slurry may be used as a more effective and less hazardous substitute which also has slight systemic properties when applied to roots (Dixon *et al.*, 1972). There is considerable interest in the use of chemical sterilants to eradicate *P. brassicae* from soil. Materials found to be effective include chloropicrin, dazomet, dichloropropane+dichloropropene, and methyl bromide. Dazomet may be applied in granular form and incorporated with a rotary cultivator, giving it an advantage over the other materials which need to be injected in gaseous form. The cost of injection was thought to limit their use to eradication of small infection foci in otherwise pathogen-free land used for high value horticultural brassicas. But the expanding use of injection machines to eradicate other pathogens such as potato cyst eelworm may reduce these costs and make them available for use against clubroot. Pentachloronitrobenzene (PCNB) is toxic to *P. brassicae* but can be phytotoxic to brassicas, but its use with hydrated lime can ameliorate this disadvantage. Control of *P. brassicae* was achieved using 4480 kg hydrated lime broadcast per hectare plus 10–20 g PCNB per square metre band applied by Anderson *et al.* (1976). Application of lime to raise pH levels above 7.0 is a traditional method of clubroot control. But very heavy rates are required; those reported include applications in excess of 45 tonnes/ha in Newfoundland (K. G. Proudfoot, personal communication) and California, USA (Welch *et al.*, 1976). Calcium cyanamide applications are also reported to reduce clubroot infestation (Mattusch, 1978).

Husbandry techniques remain a major means of clubroot control. Wide rotations with a 6 year break between any crucifer crop are essential. This applies equally to crops where resistant cultivars are used since the site of resistance is not established, and it is likely from the observations of Samuel and Garrett (1945) that the root hairs of such cultivars are invaded during the primary stages of pathogenesis to a similar extent to those of susceptible cultivars. Even wider rotations could be advocated for spring- and summer-growing brassica crops which occupy the soil in those climatic periods which provide optimal conditions for *P. brassicae* activity. Soil cultivation can be used effectively for clubroot control, in south-western Wales, for instance, continual rotary cultivation of land intended for cauliflower production but infected with *P. brassicae* lowers the rate of infestation. This is presumably because the loose, dry, friable soil permits desiccation of the resting spores. Where controls are practised, their efficacy should be monitored by the assessment of *P. brassicae* populations, for example by the methods of Melville and Hawken (1967).

5.2 VIRUSES

5.2.1 Broccoli Necrotic Yellows Virus (BNYV)

Only one species of aphid, *Brevicoryne brassicae*, has been shown to transmit BNYV. Geographical distribution is restricted to England, and the only naturally infected hosts so far identified are late heading cauliflower (*B. oleracea* var. *botrytis*) and Brussels sprout (*B.oleracea* var. *gemmifera*). Virus particles are bacilliform rods, 275 nm x 75 nm in size, although in some preparations they appear as bullet-shaped structures 266 nm x 66 nm.

Symptoms caused by BNYV are mild vein clearing and slight leaf rolling which may disappear as the host matures. Virus particles are found enclosed in membrane-bounded sacs within the cytoplasm of parenchymatous cells. These sacs form from the endoplasmic reticulum, the final stages of virus assembly appearing to take place within the sac. Mitochondria of infected cells are swollen, with few cristae. Particle size and their intracellular location resemble Lettuce Necrotic Yellows Virus (*see* section 7.2.3) but differences in host range, host reaction, geographical distribution and serological activity would suggest they are separate viruses. Seed transmission has not been established.

5.2.2 Cauliflower Mosaic Virus (CaMV)

Synonyms of CaMV are Cabbage Virus B, Chinese Cabbage Mosaic Virus, Cabbage Mosaic Virus and Broccoli Mosaic Virus. It is transmitted by some 27 species of aphid, including *Brevicoryne brassicae* (cabbage aphid), *Rhopalosiphum pseudobrassicae* (false cabbage aphid), and *Myzus persicae* (peach aphid), all of which breed on cabbage, and by *Aphis graveolens* (celery leaf aphid), *A. apigraveolens* (celery aphid), *A. middletoni* (erigeron root aphid), *A. gossypii* (cotton or melon aphid), *Cavariella aegopodis* (yellow willow aphid), *Aulacorthum circumflexum* (lily aphid) and *Hydadaphis mellifera* (honeysuckle aphid), all of which are unable to reproduce on cabbage. All instars can transmit CaMV without a latent period. Acquisition takes 1—2 min and transmission can occur immediately afterwards. Cauliflower Mosaic Virus is stylet-borne and non-persistent; the particles being spheres 50 nm in diameter. Distribution is widespread in temperate regions throughout Europe, the USA and the UK, and has been reported in New Zealand. In addition to brassica crop hosts, various cruciferous weeds can be infected by CaMV such as wild mustard (*Sinapis arvensis*), shepherd's purse (*Capsella bursa-pastoris*) and jointed charlock (*Raphanus raphanistrum*).

The expanded foliage of young cauliflower (*B. oleracea* var. *botrytis*) may remain symptomless while young leaves develop vein clearing of at least part of the leaf, especially towards the base. Enations may develop but are not a consistent symptom. Striking symptoms appear on mature plants, with vein banding beginning as a dark green coloration and loss of chlorophyll in the interveinal areas. As the syndrome progresses a vivid mosaic of light green or chlorotic areas interspersed between very dark green regions is produced. Infected brassica leaves lose their typical waxy bloom in the interveinal areas.

Systemic symptoms are typical of CaMV on inoculated cabbage (*B. oleracea* var. *capitata*), but no local lesions form. At 28 °C vein clearing becomes very prominent, with a mild diffuse mottle, loss of waxy bloom, but little necrosis or distortion. Vein clearing is slower at temperatures below 20 °C but may become prominent as chlorotic vein banding with mild mottle and sporadic enations. Slight stunting may develop.

Chinese cabbage (*B. campestris* var. *pekinensis*) typically shows systemic vein clearing beginning from the leaf base and eventually spreading over the entire leaf. After 21–28 days a coarse mottling forms on the inner leaves with irregular light and dark regions between the veins and slight distortion of the leaf surfaces. Raised green islands may gradually form on the foliage; older leaves show vein clearing but few other symptoms except for accelerated senescence and death. Mild stunting is typical of most infected plants.

Particles of CaMV are found only in the cytoplasm of infected cells, often associated with granular, electron-dense material which forms the bulk of the prominent inclusion bodies found in chronically infected plants. When fully formed these consist of compact, elliptical masses of material containing vacuoles but devoid of membranes. Randomly scattered throughout this granular matrix are virus particles, particularly near to the periphery and within vacuoles.

Cauliflower Mosaic Virus can be distinguished from the Cabbage Black Ringspot strain of Turnip Mosaic Virus (*see* section 5.2.5) by its non-transmissibility to *Nicotiana* spp. Symptoms are differentiated from Turnip Mosaic Virus (ordinary strain) by the production of cleared veins on the younger leaves of cauliflower plants followed by vein banding and necrotic spotting.

Apparently CaMV is not seed-transmitted, so that protection of new brassica crops can only be achieved by destruction of the old season's infected crops prior to the emergence of new seedlings. There should be a break of at least 1 month between destruction of old crops and brairding of new ones. Seed beds should be isolated geographically from existing brassica crops or surrounded by trap crops of kale (*B. oleracea* var. *acephala*) or rape (*B. napus*). The most satisfactory form of control is to raise transplants outside the areas of crop production.

5.2.3 Radish Mosaic Virus (RMV)

Transmission of RMV is achieved rather inefficiently by black flea beetle (*Phyllotreta* spp.), spotted cucumber beetle (*Diabrotica undecimpunctata*) and other leaf-feeding beetles such as *Epitrix hirtipennis* and *Phyllotreta cruciferae*. The virus is retained for up to 48 h after feeding. The particle is isometric, 30 nm in diameter and is grouped with Bean Pod Mottle Virus (*see* section 6.5.5), Broad Bean Stain Virus (*see* section 6.5.9) and True Broad Bean Mosaic Virus (*see* section 6.5.10). It has a wide host range covering nine genera of five Angiosperm families and has been identified in Europe, Japan and California, USA.

Symptoms on cultivated radish (*Raphanus sativus*) are initially small, roughly circular to irregular chlorotic lesions distributed between and adjacent to the veins. Lesions increase in number to form a coarse mottle which contrasts with the the healthy tissue. Within 14 days of infection healthy tissue is confined to irregularly shaped non-raised green islands set against a conspicuous yellowish-green background. Foliar distortion is limited but there is no necrosis or stunting.

Infected cauliflowers (*B. oleracea* var. *botrytis*) form diffuse chlorotic lesions developing from systemic infection.

Cabbage (*B. oleracea* var. *capitata*) shows chlorotic and necrotic lesions developing from systemic infection.

Spinach (*S. oleracea*) shows yellow lesions on infected juvenile foliage which spread systemically as the host matures. Mid rib curvature follows with marked leaf distortion, dwarfing and eventual plant death.

Within infected host cells aggregates of virus particles are found in the cytoplasm and vacuoles. Particles concentrate at cellular membranes, often in multiple rows within membrane-bounded, tube-like structures. Infected turnip (*B. campestris*) epidermal cells contain large vesicular inclusion bodies within which are aggregates of virus particles.

Control by development of resistant cultivars may be possible since Tender Green Mustard (*B. perviridis*) is heterozygous for resistance and resistance has been noted in *B. campestris* cv. Purple Top White Globe compared to the cultivars Early White Flat Dutch and Shogoin, which are susceptible.

5.2.4 Turnip Crinkle Virus (TCV)

Larvae and adult flea beetles are vectors of TCV, particularly the genera *Phyllotreta* (nine spp.) and *Psylliodes* (two spp.). The particles are isometric, 28 nm in diameter. Distribution is so far restricted to Germany, India, Yugoslavia and the UK. Both cultivated and weed brassicas are host to TCV, together with tomato (*L. esculentum*), bean (*Ph. vulgaris*), cucumber (*C. sativus*) and spinach (*S. oleracea*).

Symptoms vary depending on the strain of TCV involved:

(1) *Mild strain*   This produces crinkling of the leaves, the margins of which curl inwards together with development of indistinct, irregular, light green or yellow patches on slightly stunted plants.

(2) *Severe strain*   Symptoms are similar to those caused by the mild strain, but are of greater intensity with severe leaf distortion, crinkling, severe stunting and rosetting. The mature foliage of infected swedes (*B. napus*) dies very quickly, leaving only a tuft of apparently healthy young leaves. All host tissue is invaded by virus particles, but no inclusion bodies develop, although plastid changes may take place.

5.2.5 Turnip Mosaic Virus (TuMV)

Synonyms of TuMV include Cabbage Black Ringspot Virus, Cabbage Black Ring Virus, Horseradish Mosaic Virus and Radish P and R viruses. Transmission is via a number of aphid species including *Brevicoryne brassicae* and *Myzus persicae*. Acquisition time is less than 1 min and infection can take place in less than 1 min; all instars are able to transmit TuMV but retention time is less than 4 h. Particles of TuMV are flexuous filaments 580–574 nm long. Geographical distribution is world-wide, with most frequent reports from temperate zones of Africa, Asia, Europe and North America. Host range is very wide, covering 38 species of 12 Angiosperm families which include Cruciferae, Chenopodiaceae, Compositae and Solanaceae. Symptoms vary according to the strain of TuMV involved.

(1) *Ordinary strain (Turnip Mosaic Virus)*   The turnip host (*B. campestris*) develops conspicuous coarse systemic vein clearing with interveinal mottling leading to a yellowish discoloration. Foliage becomes markedly crinkled and dwarfed and stunting rapidly follows infection. As the leaves expand the yellow coloration may be masked by very dark green, irregular raised islands which become interspersed by yellow tissue.

On horseradish (*Armoracia rusticana*) symptoms develop from the spring onwards as a chlorotic blotchy mottling which may or may not be accompanied by vein clearing. Leaves generally become chlorotic and dwarfed. As the foliage ages, mottling becomes diffuse and the lesions less distinct. Later in the season necrotic rings form at the periphery of the chlorotic zones. There may be flecking and streaking of the petioles and leaf veins towards autumn. Flecking may extend into the roots which have a patchy chlorosis when sectioned.

Infected rhubarb (*Rheum officinale*) shows severe mottling and stunting.

Turnip Mosaic Virus causes a specific mosaic reaction with lettuce (*L. sativa*). Observations in California, USA, showed that *Bremia lactucae* (downy mildew) resistant, crisphead lettuce are very susceptible to TuMV, particularly the cultivars Calmar, Imperial 410, Imperial Triumph, Valrio, Valtemp and Valverde.

(2) *Cabbage Black Ringspot strain*   On cabbage (*B. oleracea* var. *capitata*) the chief distinction between the ordinary strain and Cabbage Black Ringspot strain is the very severe symptoms which the latter causes to cabbage. Within 20 days of infection small black necrotic rings or spots form on the leaves. Young leaves may remain totally symptomless. Following systemic infection the black ringspots are initially seen on the leaf undersurface.

Cauliflower and broccoli (*B. oleracea* var. *botrytis*) seedlings develop a diffuse systemic mottle consisting of small pale green roughly circular areas which contrast with the dark green background. Usually vein clearing and banding are not significant symptoms on cauliflower. High temperatures may accelerate symptom expression.

Cell inclusions resulting from infection are easily observed with the light microscope. In ultrathin sections of infected spinach mustard (*B. perviridis*) virus particles are associated with intracellular fibrous masses and banded structures.

5.2.6 Turnip Rosette Virus (TRV)

Transmission of this virus is thought to be by flea beetles (*Phyllotreta* spp.). It has only been identified infrequently on turnip (*B. campestris*) and swede (*B. napus*) crops in Scotland. Other hosts in the Compositae and Solanaceae have been infected artificially. Particles of TRV are isometric, 28 nm in diameter.

Symptoms on turnip include petiole and vein necrosis with severe dwarfing, leaf distortion and rosetting. Infection of young plants is usually fatal. Vein banding, rosetting and stunting are also common symptoms of infected swedes.

5.2.7 Turnip Yellow Mosaic Virus (TYMV)

A synonym of this virus is Newcastle Turnip Virus. Natural transmission occurs via flea-beetle vectors (*Phyllotreta* and *Psylliodes* spp.), both of which acquire and are reinfective after a few minutes. The mustard beetle, *Phaedon cochleariae*, and its larvae can acquire this virus within a few minutes but require a delay of 1 day before being capable of transmission. Other vectors include grasshoppers (*Leptophyes punctatissima* and *Stanroderus bicolor*) and the common earwig (*Forficula auricularia*). The particle is an isometric sphere 28 nm in diameter. Distribution is so far restricted to western Europe and the host range confined almost exclusively to the Cruciferae.

Symptoms on cauliflower (*B. oleracea* var. *botrytis*), turnip (*B. campestris*) and Chinese cabbage (*B. campestris* var. *pekinensis*) become visible about 14 days after infection. Pronounced vein clearing of the younger leaves is followed by formation of yellow patches on the older leaves. On Chinese cabbage, in particular, the mosaic is a vivid yellow with intense yellowing or bleaching interspersed with dark green. Mosaic symptoms on other hosts are less intense. During periods of low temperatures, infected plants become stunted, with yellow zones on the outer leaves which become necrotic, and abscission is accelerated. Infected plants are more susceptible to frost damage than healthy ones. Thus cauliflowers infected in the autumn either fail to survive the winter or produce inferior curds, while spring-infected plants are stunted but again with low quality curds.

Virus particles are found throughout infected Chinese cabbage plants but reach their highest concentrations in the leaf lamina. The chloroplasts of infected mesophyll cells become rounded and aggregate to form 'X' bodies. A most constant feature of infection is the appearance of numerous vesicles in the chloroplasts, especially near their surfaces.

Three categories of TYMV strain have been identified:

(1) *Cambridge Culture strain*   This is probably a mixture of types. Areas of different colour in leaves exhibiting mosaic symptoms contain different strains of the pathogen.

(2) *Northumberland Isolate*   This causes more severe symptoms than the Cambridge strain on cauliflower, cabbage and Brussels sprout (*B. oleracea* vars *botrytis, capitata* and *gemmifera* respectively), but is less severe on other hosts.

(3) *Groups of strains*   Various strains have been isolated in parts of western Europe which differ in the nucleic acid content of their RNA.

5.2.8 Mixed infections by brassica viruses

Brassica crops are likely to be infected by more than one of the viruses described above. Recent experience in the UK has shown that following a succession of mild winters, overwintered brassica crops can be devastated by these pathogens. Virus infection in Brussels sprout (*B. oleracea* var. *gemmifera*) and swede (*B. napus*) crops has been particularly severe, those mainly involved were Turnip Mosaic Virus and Cauliflower Mosaic Virus. Symptoms consisted of heavy leaf drop and yellowing of the plant apices with very dark green vein banding and stunting (figure 5.5). Variation in symptom expression can be attributed to different combinations of brassica viruses being present; up to five different particles could be recognised in some infected samples, including Cucumber Mosaic Virus (*see* section 11.3.2). Dutch white cabbages for storage have been found showing a variety of symptoms, including necrotic spotting, flecking and streaking symptoms, usually in the interior of the head. Some such symptoms may be attributed to physiological disorders, but viruses have also been implicated such as Turnip Mosaic Virus, Cauliflower Mosaic Virus and Broccoli Necrotic Virus. Cauliflower Mosaic Virus, in particular, has been found in the outer wrapper leaves of white storage cabbage. Generally, Turnip Mosaic Virus is found during the summer while Cauliflower Mosaic Virus increases towards autumn as the temperature falls. Tissue necrosis is strongly correlated with the presence of this virus.

As indicated for Cauliflower Mosaic Virus in section 5.2.2, none of these viruses is thought to be seed-transmitted, and few are persistent; consequently, geographical isolation may be used as a main means of control, keeping young plants well separated from older infected crops and using trap crops to prevent vector invasion. Breeding for resistance to Turnip Mosaic Virus is possible in Brussels sprout (*B. oleracea* var. *gemmifera*), where variations in cultivar symptom expression have been identified; only mild symptoms are found in the cultivars Achilles, Citadel and King Arthur, whereas the cultivar Fasolt is very severely affected. Similarly, in swedes (*B. napus*) the cultivar Marian develops severe symptoms while the cultivar Ruta Øtofte is only mildly affected.

Figure 5.5   Virus infection on Brussels sprout leaf. (Reproduced by permission of National Institute of Agricultural Botany, Cambridge.)

REFERENCES

In this and subsequent chapters, the references are subdivided by section for the convenience of the reader.

Section 5.1.1
Asada, Y. (1974). *Mem. Coll. Agric. Ehine Univ.*, **19**, 169–83.
Asada, Y. and Kugoh, T. (1971). *Ann. Phytopath. Soc. Japan.* **37**, 311–3.
Asada, Y. and Matsumoto, I. (1971). *Physiol. Pl. Path.* **1**, 377–83.
Asada, Y and Matsumoto, I. (1972). *Phytopath. Z.* **73**, 208–14.
Baines, G. (1975). *12th A. Rep. Kirton exp. Stn* 40.
Channon, A. G. and Turner, M. K. (1970). *A. Rept. natn. Veg. Res. Stn* **1969**, 102.
D'Ercole, N. (1975). *Informatore Fitopatologico* **25**, 21–3.
Dickinson, C. H. and Greenhalgh, J. R. (1977). *Trans. Br. mycol. Soc.* **69**, 111–6.
Fraymouth, J. (1956). *Trans. Br. Mycol. Soc.* **39**, 79–107.
Greenhalgh, J. R. and Dickinson, C. H. (1975). *Phytopath. Z.* **84**, 131–41.
Greenhalgh, J. R. and Dickinson, C. H. (1976). *Ann. appl. Biol.* **84**, 278–81.
Greenhalgh, J. R. and Mitchell, N. D. (1976). *New Phytol.* **77**, 391–98.
Ingram, D. S. (1969). *J. gen. Microbiol.* **58**, 391–401.
Klinkovskaya, I. K. (1976). *Byulleten' Usesoyuznogo Nauch no Issledovatel' skogo Instituta Zashchity Rastenii,* No. 38, 31–5.
Lebeau, F. J. (1945). *J. agric. Res.* **71**, 453–63.
McMeekin, D. (1971). *Pl. Dis. Reptr.* **55**, 877–8.
Natti, J. J., Dickson, M. K. and Atkin, J. D. (1967). *Phytopathology* **57**, 144–7.
Ohguchi, T., Yamashita, Y. and Asada, Y. (1974). *Ann. Phytopath. Soc. Japan* **40**, 419–26.
Ohguchi, T. and Asada, Y. (1975). *Physiol. Pl. Path.* **5**, 183–92.
Ryan, E. W. (1977). *Proc. 9th. Br. Crop Protect. Conf.* 297–300.
Sansome, E. and Sansome, F. W. (1974). *Trans. Br. mycol. Soc.* **62**, 323–32.
Shiraishi, M., Sakamoto, K., Asada, Y., Nagatani, T. and Hidaka, H. (1975). *Ann. Phytopath. Soc. Japan* **41**, 24–32.
Sumner, D. R., Glaze, N. C., Dawler, C. C. and Johnson, A. W. (1978). *Pl. Dis. Reptr* **62**, 51–5.
Thornton, J. D. and Cooke, R. C. (1974). *Physiol. Pl. Path.* **4**, 117–25.
Vasileva, E. D. (1976). *Nauchnye Trudy Leningradskogo S-kh Instituta* No. 297, 97–100.
Vladimirskaya, M. E., Ilina, M. N. and Klinkovskaya, I. K. (1975). *Mikologiya i Fitopatologiya* **9**, 130–2.
Yerkes, W. D. and Shaw, C. G. (1959). *Phytopathology* **49**, 499–507.

Section 5.1.2
Blumer, S. (1967). *Echt mehltaupilze (Erysiphaceae)*. Fischer, Jena.
Dixon, G. R. (1974). *Pl. Path.* **23**, 105–9.

Dixon, G. R. (1978). Powdery mildew diseases of vegetables and allied crops. In *Powdery Mildews* (D. M. Spencer, ed.). Academic Press, London.

Junell, L. (1967). *Sr. bot. Tidskr.* **61**, 209–30.

Salmon, E. (1900). *Mem. Torrey bot. Club* **9**, 1–292.

Walker, J. C. and Williams, P. H. (1965). *Pl. Dis. Reptr* **49**, 198–201.

Walker, J. C. and Williams, P. H. (1973). Crucifers. In *Breeding Plants for Disease Resistance: Concepts and Applications.* (R. R. Nelson, ed.). State University Press, Pennsylvania.

Williams, P. H., Walker, J. C. and Pound, C. S. (1968). *Phytopathology* **58**, 791–6.

Section 5.1.3

Braverman, S. W. (1971). *Pl. Dis. Reptr* **55**, 454–7.

Braverman, S. W. (1977). *Pl. Dis. Reptr* **61**, 360–2.

Campbell, R. (1972). *Trans. Br. mycol. Soc.* **59**, 153–6.

Chupp, C. (1935). *Phytopathology* **25**, 269–74.

Govshkov, A. K. (1976). *Trudy Uses. S-Kh Inst. Zaoch. Ubrazuvaniya* No. 117, 25–9.

Gupta, R. B. L., Desai, B. G. and Pathak, V. N. (1972). *Phytopath. medit.* **11**, 61–2.

Jouan, B., Lemaire, J. M. and Hervey, Y. (1972). *Annls Phytopath.* **4**, 133–55.

Kear, R. W., Williams, D. J. and Stevens, C. C. (1977). *Proc. 9th Br. Insectic. Fungic. Conf.* 179–87.

Maude, R. B. and Humpherson-Jones, F. M. (1977). *A. Rep. natn. Veg. Res. Stn* **1976**, 95–6.

Maude, R. B. and Humpherson-Jones, F. M. (1978). *A. Rep. natn. Veg. Res. Stn* **1977**, 95–7.

Nehemiah, A. K. M. and Deshpande, K. B. (1977). *Ind. Phytopath.* **29**, 55–7.

Pace, M. A. and Campbell, R. (1974). *Trans. Br. mycol. Soc.* **63**, 193–6.

Petrie, G. A. (1974*a*). *Can. Pl. Dis. Surv.* **54**, 31–4.

Petrie, G. A. (1974*b*). *Can. Pl. Dis. Surv.* **54**, 155–65.

Richardson, M. J. (1970). *Proc. int. Seed Test. Assoc.* **35**, 207–23.

Roscoe, Q. (1967). Studies of *Alternaria brassicae* and *A. brassicicola.* Ph.D. thesis, University of Exeter, Exeter.

Skipp, R. A. and Bailey, J. A. (1977). *Physiol. Pl. Path.*, **11**, 101–12.

Skoropad, W. P. and Tewari, J. P. (1977). *Can. J. Pl. Sci.* **57**, 1001–3.

Tsuneda, A., Skoropad, W. P. and Tuvari, J. P. (1976). *Phytopathology* **66**, 1056–64.

Tsuneda, A. and Skoropad, W. P. (1977). *Can. J. Bot.* **55**, 448–54.

Wood, R. K. S. (1967). *Physiological Plant Pathology.* Blackwell Scientific Publications, Oxford.

Section 5.1.4

Barbetti, M. J. (1975). *Aust. J. exp. Agric. Animal Husb.* **15**, 705–8.

Barbetti, M. J. (1978). *Am. Phytopath. Soc. Newsletter* 7, 3–5.

Bousquet, J. F., Ferezou, J. P., Devys, M. and Barbier, M. (1977). *C. r. hebd. Séanc. Sci., Paris, D* 284, 927–8.

Cruickshank, I. A. M. and Palmer, T. P. (1954). *N.Z. Jl Sci. Technol.* 36, 122–8.

Gabrielson, R. L., Mulanax, H. W., Matsnoka, K., Williams, P. H., Whiteaker, G. P. and Maguire, J. D. (1977). *Pl. Dis. Reptr* 61, 118–21.

Jacobsen, B. J. and Williams, P. H. (1971). *Pl. Dis. Reptr* 55, 934–8.

Klinkovskaya, I. K. (1976). *Byulleten Usesoyuznogo Nauchno Issledovatel' skogo Instituta Zashchity Rastenii* No. 38, 31–5.

Lacoste, L., Louvet, J., Anselme, C., Alabouvett, C., Brunin, B. and Pierre, J. G. (1969). *C. r. hebd. Séanc. Agric. Fr.* 55, 981–9.

McGee, D. C. (1977). *Aust. J. agric. Res.* 28, 53–62.

Maude, R. M., Presly, A. H. and Dudley, C. L. (1973). *A. Rep. natn. Veg. Res. Stn* 1972, 94.

Petrie, G. A. (1973). *Can. Pl. Dis. Surv.* 53, 26–8.

Sherf, A. F. (1968). *Blackleg of Cabbage and other Crucifers*. Extension Bulletin No. 1209. New York State College of Agriculture, Cornell, N.Y.

Thurling, N. and Venn, L. A. (1977). *Aust. J. exp. Agric. Animal Husb.* 17, 445–51.

Section 5.1.5

Geeson, J. D. and Robinson, J. E. (1975). *Commercial Grower* 27 June, 1245–6.

Rogers, I. S. and Wicks, I. T. (1970). *Expl Rec.* 5, 12–15.

Vanterpool, T. C. (1968). *Rapp. Activ. Cent. Rech. Agron. Etat., Gembloux* 1967, 35–42.

Welch, N. C., Greathead, A. S., Hall, D. H. and Little, T. (1969). *Calif. Agric.* 23, 17.

Wilson, G. J. (1971). *N.Z. Commercial Grower* 26, 11.

Section 5.1.6

Parmeter, J. R. (ed.) (1970). Rhizoctonia solani, *Biology and Pathology*. California University Press, Stanford, Calif.

Section 5.1.7

Anisimov, A. M. (1969). *Trudy Khar'kov sel'khoz. Inst.* 79, 21–4.

Anisimov, A. M. and Kovalchuk, N. I. (1969). *Trudy Khar'kov sel'khoz. Inst.* 79, 25–30.

Armstrong, G. M. and Armstrong, J. K. (1952). *Phytopathology* 42, 255–7.

Armstrong, G. M. and Armstrong, J. K. (1974). *Pl. Dis. Reptr* 58, 479–80.

Beckman, C. H. (1967). *Phytopathology* 57, 699–702.

Davis, D. (1967). *Phytopathology* 57, 311–4.

Gangopadhyny, S. and Kaprov, K. S. (1976). *Indian J. agric. Sci.* 45, 172–4.

Gordon, W. L. (1965). *Can. J. Bot.* 43, 1309–18.

Heitefuss, R., Buchanan-Davidson, D. J., Stahman, M. A. and Walker, J. C. (1960). *Phytopathology* 50, 198–205.

Kaszonyi, S. (1974). *Kerteszeti Egyetem Kozlemenzei* **37**, 247–57.

Reyes, A. A. (1970). *Proc. Can. Phytopath. Soc.* **37**, 21–30.

Reyes, A. A. and Chadha, K. C. (1972). *Phytopathogy* **62**, 1424–8.

Vladimirskaya, M. E., Ilina, M. N. and Klinkovskaya, I. K. (1975). *Mikologiya i Fitopatologiya* **9**, 132–32.

Walker, J. C. (1959). Progress and problems in controlling plant disease by host resistance. In *Plant Pathology Problems and Progress, 1908–1958* (C. S. Holton, G. W. Fischer, R. W. Fulton, H. Hart and S. E. A. McCallan, eds). Wisconsin University Press, Madison, Wisc.

Williams, P. H., Walker, J. C. and Pound, G. S. (1968). *Phytopathology* **58**, 791–6.

Section 5.1.8

Aist, J. R. and Williams, P. H. (1971). *Can. J. Bot.* **49**, 2023–34.

Anderson, W. C., Gabrielson, R. L., Haglund, W. A. and Baker, A. S. (1976). *Pl. Dis. Reptr* **60**, 561–4.

Ayers, G. W. and Lelacheur, K. E. (1966). *Can. Hort. Coun., Rep. Cmttee hort. Res.* 26.

Buczacki, S. T., Ockendon, J. G. and Freeman, G. H. (1978). *Ann. appl. Biol.* **88**, 229–38.

Buczacki, S. T., Toxopeus, H., Mattusch, P., Johnston, T. D., Dixon, G. R. and Hobolth, L. A. (1975). *Trans. Br. mycol. Soc.* **65**, 295–308.

Butcher, D. N., El-Tigani, S. and Ingram, D. S. (1974). *Physiol. Pl. Path.* **4**, 127–41.

Chiang, M. S. and Crete, R. (1970). *Can. J. Genet. Cytol.* **12**, 253–6.

Chiang, M. S., Chiang, B. Y. and Grant, W. F. (1977). *Euphytica* **26**, 319–36.

Colhoun, J. (1953). *Ann. appl. Biol.* **40**, 639–44.

Colhoun, J. (1958). *Club Root Disease of Crucifers Caused by* Plasmodiophora brassicae *Woron.* Phytopathology Paper no. 3. Commonwealth Mycological Institute, Kew.

Colhoun, J. (1961). *Trans Br. mycol. Soc.* **44**, 593–600.

Crute, I. R., Gray, A. R., Crisp, P and Buczacki, S. T. (1980). *Pl. Breed. Abstr.* **50**, 91–104.

Dekhuijzen, H. M. (1975). *Physiol. Pl. Path.* **6**, 187–92.

Dekhuijzen, H. M. and Overeem, J. C. (1971). *Physiol. Pl. Path.* **1**, 151–62.

Dixon, G. R. (1977). Pathogen specificity in *Plasmodiophora brassicae* (clubroot) and *Erysiphe cruciferarum* (powdery mildew) on Brassicae. Paper presented at the Brassica Fodder Crops Conference, Scottish Agricultural Development Council and Scottish Plant Breeding Station, Edinburgh.

Dixon, G. R., Doodson, J. K., Beeney, B. W., Davies, H., Jemmett, J. L. and Moxon, R. H. (1972). *J. natn. Inst. agric. Bot.* **12**, 456–63.

Gallegly, M. E. (1956). *Phytopathology* **46**, 467.

Ingram, D. S. (1969). *J. gen. Microbiol.* **56**, 55–67.

Karling, J. S. (1968). *The Plasmodiophorales.* Hafner, New York.

Katsura, K., Egawa, H., Toki, T. and Ishii, S. (1966). *Ann. Phytopath. Soc. Japan* **32**, 123–9.

Keen, N. T. and Williams, P. H. (1969). *Phytopathology* **59**, 778–85.

Keen, N. T., Reddy, M. N. and Williams, P. H. (1968). *Phytopathology* **58**, 1054.

Lammerink, J. (1967). *N. Z. Jl. agric. Res.* **10**, 109–15.

Luzny, J. (1965). *Acta Univ. agric., Brno* 619–28.

MacFarlane, I. and Last, F. T. (1959). *Ann. Bot.* **23**, 547–70.

McNaughton, I. H. (1973). *Nature, Lond.* **243**, 547–8.

Mattusch, P. (1978). *NachrBl. PflSchutzdienst., Braunschweig*, **30**, 150–2.

Melville, S. C. and Hawken, R. H. (1967). *Pl. Path.* **16**, 145–7.

Rick, C. M. and Perkins, D. Y. (1955). *Calif. Agric.* **9**, 10–11.

Samuel, G. and Garrett, S. D. (1945). *Ann. appl. Biol.* **32**, 96–101.

Sciaroni, R. H. and Welch, N. C. (1969). Club root disease of Brussels sprouts
  – breeding programme. In *Vegetable Production*, University of California
  Agricultural Extension Service.

Sterling, J. D. E. (1951). *Scient. Agric.* **31**, 253–68.

Strandberg, J. O. and Williams, P. H. (1967). *Phytopathology* **57**, 330.

Tjallingii, F. (1965). *Euphytica* **14**, 1–22.

Tommerup, I. C. and Ingram, D. S. (1971). *New Phytol.* **70**, 327–32.

Walker, J. C. and Larson, R. H. (1960). *Univ. Wisc. Agric. Exp. Stn. Bull.* No. 547,
  12–16.

Watson, A. G. and Baker, K. F. (1969). *Econ. Bot.* **23**, 245–52.

Weisaeth, G. (1976). *Qualitas plantarum* **26**, 167–90.

Welch, N., Greathead, A. S., Inman, J. and Quick, J. (1976). *Calif. Agric.* April,
  10–11.

Williams, P. H. (1966). *Phytopathology* **56**, 521–4.

Williams, P. H. and McNabola, S. S. (1967). *Can. J. Bot.* **45**, 1665–9.

Williams, P. H. and Yukawa, Y. B. (1967). *Phytopathology* **57**, 682–87.

Williams, P. H., Aist, S. J. and Aist, J. R. (1971). *Can. J. Bot.* **49**, 41–7.

Williams, P. H., Keen, N. T., Strandberg, J. O. and McNabola, S. S. (1968).
  Phytopathology **58**, 921–8.

Wit, F. (1966). *Acta agric. scand.*, Suppl. 16, 65–67.

Woronin, M. (1878). *Jb. wiss. Bot.* **11**, 548–74. Translated by C. Chupp (1934)
  in *Phytopathology Classics*, Vol. 4. American Phytopathological Society,
  St. Paul, Minn.

FURTHER READING

In this and subsequent chapters, the suggestions for further reading are
subdivided by section for the convenience of the reader.

Section 5.1.3
Ellis, M. B. (1968*a*). Alternaria brassicae. Commonwealth Mycological Institute

Descriptions of Pathogenic Fungi and Bacteria no. 162. Commonwealth Mycological Institute, Kew.

Ellis, M. B. (1968*b*). Alternaria brassicicola. Commonwealth Mycological Institute Descriptions of Pathogenic Fungi and Bacteria no. 163. Commonwealth Mycological Institute, Kew.

Weimar, J. L. (1924). *J. agric. Res.* **29**, 421–42.

Wiltshire, S. P. (1947). *Species of* Alternaria *on* Brassicae. Mycological Paper no. 20. Commonwealth Mycological Institute, Kew.

Section 5.1.4

Anon (1965). *Proc. int. Seed Test Assoc.* **30**, 1109–10.

Cook, R. J. (1975). *Diseases of Oil Seed Rape in Europe.* Ministry of Agriculture, Fisheries and Food, London.

Lacoste, L. (1965). Biologie naturelle et culturale des *Leptosphaeria* cesati et de notaris determinisme de la reproduction sexuelle. Thesis de l'Université de Toulouse.

Lucas, M. T. and Webster, J. (1967). *Trans. Br. mycol. Soc.* **50**, 85–121.

Petrie, G. A. and Vanterpool, T. C. (1974). *Can. Pl. Dis. Surv.* **54**, 119–23.

Punithalingam, E. and Holliday, P. (1972). Leptosphaeria maculans. Commonwealth Mycological Institute Descriptions of Pathogenic Fungi and Bacteria no. 331. Commonwealth Mycological Institute, Kew.

Smith, H. C. and Sutton, B. C. (1964). *Trans. Br. mycol. Soc.* **47**, 159–65.

Section 5.1.5

Punithalingam, E. and Holliday, P. (1975). Mycosphaerella brassicicola. Commonwealth Mycological Institute Descriptions of Pathogenic Fungi and Bacteria no. 468. Commonwealth Mycological Institute, Kew.

Section 5.1.6

Mordue, J. E. M. (1974). Thanetophorus cucumeris. Commonwealth Mycological Institute Descriptions of Pathogenic Fungi and Bacteria no. 406. Commonwealth Mycological Institute, Kew.

Section 5.1.7

Booth, C. (1971). *The Genus Fusarium.* Commonwealth Mycological Institute, Kew.

Gilman, J. C. (1916). *Ann. Missouri bot. Gdn* **3**, 25–84.

Subramanian, C. V. (1970). Fusarium oxysporum *f. sp.* conglutinans. Commonwealth Mycological Institute Descriptions of Pathogenic Fungi and Bacteria no. 213. Commonwealth Mycological Institute, Kew.

Sumner, D. R. (1974). *Phytopathology* **64**, 692–8.

Walker, J. C. (1952). *Diseases of Vegetable Crops.* McGraw-Hill, New York.

Sections 5.2.1–5.2.8

Campbell, R. N. (1973). *Radish Mosaic Virus.* Commonwealth Mycological Institute/Association of Applied Biologists Descriptions of Plant Viruses no. 109. Commonwealth Mycological Institute, Kew.

Campbell, R. N. and Lin, M. T. (1972). *Broccoli Necrotic Yellows Virus.* Commonwealth Mycological Institute/Association of Applied Biologists Descriptions of Plant Viruses no. 85. Commonwealth Mycological Institute, Kew.

Hollings, M. and Stone, O. M. (1972). *Turnip Crinkle Virus.* Commonwealth Mycological Institute/Association of Applied Biologists Descriptions of Plant Viruses no. 109. Commonwealth Mycological Institute, Kew.

Hollings, M. and Stone, O. M. (1973). *Turnip Rosette Virus.* Commonwealth Mycological Institute/Association of Applied Biologists Descriptions of Plant Viruses no. 125. Commonwealth Mycological Institute, Kew.

Matthews, R. E. F. (1970). *Turnip Yellow Mosaic Virus.* Commonwealth Mycological Institute/Association of Applied Biologists Descriptions of Plant Viruses no. 2. Commonwealth Mycological Institute, Kew.

Shepherd, R. J. (1970). *Cauliflower Mosaic Virus.* Commonwealth Mycological Institute/Association of Applied Biologists Descriptions of Plant Viruses no. 121. Commonwealth Mycological Institute, Kew.

Smith, K. M. (1972). *A Textbook of Plant Virus Disease.* Longmans, London.

Tomlinson, J. A. (1970). *Turnip Mosaic Virus.* Commonwealth Mycological Institute/Association of Applied Biologists Descriptions of Plant Viruses no. 8. Commonwealth Mycological Institute, Kew.

6
Pathogens of Legume Crops

Legume crops are of vital importance to world agriculture, providing essential supplies of protein especially for underdeveloped areas. In advanced countries these crops lend themselves to highly mechanised programmed cropping techniques supplying the demands of the processing industry. These techniques have doubled the yield of legume crops over the last 30 years. Both forms of culture result in particular pathogen problems, for example, *Erysiphe pisi* (powdery mildew) on the ripening crops in Asia and *Peronospora viciae* (downy mildew) on the lush, unripe processing crops of Europe and the USA. Plant breeders have been particularly active with legume crops, introducing resistance to a wide range of pathogens. This has been highly successful and durable with *Fusarium oxysporum* f. sp. *pisi* (wilt) but far less so with *Colletotrichum lindemuthianum* (anthracnose), where many physiological races have evolved in response to the introduction of monogenic resistance.

Pathogens which affect legume crops are divided in this chapter into those which mainly attack peas (*Pisum sativum*) and those of greatest importance to bean crops (*Vicia faba* and *Phaseolus* spp.). This has been done mainly for convenience in writing the chapter and it should be remembered that several pathogens, particularly viruses, are pathogenic to both crop groups. *Botrytis* spp. are dealt with in this chapter not only as pathogens of legumes but also as causal organisms of disease in many other vegetable crops.

Pea Crops

6.1 FUNGAL PATHOGENS

6.1.1 *Peronospora viciae* (downy mildew)

In the American literature this pathogen is referred to as *P. pisi* since it is thought to be morphologically distinct from *P. viciae* on *Vicia* beans and vetches (Campbell, 1935). In the English literature, however, the two species are considered identical and referred to as *P. viciae*. Peas (*Pisum sativum* and *P. arvense*) and *Vicia* beans are the major crop hosts. Downy mildew has become the major disease of the vining pea crop in the UK over the last decade and is well recognised as a significant pathogen of crops in Eire and the USA.

Symptoms of the host—parasite complex vary with host growth stage. At emergence 'systemic' symptoms are the most striking. Infected plants occur sporadically throughout the crop, the seedlings being stunted, with contorted foliage which becomes chlorotic and covered by abundant sporulation. Several workers have speculated that these symptoms represent seed-borne infections. Such plants are usually killed by the pathogen, but not before acting as primary foci for the further spread of the pathogen. Seedlings which are secondarily infected will tolerate considerable infection before being killed. The pathogen spreads to the developing foliage where it appears as discrete pustules on the leaf undersurface. The pustules are white-bluish in colour, varying from 0.5 to 3 cm in length, and are usually bounded by the veins of the leaf. On the upper surface chlorotic areas are seen in positions equivalent to those of pustules on the undersurface. In severe infections tendrils, petioles and stems may be infected.

In cool moist conditions such as those in southern Scotland, Eire and the Pacific valleys of the USA, flower and pod infections are common. On pods *P. viciae* causes blotchy brown lesions to develop. Within the pod a white felt-like proliferation of the endocarp takes place with the lesion gradually becoming brown in colour; adjacent seeds either abort or show small brown sunken spots.

Peronsporoa viciae is a Phycomycete, class Oomycetes. The mycelium is intercellular, producing branched coiling or needle-shaped haustoria. Through the host stomata asexual sporangiophores are produced in groups of between five and seven, 160—750 μm long and 8—13 μm wide, lacking branching for the first two-thirds of their length. Thereafter, dichotomous branches form carrying oval to elliptical sporangia which are 15—30 μm x 15—20 μm in size. When mature the sporangia appear pale violet to pale grey *en masse.* Germination is via a germ tube; zoospores have not been reported. In the sexual phase the coenocytic mycelium gives rise to oogonia and antheridia and, following fertilization, spherical light brown to deep yellowish-pink reticulate oospores form which are 26—43 μm in diameter.

Although there is no positive proof that seed-borne infection takes place, the scattered 'systemic' infections found in seedling stands are strongly indicative of this means of spread. Certainly diseased haulm, containing oospores, provides a reservoir of infection (Ryan, 1971), while oospores present in soil may be equally important (Dixon, 1981). Sporangia are the main means of spread within and possibly between crops. Infected leaves produce sporangia up to 6 weeks after invasion and sporulating lesions contain viable sporangia for 3 weeks. The viability of sporangia varies considerably (Pegg and Mence, 1970). These workers showed that sporangia germinated over the temperature range 1—24 °C with an optimum of 4—8 °C, but suggested that high humidity was the most important single factor governing the initiation and development of field epidemics. Maximum infection took place after 6 h of leaf wetness at 8—20 °C. Invasion was unaffected by light, but this did retard sporulation, for which the optimum temperature range was 12—20 °C. After infection an unusual feature of this host—parasite complex is the development of a hemispherical, membrane-bound, electron-dense deposit termed the penetration matrix. This was found by Hickey and Coffey (1977) to be embedded in the host cell wall and to extend into the host cytoplasm; the matrix was always in intimate association with the unilayered hyphal wall of the pathogen.

Crop losses due to *P. viciae* occur through reduction in the initial plant stand caused by 'systemic' and subsequent heavy seedling infections. Foliar infections are generally insufficient to reduce yield significantly (Pegg and Mence, 1972). The main effect of adult plant infections in vining crops in England is to cause large variations in the maturity date within an individual crop, rendering it unacceptable for processing. In other regions where floral and pod infections are frequent considerable losses in yield of pods have been recorded.

One reason for the increased importance of this pathogen in English vining pea crops may be the decreased use of dinoseb herbicides. Systemically infected plants were killed by the herbicide whereas healthy plants were unaffected since they were protected by an unruptured layer of cuticular wax (G. P. Gent, personal communication). Considerable control can be achieved by the use of resistant cultivars, for example Aries, Ajax, Fek, Sprite and Suprema (Dixon, 1981). The genetics of resistance in *Pisum* spp. to *P. viciae* has been investigated by Matthews and Dow (1972). There are three resistance systems, a single dominant gene, two complimentary recessive genes and a single recessive gene. Systemic fungicides of the acylalanine type (*see* section 4.3.2) might provide a new means of controlling this pathogen, especially when used as seed dressings.

6.1.2 *Erysiphe pisi* (*E. polygoni*) (powdery mildew)

A wide range of legume crops is attacked by this pathogen: *P. sativum* (as dry peas), *P. arvense* (field pea), *Cicer arietum* (gram), *Cajanus cajan* (pigeon pea), *Phaseolus mungo* (black gram), *Ph. aureus* (green gram) and *Lens esculentum* (lentil). There may be different strains attacking these crops, since Hammerlund (1925) was able to identify at least three biologic forms. The disease is widely reported on crops in Australia, Canada, France, India, Peru, Zimbabwe (where it caused the cessation of pea production), South Africa, the UK and the USA.

Symptoms are similar to those of other powdery mildews: a greyish-white mycelium develops as discrete lesions on the upper leaf surface; these gradually coalesce until the whole leaf is competely colonised and turns chlorotic and necrotic; from the mycelium haustoria are produced into the host epidermal cells, while the mycelium produces aerial conidiophores from which conidia are abstricted. As infection progresses the pathogen spreads to the stems and pods. This is one of the few powdery mildew fungi where seed-borne infection is well documented. Work by Crawford (1927) in Mexico showed that sulphur fungicides applied to the seed would reduce losses considerably, indicating that the fungus is carried on the seed surface.

Powdery mildew epidemics on peas are encouraged by prolonged warm dry days and nights cool enough for dew formation (Hagedorn, 1973).

As with other powdery mildews, *E. pisi* is considered as an Ascomycete of the class Plectomycetes. Mycelium is usually thinly developed on the host surface, bearing solitary barrel-shaped asexual conidia although they occasionally develop in chains, 31–38 μm x 17–21 μm in size. Globular sexual cleistothecia occur infrequently and may be either gregarious or scattered, 85–126 μm in diameter. They carry 10–30 appendages which are basally inserted, frequently of a knotty shape (but not branched), brown in colour, usually at least as long as the ascocarp diameter and often much longer. Between three and 10 asci are present whose shapes vary from ovate to subglobose and which are 50–60 μm x 30–40 μm in size. Within are between three and six ascospores, 22–27 μm x 13–16 μm in size.

Phytoalexins were demonstrated for the first time in an obligate host–parasite relationship using the *E. pisi–Pisum* complex (Oku *et al.*, 1975). The pathogenic *E. pisi* was 13 times more tolerant to pisatin than spores of *E. graminis* f. sp. *hordei*. Concentrations of pisatin were greater at the infection site than elsewhere in the leaf, and thus a role in host specificity has been suggested. Pisatin was produced in advance of susceptible cell collapse or hypersensitive necrosis. Host colonisation has been studied by Smith (1969), who defined 10 developmental stages in the colonisation of the cultivar Onward. Working with cowpeas, Paulech and Herrera (1969, 1970) identified six stages in the first 150 h of colonisation. Germ tube formation started within 1 h of inoculation. On susceptible plants colonisation continued until the whole leaf was covered by mycelium, whereas on resistant plants infection was localised to small dark spots.

There are several sources of resistance which may be exploited as a means of control. Harland (1948) identified the recessive gene *er* and subsequently another recessive gene er_2 was found by Heringa *et al.* (1969). There is considerable breeding work in progress in the USA since Gritton and Ebert (1975) showed that pod infection adversely affected total plant weight, weight of shelled peas, numbers of peas per pod, number of peas per plant, plant height, nodes per plant and led to higher tenderometer readings which thereby depressed quality. Suitable 'quick freeze' or vining cultivars have been developed using resistance from the cross Oregon State University 42 x New York 59-29. This was back-crossed to the cultivars Sprite, Dark Skinned Perfection, New Era, and New Line Early Perfection to give commercial cultivars. Breeding work in Italy (M. Cirulli, personal communication) is aimed at the artificial induction of resistant mutants from the cultivar Sprinter using irradiation techniques. Work is now in progress to incorporate resistance to *E. pisi* into pea cultivars with reduced foliage (so-called 'leafless peas') in the UK (Dow, 1978).

In India, where the pathogen is a considerable threat to a crop supplying valuable protein for subsistence farmers, control is achieved by use of sulphur fungicides. In trials, large yield increases have followed fungicide application (Vaseduva, 1962). Losses due to the pathogen have been estimated as of the order of 20–30 per cent reduction in pod number and 25 per cent reduction in pod weight.

6.1.3 *Ascochyta* spp. (leaf, pod spot and root rot)

Three species of *Ascochyta* are responsible for the disease complexes: *Mycosphaerella* blight, *Ascochyta* blight and pod spot and *Ascochyta* root rot. A confused nomenclature has arisen for these pathogens because they exist in several states and incite broadly similar symptoms (table 6.1). All three pathogens are seed transmitted and of world-wide occurrence. The disease syndrome incited by *M. pinodes* embraces most of the symptoms induced by *A. pisi* and *P. medicaginis* var. *pinodella*, consequently field identification of the three organisms is difficult.

(a) *Mycosphaerella* blight
Initially, foliar lesions start as small purplish areas which can remain restricted to less than 0.5 cm in diameter, in which case they lack a distinct margin or they enlarge, becoming black to brown with a definite outer ring. Infection usually spreads from the leaves to the petioles and thence to the stem, causing girdling lesions which may coalesce and thus give the entire stem a blue-black hue. On the flowers, infections start as pin-point lesions on the petals which senesce very quickly. On developing pods, infection leads to uneven development; the seeds may show no outward signs of infection or may have various degrees of shrinkage and discolouration. As infected seed germinates, lesions develop at the

Table 6.1 Nomenclature of *Ascochyta* spp. causing leaf, pod spot and root rot of peas.

Mycosphaerella blight	*Ascochyta* leaf and pod spot	*Ascochyta* root rot
*M. pinodes**	*A. pisi**	*Phoma medicaginis* var. *pinodella**
Sphaeria pinodes	*Sphaeria concava*	*A. pinodella*
Sphaerella pinodes	*A. pisicola*	*P. trifolii*
Didymellina pinodes		
Didymella pinodes		

* Names used in this text conform with Commonwealth Mycological Institute Descriptions of Pathogenic Fungi and Bacteria nos 340, 334 and 518, respectively.

point of cotyledonary attachment, causing a foot-rotting symptom along the length of the developing plumule and radicle. Diseased seedlings may die before emergence, but if emergence is achieved lesions become evident on the above soil portions and eventually most infected plants are killed.

The Ascomycete (order Sphaeriales) sexual stage of *M. pinodes* produces perithecia on the host stems and pods. These are globose and dark brown in colour with apical papillate ostioles 90–180 μm in diameter. Within the perithecia cylindrical to subclavate asci are produced which have either a short stem or are sessile and attached directly to the wall of the perithecium. Each ascus is eight-spored, 50–80 μm x 10–15 μm in size, surrounded by a bitunicate ascus wall. Within this the ascospores are irregularly biserate, hyaline, and ellipsoid with a constriction at the central septum and rounded ends, 12–18 μm x 4–8 μm. The asexual pycnidial stage is found on all infected host organs, either singly or in groups. At first the pycnidia are immersed in host tissue, but they emerge above the surface at maturity. They are dark brown to black, 100–200 μm in diameter, opening by papillate ostioles; the walls are composed of fungal pseudoparenchymatous tissue the cells of which tend to be thicker towards the outer layers. Within the pycnidium conidia are abstricted which are hyaline and septate with slight constriction at the septum, 8–18 μm x 3–5 μm. Five physiological races of *M. pinodes* have been identified in Czechoslovakia of which race 3 is predoninant (Ondreij, 1974).

There are four means of transmission of *M. pinodes*: water-splash of the conidia, carriage of ascospores in air currents, survival between pea crops in soil and host debris, and via seed transmission. Conidia in the soil develop into chlamydospore and sclerotial stages. Pea haulm left as trash in the field is an important source of infection by *M. pinodes* as it is capable of cycles of active saprophytic growth on this material (Sheridan, 1973). Most mycelium occurs on the outer regions of stem tissue with little penetration into sub-epidermal layers. *Mycosphaerella pinodes* is also capable of saprophytic colonisation of host roots. Twelve months after composting infected haulm the fungus was still viable (Blaumann, 1953). Work in Australia demonstrated that ascospores arising from host debris were important sources of new infection for succeeding crops (Carter and Moller, 1961). Dispersal of the ascospores occurred with diurnal rhythm, there being a peak in the afternoon. Ascospores required dry conditions for release and then 4–5 h at 20 °C and high night relative humidities for penetration (Carter, 1963). Conidia require a higher temperature, 24 °C, for germination (Sorgel, 1956).

(b) *Ascochyta* blight and pod spot

Ascochyta pisi causes light brown foliar lesions which have a prominent dark margin and pale centre. When infected seed germinates primary lesions develop on the first leaves. The pathogen can cause pre- and post-emergence damping-off and dwarfing, but essentially attacks occur on the aerial plant parts. Unlike *M.*

pinodes and *P. medicaginis* var. *pinodella, A. pisi* is not characterised by foot-rotting symptoms.

Only the asexual imperfect stage of *A. pisi* is known; globose and brown pycnidia form on the leaves and pods, initially immersed in host tissue but later erupting above the epidermis. The pycnidial wall is composed of between one and four layers of elongated yellow-brown, thin walled cells and is 100–200 μm in diameter. Within the pycnidium short hyaline conidiophores, 6–14 μm x 3–8 μm in size, arise from the wall cells. Conidia are hyaline, straight or slightly curved, usually monoseptate with a slight constriction at the septum and rounded ends; they are 10–16 μm x 3–4.5 μm in size.

A classification of *A. pisi* isolates was made by Wallen (1957) containing four physiological races (I–IV) on the basis of testing 80 isolates on seven pea cultivars (table 6.2). Isolates of the four races exhibited geographical

Table 6.2 Classification of host reactions to *A. pisi* (after Wallen, 1957).

Degree of resistance	Reaction designation		Description of reaction
	Leaves	Stems	
Highly resistant	A	1	Small flecks only
Moderately resistant	B	2	Small lesions, no pycnidia
Moderately susceptible	C	3	Necrotic lesions, pycnidia present
Very susceptible	D	4	Deep necrotic lesions, abundant pycnidia
Highly susceptible	E	5	Plants killed

differentiation in Canada; races I and II came from the Prairie Provinces, race III from the Georgian Bay area and central Ontario and race IV from the Ottawa Valley and to a lesser extent from central and western Ontario, Quebec and Nova Scotia. In the Netherlands an alphabetical classification of races (A–C) has been used (N. Hubbeling, personal communication). Resistance was shown to be governed by a pair of dominant genes either of which could give resistance (Lyall and Wallen, 1958). Work with leafless and semi-leafless peas in the UK is aimed at identifying resistance to *A. pisi* (Dow 1978).

Transmission of *A. pisi* is via rain-splashed conidia, infected host debris and contaminated seed. Unlike *M. pinodes, A. pisi* has low saprophytic ability and the formation of soil-borne chlamydospores is rare (Dickinson and Sheridan, 1968; Sheridan and Dickinson, 1968).

Penetration of host tissue from conidia is via the cuticle and stomata (Brewer and MacNeil, 1953; Blakeman and Dickinson, 1967). Optimal conidial germination takes place at 20–24 °C (Sattar, 1934; Hare and Walker, 1944; Bertini, 1956; Sorgel, 1956).

Studies of a phytoalexin produced by *P. sativum* cvs Meteor and Kelvedon Wonder showed that conidia of race 1 were significantly less tolerant of the phytoalexin than those of race 2 (Harrower, 1973).

(c) *Ascochyta* foot rot

Stem and foliar symptoms in this syndrome are similar to those of *M. pinodes* but of lower intensity. The disease is characterised by foot-rotting lesions. The symptomatology of these three organisms are summarised in table 6.3.

Table 6.3 Comparative symptomatology of *Mycosphaerella pinodes*, *Ascochyta pisi* and *Phoma medicaginis* var. *pinodella*.

Symptoms	*M. pinodes*	*A. pisi*	*P. medicaginis* var. *pinodella*
Foliar, flower and pod spotting	+	+	–
Food rot	+	–	+

+, Predominant symptom; –, unusual symptom.

As with *A. pisi*, only the asexual imperfect stage of *P. medicaginis* var. *pinodella* is known. Pycnidia are variable in shape, 200–300 μm in diameter, containing short hyaline conidiogenous cells which develop from cells lining the pycnidial cavity. The conidia are hyaline, generally unicellular, and 4.5–10 μm x 2–3 μm in size. Dark brown chlamydospores form either terminally or within the mycelium and either singly or in chains. No physiological specialisation has been reported.

Dispersal within crops is by rain-splashed conidia and infected seed is the major means of transmission between crops. Conidial germination is optimal at 20 °C, very slow at 5 °C but still significant at 35 °C (Schenck and Gerdemann, 1956).

Both *A. pisi* and *M. pinodes* produce conidia of approximately similar size but larger than those of *P. medicaginis* var. *pinodella*. Additionally, *A. pisi* can be distinguished from *P. medicaginis* var. *pinodella* by culturing on oat agar, on which the former organism produces an exudate of carrot red spore masses while the latter forms light buff to flesh-coloured spore masses. There is greater cellulase and pectinase production by *M. pinodes* than by *A. pisi* and a closer serological relationship between *M. pinodes* and *P. medicaginis* var. *pinodella* than with *A. pisi.*

The main avenues for control of all three pathogens are by use of disease-free seed and seed sanitation. Where small seed batches are required, freedom from disease can be achieved by roguing infected plants and foliar spraying. It is difficult to do this for large bulks and for these seed must be produced in very dry regions. Excellent sanitation has been achieved by the method developed by Maude (1966) using the thiram soak technique whereby pea seed is treated with 0.2 per cent suspensions of thiram for 24 h at 30 °C. Investigations of the mode of of action of this technique showed that thiram is actively taken up by the seed during imbibition (Maude and Park, 1969). An advantage of this method is that treated seed does not have to be drilled immediately but can be redried and marketed in the usual way.

Benomyl has activity against these pathogens and has been used in mixtures with thiram as a seed treatment and alone as foliar sprays. Destruction of infected pea haulm by either burning or deep ploughing is an essential aspect of cultural control. There should be at least 4 years break between pea crops and fields selected for a new crop should be spatially isolated from fields which have grown peas in the preceding 3–4 years.

6.1.4 *Aphanomyces euteiches* and *Pythium* spp. (root rots)

(a) *Aphanomyces euteiches*

Aphanomyces euteiches is a widespread pathogen of pea crops and is especially severe in areas with high soil moisture and temperatures of 22–28 °C. It is a limiting factor to pea production in the mid-western USA (Walker and Hare, 1943; Carley, 1969), also causing severe losses in Denmark, Jamaica, Norway, Sweden, Tasmania, the UK and the USSR. Crop losses in Tasmania were estimated to be from 40 per cent to total crop failure (Geach, 1936). Data on host range suggest that many crops can be infected by *A. euteiches*, but care must be exercised in interpreting the information since much of the work has been done using sterile cultures. Both pea and *Phaseolus* beans can be attacked, but the pathogen would appear to be less of a problem on beans.

Early descriptions of the disease indicated that the pathogen invades through the root cortex and basal stem leading to rotting of host tissue in which are embedded thick walled oospores (Jones and Drechsler, 1925). Peas are susceptible to root rot throughout their growing period. Symptoms first appear 3–4 days after root penetration. In the initial stages of pathogenesis the root and epicotyl tissues become water-soaked with discoloured lesions in the cortex. As the pathogen spreads the fibrous root system is destroyed. The water-soaked areas are initially pale yellow to straw-coloured, but as the tissues soften they darken, collapse and disintegrate. Root rotting may extend 2–5 cm above soil level. The lower foliage becomes yellow and brittle. If infection takes place when the plant is juvenile sudden wilting may occur. In more mature plants there may be no obvious signs of infection except for poorly filled pods and low yields,

but usually plants are stunted and weakened. The best diagnostic features are the
vascular cylinder of the root pulling out easily from the cortex, the failure of the
fungus to penetrate through the endodermis, and the presence of oospores
(25—35 μm in diameter) in diseased tissue; these oospores have a sinuous inner
surface and smooth outer surface which distinguishes them from oospores of
Pythium spp.

This pathogen is classed as a Phycomycete and is usually placed in the order
Saprolegniales. In water culture it produces a very delicate coenocytic mycelial
thallus radiating from submerged substrate (Scott, 1961). On nutrient-rich media
a whitish aerial mycelium is produced with delicate hyaline hyphae 3—10 μm in
diameter. Both sexual and asexual means of reproduction have been identified.
In the asexual stage two types of zoospores are produced — a condition known
as dimorphism. Primary zoospores are produced from a zoosporangium which
consists of axial mycelial filaments 1—2 mm long bearing between six and 10
well-developed branches. The zoospores differentiate very rapidly within the
zoosporangium, involving migration of the cytoplasm around each nucleus,
withdrawal of the plasmalemma from the hyphal wall and evagination of the
central vacuole. The contents of the central vacuole are discharged into the space
between the plasmalemma and the hyphal wall. A plasma membrane which
covers the primary spores is formed jointly from the tonoplast and plasmalemma.
The zoospores extrude from the tip of the filamentous sporangium. These
encyst for 1—3 h and then produce secondary zoospores which are 13 μm x
7—8 μm with two flagella, 24 μm long, inserted in a slight depression of the
zoospore wall. In sexual reproduction antheridia and oogonia are produced on
the vegetative mycelium. Before fertilisation the oogonia are thin walled, sub-
globose—spherical with densely granular vacuolate contents and are borne
terminally on lateral branches. Antheridia are diclinous in origin, varying from
one to five in number, large, curved and clavate-borne on a stalk 8—10 μm in
diameter and 15—18 μm long. A fertilisation tube grows out to connect
with the oogonium. After fertilisation the subsequent oospore is hyaline and
thick walled with a central oil globule. The oospore germinates to produce
zoosporangia and zoospores. Thus the infective unit of *A. euteiches* is the
zoospore.

Both the root cap and zone of elongation are invaded (Cunningham and
Hagedorn, 1962). The active zoospore comes to rest on the root surface,
encysts and then germinates, producing a simple germ tube within 1½ h. These
usually penetrate between cell walls, but occasionally into the cells. Appressoria
are produced by some germ tubes. The pathogen may survive in the field in the
absence of pea crops for longer than 10 years. The oospores provide the obvious
vehicle for this persistence (Kendrick and Zentmeyer, 1957). Spread from field
to field may occur through carriage with soil particles in wind blows, with water
and by mechanical agencies. There is no evidence as to how wider spread is
accomplished.

Repeated cropping with peas on infected land leads to a linear increase in disease, with almost 8 per cent crop loss in year 1 to 100 per cent crop loss in year 5. Disease control relies largely on cultural techniques, since so far only limited sources of host resistance have been identified; chemical seed treatments and soil-applied fungicides have had little effect on this pathogen, although Grau (1977) showed that the herbicides dinitramine and trifluralin reduced the incidence of root rot caused by *A. euteiches*. For disease avoidance and the planning of crop rotations, techniques of soil indexing for the presence of *A. euteiches* have been developed by Sherwood and Hagedorn (1958) and Reiling *et al.* (1960). Other cultural techniques include early planting, improvement of soil drainage and phosphate fertilisation. There is a suggestion that the introduction of crucifer crops into the rotation may have a suppressive effect on *A. euteiches* populations. Heavy applications of lime to the soil have been correlated with reduced incidence of root rot (Lewis, 1977).

(b) *Pythium* spp.

Pythium spp. cause a wide range of diseases on many crop plants such as damping-off of seedlings and hollow stem, root rot, stem rot and wilt; both peas and *Phaseolus* beans are attacked. The principal fungal species involved are *P. ultimum*, *P. debaryanum* and *P. aphanidermatum* but at least eight others have been associated with the root rot complex of beans in the USA.

On young plants *Pythium* spp. cause a wet rot or traditional damping-off. The host stem is invaded at or just below the soil surface and then the pathogen spreads up and down the stem, producing a soft colourless to dark brown rot. On seedlings, especially under protected cultivation, the stems may be neither softened nor discoloured but flattened and pinched, collapsing from the soil line upwards for 5–10 cm. More mature plants may survive for some time after infection, with occasional wilting, and then collapse completely. Under hot moist environmental conditions, particularly in the USA, *Pythium* spp. cause a rot of the stems and lateral branches of beans which is termed *Pythium* wilt. The stem cortex becomes soft and slimy, separating easily from the vascular cylinder. The leaves curl and become flaccid as day-time temperature rises but regain turgidity at night. Eventually the wilt becomes permanent and the host dies.

In general, however, it is the damping-off syndrome which is most often associated with *Pythium* spp. Commonly, infection takes place through the seed or developing radicle leading to seed rot and pre-emergence death of the host. Alternatively, newly emergent seedlings are attacked at ground level, leading to collapse in restricted areas. This is found in seed trays, nursery beds and row crops and is usually associated with overcrowding.

Pythium species are Phycomycetes and are placed in the Peronosporales. Sporangia are produced directly from the mycelium but their form varies with different species.

In *P. aphanidermatum* sporangia are formed from inflated lobed hyphae, whereas those of *P. debaryanum* are globose. A terminal or intercalary portion of a hypha enlarges and assumes a spheroidal shape and is cut off by a cross-wall. The sporangia contain numerous nuclei around which the asexual zoospores differentiate in a thin walled vesicle at the tip of a fine tube developed from the sporangium. The zoospores are bean-shaped with two laterally attached flagella; after release they encyst, being 9 μm diameter at this stage, and then germinate to produce a germ tube. In some varieties of *P. ultimum* the sporangium is reported to germinate directly to form a germ tube.

Sexual oogonia and antheridia develop readily from cultures derived from single zoospores, indicating that *Pythium* spp. are probably homothallic, but heterothallism has been demonstrated for *P. sylvaticum* (Campbell and Hendrix, 1967). Oogonia develop as terminal or intercalary spherical swellings which are cut off by cross-walls from adjacent mycelium, reaching 19–29 μm in size. Typically, in *P. ultimum* there is a single antheridium to each oogonium, but in *P. debaryanum* there may be several. The young oogonium is multinucleate and the cytoplasm differentiates into a multinucleate central mass – the ooplasm. Antheridia attach to the oogonial wall and penetrate via a fertilisation tube. The fertilised egg secretes a double wall and a globule of reserve food material develops in the cytoplasm. Germination of the oospore takes place after a period of dormancy either by means of a germ tube or by a vesicle in which zoospores are differentiated (Hendrix and Campbell, 1973).

Infection by *Pythium* spp. is influenced by a range of factors: inoculum density, soil moisture, soil temperature, soil pH, cation composition, light intensity and the presence and numbers of other micro-organisms. Various species have different temperature requirements for optimal growth; thus *P. ultimum* and *P. debaryanum* require cool conditions (below 20 °C), whereas *P. aphanidermatum* requires temperatures above this.

Pythium spp. are facultative pathogens capable of surviving as saprophytes in the absence of a host, but as an alternative the oospores provide a resistant resting spore mechanism. They are not vigorous competitors with other micro-organisms in the soil (Barton, 1961). High levels of soil moisture have been shown to favour the saprophytic ability of *Pythium* spp. Their survival ability would appear to be high since *P. ultimum* was viable after being held at −18 °C for 24 months and in air-dried soil for 12 years (Hoppe, 1966; Munnecke and Moore, 1969). The germination of *P. aphanidermatum* and *P. irregulare* is encouraged by the presence of seed or root exudates (Chang-Ho, 1970; Kraft and Erwin, 1968).

Once established in soil the resting spores are virtually impossible to eradicate except by wide-spectrum soil fumigants (*see* section 4.3.4). Cultural controls, such as low density planting, regulation of soil moisture and crop ventilation can be utilised, particularly for protected crops. Use of nitrate nitrogen and potassium reduced damping-off in moist soil, whereas ammonium nitrogen and phosphate did not (Yale and Vaughan, 1962). Nitrogen deficiency in cucumbers resulted in more disease as compared with plants having adequate nitrogen

(McClure and Robbins, 1942). The addition of soil amendments, for example sawdust, bark, crop residues and green manuring, can be effective for *Pythium* control (Vaartaja and Bumbieris, 1968), probably by encouraging soil flora antagonistic to *Pythium* spp. Crop rotational control is not generally effective due to the ubiquitous nature of *Pythium* spp. and their very wide host range. Some degree of control has been claimed in beans through the use of resistant cultivars (Adegbola and Hagedorn, 1969). Chemical control can be achieved by use of drazoxolon or thiram.

6.1.5 *Fusarium* spp. (wilt and root rot)

Only the asexual conidial states of most *Fusarium* spp. have been identified; they are placed in the order Moniliales of the Fungi Imperfecti. Where sexual stages have been identified, these are often characteristic of the Ascomycete genus *Nectria.* There is, however, considerable confusion in the nomenclature of *Fusarium* which has been compounded by use of the term *formae speciales.* These are defined as pathological strains which are indistinguishable from saprophytic strains of the same species but exhibit different physiological properties in their ability to parasitise specific hosts. Single *formae speciales* were originally thought to have specific pathogenicity to one host, and this was indicated by host names being used to identify them. This concept of highly selective pathogenicity led to the establishment of several *formae speciales* which were subsequently shown to be merely races of others described from different hosts. *Fusaria* described in this and other chapters are classified according to Booth (1971).

(a) *Fusarium oxysporum* f. sp. *pisi* (wilt)

This organism is also referred to in the literature as *F. vasinfectum* var. *pisi, F. orthoceras* var. *pisi, F. oxysporum* f8 and *F. oxysporum* var. *orthoceras.* Descriptions of the symptoms of pea wilt are confused since two disease syndromes have been identified: 'wilt' and 'near wilt'. Wilt is also known as 'St John's disease' because symptoms are most noticeable around St. John's Day, 24 June. Host foliage becomes yellow with the leaflets and stipules curling downwards and inwards – a typical symptom of vascular disease in hosts with compound leaves. The foliage withers from the base of the plant upwards, and death ensures before pod formation or before swelling (figure 6.1). Wilt may also be unilateral, affecting only one side of the host. The vascular tissues show a brown to orange or deep red discoloration which extends throughout the invaded root system. Fungal hyphae are restricted to the host xylem vessels and there is little or no rotting of the root cortex, although the pathogen invades from the soil through the cortex to reach the host vascular system. After death of the host the pathogen will grow out of the vessels and a white stromatic mycelium heavy with sporulation is found

Figure 6.1   Symptoms caused by *Fusarium oxysporum* f. sp. *pisi* (pea wilt). (Reproduced by permission of Manchester University.)

on the stem surface, especially under conditions of high humidity. Near wilt symptoms are similar to those of wilt but develop more slowly, frequently reaching maximum expression after the pods have developed. Consequently, what initially appears to be a healthy crop can be devastated just before maturity. Race 2 of *F. oxysporum* f. sp. *pisi* is usually attributed as the causal agent of near wilt while race 1 and some other races are the causes of wilt. This has been summarised by Hubbeling (1974):

F. oxysporum f. sp. *pisi* races	Authority
Race 1 (wilt)	Linford (1928)
Race 2 (near wilt)	Snyder (1933)
Race (near wilt) (with early) (yellowing)	Schreuder (1951), Labruyère *et al.* (1959)
Race 3A (wilt)	Buxton (1955)
Race 4 (wilt)	Bolton *et al.* (1966)
Race 5 (wilt)	Haglund and Kraft (1970)
Races 6, 7, 8, 9, 10, 11 (wilt)	Armstrong and Armstrong (1974)

The position of race 3 is obscure since Labruyère *et al.* (1959) also implicated the nematode *Rotylenchus robustus* in the syndrome.

In culture, *F. oxysporum* f. sp. *pisi* can exist in four states: septate mycelium, microconidia (2.5—4 μm x 6—15 μm), macroconidia which are typically fusiform, hyaline and multiseptate (3.5—5.5 μm x 25—22 μm) and as chlamydospores. The relative importance of these states in soil is unknown, nor is it known whether they are equally important as infective agents of the host root. Probably conidia are responsible for aerial spread of the pathogen from dead diseased hosts, but it is also possible that spread can occur from the roots of a diseased plant to a healthy one by mycelial colonisation. Considerable studies have been made of the role of host root exudates in the stimulation of chlamydospore germination and attempts were made to correlate this with host resistance (Buxton, 1957*a,b*; Doling, 1963). Such exudates would contain organic acids and Hubbeling (1966) reported that acid soil conditions were associated with increased wilt symptoms. A study by Whalley (1971), however, could show no correlation between the germination of conidia and chlamydospores and the source of root exudates.

Pea wilt was recognised to be the most important disease of dried and processing peas in the USA in the 1930s and subsequently it was found to be present throughout Continental Europe and Australia (Snyder, 1935). Resistance to race 1 is governed by gene F_n (Wade, 1929) and to race 2 by F_{nw} (Hare *et al.*, 1949); both single dominant genes are located in linkage group IV (Wells *et al.*, 1949). Resistance to races 4 and 5 has been attributed to several recessive genes (Matthews and Dow, 1972). The use of cultivars possessing these resistance genes is an illustration of the successful application of plant breeding to control a soil-borne pathogen. The pathogen became important in the UK in the 1950s when highly susceptible cultivars were grown for the pulling green pea market in Essex. Large crop losses were sustained due to the use of these cultivars. The decline of this form of production in favour of vining peas with consequent use of American and Continental resistant cultivars and the relocation of production closer to the processing factories in Lincolnshire and Norfolk has meant that the disease is now of little economic importance.

(b) *Fusarium solani* f. sp. *pisi* (root rot)

This soil-borne pathogen otherwise referred to as *E. martii* var. *pisi*. is commonly found in association with *F. oxysporum* f. sp. *pisi*, the causal agent of wilt. But the the disease syndrome is quite distinct. The cortex of the host root and hypocotyl become blackened and rotten, resulting in chlorosis and stunting of the plant (figure 6.2). Often there is a brilliant red discoloration of the root vascular system. This does not extend to the stem, as in seen in the case of the wilting syndrome.

In culture, *F. solani* f. sp. *pisi* produces macrocondia which are mostly triseptate, 4.5–5 µm x 27–40 µm in size, curved and hyaline; microconidia (9–16 µm x 2–4 µm) are produced sparsely and chlamydospores (10–11 µm x 8–9 µm) develop in a terminal or intercalary manner either singly or in chains. These appear to be a major means of perennation since Nash (1963) reported that they can exist for 5 years in soil in the absence of a host. The sexual perithecial stage has been identified as *Nectria haematococca*, which may occur as either homo- or heterothallic strains (Booth, 1975).

Figure 6.2   Symptoms caused by *Fusarium solani* f. sp. *pisi* (pea root rot). (Reproduced by permission of Manchester University.)

Root rot of peas is of very considerable economic importance in Canada, Europe (including the UK) and the USA. It has been distinguished from root rot of *Phaseolus* beans, although Kraft and Burke (1974) showed that both organisms could infect the roots of the other host. Severe root rot in peas was, however, only caused by *F. solani* f. sp. *pisi*. The question of a relationship between *F. solani* f. sp. *pisi* and *F. oxysporum* f. sp. *pisi* has been investigated by Bolton and Donaldson (1972). Isolates of both fungal species resembled each other both culturally and in their ability to produce root rot and wilting symptoms. The authors suggest that both organisms may constitute a single species. If this were the case the increased importance of root rot in comparison to wilt (D. M. Derbyshire, personal communication) might be explained as an effect of the use of of wilt-resistant pea cultivars having led to the evolution of pathogen strains with virulence characteristics which allowed them to cause root rotting rather than wilting.

Soil temperatures of 26–28 °C are optimal for disease development, with soil moisture levels of 15 per cent; there is a sharp decline in disease when moisture levels exceed 25 per cent. Soil fumigation offers a chemical means of control, but at present this is thought to be uneconomic. Breeding lines with resistance greater than that of the cultivar Dark Skinned Perfection have been identified by Kraft and Roberts (1969, 1970).

6.2 VIRUSES

6.2.1 Pea Early Browning Virus (PEBV)

Several stubby root nematodes act as vectors for this soil-borne virus. In the Netherlands these have been identified as *Paratrichodorus teres* and *P. pachydermus*, while *P. anemones, Trichodorus primitivus* and *T. viruliferus* are implicated in the UK. Seed also acts as a means of transmission. The coats of infected seeds exhibit wrinkling and greenish-grey discolouration of the testa. The virus particles are short thick rods of two distinct size ranges: 100 and 200 nm. It is thought to be distributed throughout western Europe, especially Holland and England, occurring chiefly in areas with loamy sand soils which are favoured by the nematode vectors.

Symptoms usually appear within 2 months of drilling; irregular purplish-brown necrotic discolourations develop on the stems, petioles and leaves. These start as vascular necroses and then spread to surrounding tissues. Localised wilting follows the death of the veins. Infected plants are stunted and distorted with an overall yellow hue or faint mottling. Where the plant tips are killed tillers may grow from the base. Vegetable hosts include *Beta vulgaris, Cucumis sativus, Lycopersicon esculentum, Phaseolus vulgaris* and *Vicia faba.*

Three strains of PEBV have been identified: *Dutch strain*, which is prevalent in the Netherlands and not found in UK, *British strain*, which is serologically only distantly related to the Dutch strain (two variants have been reported by Harrison (1966)) and an *Italian strain* which seems to be more akin to the UK strain than the Dutch.

6.2.2 Pea Enation Mosaic Virus (PEMV)

Spread by the aphid vectors *Acyrthosiphon pisum, Macrosiphum euphorbiae* and *Myzus persicae*, this virus was found to be of the circulative (persistent) type by Nault *et al.* (1964). The particles are isometric, about 30 nm in diameter. It has been reported in Germany, Holland, the UK and the USA.

Symptoms on pea are severe mottling, crinkling and savoying of leaves and stipules. Yellowish spots which progressively become white and transparent develop on the leaves. On very susceptible cultivars the leaves become covered in necrotic spots accompanied by proliferations (enations) on their reverse sides. Such symptoms are not found with other legume viruses and may therefore be classed as diagnostic. Where infection precedes pod formation these may become badly deformed, the pod walls developing a rough, ridged and wrinkled texture followed by stunting. The seeds of infected pods are small and yellow. This virus is the causal agent of Broad Bean Mosaic (BBM), which is characterised by an easily visible mosaic of the foliage which tends to be a spotting rather than mottling, the spots being irregular in shape and size but usually associated with the veins. Stunting may occur but is not usually severe. Large accumulations of virus occur in plant cell nuclei and the virus may multiply there; less virus is found in the cytoplasm and vacuoles.

6.2.3 Pea Seed-borne Mosaic Virus (PSBMV)

Commonly referred to a Pea Leaf Roll Virus (PLRV), this virus is both aphid- and seed-transmitted. Aphid vectors include *Myzus persicae, Macrosiphum euphorbiae* and *Acyrthosiphon pisum*. The particles are filamentous, and are 770 nm x 12 nm in size.

Some reduction in size of infected plants is found in peas, accompanied by leaf narrowing, downward rolling and some slight mosaic or mottling (Bos, 1970). More severe symptoms develop on broad beans, including yellowing and rolling of the upper foliage, which develop a bright yellow colour with rolled leaves which are thickened and brittle. This is followed by defoliation and necrosis of the plant tip. Seed only becomes infected when the plants are diseased prior to flowering. Transmission is more common with seed having split testas than with normal seed. Commercial seed lots with up to 90 per cent infected seeds have been found.

Most isolates of the virus induce pinwheel inclusions in the cytoplasm of mesophyll cells of pea and broad bean. Less common isolates induce tonoplast aggregates or dense bodies and laminated aggregates. One isolate characterised by induction of tonoplast aggregates also induced the formation of convoluted endoplasmic reticulum. Large accumulations of virus-like particles occur in the cytoplasm of parenchyma cells in pea roots.

A new virus has been discovered in Germany, Pea False Leaf Roll Virus (PFLRV) which is also aphid- and seed-transmissible. Only *Myzus persicae* appears to act as the vector. Symptoms include leaf roll, chlorotic spots on immature foliage, necrosis and glaucous leaf discolorations.

6.2.4 Pea Mosaic Virus (PMV)

Known also as Common Pea Mosaic Virus (CPMV) and Red Clover Mosaic Virus (RCMV) the vectors of this virus are *Acyrthosiphon pisum, Myzus persicae, Aphis fabae* and *Aphis rumicis.* In India it is also thought to be transmitted by *A. craccivora.* The virus has frequently been found in Australia, Europe, New Zealand and the USA. It is a long thread-like particle.

On *P. sativum* symptoms vary considerably with host age and environment. Initially there is vein clearing in young foliage followed by severe chlorosis with dark green areas randomly distributed over the leaf lamina. Generalised stunting is a characteristic symptom. Pea cultivars vary in their response to infection by PMV; the cultivars Alaska and Telephone show general chlorosis while mottling is the predominant symptom in the cultivars Alderman, World's Record and Market Surprise.

The virus also attacks broad bean, causing Broad Bean Mosaic (BBM). On this host the foliage develops a bright yellow and green mottle; affected leaves may also be narrowed and elongated. Unaffected areas of the leaf stand out as sharp green against the mottling of diseased ones. The virus prevents differentiation of the palisade and spongy parenchyma cells within the leaf leading to infected leaves being thinner than healthy ones.

Histological studies of infected pea leaves have shown that three forms of virus inclusion occur: rhombohedral crystals in the cytoplasm of 0.3–1.5 μm in cubic or hexagonal section, bands 25–75 nm wide and up to 3.5 μm long which may be associated with chloroplasts and mitochondria, and the particles of PMV associated with these bands. Severe disruption of the chloroplasts takes place which Cousin *et al.* (1969) suggest leads to the chlorotic areas on leaves.

Three strains of PMV have been recognised in the USA which may be distinguished from each other on the basis of symptoms and from PMV because they cannot be transmitted to red clover (*Trifolium pratense*).

(1) *Marble strain*   The youngest leaves show distinct vein clearing within 10 days of inoculation followed by distortion, chlorosis and reduction in size of any further leaves which may develop. This leads to a marbled type of mottling

with large chlorotic areas bounded by light green or normal tissue. Mature foliage may senesce abnormally quickly and there is dark discoloration at the point of abscission. Discoloured tissue develops in the internodal areas and may spread to girdle the stem.

(2) *Speckled strain*   This differs from the marble strain only in the degree of symptom formation. Speckling consists of small irregular areas of dark green tissue bounded by larger areas of yellowish green. Leaf distortion is rarely a major symptom, and while there may be some cortical discoloration leaf abscission is not common.

(3) *Mild strain*   Symptoms vary with some vein clearing and mild mottling but there is little or no effect on growth and development of the foliage.

6.2.5 Pea Necrosis Virus (PNV)

This so far unidentified virus has characteristics of Bean Yellow Mosaic Virus (BYMV). It has only been reported in the Netherlands (Bos, 1967), where symptoms on susceptible peas included stem and leaf necrosis. Cultivars of the 'Perfection' group were unaffected.

6.2.6 Pea Streak Virus (PSV)

Vectors of this virus are *Acyrthosiphon pisum* and *Aphis pisum.* The particle is a parallel-sided flexuous rod 620–690 nm long with square ends. So far it has only been found in the pea-growing areas of the USA (Wisconsin, Idaho and Washington states), but it has been reported on clover in Canada, West Germany and the USA.

Symptoms are characterised by light brown purplish necrotic lesions of varying sizes on the stems and petioles of peas. Such lesions may extend along several internodes, often accompanied by stem girdling. The upper edge of infected pods may exhibit a brownish colouration with streaking of the peduncle. Leaves and pods may have a roughened appearance due to the presence of sunken necrotic light brown lesions. When plants are infected at a juvenile state the pods may fail to fill out. Stunting of the plant apex occurs due to contraction of the internode length with leaf wrinkling and curling. Sometimes there is mild chlorosis of the plant generally, but without vein clearing or mottling. Often extra tillering may accompany stunting, and premature death of the plants is frequent. On test plants under glass necrotic symptoms may fail to develop fully, but the plants wilt progressively and have a steel grey discolouration of the stem. Small brown necrotic streaks are reported by Hagedorn and Walker (1949) on the veins of leaves, stipules and stems of infected peas. In pea epidermal cells extensive parts of the cytoplasm are often stainable with phloxine and sometimes contain well-defined granular and vacuolated inclusion bodies. Negatively stained pea leaf sap preparations contain large amounts of non-aggregated particles, often attached to cell organelles. In ultrathin sections, particles occur separately or more frequently in bundles attached to membranes, for example around vacuoles (Bos and Rubio-Huertos, 1972).

Many other viruses are known to cause necrotic streak diseases in pea; these include Alfalfa Mosaic, Bean Yellow Mosaic, Beet Mosaic, Broad Bean Wilt, Cucumber Mosaic, Lettuce Mosaic, Pea Early Browning, Pea Necrosis, Tobacco Ringspot, Tomato Spotted Wilt and White Clover Mosaic viruses. They may be identified with certainty only on the basis of different particle morphology and the ability to infect some or several non-legumes.

Bean Crops

6.3 BACTERIAL PATHOGENS

6.3.1 *Pseudomonas phaseolicola* (halo blight)

Widely distributed in all regions growing *Phaseolus* beans, this seed-borne bacterial disease causes very considerable crop losses. Halo blight disease is often referred to as grease spot disease because of the greasy water-soaked lesions found on infected organs. Generally, in the early stages of infection, the plants have a yellowish colour to the leaves, but as the pathogen is established systemically symptoms may vary. Infection is often initiated in the minor veins, progressing to the main vein. Reddish discolorations develop in the interveinal areas; if infection starts in the petiole this and the adjacent main veins first take on a reddish appearance. On young plants stem lesions start as water-soaked spots which enlarge and appear as reddish streaks, expanding along the length of the stem. The stem epidermis and cortex may split and bacterial slime is exuded. Where symptoms appear as water-soaked spots they start as small isolated spots on the undersurface of leaves and leaflets which gradually enlarge and coalesce. Later a halo-like zone of greenish-yellow tissue develops outside the water-soaked region. Single halos may be 2–3 cm in diameter. Bacterial slime generated by *P. phaseolicola* is light cream to silver-coloured.

Where plants develop from infected seed a common symptom is stem girdling or 'joint rot'. Symptoms start at the primary node above the cotyledons as a small water-soaked amber-coloured lesion which girdles the stem. Girdling is usually complete when the pods are semi-mature and the increasing weight of swelling pods causes the plant to break at the weakened node. Pod infections are often zonate, having a small brown to red region of tissue surrounding the lesion. Lesions are common on the pod sutures, leading to invasion of the vascular system and the seed via the funiculus. Wilting is common in plants grown from infected seed; leaflets wilt from the pulvinus in the day-time but recover their turgor at night. If young pods are infected the seed may rot and fail to mature. If penetration is through the funiculus alone, only the hilum may be discoloured, which is difficult to detect on dark coated cultivars. The plumules of seedlings grown from infected seed may be destroyed. This condition is known as snake's head and can lead to a proliferation of lateral shoots, but the plants are very dwarfed.

Halo blight symptoms are expressed to the maximum at 16–20 °C; under higher temperatures (28–32 °C) symptomatology is modified and the halo may disappear. However, some experiments have shown that the population of bacteria in infected plants is greater at higher temperatures.

The causal agent, *P. phaseolicola*, is an aerobic, Gram-negative, rod-shaped bacterium which occurs singly or in pairs and is motile, possessing between one and six polar or bipolar flagellae. Acid but no gas is produced oxidatively from galactose and glycerol, but not from lactose, maltose, cellobiose, mannitol, sorbitol, dulcitol, *meso*-inositol, inulin, and methyl-D-glucoside or salacin. In culture the organism may undergo smooth to rough colony variation. Storage of cultures under oil has shown pathogenicity and viability to be retained for 13–18 months. An agar medium containing 2, 3,5-triphenyltetrazolium chloride has been used to differentiate pathogenic from non-pathogenic colonies. Host range includes *Ph. vulgaris, Ph. coccineus, Ph. lunatus* var. *macrocarpus, Ph. multiflorus, Ph. atropurpureus, Pueraria thunbergiana* and *Glycine max*, the last-mentioned on artificial inoculation.

Host invasion takes place through the stomata or at sites of mechanical injury. Once inside the host the whole vascular system becomes invaded and the host is systemically infected. Bacteria migrate through the intercellular spaces of parenchyma tissue, dissolving the middle lamella slightly in advance; affected cells collapse and are invaded. This tissue breakdown leads to the development of lysigenous cavities. Large bacterial masses form in the xylem cells as a result of multiplication and the cell walls either rupture or are dissolved enzymically and the pathogen passes into the parenchyma tissues again. In an ultrastructural study of leaves from infected and susceptible bean cultivars, Sigee and Epton (1975) found that *P. phaseolicola* cells had small surface protuberances which disappeared 48 h after inoculation. In susceptible leaves the bacteria formed a well-defined nuclear region and densely ribosomal aggregations developed. Between 4 and 7 days after infection bacteria in susceptible leaves produced large surface vesicles; some of these ruptured, liberating their contents and membrane fragments into the intercellular spaces. Additionally, some bacteria had large irregular projections with dense cytoplasmic contents.

Spread within crops can take place by wind-driven rain-splash, which will carry the organism up to 25 m from a point source. Overhead irrigation will disseminate *P. phaseolicola* but not furrow irrigation. Apparently *P. phaseolicola* cannot survive colder seasons in soil or plant debris. Transmission between crops is on the surface of seed or beneath the testa and between the cotyledons.

Two distinct physiological races (1 and 2) of *P. phaseolicola* have been well documented and sources of host resistance identified (Patel and Walker, 1965, 1966). Subsequently, two further races, possibly three, have been identified. These come from France, Zimbabwe and Rumania. Tests for resistance need to be made at several growth stages because plants can be resistant in the seedling stage but susceptible at the pod stage. Resistance can be expressed by the development of necrotic lesions which none the less contain viable bacteria. Additionally, symptoms may fail to be expressed due to lack of multiplication by the bacterial cells; this could be an expression of resistance or due to there being a minimal concentration level below which bacteria do not multiply. The rate of invasion has been shown to vary with the host cultivar. Studies of individual sources of resistance indicated that the cultivar Mexican Red contained one or two recessive genes for resistance while its progeny cultivar Red Mexican possessed resistance governed by a single dominant gene. The most important source of resistance to *P. phaseolicola* races 1 and 2 is PI 150414, used in breeding programmes in Holland, the UK and the USA. Resistance to both races is governed by a single recessive gene (Patel and Walker, 1966; Dickson and Natti, 1966). More recent work (Hill *et al.*, 1972) suggests that the leaf resistance of this line is controlled by a single dominant gene. These authors also showed that resistance to leaf and pod symptoms and non-systemic chlorosis were controlled by different major dominant genes. Coupling linkage was detected between the genes controlling leaf and systemic chlorosis symptoms. This is claimed to be the first report of separate control of the expression of halo blight reaction in different plant organs, that is a susceptible water-soaked reaction on pods and leaves and systemic chlorosis of leaves. Work by Taylor *et al.* (1978) also showed that resistance in PI 150414 is controlled by a single recessive factor, but in crosses with the cultivars Cascade and Seafarer results suggested that resistance could be detected in the heterozygous condition and is therefore partially dominant. Resistance expression may be affected by the genetic background and environmental conditions. An alternative resistance source is OSU 10183, which has complex parentage but contains germplasm from *Ph. vulgaris, Ph. coccineus* and the commercial cultivars Bush Blue Lake , Tendercrop and Puregold. Although not intentionally bred for halo blight resistance, OSU 10183 may be resistant due to an accumulation of polygenes, especially from the Bush Blue Lake progenitors.

As with anthracnose (*Colletotrichum lindemuthianum, see* section 6.4.4), the value of pathogen-free seed as a means of combating this disease cannot be over-emphasised. A policy of seed production in arid sections of the inter-mountain, south-western and Pacific coastal states of the USA has ensured freedom from *P. phaseolicola* in seed used for first year crop production in areas where the disease is endemic.

Roguing bean seed crops for infected plants has been a successful means of obtaining disease-free seed in New Zealand.

Chemical control is limited by a lack of suitable materials (*see* section 4.3.5). Traditional materials such as Bordeaux mixture, copper oxychloride and copper sulphate will give some measure of control for limited time periods. Antibiotics should offer a longer lasting method of control, but, as Taylor (1972) showed, to reduce pod and foliar infection by 90 per cent sprays of both streptomycin sulphate and copper oxychloride needed to be applied at 10 day intervals from seedling emergence to flowering time. When applied as single sprays at pod set copper was more effective than streptomycin, reducing infection 50 per cent (Taylor and Dudley, 1977a). Reductions of this magnitude are, however, insufficient to render an infected crop suitable for processing since crops with more than 5 per cent infected pods are usually rejected by the processors. Treatment of systemically or externally infected bean seed with slurries of streptomycin or kasugamycin reduced the level of primary field infection developing from infected seed by 98 per cent (Taylor and Dudley, 1977b). The efficacy of kasugamycin is significant in that it has no medical uses and consequently could be exploited for crop protection without risks to human health. There is a possibility, however, that antibiotic resistant strains of P. phaseolicola could become common if kasugamycin alone were used to control this pathogen.

6.4 FUNGAL PATHOGENS

6.4.1 *Uromyces* spp. (rust)

Most *Phaseolus* species are susceptible to *U. phaseoli* var. *typica* (*U. appendiculatus*). This rust was first reported in Germany (1795) and since then has achieved world-wide distribution. Very serious crop losses can occur in some seasons, but the pathogen requires high humidities for 8–10 h for infection and is therefore rare in localities where the RH does not reach 95 per cent for extended periods.

Commonly, symptoms develop on leaves and pods but not the stem and branches. Pustules develop within 5 days of infection on the leaf undersurface as small white slightly raised spots (sori). In the infection process a germ tube grows into the stoma and from it mycelium develops intercellularly, eventually erupting as a uredosorus. The primary sorus is 1–2 mm in diameter; secondary sori develop outside the infection site as a ring. As the host ages the uredosorus may be replaced by a teliosorus which is black-brown in colour. *Phaseolus* bean rust has an autoecious life cycle, that is a life cycle completed on one host, generally producing only uredo- and teliospores. The latter may act as a perennation stage. Aecia are rarely seen. Uredospores serve to disseminate the pathogen over wide areas; they are catenulate, brown, spiny, unicellular and thin walled, being 8–24 μm x 20–37 μm in size. There are two equitorial or subequitorial pores. Teliospores are amphigenous, globoid to ellipsoid and 20–28 μm x 25–35 μm in size with a wall 3–4 μm thick, generally with a hyaline papilla over the pore and smooth coated. Uredo- and teliospores can be found in the same sorus.

Temperature, light intensity and physiological age of the host influence the formation of teliospores. It would appear that some physiological races form teliospores more easily than others. Tropical races of *U. phaseoli* var. *typica* which do not form teliospores can be induced to do so if grown in temperate latitudes. They require a dormancy period before germination. Darkness stimulates germination but retards mycelial growth. Host nutrition also affects infection; increased infection occurred where bean plants were given extra nitrogen; extra potassium retarded infection and phosphate had an indeterminate effect.

More then 30 physiological races have been identified in Australia, Brazil, Hawaii and the USA, often with different differential series being used. Several programmes of breeding for resistance have been limited in their effectiveness by new cultivars succumbing to new virulences as soon as they were grown on an extensive area. Pustule size has been used as a criterion of resistance and it is possible to group cultivars into three classes: immune (resistant), those showing severe flecking but no spore production, and those with numerous sori and abundant spores. Histologically resistance operates through a hypersensitive mechanism. As with most rusts, it is possible to divide infection types into five categories, where 0, 1 and 2 are resistant and 3 and 4 susceptible (Wei, 1937). Effective chemical control has been achieved with sulphur dusts.

Broad bean, pea and lentil are attacked by *U. viciae-fabae*. Although widespread geographically, the pathogen usually only causes slight injury. As with *U. phaseoli* var. *typica*, high atmospheric humidity is required for spread. Aeciospores are spherical and of 18–26 μm in diameter with a verrucose hyaline wall; uredospores are elliptical to obovoid, measuring 22–28 μm x 19–22 μm and having a finely echinulate wall which is yellow to sienna in colour, 1–2.5 μm thick and containing three or four equitorial pores; teliospores may be similar in shape to uredospores or cylindrical, of 25–40 μm x 18–26 μm, and having walls which are chestnut-coloured and 1–2 μm thick borne on yellow or sienna pedicels 100 μm long. Considerable physiological specialisation occurs and nine races were separated on pea cultivars (Laundon and Waterston, 1965). Dissemination by seed infection has been reported, short-term spread is via aecio- and uredospores while teliospores, which can remain viable for 2 years at 3–18 °C, are a major means of perennation.

6.4.2 *Ascochyta fabae* (leaf spot)

Largely specialised on *Vicia* beans, this pathogen has achieved world-wide spread presumably through seed infection. Symptoms are seen first on the primary foliage leaves of seedlings developing from infected seed. They appear as elongated lesions up to 1 cm long with chestnut-brown margins and greyish centres. Lesions develop first on the tips and margins of leaves, gradually spreading towards the main veins of the compound leaf and petiole. Elongated red-brown stem lesions develop which weaken the stem and may cause lodging. In severe attacks the foliage is totally destroyed and the growing pods become covered in lesions. Pod lesions are usually darker and more deeply sunken than those on leaves. Infected seeds are covered in circular dark brown spots. The main seat of infection is the seed testa rather than the cotyledons. The pathogen remains viable on the seed for up to 3 years and for 4–5 months on infected trash.

The causal agent is an imperfect fungus (order Sphaeropsidales) which produces prominent yellow-brown pycnidia possessing a papillate ostiole. Hyaline conidia are formed within each pycnidium; these may be straight or slightly curved and mono- to triseptate with no constrictions at the septa; they are 16–24 μm x 3.5–6 μm in size. It takes 12–18 days for pycnidia to form following initial infection. Short-range spread of the pathogen occurs by rain-splash transmission of the conidia which ooze from the pycnidia in wet weather. For successful re-infection of the seed there must be rain early in the development of the crop so that the pathogen is carried sufficiently high in the leaf canopy to re-infect the pods and seeds as they develop (Hewett, 1973). Spread within crops is limited to within 6–10 m from a primary focus established from an infected seed. This means that foci arising from a 0.1 per cent level of seed infection would rarely meet within a crop. From field sowings of infected seed, only 2–15 per cent produced seedlings with leaf lesions. The amount of infection from a single batch of infected seed was shown to vary widely when sown at a range of centres from the eastern to the western sides of England (Hewett, 1973). It is thought that the wetter environment in the west and south of England is the main factor in the increased severity of disease in *Vicia* bean crops grown in those areas.

Introduction of a seed certification scheme in the UK in which 0 and 0.2 per cent infection levels were set for basic and certified seed, respectively, has had the effect of greatly reducing the levels of infection in field-grown seed. It is claimed that the cultivar Minor was freed from the disease.

Seed treatment techniques are only partially effective in controlling *A. fabae* and usually reduce seed viability very considerably. This is due to swelling and cracking of the testa in the drying process after disinfection. Use of benomyl and thiram in a slurry technique reduced infection to less than 0.1 per cent of seeds but impaired subsequent germination. Fungicidal sprays applied to standing crops have had limited success; compounds used included manganese dithiocarbamates.

There are no reports of physiological specialisation in *A. fabae* and inoculations on legumes nearly related to *Vicia* have been mostly unsuccessful. In the few instances where lesions developed on pea (*P. sativum*), the pathogen retained its specific character and was quite distinct from *A. pisi* (*see* section 6.1.3). There are reports of resistant cultivars being available in Russia, but tests in western Europe have shown no evidence of resistance in *V. fabae.*

Phaseolus beans are susceptible to *A. boltshauseri*, which causes dark zonate lesions on leaves and is occasionally reported on crops in Europe and the USA.

Reproduction, as with *A. fabae*, is via conidia produced in pycnidia. Conidial size varies with the degree of septateness, non-septate spores being 6–11μm x 2–3 μm and multiseptate spores being 16–34 μm x 4–7 μm.

Separated from *A. boltshauseri* by some authorities is *A. phaseolorum* on account of its larger (13–16.5 μm x 3.5–5 μm)) and only monoseptate conidia. *Ascochyta phaseolorum* is widely distributed geographically; symptoms are foliar target spotting of many leguminous genera – *Glycine, Lablab, Phaseolus* and *Vigna*. Symptoms develop as irregularly circular leaf spots with grey to brown centres surrounded by a border of light green-yellow tissue. Other lesions are zonate, light to dark brown at the leaf edges and 0.5–5 cm in diameter, which crack in the centre with the dried tissue often falling out to give a target spotting effect. Formation of lesions on the pulvini frequently leads to severe defoliation. Lesions can also be found on the pods, stems and roots of plants which develop from infected seed. This pathogen is reported to cause considerable losses on green gram (*Ph. aureus*) and black gram (*Ph. mungo*) in the Punjab area of India and on cowpea (*V. sinensis*) in Zimbabwe. Most cultivars of green beans (*Ph. vulgaris*) are susceptible, but breeding for resistance is reported from the USSR. Zineb dusts or sprays can give satisfactory chemical control while cultural controls can be achieved by the use of pathogen-free seed and roguing of infected plants.

6.4.3 *Botrytis* spp. (grey mould and chocolate spot)

The causal agent of grey mould is *Botrytis cinerea*, which attacks a very wide range of vegetable crops. Chocolate spot, on the other hand, is mainly confined to *Vicia* beans and the causal agent predominantly shown to be *B. fabae*, although *B. cinerea* does contribute to the syndrome.

(a) *Botrytis cinerea*
As with other pathogens which invade a number of crop genera, the main diseases caused are considered in a single section.

Phaseolus beans and peas
Botrytis cinerea is possibly one of the most easily identified of pathogens. This is due to the profuse production of off-white to grey mycelium covered with dark conidia on any infected organ (figure 6.3). Beans and peas may be attacked before maturity, in which case general wilting results from destruction of the stem tissue. The prime sites of infection, however, are the foliage and pods. *Botrytis* spp. are weakly penetrating pathogens usually invading through a site of injury, mechanical damage or via thin walled tissue such as floral organs. Following fertilisation the latter often abscise and drop on the leaves, forming a focus of moribund tissue which becomes colonised by *B. cinerea* and from where a lesion spreads out on to the leaf tissue. Once established the pathogen is

Figure 6.3   Lesions caused by *Botrytis cinerea* (grey mould) on dwarf French
bean. (Reproduced by permission of National Institute of
Agricultural Botany, Cambridge.)

capable of rapidly destroying the leaf, reducing it to a water-soaked mass of
slimy tissue covered in grey mould fructifications.

    Water soaking is due to the effects of macerating enzymes. Pods are similarly
infected, either through the invasion of senile flower parts or at a point of

damage. Spreading dark elliptical lesions form on the pod which are a mass of mycelium with the tissue beneath becoming softened and rotten. Pods in contact with the soil generally rot from the tip upwards, but invasion mid-way along the pod is also common. Under warm (15–20 °C) and moist (90–95 per cent RH) conditions the pathogen can rapidly destroy a whole crop. It is particularly important as a storage and transit pathogen. Under these conditions an initial inoculum from a few infected pods can spread rapidly to contaminate a large proportion of a consignment. Beans intended for freezing and canning will be refused by the processors on the basis of *Botrytis* infection since diseased pods would have to be removed by hand before processing.

Brassica crops
Usually crops such as Brussels sprouts, cabbages and cauliflowers are attacked following infection by other pathogens or in periods of adverse environmental conditions. Sprout buds, cabbage hearts and cauliflower curds become covered in sporulating grey mould lesions following extended periods of rain. This eventually reduces these crops to a slimy mass.

Carrot and parsnip
Considerable storage losses are caused to carrots and parsnips by *B. cinerea*. Injured roots when stored without environmental controls form the focus for infection. The moribund roots become covered in grey mould, turning rotten due to the effects of macerating enzymes.

Lettuce
Major crop losses are experienced from *B. cinerea* in lettuce crops. Lettuce leaf tissue is composed of thin walled parenchyma cells with very little thickening, consequently these provide a ready site for penetration. The plants can be invaded at any growth stage, but the base of the plant and outer leaves, especially in butterhead types, which are in contact with the soil, usually are the first regions to become infected. Thereafter, the whole heart is invaded, becoming covered in sporulation and turning into a water-soaked mass.

Cucurbit crops
As with beans, the fruits are often invaded from the distal end with a grey soft rot spreading gradually over the whole organ. Leaves and pruning scars are also prime sites for invasion, as indeed are any plant parts which are injured or in contact with the soil.

Tomato
Two syndromes caused by *B. cinerea* occur in tomatoes:

(1) *Soft rot* This will affect stem, leaves and fruits (figure 6.4). Invasion of the leaves generally succeeds where calyces have lodged on them to form foci of

Figure 6.4   Lesions on stem, leaves and floral organs of tomato caused by
Botrytis cinerea (grey mould). (Reproduced by permission of
National Institute of Agricultural Botany, Cambridge.)

infection; stem penetration takes place at badly made pruning scars. These give
rise to elliptical lesions up to 10 cm long which can girdle the stem and cause
collapse of the plant. Where this happens the pathogen may succeed in colonising
the vascular tissue and become distributed systemically. Fruit rot starts as a
primary invasion of the caylx or pistil progressing over the developing fruit.

(2) *Ghost spotting*   This results from *B. cinerea* spores germinating on
tomato fruit under conditions of high humidity but failing to penetrate and
establish a full infection process because of a fall in humidity. The spots are
usually up to 1 cm in diameter, having a pale green halo and silvery centre,
making the fruit unsightly and reducing its quality grading. The symptoms are
attributed to pectinase enzymes diffusing from the germ tubes and dissolving the
middle lamella of the epidermal walls.

Botrytis cinerea is the conidial or imperfect state of the Ascomycete (order
Helotiales) *Sclerotinia fuckeliana.* Sclerotial size is extremely variable,
depending on media and cultural conditions; they are black and generally
smaller and thinner than those of *S. sclerotiorum* (*see* section 6.4.5).
Macroconidia, which are ellipsoidal to obovoid, often with a pronounced hilum,
are colourless to brown, measuring 6–18 µm x 4–11 µm, and are produced on
long conidiophores. These conidiophores are up to 2 mm in length and 16–30 µm
thick, dark in colour, with branched ends the tips of which have a very rounded
appearance; they are thin walled and bud outwards to form the conidia, which
are easily detached by wind currents or thrown off as the conidiophores twist
hygroscopically. Microconidia develop from clusters of phialides and are involved
as factors in the sexual reproduction process. Microconidia of one mating type
must fall on sclerotia of the opposite mating type before apothecia will develop;
this is known as physiological heterothallism (Whitehouse, 1949) (*see* figure 6.5).
　　This fungus has a highly developed ability to exist as both a parasite and as a
saprophyte. It is distributed world-wide, but is most prevalent in humid
temperate and sub-tropical areas.
　　Attempts have been made to group strains of the organism according to
sporulation, sclerotial formation, mycelial characters, pectolytic enzyme activity
and host range, but in the main these have tenuous validity. The definition of
strains or races of *B. cinerea* is difficult because the mycelium and conidia

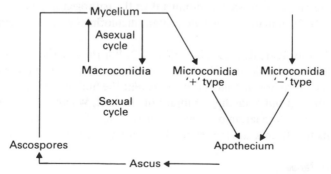

Figure 6.5   Developmental cycle of *Sclerotinia fuckeliana* (*Botrytis cinerea*,
　　　　　　grey mould).

contain nuclei of different genetic constitution (heterocaryosis) and the numbers of nuclei per conidium are irregular.

Dissemination is by the carriage of conidia in wind currents or by rain-splash from crop to crop and plant to plant. Perennation between crops occurs as a saprophytic mycelial or sclerotial stage on plant debris. Spores and mycelium are thought to be seed-borne on some hosts. The optimum temperature for growth, sporulation and spore germination is 25 °C, but the fungus can be very active at temperatures well below this.

The phenomenon of spore latency is well illustrated by the penetration process in *B. cinerea*. Latency is defined as a period of quiescence between spore deposition and germination. Given favourable environmental conditions the spore rapidly moves from quiescence to penetration, resulting in the establishment of an aggressive infection in which all the typical symptoms of the grey mould syndrome develop. A range of factors will influence the speed of this transition, for example physiological age of the host, effects of host nitrogen nutrition, carbohydrate and pectin levels. Pollen is a potent activator of the aggressive stage (Chu-Chou and Preece, 1968), the active agent being water-soluble, dialysable, non-protein and heat-stable. Similar effects could not be obtained with amino acids, sugars, organic acids, mineral salts, vitamins, indole auxins, gibberellins or abscissic acid.

Control of *B. cinerea* rests largely with the use of chemical and cultural methods. Genetic variability within the fungus precludes breeding along traditional lines utilising monogenic resistance. Although it may be possible to accumulate polygenes to produce lines with improved levels of tolerance. Studies of commercial French bean (*Ph. vulgaris*) cultivars (Dixon, 1975) showed that some cultivars were less badly infected than others (table 6.4).

Chemicals are the most effective method of control. Thus *B. cinerea* is a good example of the role which this form of control should play, being utilised when other methods are inadequate. The main materials used over the last 10 years have been benomyl and carbendazim. But to be successful a spray programme should include other materials, preferably of a non-systemic nature, otherwise chemically resistant races become dominant in the pathogen population (*see* section 4.3.3). Such materials include captan, dichlofluanid, iprodione and thiram.

Cultural controls are discussed in section 4.2. For the specific control of this pathogen they must include methods which maintain low relative humidity within the plant canopy and measures to prevent the build-up of disease-ridden detritus in the soil and wounding or injury of the host. Where such wounding is unavoidable, as in defoliation of tomatoes or training of cucumbers, clean pruning cuts free from snags are essential to minimise the sites for colonisation.

(b) *Botrytis fabae*

Chocolate spot on *Vicia* beans was initially attributed to *B. cinerea*, but the major causal organism is now accepted as *B. fabae*. At any stage in the

Table 6.4 Reaction of dwarf French bean
cultivars to infection by *B. cinerea*
(after Dixon, 1975).

Cultivar	Diseased pods per plot (per cent)
Bush Blue Lake Supreme	40.5
Cascade	40.9
Chicobel	28.3
Dorco	12.5
Lake Shasto	34.3
Loch Ness	51.8
Roma	59.4
Simato	25.1
Slenderette	23.7
Sunglo	25.3
Supernor	26.2
Bush Blue Lake 274	30.1
XPR 35	34.1
Standard error	4.5
Significant difference ($P = 0.01$)	13.0

development of the crop small scattered lesions develop on the foliage, stems and pods: these are the non-aggressive stage. Under conditions of high humidity this quickly changes to an aggressive stage where the lesions begin to sporulate, coalesce and cause a black blight with a typically fluffy grey-white mycelium covering the lesions and producing copious conidia. As a consequence, leaf tissue is rapidly macerated by enzymes of the polygalacturonase type produced by the fungus; this leads to defoliation. Infected young pods are stunted and the ovules develop irregularly or not at all. Mature pods when infected become blackened, with the discoloration extending to the seeds, which renders them unfit for processing. In epidemic years considerable yield losses can be attributed to *B. fabae*. *Vicia* beans are most prone to infection if grown in soils deficient in phosphate and potassium and with impeded drainage.

Sclerotia of *B. fabae* are rarely formed under field conditions, but in culture range in size from 1 to 3 mm; conidia are large than those of *S. fuckeliana* (*B. cinerea*), being 14–29 μm x 11–20 μm. Cultural variants intermediate between the two species have been reported. The pathogen is widely distributed wherever *Vicia* beans are grown. Characters such as physiological specialisation, transmission and control are similar to those of *B. cinerea.*

(c) The mechanism of *Botrytis* infection

Considerable studies of the physiology of infection have been made using *B. fabae* and *B. cinerea* largely because these pathogens, and in particular their legume hosts, are highly amenable to laboratory-scale investigations.

Initial infection is controlled by the fungistatic properties of epiphytic bacteria and epicuticular waxes which can inhibit conidial germination and germ tube growth. The process of penetration was well established in the 1920s. Conidia become fixed to the leaf by the outer layers of the germ tube, becoming mucilaginous following water absorption about 18 h after deposition. Hyphae developing from the germ tube do not penetrate through stomata of uninjured leaves but grow across the leaf surface; the hyphal tip then turns down towards the leaf, attaching to it in the region just behind the tip again by a mucilaginous layer. The host cuticle is indented and a projection develops from the germ tube. This penetrates the cuticular and sub-cuticular layers and the germ tube grows directly into the lumen of epidermal cells or horizontally beneath the cuticle. In either case the cuticle is caused to swell away from the epidermal layer. Where epidermal cells are penetrated by infection hyphae this occurs prior to death of the cells (Wood, 1967). Further penetration can be prevented by deposition of reaction material between the epidermal cell wall and the plasmalemma. Reaction material is initially colourless, but with time the granular deposit at the penetration site and adjacent cell walls turns red-brown.

The initial leaf reaction to epidermal penetration is cell necrosis leading to the development of a small brown lesion. In leaves of *Vicia* beans *B. cinerea* may be isolated within such a lesion whereas *B. fabae* spreads within the dead cell and into surrounding tissue. Around the necrotic cells there is a concentration of the phytoalexins wyerone and wyerone acid. It is likely that these compounds are produced by living cells adjacent to those which have been invaded and turned necrotic since the fluorescence spectra of the vacuoles of live *Vicia* bean cells adjacent to necrotic cells are similar to those of pure solutions of wyerone and wyerone acid (*see* figure 6.6 for formulae). It is therefore thought that these compounds are synthesised in the living tissue surrounding the lesion and do not diffuse out from the cells which have died. Furthermore, it is thought that these compounds accumulate and limit further growth of the pathogen. Support for this comes from the finding that wyerone acid rapidly declines in concentration as *B. fabae* spreads out from the initial infection site. *In vitro* the fungus can degrade wyerone acid by reduction of the acetylenic and keto groups. This may also occur *in vivo*. The effects of pollen exudates in promoting growth of *B.*

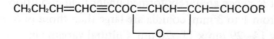

Figure 6.6   Structural formulae of wyerone (R = CH$_3$) and wyerone acid (R = H).

cinerea may be due to prevention of the pathogen from metabolising the antifungal wyerone acid (Deverall, 1977).

6.4.4 *Colletotrichum lindemuthianum* (anthracnose)

Anthracnose has been recognised as a serious disease of *Phaseolus* beans for at least least 150 years and is present in all countries where the crop is produced. The pathogen is seed-borne, and infected seed is covered with yellow to brown sunken cankers. If infected seeds germinate, the cotyledons develop similar cankers from which conidia wash down on to the hypocotyl. Here lesions 1—2 cm long develop, initially as small flesh to rust-coloured specks which then elongate, destroying the epidermal and cortical tissue; often girdling of the growing stem occurs, causing it to collapse. Invasion of the petiole and leaf veins occurs progressively, and when the petiole is badly attacked the leaf droops. Lesions develop along the veins on the leaf undersurface, starting with a dark brick-red colour and later turning dark brown or black. Symptoms are most clearly defined on pods, beginning as flesh to rust-coloured spots but spreading to become elongated, dark, deeply sunken, black lesions. These extend through the endocarp to the seed. If infection takes place early the pod may fail to develop, becoming shrivelled and eventually dying. Lesions on mature pods are marked at the edge by a slightly raised black ring with a reddish to chestnut border. The centre of the lesion is light buff-coloured with flesh-coloured acervuli which become grey-brown to black as they dry out.

Acervuli of this Fungus Imperfectus (order Melanconiales) are found on pods, leaves and stems. They are rounded to elongated up to 300 μm in diameter, borne sub-epidermally but disrupting the epidermis as they mature. Within the acervulus there is sparse development of setigerous cells which are brown, septate, with little or no swelling at the base but slightly tapering towards the apex, and measuring 4—9 μm in width and up to 100 μm in length. Conidia produced within the acervulus are cylindrical with rounded ends; they are non-septate, measure 11—20 μm x 2.5—5.5 μm, and are borne on hyaline or slightly brown cylindrical conidiophores.

Dissemination within the bean crop is by means of conidia carried by rain-splash, air currents or mechanical contact with adjacent healthy plant tissue. Perennation takes place on infected seed or crop residues. The fungus is viable for at least 2 years on seed and capable of withstanding temperatures of −20 °C for short periods. Survival in seed takes place as dormant mycelium within the seed coat or in the cells of the cotyledons and elsewhere in the seed. Susceptibility is largely restricted to French or snap bean types (*Ph. vulgaris*) and tepary bean (*Ph. acutifolius* var. *latifolius*), scarlet flowered runner or stick beans (*Ph.coccineus* formerly *Ph. multiflorus*), lima bean (*Ph. lunatus*) and the mung bean (*Ph. aureus*) are less susceptible.

The main avenue for controlling this pathogen has been by the use of resistant cultivars. This is despite the high degree of variability and in consequence the large numbers of physiological races present in *C. lindemuthianum* populations. Success with this form of control is probably due to the nature of pathogen dissemination as water-borne conidia, in consequence of which it approximates to the simple interest model (*see* section 3.1). Races of *C. lindemuthianum* have been formed into virulence groups using letters of the Greek alphabet, viz. alpha, beta, gamma, delta, etc. Groups alpha and beta were recognised in the 1930s and resistance in the cultivars then in use was shown to be due to at least eight dominant genes. Later Andrus and Wade (1942) proposed a system of 10 genes in three allelomorphic series with both duplicate and complementary genes for resistance, one dominant gene for susceptibility and gene interactions at three points to co-ordinate the data then available for the inheritance of resistance to beta and gamma races. Three independent genes were proposed for resistance to race delta. In Europe, Hubbeling (1961) proposed eight dominant allelic genes for resistance to races alpha, beta, gamma and delta. A new source of dominant resistance, gene ARE was identified in the line Cornell 49/242 which gave resistance to all four races of *C. lindemuthianum* (Masterbroek, 1960). Previously, resistance genes had to be introduced into at least 10 sites in the chromosomes to give resistance to the four races of *C. lindemuthianum*, and with the probability that different loci were involved this made breeding difficult. Use of the ARE gene could provide resistance with only a single gene involved. Additionally the ARE gene gave resistance to the newly identified race epsilon. Further resistance testing could employ a mutant form of race alpha, later named lambda, which was virulent to all previously known resistant genes. Consequently, most new cultivars incorporated resistance from Cornell 49/242, but further sources of resistance were identified from two Mexican bean lines No. 222 and No. 227 (Hallard and Trebuchet, 1976); this resistance is controlled by two separate single dominant genes. As might be expected, further races have been identified, race kappa (or Ebnet) in Germany (Kruger *et al.*, 1977), which is virulent to gene ARE, and race jota (N. Hubbeling, personal communication found in the Netherlands following experiments in which mixtures of races kappa, gamma, delta and lambda were inoculated on test plants in the field. Differentials for these races are shown in table 6.5.

Australian races of *C. lindemuthianum* differ from those reported in Europe and the USA, but the ARE gene has proved resistant to all isolates collected so far (Zaumeyer and Meiners, 1975). Shortly after the kappa race was identified in Europe, a race capable of overcoming the ARE gene was isolated in Brazil. This has been named alpha-Brazil; fortunately resistance to it is available in the line Mexique 222. Work in Uganda (Leakey, 1970) has used the *ARE* gene, although two races have been identified which are virulent to it.

The relationships between races have been summarised by Fouilloux (1976) based on earlier dendrographic studies by Charrier and Bannerot (1970), suggesting two relationships between the newly recognised races (figure 6.7).

Table 6.5   Races of *Colletotrichum lindemuthianum* (after Hubbeling, 1976).

Bean cultivar	Races of *C. lindemuthianum*						
	Epsilon	Alpha	Beta	Gamma	Delta	Kappa	Lambda
Processor	R	S	S	S	S	S	S
Michigan Dark Red Kidney	R	R	S	S	S	S	S
Perry Marrow	R	R	R	S	S	S	S
Centrum and Widusa	R	S	R	R	S	S	S
Kaboon	R	R	R	S	R	R	S
Mitchelite and Robust	S	S	R/S	R/S	S	S	S
Samlac and Emerson 847	R	R	R/S	R/S	S	S	S
Prelude	S	S	R	R/S	S	S	S
Cornell 49/242	R	R	R	R	R	S	R

R, resistant; S, susceptible, R/S, mixed reaction.

The alternative method of control to cultivar resistance is through the use of pathogen-free seed. This has been successful in the USA, where seed production moved to more arid western states where *C. lindemuthianum* does not exist. Clean seed regulations in the UK have similarly rendered this pathogen of minor significance, whereas in all other areas it is a major limiting factor facing bean production.

Considerable studies have been made of the physiology of this host—parasite relationship. The phytoalexin phaseollin and other phenols accumulated in bean pod tissue which underwent browning in both resistant and susceptible reactions. Browning took place several days earlier in resistant reactions as a hypersensitive response developed with incompatible races of *C. lindemuthianum* (Rahe *et al.*, 1969). Germination and germ tube growth of races beta, gamma and delta were equally sensitive to less than 10 μg/ml of phaseollin. Mycelium was less sensitive and phaseollin may be metabolised by hyphae (Bailey and Deverall, 1971). Isolates of *C. lindemuthianum* races placed on hypocotyl tissue formed appressoria and penetrated the epidermal cells regardless of the susceptibility or resistance of the cultivar (Skipp and Deverall, 1972). Two types of cellular response were found, however, dependent on the pathogen race used. In incompatible combinations hyphal growth slowed soon after the penetrated cells

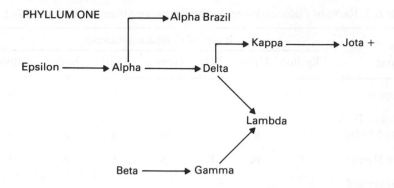

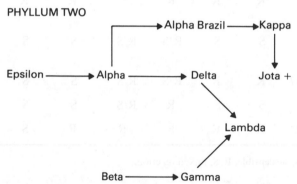

Figure 6.7   Relationships between physiological races of *Colletotrichum lindemuthianum* (anthracnose) (After Fouilloux, 1976). The + sign indicates an addition by the present author.

became necrotic, but continued for several days thereafter. Susceptible tissue remained visibly unaffected for at least 3 days while fungal colonisation took place. Necrosis then followed and brown lesions developed. Albersheim *et al.* (1969) suggested that *C. lindemuthianum* fails to invade resistant cultivars due to an inability on the part of the pathogen to remove sugar moieties from the host cell wall hemicellulose, while Skipp and Deverall (1972) contended that resistance is due to changes in the cell following penetration, which leads to the hypersensitive response. These changes are of two types: (1) loss of semi-permeability accompanied by shrinkage of the nuclear membrane and plasmalemma, and (2) cytoplasmic streaming becoming more active and resulting in the accumulation of newly visible particles at the site of penetration. Eventually cellular activity and cell organisation deteriorated as movement slowed, then ceased, and coagulation of the cytoplasm spread into the cell. With both reaction types, browning occurred after the cells had lost their vital properties. Further work in the USA (Anderson and Albersheim, 1972) indicated that cell wall-degrading endopolygalacturonases produced by *C. lindemuthianum* races alpha, gamma and delta could be inhibited equally by proteins present in the host cell wall. From this they suggested that the differential resistance/susceptibility reactions were due to the ability of the pathogen to produce excess endopolygalacturonase such that it exceeded the quantities of protein inhibitor formed by the host. Where such an excess of pathogen-produced enzyme was produced, then penetration proceeded and the susceptible reaction took place. The presence of cross-protection factors has also been studied in this host–parasite combination as a possible means of resistance. Bean hypocotyls could be protected against pathogenic races of *C. lindemuthianum* by a diffusable factor from incompatible reactions (Berard *et al.*, 1972). The factor was cultivar specific and hypersensitive flecking did not occur in the protected area. Conidia of a challenge inoculum germinated, formed appressoria and penetrated protected host tissue, but mycelium was contained within the single epidermal cell penetrated. If the factor was placed on another cultivar it did not alter the susceptible or resistant response, but the response depended on the cultivar and race of *C. lindemuthianum* used. Studies of incompatibility using Cornell 49/242, which is resistant to gamma and delta races (Allard, 1974), showed that resistance was due to delay in appressorial activity and subsequent cell necrosis which inhibited growth of the primary hyphae. In isogenic material derived from Cornell 49/242, infection failed due to localised deposition of intracellular callose. Similar evidence was obtained by Mercer *et al.* (1974), who suggested that hypersensitive death of cells appeared to be the most important cause of resistance. Granulation of walls of killed cells did not extend beyond the middle lamella, and the pits between killed and adjacent living cells became occluded. Reaction material which may be similar to the callose referred to by Allard (1974) was found in the lumen of cells which restrained hyphal growth in the combination of the cultivar Immuna and *C. lindemuthianum* race gamma. Fine structure studies showed that reaction material developed shortly before and after penetration of hyphae into the lumen of epidermal cells (Mercer *et al.*, 1975). But the cytoplasm of infected cells remained viable, increasing in volume compared to corresponding cells in uninfected plants. Penetrating hyphae did not grow through the cytoplasm but between it and the adjacent cell wall. Reaction material did not develop in cortical cells when they were invaded.

It is likely that resistance mechanisms will vary depending on the genetic source of resistance, the race of *C. lindemuthianum* and the experimental environment used. Consequently, it is not surprising that several workers have postulated a variety of means by which resistance operates in this host–parasite combination.

6.4.5 *Sclerotinia* spp. (white rot)

These pathogens are geographically universally distributed and attack a very wide host range. Symptoms on major crop hosts are described below.

(a) Asparagus, cucurbits, pea, *Phaseolus* bean, Solanaceae

Disease starts as irregular water-soaked areas on the stems which spread rapidly to the rest of the plant, forming a soft watery rot. This may dry out to become lighter in colour. Warm (23 °C) and moist (95 per cent RH) conditions encourage fungal growth, which develops as a white cottony mat of mycelium on the leaves, stems and pods. Within the superficial mycelium hard, dark, black sclerotia are formed.

(b) Carrot and parsnip

Major damage is caused to the swollen roots, leading to a watery decay accompanied by external white mycelial stroma with black sclerotia. Optimal decay takes place at 23 °C. In store the disease can be controlled by temperature manipulation.

(c) Celery and parsley

Damping-off of seedlings is a prime symptom caused by penetration of the hypocotyl and subsequent rapid invasion of the cortex accompanied by formation of white mycelial masses. Celery can also be infected at more mature stages, giving rise to a pink rot of the basal crown and petioles, again associated with the production of copious white mycelium embedded in which are black sclerotia.

(d) Crucifers

Sclerotinia rot is usually associated with semi-mature crops where the cortex of the main stem becomes soft and rotten with masses of white cottony mycelium and black sclerotia.

(e) Lettuce

Damping-off will take place with infected lettuce seedlings, but on more mature plants a progressive wilt develops, starting with the oldest leaves. Mycelium is found at or near soil level and extends upwards through the main stem. Severe rotting can lead to considerable losses in transit.

Sclerotinia spp. are classed as Ascomycetes of the order Helotiales; this means that they produce sclerotia which germinate to produce cup-shaped apothecia from which ascospores are produced. No true asexual conidia are formed, but microconidia or spermatia grow in chains from the tips of short lateral branches of the vegetative mycelium or from sclerotia or the discs of over-mature apothecia. Microconidia are involved in sexual reproduction by, in this instance, simple self-fertilisation, since the fungus is homothallic. Transfer of microconidia to sclerotia of the same mycelium results in the formation of apothecia (figure 6.8).

White rot has been attributed to three causal organisms: *S. sclerotiorum* (*Whetzelinia sclerotiorum*), *S. minor* and *S. intermedia*. These organisms are distinguishable by the sizes of sclerotia, asci and ascospores (table 6.6).

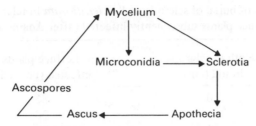

Figure 6.8   Developmental cycle of *Sclerotinia sclerotiorum* (white rot).

Sclerotial size is dependent on temperature since larger sclerotia are produced by *S. intermedia* and *S. minor* at 25 °C while smaller ones developed at 10 °C. No dormancy period is required before sclerotia will germinate to form apothecia, but moist conditions (90–95 per cent RH) and temperatures below 25 °C are necessary together with a light requirement; in continuous darkness the apothecia abort.

Table 6.6 Size ranges of sclerotia, asci and ascospores in *Sclerotinia* spp.

Organ	*S. sclerotiorum*	*S. intermedia*	*S. minor*
Sclerotia (mm)	2.5–6	1–3	0.5–1
Asci (μm)	8–10 x 125–160	7–8 x 127	9 x 140
Ascospores (μm)	6–7 x 12–15	5 x 13	7 x 14

Sclerotia are the principle means of perennation from one crop to the next on the same land and can be distributed to new sites by implements, animal agencies, irrigation water and mixed with seed. They will germinate to form mycelium which can invade young seedlings, causing the damping-off syndromes referred to for celery, parsley and lettuce. Ascospores produced from apothecia are the primary means of foliar infection, which can take place at any stage in the growth of crops. Ascospores can be dispersed several miles by wind in a viable condition.

Sclerotia have been shown to survive up to 15 months in soil when buried to depths of 30 cm, but viability was reduced by burial at 60 cm. Viability also declined if the soil was air-dried and then remoistened (Adams, 1975). Only sclerotia present in the upper 5 cm of soil are important in the initiation of infection (table 6.7).

Control of this pathogen is extremely difficult because of its wide host range and persistent sclerotia. There are some suggestions of sources of resistance (Abawi et al., 1975), but these are unlikely to give complete control. Systemic fungicides of the benomyl type provide a means of limiting the pathogen, but resistant strains are likely to develop. Cultural controls such as soil cultivation

Table 6.7 Depth of burial of sclerotia of *S. sclerotiorum* in relation to numbers
of lettuce plants subsequently infected (after Adams and Tate, 1975).

Depth of sclerotia in soil (cm)	Lettuce plants infected (per cent)
0	86
1	20
2	22
4	10
8	2
12	0

and aeration to kill sclerotia or flooding infected land so that the sclerotia rot
are amongst the most effective techniques. Control of storage rots due to
S. sclerotiorum in carrots during shipment to the UK has been achieved by
maintaining the roots in a turgid condition; cool storage will also limit the spread
of this pathogen. Encouraging results have been obtained (H. Tribe and J. Turner,
personal communication) for the biological control of *S. sclerotiorum* using
Coniothyrium spp. which parasitise the sclerotia.

Although principally a major pathogen of clover (*Trifolium* spp.),
S. trifoliorum (clover rot) will attack *Vicia* beans. Infection is via ascospores
invading the foliage of overwintered beans and leading to systemic colonisation
of the whole plant, or from soil-borne sclerotia from which mycelium enters the
upper roots and lower stem regions. There is no profuse production of mycelium
on the outside of the plant, as with *S. sclerotiorum*. Once infected the host wilts,
becomes necrotic and slowly dies through starvation. Large black sclerotia (1–10
mm) form within the medullary cavity. A sub-specific status, *S. trifoliorum* var.
fabae, has been proposed for the pathogen on *Vicia* beans, but this may be
unnecessary since the strain which attacks clover will also infect beans. The life
history is similar to other *Sclerotinia* spp.: spermatia (microconidia) function as
fertilising male cells during the development of apothecia, subsequently leading
to the production of ascospores which are hyaline, unicellular, elliptical,
12–8 μm x 8 μm in size, and wind-dispersed.

6.4.6 *Fusarium solani* (root rot)

Serious root rot of broad bean (*V. faba*) and French bean (*Ph. vulgaris*) are
caused by *F. solani* f. sp. *fabae* and *F. solani* f. sp. *phaseoli*, respectively. On both
hosts symptoms consist of a dry rotting of the upper tap root region and stem
collar at or just above soil level (figure 6.9). The stem tissue takes on a reddish
discoloration which may gradually darken and eventually become necrotic,
particularly on *Vicia* beans. In sub-lethal attacks secondary roots are produced

Figure 6.9   Destruction of the root system and subsequent foliar wilting of
Vicia bean caused by *Fusarium solani* (root rot). (Reproduced by
permission of National Institute of Agricultural Botany,
Cambridge.)

by *Phaseolus* plants. The foliage usually shows slow chlorosis and desiccation
due to the loss of water-absorptive capacity by the root system. Within the stem
there is usually discoloration of the cortical tissue.

As with other *Fusaria* (*see* section 6.1.5), three forms of spores are produced
by the imperfect stage: microconidia borne on elongated phialides, which are

hyaline, cylindrical, monoseptate, and measure 9—16 μm x 2—4 μm; macroconidia, which are cylindrical, often slightly wider towards the apex, and with a well marked foot cell, and measure 40—100 μm x 5—7.5 μm; and chlamydospores, which vary from globose to oval, are smooth to rough walled, and measure 10—11 μm x 8—9 μm. The perfect Ascomycete stage is identified as *Nectria haematococca*.

Perennation occurs on decaying debris as a saprophyte. Although *F. solani* f. sp. *phaseoli* grows hardly at all in soil alone, it has been shown to grow in the rhizosphere of non-hosts (Schroth and Hendrix, 1962) and the chlamydospores will germinate in the presence of root exudates from many non-susceptible plants as well as *Phaseolus* beans, in which there is a saprophytic growth phase prior to penetration of the root cortex. It can infect peas (*see* section 6.1.5) but does not cause severe symptoms. Dissemination occurs through the movement of infected debris and drainage water. In the UK the pathogen has been noted as occurring on *Vicia* beans grown on heavy clay soils with impeded drainage. Symptoms can be found at most stages in the life of a crop, but winter-sown beans in particular exhibit symptoms in the late spring (April—May) or just before maturity (late July or August). There are no adequate control measures, but the use of long rotations (6—8 years) avoiding the use of all other legumes has been advocated. Incorporation of barley straw into infected soil increased the lysis of germ tubes and reduced the saprophytic growth of *F. solani* f. sp. *phaseoli* on the host root; also, the number of thalli found on roots was less in soils amended with barley, and those which did form were smaller than in unamended soil. Biological control brought about by crop residues can, therefore, have an effect up to and even following penetration of the host root. *Bacillus cereus, B. megaterium* and species of *Pseudomonas* are affected antagonists of *F. solani* f. sp. *phaseoli* and reduced the disease in beans after the addition of chitin to soil (Mitchell and Alexander, 1961). Where crops are infected, only shallow cultivation should be practised; this enables any residual healthy root system to grow undisturbed. Also, soil aeration increases the numbers of chlamydospores formed. Patrick and Tousson (1965) report that 25 per cent of microconidia added to unaerated soil converted to chlamydospores, whereas in aerated soil the figure rose to 40 per cent.

6.5 VIRUSES

This section divides naturally into two groups: in sections 6.5.1—6.5.7 the viruses infecting *Phaseolus* beans are discussed; the viruses which attack *Vicia* beans are dealt with in sections 6.5.8—6.5.11.

6.5.1 Bean Common Mosaic Virus (BCMV)

More than 14 aphid species have been reported as vectors of this virus. Of these the most important are *Aphis rumicis, Macrosiphum gei* (*solanifolii*) and *Macrosiphum pisi*. Seed infection plays an important role in the world-wide distribution of BCMV and is probably the principal source of inital crop infections. Plants which are infected after flowering do not pass on the virus to the seed. Also, the distribution of infected seeds in pods is erratic. The virus is found in the embryo and cotyledons but seldom in the testa. It is also thought that the virus can be transmitted via infected pollen. Virus particles are flexuous filaments 750 nm long by 15 nm wide.

Symptoms induced by BCMV in *Phaseolus* spp. vary with the cultivar involved, the host growth stage and the environment. In general, the leaves of infected plants are mottled and chlorotic with a downward cupping of the laminae, giving the leaflets an arched, puckered and blistered appearance. Usually there is a reduction in the size of infected leaves associated with this contortion. On moderately susceptible cultivars, leaf crinkling is a typical symptom and often is accompanied by yellowing and pronounced venation. Some distinction can be drawn between symptoms developed on plants infected by aphids and those infected via the seed. This is complicated because symptoms vary on mature leaves and those which are in a juvenile state at the time of infection. The leaves of aphid-infected plants are crinkled, chlorotic and stiff, tend to droop and have shortened petioles, but there is no downward rolling of the leaf margins or mosaic mottling. Where infection is derived from seed the leaves often develop a pattern of light green and dark green areas, the former often concentrated at the leaf margin. Also, there is a distinct downward rolling of the leaf margin. A characteristic symptom on the first compound leaf is a dark green blistering of areas of the lamina. Symptoms tend to lessen in intensity as the season advances.

Infection is usually associated with the production of excessive numbers of lateral shoots. Symptom severity varies with cultivar susceptibility, while highly susceptible ones are affected as described above; more tolerant cultivars are as easily infected but do not develop marked symptoms, although the virus can be readily recovered. Some resistant cultivars have been identified on which no symptoms develop following inoculation and virus cannot be re-isolated. The major diagnostic character of BCMV in the field is downward curling of the foliage and this may be used to distinguish it from Bean Yellow Mosaic Virus.

The chlorotic areas of mosaic symptoms show chloroplast degeneration; in such areas islands of chlorotic cells are surrounded by normal cells. In the former the plastic stroma is flattened, enlarged in diameter and ultimately collapses in a viscous pale yellow or colourless mass. Sometimes the stroma is vacuolated, often with hyaline granules present. Two types of cell inclusion have been found: filamentous inclusions which may be concentrations of virus particles and lamellar inclusions in various configurations.

Disease is caused by this virus in a wide range of *Phaseolus* spp. and in *Vicia faba* (broad bean). It has a world-wide distribution and was one of the earliest viruses to be recognised, being reported by Ivanowski in Russia in 1899. A number of strains have been identified in America and Holland which are differentiated on the basis of reactions by a range of cultivars.

6.5.2 Bean Double Yellow Mosaic Virus (BDYMV) and Bean Golden Mosaic Virus (BGMV)

Both viruses are spread by the whitefly *Bemisia tabaci*. The foliage of infected plants develops scattered discoloured patches which slowly turn bright yellow. There is no dwarfing but pod production is impaired. A bright golden leaf mosaic is typical of BGMV.

6.5.3 Bean Local Chlorosis Virus (BLCV)

Transmitted by *Aphis craccivora*, seven strains of this virus have been identified. Strain C causes puckering and small chlorotic spots with some stunting on the leaves of *Ph. vulgaris* cv. Black Wonder. Strain E causes mottling, puckering of leaves, stunting and excessive growth of side shoots on *Glycine max*. Strain F causes curling mottling and general foliar malformations with necrotic marking of stems and pods of a range of *Ph. vulgaris* cultivars. Bean Necrotic Speckle Virus (BNSV) may be associated with BLCV causing small local necrotic lesions on beans.

6.5.4 Bean Necrosis Virus (BNV)

Differentiated from BLCV by not being transmitted by *Aphis craccivora*, this virus causes severe local and systemic necrosis of *Ph. vulgaris*.

6.5.5 Bean Pod Mottle Virus (BPMV)

Transmitted mainly by the bean leaf beetle *Ceratoma trifurcata*, this virus is restricted to Europe and the USA. Virus particles are isometric, about 30 nm in diameter. *Vigna sinensis* (cowpea) is not infected by BPMV but is infected by Southern Bean Mosaic Virus (SBMV), thereby providing a means of distinguishing between these two viruses. As with SBMV, Pod Mottle Virus causes local lesions on some bean cultivars and systemic infection of others. Those cultivars which suffer from local lesions are resistant to systemic infection and *vice versa*. Local lesions are light brown, round, produced in a diffuse pattern and apparently subepidermal. Systemic symptoms are more intense, the foliage being malformed and mottled, often with intense chlorosis. Infected pods are badly mottled, with the green areas having a deep green colour. They contain aborted ovules while the pod walls are roughened and warty, often curled and twisted. Lima beans and soybean are hosts of this virus as well as French beans.

6.5.6 Southern Bean Mosaic Virus (SBMV)

Although detectable in newly ripened seed, this virus does not appear to be able to survive storage for longer than 7 months. Both beans and cowpeas are hosts, but strains from one may not attack the other. The main vector of the cowpea strain is the bean leaf beetle *C. trifurcata*. The virus particles are isometric 25 nm diameter.

Symptoms on *Ph. vulgaris* (French bean), as with PMV, vary according to the susceptibility of the cultivar to systemic or local lesion development. Where local lesions develop they appear within 3 days of infection as brownish red circles with lighter centres ranging from 1 to 3 mm in diameter. Systemic infection starts as mild mottling, increasing in intensity with vein banding where the interveinal areas are lighter green than the tissue close to the veins. Some puckering and blistering may develop. In severely infected cultivars veinal necrosis and early leaf abscission occur. Symptoms appear on pods as dark green irregularly shaped water-soaked blotchy areas on green podded beans and as greenish yellow areas on wax podded beans. Small-seeded lima bean (*Ph. lunatus*) cultivars showed only local lesions, whereas large-seeded types appeared resistant. Only mild leaf mottling developed on infected soya bean (*Glycine max*).

Two variants have been reported: Southern Bean Mosaic Virus 2, which causes larger more distinct local lesions with stunting, curling, malformation and reductions of leaf size with systemic infections; and a Yellow Variant which causes a characteristic yellow mottling. Resistance to systemic symptoms could be achieved by selecting only breeding material showing local lesions. Recently, another mosaic virus (Bean Western Mosaic Virus, BWMV) has been identified which is seed-borne, causing leaf mottle, stunting and necrosis.

6.5.7 Bean Yellow Mosaic Virus (BYMV)

Conflicting evidence on the seed transmission of this virus has been produced; insect vectors include the aphids *Acyrthosiphon pisum, Aphis fabae, Megoura viciae* and *Myzus persicae*. The virus is stylet-borne (non-persistent). The particle is a flexuous rod 750 nm long and 13—14 nm wide. Distribution extends over Africa, Europe, India, Japan, North and South America and the UK.

Symptoms induced by BYMV vary with the host species. On *Ph. vulgaris* (French bean) all leaflets curl downwards and point down from the point of attachment to the petiole. The leaf surfaces are irregular with small light yellow areas standing against a green background. Chlorosis spreads until most of the foliage is yellowed. In the early stages the plant is very brittle. In distinction from Common Bean Mosaic Virus (CBMV) the symptoms of BYMV become greater as the season advances. Internode length is reduced and lateral shoots proliferate, giving the plants a bushy, stunted appearance. Many fewer pods are produced on infected plants. Symptoms on *P. sativum* (garden pea) resemble those of PEMV and PMV, but are milder. Initially there is faint mottling which intensifies with the presence of numerous dark green areas having irregular outlines and lying close to the main veins. Vein clearing may develop, with the areas between the veins remaining green but of a lighter shade than in healthy plants. There is some reduction of leaf size, with slight upward curling of the leaf edges and wrinkling.

Mild chlorosis, slight leaf contusion and plant stunting are typical symptoms of BYMV on *V. faba* (broad bean). It is characteristic that crystalline inclusion bodies are found in the nuclei, cytoplasm and guard cells of stomata. Inclusions are of three types: aggregates resembling virus particles, elongated particles 13–15 nm wide and particles 7 nm wide. The mitochondria become opaque with electron-transparent block-shaped cristae.

The virus can be distinguished from CBMV in that it is transmissible to *P. sativum* (garden pea). Five strains have been identified:

(1) *Pod Distorting strain*   This strain causes the pods to become severely warted, mis-shapen and disfigured. There is considerable variation in the response of bean cultivars to this strain.

(2) *Black Root or X-Disease strain*   The most frequent symptom on *Ph. vulgaris* is purpling of the leaf bases of the lower leaves accompanied by tissue death. The leaves often have dark irregular spots and necrotic veins with the interveinal walls of the pods turning black. Alternatively, the roots may become affected and the plants wilt and die prematurely.

(3) *Necrotic Lesion strain*   This strain induces both necrotic local lesions and intense mottling symptoms.

(4) *Severe Yellow Mosaic strain*   This causes strong epinasty, chlorosis and veinal necrosis in the primary leaves of *Ph. vulgaris*. In some cultivars this is followed by top necrosis and plant death; in others by severe yellow mosaic.

(5) *Sweet Pea Streak Virus*   On *Ph. vulgaris* a few local lesions occur which are pale green spots surrounded by a fine necrotic rim; later a general veinal chlorosis may develop. Reddish-brown local lesions develop on *V. faba* (broad bean) with slight vein clearing of younger leaves and necrotic spots on older leaves.

Infected *Trifolium pratense* (red clover) is a prime source of infection for BYMV. Beans should not be planted near clover crops and should be rogued when infections are first noticed.

6.5.8 Broad Bean Mottle Virus (BBMV)

This virus has been detected only on a few crops in England and Germany. Its vectors are unidentified but it is known not to be seed-borne. The virus particles are isometric, 26 nm in diameter.

Symptoms on *V. faba* (broad bean) begin with vein clearing of the youngest leaves; this then fades to be replaced by bright interveinal mottling. Under cold conditions, marginal leaf blackening followed by death of the main and lateral shoots are typical symptoms. Usually there is general stunting of the plant.

Amorphous inclusions develop in the cells of chlorotic areas; these are small in recently infected cells but may vacuolate and enlarge until they are several times the size of the nuclei. The inclusions are mainly composed of virus particles. Infection of *P. sativum* (pea) is usually lethal. At first infected leaves turn necrotic and shrivel, then the rest of the plant collapses and wilts. Young foliage may exhibit mottling prior to wilting. Bright yellowing of the veins is a first indication of infection of *Ph. vulgaris* (French bean). This is followed by interveinal mottling.

6.5.9 Broad Bean Stain Virus (BBSV)

The weevils *Apion vorax* and *Sitona lineatus* are vectors of this virus, which is also seed-borne and will spread widely within a crop once infection has started (Gibbs *et al.*, 1968). Distribution extends through Europe and north-western Africa. The particle is isometric, 25 nm in diameter.

Symptom severity is extremely variable even on an individual plant. Some leaves show mild green mosaic or chlorosis with patches of green tissue while others are apparently healthy. Eventually the chlorotic areas become puckered with irregular outlines. Symptoms are worse in cold than hot weather. Infected seeds have a distinct dark brown stain often forming a band which encircles the seed. The virus also causes chlorotic mottling, wilt and necrosis of *P. sativum* (pea) and *Ph. vulgaris* (French bean).

6.5.10 Broad Bean True Mosaic Virus (BBTMV)

Symptoms are similar to those caused by BBSV. (Broad Bean True Mosaic Virus is also known as Echtes Ackerbohne Mosaik-virus, EAMK) and spread by the same vectors, *A. vorax* and *S. lineatus* (weevils). This virus is seed-borne and spreads easily within crops. The particles are isometric, 25 nm in diameter, and it is found in Europe and north-western Africa. Systemic mottling and mosaic develop on infected *V. faba* (broad bean), often becoming more severe with shoot necrosis in cold weather. On *P. sativum* (pea) the plants are stunted with severe systemic chlorotic mosaic, which occasionally becomes necrotic. Distinction may be drawn from BBSV in that BBTMV does not cause chlorosis and necrosis of *Ph. vulgaris* (French bean).

6.5.11 Broad Bean Vascular Wilt Virus (BBVWV)

Transmitted by the aphids *Myzus persicae, Aphis craccivora, Macrosiphum euphorbiae* and *Acyrthosiphon onobrychis*, this virus does not appear to be seed-borne. It has been identified in Europe, Japan, south-eastern Australia and the USA (New York state). The particle is isometric, 25 nm in diameter.

Under field conditions, *V. faba* (broad bean) plants develop a lateral bending of the apical tip with the younger leaves inrolled and necrotic. After a few days, rosetting and flattening of the apex is apparent. Slowly the whole plant wilts, with the growing tip becoming blackened. In the collar region, just above soil level, the stem is blackened; the root system is destroyed with intense discolouration of the vascular cylinder. No local lesion development has been observed. Secondary symptoms in plants which survive the wilting stage include leaf distortion with blistered dark green regions between the veins, which become blistered. Later still, the plants have a stiffened appearance with small leathery, chlorotic and inrolled leaves, the veins of which are purplish. Four strains have been reported; of these, Pea Streak Virus produced local lesions followed by systemic necrosis on *V. faba* (broad bean). Closely related to BBVWV are Nasturtium Ringspot Virus (NRV), Petunia Ringspot Virus (PRV) and a virus isolated from parsley (*Petroselinum crispum*). When inoculated on *V. faba* (broad bean), both NRV and PRV induced cellular inclusions. In Australia control is achieved by roguing and late sowing to avoid the early winter infection period.

REFERENCES

Section 6.1.1

Campbell, L. (1935). *Downy Mildew of Peas Caused by* Peronospora pisi (*DeB.*) *Syd*. Technical Bulletin no. 318. Agricultural Experiment Station Washington.

Dixon, G. R. (1981). Downy mildews of peas and beans, In *The Downy Mildews* (D. M. Spencer, ed.). Academic Press, London.

Hickey, E. L. and Coffey, M. D. (1977). *Can. J. Bot*. **55**, 2845–58.

Matthews, P. and Dow, P. (1972). *A. Rep. John Innes Inst*. **1971**, 36–8.

Pegg, G. F. and Mence, M. J. (1970). *Ann. appl. Biol.* **66**, 417–28.

Pegg, G. F. and Mence, M. J. (1972). *Ann. appl. Biol.* **71**, 19–31.

Ryan, E. W. (1971). *Ir. J. agric. Res.* **10**, 315–22.

Section 6.1.2

Crawford, R. F. (1927). *Powdery Mildew of Peas*. Bulletin no. 163. Agricultural Experiment Station, New Mexico.

Dow, P. (1978). *A. Rep. John Innes Inst.* **1977**, 31–2.

Gritton, E. T. and Ebert, R. D. (1975). *J. Am. Soc. hort. Sci.* **100**, 137–42.

Hagedorn, D. J. (1973). Peas. In *Breeding Plants for Disease Resistance: Concepts and Applications* (R. R. Nelson, ed.). State University Press, Pennysylvania.

Hammerlund, C. (1925). *Hereditas* **6**, 1–26.

Harland, S. C. (1948). *Heredity* **2**, 263–9.

Heringa, R. J., van Norel, A. and Tazelaar, M. F. (1969). *Euphytica* **18**, 163–9.

Oku, H., Ouchi, S., Shiraishi, T. and Baba, T. (1975). *Phytopathology* **65**, 1263–7.

Paulech, C. and Herrera, S. (1969). *Biol. Bratisl. A* **24**, 720–7.

Paulech, C. and Herrera, S. (1970). *Biol. Bratisl. A* **25**, 3–10.

Smith, C. G. (1969). *Trans. Br. mycol. Soc.* **53**, 69–76.

Vaseduva, R. S. (1962). *Rep. agric. Res. Inst. New Dehli*, **1958–1959**, 131–47.

Section 6.1.3
Bertini, S. (1956). *Annali sper. Agric*. **10**, 957–81.
Blakeman, J. P. and Dickinson, C. H. (1967). *Trans. Br. mycol. Soc*. **50**, 385–96.
Blaumann, G. (1953). *Kühn-Arch*. **67**, 305–83.
Brewer, D. and MacNeil, B. H. (1953). *Can. J. Bot*. **31**, 739–44.
Carter, M. V. (1963). *Aust. J. biol. Sci*. **16**, 800–17.
Carter, M. V. and Moller, W. J. (1961). *Aust. J. agric. Res*. **12**, 879–88.
Dickinson, C. H. and Sheridan, J. J. (1968). *Ann. appl. Biol*. **62**, 473–83.
Dow, P. (1978). *A. Rep. John Innes Inst*. **1977**, 31–2.
Hare, W. W. and Walker, J. C. (1944). Asocochyta *Disease of Canning Peas*.
    Research Bulletin no. 150. Agricultural Experiment Station, Wisconsin.
Harrower, K. M. (1973). *Trans. Br. mycol. Soc*. **61**, 383–6.
Lyall, L. H. and Wallen, V. R. (1958). *Can. J. Pl. Sci*. **38**, 215–8.
Maude, R. B. (1966). *Ann. appl. Biol*. **57**, 193–200.
Maude, R. B. and Park, A. M. (1969). *An. Rep. natn. Veg. Res. Stn* **1968**, 93.
Ondreij, M. (1974). *Knizni a Dokunientacni Zpavodaj* **8**, 36.
Sattar, A. (1934). *Trans. Br. mycol. Soc*. **18**, 276–301.
Schenck, N. C. and Gerdemann, J. W. (1956). *Phytopathology* **46**, 194–200.
Sheridan, J. J. (1973). *Ann. appl. Biol*. **75**, 195–203.
Sheridan, J. J. and Dickinson, C. H. (1968). *Ir. J. agric. Res*. **7**, 335–42.
Sorgel, G. (1956). *Phytopath. Z*. **28**, 187–204.
Wallen, V. R. (1957). *Can. J. Pl. Sci*. **37**, 337–41.

Section 6.1.4
Adegbola, M. O. K. and Hagedorn, D. J. (1970). *Phytopathology* **60**, 1477–9.
Barton, R. (1961). *Trans. Br. mycol. Soc*. **44**, 105–18.
Campbell, W. A. and Hendrix, F. F. (1967). *Mycologia* **59**, 274–8.
Carley, H. E. (1969). Factors affecting the epidemiology of pea (*Pisum sativum*) root rot caused by *Aphanomyces euteiches* Drechs. Ph.D. thesis, University of Minnesota, St. Paul, Minn.
Chang-Ho, Y. (1970). *Can. J. Bot*. **48**, 1501–14.
Cunningham, J. L. and Hagedorn, D. J. (1962). *Phytopathology* **52**, 827–34.
Geach, W. L. (1936). *Tasmanian J. Agric*. **32**, 132–43.
Grau, C. R. (1977). *Phytopathology* **67**, 551–6.
Hendrix, F. F. and Campbell, W. A. (1973). *A. Rev. Phytopath*. **11**, 77–98.
Hoppe, P. E. (1966). *Phytopathology* **56**, 1411.
Jones, F. R. and Drechsler, C. (1925). *J. agric. Res*. **30**, 293–325.
Kraft, J. M. and Erwin, D. C. (1968). *Phytopathology* **58**, 1427–8.
Kendrick, J. B. and Zentmyer, G. A. (1957). Recent advances in control of soil fungi. In *Advances in Pest Control* (R. L. Metcalf, ed.). Interscience Publishers, New York.
Lewis, J. A. (1977). *Pl. Dis. Reptr* **61**, 762–6.
McClure, T. T. and Robbins, W. R. (1942). *Bot. Gaz*. **103**, 684–97.

Munnecke, D. E. and Moore, B. J. (1969). *Phytopathology* **59**, 1517–20.
Reiling, T. P., King, T. H. and Fields, R. W. (1960). *Phytopathology* **50**, 287–90.
Scott, W. W. (1961). *A Monograph of the Genus* Aphanomyces. Technical Bulletin no. 151. Agricultural Experiment Station, Virginia.
Sherwood, R. T. and Hagedorn, D. J. (1958). *Determining the Common Root Rot Potential of Pea Fields*. Technical Bulletin no. 531. Agricultural Experiment Station, Wisconsin.
Vaartaja, O. and Bumbieris, A. J. (1968). *Aust. J. biol. Sci.* **17**, 436–45.
Walker, J. C. and Hare, W. W. (1943). *Pea Diseases in Wisconsin in 1942*. Technical Bulletin no. 145. Agricultural Experiment Station, Wisconsin.
Yale, J. W. and Vaughan, E. K. (1962). *Phytopathology* **52**, 1285–7.

Section 6.1.5
Armstrong, G. M. and Armstrong, J. K. (1974). *Phytopathology* **64**, 849–57.
Bolton, A. T. and Donaldson, A. G. (1972). *Can. J. Pl. Sci.* **52**, 189–96.
Bolton, A. T., Nuttal, V. W. and Lyall, L. H. (1966). *Can. J. Pl. Sci.* **46**, 343–7.
Booth, C. (1971). *The Genus* Fusarium. Commonwealth Mycological Institute, Kew.
Booth, C. (1975). *A. Rev. Phytopath.* **13**, 83–93.
Buxton, E. W. (1955). *Trans. Br. mycol. Soc.* **38**, 309–16.
Buxton, E. W. (1957*a*). *Trans. Br. mycol. Soc.* **40**, 145–54.
Buxton, E. W. (1957*b*). *Trans. Br. mycol. Soc.* **40**, 305–16.
Doling, D. A. (1963). *Trans. Br. mycol. Soc.* **46**, 577–84.
Haglund, W. A. and Kraft, J. M. (1970). *Phytopathology* **60**, 1861–2.
Hare, W. W., Walker, J. C. and Delwiche, E. J. (1949). *J. agric. Res.* **78**, 239–50.
Hubbeling, N. (1966). *Neth. J. Pl. Path.* **72**, 206.
Hubbeling, N. (1974). *Meded. Fakulteit Landbouwwetenschappen, Gent* **39**, 991–1000.
Kraft, J. M. and Burke, D. W. (1974). *Pl. Dis. Reptr* **58**, 500–4.
Kraft, J. M. and Roberts, D. D. (1969). *Phytopathology* **59**, 1036.
Kraft, J. M. and Roberts, D. D. (1970). *Phytopathology* **60**, 1814–7.
Labruyère, R. E., Ouden, H. and Seinhorst, J. W. (1959). *Nematologica* **4**, 336–43.
Linford, M. B. (1928). Fusarium *Wilt of Peas in Wisconsin*. Technical Bulletin no. 85, Agricultural Experiment Station, Wisconsin.
Matthews, P. and Dow, P. (1972). *A. Rep. John Innes Inst.* **1977**, 36–8.
Nash, S. M. (1963). *Diss. Abstr.* **24b**, 2211–2.
Schreuder, J. C. (1951). *Tijdschr. PlZiekt.* **57**, 175–206.
Snyder, W. C. (1933). *Science, N.Y.* **77**, 327.
Snyder, W. C. (1935). *Zentbl Bakt.* **91**, 449–59.
Wade, B. L. (1929). *Inheritance of* Fusarium *Wilt Resistance in Canning Peas*. Technical Bulletin no. 97, Agricultural Experiment Station, Wisconsin.

Wells, D. G., Walker, J. C. and Hare, W. W. (1949). *Phytopathology* **39**, 907–12.
Whalley, W. M. (1971). Studies of *Fusarium oxysporum* f. *pisi* (Linf.) Snyder and Hansen in relation to host resistance. Ph.D. thesis, University of Manchester.

Sections 6.2.1–6.2.6
Bos, L. (1967). *Proc. 6th Conf. Czechoslovak Virologists, Olomonc*.
Bos, L. (1970). *Neth. J. Pl. Path.* **71**, 8–13.
Bos, L. and Rubio-Huertos, M. (1972). *Neth. J. Pl. Path.* **78**, 247–257.
Cousin, R., Maillet, P. L., Allard, C. and Staron, R. (1969). *Ann. Phytopath.* **1**, 195–200.
Hagedorn, D. J. and Walker, J. C. (1949). *Phytopathology* **39**, 837–47.
Harrison, B. D. (1966). *Ann. appl. Biol.* **57**, 121–9.
Nault, L. R., Gyrisco, G. G. and Rochow, W. F. (1964). *Phytopathology* **54**, 1269–72.

Section 6.3.1
Dickson, M. H. and Natti, J. J. (1966). *Farm Res.* **32**, 4–5.
Hill, K., Coyne, D. P. and Schuster, M. L. (1972). *J. Am. Soc. hort. Sci.* **97**, 494–8.
Patel, P. N. and Walker, J. C. (1965). *Phytopathology* **55**, 889–94.
Patel, P. N. and Walker, J. C. (1966). *Phytopathology* **56**, 681–2.
Sigee, D. C. and Epton, H. A. S. (1975). *Physiol. Pl. Path.* **6**, 29–34.
Taylor, J. D. (1972). *Ann. appl. Biol.* **70**, 191–7.
Taylor, J. D. and Dudley, C. L. (1977*a*). *Ann. appl. Biol.* **85**, 217–21.
Taylor, J. D. and Dudley, C. L. (1977*b*). *Ann. appl. Biol.* **85**, 223–32.
Taylor, J. D., Innes, N. L., Dudley, C. L. and Griffiths, W. A. (1978). *Ann. appl. Biol.* **90**, 101–110.

Section 6.4.1
Laundon, G. F. and Waterston, J. M. (1965). Uromyces viciae-fabae. Commonwealth Mycological Institute Descriptions of Pathogenic Fungi and Bacteria no. 60. Commonwealth Mycological Institute, Kew.
Wei, C. T. (1937). *Phytopathology* **27**, 1090–1105.

Section 6.4.2
Hewett, P. D. (1973). *Ann. appl. Biol.* **74**, 287–95.

Section 6.4.3
Chu-Chou, M. and Preece, T. F. (1968). *Ann. appl. Biol.* **62**, 11–22.
Deverall, B. J. (1977). *Defence Mechanisms in Plants*. Cambridge University Press, London.
Dixon, G. R. (1975). *J. natn. Inst. agric. Bot.* **13**, 338–41.
Whitehouse, H. L. K. (1949). *Biol. Rev.* **24**, 411–77.

Wood, R. K. S. (1967). *Physiological Plant Pathology*. Blackwell Scientific
   Publications, Oxford.

Section 6.4.4

Albersheim, P., Jones, T. M. and English, P. D. (1969). *A. Rev. Phytopath.* 7,
   171–94.
Allard, C. (1974). *Ann. Phytopath.* 6, 359–83.
Anderson, A. J. and Albersheim, P. (1972). *Physiol. Pl. Path.* 2, 339–46.
Andrus, C. F. and Wade, B. L. (1942). *The Factorial Interpretation of
   Anthracnose Resistance in Beans*. Technical Bulletin no. 810. United States
   Department of Agriculture, Washington, D.C.
Bailey, J. A. and Deverall, B. J. (1971). *Physiol. Pl. Path.* 1, 435–49.
Berard, D. F., Kuć, J. and Williams, E. B. (1972). *Physiol. Pl. Path.* 2, 123–27.
Charrier, A. and Bannerot, H. (1970). *Ann. Phytopath.* 2, 489–506.
Fouilloux, G. (1976). *Annls amelior. plantes* 26, 443–53.
Hallard, J. and Trebuchet, G. (1976). *Rep. Bean Improvement Co-op.* no. 19,
   44–46.
Hubbeling, N. (1961). *Recent Adv. Bot.* 1, 438–43.
Hubbeling, N. (1976). *Rep. Bean Improvement Co-op.* no. 19, 49–50.
Kruger, J., Hoffman, G. M. and Hubbeling, N. (1977). *Euphytica* 26, 23–5.
Leakey, C. L. A. (1970). *Rep. Bean Improvement Co-op.* no. 13, 60–1.
Masterbroek, C. (1960). *Euphytica* 9, 177–84.
Mercer, P. C., Wood, R. K. S. and Greenwood, A. D. (1974). *Physiol. Pl. Path.*
   4, 291–306.
Mercer, P. C., Wood, R. K. S. and Greenwood, A. D. (1975). *Physiol. Pl. Path.*
   5, 203–14.
Rahe, J. E., Kuć, J., Chuang, C. M. and Williams, E. B. (1969). *Neth. J. Pl. Path.*
   75, 58–71.
Skipp, R. A. and Deverall, B. J. (1972). *Physiol. Pl. Path.* 2, 357–74.
Zaumeyer, W. J. and Meiners, J. P. (1975). *A. Rev. Phytopath.* 13, 313–34.

Section 6.4.5

Abawi, G. S., Providenti, R. and Hunter, J. E. (1975). *Proc. Am. Phytopath. Soc.*
   2, 50 (abstract).
Adams, P. B. (1975). *Pl. Dis. Reptr* 59, 599–603.
Adams, P. B. and Tate, C. J. (1975). *Pl. Dis. Reptr* 59, 140–3.

Section 6.4.6

Mitchell, R. and Alexander, M. (1961). *Nature, Lond.* 190, 109–10.
Patrick, Z. A. and Tousson, T. A. (1965). Plant residues and organic amendments
   in relation to biological control. In *Ecology of Soil Borne Plant Pathogens*
   (K. F. Baker and W. C. Snyder, eds). John Murray, London.
Schroth, M. N. and Hendrix, F. F. (1962). *Phytopathology* 52, 751.

Section 6.5.9
Gibbs, A. J., Giussani-Belli, G. and Smith, H. G. (1968). *Ann. appl. Biol.* **61**, 99–107.

FURTHER READING

Section 6.1.1
Mukerji, K. G. (1975). Peronospora viciae. Commonwealth Mycological Institute Descriptions of Pathogenic Fungi and Bacteria no. 455. Commonwealth Mycological Institute, Kew.

Section 6.1.2
Dixon, G. R. (1978). Powdery mildews of vegetables and allied crops. In *The Powdery Mildews* (D. M. Spencer, ed.,), Academic Press, London.
Kapoor, J. N. (1967). Erysiphe pisi. Commonwealth Mycological Institute Descriptions of Pathogenic Fungi and Bacteria no. 155. Commonwealth Mycological Institute, Kew.

Section 6.1.3
Punithalingam, E. and Holliday, P. (1972). Mycosphaerella pinodes. Commonwealth Mycological Institute Descriptions of Pathogenic Fungi and Bacteria no. 340. Commonwealth Mycological Institute, Kew.
Punithalingam, E. and Holliday, P. (1972). Ascochyta pisi. Commonwealth Mycological Institute of Pathogenic Fungi and Bacteria no. 334. Commonwealth Mycological Institute, Kew.
Punithalingam, E. and Gibson, I. A. S. (1976). Phoma medicaginis *var*. pinodella. Commonwealth Mycological Institute Descriptions of Pathogenic Fungi and Bacteria no. 518. Commonwealth Mycological Institute, Kew.

Section 6.1.4
Matthews, V. D. (1931). *Studies on the Genus* Pythium. North Carolina University Press, Raleigh, N.C.
Middleton, J. T. (1943). *Mem. Torrey bot. Club* **20**, 1–171.
Papavizas, G. C. and Ayers, W. A. (1974). Aphanomyces *Species and Their Root Diseases in Pea and Sugarbeet*. Technical Bulletin no. 1485. United States Department of Agriculture, Washington, D.C.
Waterhouse, G. M. and Waterson, J. M. (1964). Pythium aphanidermatum. Commonwealth Mycological Institute Descriptions of Pathogenic Fungi and Bacteria no. 36. Commonwealth Mycological Institute, Kew.
Waterhouse, G. M. (1967). *Key to* Pythium *Pringsheim*. Mycological Papers no. 109. Commonwealth Mycological Institute, Kew.
Waterhouse, G. M. (1968). *The genus* Pythium *Pringsheim*. Mycological Papers no. 110. Commonwealth Mycological Institute, Kew.

Sections 6.2.1—6.2.6

Bos, L. (1973). *Pea Streak Virus*. Commonwealth Mycological Institute/
    Association of Applied Biologists Descriptions of Plant Viruses no. 11.
    Commonwealth Mycological Institute, Kew.
Hampton, R. O. and Mink, G. I. (1975). *Pea Seed Borne Mosaic Virus*.
    Commonwealth Mycological Institute/Association of Applied Biologists
    Descriptions of Plant Viruses no. 146. Commonwealth Mycological Institute,
    Kew.
Harrison, B. D. (1973). *Pea Early Browning Virus*. Commonwealth Mycological
    Institute/Association of Applied Biologists Descriptions of Plant Viruses no.
    120. Commonwealth Mycological Institute, Kew.
Shepherd, R. J. (1970). *Pea Enation Mosaic Virus*. Commonwealth Mycological
    Institute/Association of Applied Biologists Descriptions of Plant Viruses No.
    25. Commonwealth Mycological Institute, Kew.
Smith, K. M. (1972). *A Textbook of Plant Virus Diseases*. Longman, London.

Section 6.3.1

Hayward, A. C. and Waterston, J. M. (1965). Pseudomonas phaseolicola.
    Commonwealth Mycological Institute Descriptions of Pathogenic Fungi
    and Bacteria no. 45. Commonwealth Mycological Institute, Kew.
Zaumeyer, W. J. and Thomas, R. H. (1957). *A Monographic Study of Bean
    Diseases and Methods for Their Control*. Technical Bulletin no. 868, United
    States Department of Agriculture, Washington, D.C.
Zaumeyer, W. J. and Meiners, J. P. (1975). *A. Rev. Phytopath*. **13**, 313—34.

Section 6.4.1

Zaumeyer, W. J. and Thomas, H. R. (1957). *A Monographic Study of Bean
    Diseases and Methods for Their Control*. Technical Bulletin no. 868. United
    States Department of Agriculture, Washington, D.C.

Section 6.4.2

Punithalingam, E. and Holliday, P. (1975). Ascochyta fabae. Commonwealth
    Mycological Institute Descriptions of Pathogenic Fungi and Bacteria no. 461.
    Commonwealth Mycological Institute, Kew.
Sutton, B. C. and Waterston, J. M. (1966). Ascochyta phaseolorum. Common-
    wealth Mycological Institute Descriptions of Pathogenic Fungi and Bacteria
    no. 81. Commonwealth Mycological Institute, Kew.

Section 6.4.3

Ellis, M. B. and Walker, J. M. (1974*a*). Sclerotinia fuckeliana (*Conidial State*:
    Botrytis cinerea). Commonwealth Mycological Institute Descriptions of
    Pathogenic Fungi and Bacteria no. 431. Commonwealth Mycological Institute,
    Kew.

Ellis, M. B. and Walker, J. M. (1974*b*). Botrytis fabae. Commonwealth
Mycological Institute Descriptions of Pathogenic Fungi and Bacteria no. 432.
Commonwealth Mycological Institute, Kew.

Jarvis, W. R. (1977). Botryotinia *and* Botrytis *Species: Taxonomy, Physiology
and Pathogenicity – A Guide to the Literature*. Monograph no. 15.
Department of Agriculture, Ottawa, Canada.

Section 6.4.4

Mordue, J. E. M. (1971). Colletotrichum lindemuthianum. Commonwealth
Mycological Institute Descriptions of Pathogenic Fungi and Bacteria no. 316.
Commonwealth Mycological Institute, Kew.

Zaumeyer, W. J. and Thomas, H. R. (1957). *A Monographic Study of Bean
Diseases and Methods for Their Control*. Technical Bulletin no. 868. United
States Department of Agriculture, Washington, D.C.

Section 6.4.5

Mordue, J. E. M. and Holliday, P. (1976). Sclerotinia sclerotiorum. Commonwealth Mycological Institute Descriptions of Pathogenic Fungi and Bacteria
no. 513. Commonwealth Mycological Institute, Kew.

Walker, J. C. (1952). *Diseases of Vegetable Crops*. McGraw-Hill, New York.

Zaumeyer, W. J. and Thomas, H. R. (1957). *A Monographic Study of Bean
Diseases and Methods for Their Control*. Technical Bulletin no. 868. United
States Department of Agriculture, Washington, D.C.

Section 6.4.6

Booth, C. and Waterston, J. M. (1964). Fusarium solani. Commonwealth
Mycological Institute Descriptions of Pathogenic Fungi and Bacteria no. 29.
Commonwealth Mycological Institute, Kew.

Sections 6.5.1–6.5.11

Bos, L. (1970). *Bean Yellow Mosaic Virus*. Commonwealth Mycological
Institute/Association of Applied Biologists Descriptions of Plant Viruses no.
40. Commonwealth Mycological Institute, Kew.

Bos, L. (1971). *Bean Common Mosaic Virus*. Commonwealth Mycological
Institute/Association of Applied Biologists Descriptions of Plant Viruses
no. 73, Commonwealth Mycological Institute, Kew.

Gibbs, A. J. (1972). *Broad Bean Mottle Virus*. Commonwealth Mycological
Institute/Association of Applied Biologists Descriptions of Plant Viruses no.
101. Commonwealth Mycological Institute, Kew.

Gibbs, A. J. and Paul, H. L. (1970). *Echtes Ackerbohne mosai-virus* (*Broad
Bean True Mosaic*). Commonwealth Mycological Institute/Association of
Applied Biologists Descriptions of Plant Viruses no. 29. Commonwealth
Mycological Institute, Kew.

Gibbs, A. J. and Smith, H. G. (1970). *Broad Bean Stain Virus*. Commonwealth Mycological Institute/Association of Applied Biologists Descriptions of Plant Viruses no. 20. Commonwealth Mycological Institute, Kew.

Semancik, J. S. (1972). *Bean Pod Mottle Virus*. Commonwealth Mycological Institute/Association of Applied Biologists Descriptions of Plant Viruses no. 108. Commonwealth Mycological Institute, Kew.

Shepherd, R. J. (1971). *Southern Bean Mosaic Virus*. Commonwealth Mycological Institute/Association of Applied Biologists Descriptions of Plant Viruses no. 57. Commonwealth Mycological Institute, Kew.

Smith, K. M. (1972). *A Textbook of Plant Virus Diseases*. Longman, London.

Taylor, R. H. and Stubbs, L. L. (1972). *Broad Bean Wilt Virus*. Commonwealth Mycological Institute/Association of Applied Biologists Descriptions of Plant Viruses no. 81. Commonwealth Mycological Institute, Kew.

7
Pathogens of Composite Crops

Relatively few pathogens are considered in this chapter and are mainly those which invade lettuce (*Lactuca sativa*), which is the principal vegetable crop in the family Compositae. *Bremia lactucae* (downy mildew) has received very considerable attention from agronomists, pathologists, plant breeders and physiologists in the last 30–40 years. Breeding has been directed solely at the utilization of monogenic resistance, with a concomitant upsurge of pathogen virulences capable of overcoming each resistance as it was used for commercial lettuce cultivars. Recent discoveries concerning the sexuality of *B. lactucae* and clarification of the host resistance–pathogen virulence picture may eventually lead to more stable forms of host resistance being available. In the meanwhile effective chemical control of this Phycomycete pathogen has become a real possibility (*see* section 4.3.2). Under glasshouse conditions especially, *Botrytis cinerea* (grey mould) is a major problem for those producing lettuce crops. This pathogen is dealt with in section 6.4.3. Powdery mildew (*Erysiphe cichoracearum*) is included since it presents an excellent example of the evolution of a pathogen capable of invading the lettuce crop (*L. sativa*), whereas previously it was confined to wild lettuce (*L. serriola*). A range of virus pathogens are also described since they present major barriers to the production of a crop where there is a zero tolerance to blemish on the part of the eventual purchaser.

7.1 FUNGAL PATHOGENS

7.1.1 *Bremia lactucae* (downy mildew)

Over the last 30 years *B. lactucae* (downy mildew) has become the major pathogen of glasshouse and field-grown lettuce crops. This is especially so in western Europe and Israel. Previously it was reportedly important only on autumn field crops and spring-grown protected crops in these regions. In the USA the disease caused considerable losses for several decades. Reasons for this increased importance are: the breeding of large numbers of lettuce cultivars in the Netherlands, mostly with similar genetic backgrounds, which have been used in all areas of lettuce production in Europe; intensification of production, such that more crops could be obtained from the same land each year at a greater population density per crop; and the lack of any really effective chemical to control the pathogen on susceptible cultivars which possessed desirable agronomic characteristics and were therefore used extensively by growers. This host—pathogen complex is reviewed by Crute and Dixon (1981).

The pathogen will colonise at any growth stage from seedling to mature plant (*see* section 2.1.2). Once inside the leaf, an intercellular mycelium is established with haustoria protruded into the surrounding parenchyma cells. Sporangiophores are produced through the stomata and become the first visible symptom of this disease. They are seen as large numbers of discrete projections bearing sporangia, easily visible to the naked eye, on the undersurface of the leaves of mature plants, but will completely cover cotyledonary and primary leaves (figure 7.1). On mature foliage chlorotic patches develop opposite the areas of sporulation on the undersurface. In severe infections the sporangiophores can be produced so densely as to give a felt-like appearance. As the leaf ages the chlorotic regions become necrotic and brittle, especially around the leaf margins. Usually the outer foliage of mature plants becomes infected and the fungus gradually spreads towards the central leaves. Usually the outer seven leaves are most badly damaged by *B. lactucae*. Where infected plants produce a flower stalk, this and the bracts will become infected. Systemic infection may cause a brown-black

Figure 7.1   Sporulation of *Bremia lactucae* (lettuce downy mildew) on lettuce leaf. (Reproduced by permission of National Vegetable Research Station.)

discoloration in the upper centre of stem tissue and in the leaf bases near the shoot tip; infected plants are slightly stunted.

Bremia lactucae is a Phycomycete (order Oomycetes). It produces coenocytic hyphae which vary in diameter from 5 to 12 µm, and saccate haustoria 15 µm long and 10 µm in diameter. Between one and three asexual sporangiophores are formed from the mycelium in the sub-stomatal cavities. These constrict slightly at the point where they pass the guard cells, but at the leaf surface they are approximately 11 µm in diameter, restricting to 9 µm at the first division. The sporangiophores branch dichotomously between three and six times and are ultimately terminated by a clavate swelling on which are borne four or five sterigmata, each producing a single sporangium. Sporangiophore length varies with environmental humidity from 200 to 1200 µm. The sporangia are hyaline, ovoid-ellipsoidal to globose and 20 µm x 18 µm in size, with a thick smooth wall. Germination is by the direct production of a germ tube, although germination via the production of eight or more swarm spores was reported in the 1920s (Verhoeff, 1960).

Sexual reproduction is by the formation of oospores, a process only recently discovered in this organism (Tommerup *et al.*, 1974). Female oogonia are formed as swollen tips of intercullular hyphae containing up to six nuclei. Potential male antheridia arise in clusters of two or more and contain two or three nuclei. After 4–5 days the oogonium has enlarged to contain up to 12 nuclei and is filled with small lipid droplets. The antheridium with between four and six nuclei becomes perigynously adpressed to the oogonium and a septum forms at the base of each structure. Meiosis probably takes place at this stage, indicating that the vegetative mycelium of *B. lactucae* is diploid. The oogonia reach a maximum size of 30 µm and a fertilisation tube develops between the antheridium and the oogonium, the latter taking on the character of a developing oosphere, having a single large nucleus and large liquid droplets. A single antheridial nucleus passes through the fertilisation tube and is thought to fuse with the oosphere nucleus, forming the oospore or resting spore.

Rapid spread of *B. lactucae* occurs by means of the sporangia, probably in air currents and by splash transfer from one plant to another. Oospore production permits perennation on old host leaves and other plant debris between lettuce crops. Oospores are formed more abundantly in leaves of mature plants than in cotyledonary tissue. Their occurrence appears to be highly random, either in groups or thinly scattered, and not restricted to any specific region of infected leaves, being equally abundant in the green central areas of lesions as the outer necrotic zones.

Environmental conditions influencing oospore germination are unknown, but there is considerable information on the germination of sporangia. Various values for the optimal temperature for germination have been quoted, but between 15 and 21 °C the germination percentage and length of germ tubes increase in direct proportion to time. The temperature at which sporangia are produced also influences their ability to germinate, those formed at high temperatures being less viable than those produced at low temperatures. Optimal penetration, subsequent growth of hyphae and formation of haustoria occurs at 15–17 °C; 24 h after inoculation at these temperatures, hyphae 34–46 μm long are present within the leaf tissue. As might be expected with a Phycomycete fungus, sporangial germination, penetration and the development of mycelium within the leaf are favoured by high relative humidity. Sporangiophore production is also influenced by high humidity; indeed it has been shown that before sporangiophores can be produced the leaf surface needs to be covered by a film of water, but this process is tolerant of a wide temperature range, namely 6–23 °C. Sporangial germination is also influenced by relative humidity, for it is claimed that complete immersion in water is required. Two types of sporangia have been identified: those with hyaline, minutely granular contents and those with opaque, coarsely granular contents, the latter being non-viable. These environmental requirements are summarised in table 7.1.

Table 7.1 Summary of environmental requirements of *B. lactucae* (after Verhoeff, 1960)

Physiological process	Relative humidity	Temperature (°C)
Sporangial germination	Water droplets	2–10
Growth of germ tubes	Water droplets	15
Penetration via epidermal cells	Water droplets	10–22
Spread of mycelium, formation of haustoria, filling substomatal cavities	High humidity	20–22
Production of sporangiophores	Water film	6–23

Control of *B. lactucae* has largely rested on the use of resistant cultivars. Over the last 50 years, more than 100 cultivars have been produced possessing race-specific resistance and at least 30 distinct physiological races of the pathogen identified. Considerable confusion has arisen because these races have been given varying nomenclature by different workers. Thus, in different countries, they have been labelled as follows: Israel, IL1–IL3; Netherlands, NL1–NL7; UK, W1–W9; USA, races 1–5. For growers, particularly outside the Netherlands, there has been the additional problem of interpreting the resistance description given to Dutch-bred cultivars in terms of the races of *B. lactucae* present in areas where they wished to grow the cultivar, since no direct parallel was available between the resistance as cited in terms of Dutch races of *B. lactucae* and the races in their own country. Utilising the data obtained from cultivar testing by many workers and some independent testing, Johnson *et al.* (1977) identified five different dominant resistance genes of major effect in *L. sativa*: *Dm 2*, *Dm 3*, *Dm 4*, *Dm 6* and *Dm 8* and a pair of dominant genes with complementary effect, *Dm 7/1* and *Dm 7/2*. Sources of this resistance are summarised in table 7.2. It is possible to equate these with some of the 10 virulence factors in *B. lactucae* and postulate a gene-for-gene relationship between host resistance and pathogen virulence. Using this model it should be possible to study the frequency of virulence factors and identify those with low frequency, thereby indicating resistance genes which might be incorporated into a breeding programme. A considerable survey of *B. lactucae* virulences was mounted in the UK (Dixon and Wright, 1978; Dixon, 1978). Samples of lettuce infected with *B. lactucae* were collected from seven areas of the UK during 1973–77 and tested on a range of differentially resistant cultivars to determine the frequency

Table 7.2 Putative sources of resistance to *Bremia lactucae* (Crute and Johnson, 1976).

Postulated resistance gene	Source	Lettuce type	Primary reference
1	Blondine	No information of origin, spring butterhead	Tjallingii and Rodenburg (1967)
2	Meikoningen	Winter forcing butterhead, 1902	Schultz and Roder (1938)
3, 4	Gotte à forcer types	French winter forcing	Ogilvie (1944)
5	*L. serriola* PI 167150	Wild collection from Turkey	Zink (1973)
6	Grand Rapids	Oak leaf	Verhoeff (1960)
7	Romaine blonde lente à monter	French 'Romaine'	Jagger and Chandler (1933)
8	*L. serriola* PI 91532	Wild collection from the USSR	Jagger and Whitaker (1940)
9	Bourgiugnonne grosse blonde d'hiver	French winter forcing butterhead	Jagger and Whitaker (1940)
10	Sucrine	Cos, 1880	Channon and Smith (1970)

Table 7.3 Occurrence of virulence factors in *Bremia lactucae* samples during 1973–77.

Year	Virulence factors								
	1	2	3	4	5	7	8	9	10
1973	–	92	50	62	–	36	50	–	–
1974	–	76	86	88	–	58	51	–	–
1975	100	65	66	70	65	72	60	41	51
1976	100	71	79	79	62	85	49	64	63
1977	100	85	94	100	52	92	39	44	37
Mean	100	78	75	80	60	69	50	50	50

Data are the percentages of samples containing each virulence at high frequency, that is where more than 50 per cent of cotyledons of a differential test cultivar showed sporulation following inoculation.
– , no suitable differential available.

of virulence factors in each pathogen population. A summary of results is given in table 7.3.

The major feature revealed by this survey was the high frequency in most areas of the UK of all virulence factors compatible with the resistances used in most breeding programmes. This indicated that without a major change in direction towards new sources of resistance, for example interspecific hybridisation with other *Lactuca* species containing resistances for which the *B. lactucae* population contained no comparable virulences, further breeding using major genes would prove ineffective because the pathogen had the capacity to overcome all known resistances in most samples tested. Even use of close relatives of *L. sativa* is insufficient to provide resistant material, since *L. sativa* cv. Hilde x *L. serriola* crosses to give cultivars such as Capitan and Mantilla were susceptible to the pathogen before their release into commerce. It is possible that use can be made of resistance identified in *L. saligna*, which is thought to be controlled by a complex pattern of recessive genes (Netzer *et al.*, 1976). The alternative avenue would be to use non-specific resistance, but this implies that there would be a certain level of infection present on the host. This may not be an acceptable alternative with vegetable crops such as lettuce, where the concept of zero damage is applied to the product being sold and consumed. Differences between the levels of infection on cultivars in field trials with apparently no specific resistance which might indicate some form of non-specific resistance were noted by Dixon *et al.* (1973).

Husbandry control relies on the maintenance of low relative humidity under glass. Experiments whereby the land to be used for lettuce production has been brought to field capacity prior to planting out seedlings in peat blocks and thereafter little or no irrigation applied have considerably reduced the levels of infection. Also, placing the blocks on the soil surface rather than planting them in the border soil, thereby ensuring a free flow of air around the young seedlings, will reduce disease incidence. In the Westland region of Holland, use is made of the 'quiet growing system' in an attempt to overcome B. lactucae, with day temperatures of 12 °C and 5 °C at night, the night regime starting at 15.00 but the ventilators remaining open until the glasshouse temperature has fallen to the night temperature. It is essential to remove moisture from the crop at the end of the day, and if necessary the grower will raise the temperature to lower relative humidity. Since oospores have been shown to be a significant means of perennation it is essential to remove all debris after the crop. On the open field scale rotations should be practised. Composite weeds are also hosts to B. lactucae, but their significance as a reservoir of infection is unknown since attempts to cross-inoculate between weeds and lettuce have generally been unsuccessful.

Chemical control of this pathogen requires frequent applications of large amounts of material. Dust formulations are preferred as they do not increase the relative humidity. In the Netherlands applications of zineb and thiram dusts are made every 7 days at the propagation stage; thereafter three or four applications are made post-planting with at least 14 days clearance between the last application and cutting. In the UK zineb and mancozeb are used either individually or in combination, the first spray or dust being applied when half the seedlings have germinated and repeated every 7 days. This is decreased to every 3 days if there is a nearby source of infection. When used as dusts, some phytotoxicity can occur at low temperatures, so that a minimum night temperature of 6 °C is required on the night following application. The advent of acylalanine derivatives which have systemic activity against B. lactucae should improve chemical control (see section 4.3.2). These materials can be incorporated into the blocking compost, thereby protecting the plant from germination onwards.

Studies by Zink and Duffus (1969, 1970, 1973) into the relationship between resistance to B. lactucae in L. sativa and L. serriola and resistance to Turnip Mosaic Virus (TuMV, see section 5.2.5) showed that resistance to TuMV and B. lactucae are each controlled by single dominant genes designated Tu and Dm. The TuMV-susceptible gene tu is linked with the downy mildew resistant gene Dm. A survey of cultivated lettuce (L. sativa) cultivars indicated that TuMV susceptibility is restricted to downy mildew-resistant crisphead types such as Calmar, Imperial 410, Imperial Triumph, Valrio, Valtemp and Valverde, while resistance to TuMV and downy mildew is present in butterhead-type cultivars such as May King, Meikoningen, Proeftuin's Blackpool, Ventura; leaf types Red Salad Bowl, Salad Trim; and cos type Valmaine. Crosses between TuMV-susceptible/downy mildew-resistant L. serriola and TuMV-susceptible/downy mildew-resistant *L. sativa* cultivars of the Calmar and Imperial type indicated that they possess the same dominant allele for downy mildew resistance and the same recessive allele for TuMV susceptibility. This relationship arises from the use of *L. serriola* (PI 91532) in the breeding of *L. sativa* cvs Calmar and Imperial.

7.1.2 *Erysiphe cichoracearum* (powdery mildew)

Most Compositae are hosts to *E. cichoracearum*, including vegetables such as lettuce (*L. sativa*), artichokes (*Cynara scolymus, Helianthus tuberosus*), chicory (*Cichorum intybus*) and endive (*C. endivia*). The fungus colonises seedling and mature leaves and stems appearing on the upper surface as white lesions which are initially discrete but gradually enlarge and coalesce. Under conditions of heavy infection the undersurface of the leaf will also be colonised. Affected foliage loses lustre, curls, becomes chlorotic, then brown and dies. Diseased lettuce plants have a dusty, off-colour appearance, with yellowing and browning of diseased leaves and a perceptible odour. This Ascomycete (order Plectomycete) produces a well-developed mycelium, with conidia borne in long chains which are elliptical to barrel-shaped and 25–45 μm x 14–26 μm in size. Large cleistothecia (90–135 μm in diameter) are formed in autumn with unbranched external appendages up to 500 μm long. Internally the asci are ovate and borne on a short stalk and measure 60–90 μm x 25–50 μm; ascospores are produced in pairs. Both *E. cichoracearum* and *Sphaerotheca fuliginea* cause powdery mildew of cucurbits and closely resemble each other morphologically and anatomically. They can be distinguished by the characters shown in table 7.4.

The minimum temperature for infection by *E. cichoracearum* is 6–10 °C and the maximum is 27 °C. Highest percentage germination takes place with a relative humidity of 95–98 per cent, but a totally saturated atmosphere inhibits germination. The pathogen has world-wide distribution. A most interesting feature has been the evolution of strains attacking wild (*L. serriola*) and cultivated lettuce (*L. sativa*) in California and neighbouring states of the USA.

Table 7.4 Differentiation of *Erysiphe cichoracearum* and *Sphaerotheca fuliginea*.

Character	*E. cichoracearum*	*S. fuliginea*
Colour of mycelium	Floury white	Rusty brown
Conidia	Form well-differentiated appressora	Produce forked germ tubes
Number of asci	10–25 per cleistothecium	1 per cleistothecium

Initially *E. cichoracearum* was found on wild lettuce in the Salinas Valley, then a physiologically distinct strain was identified on commercial cultivated lettuce. Later, mixed infections of both strains were found on wild lettuce in the field, and it is suggested that the wild attacking strain mutated to produce a strain capable of colonising cultivated lettuce which are grown close to *L. serriola* populations in the Salinas Valley. The strain pathogenic to *L. sativa* is now spreading north and south of the Salinas Valley and may have reached Arizona. Initially only the asexual stage was found on *L. sativa*, with perithecia on *L. serriola*, but in the 1950s perithecia were found in abundance on a crop of the cultivar Great Lakes. Subsequent testing for resistance showed that none of the crisphead and non-heading leafy types were resistant, and only butterheads such as Arctic King, Big Boston, Salad Bowl and Bath Cross (a red-leaved cos type) possessed resistance. Chemical control can be achieved with materials such as karathane, benomyl, carbendazim and thiophanate-methyl.

7.2 VIRUSES

7.2.1 Lettuce Big Vein Virus (LBVV)

Several viruses are known to be transmitted by soil-borne fungi, one of which is LBVV with the vector *Olpidium brassicae*. The virus is carried within the fungal zoospores which are released from resting spores into the soil moisture films. Penetration of the root cells is accomplished by the zoospore attaching to the outer cell wall, forming a cyst and then producing a projection tube. Through this the contents of the encysted zoospore pass into the root cell. The virus has not been isolated and characterised, nor can the vector be grown in pure culture. Soil transmissibility of LBVV is lost when the virus is transmitted by grafting to lettuce plants free from *O. brassicae*. When virus-free *O. brassicae* are introduced into such plants soil transmissibility is restored. Isolates of *O. brassicae* free from LBVV acquire the virus from roots of graft-inoculated plants during the first vegetative generation of the fungus in the roots. Soil containing *O. brassicae* carrying LBVV can be air-dried and retain infectivity for at least 8 years.

Initial symptoms include a very marked vein clearing followed by enlargement and bleaching of the vascular regions of petioles and leaf blades. Further vein banding and pronounced savoying of the leaves takes place as the host matures until the lettuce has a stark appearance with whitened veins standing out against the greener interveinal tissue. Host range is considered to be limited to the Compositae family. So far this disease has been reported only in western Europe, New Zealand and lettuce-producing states of USA, especially California. Control can be achieved only by means of soil sterilisation (*see* section 4.3.4).

7.2.2 Lettuce Mosaic Virus (LMV)

This virus is transmitted mechanically, through seed and by aphid vectors, particularly *Myzus persicae, Macrosiphum euphorbiae* and *Acyrthosiphon scariolae-barri*. Alate instars of *M. persicae* are less efficient vectors than the apterae. The virus is stylet-borne (non-persistent), transmission efficiency rises with increasing acquisition access time from 5 to 120 min. The incidence of seed-borne virus ranges from 1 to 8 per cent in different lettuce cultivars, but seed transmission does not occur in the cultivar Cheshunt Early Giant because the primary flower heads are killed by the pathogen, and later flowers produce normal seed. Transmission occurs through both the pollen and ovules of infected plants. The virus particle is a flexuous rod 750 nm long and 13 nm wide.

Symptoms on mature butterhead lettuce (*L. sativa*) consist of dwarfing, malformed hearts, mottling, yellowing, necrosis and leaf distortion. Mottling and yellowing are more prominent in the early season while necrosis and scorching become evident in summer. Vein clearing is common in both infected seedlings and mature plants together with irregular pale blotching, and the whole leaf may take on a hard yellow appearance similar to wind damage. Leaf morphology is changed with increased blistering and ballooning, while marginal serrations typical of some cultivars disappear when infected by LMV. Necrosis begins as small lesions between the veins or as definite veinal necrosis and marginal leaf scorch. Mosaic becomes evident when the flower stalk is produced. The leaves on the stem and inflorescence exhibit pronounced mottling, possibly accompanied by necrosis, and the whole plant may be stunted. In some cultivars necrotic lesions form on the stem, bracts and flower buds, while the flowers may fail to open. Seed production is reduced. Once infected the virus is distributed systemically within the lettuce plant.

Vein clearing is the primary symptom on cos cultivars (*L. sativa*) with more or less intense mottling. The plants tend to be stunted with leaf scorching, but veinal chlorosis is less frequent. Failure to produce a dense compact heart is a useful diagnostic symptom if mottling is not expressed. Other vegetable hosts include pea (*P. sativum*) and endive (*Cichorium endivia*). Four strains of the virus have been characterised in California, USA, by symptoms produced on lettuce and pea. The virus has world-wide distribution but is of particular economic significance in California and Europe.

Spread occurs through seedlings grown from infected seed and from neighbouring infected crops. This led to suggestions for cultural control in which over-wintered plants or the seed beds from which winter crops are transplanted should not be sited close to other lettuce crops. Crops of similar age should not be scattered about a holding but planted in blocks and separated from others spatially. New drillings or plantings should not adjoin older crops. Open sites are preferred to enclosed ones and seed beds should be away from hedges, woods and buildings.

The use of virus-free seed, however, would provide an efficient means of control. Because of the widespread distribution of the virus this is difficult to achieve, but by use of isolation and roguing it is feasible to produce seed with less than 0.1 per cent infected seeds, and this provides an efficient control measure for early summer field crops. Most reputable seed houses index their seed for virus content by growing samples of seed and visually examining young seedlings for signs of infection. So far no methods of inactivating the virus in seed or of separating infected from uninfected seed have been developed, although diseased seed has been shown to be lighter than healthy. Seed with contamination greater than 0.1 per cent constitutes a considerable economic risk to the grower.

Some Dutch lettuce cultivars have been developed with tolerance to LMV, for when infected they remain symptomless. There is a lower rate of LMV multiplication in tolerant cultivars compared to susceptible ones (table 7.5). Tolerant cultivars present a considerable risk in that the particles which do multiply may be mutant strains capable of causing more severe outbreaks of the disease.

Table 7.5 Lesion development on *Chenopodium quinoa* when inoculated with sap from Lettuce Mosaic Virus-tolerant and -susceptible lettuce cultivars (after Tomlinson and Faithfull, 1975a).

Cultivar	No. lesions on *C. quinoa*	
Cil	2	Tolerant
Obo	5	Tolerant
Avira	1	Tolerant
Suzan	107	Susceptible
Hilde	128	Susceptible
Unrivalled	114	Susceptible

7.2.3 Lettuce Necrotic Yellow Virus (LNYV)

This virus is transmitted by the aphids *Hyperomyzus persicae* and *H. carduellinis*, the former being the major vector. The virus persists through a moult of the vector and is of the circulative (persistent) type. Sowthistle (*Sonchus oleraceus*) is the main field source of both virus and vector; lettuce which is not a host of the aphid probably becomes infected when probed by migrating aphids. The host range is limited, and geographical distribution is restricted to Australia and South Island, New Zealand. Virus particles are baccilliform, 230 nm long and 65 nm wide. The particle has an outer envelope covered with uniformly arranged projections enclosing an internal component consisting of a long filament coiled in a regular shallow helix of pitch 4.5 nm.

Following infection of lettuce (*L. sativa*) there is a change from the normal vivid green of healthy plants to a dull green, some foliage becoming bronzed and necrotic, and accompanied by severe chlorosis, flattening of the developing heart, wilting and death. Symptoms on older leaves are reminiscent of mineral deficiency, with strong chlorotic mottling. Wilting and mortality are increased by high temperatures but recovery may occur at low temperatures.

Where infection takes place before hearting, segments of the primary and secondary veins become reddened, particularly on leaves close to the growing point; this leads to internal chlorosis.

On spinach (*Spinacia oleracea*), primary vein netting occurs about 40 days after infection. This is followed by leaf distortion, which may be confused with genetic abnormalities.

Tomatoes (*Lycopersicon esculentum*) may also act as hosts to LNYV. Symptoms are slight interveinal chlorosis, with rusting, bronzing and interveinal mottling of mature foliage. Although infected plants are stunted, flowers and fruit are produced normally and no symptoms appear on the fruit.

In the weed host *S. oleraceus*, virus particles have been identified in the cytoplasm of mesophyll cells, epidermal cells, hair cells, immature xylem and sieve tubes. These particles are usually enveloped in a membrane. Subsequent to symptom development there is degradation of nuclei, chloroplasts and mitochondria and loss of some types of chloroplast ribosomes.

The major avenue of control is to eradicate sowthistle (*S. oleraceus*) weeds from lettuce crops. This may be done with the pre-emergence herbicide mixture propham with diuron and methylisopropylphenyl carbamate; alternatively, use can be made of propyzamide, a soil-acting herbicide, on land being prepared for lettuce, but well in advance of planting or drilling.

7.2.4 Beet Western Yellows Virus (BWYU)

Synonyms of this virus include Turnip Yellow Virus (TYV), Radish Yellow Virus (RYV) and Turnip Mild Yellow Virus (TMYV). The main vector is the aphid *Myzus persicae* and in Germany *Dysaulocorthum vincae* and *Rhopalomyzus ascalonicus*. Vectors retain an ability to transmit after moulting, but the virus is not passed on to progeny. Transmission is of the circulative type and persists in the vector for up to 50 days. Some differences have been found in the efficiency with which virus isolates are transmitted by the vectors and these relate to virus concentrations in the host. Particles are isometric and of approximately 26 nm in diameter. The pathogen has been reported in North America, Europe and Asia, but is probably common throughout the world. Host range is wide, some 100 species of 21 dicotyledonous families being susceptible. Variant strains have been distinguished on the basis of host range and virulence. These strains predominate in particular plant species, thus the Turnip Yellow strain is most common in turnip (*B. campestris*). The variants will not cross-protect when inoculated into the same plant.

The most common symptom is interveinal yellowing of the older or intermediate leaves especially under high light intensity. In turnips symptoms first develop on maturing crops from September onwards as a red discoloration of the leaf followed by rapid chlorosis of the entire lamina, which becomes hard and brittle. Plants are dwarfed and the root yield severely reduced. Internally, gummosis occurs in the phloem and starch accumulates in the shoots. Virus particles appear to be confined to the phloem and are associated with phloem degradation. They are found in the nuclei of phloem parenchyma cells.

In England the virus causes a serious yellowing syndrome on butterhead, crisp and cost lettuce crops with intense outer leaf chlorosis. This is caused by chloroplast degeneration, during which there is disappearance of grana stacks, stroma lamellae and the appearance of abnormally large starch grains in the chloroplasts followed by increased numbers of lipid granules (Tomlinson and Webb, 1978). Symptoms on lettuce resemble those caused by magnesium deficiency; Tomlinson and Walker (1973) showed that tissue from infected plants contained significantly less magnesium, potassium, calcium, nitrogen and phosphorus compared to healthy plants. Trials indicate that the cultivar Merida expresses symptoms more severely than other outdoor butterhead types such as Avondefiance, Cobham Green, Hilde and Suzan. Applications of the systemic fungicide carbendazim to lettuce plants after inoculation with BWYV led to almost total symptom suppression, although the virus titre in these plants was unaffected (Tomlinson and Faithfull, 1975*b*).

The lettuce strain does not cause symptoms when inoculated on red beet plants. This host, when infected by its own strain of BWYV, is more susceptible to attack by *Alternaria* spp.

REFERENCES

Section 7.1.1

Channon, A. G. and Smith, Y. (1970). *Hort. Res.* **10**, 14–19.

Crute, I. R. and Johnson, A. G. (1976). *Ann. appl. Biol.* **83**, 125–37.

Crute, I. R. and Dixon G. R. (1981). Downy mildew diseases caused by *Bremia* Regel. In *The Downy Mildews* (D. M. Spencer, ed.). Academic Press, London.

Dixon, G. R. (1978). Monitoring vegetable diseases. In *Plant Disease Epidemiology* (P. R. Scott and A. Bainbridge, eds). Blackwell Scientific Publications, Oxford.

Dixon, G. R., Tonkin, M. H. and Doodson, J. K. (1973). *Ann. sppl. Biol.* **74**, 307–13.

Dixon, G. R. and Wright, I. R. (1978). *Ann. appl. Biol.* **88**, 287–94.
Jagger, I. C. and Chandler, N. (1933). *Phytopathology* **23**, 18–19.
Jagger, I. C. and Whitaker, T. W. (1940). *Phytopathology* **30**, 427–33.
Johnson, A. G., Crute, I. R. and Gordon, P. L. (1977). *Ann. appl. Biol.* **86**, 87–103.
Netzer, D., Globerson, D. and Sacks, J. (1976). *Hort. Sci.* **11**, 612–13.
Ogilvie, L. (1944). *A. Rep. Agric. Hort. Res. Stn Bristol Univ.* **1943**, 90–4.
Schultz, H. and Roder, K. (1938). *Züchter* **10**, 185–94.
Tjallingii, F. and Rodenburgh, C. M. (1967). *Zaadbelangen* **21**, 104–5.
Tommerup, I. C., Ingram, D. S. and Sargent, J. A. (1974). *Trans. Br. mycol. Soc.* **62**, 145–50.
Verhoeff, K. (1960). *Tijdschr. PlZiekt.* **66**, 133–203.
Zink, F. W. (1973). *J. Am. Soc. hort. Sci.* **98**, 293–5.
Zink, F. W. and Duffus, J. W. (1969). *J. Am. Soc. hort. Sci.* **94**, 403–7.
Zink, F. W. and Duffus, J. E. (1970). *J. Am. Soc. hort. Sci.* **95**, 420–2.
Zink, F. W. and Duffus, J. E. (1973). *J. Am. Soc. hort. Sci.* **98**, 49–51.

Sections 7.2.1–7.2.4
Tomlinson, J. A. and Faithfull, E. M. (1975*a*). *A. Rep. natn. Veg. Res. Stn* **1974**, 119.
Tomlinson, J. A. and Faithfull, E. M. (1975*b*). *A. Rep. natn. Veg. Res. Stn* **1974**, 118–9.
Tomlinson, J. A. and Walker, V. M. (1973). *A. Rep. natn. Veg. Res. Stn* **1972**, 97–9.
Tomlinson, J. A. and Webb, M. J. W. (1978). *Physiol. Pl. Path.* **12**, 13–18.

FURTHER READING

Section 7.1.2

Dixon, G. R. (1978). Powdery mildews of vegetable and allied crops. In *The Powdery Mildews* (D. M. Spencer, ed.). Academic Press, London.
Kapoor, J. N. (1967). Erysiphe cichoracearum. Commonwealth Mycological Institute Descriptions of Pathogenic Fungi and Bacteria no. 152. Commonwealth Mycological Institute, Kew.

Sections 7.2.1–7.2.4

Duffus, J. E. (1972). *Beet Western Yellows Virus*. Commonwealth Mycological Institute/Association of Applied Biologists Descriptions of Plant Viruses no. 26. Commonwealth Mycological Institute, Kew.
Franki, R. I. and Randless, J. W. (1970). *Lettuce Necrotic Yellows Virus*. Commonwealth Mycological Institute/Association of Applied Biologists Descriptions of Plant Viruses no. 26. Commonwealth Mycological Institute, Kew.

Smith, K. M. (1972). *A Textbook of Plant Virus Diseases*. Longman, London.
Tomlinson, J. A. (1970). *Lettuce Mosaic Virus*. Commonwealth Mycological
    Institute/Association of Applied Biologists Descriptions of Plant Viruses
    no. 9. Commonwealth Mycological Institute, Kew.

8

Pathogens of Umbelliferous Crops

The most significant Umbelliferous crops, carrot (*Daucus carota*) and parsnip (*Pastinaca sativa*), are grown for their edible roots while with celery (*Apium graveolens*) the edible petioles are blanched, by earthing up, especially in the UK but to a lesser extent in Europe and the USA. In consequence, some of the most important pathogens are those which disfigure or cause the decay of roots or petioles. Also these crops provide excellent examples of storage rots, for example *Mycocentrospora acerina*. Violet root rot caused by *Helicobasidium purpureum* is of interest in relation to control by rotation. It is now evident, particularly in East Anglia (UK), that carrots and sugar beet are important hosts and must be widely separated in the rotation. Foliar blights can cause considerable damage to the growing phases of these crops and also to herb crops. Although the latter are produced on small areas their profitability is such as to warrant more attention from pathologists. The recent study of parsnip canker provides an example of the elucidation of a complex disease syndrome and its partial control by plant breeding. The sections covering virus pathogens are divided on the basis of whether the principal host is carrot, celery or parsnip, but several viruses have wider host ranges and extensive numbers of insect vectors – *see* especially Celery (Western) Mosaic Virus (section 8.2.5). Some disease syndromes require several viruses to be present in the host, for example Carrot Motley Dwarf, while the phenomenon of 'helper' viruses is exemplified by Carrot Mottle Virus.

8.1 FUNGAL PATHOGENS

8.1.1 *Septoria apiicola* (leaf spot)

Synonyms for this pathogen are *S. apii*, *S. apii-graveolentis* and *S. petroselenii*, while the disease is also referred to as late blight of celery (*A. graveolens*) and celeriac (*A. graveolens* var. *rapaceum*). The fungus is seed-borne and has world-wide distribution. It is the most important disease of celery and *S. apiicola* is rated as the most destructive of *Septoria* parasites.

In early literature distinction was made between *S. apii-graveolentis*, causing small leaf lesions, and *S. apii*, causing large leaf lesions. Following extensive studies by Gabrielson and Grogan (1964), using a world-wide collection of isolates, only one species (*S. apiicola*) is now recognised. The fungus penetrates directly into host leaves and petioles to establish an intracellular mycelium. Symptoms begin as chlorotic spots or flecks which later turn necrotic. Lesions may remain less than 3 mm in diameter (figure 8.1) or expand up to 10 mm, with several lesions coalescing together. The necrotic areas have a definite margin and are surrounded by a chlorotic halo which merges gradually into uninfected

Figure 8.1   Lesions on a celery leaf caused by *Septoria apiicola* (leaf spot). (Reproduced by permission of National Institute of Agricultural Botany, Cambridge.)

tissue. Mycelium is not restricted to the lesion but ramifies into apparently uninfected tissue around the lesion. Asexual pycnidia form quickly after infection is established, appearing as conspicuous small black bodies. Where the lesions remain small, pycnidia are numerous and scattered throughout the lesion, but in larger lesions the pycnidia are concentrated near the centre and are few in number. The necrotic tissue is reddish-brown towards the lesion centre and a darker reddish-brown at the periphery. Numbers of pycnidia produced have been inversely related to high levels of peroxidase activity in the host cells. Greater peroxidase production is associated with low light intensity and chlorosis is related to reduced peroxidase activity. Numbers of pycnidia were high on infected older leaves exposed to green light (of wavelength 515 nm) at about $12 \, J \, m^{-2} \, s^{-1}$ compared to infected controls grown under white light of $35.5 \, J \, m^{-2} \, s^{-1}$. On young leaves, however, exposed to orange light (640 nm) with little chlorotic tissue and low peroxidase levels there were large numbers of pycnidia and these were clustered together (Benedict, 1973). These effects of enzyme activity and light may go some way towards explaining the types of symptom development originally used to separate different species of *S. apiicola*.

The brown-black, globular pycnidia form immersed within the leaf or petiole tissue and are 75–195 μm in diameter. The pycnidial walls are up to three cells thick. These cells have thin cell walls of pale-brown pseudoparenchymatous tissue; the cells are darker and thickened towards the pycnidial ostiole. Asexual conidia within the pycnidium are hyaline, needle-shaped and have between one and four septa, tapering slightly towards the apex; they measure 22–56 μm in length and 2–2.5 μm in width. Conidia form as phialospores from hyaline aseptate conidiophores which develop from the innermost layer of cells in the pycnidium; the dimensions of the conidiophore are 8–10 μm x 3–3.5 μm. *Septoria apiicola* is classed as a Fungus Imperfectus (order Sphaeropsidales).

The extent of specialisation within *S. apiicola* is ill defined; some authors state that isolates from celery and celeriac are unable to infect parsley and vice versa, whereas others claim to have achieved cross-infection. Successful infections have been established on celery with isolates from *A. australe*. Weed hosts may therefore form a reservoir of infection from which spread takes place to cultivated celery.

The major means of transmission of *S. apiicola* is via infected seed, but infected debris is an important means of perennation and local dissemination. The disease is not usually seen on crops until late in the season, but may occasionally appear in the seed bed, usually resulting in death of the seedlings. Conidia have survived up to 10 months on celery leaves under laboratory conditions and for at least 4 months on debris in soil. Pycnidia, mycelium and conidia are found on infected seed; the pathogen is absent from seed embryos and endosperms, but mycelium penetrates pericarps and testas. Infected seed carried viable conidia for up to 15 months at room temperature and for longer periods at -20 °C (Sheridan, 1966). Conidia will germinate over the temperature range 9–28 °C with the optimum being at 20–25 °C. Rainy weather favours dissemination and epidemic development, as conidia transmitted from plant to plant by rain-splash or irrigation water. The latter is especially important in this crop, which it is derived from bog land progenitors and requires large quantities of irrigation water. Crop rotation is a significant means of control since Maude and Shuring (1970) showed that celery transplanted in June could be infected from crop debris carrying *S. apiicola* put into the soil 9 months earlier. Viable conidia were extracted from buried debris for as long as visible plant material persisted. From this work it is recommended that there should be at least a 2 year break between plantings of celery on the same land.

Hot water treatment of celery seed, 25 min at 50 °C, developed by Bant and Storey (1952), gives almost complete control of seed-borne infection but tends to depress germination. Complete control without this defect is obtained by soaking the seed for 24 h at 30 °C in an aqueous suspension of 0.2 per cent thiram (Maude, 1970).

Chemical control can be achieved where field infection becomes established. In Germany control on celeriac (*A. graveolens* var. *rapaceum*) was greatest with tin plus maneb mixtures compared to benomyl, copper oxychloride and mancozeb. The usefulness of organotin for control of *S. apiicola* has been extensively studied by Ryan and co-workers in Eire. For this work assessment techniques involving measurement of leaf and petiole infection and numbers of diseased petioles per plant, together with gross and marketable yields, were used. In New Zealand, captafol has been found more effective than maneb or captan, while benomyl and carbendazim gave only poor control.

Some sources of resistance are reported in celery cultivars grown in Egypt, Switzerland and the USA.

8.1.2 *Erysiphe heraclei* (powdery mildew)

Most umbelliferous crops are susceptible to this pathogen, which is also referred to as *E. umbelliferarum*. Hosts include angelica (*Angelica archangelica*), carrot (*Daucus carota*), celery (*Apium graveolens*), coriander (*Coriandrum sativa*), dill (*Anethum graveolens*), fennel (*Foeniculum vulgare*), parsnip (*Pastinaca sativa*) and parsley (*Petroselinum crispum*). Symptoms are typical of powdery mildew infection on other crops, including the development of a white mycelial cobweb on the upper leaf surface (figure 8.2). The outer, more mature leaves are attacked first and then infection spreads to more juvenile foliage. When young plants are attacked they are either killed or their vigour is greatly reduced. Infection is usually associated with foliar senescence. The use of fungicides to control *E. heraclei* on parsnips in the UK, however, gave no significant yield response, but there was a trend towards increased total weight and larger root sizes in the sprayed plots.

Powdery mildew is particularly important as a pathogen of crops produced in Mediterranean regions and in India. Epidemics are severe on winter-sown carrots

Figure 8.2 Foliage of carrot showing infection by *Erysiphe heraclei* (powdery
mildew). (Reproduced by permission of National Institute of
Agricultural Botany, Cambridge.)

in Israel when the crop reaches the 10–12 week stage and was estimated by
Netzer and Katzir (1966) to be one of the two major foliar diseases of Israeli
carrots. Outbreaks of the disease also occur in the Turin area of Italy on the
types Nantes, Palesean and Nantes x Palesean hybrids; France; Jersey; and
occasionally in dry summers on carrots grown in the black fen areas of East
Anglia (UK). Herb and celery crops are reported to be sporadically infected in
Italy with severe crop losses in certain seasons. Indian coriander (*C. sativa*) crops
are frequently infected in March. On this host the fungus spreads rapidly,
affecting leaves, stems and peduncles; development of the flowers and fruits is
retarded so that they remain immature. Losses of up to 80 per cent of seed yield
are reported for late season crops. Infection leads to losses of seed yield, colour
and quality.

A typical Ascomycete (order Plectomycetes), *E. heraclei* forms a well-
developed extracuticular mycelium with lobed haustoria produced into the
epidermal cells. Cylindrical conidia develop either singly or in chains; the conidia
measure 34–46 μm x 14–20 μm. The sexual cleistothecia are initially globular
in shape but then become flattened, produced in a scattered or thinly grouped
manner; they measure 85–120 μm in diameter. Appendages on the cleistothecia
are formed largely from the base in large numbers; these are narrow to rather
coarse, mycelium-like and are often interlaced with the mycelium. They grow

up to 200 μm in length and branch at least once (but generally more frequently) to give a coral-like appearance. Within the cleistothecium are formed between three and 10 elliptical or globular asci, of 55—70 μm x 30—45 μm, each containing between three and six ascospores. Each of these ascopores is ovate to elliptical in shape and 20—28 μm x 10—15 μm in size. *Erysiphe heraclei* can be distinguished from other *Erysiphe* species by the possession of irregularly branched appendages in large numbers and elongate cylindrical conidia. Some physiological specialisation is thought to occur, three host-specialised strains on carrot, fennel and parsley, respectively, having been separated on the basis of conidial measurements (Marras, 1962). The total host range covers at least 85 umbelliferous genera with widespread geographical distribution in Mediterranean and semi-tropical areas. Reports of transmission on carrot seed have been made in the Netherlands and India and on parsley seed in Hungary.

Chemical control can be achieved by the use of systemic materials such as benomyl, carbendazim and thiophanate-methyl or protectants such as maneb plus morestan, triphenyltin acetate or triphenyltin hydroxide. Some levels of field resistance have been noted with carrot and parsnip cultivars. In carrots this was related to maturity class while the parsnip cultivar Avonresister showed particular freedom from disease in UK trials (G. R. Dixon, unpublished data).

8.1.3 *Alternaria, Cercospora* and *Phoma* spp. (foliage blights and root rots)

Several species of these imperfect fungal genera incite similar diseases on various members of the Umbelliferae. Each pathogen is dealt with separately, together with host symptoms and host range, but control techniques are covered collectively at the end of the section.

(a) *Alternaria dauci* (foliar blight)

Symptoms caused by *A. dauci* and *Cercospora carotae* are similar. Both attack the leaves but the lesions caused by *A. dauci* tend to be more elongated, irregular in shape and lack a definite margin. Usually *A. dauci* infects older leaves, often causing single leaflets to collapse and die. Generally it appears later in the season than *C. carotae*. Asexual conidia are produced superficially in the lesion; these are 30—100 μm long and have the multiseptate character typical of *Alternaria* spp., they are dark coloured, club-shaped, with a long appendage at the distal end borne on short dark conidiophores. The broadest end of the conidium is attached to the conidiophore. Taxonomically it is placed in the order Moniliales.

Generally found on carrot crops in temperate and Mediterranean regions, *A. dauci* has been studied in particular in Israel. *Alternaria dauci* is seed-borne, mycelium being found both on the 'seed' surface and as a compressed layer between the pericarp and testa (Netzer and Kenneth, 1969). Apparently it is unable to infect parsley (*Petroselinum crispum*), celeriac (*Apium graveolens* var. *rapaceum*) and fennel (*Foeniculum vulgare*) but is found on weed hosts: *Daucus maximus, Ridolfia segetum* and *Caucalis tenella*. Saprophytic perennation occurs between carrot crops on discarded foliage; viability on such debris is reduced where there is alternate wetting and drying, as happens following winter and early spring harvests in Israel, but is prolonged for at least 3 months when there is no rain, as with late spring and summer harvests. Also *A. dauci* remains viable longer if infected debris remains on the soil surface rather than if it is buried to a depth of 20 cm.

Auxotrophic (thiamine-deficient) and prototrophic pathogenic cultures of *A. dauci* were isolated from natural lesions (Netzer and Kenneth, 1970). Individual hyphae, when separated from germinating conidia, behaved in accordance with their origin, indicating that the multinucleate conidium is homokaryotic. When proto- and auxotrophic conidia were plated together, apparently heterokaryotic hyphae were produced but subsequent daughter conidia segregated into the original parental types. Elsewhere strains of *A. dauci* which only synthesise indoleacetic acid (IAA) in the presence of tryptophan precursor have been isolated.

(b) *Alternaria radicina* (black root rot)

Commonly referred to in the literature as *Stemphyllium radicinum, A. radicina* causes black rot of carrot (*Daucus carota*) but is also pathogenic to parsley (*Petroselinum crispum*), parsnip (*Pastinaca sativa*) and dill (*Anethum graveolens*). Symptoms produced on carrot leaves and petioles are similar to those of *A. dauci* but with more widely distributed lesions. Generally *A. radicina* causes pre- and post-emergence damping-off. Primary taproot lesions on older plants begin at the petiole base, developing into a dark shallow black lesion which spreads into the crown and on to the root shanks. Lesions are irregular to circular in outline, slightly depressed, but not more than 3 mm deep. Decayed tissue is greenish to jet black and the surface is covered in conidiophores bearing conidia. Secondary lesions can form below ground level, often coincident with cracks and splits which develop for nutritional or other reasons. In storage infected roots develop a dry mealy rot. The pathogen has widespread distribution throughout temperate and Mediterranean areas.

Colonies of *A. radicina* (order Moniliales) are dark blackish-brown to black, containing conidiophores which arise singly or in groups. These are usually simple and unbranched, up to 200 μm long and 3–9 μm thick with one to several conidial scars. Conidia are solitary or borne in chains of two or three; they are of variable shape from elliptical to pear-shaped, with the broadest end attached to the conidiophore.

Each conidium is divided by between three and seven transverse and one to several longitudinal or oblique septa, possibly with a constriction at each septum; size ranges are 27–57 μm long x 9–27 μm at the broadest part. No physiological specialisation has been noted.

As with *A. dauci, A. radicina* is seed-borne and perennates on carrot debris in the soil. The fungus was shown by Maude and Moule (1972) to have a longevity of at least 8 years in mineral soil. Infection is thought to develop first on the foliage and then progress to the root. Contamination of healthy roots takes place from infected foliage during harvest leading to decay in store. The fungus is tolerant of a wide temperature range (−0.5−34 °C) with optimal growth at 28 °C. Russian workers have shown that the pathogen is borne both superficially and within the 'seed', and that sporulation is enhanced by darkness. Viability on infected debris is lost more quickly when this is buried rather than left on the soil surface.

(c) *Cercospora carotae* (foliar blight)

A widespread carrot pathogen, *C. carotae* is rated as the main foliar disease of carrots, affecting both cultivated and wild forms of *Daucus*. Elongate lesions form at the leaflet margins, giving rise to unequal growth of the leaflet and consequent curling. Lesions elsewhere on the lamina appear as pin-sized chlorotic spots developing a necrotic centre and a more diffuse border. Lesion colour varies with relative humidity; when this is low lesions tend to be tan-coloured, becoming darker under moist conditions. Coalescence between spots is common.

Cercospora carotae (order Moniliales) forms a mycelium within the leaf and petiole tissue from which conidiophores erupt through the stomata or burst in clusters from the epidermis. Conidiophores are dark and unbranched, carrying successive hyaline conidia which are multiseptate and of 2.2−2.5 μm x 40−100 μm in dimension. Perennation between crops is on seed or infected debris. Penetration takes place through the stomata, with optimal germination at 28 °C.

The conidia are usually wind transmitted. In contrast to *A. dauci* the pathogen infects younger foliage rather than older leaves.

(d) *Cercospora apii* (foliar blight)

Known as 'early blight' of celery in contrast to 'late blight' caused by *Septoria apiicola*, this pathogen is of major importance on celery crops in both southern and northern states of the USA.

Symptoms appear as round chlorotic spots which rapidly become 1 cm or more in diameter and darken in colour. At the centre of such lesions conidiophores erupt through the epidermis from the mycelium which has colonised within the leaf tissue. On petioles the lesions are elongated, developing parallel to the longitudinal axis of the organ.

Mycelium of *C. apii* (order Moniliales) is pale brown and torulose. Aggregations of mycelium into sclerotial-like structures 20−50 μm in diameter form in the substomatal cavities. From these structures, brown septate conidiophores of 3.5−5.5 μm x 40−180 μm develop in groups. Several conidia are produced separately on each conidiophore; a scar is left where the ripe conidium is detached. Conidia are multiseptate and club-shaped with the broadest end attached to the conidiophore and tapering towards the apex; they measure 3.5−4.5 μm x 22−290 μm. The fungus is both seed- and soil-borne, perennating between crops on infected celery debris. Conidia are wind and rain-splash distributed. Sporulation is greatest with more than 8 h of high relative humidity and temperatures of less than 15 °C. In epidemic conditions, in excess of 6000 conidia were trapped per day, with numbers reaching a peak at noon and being at their lowest at night. The celery—*C. apii* host—parasite complex has been studied for many years in Florida, USA, leading to the development of disease-tolerant lines. Recently, Berger (1973) used these to examine the effects of mixed susceptible and tolerant host populations on the development of epidemics of this compound interest disease. Disease incidence and infection rates (*see* section 3.1) of *C. apii* on susceptible celery plants decreased as the percentage of blight-tolerant plants in the population was increased. This effect was largely lost when disease incidence rose above 25 per cent. There were no significant differences in the infection rates of susceptible and tolerant celery lines for a major portion of the epidemic, suggesting that tolerance was only effective at low inoculum densities.

(e) *Phoma apiicola* (root and crown rot)
Celery (*Apium graveolens*) and celeriac (*A. graveolens* var. *rapaceum*) are the principal hosts of *P. apiicola*, but parsnip (*Pastinacea sativa*), parsley (*Petroselinum sativum*), carrot (*Daucus carota*) and caraway (*Carum carvi*) are also found to be susceptible. It is primarily a cause of storage rotting, but infections are initiated in the field.

A light-coloured lesion which forms into an irregular red blotch is found on the foliage and has been reported on the floral organs of celeriac (*A. graveolens* var. *rapaceum*). In moist conditions pycnidia develop on the lesions. Where the outer petioles of mature plants are penetrated, the fungus usually progresses into the crown. Invaded areas are initially blue-green, but turn black and have a scurfy texture as the disease develops. Death of the epidermal tissue leads to cracking of the crown. Infection may lead to the root system near the crown being destroyed, after which the plant will topple over due to lack of anchorage or in milder cases be badly stunted.

Initially the mycelium of *P. apiicola* (order Sphaeropsidales), which grows internally, is hyaline, but it darkens with age. Very old mycelium may be torulose and resemble that of *Mycocentrospora acerina* (*see* section 8.1.6). Asexual pycnidia form immersed in host tissue, but on maturity they erupt with a short beak piercing the epidermis. Pycnidia vary in size, measuring $70-175$ μm x $180-420$ μm. The pycnospores are almost oblong in shape and measure $1-1.6$ μm x $3-3.8$ μm. The temperature range of fungal growth is $-5-30$ °C, with an optimum of $16-18$ °C for mycelial growth, pycnidial formation and spore germination. *Phoma apiicola* is seed-borne and also persists on infected debris.

All five pathogens discussed in this section are seed-borne; consequently seed treatment is of utmost importance for their control, either by use of hot water treatment (50 °C for 25 min) or using a thiram soak (24 h at 30 °C in

0.2 per cent aqueous thiram suspension). Fungicidal sprays may be used to control field infections using materials such as thiram or zineb. The latter reduced disease incidence due to *A. radicina* by 45 per cent in Russian trials. However, numerous sprays may be required; for instance Florida celery growers apply 25–40 sprays to control *C. apii* over the 3–4 month life of the celery crop. Since soil-borne trash is an important element in the perennation of these pathogens, use of soil sterilant chemicals such as quintozene and dazomet will give control and may be economical for high value crops such as celery and some herb crops. Cultural control is essential, using wide rotations and avoiding land where previous crops have been attacked by these pathogens for up to 10 years. Deep cultivation to place infected debris well down in the soil will also reduce future levels of inoculum. Breeding for resistance appears to have been attempted only for celery against *C. apii*. This resulted in only tolerant cultivars, suggesting a lack of strong sources of resistance; the resistance source used was a hollow stemmed Turkish celeriac (*A. graveolens* var. *rapaceum*).

8.1.4 *Helicobasidium purpureum* (violet root rot)

Violet root rot was first described in 1728 and has since been identified on a wide range of crop plants such as asparagus (*Asparagus officinalis* var. *altis*), celery (*Apium graveolens*), beet (*Beta vulgaris*), carrot (*Daucus carota*), parsnip (*Pastinacea sativa*), parsley (*Petroselinum crispum*) and potato (*Solanum tuberosum*) and on weeds such as yarrow (*Achillea millefolium*), couch-grass (*Agropyron repens*), sweet vernal grass (*Anthoxanthemum odoratum*), thistle (*Cirsium* spp), silverweed (*Potentilla anserina*), creeping buttercup (*Ranunculus repens*), sheep's sorrel (*Rumex acetosella*) and dock (*Rumex* spp.). Distribution of the pathogen is widespread throughout Europe and the USA.

Symptoms on the aerial parts of plants infected by *H. purpureum* are not distinctive; the foliage turns chlorotic, wilts and eventually dies. Subterranean regions of the host, on the other hand, bear a characteristic external mat of mycelium which is initially pale buff to violaceous and gradually turns red-violet to violet-brown. The dense mycelial mat contains numerous closely aggregated papillae which resemble sclerotia and are somewhat darker than the rest of the mycelium. Internally rotting of the host organ may proceed until little is left of the original tissue except the outer 'skin'. Where a number of infected roots occur in close proximity, the pathogen may grow over the soil surface as a thick chocolate brown mat up to 30 cm long and 15 cm wide; in severe cases this mat may extend upwards around the plant base.

Helicobasidium purpureum is a Basidiomycete (order Hymenomycetes) characterised by the production of curved basidia growing directly on the mycelium. Hyphal branches arise at right angles with a septum not more than 10 μm from each junction. The mycelium is branched septate and evenly distributed over the host surface. Aggregations into papillae are easily visible to the naked eye, being rounded, flattened and covered with a thick velvety felt; these aggregations vary in size from a few millimetres to several centimetres. Such aggregations serve as infection cushions from which penetration into the host tissues is achieved (*see also Thanetophorus cucumeris*, section 5.1.6). The perfect basidial stage is found only during limited periods in spring, the hymenium being purplish-violet in colour. On this hymenium there develop hyaline septate basidia. From each basidium there arise two or four sterigmata which are 10–35 μm long and carry hyaline basidiospores varying in shape from oval to reniform and 10–12 μm x 6–7 μm in size. Initially the mycelial stage was grouped in the imperfect genus *Rhizoctonia*, and in French literature is often still referred to as *R. violacea.*

The pathogen is soil-borne and infection develops sporadically throughout a crop grown on infected land. Spread through the soil is slow. Byford and Prince (1976) showed that severe infection of sugar beet reduced both root weight and sugar yield; indeed the sugar content of heavily diseased roots fell by 30 per cent compared to that of healthy controls.

Crop rotation is the main means of control, and in this context cereal break crops are valuable. Where susceptible crops such as beet and carrots are allowed to succeed each other on infected land, losses can be high. It is preferable to lift and store such crops in the autumn rather than allow them to stand for prolonged periods. Experiments in the UK showed that carrot crops with only 1 per cent of infected roots in June contained 86 per cent of infected roots by December. Soil fumigation has been advocated in France for small areas which are to be cropped with high value plants such as asparagus, but for others this would be uneconomic at present. Debris from diseased crops should be disposed of, not left to form foci for further infection and, care should be exercised to prevent machinery from spreading the pathogen to uninfected land.

8.1.5 Canker

Canker is the major disease of parsnips in the UK and has been reported on crops in Australia and the USA. The cause of this syndrome has been attributed to a range of fungal pathogens and physiological disorders, but work by Channon and co-workers elucidated the major causal organisms. Two types of canker are found: black canker, caused by *Intersonilia pastinacae*, a *Phoma* sp. or *Ascochyta* sp. and *Mycocentrospora acerina* (*see* section 8.1.6), and orange-brown canker. The cause of the latter is uncertain, it is less common than the black type and may have a physiological origin.

(a) Black canker
On parsnip roots *I. pastinacae* causes dark brown or purplish-black rotting lesions which vary from a few millimetres to several centimetres in diameter. Where the root surface is unbroken the lesions are sunken and somewhat obscured, but if the underlying tissue is exposed it has a rough scurfy appearance. With more advanced cases rotting extends into the cambial zone, but more often penetration

is restricted to within 5 mm of the root surface. Lesions most frequently occur on the root shoulder and crown, sometimes developing on the shank, and are frequently centred on lateral root bases. At the same time as black cankers form on the roots in autumn, brown or orange-brown lesions of 1 mm diameter surrounded by pale green halos form on the leaves. These may coalesce or enlarge to form necrotic areas in the centres or margins of leaflets. Extensive lesion formation on the petioles and inflorescences have been reported by Channon (1969) as caused by *I. pastinacae*. Seeds are also infected both superficially and more deeply.

Intersonilia pastinacae is a Basidiomycete (order Hymenomycetes), identified by ballistospore reproduction and possession of mycelium in which frequent clamp connections are found. On agar the mycelium is 2.0–2.7 μm in diameter with clamp connections at most septa, producing hyaline, sub-reniform or pyriform ballistospores of 11.4–20.0 μm x 7.2–11.4 μm borne singly on sporophores which develop from terminal inflations measuring 10.6–12.9 μm x 7.4–9.3 μm. Abundant, thick-walled, spherical chlamydospores 8.9–11.7 μm in diameter are formed in clusters or chains throughout the mycelium (Channon, 1963).

Perennation of *I. pastinacae* in soil probably occurs by the chlamydospores or on infected parsnip roots. Spread within crops is likely to take place by movement of ballistospores, which infect the leaves and thereby give rise to root infections. Trapping experiments showed that most ballistospores were released at about 10.00 in parsnip crops. Some spread of the pathogen may take place through infected seed.

An unidentified *Phoma* or *Ascochyta* sp. is also thought to contribute to the canker syndrome. Characteristically, this produces pycnidia which bear ostioles with short papillae; pycnospores measure 5.8–7.8 μm x 2.0–2.5 μm. The outer wall of each pycnidium is formed of one or two layers of dark cells and the pycnospores are unicellular, indicating a *Phoma* sp., but some are bicellular and might therefore be an *Ascochyta* sp. Artificial inoculation of parsnip foliage with isolates of this fungus gave risk to dark brown or purplish-brown necrotic lesions with yellow-green halos.

(b) Orange-brown canker

Lesions of this disorder vary in size but are usually shallow, with the periderm sloughed off, giving·a scurfy appearance to exposed tissue. Initial development of orange-brown canker may be associated with horizontal growth cracks in the periderm. Orange-brown canker is usually restricted to the shoulders of the root and is less common than black canker. No causal organism has been identified with this disorder.

Canker can be controlled by treatment of infected seed for 24 h at 30 °C in 0.2 per cent aqueous thiram and by soil sterilisation, although the latter is not economic on large areas. A major effort was made in the 1950s to develop the canker-resistant cultivar Avonresister (Channon *et al.*, 1970). Resistance was found to be expressed in a non-specific manner as either a smaller proportion of infected roots or reduced lesion size or both when compared to a susceptible commercial cultivar. This was achieved by continuous field selection on a range of mineral and organic soil types over several seasons. Parsnips are both partially self-fertilised and cross-fertilised, therefore the breeding technique involved the establishment of several basic seed lines which were selected for freedom from canker and other agronomic attributes. The best roots from the best lines were grown in separate groups and allowed to mass pollinate in isolation from the other groups, seed from each plant being separately harvested and grown as progeny rows. The resultant best roots were reselected and, after three cycles of line breeding, lines were multiplied by mass pollination, with some lines being bulked together. This programme resulted in a more resistant cultivar with improved uniformity of root size and shape with less lateral root formation. But Avonresister possesses two defects: the overall root size tends to be small and has a very thin skin which ruptures easily. These factors have prevented it from becoming widely grown, but it does form the basis for further commercial breeding.

8.1.6 *Mycocentrospora acerina* (storage rot)

In the literature this pathogen is commonly referred to as *Centrospora acerina*; however, this generic name has now been adopted for an algal genus and *Mycocentrospora* should be applied to the fungus. A major cause of deterioration of celery under cool storage, *M. acerina* causes the disease liquorice rot; on carrots it is known as black rot, while it has also been implicated in the parsnip canker syndrome (*see* section 8.1.5).

Large, black, sunken lesions which contain torulose mycelium are found on the shoulders, shanks and root tips of carrots attacked by *M. acerina*. Rotting at the tap root tip is a very characteristic symptom, particularly if the tap root has been damaged or broken in the harvesting operation. If such roots are incubated under moist conditions an aerial mycelium possessing a pinkish tinge develops. This coloration can be used to distinguish rotting caused by *M. acerina* from that due to *Alternaria* and *Stemphylium* spp., which give rise to dark mycelium and spores. Other pathogens which cause storage rots of carrot and celery are *Botrytis cinerea* (*see* section 6.4.3) and *Sclerotinia sclerotiorum* (*see* section 6.4.5).

Liquorice rot caused by *M. acerina* is thought to be the major factor limiting the storage potential of celery in the UK and the USA. During storage infected celery heads develop spreading black lesions centred at the junctions between petiole bases and the celery stem (butt). Within each lesion is a torulose mycelium characteristic of *M. acerina*. When infection is severe the whole region of attachment between the petiole and butt collapses as a black rotten mass with the remains of the petiole being left loosely attached to the stem (Derbyshire and Crisp, 1971). Infection is usually centred on those parts of the petioles which have been below soil level in the field, and lesions contain chlamydospores, mycelium but rarely conidia. Chlamydospores are common on necrotic areas of the petiole, around leaf scars and on attached soil particles. Rotting usually starts after 8–10 weeks of storage at 2 °C. The infection process has been described by Day et al. (1972). Germinating conidia and chlamydospores produce a single germ tube. These grow randomly over the epidermis, penetrating intact cuticle or damaged areas but rarely through stomata. Two types of appressorium are formed from the germ tube, either a simple pyriform structure 50 μm long and 30 μm wide or a bifurcate structure with equal lobes 30 μm long and 20 μm wide. From beneath the appressorium an infection peg, about 10 μm in diameter. grows through the cuticle and into the epidermal cell. Following penetration the hypha grows to 10–15 μm in diameter, passing across the cell lumen and out through the opposite wall. Further colonisation is both inter- and intracellular. Behind the developing lesion large numbers of chlamydospores form. Tissue in front of the advancing lesion edge is macerated and infected cells collapse. Initially the lesions are cinnamon-coloured, but turn black as chlamydospores are formed. Lesions tend to be longitudinal since the invasion process is impeded by host cells thickened by collenchyma. Most lesions develop at the sides of petioles and in the centre of petiole bases. Infection was found to be randomly distributed in stored plants, indicating that spread from plant to plant was rare.

A long phase of 5–6 weeks occurs between the commencement of storage and development of infection. Only when host tissue has begun to senesce is infection successful.

Mycocentrospora acerina is a Fungus Imperfectus (order Hyphomycetes) producing multiseptate needle-shaped conidia 110–200 μm long x 10–12 μm wide; these have a characteristic whip-like terminal appendage and a second lateral appendage somewhat resembling a germ tube arising from the basal cell. Conidia develop from torulose mycelial fragments (Iqbal and Webster, 1969).

The major source of infection is from soil fragments, and invasion is thought to take place from soil while the crop is in the field or to be transferred to uninfected plants during trimming preparatory to storage. But water has been shown to contain *M. acerina*, consequently infection could occur where celery is irrigated or washed with unchlorinated water. The fungus rarely causes disease in the field. In artificial inoculation tests parsnip seedlings died quickly but carrots only developed leaf spotting symptoms. Work in Norway has related high levels of potassium fertiliser to increased incidence of *M. acerina* on celery.

Fungicidal control has been achieved on celery with either 1 per cent benomyl dips or soaking for 15 min in 1 per cent benomyl. Similar treatment of carrots, while not eradicating black root rot, reduced its incidence considerably. But these techniques should be viewed as additions to the storage process; only high quality produce should be put into store and it must be handled carefully at all stages.

8.2 VIRUSES

8.2.1 Carrot Mosaic Virus (CMsV)

This virus is transmitted by the aphids *Acyrthosiphon pisum, Cavariella aegopodii* and *Myzus persicae*. The dimensions of the filamentous virus particle are 752 nm in length and 15 nm in diameter.

Mosaic symptoms develop on the outer leaves but not on younger foliage. Large spots of 1−2 mm diameter without a distinct outer limit are distributed over the leaf blade. Older leaves become curled, possibly with red or orange spots. Lesions forming on the umbelliferous flower stalks may lead to lodging, but the developing seeds are uninfected.

8.2.2 Carrot Mottle Virus (CMtV)

The aphid *Cavariella aegopodi* is the principal vector of CMtV, although *Hemaphis heraclei* has been reported as transmitting the virus under artificial conditions in Japan. Although the virus is circulative and retained by its vector for some time, being passed through moults, transmission can take place only in the presence of a 'helper' virus, which in this case is Carrot Red Leaf Virus. Together these viruses give rise to the syndrome Carrot Motley Dwarf. Carrot Mottle Virus ceases to be aphid-transmissible if mechanically inoculated or transmitted by *C. aegopodii* to host plants which are not also hosts to Carrot Red Leaf Virus. The requirement for a 'helper' virus is thought to be due to encapsidation of the nucleic acid of CMtV by protein from CRLV, and this permits aphid transmission of the dependent virus. Particles of CMtV are approximately spherical, 52 nm in diameter.

Under natural conditions CMtV probably occurs only in mixed infections with CRLV − *see* Section 8.2.3 for the symptoms of Carrot Motley Dwarf. Where coriander (*Coriandrum sativum*) is used as a test plant the symptoms caused by CMtV are mild systemic chlorotic mottle or yellowing with slight necrotic spotting and some dwarfing. Symptomless systemic infection has been reported for carrot (*Daucus carota* cv. Gold Pak) and celery (*Apium graveolens* cv. Spartan).

Cytological changes attendant on infection by CMtV have been described only for leaf tissue of the indicator plant *Nicotiana clevelandii* when systemically infected. Eight to nine days after inoculation the concentration of virus particles reaches its maximum in the cell vacuoles. Starting 6 days after inoculation, tubules appear in the cytoplasm associated with the plasmodesmata. Some tubes become enclosed in cell wall material, forming outgrowths of the plasmodesmata and extended towards the cell vacuole, while others extended towards the nucleus, leading to invaginations of the nuclear membrane.

The virus has been reported from Australia, California (USA), Japan, New Zealand and the UK.

8.2.3 Carrot Red Leaf Virus (CRLV)

As well as being transmitted by the aphid *Cavariella aegopodii*, there is a possibility that CRLV can be seed-borne. As with CMtV, it is circulative (persistent), being retained for 1–2 weeks and passed through moults. Vector efficiency rises when feeding times are extended to several days. By acting as a 'helper' virus to CMtV the latter becomes aphid-transmissible. In combination CMtV and CRLV give rise to the syndrome known as Carrot Motley Dwarf disease.

Symptoms incited by CRLV alone are reddening and chlorosis of foliage; the whole plant may become crimson or there may be only slight discoloration of the more mature leaves. Host range is confined to the Umbelliferae and so far the virus has been reported only in Australia and the UK.

Carrot Motley Dwarf symptoms start with stunting of semi-mature foliage accompanied by twisting of the petioles, which particularly on older leaves can lead to the lower leaf surface being turned upwards. The central groove of the leaf is accentuated, while individual leaflets become distorted and stunted. Irregular chlorotic mottling is a primary symptom, often followed by yellowing of the leaf margin; leaf reddening develops later.

Care must be exercised in identifying the cause of this disease since reddening of carrot foliage can arise for a variety of reasons. Similar symptoms have been attributed by German workers to a complex of three viruses, Carrot Mottle Virus, Carrot Red Leaf Virus and Parsnip Mottle Virus. The CMtV component of Motley Dwarf can be identified with reasonable certainty since it is the only carrot virus which is persistent in the vector and also manually transmissible by sap. Apparent tolerance to Carrot Motley Dwarf has been reported in the parsley (*P. crispum*) cultivars Claudia and Bravour, but tests on the mode of inheritance gave confusing results.

8.2.4 Celery Latent Virus (CLV)

Identified only in Italy, so far only mechanical transmission of this virus has been achieved. Its particles are flexible rods, 860 nm long. Inoculated celery (*A. graveolens*) seedlings remained symptomless but celeriac (*A. graveolens* var. *rapaceum*) sometimes developed chlorotic lesions.

8.2.5 Celery (Western) Mosaic Virus (CeMV)

Many aphids are vectors of CeMV, including *Aphis graveolens, A. fabae, A. gossypii, A middletoni, Aulacorthum circumflexum, Cavariella aegopodii, C. pastinacea, Dysaphis apiifolia, Hyadaphis mellifera, Myzus circumflexus, M. convulvuli* and *M. persicae*. Particles of CeMV are rod-shaped, varying from 760 to 780 nm in length.

Initially infected plants bear their leaves parallel to the soil instead of in an upright position; this is accompanied by foliar chlorosis and dwarfing of developing petioles. There is vein clearing and puckering of young leaves with speckling of older foliage, the margins of which may turn chlorotic. Later, necrotic rust-coloured specks occur on the upper surface of outer leaves. These may enlarge, forming necrotic sunken areas which combine into streaks or irregular lesions on the leaf margins. Following this the leaflets become narrowed, twisted and cupped. Alternating white and green streaks form on the petioles, often accompanied by bleached spots. This syndrome can be differentiated from Cucumber Mosiac Virus (Celery (Southern) Mosaic Virus – *see* section 11.3.2) by the absence of necrotic lesions and irregular zones on the upper surface of mature foliage, these being typical of secondary systemic symptoms of CeMV. In the UK, CeMV has been reported as responsible for chlorosis and stunting of coriander (*C. sativum*) and golden-yellow chlorosis and necrotic spotting of parsley (*Petroselinum crispum*).

A Crinkle-Leaf strain has been differentiated from the type strain of CeMV on the basis of symptomatology and host range. On celery (*A. graveolens*) symptoms consist of a yellow mottle with raised blister-like areas and a pronounced crinkling of the foliage which distinguishes this variant from true CeMV. Initial symptoms are vein clearing on the most juvenile foliage followed by yellow vein banding which leaves the interveinal areas remaining green. These bands are narrow to begin with but slowly spread out, becoming diffuse. Such symptoms may be confined to the basal part of the leaf. Although both the type strain of CeMV and Crinkle-Leaf variant are restricted in host range to the Umbelliferae, the variant will cause symptom development on Long Smooth Parsnip (*Pastinaca sativa*) and anise (*Pimpinella anisum*), whereas the type strain will not. Further strains related to CeMV have been isolated from parsley (*Petroselinum crispum*) in California (USA) and distinguished from the type strain by serological tests. Cytological studies have indicated the presence of pinwheel and tubular inclusions in cells infected by CeMV.

Control of CeMV was achieved in California (USA) by the enforcement of a celery-free period, thereby eliminating the largest source of virus inoculum. Such a policy is unlikely to be effective in other celery-growing regions, such as the UK, where weed hosts like wild hemlock (*Conium maculatum*) provide a reservoir of inoculum. This is the commonest umbelliferous weed in the celery-growing fenland areas of East Anglia (UK). Other significant weed hosts of CeMV are hogweed (*Heracleum spondylum*), cow parsley (*Anthriscus sylvestris*) and wild parsnip (*Pastinaca sativa*). Field trials with the celery cultivars Lathom Blanching, Ely White, New Dwarf White and Fenlander showed that there was 30 per cent reduction in yield of the fourth-mentioned cultivar following infection by CeMV but no detectable effect on the other three cultivars.

8.2.6 Celery Ring Spot Virus (CeRSV)

Two separate viruses are thought to give rise to this disease syndrome, Celery

Ring Spot Virus and Hemlock (Poison) Ring Spot Virus. The former has been transmitted only mechanically and even then with difficulty. When infected with CeRSV, pale green and yellow rings or ring patterns develop on celery leaves. When these occur as local lesions they are up to 3 mm in diameter. If infection becomes systemic the rings are paler and may be diamond-shaped, and stunting may take place. Hemlock (Poison) Ring Spot Virus can be mechanically transmitted from parsley to parsley (*P. crispum*) but not from poison hemlock (*C. maculatum*) to celery (*A. graveolens*). insect transmission occurs through the aphid *Rhopalosiphum conii* in which the virus is non-persistent.

Symptoms on parsley (*P. crispum*) are a vivid pattern of ringspots, broken yellow lines and green or chlorotic vein banding. The spots have an outer chlorotic halo and an inner green rim within which is a chlorotic centre. Mature celery (*A. graveolens*) foliage, but not the juvenile foliage, shows symptoms. These develop as pale green lines or bands which may later turn chlorotic. Four types of ringspotting have been described: yellow or band-encircling green tissue, greening enclosing a chlorotic centre, concentric alternating yellow and green lines surrounding a green area, possibly surrounded by a pale yellow halo. Other hosts include chervil (*Anthriscus cerefolium*), on which as well as chlorotic banding there is a development of necrotic spots and purpling or browning of the foliage; coriander (*C. sativum*), where typically the leaf tips turn yellow; carrot (*D. carota*), the leaves of which develop sunken chlorotic areas. There may be chlorotic rings either with or without a green centre and cleared veinlets, and in parsnip (*P. sativa*) usually the ring symptoms are absent, with only the outer leaves developing pale green zones.

Hemlock (Poison) Ring Spot Virus can be differentiated from CeRSV in that the former is transmissible to parsley (*P. crispum*) and has an aphid vector whereas CeRSV posesses neither of these attributes.

8.2.7 Celery Yellow Net Virus (CeYNV)

As with CeRSV this virus has only been shown to be mechanically transmissible, and with difficulty. In the field, infected celery (*A. graveolens*) has bright yellow flecks and bands which are most conspicuous along the main veins. Plants are stunted and mis-shapen; the petioles show necrotic streaks which may lead to the death of the outer leaves, and this may eventually be followed by death of the inner leaves and crown. Seedlings have been infected artificially and the primary symptom was systemic vein clearing followed by stunting, rosetting, yellow veinal flecks, leaf buckling and eventual plant death. Parsley (*P. crispum*) and carrot (*D. carota*) have been infected artificially, symptoms being systemic pale green spotting of young foliage, which in parsley (*P. crispum*) was followed by sparse ringspotting which later turned necrotic.

8.2.8 Celery Yellow Spot Virus (CeYSV)

Transmitted by the aphid *Rhopalosiphum conii*, this virus is circulative (persistent). Vegetable hosts include celery (*A. graveolens*) and parsnip (*P. sativa*). On celery, symptoms are irregular pale green areas which turn chlorotic, with spotting and striping concentrated along the veins and randomly scattered over the leaf lamina. The small spots may eventually coalesce and their yellow colour change to a bleached effect. Similar bleached lesions can form on the petioles. Beneath the epidermis of such lesions are brown flecks. Infected parsnips (*P. sativa*) show only mild mottling.

8.2.9 Parsnip Mosaic Virus (PMV)

Non-persistently transmitted by the aphids *Cavariella aegopodii*, *C. theobaldi* and *Myzus persicae*, particles of this virus are flexuous rods 736 nm long by 14 nm wide. Reports of this virus are so far confined to the UK, where it is commonly found in field crops. Symptoms include a mild mosaicing of the foliage, but the syndrome is often complicated by the presence of Parsnip Yellow Fleck Virus. Artificial inoculation of parsnip (*P. sativa*) led to chlorotic systemic vein banding, while on coriander (*C. sativum*) severe systemic veinal necrosis and distortion of juvenile foliage developed. Abundant pinwheel and bundle inclusions developed in leaf cells of infected coriander (*C. sativum*) plants.

8.2.10 Parsnip Yellow Fleck Virus (PYFV)

Although carried by the aphid *Cavariella aegopodii*, infection cannot take place directly to parsnip (*P. sativa*) without the presence of the 'helper' virus Anthriscus Yellows which comes from chervil (*Anthriscus cerefolium*). Transmission by *C. pastinacae* does not apparently require the presence of a 'helper' virus. Differentiation between the two viruses can be achieved on the basis that PYFV is mechanically transmissible whereas Anthriscus Yellows is not. The particles of PYFV are isometric, 30 nm in diameter. Symptoms of PYFV on parsnip (*P. sativa*) are a systemic veinal necrosis or chlorosis possibly associated with faint chlorotic mottle and flecking. On chervil (*A. cerefolium*) and coriander (*C. sativum*) localised necrotic lesions form with blackening and shrivelling of juvenile foliage, which first develops at the distal ends of leaves, progressing back to the petiole and into the swollen tap-root. Spinach (*Spinacia oleracea*) is also host to PYFV on which chlorotic local lesions develop followed by systemic chlorotic and necrotic flecks and distortion. Inclusion bodies composed of vesicles develop in infected spinach cells. Such cells also contain plasmodesmatal and cytoplasmic tubules in which are virus particles, the tubules being ensheathed by cell wall out-growths. The lumen of phloem sieve tubes have also been found to contain these tubules.

Other hosts include celery (*A. graveolens*), carrot (*D. carota*) parsley (*P. crispum*), beet (*Beta vulgaris*), cucumber (*Cucumis sativa*) and tomato (*L. esculentum*). On non-umbelliferous hosts local necrotic or chlorotic lesions form

without systemic invasion. Reservoirs of wild inoculum occur in hogweed
(*Heracleum sphondylium*).

REFERENCES

Section 8.1.1
Bant, J. H. and Storey, I. F. (1952). *Pl. Path.* **1**, 81–3.
Benedict, W. G. (1973). *Physiol. Pl. Path.* **3**, 69–78.
Gabrielson, R. L. and Grogan, R. G. (1964). *Phytopathology* **54**, 1251–7.
Maude, R. B. (1970). *Ann. appl. Biol.* **65**, 249–54.
Maude, R. B. and Shuring, C. G. (1970). *Pl. Path.* **19**, 177–9.
Sheridan, J. E. (1966). *Ann. appl. Biol.* **57**, 75–81.

Section 8.1.2
Marras, F. (1962). *Studi Sassaresi Sez. III*, **9**(2), 12.
Netzer, D. and Katzir, R. (1966). *Pl. Dis. Reptr* **50**, 594–5.

Section 8.1.3
Berger, R. D. (1973). *Phytopathology* **63**, 535–7.
Maude, R. B. and Moule, C. G. (1972). *A. Rep. natn. Veg. Res. Stn 1971*, 76.
Netzer, D. and Kenneth, R. G. (1969). *Ann. appl. Biol.* **63**, 289–94.
Netzer, D. and Kenneth, R. G. (1970). *Can. J. Bot.* **48**, 831–5.

Section 8.1.4
Byford, W. J. and Prince, J. (1976). *Ann. appl. Biol.* **83**, 61–7.

Section 8.1.5
Channon, A. G. (1963). *Ann. appl. Biol.* **51**, 1–15.
Channon, A. G. (1969). *Ann. appl. Biol.* **64**, 281–8.
Channon, A. G., Dowker, B. D. and Holland, H. (1970). *J. hort. Sci.* **45**, 249–56.

Section 8.1.6
Day, J. R., Lewis, B. G. and Martin, S. (1972). *Ann. appl. Biol.* **71**, 201–10.
Derbyshire, D. M. and Crisp, A. F. (1971). *Proc. 6th Insectic. Fungic. Conf.* **1**, 167–72.
Iqbal, S. H. and Webster, J. (1969). *Trans. Br. mycol. Soc.* **53**, 486–90.

FURTHER READING

Section 8.1.1
Sutton, B. C. and Waterson, J. M. (1966). Septoria apiicola. Commonwealth
    Mycological Institute Descriptions of Pathogenic Fungi and Bacteria no. 88,
    Commonwealth Mycological Institute, Kew.

Section 8.1.2

Dixon, G. R. (1978). Powdery mildews of vegetables and allied crops. In *The Powdery Mildews* (D. M. Spencer, ed.). Academic Press, London.

Kapor, J. N. (1967). Erysiphe heraclei. Commonwealth Mycological Institute Descriptions of Pathogenic Fungi and Bacteria no. 154. Commonwealth Mycological Institute, Kew.

Section 8.1.3

Ellis, M. B. and Holliday, P. (1972). Alternaria radicina. Commonwealth Mycological Institute Descriptions of Pathogenic Fungi and Bacteria no. 346. Commonwealth Mycological Institute, Kew.

Sections 8.2.1–8.2.10

Murant, A. F. (1972). *Parsnip Mosaic Virus.* Commonwealth Mycological Institute/Association of Applied Biologists Descriptions of Plant Viruses no. 91. Commonwealth Mycological Institute, Kew.

Murant, A. F. (1974*a*). *Carrot Mottle Virus.* Commonwealth Mycological Institute/Association of Applied Biologists Descriptions of Plant Viruses no. 137. Commonwealth Mycological Institute, Kew.

Murant, A. F. (1974*b*). *Parsnip Yellow Fleck Virus.* Commonwealth Mycological Institute/Association of Applied Biologists Descriptions of Plant Viruses no. 129. Commonwealth Mycological Institute, Kew.

Shepard, J. F. and Grogan, R. G. (1971). *Celery Mosaic Virus.* Commonwealth Mycological Institute/Association of Applied Biologists Descriptions of Plant Viruses no. 91. Commonwealth Mycological Institute, Kew.

Smith, K. M. (1972). *A Textbook of Plant Virus Diseases.* Longman, London.

9
Pathogens of Chenopodiaceous Crops

This chapter highlights the benefits which have come for horticultural crops through the study of a more extensively grown agricultural crop, sugar beet. Many of the pathogens of chenopodiaceous crops are similar, and the close botanical relationship between sugar beet and red beet and spinach enables research from one crop to be easily applied to the others. This is especially the case for pathogens such as *Peronospora farinosa* (downy mildew), *Erysiphe betae* (powdery mildew) and virus pathogens such as Beet Yellows Virus. The sugar beet breeders have successfully avoided use of monogenic resistance to *P. farinosa*; unfortunately horticultural plant breeders have failed to follow their example, with predictable results. Development of fungal races with resistance to systemic fungicides first became evident on a wide scale with the beet pathogen *Cercospora beticola* and has given rise to interesting studies in Greece and the USA. Studies of the bacterial gall-forming pathogen *Agrobacterium tumefasciens* are of fundamental significance to our understanding of the manner in which plant, and perhaps animal, tumours are initiated.

9.1 BACTERIAL PATHOGENS

9.1.1 *Agrobacterium tumefasciens* (crown gall)

This parasite has the widest host range and geographical distribution of any bacterial plant pathogen, affecting 140 genera of 61 Angiosperm families in all five continents. It is, however, largely restricted to dicotyledonous hosts. Symptoms were first recorded as crown gall on grapes in Europe in 1853 and *A. tumefasciens* first isolated in the USA in 1904. Symptoms are very characteristic and definitive, the galls are usually rounded, with an irregular rough surface (figure 9.1), ranging in size up to several centimetres, usually developing near the soil line but sometimes on roots or aerial organs. The bacterium stimulates the host parenchyma cells to abnormal growth, resulting in gall formation. Prerequisites to crown gall tumour formation are host tissue

Figure 9.1   Galling of beet root caused by *Agrobacterium tumefasciens* (crown
gall). (Reproduced by permission of National Institute of
Agricultural Botany, Cambridge.)

wounding or entry via lenticels, and viable *A. tumefasciens* cells. It is thought
that the bacterial cells may become attached to the host cell surface where a
tumourigenic substance is elaborated and in turn this initiates host cell
conversion or transformation. Once this process has commenced, bacterial
cells are no longer necessary to maintain the tumourous state. When tumourous,
bacteria-free cells are grafted on to healthy tissue new tumours are initiated.
Five hypotheses have been advanced as to the nature of the tumour-inducing
substance: (1) metabolic products of *A. tumefasciens*; (2) normal host

constituents which are converted by the bacterium into tumourigenic substances; (3) a fraction of the bacterial cell such as DNA; (4) a virus or other agent present in association with *A. tumefasciens*; (5) *A. tumefasciens* cells altered in their morphology and physiology. Currently hypothesis (3) is receiving most favour; it is suggested that large DNA molecules (plasmids) confer tumourigenic and virulence properties on *A. tumefasciens*. The surface components of *A. tumefasciens* alter when they carry plasmids and such changes permit the bacteria to attach to specific target sites in wounded host tissues, subsequently permitting the transfer of still further unidentified tumourigenic substances. These latter may be only a few pathogen genes which can change the genetic structure of the host. At present it is thought that the actual tumours result from host cells producing at least two uncommon amino acids, octopine and nopaline (Kado, 1976).

Agrobacterium tumefasciens is an aerobic, Gram-negative rod, $0.4-0.8$ μm x $1.0-3.0$ μm; it is motile, with between one and five laterally inserted flagellae. Some non-motile variants have been reported. In culture the colonies are white, convex, circular, glistening and translucent. Chemical properties include the production of acid, but not gas, by oxidation of glucose, fructose, arabinose, galactose, mannitol and salicin. The organism is non-proteolytic and non-lipolytic and cannot hydrolyse starch. Strains vary in their ability to produce nitrite from nitrate; ammonia is evolved from media containing arginine while most isolates produce 3-ketolactose from lactose and utilise tryptophan to form β-indoleacetic acid. Growth is optimal at temperatures of 25–30 °C. Four races were identified in the UK, differing in their capacity to cause gall development on a range of hosts. Some host specificity has been identified in that isolates from one host will not necessarily induce symptoms on another. Virulence and pathogenicity are retained for more than 20 years in culture, such stability being unusual for bacterial pathogens.

Entry to the host is through wounds or lenticels. In the absence of a host, saprophytic growth takes place in soil or on infected debris. Control techniques are largely aimed at disease avoidance, ensuring that only land known to be free from the bacterium is used. Treatment of infested soil with sulphur to lower pH reduces the numbers of *A. tumefasciens* in soil, fumigants and antibiotic drenches have been used experimentally. Soil may be assayed for the presence of *A. tumefasciens* by burying carrot slices which become galled in infected soil.

9.1.2 *Corynebacterium betae* (silvering disease)

Reported only in Eire and the UK, *C. betae* causes silvering disease of red beet (*B. vulgaris*). Young plants, 6–8 weeks old, first show silvering along the veins of a few leaves. The epidermis becomes cracked, exposing the underlying palisade layers to give a scurfy appearance. As symptoms intensify, the plants wilt and die. Localised lesions, 1–5 mm in diameter, with cracked and silvery centres and surrounded by a cracked halo, develop on adjacent plants as the pathogen spreads. Symptoms spread to the bracts and seed clusters as the inflorescences are formed. No consistent internal symptoms are found in the petioles, stems or roots. Silvery symptoms are due to increased numbers of air spaces between the epidermal cells (Keyworth and Howell, 1961) and are similar to the effects of the fungal pathogen, *Stereum purpureum*, which causes silver leaf of plum. In the latter, symptoms have been attributed to a toxin, but no such agent has been isolated for *C. betae*.

Corynebacterium betae is an anaerobic, Gram-positive rod bacterium, 0.3–0.5 μm x 0.8–1.6 μm in size, usually found singly but occasionally in pairs; it is motile, with three peritrichous flagellae. Colony appearance is circular, convex, pale yellow and transparent. Chemical properties include the liquification of gelatin, hydrolysis of starch and reduction and peptonisation of litmus milk. The bacterium cannot reduce nitrate to nitrite nor can it produce hydrogen sulphide and indoles. Acid, but no gas, is produced from glucose, lactose, maltose, sucrose, glycerol and salicin. Host range is confined to *Beta vulgaris*, principally red beet and mangold but occasionally sugar beet. No data are available on physiological specialisation.

The pathogen is seed-transmitted, infected seed giving rise to 1–2 per cent of diseased plants. Local transmission from plant to plant is by wind-blown moisture droplets, principally in wet autumns. Considerable losses are caused to seed crops, but the pathogen is of limited economic importance in ware crops. In the early 1960s control was achieved by soaking seed for 24 h in solutions of ethromycin (200 μg/ml) or streptomycin (400 μg/ml). Such techniques are now known to be biologically unacceptable.

9.2 FUNGAL PATHOGENS

9.2.1 *Peronospora* spp. (downy mildew)

(a) *Peronospora farinosa* f. sp. *betae*
The host range of this pathogen is restricted to red beet, sugar beet and mangolds (*B. vulgaris*) and sea beet (*B. maritima*). In the older literature it is referred to as *P. schaactii*. Foliage of all ages can be affected by the pathogen but the most severe symptoms develop on younger leaves, particularly in cool, moist conditions. Attacks usually take place on plants with between four and 10 leaves, seldom killing the host but severely checking growth, with subsequent development of accessory buds giving rise to a rosette of small spindly leaves. These become extensively chlorotic and curl downwards. Distortion and swelling of the lamina are characteristic symptoms on young leaves (figure 9.2). The fungus invades through the cuticle, giving rise to an intercellular mycelium which produces haustoria into the leaf palisade and mesophyll cells. Eventually sporulation takes place from the leaf undersurface, which becomes covered in a

Figure 9.2 Infection of beet leaves by *Peronospora farinosa* f. sp. *betae* (downy mildew). Note the thickening and distortion of the apical leaves. (Reproduced by permission of National Institute of Agricultural Botany, Cambridge.)

purplish weft of sporangiophores. Under very moist conditions sporulation extends to the leaf upper surface. In dry environments lesions become necrotic, which together with the chlorotic symptoms is reminiscent of the effects of Beet Mild Yellowing Virus (*see* section 9.3.3). Typical symptoms on older foliage are orange discoloration, thickening and the brittleness of the lamina. Where seed crops are infected the inflorescence stalk is dwarfed and distorted, sepals and bracts become swollen and sporulation takes place on all infected organs. The entire inflorescence is compacted with excessive leaf development giving a 'witch's broom' effect. Seed clusters are shrivelled, with many of the flowers being sterile. The fungus invades the pericarp and sepals of the developing cluster and the integuments of the ovule, probably through the funiculus, in which sexual oospores may be found. Infected seed is a primary means of transmission for *P. farinosa* f. sp. *betae*, although seed from infected plants seldom produces more than 1 per cent infected seedlings. Severe attacks usually take place only where beet is grown in a maritime climate, such as the coastal areas of California, USA, and the beet seed-producing states of Washington and Oregon, USA. In the UK large areas of beet are grown in East Anglia, where cool, moist conditions can prevail in spring, and severe epidemics are reported from southern USSR, where the conditions are similar.

The causal organism *P. farinosa* f. sp. *betae* is a Phycomycete (class Oomycete) which produces multibranched asexual sporangiophores, which emerge from stomata either singly or in groups of two or three. Sporangiophores are about 11 μm in diameter at the base tapering to 6 μm at the first branch. Sporangia are hyaline, 20–28 μm x 17–24 μm, oval and germinate directly by a germ tube. In consequence they may also be termed conidia. Sexual oospores, 26–36 μm in diameter, form within the host tissues during cool, moist conditions. These are reported to germinate either by germ tube or by production of zoospores. Sporangial germination is stimulated by the reduction of temperature to just above freezing and by washing in deionised water. Indeed, sporangia are resistant to exposure to -12 °C for 24 h. The optimum temperature for oospore germination is 8 °C.

Perennation is by oospores and mycelium in trash from infected crops, but infected seed crops will provide a major source of infection for newly emergent ware crops. For this reason ware and seed crops are separated geographically in the USA and the UK. Seed-borne infection will provide a means of entry into previously uninfected regions. In Byelorussia, where there is a series of short dry periods in summer, there is a tendency for two outbreaks of disease to develop, one in early summer and the other in early autumn (Shukanan, 1974).

Fungicidal control can be achieved by regular dithiocarbamate (for example zineb) sprays every 10–12 days. Such a control programme becomes culturally unacceptable once the canopy is closed unless facilities are available for aerial application.

Cultural control is through the separation of seed and ware crops, destruction of infected debris and use of wide rotations. Considerable use can be made of host resistance providing it is carefully managed. Two forms of resistance, specific and non-specific, have been identified. Specific resistance is manifested as an hypersensitive reaction to invasion and is found in American sugar beet material. Resistance is due to a single dominant gene which gives spectacular control, inoculated plants showing only a few translucent 'pin-prick' lesions (Russell, 1969). But use of such resistance was avoided in the UK since it could have caused the segregation of pathogen virulences capable of overcoming the monogenic resistance, thereby leading to the circular physiologic race-resistant cultivar cycle (*see* section 3.3). Instead non-specific resistance, thought to be due to several genes which reduce levels of sporulation, has been utilised. Non-specific resistance is very sensitive to environmental conditions. The expression of resistance by reduced sporulation can be decreased by shading the host plant and increased by spraying the leaves with sucrose solution prior to inoculation. Partial defoliation increased susceptibility of apical leaves to infection and subsequent sporulation. Application of potassium iodide to beet roots decreased the numbers of infected plants. Some correlation was found (Russell and Evans, 1972) between the levels of monosaccharides in the four youngest leaves of sugar beet plants and their susceptibility in comparison with older less susceptible foliage.

To allow plant breeders to utilise non-specific resistance and to test their material in the field, trials were organised (Dixon, 1976) about 400 km from the main UK production area but in an environment favourable to the pathogen. In these trials strips of a cultivar known to be highly susceptible, for example Maris Vanguard or Vytomo, were artificially inoculated and then the pathogen allowed to spread naturally to plots of breeders' material. By recording the levels of infection within these plots and selecting plant material from them, UK and Irish breeders have been able to maintain a high level of non-specific resistance within the commercially available sugar beet cultivars.

The techniques of tissue culturing have been applied to the study of this host–parasite combination by Ingram and Joachim (1971). On sugar beet callus *P. farinosa* f. sp. *betae* produced normal intercellular hyphae with digitate haustoria, sporangiophores and sporangia and remained pathogenic for 2 years. The fungus grew short distances away from infected calluses on the surface of an agar medium but did not grow axenically when connections with these calluses were severed. Calluses grown from monogenically resistant sugar beet lines lost their resistance to isolates of *P. farinosa* f. sp. *betae*.

(b) *Peronospora farinosa* f. sp. *spinaciae*
This form of species is restricted to spinach (*S. oleracea*). In the literature the names *P. effusa* and *P. spinaciae* are also used. Symptoms are similar to those described for beet downy mildew except that mature foliage is as susceptible as young leaves. Likewise, the fungus is favoured by cool, moist conditions and optimal temperatures for epidemic development are between 10 and 18 °C. The pathogen has world-wide distribution, causing severe damage to spinach crops. It is seed-borne, with mycelium colonising the seed coat, and oospores are found in the seed surface.

An ultrastructural study of the host–parasite combination was made by Kajiwara (1973). An electron-dense substrate was deposited on the cell wall of an incipient haustorium of *P. farinosa* f. sp. *spinaciae* which appeared to consist of lipid material. A conspicuous sheath with an electron-transparent matrix with electron-dense particles was present in the periphery of the electron-dense zone. A fibrilar or fibre-like structure in the outermost part adjacent to the host plasmalemma was named the fibroid sheath and was continuous with the inner layer of the host cell wall. Fibroid sheath material may be deposited inside the host cell wall as a defence mechanism. The mature haustorium came into direct contact with the host plasmalemma or cytoplasm, which partly disappeared in association with haustorial growth.

Chemical and cultural controls are similar to those for beet downy mildew, but the approach to the use of resistance illustrates the constraints which eventual crop use can put on plant breeders. Non-specific resistance inevitably implies that there will be some disease present on resistant plants: this is acceptable for beet, where the root is the portion to be eaten or processed; with spinach, on the other hand, the leaves are the part of the plant presented to the consumer and these need to be free from blemishes. This — at least with the present state of knowledge—implies the use of specific resistance. Studies by Eenink (1976) in the Netherlands have identified resistance to physiological races 1 and 2 of the pathogen. Resistance is governed by two separate but closely linked genes.

9.2.2 *Erysiphe betae* (powdery mildew)

This pathogen is widely distributed in most areas where beet (*B. vulgaris*) is grown, with the possible exception of South America, Australia and eastern Asia. *Erysiphe betae* causes symptoms similar to those of other extracuticular powdery mildews. These begin with single, rounded, white, mealy specks of mycelium, usually on the upper leaf surface. Gradually these lesions expand and coalesce until the whole leaf surface is covered by a dense layer of mycelium, from which are produced copious numbers of conidiophores. Usually the older and more mature foliage is colonised; only rarely and under conditions of severe epidemic are young leaves infected. At any point after the first lesions form, sexual perithecia develop as small dark round structures easily visible to the naked eye and randomly arranged on the mycelium. Within the space of 24 h each sexual conidiophore forms a conidium which is fully differentiated and ripe by midday. At this time the conidia are released and carried on air turbulences to uninfected foliage. Germination is rapid, appressoria form and the infection process is completely by late afternoon. At the optimal temperature, 25 °C, the incubation period is completed in 5 days. A close correlation exists between temperature and successful infection, such that with a rise in temperature from 3 to 18 °C the increase in infection rose from 40 to 100 per cent.

The conidial form of this Ascomycete (class Plectomycete) is the most widespread; conidia are cylindrical, although elongated ellipsoidal forms are known. Conidial size is dependent on temperature and relative humidity. Smaller conidia are formed at low temperatures (40.1 μm x 14.2 μm) in dry atmosphere (45.1 μm x 15.3 μm) and larger conidia at high temperature (47.9 μm x 17.4 μm) and in moist air (49.4 μm x 17.7 μm). A high percentage of *E. betae* conidia are viable, producing a germ tube and appressorium. Perithecia are found scattered throughout the ectoparasitic mycelium. Initially these are white but darken on maturity; they are rounded, with numerous basally inserted appendages. Perithecial size depends on their density on the leaf surface; at greater densities smaller perithecia are formed. Size ranges from 95 to 120 μm and the appendages are 100–250 μm in length with four to six asci per perithecium, each ascus being 50–70 μm long and 30–40 μm wide. Up to four ascospores are found in each ascus, these being 20–30 μm long and 14–16 μm wide. The function of perithecia is probably to provide a vehicle for perennation and also a means for genetic recombination.

This pathogen is well adapted to the conditions of semi-arid, arid and continental climates. The conidia have a high water content (about 60 per cent), which permits germination to proceed even at low air humidities. But *E. betae* is specialised to *Beta* spp., infecting only *B. cicla, B. diffusa, B. maritima, B. patellaris, B. patula, B. rapa, B. trigyna* and *B. vulgaris.*

The extent and importance of *E. betae* epidemics can be classified into three groups related to climate:

(1) Regular, vigorous development of powdery mildew epidemics takes place where the average monthly temperature rises to over 20 °C in the growing period and there are drought periods of 4–5 months, for example eastern Mediterranean areas, Turkey and the southern steppe region of the USSR.

(2) Occasional vigorous epidemics develop when average monthly temperatures are 15–20 °C during the growing period and there is a short drought or dry period and frost and cold spells play only a minor part, for example central and southern France.

(3) Slight mildew epidemics develop which are of only low economic significance in areas with normal average monthly temperatures of 10–20 °C and no dry period, for example the UK (Drandarevski, 1978).

Some differences in cultivar resistance to *E. betae* have been found, but none appears to have specific resistance to the pathogen. In high risk areas, such as Lebanon, chemical control with materials such as sulphur, dinocap and quinomethionate gave increases in beet yield of 23 per cent, in leaf mass of 50 per cent and in sugar of 24 per cent, but applications had to be made every 14 days. Systemic materials such as benomyl and thiophanate-methyl needed to be applied every 25–30 days to achieve yield increases of 19.6 per cent in root weight, 20.7 per cent of leaf mass and 27.2 per cent of sugar in Russian trials.

9.2.3 *Cercospora beticola* (leaf spot)

In warm temperate areas *C. beticola* is the most devastating foliar pathogen of beet crops; epidemics occur annually in southern Europe, Japan, Russia and the USA, but northern European crops are affected only rarely.

Symptoms consist of circular lesions up to 2 mm in diameter in vast

Figure 9.3   Infection of beet leaves by *Cercospora beticola* (leaf spot).
(Reproduced by permission of National Institute of Agricultural
Botany, Cambridge.)

numbers scattered over the entire leaf lamina (figure 9.3). Each lesion has a
well-defined halo which is darker than the remainder of the lesion. The centre is
tan to brown in colour but turns greyish when sporulation takes place.

When petioles are affected the lesions become elongated. Leaf senescence is
accelerated when the concentration of lesions is high; the foliage becomes
chlorotic and falls off. More mature foliage is more susceptible than younger
leaves, but as an epidemic develops there is progressive defoliation. In seed crops
all parts of the inflorescence become infected, including the seed clusters,
leading to seed-borne infection which in the next generation provides a primary
source of inoculum. Effects on ware crops include reduction of root growth and
consequent loss of sugar yield. Trials in Russia, when the pathogen was
controlled by spraying, reduced infection levels six- to eightfold and increased
root yield by 40–70 per cent with improved juice purity.

Cercospora beticola is a Fungus Imperfectus (order Moniliales) with no known
sexual stage. The mycelium is dark, septate and grows intracellularly in the host.
Mycelial clusters, termed 'sclerotia', form within the leaf tissue and dark coloured
conidiophores grow from these through the epidermal surface. Conidiophore
growth is continuous, with successive conidia produced as mature ones are
dehisced. These are hyaline, elongated and multiseptate; they are slim but

broadly rounded at the point of attachment to the conidiophore and tapering towards the distal end. Conidiophores are 4–6 μm in diameter at the apex and 60–190 μm long; conidia vary from 78 to 228 μm in length, being 4.4–6.3 μm wide at the base and 1.6–3.2 μm wide at the tip. Some authorities believe that *C. beticola* and *C. apii* (*see* section 8.1.3) are synonymous organisms. Indeed, it has been shown (Lynch, 1974) that many *Cersospora* species are so closely related that they may merely represent variants of a species cluster, differentiated by environmental factors and by interations with the host plant.

Conidia are largely disseminated by wind currents but may also be carried in irrigation water. High relative humidity is an essential prerequisite to sporulation. Profuse conidia are formed when day-time temperatures remain above 16 °C. Penetration may take place through closed stomata at night (Rathaiath, 1976). An appressorium is usually formed over the closed stoma, but not over an open stoma, during daylight. Penetration and disease development are higher under night-time wetting and day-time drying than in the reverse conditions. Lesions generally appear on beet leaves 9–10 days after inoculation (Dumitras, 1975). Precise investigations by Rathaiath (1977) showed that penetration of beet leaves was enhanced by interruption of leaf wetting with daily dry intervals of 1–6 h duration, but 6 h drying was more effective. Three phenomena differentiated the interrupted wetting process from continuous wetting: (1) initiation of penetration hyphae from germ tubes over the stomata; (2) production of side branches directed positively towards stomata from germ tubes near stomatal openings; (3) formation of secondary conidia which frequently effected penetration. The enhanced penetration under interrupted wetting is probably due to hydrotrophism. The frequency of penetration was similar in resistant and susceptible cultivars, but more leaf lesions were formed on the latter. Optimal incubation conditions when *C. beticola* is within the host leaf are 72 h at 28 °C with 95–100 per cent relative humidity. Where temperatures ranged from 12 to 20 °C or from 30 to 35 °C, fewer lesions formed and their appearance was delayed for at least 20 days. High relative humidity favoured lesion formation even when the original inoculum density was low.

Overwintering by *C. beticola* is chiefly on infected debris as mycelial 'sclerotia' within infected leaves. Cultural controls are, therefore, aimed at the destruction of infected debris by deep ploughing and use of wide rotations to prevent an accumulation of soil-borne inoculum. Infection may also be carried with seed clusters, and this gives rise to primary disease foci in the field. Attempts have been made to breed sugar beet cultivars for resistance to *C. beticola*, but information on the inheritance of resistance is sparse. There would appear to be both specific and non-specific resistance. Non-specific resistance is quantitative and controlled by four or five alleles (Smith and Gaskill, 1970). More recently it has been shown that environmental variation accounts for at least 50 per cent of the resistance expressed by beet plants selected for resistance to *C. beticola* (Smith and Ruppell, 1974). It was concluded that there was significant additive gene action for resistance, and selection to increase resistance could be based on the mean disease levels present in F_3 progeny. Some information is available on physiological specialisation in *C. beticola* and its relationship to specific host resistance. Several races have been identified in Germany, Israel and the USA. Two races identified in Texas and Colorado have been named C1 and C2. Work with the latter (Lewellen and Whitney, 1976) suggests resistance is controlled by a single dominant gene, designated *Cb*, which has no effect on race C1. Resistance is expressed either by the absence of host reaction or by foliar flecking. The flecks are generally 1 mm or less in diameter but occasionally develop into a chlorotic reaction 1–2 mm in size. Flecking reactions are more prevalent with heterozygous than homozygous resistant plants. The homozygous recessive genotype is susceptible to both races.

The sugar beet–*C. beticola* host–parasite relationship provides one of the most vivid examples of rapidly developing resistance by a pathogen to fungicides. Benomyl provided an excellent control of *C. beticola* and was used extensively on a world scale. In 1972 this control began to fail in sugar beet crops grown in northern Greece. Surveys showed there was a widespread occurrence of benzimidazole-resistant *C. beticola* strains. Analysis of isolates in subsequent years (Dovas *et al.*, 1976) showed there was no decline in frequency of benzimidazole-resistant strains within the *C. beticola* population. Fungicide-resistant and fungicide-susceptible strains were apparently equally fit to survive under field conditions. In Texas, USA, tolerance to benomyl was similarly developed after three seasons' use. The mode by which such resistance develops is open to specualtion; Kappas *et al.* (1974) thought that benzimidazole caused mutagenic effects and affected the ploidy of *Aspergillus nidulans*, causing increased numbers of haploid and diploid segregants in the fungal colonies. Additionally, there was induced genetic segregation, probably by chromosomal non-disjunction. But whether *C. beticola* is susceptible to similar benzimidazole-induced mutagenesis is questioned by Ruppell (1975), who was unable to develop fungicide-resistant strains by growing isolates on media containing increased levels of benomyl.

The development of resistance to systemic fungicides has meant that chemical control has reverted to the use of protectant materials such as triphenyltin hydroxide and maneb.

9.2.4 *Uromyces betae* (rust)

The most characteristic symptom of *U. betae* on *Beta vulgaris* is the formation of tiny cinnamon-brown lesions distributed over the upper leaf surface. This is the uredial stage and uredospore germination is optimal at temperatures of 10–22 °C, when rapid colonisation of the entire foliage takes place. Mature leaves begin to wilt, become desiccated and die prematurely. Infected younger leaves tend to remain upright but there is considerable contusion of the leaf surface and attendant chlorosis. Where infection is severe the entire plant may collapse. This pathogen is thought to be seed-borne and has world-wide distribution.

Rust fungi are classed as Hemibasidiomycetes. *Uromyces betae* is a long-cycle autoecious type found only on *B. vulgaris, B. ciela* and *B. rapa.* Pycnial and aecial stages are found infrequently and then only in the spring when the air temperature is between 10 and 13 °C. Aecia develop about 30 days after spermogonia are first visible, and the optimal temperature for aeciospore germination is 15 °C. Aeciospores are 17–21 μm x 23–26 μm in size with a colourless wall 1.5–2 μm thick and finely verrucose. The cinnamon-brown uredial stage is commonly found only on beet foliage, producing elliptical to oval urediospores measuring 19–24 μm x 26–33 μm and having a golden-brown wall up to 2 μm thick and covered with spines and equipped with three or four equitorial germ pores. Chestnut-brown telia containing elliptical to oval teliospores may develop either on very senescent foliage or at the end of the growing season; these teliospores measure 18–22 μm x 26–30 μm and have a dark golden-brown wall 1.5–2 μm thick with a hyaline papilla covering the germ pore. Differences in the susceptibility of beet cultivars to *U. betae* have been reported, but little is known of physiological specialisation by this pathogen.

Spread occurs principally by wind-blown uredospores, while overwintering is accomplished on seed crops, stecklings, groundkeeping beet and mangolds. Reports from the USSR suggest that the teliospore stage is involved in over-wintering, viable spores being found on the soil surface after 1 year and on seed clusters after 2 years. Cultural control is achieved by removal of infected debris and deep ploughing. In parts of the USSR late sowing is used as a means of disease avoidance. Some degree of chemical control can be achieved with materials such as Bordeaux mixture, thiram and zineb; the recently developed systemic fungicides active against rust fungi, such as benodanil, may also be used. Resistance to *U. betae* is reported by Coons (1953) in the sugar beet cultivar US 15; more recently Russell (1970) suggested that resistance is present in some UK sugar beet cultivars.

A second rust, *Puccinia aristidae*, affects both beet (*B. vulgaris*) and spinach (*Spinacia oleracea*). Although of only minor significance on beet this pathogen has been known to cause serious damage to spinach crops, particularly in the USA. This is a dioecious rust with the pycnial and aecial stages found on beet and spinach. Symptoms appear as light yellow-green lesions 2 mm in diameter which turn orange as the aecidial cups rupture the leaf surface and open. The aeciospores are globular, measuring 13–20 μm x 15–23 μm and having finely verrucose walls. Uredial and telial stages form on graminaceous species such as *Distichlis spicata.*

9.2.5 *Aphanomyces cochlioides* and *Pleospora bjorlingii* (damping-off and root rot)

(a) *Aphanomyces cochlioides*
The disease syndrome caused by *A. cochlioides* is known as 'black root'. Symptoms begin early in the seedling stage of beet (*Beta vulgaris*) plants.

Initially a pre-emergence damping-off results in the death of germinating seedlings and is recognised only by the resultant poor stands of seedlings. Diagnosis of the exact causal organism is difficult at this stage since similar effects are caused by *Pleospora betae* (*see below*), *Pythium* spp. (*see* section 6.1.4) and *Thanetophorus cucumeris* (*see* section 5.1.6). This phase may be followed by post-emergence damping-off, resulting from spread of the pathogen from seedlings which have been killed below ground to those which have so far managed to escape infection. Penetration of the hypocotyl starts at ground level as a water-soaked area which extends up and down the hypocotyl. This discoloration may latter extend up into the cotyledonary petioles. The invaded area rapidly turns brownish and then jet black, hence the term 'black root'. Gradually the hypocotyl cortex dries and stem and hypocotyl become shrunken to a dark slender thread. Oospores are readily found within this collapsed tissue. Under warm (15 °C and over) and moist conditions, entire stands of beet can be destroyed within 3–4 days. At lower temperatures infected plants may survive for 10–14 days. As the pathogen invades further up the stem the leaves take on a bluish tinge which slowly changes to yellow. If the attack is less severe and the host is able to produce between three and five true leaves, then the infected hypocotyl cortex may crack and be sloughed off, resulting in normal growth for some time. But disease symptoms re-appear later, usually in June–August. In these more mature plants stunting is the first visible symptom, followed by yellowing of the older leaves and wilting. A greenish-yellow discoloration of the swollen hypocotyl develops which turns through brown to almost black. Infected tissues are slightly soft and water-soaked and eventually shrivel. Where soil moisture contents are high the tap root tip and lateral rootlets rot, causing a growth reduction. Infected sugar beet plants usually have low sucrose content and high levels of juice impurities. All forms of *B. vulgaris* (sugar beet, red beet and mangel) are susceptible to *A. cochlioides* as well as chard (*B. vulgaris* var. *cicla*) and spinach (*S. oleracea*) together with a wide variety of weeds belonging to 10 Angiosperm families. The pathogen has been widely reported on sugar beet crops in Europe and the USA. In South America the disease is called 'caida' and in Chile is responsible for considerable losses at the post-emergence stage.

The biology and epidemiology of *Aphanomyces* spp. is dealt with in the section devoted to *A. euteiches* (*see* section 6.1.4). Here only characteristics differentiating between *A. cochlioides* from *A. euteiches* are presented.

Asexual characters of *A. cochlioides* differentiating it from *A. euteiches* are as follows:

(1) Zoosporangia are longer, being 3–4 mm; they are also sinuous, irregular in diameter and involve large segments of the vegetative thallus.

(2) The apex of the zoosporangium, although tapered, is not attenuated to the same extent as with *A. euteiches*,

(3) Primary zoospore cysts are more variable in size, being 6–15 μm.

(4) The papilla through which encysted zoospores are evacuated is smaller.

Sexual characters of *A. cochlioides* differentiating it from *A. euteiches* are four in number:

(1) Antheridia are smaller, being 6–10 μm x 9–18 μm in size.
(2) The basal septum delimiting the oogonium does not develop into a columella-like structure.
(3) The oogonial wall is less sculptured internally.
(4) Oospores are hyaline to yellow, filling the oogonia more completely, but the average size is smaller, being 20–23 μm.

The infection process of beet by *A. cochlioides* is less well elucidated than that of pea by *A. euteiches*. In beet mycelium is found only in the intercellular spaces of the hypocotyl and root tissue. Hyphae are scant in infected tissue and occupy a relatively small proportion of the intercellular spaces. The pathogen appears to spread slightly in advance of visible symptoms. Cell walls adjacent to the mycelium become dark brown to black, with considerable amounts of dark granular material surrounding the hyphae in the intercellular spaces. The initial site of infection is thought to be the hypocotyl at soil level. Here open stomata may be the portals for entry by germinated zoospores since the sugar beet plant has a thick hypocotyl and the pathogen always appears to be intercellular. Under conditions of artificial infection numbers of infected sugar beet plants increased logarithmically with the inoculum density of *A. cochlioides* zoospores, and a minimum number of zoospores was required to induce typical symptoms. Information on the effect of environment on this host–parasite complex is limited, but McKeen (1949) found that on sugar beet at 13 °C black root development was slight, became more severe at 17 °C and was very serious at 21–25 °C. The age at which seedlings are infected has a considerable effect on the resultant symptoms; more mature seedlings have a lower incidence and a lower amount of black root. Little is known either of the mechanism of survival of *A. cochlioides* in soil, but infectivity is retained for up to 10 years, possibly as resting spores or by invasion of alternate hosts.

Manipulation of crop rotation has been shown to be an effective means of reducing crop losses due to *A. cochlioides*. Attacks are far less severe when beet is preceded by maize, small grain cereals or by soybean, but rotations containing lucerne (alfalfa), beans or clover may encourage *A. cochlioides*. The effects of maize in reducing soil-borne levels of *A. cochlioides* are associated with increased microflora containing *Penicillium* spp., *Aspergillus fumigatus* and *Trichoderma viride*. Phosphate added to the beet seed bed reduced the level of damage due to *A. cochlioides*, especially on light soils compared to heavy ones. Infection was also less where nitrate rather than ammonium was used as the source of nitrogen or where the potassium to nitrogen ratio was unbalanced.

Attempts have been made to breed sugar beet for resistance to *A. cochlioides* in the USA (Doxtator and Finkner, 1954) with the following results:

(1) Resistance could be improved in monogerm sugar beet by back-crossing and selection; at least 50 per cent of selected plants produced progenies more resistant to *A. cochlioides* than their parent lines, but this was less with F_1 hybrid lines than with open pollinated lines.

(2) Susceptibility to *A. cochlioides* tends to be associated with susceptibility to *Thanetophorus cucumeris* (*see* section 5.1.6). Red beet tends to be less susceptible to both pathogens than sugar beet.

(3) From this programme resistance has been incorporated into several American monogerm hybrids developed from the breeding lines US H7, US H8 and US H20.

(b) *Pleospora bjorlingii*
Synonyms of this pathogen include *Pleospora betae, Phoma betae* and *Phyllosticta betae*. It is a common facultative parasite of *Beta* spp., causing seedling black root (*see above*), leaf spot and stem and root rots. Beet seed grown in cool moist conditions is commonly infected with *P. bjorlingii*. Its main significance is therefore as a seed-borne cause of black root; in contrast to *A. cochlioides* which is principally soil-borne. Symptoms are similar to those described under *A. cochlioides*; dark brown or black, well-defined lesions form usually near the soil line and there is often considerable pre-emergence damping-off. On more mature plants infection is usually restricted to older leaves and to the pedicel of the inflorescence. Such foliar spots have a poorly defined margin, are coloured light brown and are up to 2 cm in diameter. Asexual pycnidia are commonly found scattered throughout the lesion in concentric rings. On seedstalks brown to black necrotic streaks develop which have greyish centres. If the host is not killed soon after infection a dry black root rotting syndrome develops. Where beet are lifted and stored this can lead to serious storage losses.

Pleospora bjorlingii is an Ascomycete (class Loculoascomycete). Sexual pseudothecia form within the host cortex which are globose, and bear a short apical papilla which terminates in an ostiole. The pseudothecia are 260–400 μm in diameter and 200–600 μm long with a wall 35–40 μm thick. The asci are club-shaped with two walls and a rounded apex measuring 85–120 μm x 14–16 μm; these asci each contain eight ascospores which are brown and are divided by three transverse septa and by a single longitudinal septum in each of the two central cells. At each transverse septum the ascospore wall is constricted; ascospore size range is 18–25 μm x 7–10 μm. The asexual pycnidia are found in the host cortex adjacent to the pseudothecia, being 150–250 μm in diameter and 200–230 μm high with an outer wall of two or three layers of irregular pseudoparenchyma cells and an inner wall of one or two layers of thin hyaline cells from which phialides form; these phialides measure 6–8 μm x3.5 μm. Pycnospores bud off from the phialides as hyaline oval to sub-cylindrical cells 5—8 μm × 3—4.3 μm in size. Geographical distribution, as with most seed-borne diseases, is world-wide.

Although seed is the major means of dissemination, localised spread can take place via agencies such as wind, rain, irrigation water and on diseased refuse. Close topping of sugar beet during harvesting can provide a means of entry for *P. bjorlingii* leading to rotting of previously healthy mature roots. Rotting is favoured with temperatures in excess of 15 °C. Clean seed is the major means of control. Hot water treatment will eradicate the pathogen but is not acceptable for commercial reasons. Rubbing the seed will remove some superficial infection (Gambogi and Byford, 1976). But infection can be more deep seated, especially if there has been rainfall just before or during the seed harvesting operation. Cultivar resistance may be a factor in influencing the initial level of seed infection; Byford (1978) inferred that resistance is to the spread of *P. bjorlingii* within the crop rather than to penetration of the seed cluster. Seed dressings such as ethyl mercury phosphate which are regularly applied to sugar beet are probably the main and simplest method of control, but crop rotation and maintenance of soil fertility are important avenues of cultural control. As with *A. cochlioides*, phosphate deficiency has been related to the incidence of root rots caused by *P. bjorlingii*, as have shortages of other nutrients such as potassium, manganese and boron.

9.3 VIRUSES

9.3.1 Beet Leaf Curl Virus (BLCV)

Transmission of BLCV is by adult lacebugs (*Piesma quadratum*), whose nymphal stages can acquire the virus but not transmit it. The virus is present in the salivary glands, intestinal wall and haemolymph, but it is not transmitted from adults to the next generation. No information is available about particle size and shape. Beet (*Beta* spp.), spinach (*Spinacia* spp.) and beans (*Phaseolus* spp.) are hosts of BLCV; geographical distribution appears to be confined to western Europe.

Symptoms on beet commence as a glassy or translucent appearance to the veins, which swell but fail to elongate, thereby giving rise to leaf curling. Proliferation of small leaves from the root crown causes the whole plant to take on a cabbage-like appearance. These small leaves remain immature, curving inwards towards the plant centre. Crinkling of the foliage is accompanied by inflation of the parenchyma cells, which as the leaves age turn necrotic and die. High temperatures increase the severity of symptoms. Three types of disease syndrome have been described: a very progressive and severe form which starts in early summer; a similarly severe form but which fluctuates allowing some periods of normal host growth; and a mild form which begins in late summer.

Control techniques using trap crops have been successful in Silesia, whereby early sown strips of beet are grown around the edges of fields which catch overwintering lacebugs as they migrate from hedgerows. Once these strips are infected they are ploughed in.

9.3.2 Beet Marble Leaf Virus (BMLV)

Although the aphids *Myzus persicae, Aphis fabae* and *Macrosiphon euphorbiae* are vectors of BMLV, transmission is very inefficient. Host range is confined to the family Chenopodiaceae and geographical distribution to the western USA.

Systemic symptoms are found first and are then succeeded by local lesions. Young infected leaves have a vein chlorosis or mottling with chlorotic patterning as they mature. Generally the leaves yellow prematurely, but without thickening of the lamina which is typical of plants infected by Beet Yellows Virus (BYV) (*see* section 9.3.12), although the leaves do become papery and dry.

9.3.3 Beet Mild Yellowing Virus (BMYV)

The chief aphid vector is *Myzus persicae*, but in contrast to Beet Yellows Virus (BYV) (*see* section 9.3.12) it is circulative. The particle is possibly isometric and larger than BYV. The virus is found widely distributed in the UK and the USA, affecting *Beta* spp. and spinach (*Spinacia oleracea*).

An orange-yellow colour develops on the foliage of infected plants, but there is no brown or red necrotic spotting or vein etching which is typical of Beet Yellows Virus (BYV) (*see* section 9.3.12).

Applications of an 0.01 per cent solution of thiabendazole lactate reduced the vector reproduction rate and can be used as an indirect means of chemical control.

9.3.4 Beet Mosaic Virus (BMV)

Several aphids transmit BMV, including *Myzus persicae, Aulacorthum circum-flexum, A. solani* and *Aphis fabae*; acquisition time varies with the vector species but in all cases the virus is non-persistent. The host range includes members of the Chenopodiaceae, Leguminosae and Solanaceae. Distribution of BMV is world-wide, wherever beet are grown. Particles are flexuous and filamentous rods 730 nm long and 13 nm wide.

Initially signs of infection on beet (*B. vulgaris*) are seen on some of the innermost leaves as small chlorotic flecks or irregular markings with slight puckering of the lamina around them. These are followed by bright mottling with pale green or yellow discoloration against the darker green of the healthy lamina. On older leaves pale green speckling and mottling develops. A characteristic symptom is backward bending of the leaf tip, which is frequently accompanied by curling and crinkling of the leaf tip. When the disease is severe, juvenile foliage rolls inward; plant stunting and deformation may also be evident. Palisade tissue within infected leaves is less differentiated from the mesophyll than normal and there is a reduction in the number of intercellular spaces. Nuclear size is reduced, but the numbers of chloroplasts increases. Sometimes intracellular 'X' bodies are found as well as pinwheels, bundle inclusions and enlarged sprouting nucleoli.

Infected spinach (S. oleracea) may take up to 3 weeks to exhibit symptoms but these then appear suddenly first as a backward arching of the young foliage together with the development of bright golden flecks. These are circular or irregular in outline, possibly with a dark central point. Frequently the flecks coalesce to produce large chlorotic areas. Unlike the symptoms of Cucumber Mosaic Virus (see section 11.3.2), there is no overall foliar chlorosis at this stage. As plant growth ceases and stunting begins, however, a yellow discoloration spreads over the foliage. Mature leaves may then become necrotic, with leaf death advancing from the tip and spreading to the inner foliage, and eventually the plant is reduced to a whorl of small mottled and puckered leaves.

The yellow mosaic and blotching symptoms could be confused with those caused by the nematode-transmitted Tomato Black Ring Virus (see section 12.3.2), but this virus can be distinguished from BMV by particle morphology and the range of diagnostic hosts. Cucumber Mosaic Virus (see section 11.3.2) and Beet Ring Mottle Virus (see section 9.3.6) also cause mottling, pronounced chlorosis, narrowing and distortion of the leaves and severe stunting. Beet Yellows Virus (see section 9.3.12), Beet Mild Yellowing Virus (see section 9.3.3) and Beet Western Yellows (see section 7.2.4) all cause chlorosis of the older leaves but not mottling or chlorotic flecking.

Weeds such as docks (Rumex spp.), poppies (Papaver spp.), sowthistle (Sonchus spp.) and goose foot (Chenopodium spp.) act as hosts to Aphis fabae and as reservoirs of BMV and should be eradicated from beet and spinach crops. Phosphate deficiency has been correlated with symptom severity.

9.3.5 Beet Pseudo-Yellows Virus (BPYV)

The whitefly Trialeurodes vaporariorum is the vector but loses infectivity very quickly. Geographical distribution is restricted to the Salinas Valley, California, USA. There is a wide host range including crops such as beet (B. vulgaris), carrot (Daucus carota), cucumber (Cucumis sativus), lettuce (Lactuca sativa and L. serriola) and spinach (Spinacia oleracea). Symptoms on beet include yellow spotting of mature leaves with small scattered islands of green tissue. The bright chlorotic areas are 1—1.5 cm in diameter and the leaves become thickened and brittle. In contrast to Beet Yellows Virus (see section 9.3.12) and Beet Western

Yellows Virus (*see* section 7.2.4), chlorosis is more uniform and there is less sectoring and green veining.

9.3.6 Beet Ring Mottle Virus (BRMV)

This virus is stylet-borne (non-persistent) and transmitted by the aphids *Acyrthosiphon latucae, Aphis favae, A. helianthi, A. pomi, Brachycaudus helichrysi, Myzus ornatus, M. persicae, Pentratrichopus fraggaefolii* and *Sitobion avenae.* Geographical distribution is restricted to the Salinas Valley, California, USA.

Symptoms on beet (*B. vulgaris*) start as local chlorotic rings, 2–3 mm in diameter which expand to 4–5 mm and then coalesce. Systemic symptoms begin 14–30 days after infection as distortion of the young leaves and the blades become stunted and narrowed. Margins of the leaves take on a characteristic wavy appearance. There may be uneven growth of the leaf blades which leads to twisting. Infected spinach (*S. oleracea*) shows no local lesions, but systemic symptoms are expressed as interveinal chlorosis accompanied by dark green islands which have an indefinite margin. A mottling symptom may develop on more mature foliage and as in beet the leaves become stunted and twisted.

9.3.7 Beet Rosette Disease Virus (BRDV)

No vector has been identified; its distribution extends through southern and central California and possibly into other western states of the USA. In the field, leaves of infected beet (*B. vulgaris*) are deformed leading to marked rosetting, and the older foliage dies, leaving clusters of terminal and axillary shoots with narrow leaves. Under artificial conditions, chlorosis and twisting of the young leaves is accompanied by down-bending of the mid rib about half way along the lamina. There may be enations of the veins on the leaf undersurface. The larger veins of such leaves exude a sticky fluid.

9.3.8 Beet Savoy Virus (BSV)

Beet Savoy Virus is thought to overwinter within its vector, the lacebug *Piesma cinereum*. Distribution is widespread in the USA, extending through Colorado, Michigan, Minnesota, Nebraska, South Dakota and Wyoming and into south-western Ontario in Canada.

Infected beet (*B. vulgaris*) plants are dwarfed with downcurled and savoyed leaves. Veinlet clearing precedes thickening of the veinlets, leading to a net-like appearance on the upper leaf surface. Roots of infected plants exhibit phloem necrosis and flesh discoloration; in sugar beet the sucrose content is reduced.

Control can be achieved by avoiding the use of land near woodland or uncultivated areas for beet production and by using barrier crops between beet and such reservoirs of infection.

9.3.9 Beet Yellow Net Virus (BYNV)

In nature the main vector is *Myzus persicae*, but other aphids such as *Aphis rumicis, Aulacorthum solani* and *Macrosiphum solanifolii* have acted as vectors of BYNV under artificial conditions. Acquisition of BYNV by a vector was increased by allowing extended feeding times of up to 24 h. Records of the pathogen come from northern California in the USA, and from the UK and Germany.

Characteristic symptoms include the development of a chlorotic network of veins against a green background of interveinal tissue. Young foliage shows symptoms about 9 days after infection, when only the main veins may be chlorotic. This increases as the leaf matures. The formation of small yellow spots on young leaves is thought to be an initial reaction to infection. Virus particles are confined to the host phloem tissue. Spinach (*Spinacia oleracea*) is not a host to BYNV. A strain of the virus known as Beet Yellow Net Mild strain was found in sugar beet in Lincolnshire, UK, which was more easily transmitted by aphids. Another variant known as Beet Yellow Net Mild Yellows, which causes symptoms indistinguishable from other beet yellowing viruses, was described in the 1960s. It is thought that Yellow Net Mild Yellows may act as a 'helper' virus for the transmission of Yellow Net Virus.

9.3.10 Beet Yellow Stunt Virus (BYSV)

Since this virus is circulative it can be distinguished from Beet Western Yellows Virus (*see* section 7.2.4); vectors include the aphids *Hyperomyzus latucae Macrosiphum euphorbiae* and *Myzus persicae*. A destructive yellows type of syndrome develops on beet (*Beta vulgaris*) and lettuce (*Lactuca sativa*); other hosts include sowthistle (*Sonchus oleraceus*), *Beta macrocarpa, Chenopodium capitatum, Claytonia perfoliata, Geranium dissectum, Lactuca serriola* and *Nicotiana clevelandii*. Distribution is restricted to the Salinas Valley, California, USA.

9.3.11 Beet Yellow Vein Virus (BYVV)

No vector has been identified for BYVV. Very young leaves at first exhibit chlorosis of the main vein and become dwarfed. As the syndrome advances the host becomes severely stunted. Yellowing extends beyond the vein into adjacent parenchyma tissue. Chlorotic stripes and spots develop on both leaf surfaces. It can be distinguished from Beet Yellow Net Virus (*see* section 9.3.9) by the greater degree of stunting but more limited yellowing and lack of an aphid vector.

9.3.12 Beet Yellows Virus (BYV)

Synonyms of BYV are Crackly Yellows Virus, Beet Etch Yellows Virus and Beet Romagna Yellows Virus. Transmission is principally by the aphid *Myzus periscae* and to a lesser extent by *Aphis fabae*, but the root-feeding aphid *Hyperomyzus staphyleae* may also act as a vector. The virus particle is filamentous, 10 nm in diameter and 1250 nm long.

In distinction to most beet (*Beta vulgaris*) viruses, symptoms begin on the older foliage, which becomes yellow, thickened and brittle. Chlorosis starts at the leaf tips, developing interveinally, varying from pale watery to a greenish-yellow hue and then becoming yellow and deep orange. Affected areas have a waxy feel and break up when crushed. Necrosis rapidly follows chlorosis, developing down the lamina from the leaf tip. Cold, dull weather tends to accelerate necrosis and to retard chlorosis. Internally the phloem tissues degenerate and virus particles are found in the chloroplasts.

Symptoms on spinach (*Spinacia oleracea*) are more variable in severity but chlorosis of mature leaves is frequent. Vein clearing and curling may develop together with necrosis of the growing apex and death of the host. New Zealand spinach (*Tetragonia expansa*), when infected, exhibits distinct vein clearing of the young leaves, but these tend to expand normally. More mature leaves senesce prematurely and may be stunted. Brown, sunken, necrotic lesions, 1.5 mm x 4 mm, may develop on the petioles.

Virus particles are found within the cytoplasm either as inclusion bodies or as dispersed particles. Generally these are in the phloem sieve elements. Numbers of ribosomes increase and they are packed tightly together. Characteristically the cytoplasmic components become vesiculated, the vesicles being 100 nm in diameter with small fibrils radiating from the centre, which is electron-opaque. Virus particles are found within the pores of the sieve plates, in plasmodesmata between sieve elements and parenchyma cells and between parenchyma cells themselves. This is thought to indicate that virus particles move from cell to cell. Host range is wide, covering 11 Angiosperm families, and geographical distribution extends through Australia, Europe, Iran, Syria, Turkey, the USA and the USSR.

Two strains of BYV have been identified: (1) Mild Yellows or Irish Mild Yellows, which lacks the ability to cause necrotic or 'etch' symptoms; (2) Necrotic strain, as a result of which necrotic symptoms are extremely persistent, being found throughout the growing season and remaining during the winter on overwintered seed crops.

In the UK a vector monitoring and forecasting system has been used effectively to control the spread of BYV in sugar beet. Aphid numbers are monitored by suction traps placed in the areas of beet production and the level of symptoms is assessed by fieldsmen of the British Sugar Beet Corporation. When 20 per cent of the crop is showing symptoms or there is a rapid increase in aphid numbers, warning cards are issued to beet growers advising them to spray with aphicidal organophosphorus insecticides. Recently the scheme has been jeopardised by a build-up of vectors resistant to organophosphorus insecticides, and other compounds are being evaluated, such as aldicarb, which is particularly useful as it may be applied in granular form at the same time as fertiliser applications. Other control techniques involve removal of weed hosts, which act as reservoirs of virus infection, and the removal of seed crops, which being biennial are more prone to infection, from areas of ware crop production.

Attempts have been made to breed for tolerance to 'virus yellows', which is a syndrome caused by a mixture of Beet Mild Yellowing Virus (see section 9.3.3) and BYV. Tolerance in this context is defined as a repression of symptom development in hybrid lines. Genetical control of tolerance may be governed by a single gene, which is thought to be dominant, and by a series of polygenes, which are both dominant and recessive (Cleij, 1970).

A relationship exists between susceptibility to BYV and infection by *Erysiphe betae* (powdery mildew). Field experiments have been carried out with a range of sugar beet cultivars which were allowed to become naturally infected with *E. betae* following artificial infection with BYV and sub-treatments to control BYV using dementon-S-methyl and aldicarb (table 9.1).

Virus control in the BYV-susceptible cultivars Hilleshog Monotri, Sharpes Klein Monobeet, Sharpes Klein Poly Beet, Bush Mono G and Cora significantly reduced the levels of *E. betae* infection, whereas there was little or no effect in the cultivar Vytomo, which is tolerant.

9.3.13 Beet Necrotic Yellow Vein Virus (BNYVV)

Transmission of this virus is particularly interesting in that it is spread by the soil-borne Plasmodiophoromycete fungus *Polymyxa betae*. Virus infection is correlated with the level of *P. betae* in the rootlets. Fungal resting spores apparently carry the virus internally since infectivity was retained for 4 years by air-dried soil. Particles of BNYVV are straight rods, 20 nm wide and of three length ranges: 390, 270 and 65–105 nm.

Diseased beet (*B. vulgaris*) plants show a range of symptoms including chlorosis, necrosis, vein yellowing, crinkling, wilting and stunting. Otherwise known as 'rhizomania' disease, it is characterised by the abnormal proliferation of rootlets. Root damage is due to the effects of the virus, not to those of the vector. Virus particles are found in the root, stem and leaf cells of infected beet plants and in zoospores of *P. betae*. Spinach (*Spinacia oleracea*), when

Table 9.1 Relationship between Beet Yellows Virus and powdery mildew (*Erysiphe betae*) infection in sugar beet cultivars (G. R. Dixon, unpublished data).

Cultivar	Percentage leaf area infected by powdery mildew (*E. betae*) expressed as angles		
	BYV-infected	BYV-infected and then treated with	
		Dementon-S-methyl	Aldicarb
Bush Mono 'G'	43.3	28.0	25.9
Cora	40.0	19.4	21.2
Hilleshog Monotri	50.7	31.1	34.7
Sharpes Klein Monobeet	40.6	30.4	29.5
Sharpes Klein Poly Beet	51.3	32.4	28.8
Vytomo	45.4	38.8	32.4

Significant difference between treatments, 9.434 ($P = 0.5$).
Significant difference between cultivars, 6.70 ($P = 0.01$).

infected, shows symptoms of yellow mottling and stunting. Geographically the disease has been reported from France, Italy and Japan. On the basis of lesion types developed on the diagnostic species *Tetragonia expansa*, four strains of BNYVV have been identified, causing concentric rings, yellow spots, pale chlorotic spots or rings and necrotic spots or rings on leaves.

REFERENCES

Sections 9.1.1 and 9.1.2
Kado, C. I. (1976). *A. Rev. Phytopath.* **14**, 265–308.
Keyworth, W. G. and Howell, J. S. (1961). *Ann. appl. Biol.* **49**, 173–94.

Section 9.2.1
Dixon, G. R. (1976). *Ann. appl. Biol.* **84**, 271–303.
Eenink, A. H. (1976). *Euphytica* **25**, 713–5.
Ingram, D. S. and Joachim, I. (1971). *J. gen. Microbiol.* **69**, 167–78.
Kajiwara, T. (1973). *Shokubutsu Byogai Kenkyu* **8**, 211–20.
Russell, G. E. (1969). *Br. Sugar Beet Rev.* **38**, 27–35.

Russell, G. E. and Evans, G. M. (1972). *A. Rep. Pl. Breed. Inst.* **1971**, 103.
Shukanan, A. S. (1974). *Vesti Akademii Navuk BSSR Biyalagichinykh Navvk*
   5, 59–62.

Section 9.2.2
Drandarevski, C. A. (1978). Powdery mildew of beet crops. In *The Powdery
   Mildews* (D. M. Spencer, ed.). Academic Press, London.

Section 9.2.3
Dovas, C., Skyiakakis, G. and Georgopoulos, S. G. (1976). *Phytopathology*
   66, 1452–6.
Dumitras, L. (1975). *Analele Institutilini de Cercetari pentra Protectia
   Plantelar* **11**, 73–9.
Kappas, A., Georgopoulos, S. G. and Hastie, A. C. (1974). *Mutation Res.* **26**,
   17–27.
Lewellen, R. T. and Whitney, E. D. (1976). *Crop Sci.* **16**, 558–61.
Lynch, F. J. (1974). *Proc. Soc. gen. Microbiol.* **2**, 6.
Rathaiath, Y. (1976). *Phytopathology* **66**, 737–40.
Rathaiath, Y. (1977). *Phytopathology* **67**, 358–62.
Ruppell, E. G. (1975). *Phytopathology* **65**, 785–9.
Smith, G. A. and Gaskill, J. O. (1970). *J. Am. Soc. Sugar Beet Technol.* **16**,
   172–80.
Smith, G. A. and Ruppell, E. G. (1974). *Crop Sci.* **14**, 113–5.

Section 9.2.4
Coons, G. H. (1953). *Some Problems in Growing Sugar Beets*. Year Book for
   1953. United States Department of Agriculture, Washington, D.C.
Russell, G. E. (1970). *A. Rep. Pl. Breed. Inst.* **1969**, 99–101.

Section 9.2.5
Byford, W. J. (1978). *Ann. appl. Biol.* **89**, 15–19.
Doxtator, C. W. and Finkner, R. E. (1954). *Am. Soc. Sugar Beet Technol. Proc.*
   8 (3), 94–8.
Gambogi, P. and Byford, W. J. (1976). *Ann. appl. Biol.* **82**, 31–40.
McKeen, W. E. (1949). *Can. J. Res. C* **27**, 284–311.

Section 9.3.12
Cleij, G. (1970). *Inst. int. Rech. Betteravieres* **4**, 225–36.

FURTHER READING

Sections 9.1.1 and 9.1.2
Bradbury, J. F. (1973). Corynebacterium betae. Commonwealth Mycological

Institute Descriptions of Pathogenic Fungi and Bacteria no. 374. Common-
wealth Mycological Institute, Kew.
Butcher, D. N. (1977). Plant tumour cells. In *Plant Tissue and Cell Culture*
(H. E. Street, ed.). Blackwell Scientific Publications, Oxford.
Hayward, A. C. and Waterston, J. M. (1965). Agrobacterium tumefasciens.
Commonwealth Mycological Institute Descriptions of Pathogenic Fungi and
Bacteria no. 42. Commonwealth Mycological Institute, Kew.
Lippincott, J. A. and Lippincott, B. B. (1975). *Ann. Microbiol.* **29**, 377–405.

Section 9.2.1
Richards, M. C. (1939). *Downy Mildew of Spinach and its Control.* Bulletin
no. 178. Agricultural Experiment Station, Cornell, N.Y.

Section 9.2.2
Kapoor, J. N. (1967). Erysiphe betae. Commonwealth Mycological Institute
Descriptions of Pathogenic Fungi and Bacteria no. 151. Commonwealth
Mycological Institute, Kew.

Section 9.2.3
Chupp, C. (1953). *A Monograph of the Fungus Genus* Cercospora. Cornell
University Press, Cornell, N.Y.

Section 9.2.4
Pozhar, Z. A. and Assaul, B. D. (1971). *Mikol. i Fitopatol.* **5**, 166–71.
Punithalingam, E. (1968). Uromyces betae. Commonwealth Mycological
Institute Descriptions of Pathogenic Fungi and Bacteria no. 177. Common-
wealth Mycological Institute, Kew.

Section 9.2.5
Booth, C. (1967). Pleospora bjorlingii. Commonwealth Mycological Institute
Descriptions of Pathogenic Fungi and Bacteria no. 149. Commonwealth
Mycological Institute, Kew.

Sections 9.3.1–9.3.13
Russell, G. E. (1970). *Beet Yellow Virus.* Commonwealth Mycological Institute/
Association of Applied Biologists Descriptions of Plant Viruses no. 13.
Commonwealth Mycological Institute, Kew.
Russell, G. E. (1971). *Beet Mosaic Virus.* Commonwealth Mycological Institute/
Association of Applied Biologists Descriptions of Plant Viruses no. 53.
Commonwealth Mycological Institute, Kew.
Smith, K. M. (1972). *A Textbook of Plant Virus Diseases.* Longman, London.
Tannada, T. (1975). *Beet Necrotic Yellow Vein Virus.* Commonwealth
Mycological Institute/Association of Applied Biologists Descriptions of
Plant Viruses no. 144. Commonwealth Mycological Institute, Kew.

10
Pathogens of Monocotyledon Crops

This chapter brings together several diverse Angiosperm families, Graminaeae (*Zea* sp. – sweet-corn), Amaryllidaceae (*Allium* spp. – onion and leek) and Liliaceae (*Asparagus* sp.). Pathogens affecting these crops are similarly diverse, ranging across the whole spectrum of micro-organisms. As with some other horticultural crops, research into agricultural crop pathogens has particular relevance to some monocotyledon horticultural crops. This is especially the case with pathogens which affect maize or corn crops such as the bacterium *Erwinia stewartii* (wilt), the fungus *Ustilago maydis* (smut) and the complex of *Fusarium* spp. which cause stalk rot, and many of the viruses. Work on these pathogens in agricultural crops is essential for an understanding of their biology and control which can be applied to horticultural crops. Other notable and recent developments have included the unravelling of the life cycle of *Botrytis allii* (onion neck rot), which is now known to be seed-borne. Control may be achieved even at the dry bulb storage stage by use of systemic fungicides applied as seed dressings. The causal agent of white tip of leek (*Phytophthora porri*) is found to incite a necrotic flecking of white storage cabbage, thereby providing a rationale for some of the losses which take place with this product in the field and in store. The importance of ornamentals as alternative hosts to pathogens of vegetable crops is emphasised by the bacterium *Pseudomonas alliicola* and viruses such as Onion Yellow Dwarf Virus. Considerable work is still required to understand some virus pathogens, particularly those which affect the asparagus crop. Although this crop is only produced on small land units, the financial returns per unit of land area are very high and crop productivity could be raised significantly for utilisation in soup production by processing factories.

10.1 BACTERIAL PATHOGENS

10.1.1 *Pseudomonas alliicola* (soft rot of bulb onion)

Probably *Ps. alliicola* is synonymous with *Ps. marginata*, which was identified as a pathogen of corm-forming ornamentals such as *Gladiolus* and *Freisia* (Stapp,

1961). The organism causes a severe rotting of the outer fleshy scales of onion bulbs and, although described as affecting sets imported from Spain (Taylor, 1975), it is now recognised as having been the cause of similar decay in UK-produced crops. Infection causes the outermost scales to become severely softened and turn grey-green; inner scales are also infected, containing considerable populations of *Ps. alliicola*.

The bacterium is a non-fluorescent, motile, Gram-negative rod, possessing a multitrichous polar flagellum. It is oxidative, reduces nitrates to nitrites and grows at 41 °C, giving a weak oxidase reaction. Isolates are able to utilise nicotinate, (+)-tartrate, (−)-tartrate, *meso*-tartrate, mesaconitase, γ-aminovalerate, citraconate and laevulate, but not putresceine, glutarate, erythiritol or glycollate (Roberts, 1973). It has wide geographical distribution, including Australia, Europe, the USA and the USSR.

10.1.2 *Erwinia stewartii* (bacterial wilt of maize)

Symptoms caused by *E. stewartii* are dwarfing of infected plants with the development of pale stripes on the leaves, which progressively wilt from the base of the plant upwards. The vascular system becomes plugged with a bright yellow slime which exudes from cut stems. Generally, infected plants die before maturation, but if seed is produced this too may be infected. Bacterial cells are found in the vascular system of infected seeds in the chalazal region between its outermost layer and the aleurone layer and between the endosperm cells. Plants grown from infected seed are systematically infected.

Erwina stewartii is a facultative, aerobic, non-motile rod occurring singly or in short chains. Colonies grown on nutrient agar are small, yellow, round and slow growing. Growth on gelatin is also slow but without causing liquifaction; nitrate is not reduced, nor is hydrogen sulphide evolved; litmus milk is slightly acidified and decolorised but there is no coagulation or peptonisation. Some of these characters vary according to the aggressiveness of the isolate. Acid, but not gas, is produced from glucose, galactose, sucrose, fructose, arabinose, xylose, lactose, mannose, mannitol and glycerol. No acid or gas is produced from maltose, rhamnose or dulcitol. The organism has an optimal growth pH of 6.0–8.0 and temperature of 30 °C.

The host range includes maize (*Zea mays*) and *Euchlaena mexicana*. It has been recorded in North, Central and South America, Europe, Thailand and the USSR. In addition to seed transmission, the insect *Chaetocnema pulicaria* acts as a vector, carrying the bacterial cells from leaf to leaf and retaining them during hibernation.

Sweet-corn (*Z. mays* var. *saccharata*) cultivars are highly susceptible to *E. stewartii*. Resistance to the pathogen is available and thought to be controlled by two dominant genes, with possibly a third modifying factor. Control measures include use of clean seed, insecticides to eradicate the insect vector and limitation of nitrogen fertiliser applications.

10.2 FUNGAL PATHOGENS

10.2.1 *Peronospora destructor* (downy mildew)

This pathogen causes widespread damage on a world-wide basis wherever onions are produced under cool, moist conditions. All *Allium* species are susceptible, but infection is most commonly found on *A. cepa.*

Infections develop from three sources: systematically infected leaves of overwintered crops; plants grown from infected onion bulbs; or from local lesions resulting from air-borne inoculum. Foliar symptoms develop as elongated yellowish lesions on both sides of the leaf, which are covered in greyish-violet sporulation. Gradually, the leaf tips shrivel and dry, starting with the outer foliage and progressing to the younger leaves, eventually killing them. Where infection is of systemic origin sprouting is delayed. Dwarfing and distortion may precede lesion formation and sporulation.

Under conditions of low humidity the lesions may be restricted to small, white spots devoid of sporulation, but eventually becoming necrotic. Local lesions are oval to cylindrical in shape, consisting of concentric areas of chlorotic and green tissue. Similar lesions form on the inflorescence, particularly on the upper regions, frequently causing twisting and lopsided growth. Such inflorescences are weakened by fungal activity and collapse as the umbel matures, preventing seed development. Lesions caused by *P. destructor* are often colonised by saprophytic or mildly facultative organisms such as *Alternaria porri* which produce profuse dark coloured spores on the lesion surface.

Peronospora destructor is a Phycomycete (class Oomycetes). The non-septate mycelium, 4—13 μm in diameter, grows intercellularly within the host leaf tissue, producing filamentous haustoria of 1.3—5.0 μm diameter coiled within the cells. Asexual sporangiophores are produced through the stomata; these sporangiophores are non-septate, violet-coloured, swollen to a diameter of 7—18 μm at the base and tapering to acute sterigmata at the tips; their total length varies from 122 to 150 μm. Sporangia branch monopodially up to six times and carry between three and 63 sporangia. These are pyriform to fusiform in shape, attached to the fruiting structure by the pointed end; their size range is 18—29 μm x 40—22 μm. The sporangium is thin walled with a small papilla at the proximal end and germinates by use of one or two germ tubes. Sexual reproduction is by formation of antheridia and oogonia, the latter being 43—54 μm in diameter and forming numerous globular oospores 30—44 μm in diameter. Physiological specialisation has been confirmed only in Japan, but Walker (1952) speculates on its wider occurrence. Studies in Hungary (Viranyi, 1974a) show that the main source of primary infection by *P. destructor* is over-wintering mycelium in infected onion bulbs. Short hyphae penetrated the compressed tissues of the onion neck and fleshy scales in which during storage oogonia, antheridia and oospores form (Blotnicka, 1974). On transfer of systemically infected bulbs to moist chambers or planting in moist soil the oospores germinate to produce needle-shaped hyphae which penetrate from the old stem plate into the newly developing one and into the outermost fleshy scales. Seedling leaves inoculated with a spore suspension are easily infected and the pathogen penetrated from the leaves into the leaf sheaths, stem plate and inner fleshy scales. The fungus may also overwinter as mycelium and oospores on crop debris. Sporangia are produced under high humidity (95 per cent RH) over a wide temperature range, 4–25 °C, with an optimum of 13 °C. Viability is maintained for 3 days when attached to the sporangiophore, or even longer in the dark, but for shorter periods when detached. Germination occurs only in free water between 6 and 27 °C with an optimum of 10–12 °C and germ tubes form in 2–4 h (Viranyi, 1974b). The germ tube usually forms an appressorium over the stomatal opening, penetrates through the stomata, and forms a substomatal vesicle from which the intercellular mycelium arises and sends filamentous haustoria into the host cells. The incubation period lasts 11–14 days (Viranyi, 1975). Epidemiological studies indicate that infection depends on the frequency and length of humid periods and on a requirement for free surface water. Under field conditions two humid nights are needed for the whole infection process, including sporulation, sporangial dissemination, germination and penetration. Sporangial movement is mainly effected by local air convection at 0.5 m above ground level. On a wider scale, Weihle (1975) found that westerly circulation patterns led to the fulfilment of infection criteria and that regional warning programmes could be constructed from physical data, but threshold values needed to be incorporated to take account of actual inoculum potential. In the Krasnodar region of the USSR environmental conditions favour epiphytotics every 2–3 years, and sometimes in successive years.

Control of bulb infection can be achieved in areas with hot, dry autumns by exposing bulbs in the sun for 12 days if the temperature reaches 41 °C for 4 h; this destroys the pathogen but does not affect the viability of the bulbs. In Poland conventional hot water treatment is used to control the pathogen. Disease incidence in Israeli crops (Palti et al., 1972) was affected by relative humidity and conditioned by stand density, direction of rows and plant age. Sprinkle irrigation favoured infection more than furrow irrigation. Autumn-sown crops were attacked in December–January when the mean maximum temperature in November did not exceed 12 °C and there were at least seven rainy days in October–November. In November-sown crops the disease appeared in February but temperatures of 3–4 °C in December delayed disease onset. Wild Allium species have been shown to provide a means for mycelial perennation.

Chemical control can be achieved with between two and nine sprays of captan, mancozeb or zineb, the number depending on rainfall.

Some slight differences in cultivar resistance to P. destructor have been noted. Susceptible bulbs have higher levels of indoleacetic and chlorogenic acids and infection causes increased oxidation levels. Resistant onions tend to have flat leaves, xeromorphic tissue structures with small cells, thick walls and high lignification; susceptible ones are characterised by fistular leaves, swollen flower stalks, large cells with thin walls and limited lignification. There is also correlation between resistance and the acid content of the host cuticular wax.

10.2.2 Puccinia spp. (rust)

(a) Puccinia allii (leek rust)

At least 18 species of *Puccinia* and *Uromyces* have been recorded as parasites of *Allium* spp., but the most significant pathogen is the autoecious *P. allii*. This nomenclature includes *P. mixta* and *P. porri*, which are found in the literature (Wilson and Henderson, 1966).

Only uredosori are found on leeks (*A. porrum*); these erupt as bright orange circular to elongate pustules between the veins of the leek leaf (figure 10.1). An apparently additional symptom is chlorotic spotting of the leaf (Dixon, 1976). This is found on plants irrespective of the presence of uredosori as lesions which are more or less circular up to 5 mm in diameter; initially a lighter green in colour than the rest of the leaf, they gradually take on a yellowish hue. This symptom is thought to be caused by unsuccessful invasion of the leaf by uredospores causing a 'ghost spotting' reaction. The pathogen has world-wide distribution.

Within the uredosori spherical to elliptical uredospores are formed, measuring $23-32 \mu m \times 20-26 \mu m$, and the walls of which are hyaline to yellow and spiny and have a thickness of $1-2 \mu m$. Teliosori are found on onion (*A. cepa*), usually scattered among the uredosori; these initiate below the host epidermal surface and erupt to expose chestnut-brown teliospores which are elliptical to obovoid and measure $28-45 \mu m \times 20-26 \mu m$ with a wall $1-2 \mu m$ thick. The pedicels carrying the teliospores are nearly colourless, fragile and short. Other spore forms in the life cycle of *P. allii* have been identified on the hosts *A. shoenoprasium, A. flavum* and *A. fistulosum*. Spermogonia and aecidia are found together with the aecidiospores, being globoid, of $19-28 \mu m$ in diameter, and having a yellow wall $1-2 \mu m$ thick. Similarly shaped mesospores have also been reported, $22-36 \mu m \times 15-23 \mu m$ in size. Physiological specialisation is thought to occur since onions (*A. cepa*) grown near infected garlic (*A. sativum*) in California, USA, remained free from infection.

Seed transmission of *P. allii* has been reported but not investigated thoroughly. The pathogen has become a particular problem for leek growers in Europe due to intensification of production within small land areas with crops present in the ground for nearly the whole year. Uredial lesions and chlorotic leaf spotting symptoms considerably reduce the value of the crop, especially where it is directed to supermarket and processing outlets. Considerable losses are caused on other *Allium* crops: in Chile 83 per cent losses are reported in garlic (*A. sativum*); production of garlic in Israel and of bunching onions (*A. fistulosum*) in Japan is also limited; the pathogen is reported as a severe problem on chives (*A. schoenoprasum*) in Norway and on onions (*A. cepa*) and garlic (*A. sativum*) in Tanzania.

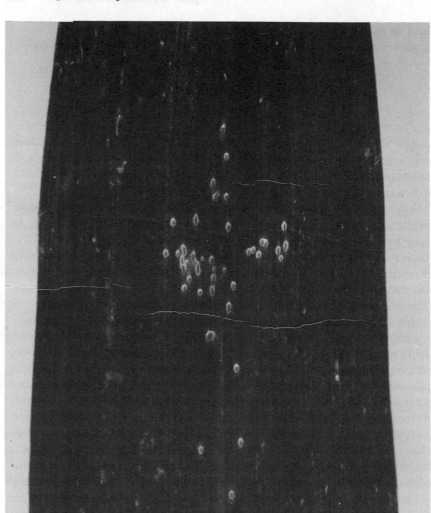

Figure 10.1   Section of a leek leaf infected by *Puccinia allii* (rust). (Reproduced
by permission of National Institute of Agricultural Botany,
Cambridge.)

Assessments of cultivar trials showed there were significant differences in the
levels of chlorosis and uredial formation on leeks (*A. porrum*) in the UK. The
fungus is favoured by high RH, moderate to low temperatures, dense planting,
excessive soil nitrogen and deficiencies of potassium. Wide rotations will help to
prevent the build-up of *P. allii*. Some success has been achieved with chemical
control using materials such as benodanil in the UK and maneb/mancozeb in
Italy. Potential biological control has been demonstrated by Doherty and Preece

(1978), who found that *Bacillus cereus* would completely inhibit germination of uredospores.

(b) *P. asparagi* (asparagus rust)
This autoecious rust is the main pathogen of asparagus (*A. officinalis*). Symptoms first develop in spring as oval yellowish lesions containing pycnia in the centre and aecia distributed around the periphery. At this stage the disease may be overlooked. Further phases of the rust life cycle form on the foliage, which develops after the edible spears have been cut. Uredial pustules form as blisters on stalks, stems, twigs and leaves; these blisters eventually break open, exposing brown powdery spore masses (Kontaxis, 1977). The blisters are followed by telia containing black teliospores. Under conditions of heavy infection the foliage turns yellow to brownish, losing vigour and senescing early. There is a failure to replenish nutrient reserves in the crown, consequently spear production in the following season is reduced. Other hosts include *Asparagus maritimus, A. plumosus*, onion (*Allium cepa*), shallot (*A. ascolonicum*), chives (*A. schoeno-prasum*) and Egyptian tree onion (*A. cepa* var. *aggregatum*).

Initially the pycnia are brownish, preceding the aecia but then surrounded by them. Aecia are white-creamy, scattered often in elongate groups containing aeciospores which are globular to oval and measure 15–21 μm x 18–27 μm with a hyaline wall 1 μm thick covered with fine spines. Uredia have a powdery texture and are cinnamon-brown, containing globular to elliptical urediospores of 19–30 μm x 18–25 μm with a golden wall 2 μm thick and four equitorial pores. Telia are blackish-brown and the teliospores are 30–50 μm x 19–26 μm, rounded at the top, with a slight constriction at the septum, and equipped with a chestnut-brown wall 10 μm thick and a pedicel usually about twice as long as the spore. Occasionally mesospores form which are 35 μm long. Indirect evidence of physiological specialisation is available since resistant cultivars bred in USA in the 1920s are now susceptible. Resistance is thought to be determined by four or five genes. The fungus is distributed throughout the asparagus-growing areas of the world.

Perennation is thought to occur by means of the teliospores, which germinate in the spring to form basidia and sporidia which are aerially disseminated. Haploid mycelium from the sporidia penetrates directly, leading to pycnia production, and the pycnospores are discharged from the foliage surface. Heterothallism may occur and mating takes place either by dispersion of pycnospores or by mating of internal haploid mycelium. Aecia develop in the same lesion as the pycnia, usually around the outside, while pycnia form at the centre. Aeciospores are air-borne and after germination penetrate through the host stomata to form an inter-cellular mycelium with haustoria developed into the cells. From this mycelium uredia develop producing 'summer spores' or uredospores which are responsible for the main disease-causing phase of the pathogen life cycle. Dew is essential for urediospore germination since they require soaking for at least 3 h before germination. Towards autumn telia with teliospores develop in increasing numbers.

Cultivars were developed early in this century with resistance to the dikaryotic stages of the rust arising from aeciospores or urediospores but were very susceptible to the haploid stages arising from sporidial infection.

The main means of control are to remove weed hosts and volunteer plants and keep seedling beds isolated from those mature enough to be in production. The latter should not become infected if spears are harvested up to early summer, thereby preventing sporidial infection from taking place. Some success has been achieved with chemical control using sulphur, Bordeaux mixture or dithio-carbamate materials.

10.2.3 *Phytophthora porri* (white tip)

In addition to causing white tip of leek (*A. porrum*) this fungus is responsible for leaf blight, bulb and root rots of several onion spp.: bulb onion (*A. cepa*), garlic (*A. sativum*), spring onion (*A. shoenoprasum*), *A. bakeri, A. grayi, A. hipponicum, A. tuberosum* and *A. wakeyi*. Genera of other families can be infected by *P. porri* after injury; recently a form of post-harvest deterioration in winter white cabbage (*B. oleracea* var. *capitata*) has been demonstrated to be caused by *P. porri*.

Symptoms on leek foliage are a water-soaked marking, particularly towards the leaf tip. This becomes chlorotic and then white with the leaves turning backwards and twisting. Initially the symptoms are similar to frost damage but are persistent and become more severe. Affected leaves of mature leeks become rotten, and growth is generally stunted. Younger plants may be killed by the pathogen.

On stored cabbage symptoms are desiccation and browning of the outer wrapper leaves with dark brown discoloration spreading upwards from the stem base into the heart leaves. Rotted tissue is not softened and there is limited development of hyphae within the stem cavities (Geeson, 1976).

Phytophthora porri is classed as an Oomycete. Asexual sporangia are formed successively on aerial sporangiophores, which are pear-shaped, hyaline and may possess an apical papilla; these sporangia are 31–48 μm x 37–75 μm in size. Sporangia germinate either directly, by production of germ tubes, or by zoospore formation. In the latter case, 20 motile zoospores, 10–12 μm in diameter, emerge and germinate by germ tube formation. Sexual antheridia, measuring 7–10 μm, and oogonia, measuring 29–44 μm, form, which after mating form spherical light yellow oospores of 19–36 μm in size. At maturity the oogonial wall has been demonstrated to collapse around the oospore.

Fungal perennation takes place in the soil as either oospores or chlamydospores. Infection of cabbage heads is thought to take place via contaminated soil particles carried by rain-splash or harvesting knives. Chlamydospores, measuring

20–30 μm, have been shown to form after prolonged incubation, their rate of development depending on the source of the isolate and the environment. Temperature requirements of *P. porri* are wide, mycelium growing between 0 and 25 °C but with an optimum between 15 and 20 °C. In Japan losses of 70–80 per cent of onion crops are caused by *P. porri*. Disease occurrence is much affected by temperature and rainfall. From regression equations using assessments of disease amount and temperature and rainfall indices, outbreaks have been forecast with 75 per cent probability (Yokoyama, 1976). In Europe considerable crop losses due to *P. porri* have been reported from the Netherlands, Norway and the UK. Chemical control has been achieved with the use of dithiocarbamate materials.

10.2.4 *Alternaria porri* (purple blotch)

The nomenclature used for this pathogen in eastern European literature is *Macrosporium porri*. Most cultivated *Allium* spp. are susceptible to *A. porri*, which attacks all parts of the host and has world-wide distribution. Initially symptoms develop as small, white, foliar lesions with elliptical centres which quickly expand, girdling the leaf or stem. Often the lesion has a yellowish outer border. At RH less than 70 per cent the lesions fail to spread, but under moist conditions the leaves collapse within 3–4 weeks of infection and the bulb is affected by a yellow-reddish watery rot. This commences at the neck and then spreads to the whole bulb. If young plants are infected their growth is inhibited and they may fail to produce a bulb.

Alternaria porri is a Fungus Imperfectus of the order Moniliales. Asexual conidiophores develop in the purplish centres of the lesions under moist conditions, either singly or in groups; these conidiophores are pale to mid brown in colour, up to 120 μm long and 5–10 μm thick, with well-defined conidial scars. The conidia, which are borne singly, are straight or slightly curved, club-shaped and taper to a beak which is often as long as the main body of the conidium; these conidia are pale to golden-brown in colour, 100–300 μm long, 15–20 μm thick and have eight to 12 transverse septa and none to several longitudinal or oblique septa. The beak is flexible, 2–4 μm thick and tapered. No physiological specialisation of *A. porri* has been reported.

Invasion takes place either through stomata or directly through the cuticle (Fahim and El-Shehedi, 1966), to form an intercellular mycelium. *In vitro* studies (Fahim, 1966) showed that the optimum temperature for sporulation is 25 °C at 90 per cent RH. Sporulation is favoured by a 2 h exposure to light, preferably sunlight, followed by 48 h of darkness. Optimal mycelial growth occurs at 23–30 °C. Conidial germination takes 45–60 min at 28–36 °C. Release of conidia is maximal between 08.00 and 14.00 and dispersal is by wind or rain splash (Meredith, 1966). Perennation is thought to occur as mycelia and conidia in diseased crop debris.

Trials of leeks (*A. porrum*) in the USSR failed to identify any sources of resistance, but some Kenyan and Brazilian onion (*A. cepa*) cultivars are resistant, possibly due to the possession of thick cuticles. Breeding for resistance to *A. porri* in the USA is utilising resistant Italian material hybridised with susceptible Spanish onions.

Chemical compounds such as dithane and mancozeb will control this pathogen if applied regularly at 7 day intervals. In India benomyl is claimed to be an effective fungicide against *A. porri*. Potential biological control is reported by Fokkema and Lorbeer (1974), who found that mycelial development following conidial germination of *A. porri* is inhibited by cells of *Aureobasidium pullulans.*

10.2.5 *Botrytis* spp. (neck rot, leaf fleck and blast)

All *Allium* species are susceptible to a range of *Botrytis* species on a world-wide scale. At least two disease syndromes develop which may be interrelated: (1) neck rot, which until recently was thought to develop from infections just before or during storage, but has now been shown to be due to latent infections which are present in the seed but only expressed as a harvest and storage disease; (2) leaf fleck and blast, which appear during the growing season in certain areas and may be manifestations of latent *Botrytis* infection which show up due to unfavourable environments for the crop during growth.

(a) Neck rot
Three *Botrytis* species cause neck rot, each inciting slightly different syndromes: *B. allii* (grey mould neck rot), *B. byssoidea* (mycelial neck rot), and *B. squamosa* (small sclerotial neck rot). Of these *B. allii* is most commonly found and is the main cause of deterioration of bulb and pickling onions in store. Although symptoms only become apparent at or after harvest, Maude and Presly (1977a) have shown the main source of infection is diseased seed.

Botrytis allii is carried within the seed and is viable for at least $3\frac{1}{2}$ years in seed stored at 10 °C and 50 per cent RH. Seedlings grown from infected seed are invaded by mycelium from the seed coat which passes into the cotyledonary leaf tips. The fungus attacks these leaves without causing symptoms as the seedlings emerge through the soil. Conidiophores are produced only after the leaf tissue has senesced and become necrotic. Leaves are invaded successively, infection developing at the tip of each leaf and the fungus then growing downwards into the tissues, eventually invading the neck of the onion bulb via those leaves which emerge directly from the top of the neck. By harvest *B. allii* mycelium is situated deeply within the neck tissues of the mature bulb. Initial signs of infection are a softening of invaded scale tissue, which becomes sunken with an outer advancing region of decay. Infected tissue turns greyish in colour due to growth of the mycelium, which forms a spreading mat of hyphae and conidiophores on the surface of the bulb scales. When infected bulbs are sectioned there is an area of partially rotted parenchyma tissue with a water-soaked appearance. Sclerotia form on the older decayed tissue as compacted whitish masses of mycelium which then darken with age to become hard, black, irregularly shaped bodies 1–5 mm in length. These may form either on the bulb surface or be slightly embedded within the decayed tissue. Mycelial neck rot (*B. byssoidea*) is distinguished from grey mould neck rot (*B. allii*) by the production of more external mycelium on the bulb but less sporulation. Small sclerotial neck rot (*B. squamosa*) is almost entirely confined to white-bulbed onion cultivars. First signs of infection of this pathogen appear at the bulb neck some while after harvesting. Thin scale-like circular sclerotia, 0.5–1.5 mm in diameter, adhere to the dry scales. Initially they are light in colour but turn black with age. Decay due to *B. squamosa* is similar to that caused by *B. allii* and *B. byssoidea*, but spread is slower.

(b) Leaf flecking and blast

Botrytis species involved in these syndromes are *B. allii*, *B. cinerea* and *B. squamosa*. The first causes only limited foliar spotting and it is likely that *B. allii* usually remains in a latent state until the development of neck rot on mature bulbs. It was suggested by Tichelaar (1967) that *B. allii* mycelium is restricted to the colourless epidermal cells during the growing stages of the host, only becoming apparent after harvest. *Botrytis cinerea* is only weakly pathogenic to onion leaves, causing superficial flecking of the surface without lesion formation or dieback of the leaf (Hancock and Lorbeer, 1963). Foliar lesions are, however, caused by *B. squamosa*; these lesions are elliptical and extended through the entire cross-section of the leaf and are followed within 5–12 days of infection by withering of the leaf tip, frequently preceded by wilting of the apical area.

Mycological details of *B. cinerea* are given in section 6.4.3, many of which are applicable to these other *Botrytis* species. Where no sexual stages have been found, they are by association included in the Ascomycetes (class Discomycetes). Pseudoparenchymatous sclerotia are the resting stages which either germinate to produce mycelium or form asexual conidiophores directly. These conidiophores have an indeterminate habit resulting in profuse conidial production. Conidia are aerially dispersed and germinate immediately they are immersed in water. Conidia are elliptical, hyaline and non-septate; the size ranges are as follows: *B. allii*, 4–8 μm x 6–16 μm; *B. byssoidea*, 5–11 μm x 8–20 μm; *B. squamosa*, 9–18 μm x 14–24 μm. Microconidia have been reported but are not common; they are globose, hyaline, about 3 μm in diameter and are borne on very short conidiophores. Physiological specialisation on onion hosts has not been reported.

The leaf spotting syndrome is critically affected by environment, requiring 24 h at 100 per cent RH and 27 °C for symptom development (Segall and Newhall, 1960). A direct relationship between spore load and number of lesions has been established and individual spots are largest when the concentration of spores was highest. Alternate periods of 12 h light and 12 h dark at 24 °C favoured lesion number development. The optimum temperature for fungal growth is 21 °C. Greatest epidemics of neck rot occur in cool moist seasons. Conidial production, germination and mycelial growth occur over a wide temperature range but infection and post-infection bulb decay are favoured by temperatures of 15–20 °C. Rotting is brought about by production of pectinases and cellulases formed by the fungus in advance of mycelial colonisation.

In the storage phase no bulb to bulb spread of disease could be detected in store (Maude and Presly, 1977b). A direct linear relationship between number of bulbs with neck rot in store and number of plants in the field with B. allii-infected necks was established. Further, since the pathogen is seed-borne the storage phase is directly related to the initial level of seed infection. However, the rate of bulb infection developed from similar levels of seed infection was subject to modification by environmental conditions during the field growth phase, but despite this the ratio of seed to bulb infection for seed with different percentages of infection remained constant. Seeds carrying 10 per cent infection resulted in losses greater than 10 per cent in both wet and dry seasons, while 1 per cent seed infection caused significant storage losses only in wet years.

Almost total control of neck rot has been achieved by chemical seed treatment using a slurry formulation containing benomyl and thiram at 30 per cent a.i. This has virtually eliminated the seed-borne source of B. allii in the UK (Maude and Presly, 1977b). Use of the systemic material benomyl as a seed treatment is thought unlikely to lead to the evolution of chemically tolerant races of B. allii provided no growing season sprays are required. If leaf fleck and blast are also a problem, use should be made of alternative chemicals such as iprodione. Cultural controls include destruction of diseased debris by deep ploughing, and of wild weed hosts (Allium vineale and A. ursinum) by herbicides; avoidance of the use of excessive nitrogen fertilisers, which give rise to succulent leaf growth more easily invaded by Botrytis spp.; careful handling of harvested bulbs before and during storage; and use of stores which are cool, dry and well ventilated.

10.2.6   Sclerotium cepivorum (white rot)

All Allium species are susceptible to S. cepivorum, which is regarded as a common and destructive pathogen wherever onions are grown. The host range includes onion (A. cepa), leek (A. porrum), shallot (A. ascalonicum), chive (A. shoeno-prasum), garlic (A. sativum) and the weeds crow garlic (A. vineale) and ramsons (A. ursinum). Its economic significance in the UK is as a pathogen of the overwintered and summer salad onion crop and of the dry bulb ware crop. Overall losses are estimated at 1–5 per cent, but individual crops can be completely killed by the pathogen (Entwistle and Munasinghe, 1978).

The first sign of infection is yellowing and death of the foliage, commencing at the leaf tips and progressing downwards. In young plants wilting and collapse are common, whereas more mature plants may decline over a period of weeks.

Typical symptoms on bulbs and adventitious roots are an abundant, superficial, fluffy white mycelium which eventually lyses to reveal copious spherical black sclerotia. Roots and bulb scales decay to a semi-watery state either in the field or in store. Sclerotia and mycelium are the main components of the life cycle of *S. cepivorum* (*see* figure 10.2) which is an Ascomycete (class Discomycete) fungus. The sclerotia are 200–500 μm in diameter possessing an outer rind of one or two layers of much thickened, heavily pigmented, rounded cells enclosing a large medullary region consisting of closely packed, elongated hyphae. The first signs of sclerotial germination are the formation of bulges on the sclerotial surface. Following this the rind ruptures and a dense plug of mycelium is extruded. This plug originates from the medullary cells, from which hyphae form and anastomose freely, growing up to several millimetres from the sclerotium. 'Microconidia' are borne on the germination hyphae. These are hyaline, spherical,

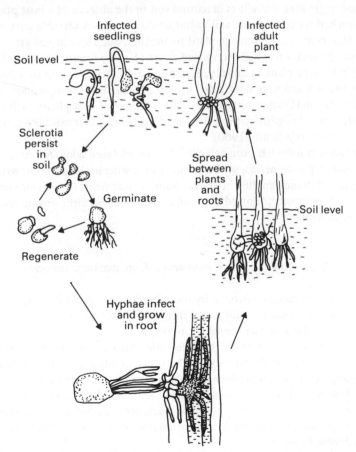

Figure 10.2   Developmental cycle of *Sclerotium cepivorum* (white rot) on onions. (Reproduced by permission of National Vegetable Research Station and Agricultural Research Council, UK.)

and 1.6–2.0 μm in diameter, borne in chains on flask-shaped phialides which occur in verticils on short side branches or in tufts directly upon a hypha. 'Microconidia' have not been observed to germinate, and their function is not known (Coley-Smith, 1960).

This pathogen is thought to persist for long periods in the soil without any functional or sporulation stage. Sclerotial germination, root infection and disease development are all optimal at 15–20 °C, declining at 5–10 °C and 25 °C. Sclerotial germination was highest at 15 per cent soil moisture but tended to be inhibited at higher moisture levels (Entwistle and Granger, 1977). In over-wintered crops disease losses are high in the autumn and spring periods when temperatures are suited to infection, whereas in summer crops the disease is of fluctuating importance dependent on the levels to which soil temperatures rise.

Studies by Scott (1956a) showed that S. cepivorum was incapable of persisting as growing mycelium in natural soil in the absence of a host plant. The mycelium had no saprophytic ability but could play a considerable part in the spread of S. cepivorum from one plant to another. Such spread was greater where the planting density was highest; indeed Scott (1956b) found that spread was directly related to planting density. Sclerotia could survive for up to 4 years in undisturbed soil and were unaffected by soil pH, nutrient status or inorganic supplementation (Coley-Smith, 1959). The presence of host plants (Allium spp.) stimulated sclerotial germination, the stimulant being a thermostable exudate of Allium roots (Coley-Smith, 1960).

Significant control has been achieved on overwintered salad onions by application of iprodione as a seed treatment at sowing in the autumn, with an additional soil drench applied in March. Similar treatments to the summer crop using a seed treatment followed by a soil drench 5 weeks after sowing also gave complete control.

10.2.7 Colletotrichum dermatium f. sp. circinans (smudge)

This pathogen has been controlled by use of resistant, coloured-skinned onion (A. cepa) cultivars. But it is still found infrequently affecting white bulb onions, shallots (A. ascalonicum) and leeks (A. porrum).

Small stromata form beneath the bulb scale cuticle; these stromata are initially green but turn black with maturity. Under moist conditions they enlarge into dark smudgy spots which produce asexual acervuli bearing characteristic black setae. Where infection becomes more deeply seated within the bulb, yellow sunken lesions form. These may produce black acervuli, but more frequently the lesions simply enlarge without fructification; this enlargement still disfigures the bulb, reducing its value.

Only the Imperfect stage of C. dermatium f. sp. circinans has been identified and is placed in the order Melanconiales. The septate mycelium is initially hyaline but darkens and thickens with age. The black or dark green stromata forming from the intertwining of thick walled hyphae. Acervuli develop from the stromata within the host cuticle; they contain hyaline conidiophores and numerous thick walled, dark setae which are usually triseptate and 80–315 μm long. As the acervulus matures it bursts through the host cuticle and conidia are budded off one at a time. These are fusiform, non-septate, hyaline to light yellow, slightly curved with an obtuse apex, and measure 3–4 μm x 18–28 μm. Under moist conditions they appear as creamy gelatinous masses. Conidial germination takes place through between one and three germ tubes, which form appressoria up to 8 μm in size on the surface scales of the host. From a germ tube an infection hypha grows through the cuticle by mechanical pressure and mycelial colonisation develops between the cuticle and epidermis. Further penetration is effected by enzymic action, which softens the host cell wall in advance of the invading mycelium. This leads to changes in host cell permeability and resultant cellular degeneration followed by mycelial invasion of the cell lumen.

Conidial germination is optimal at 20 °C and mycelial growth and symptom development at 26 °C. High RH is essential for conidial formation. Conidia are disseminated by rain-splash. Stromata within the soil act as a perennation mechanism in the absence of a host, but this fungus may also exist as a free-living saprophyte.

Highly effective control has been achieved by using coloured-skinned onion cultivars which are resistant to *C. dermatium* f. sp. *circinans*. The genetic nature of this resistance is discussed in section 4.1.2. The mechanism of resistance depends on the presence of *o*-dihydroxyphenols, catechol and protocatechuic acid in the outer bulb scales, not on the presence of the anthocyanin pigments which give the scales colour. These phenolic compounds prevent infection by inhibiting spore germination (Pierpoint, 1971). Where it is essential to grow white-fleshed cultivars, protection of the harvested bulbs from rain, and rapid drying, are essential. Drying is achieved by forced circulation of air at up to 48 °C through bulbs laid out in shallow slatted crates to dry the outer scales thoroughly. Storage should be at 1 °C with about 65 per cent RH.

10.2.8 *Urocystis cepulae* (smut)

This pathogen is also classified as *U. colchici* var. *cepulae*. All cultivated *Allium* spp. are susceptible to *U. cepulae*, but resistance is present in the wild species *A. altaicum*, *A. obliquum*, *A. nitans* and *A. odoratum* (Semehov, 1977). The fungus is found in onion-growing areas of Australia, Europe, the Middle and Far East and North and South America.

Dark lesions form on the onion cotyledons as they emerge, developing into thickened zones several millimetres in size. These may be associated with abnormal growth curvatures of infected foliage. As the lesions break open masses of dark spores are released. On more mature plants numerous dark black blisters are found on foliage and bulb scales. Most infected plants are killed within 3–4 weeks of emergence. Where mature infected bulbs are stored the pathogen does not cause direct losses but can lead to invasion by secondary pathogens.

This fungus is classed as a Hemibasidiomycete. The lesions contain chlamydospores which are otherwise known as brand spores, teleutospores or smut spores. These consist of a central reddish to dark brown, thick walled cell, 12–15 μm in diameter, surrounded by hyaline, thin walled appendage cells which are sterile and 4–6 μm in diameter. Chlamydospores develop from terminal cells of sporogenous hyphal branches which curve back upon themselves and the surrounding hyphal cells to become appendage cells of the chlamydospore. Both appendage cells and the central spores of the young chlamydospore are initially diakaryotic, but the central spore nuclei undergo karyogamy, becoming diploid before maturity. Appendage cells are initially binucleate but become mononucleate by disintegration of one nucleus. Nucleoli are found in both haploid and diploid nuclei. The central spore walls are differentiated into three distinct layers. Appendage cells contain organelles similar to those found in the central spore but with fewer lipid bodies. They have two wall layers and are attached to the central spore by an amorphous matrix (Grayson and Lacy, 1975). Only the central cell germinates, giving rise to a short hemispherical basidium. No basidiospores are formed; mycelial branches develop directly from the basidium which becomes septate with age and breaks up into hyphal fragments which in turn produce new thalli. Physiological specialisation has not been reported.

The chlamydospores are soil-borne, invading the onion at the seedling stage usually through the cotyledon prior to emergence. Onion plants are only susceptible to invasion by *U. cepulae* at the seedling stage. The leaves of an onion are produced successively in the embryonic transition region between root and leaf, remaining enclosed within the preceding leaf until they emerge above ground. Each leaf goes through a susceptible phase, but if the preceding leaf has remained uninfected the next leaf is protected by it until it too passes into the resistant phase. Deep planting of onion seed in artificially infected soil resulted in greater infection at standardised levels of inoculum due to increased amounts of susceptible tissue being exposed and longer exposure of susceptible tissue to the inoculum (Stienstra and Lacy, 1972).

Optimal temperatures for chlamydospore and hyphal fragment germination are from 13 to 22 °C. There is no appressorium formation in the infection process, the germ tube penetrates directly into the cotyledonary epidermis. Infection is abundant at 10–12 °C. The chlamydospores are of two mating types and both are required for infection to develop. *Urocystis cepulae* can be grown in axenic culture requiring malt extract, peptone and inorganic salts and an optimal pH 5.5–6.5 (Lacy, 1968; Dow and Lacy, 1969).

Development of some resistant cultivars has been achieved by hybridising *A. cepa* with *A. fistulosum* (Welsh onion), which possesses a level of resistance. The initial progeny were sterile but an amphidiploid form was fertile and resistant. Chemical control is obtained by dressing seed with thiram or by methyl bromide soil sterilisation.

10.2.9 *Ustilago maydis* (smut)

The host range of *U. maydis* is restricted to maize or corn *Zea mays* and its close relative *Euchlaena mexicana*. Literature on this host—parasite complex is voluminous and mainly directed towards the effects on agricultural crops (Christensen, 1963). In this present work consideration is primarily directed at the disease on sweet- or sugar-corn (*Z. mays* var. *saccharata*).

Symptoms are spectacular and distinctive, with the development of large dark brown or black galls on all parts of the host at any growth stage. These smooth, rounded structures (sori) result from neoplastic activity incited by the *U. maydis* mycelium growing internally within the plant, and vary in size from a few millimetres to several centimetres. Initially they are covered with a whitish green skin which at maturity bursts to liberate vast numbers of chlamydospores (otherwise known as teleuto-, brand- or smut-spores). These issue from the ruptured gall as a powdery, dark brown-black spore mass.

An additional symptom is the development of chlorotic lesions on the leaf laminae (Callow and Ling, 1973). Within these lesions the mesophyll cells are shrunken and lose their characteristic irregular form. At the centre of the lesion both mesophyll and bundle sheath plastids degenerate, but at the margins plastids are still present. Chlorotic lesions develop in the absence of systemic mycelium at the leaf tips. Galls on leaf sheaths and laminae result from hyperplasia of the host cells and are composed of thin walled parenchyma cells. Branched inter- and intracellular hyphae are present in the gall and chlamydospores develop within large aggregates of intercellular hyphae. Gall formation involves a temporary synthesis of starch in the mesophyll plastids accompanied by nuclear and nucleolar hypertrophy. There is a reduction of phenolic production in infected plants with only scant lignification of neoplastic cells. Cell proliferation in gall meristems is continuous during sorus production. Investigations of the neoplastic zones (Callow, 1975) demonstrated two distinct types of tissue within the leaf sheath. Small cells around the vascular stele contained nuclei with double and fourfold DNA content. Additionally there were larger vacuolate cells forming the bulk of the tissue with nuclei containing 16-, 32- and 64-fold increased levels of DNA, indicating substantial endopolyploidy. Nucleolar dry mass was also substantially increased in infected cells, rising up to 10-fold compared to controls, indicating substantial ribosomal synthesis.

The dry weight of galled organs gradually increased in parallel with decreased dry weight in uninfected areas of the plant (Billett and Burnett, 1978*a*). As infection progressed, unfolding of leaves from the meristem was delayed and eventual maximal leaf area reduced. Root dry weight reduction was greater than that taking place in the shoot. Infected areas of the leaf blade became chlorotic within 3—5 days of infection, losing 60 per cent of their chlorophyll, and eventually it all disappeared. Studies of the fate of assimilates indicated that importation into infected areas was enhanced at the expense of healthy parts of the plant (Billett and Burnett, 1978*b*). Accumulation increased before symptoms became visible and was greatest when fungal growth was at its highest. Within a galled leaf most imported assimilates were localised in the galled area. Loss of root dry weight was correlated with a 50 per cent reduction in movement of carbon compounds into the root. Within infected plants there was stimulation of invertase activity (Billett *et al.*, 1977) which may correlate with the changes in movement of the products of photosynthesis.

Ustilago maydis is classed as a Hemibasidiomycete fungus. The chlamydospores are globular to elliptical with prominent blunt spines and measure 8−12 μm in diameter. These arise from the dikaryotic mycelium within the host, which produces no haustoria but short branches of mycelium enter the host cells. The two nuclei within each chlamydospore fuse, and at maturity the spore contains a single diploid nucleus. At this stage the spores are dispersed from the gall either by wind or insects such as frit fly (*Oscinella frit*). During germination a promycelium or germ tube is produced and the diploid nucleus undergoes meiosis. Thereafter three septa form, isolating each single haploid nucleus. These divide and the daughter nuclei pass into sporidia formed on the promycelium. Further mitotic divisions result in more sporidia being produced. In most *Ustilago* spp. this stage is capable of saprophytic but not parasitic growth. Normally there must be fusion with a sporidium of an opposite mating type (heterothallism) by means of a short conjugation tube to initiate the new systemic dikaryotic mycelium. It is thought, however, that at least some *U. maydis* mycelium is derived from individual monokaryotic sporidia.

There is a complex form of heterothallism in *U. maydis* with incompatibility being controlled by two loci at one of which there are multiple alleles. In addition, parasexual recombination has been demonstrated in *U. maydis*. As a result the fungal population consists of an infinite number of biotypes differing in pathogenicity and other characters. The practical result of this is to render breeding for resistance by the use of monogenic systems doomed to rapid failure because the pathogen population will quickly evolve to overcome such resistances. The life cycle of *Ustilago* spp. is shown in figure 10.3.

Distribution of *U. maydis* is world-wide. The pathogen is seed-borne, being carried on the surface of the seed; it is also soil-borne where the chlamydospores retain viability for considerable time periods − in excess of 8 years in dry sand. Invasion can take place through any actively growing part of the host. The optimal temperature range for fungal growth is from 25 to 30 °C. It can be grown in axenic culture, and shake cultures are an excellent means of producing sporidial inoculum which can be injected with an hypodermic syringe in a test plant with symptoms developing in 5−11 days.

Control in agricultural crops may be achieved by use of rotation, with wheat (*T. aestivum*) and barley (*H. vulgare*) providing efficient break crops. With horticultural sweet-corn crops land areas available for rotation may be more limited. The effects of *U. maydis* on the yield of sweet-corn is more devastating than on grain or forage maize. Once sweet-corn cobs are disfigured they are rendered unsaleable; also, only one or two cobs are produced per plant compared

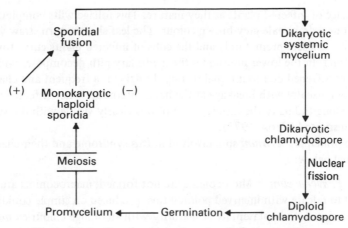

Figure 10.3   Developmental cycle of *Ustilago* spp.

to the five to eight cobs produced by agricultural maize. It has been demonstrated that the use of irrigation, which is a frequent practice with sweet-corn crops, increases the numbers of infected plants and the severity of symptoms.

Some chemical controls are available, such as treatment of seed with vitavax, thiram and benomyl. Carboximide fungicides are active against this group of pathogens due to their effects on the mitochondrial succinic dehydrogenase complex found in basidiomycetes. Breeding for resistance will need to utilise polygenic characters, and this is demonstrated by the work of Dikaneva (1973). Sweet-corn lines were classified as 'resistant' (no more than 10 per cent infected), 'moderately resistant' (11–20 per cent infected), 'susceptible' (up to 50 per cent infected) and 'very susceptible' (50 per cent or more infected). Those lines with high borne cobs and greater numbers of reproductive buds were most severely infected; late and very late ripening lines were less affected. Following up this work, Shinaraev and Dikaneva (1975) found that direct crosses of lines of *Z. mays* var. *saccharata* resistant to *U. maydis* when made with other resistant lines produced F_1 hybrids where the level of resistance was maintained. If, however, resistant lines were crossed with susceptible lines then the resultant progeny had an intermediate level of resistance.

10.2.10 *Fusarium* spp. (stalk rot)

Several *Fusarium* spp. cause root, stem and ear diseases of *Zea mays*, constituting the most serious disease problem for this crop on a world scale. The stalk rot syndrome has been reviewed in detail by Christensen and Wilcoxson (1966) and is only dealt with in outline here. Initial signs of infection are a greyish sheen on the foliage of infected plants as they mature. This foliage wilts completely, exhibiting a drab, pale grey-brown colour. The leaf sheaths turn straw-yellow, the plant senesces prematurely and the cobs of infected plants curve towards the ground. In the lower internodes the medullary pith decomposes and the stem becomes softened due to internal rotting. Lodging is a frequent and characteristic symptom, usually with breakage at the basal internode. When infected stems are opened longitudinally the disintegrated pith is clearly visible with the vascular tissue disrupted (Cook, 1973).

The principle *Fusarium* spp. involved in this syndrome and their characters are listed below:

(1) *F. avenaceum*   Microconidia are not formed; macroconidia are needle-shaped to falcate with incurved pointed tips, produced on simple conidiophores. Conidia are tri- to heptaseptate at maturity with an orange colour *en masse*; the conidia size ranges are as follows: aseptate to monoseptate, 10–15 μm x 3.5–4 μm; triseptate, 21–38 μm x 3.5–4 μm; tetra- to hexaseptate, 44–70 μm x 4–5 μm. Chlamydospores form only rarely. The fungus is both seed- and soil-borne with mycelium and wind-borne conidia produced on overwintered crop debris.

(2) *F. culmorum*   Microconidia are absent; macroconidia are produced occasionally from conidiophores which develop laterally on aerial mycelium, but more frequently from loose sporodochia. Macroconidia are tri- to pentaseptate, slightly curved fusoid in shape, with the apical cell constricted; conidial size ranges are as follows: triseptate, 26–36 μm x 4–6 μm; pentaseptate, 34–40 μm x 5–6 μm. Chlamydospores develop which are oval to globular, growing either intercalary or sometimes terminally; they are smooth or rough walled, borne singly in chains or clumps. This fungus is mainly soil-borne, persisting for several years on buried crop debris. In the UK it is the most frequent pathogen associated with stalk rot.

(3) *F. poae*   Microconidia develop which are ampule shaped, 8–12 μm x 7–10 μm or globular, 7–10 μm in diameter. Macroconidiophores are slender, much branched at the apex, bearing between one and four phialides, and measuring 15–20 μm x 2.5 μm. Macroconidia are curved, falcate and slightly wider above the median septum; they are triseptate and measure 20–40 μm x 3–4.5 μm. *Fusarium poae* is seed-borne but also transmitted by water-splash and mite vectors.

(4) *Gibberella fujikuroi* (*F. moliniforme*)   The sexual *Gibberella* stage produces perithecia which are dark blue, globular to conical, 250–350 μm high by 200–300 μm in diameter with a rough outer wall. Asci within the perithecia are ellipsoid to clavate with four to eight obliquely uniseriate to biseriate ascospores. These are hyaline, elliptical, mostly monoseptate but occasionally triseptate, and measure 14–18 μm x 4.5–6 μm. Asexual microconidia develop in chains usually without septa but are occasionally monoseptate; they measure 5–12 μm x 1.5–2.5 μm and are fusiform to club-shaped. Macroconidia are thin walled, straight or curved, narrowing at both ends; they are tri- to heptaseptate; their size ranges are as follows: triseptate, 25–36 μm x 2.5–3.5 μm; pentaseptate,

30–50 μm x 2.5–4 μm; heptaseptate, 40–60 μm x 3–4 μm. Chlamydospores do not form, but dark blue globular sclerotia are found. Air-borne conidia are produced from overwintered debris and the fungus is both seed- and soil-borne. It can retain its viability in soil for several years.

(5) *G. fujikuroi* var. *subglutinans* (*F. molinforme* var. *subglutinans*)   This form is distinguished from *G. fujikuroi* by the thinner ascospores; microconidia do not develop in chains and macroconidia are smaller with fewer septa. The asci contain eight ascospores which measure 12–15 μm x 4.5–5 μm and the sexual macroconidia are 32–50 μm x 3–3.5 μm.

(6) *G. zeae* (*F. graminearum*)   Sexual perithecia are superficial, developed from a thin stroma in clusters around the lower nodes of the host stem. They are ovoid with a rough outer wall and measure 140–150 μm in diameter. The wall is formed of two layers, an outer stromatic layer 17–31 μm wide of globular cells which are 5–12 μm x 1.5–3.5 μm and a thin inner layer of compressed thin walled cells. The asci are 60–85 μm x 8–11 μm, club-shaped with a short stalk (stipe) containing eight but sometimes fewer ascospores which are hyaline to light brown, curved needle-shaped with rounded ends and at maturity have three septa, size 19–24 μm x 3–4 μm. No microconidia form, macroconidia develop on doliiform phialides which are 10–14 μm x 3.5–4.5 μm developing from stubby multibranched conidiophores. The conidia are tri- to heptaseptate, 25–50 μm x 3–4 μm often with a pedicellate foot cell. Infections develop from seed- and soil-borne sources with secondary infections arising via rain-splashed conidia or by ascospore discharge.

The stalk rot syndrome reduces 1000 grain weight by 10 per cent and cob weight by 20 per cent in grain maize (Cook, 1977). Its effects on yield of sweet-corn (*Z. mays* var. *saccharata*) have not been elucidated, but there must be direct quantifiable reduction in yield plus loss of visual appeal of the cobs. Disease incidence is increased by high plant densities.

Control measures are primarily aimed at the destruction or removal of infected crop debris, which provides the main means of perennation. If debris must be ploughed in, it should first be chopped up to encourage more rapid decomposition and buried at 20–25 cm below the soil surface, where it will constitute only a limited risk to succeeding crops. Experiments with a range of fungicides have been singularly unsuccessful in producing a means of practical chemical control. It may be possible to breed sweet-corn hybrids with resistance to this wide range of *Fusarium* spp., but the aim should be for non-specific resistance.

10.3 VIRUSES

10.3.1 Onion Yellow Dwarf Virus (OYDV)

In excess of 50 aphid species are potential vectors of OYDV. Under field conditions those of prime importance are *Aphis rumicis, A. maidis* and

Rhopalosiphum prunifoliae. Although OYDV has been detected in pollen grains it is not thought to be seed-borne. The virus is stylet-borne, non-persistent and reported to occur in most countries where onion (*A. cepa*) and shallots (*A. ascalonicum*) are produced. Virus particles are flexuous, filamentous rods 755 nm long and 16 nm wide.

First signs of infection in onions grown from infected bulbs are the development of short yellow streaks on the primary leaf. As further leaves expand they also exhibit yellow streaks. Crinkling and flattening accompany these symptoms, with the leaves eventually losing their erect habit. Streaks also develop on the flower stalks with characteristic twisting and curling which gives the plants a dwarfed appearance. Bulbs formed from infected sets are undersized and the resultant yield is poor. Where the inflorescence is infected the flower clusters are reduced in size with fewer florets. If plants remain symptomless in the first year, growth in succeeding seasons is reduced and symptoms are usually well developed.

Epidermal cells taken from infected onion plants often contain from one to several round or elongated inclusions similar to nuclei in size but consisting of numerous rod-shaped structures. Infected cells are found to contain pinwheels, scrolls and virus-like particles associated with the cellular vesicles. There are several strains of OYDV; those isolated from shallot are more virulent than those from garlic (*A. sativum*) or narcissus (*Narcissus pseudonarcissus*).

Host range includes one-year onion (*A. cepa*), shallot (*A. ascalonicum*), garlic (*A. sativum*), leek (*A. porrum*), topset onion (*A. cepa* var. *viviparum*), multiplier onion (*A. cepa* var. *solanium*), Welsh onion (*A. fistulosum*), various ornamental *Allium* species, daffodil (*Narcissus pseudonarcissus*), polyanthus narcissus (*N. tazetta orientallis*) and the jonquil (*N. odorus regulosus*).

Large losses due to OYDV occur in the USA but control has been achieved by indexing, production of virus-free stock in disease-free areas, and removal of infected volunteer plants. In New Zealand enforcement of an *Allium*-free period has eradicated the pathogen.

Other viruses pathogenic to *Allium* species include Leek Yellow Stripe Virus (LYSV) and Shallot Latent Virus (SLV), neither of which has been described adequately.

10.3.2 Maize Leaf Fleck Virus (MLFV)

Vectors include the aphids *Myzus persicae, Rhopalosiphum prunifoliae* and *R. maidis.* The virus is circulative and persistent, retained by *M. persicae* and *R. prunifoliae* throughout their life. The virus is so far restricted to parts of California, USA, and the host range to *Z. mays* and some grass species.

Initial symptoms are the development of pale circular spots between the veins at the tips of older leaves; these gradually enlarge, taking on a yellow colour. Lesions then appear at the bases of older leaves with the tips turning necrotic. This is usually restricted to the outer edges of the leaves and is preceded by chlorosis. There is no coalescence of lesions to form streaks.

10.3.3 Maize-corn Mosaic Virus (MMV)

The leaf hopper, *Peregrinus maidis*, is the vector of MMV, virus particles being found in the salivary glands and epithelial cells of the intestinal wall. A latent period of up to 30 days occurs after virus acquisition and thereafter it is persistent. Particles resemble certain viruses infecting animals, being bullet-shaped, 250 nm x 80 nm in size, and consisting of an outer coat enclosing a thread of knob-like protrusions within which is an helix of beaded units. Crops grown in the Caribbean, parts of Central America, East Africa (Tanzania) and India are at risk from the pathogen.

Symptoms vary with different cultivars of *Z. mays* but usually commence as small elongated white spots on the mid rib near to the base of the youngest leaf. These extend to form diffuse stripes which may coalesce forming continuous stripes. Under some conditions the stripes are coarse, radiating from the mid rib, or may form yellow bands on the leaves. Symptoms have been classified into three groups:

(1) Stripes are associated with foliar bleaching along the entire length of the leaf, sometimes fading to spots and dots which vary in intensity. Under extreme conditions necrosis develops and stripes are found on the sheaths, ear husks and stalks.

(2) Bleaching of the main veins occurs with attendant coarse parallel streaks, but with the small veins and interveinal tissue remaining green.

(3) Broad chlorotic bands are observed with fewer stripes, but affecting the veins and interveinal areas. Banding may cover the whole length of the leaf or may fade to become dots, stipples and stripes.

Discolorations are due to changes in the chloroplasts. Within the palisade tissue the plastids disintegrate into granular masses with dissolution of some mesophyll cell walls. Phloem necrosis develops within the vascular tissue and there may be thickening of epidermal cell walls. Wall thickening and phloem necrosis are, however, independent processes. Numbers of chloroplasts are reduced, especially in the sheath cells of vascular bundles and vascular parenchyma cells. Virus particles have been found to bud at the inner nuclear membrane and accumulate in the perinuclear space. They are also found in the stamens of male flowers.

10.3.4 Maize-sweet-corn Mosaic Virus (MSCMV)

No vector has been identified for this virus, but it is known not to be seed-borne. It is reported from North America affecting a range of sweet-corn cultivars, barley (*Hordeum* spp.), wheat (*Triticum* spp.) and wild foxtail grass (*Setaria viridis*).

Initial symptoms are small broken chlorotic streaks on the apical leaves. As the virus becomes systemic all foliage is affected by broken or continuous interveinal chlorotic streaks which extend as far as the leaf sheath but not into the stalk. Infected plants are reduced in size and yield is severely depressed.

10.3.5 Maize Rough Dwarf Virus (MRDV)

The only natural vector of MRDV so far identified is the plant hopper *Laodelphax striatellus*, although various other members of the Delphacidae have been infected experimentally. Within the vector virus particles are found in the cytoplasm of fat bodies, mycetome, salivary glands, gut hypodermis, muscles and trachaea. The virus multiplies within its vector and is also pathogenic to it since progeny from infected females die during embryonic development. Virus particles are isometric, 55–60 nm in diameter; in some particles there is a central core some 34 nm in diameter. The virus is widely reported from southern and south-eastern Europe, as far as Israel.

First recognisable symptoms are dwarfing followed by reddening chlorosis and withering of the leaf tips. Typically, small neoplastic enations develop on the leaf undersurface, giving it a roughened texture from which the syndrome name is derived. Enations are also found on the bracts, appearing as white pustules. The adventitious roots fail to form secondary roots and are short and thickened with longitudinal cracks; eventually the root system becomes discoloured and secondary rotting takes place. If ears are formed at all they are reduced in size, with the distal portions being atrophied. Often infected plants remain sterile; the male inflorescence may emerge but the female remains rudimentary. The host chloroplast lamellae of the parenchyma cells are disarranged, with the grana and intergrana lamellae becoming randomly placed rather than occurring in an orderly pattern. Virus particules may be found within phloem cells. Where tumours develop one of the first indications is a development of vesicles at the edge of the chloroplasts. The cell wall of old tumour cells forms finger-like projections into the cell lumen and tubules appear within the cytoplasm with virus particles found in association. Virus particles are of two types, immature and mature, being 50 and 70 nm in diameter, respectively. There is some evidence to suggest the existence of two strains causing dwarfing and non-dwarfing symptoms. Many of the properties are similar to those viruses causing disease in animals.

Satisfactory control is obtained by delayed sowing and by killing grass weed hosts in and around fields 20–30 days before sowing sweet-corn. It is also suggested that Old World maize cultivars are less susceptible than some of the newer American dent hybrids.

10.3.6 Maize Streak Virus (MSV)

Three species of leaf hopper, *Cicadulina mbila, C. zea* and *C. nicholsi* are vectors of MSV. Detailed studies of vector transmission were made by Storey in the period 1925–40. All five nymphal instars of *Cicadulina* spp. are able to acquire and transmit MSV; it is retained during moulting but not transmitted through the egg. Vector races which differ in their ability (activity) to transmit MSV are known. The gut wall of those unable to transmit (inactive) is impermeable to the passage of MSV, but the vector may be rendered able to transmit by injecting virus into the abdomen or by puncturing the gut wall. Employing conventional notation (A = major gene for activity, a for inactivity) we can write the constitutions of active males, $(AX)(Y)$; inactive males, $(aX)(Y)$; active females, $(AX)(AX)$ or $(AX)(aX)$; and inactive females, $(aX)(aX)$. Individual insects of an active race are not equally efficient vectors and there is evidence that a second gene, not sex linked, modifies the effect of the major gene for activity.

This virus occurs in Africa south of the Sahara, Mauritius, Madagascar, India and probably other parts of South East Asia but not in America. The particles are isometric, about 20 nm in diameter, and usually occur in pairs 30 nm x 20 nm. Host range includes maize (*Z. mays*), sugar cane (*Saccharum officinarum*), millet (*Eleusine coracana*), wheat (*Triticum aestivum*) and a range of grasses.

Initial symptoms are a development of colourless circular spots, 0.5–2 mm in diameter, on the youngest exposed leaves. As the frequency of such spots increases they become elongated and generalised over all young leaves. Once the chlorotic areas are formed on the young leaf there is no change in their size or shape as the leaf attains its full size. Virus particles are restricted to the chlorotic leaf areas. On maize characteristic symptoms are distinct foliar chlorosis in narrow lines parallel to the veins, these vary from 0.5 to 1 mm in width, often fusing into broad bands. In transmitted light these bands appear opaque yellow in contrast to the green of the healthy parts of the leaf. As the syndrome advances the chlorotic bands become sunken.

Successful infection depends on the stylet of the leaf hopper penetrating the phloem of the plant. There is rapid passage of the virus down from the point of inoculation; this can exceed 40 cm in 120 min. Within infected cells crystalline nuclear inclusions develop which contain particles 18–20 nm in diameter. There are various strains of MSV which exhibit host adaptation; the maize forms may be differentiated into a severe (A) strain and a mild (B) strain; sugar cane and various wild grasses are affected by other strains.

10.3.7 Maize Wallaby-ear Virus (MWEV)

The jassid species *Cicadula bimaculata* is the only known vector of MWEV. Distribution is limited to south-eastern Queensland, Australia. Symptoms are first seen in January; fully mature crops are barely affected by infection but newly sown ones can be severely affected. Enations form on secondary veins of the upper leaves which swell rapidly from the distal to the proximal ends of the leaf. Dwarfing occurs and affected plants turn a vivid dark green colour. Pollen yield is lowered and growth of the silk is slow which results in reduced grain production.

10.3.8 Asparagus Latent Virus (ALV)

There is no known vector of ALV, but it can be seed-borne. It is found principally in Germany and Denmark. Differential hosts such as bean (*Ph. vulgaris*) develop local lesion symptoms and systemic infection occurs on *Nicotiana clevelandii* and *N. glutinosa*. No symptoms develop on infected asparagus (*Asparagus officinalis*).

10.3.9 Asparagus Stunt Virus (ASV)

This is only found on asparagus (*A officinalis*) in New Zealand, causing growth reduction, browning of the foliage and chlorotic to brown stem streaks. Other information on ASV is very limited.

REFERENCES

Sections 10.1.1 and 10.1.2
Roberts, P. (1973). *Pl. Path.* 22, 98.
Stapp, C. (1961). *Bacterial Plant Pathogens*. Oxford University Press, London.
Taylor, J. D. (1975). *A. Rep. natn. Veg. Res. Stn* 1974, 116–7.

Section 10.2.1
Blotnicka, K. (1974). *Hodowla Roslin Aklimatyzacja i Nasiennictivo* 18, 131–50.
Palti, J., Brosch, S., Stettiner, M. and Zilkha, M. (1972). *Phytopath. Med.* 11, 30–3.
Viranyi, F. (1974*a*). *Acta phytopath. hung.* 9, 311–4.
Viranyi, F. (1974*b*). *Acta phytopath. hung.* 9, 315–18.
Viranyi, F. (1975). *Acta phytopath. hung.* 10, 321–8.
Walker, J. C. (1952). *Diseases of Vegetable Crops*. McGraw-Hill, New York.
Weihle, G. A. de (1975). *Meded. Verhandelingen Koninklyk Nederlands Meteorologisch Instituut* 97, 33.

Section 10.2.2
Dixon, G. R. (1976). *J. natn. Inst. agric. Bot.* 14, 100–4.
Doherty, M. A. and Preece, T. F. (1978). *Physiol. Pl. Path.* 12, 123–32.
Kontaxis, D. G. (1977). *Pl. Dis. Reptr* 61, 503.

Wilson, M. and Henderson, D. M. (1966). *British Rust Fungi.* Cambridge University Press, London.

Section 10.2.3
Geeson, J. D. (1976). *Pl. Path.* **25**, 115–6.
Yokoyama, S. (1976). *Studies on the Leaf Blight of Onion (Tamanegi Shiroiro Ekibyo) caused by* Phytophthora porri *Foister.* Bulletin no. 22. Agricultural Experiment Station, Fukuoka.

Section 10.2.4
Fahim, M. M. (1966). *Trans. Br. mycol. Soc.* **49**, 73–8.
Fahim, M. M. and El-Shehedi, A. (1966). *Trans. Br. mycol. Soc.* **49**, 79–80.
Fokkema, N. J. and Lorbeer, J. W. (1974). *Phytopathology* **64**, 1128–33.
Meredith, D. S. (1966). *Ann. appl. Biol.* **57**, 67–73.

Section 10.2.5
Hancock, J. G. and Lorbeer, J. W. (1963). *Phytopathology* **53**, 669–73.
Maude, R. B. and Presly, A. H. (1977*a*). *Ann. appl. Biol.* **86**, 163–80.
Maude, R. B. and Presly, A. H. (1977*b*). *Ann. appl. Biol.* **86**, 181–88.
Segall, R. H. and Newhall, A. G. (1960). *Phytophathology* **50**, 76–82.
Tichelaar, G. M. (1967). *Neth. J. Pl. Path.* **73**, 157–60.

Section 10.2.6
Coley-Smith, J. R. (1959). *Ann. appl. Biol.* **47**, 511–18.
Coley-Smith, J. R. (1960). *Ann. appl. Biol.* **48**, 8–18.
Entwistle, A. R. and Granger, J. (1977). *A. Rep. natn. Veg. Res. Stn* **1976**, 97–8.
Entwistle, A. R. and Munasinghe, H. L. (1978). *Agric. Res. Coun. Res. Rev.* **4**, 27–30.
Scott, M. R. (1956*a*). *Ann. appl. Biol.* **44**, 576–83.
Scott, M. R. (1956*b*). *Ann. appl. Biol.* **44**, 584–9.

Section 10.2.7
Pierpoint, W. S. (1971). *A. Rep. Rothamsted. Exp. Stn* **1970** (2), 199–218.

Section 10.2.8
Dow, R. L. and Lacey, M. L. (1969). *Phytopathology* **59**, 1219–22.
Grayson, R. L. and Lacey, M. L. (1975). *Phytopathology* **65**, 994–9.
Lacey, M. L. (1968). *Phytopathology* **58**, 1460–3.
Semenov, V. A. (1977). *Byulleten Vsesoyuznogo Ordena Lenina i Ordena Druzhby narodov Instituta Rastenievodstva Imeni N.I. Vavilova* no. 70, 60–2.
Steinstra, W. C. and Lacey, M. L. (1972). *Phytopathology* **62**, 282–6.

Section 10.2.9
Billett, E. E. and Burnett, J. H. (1978*a*). *Physiol. Pl. Path.* **12**, 93–102.

Billett, E. E. and Burnett, J. H. (1978*b*). *Physiol. Pl. Path.* 12, 103–12.
Billett, E. E., Billett, M. A. and Burnett, J. H. (1977). *Phytochemistry* 16, 1163–6.
Callow, J. A. (1975). *New Phytol.* 75, 253–57.
Callow, J. A. and Ling, I. T. (1973). *Physiol. Pl. Path.* 3, 489–94.
Christensen, J. J. (1963). *Corn Smut Caused by* Ustilago maydis. Monograph no. 2. American Phytopathology Society, St. Paul, Minn.
Dikaneva, L. A. (1973). *Trudy prikl. Bot. Genet. Selek.* 51, 184–7.
Shinarev, G. E. and Dikaneva, L. A. (1975). *Byulleten Vsesoyuznogo Nauchno Issledovteliskogo Instituta Rastenievodstva imeni N.I. Vavilova* no. 50, 88.

Section 10.2.10
Christensen, J. J. and Wilcoxson, R. D. (1966). *Stalk Rot of Corn.* Monograph no. 3. American Phytopathological Society, St. Paul, Minn.
Cook, R. J. (1973). *Agric. Devmt Advisory Service Qtly. Rev.* 11, 113–7.
Cook, R. J. (1977). *Ann. appl. Biol.* 87, 266–70.

FURTHER READING

Sections 10.1.1 and 10.1.2
Bradbury, J. F. (1967). Erwinia stewartii. Commonwealth Mycological Institute Descriptions of Pathogenic Fungi and Bacteria no. 123. Commonwealth Mycological Institute, Kew.
Dowson, W. J. (1957). *Plant Diseases due to Bacteria.* Cambridge University Press, London.

Section 10.2.1
Palti, J. (1975). Peronospora destructor. Commonwealth Mycological Institute Descriptions of Pathogenic Fungi and Bacteria no. 456. Commonwealth Mycological Institute, Kew.

Section 10.2.2
Laundon, G. F. and Waterston, J. M. (1965). Puccinia-allii. Commonwealth Mycological Institute Descriptions of Pathogenic Fungi and Bacteria no. 52. Commonwealth Mycological Institute, Kew.
Waterston, J. M. (1965). Puccinia asparagi. Commonwealth Mycological Institute Descriptions of Pathogenic Fungi and Bacteria no. 54. Commonwealth Mycological Institute, Kew.

Section 10.2.4
Ellis, M. B. and Holliday, P. (1970). Alternaria porri. Commonwealth Mycological Institute Descriptions of Pathogenic Fungi and Bacteria no. 248. Commonwealth Mycological Institute, Kew.

Section 10.2.5
Ellis, M. B. and Walker, J. M. (1974). Botrytis allii. Commonwealth Mycological
    Institute Descriptions of Pathogenic Fungi and Bacteria. no. 433. Common-
    wealth Mycological Institute, Kew.

Section 10.2.8
Mielder, J. L. and Holliday, P. (1971). Urocystis cepulae. Commonwealth
    Mycological Institute Descriptions of Pathogenic Fungi and Bacteria no. 298.
    Commonwealth Mycologocial Institute, Kew.

Section 10.2.9
Ainsworth, G. C. (1965). Ustilago maydis. Commonwealth Mycological Institute
    Descriptions of Pathogenic Fungi and Bacteria no. 79. Commonwealth
    Mycological Institute, Kew.
Holliday, R. (1974). *Ustilago maydis.* In *Handbook of Genetics*, Vol. 1, *Bacteria,
    Bacteriophages and Fungi.* Plenum Press, New York.

Section 10.2.10
Booth, C. (1971). *The Genus* Fusarium. Commonwealth Mycological Institute,
    Kew.
Booth, C. (1971). Fusarium poae. Commonwealth Mycological Institute
    Descriptions of Pathogenic Fungi and Bacteria no. 308. Commonwealth
    Mycological Institute, Kew.
Booth, C. (1973). Gibberella zeae (*Conidial State*: Fusarium graminearum).
    Commonwealth Mycological Institute Descriptions of Pathogenic Fungi and
    Bacteria no. 384. Commonwealth Mycological Institute, Kew.
Booth, C. and Waterston, J. M. (1964). Fusarium avenaceum. Commonwealth
    Mycological Institute Descriptions of Pathogenic Fungi and Bacteria no. 25.
    Commonwealth Mycological Institute, Kew.
Booth, C. and Waterston, J. M. (1964). Fusarium culmorum. Commonwealth
    Mycological Institute of Pathogenic Fungi and Bacteria no. 26. Commonwealth
    Mycological Institute, Kew.
Booth, C. and Waterston, J. M. (1964). Gibberella fujikuroi. Commonwealth
    Mycological Institute Descriptions of Pathogenic Fungi and Bacteria no. 22.
    Commonwealth Mycological Institute, Kew.
Booth, C. and Waterston, J. M. (1964). Gibberella fujikuroi *var.* subglutinans.
    Commonwealth Mycological Institute Descriptions of Pathogenic Fungi and
    Bacteria no. 23. Commonwealth Mycological Institute, Kew.

Sections 10.3.1—10.3.9
Bock, K. R. (1974). *Maize Streak Virus.* Commonwealth Mycological Institute/
    Association of Applied Biologists Descriptions of Plant Viruses no. 133.
    Commonwealth Mycological Institute, Kew.
Bos, L. (1976). *Onion Yellow Dwarf Virus.* Commonwealth Mycological

Institute/Association of Applied Biologists Descriptions of Plant Viruses no. 158. Commonwealth Mycological Institute, Kew.

Herold, F. (1972). *Maize Mosaic Virus.* Commonwealth Mycological Institute/ Association of Applied Biologists Descriptions of Plant Viruses no. 94. Commonwealth Mycological Institute, Kew.

Lovisolo, O. (1971). *Maize Rough Dwarf Virus.* Commonwealth Mycological Institute/Association of Applied Biologists Descriptions of Plant Viruses no. 72. Commonwealth Mycological Institute, Kew.

Smith, K. M. (1972). *A Textbook of Plant Virus Diseases.* Longmans, London.

11
Pathogens of Cucurbit Crops

The final two chapters in this book deal with cucurbit and solanaceous crops which are produced as field vegetables and under protected culture. Cucurbit crops cover a wide range of uses from tropical water melons (*Citrullis vulgaris*) to temperate glasshouse cucumbers (*C. sativus*). They are of considerable importance to the agricultural economies of both underdeveloped and developed countries. There are also industrial uses for the production of pickled or preserved cucumber, gherkins and chutneys. Control of pathogens of these crops has been achieved by breeding for resistance; utilizing polygenic systems to combat the bacterium *Pseudomonas lachrymans* (angular leaf spot), the fungus *Pseudoperonospora cubensis* (downy mildew) and major gene resistance to *Sphaerotheca fuliginea* (powdery mildew) and *Didymella bryoniae* (black rot). Resistance has been reinforced by use of systemic fungicidal control especially with *S. fuliginea* (powdery mildew) and *Colletotrichum lagenarium* (anthracnose). By virtue of the economic significance of cucurbit crops considerable studies of host—parasite physiology have been stimulated. This also results from the suitability of cucurbit seedlings for culture under controlled conditions and of their foliar pathogens for application at controlled levels of inoculum. Such combinations of host and parasite present the experimenter with a controllable system with which to work.

Biological control may emerge for some cucurbit pathogens, especially soil-borne *Fusarium* spp., since French research has indicated that certain soils contain factors which inhibit pathogen development. Similarly, some other pathogens are inhibited by cross-protection mechanisms stimulated by non-compatible fungal strains. Viral pathogens such as Cucumber Green Mottle Mosaic Virus and the ubiquitous Cucumber Mosaic Virus are composed of an array of strains. Cucumber Mosaic Virus has a very wide host range covering diverse Angiosperm families.

11.1 BACTERIAL PATHOGENS

11.1.1 *Pseudomonas lachrymans* (angular leaf spot)

The name for this pathogen is derived from the tear-like droplets of bacterial slime which exude from invasion sites. Although the primary host is cucumber (*Cucumis sativus*) grown under field conditions in humid and semi-humid climates, a range of other cucurbits is susceptible.

Symptoms appear first on the young cotyledons as soft, transparent, rounded or irregular lesions. On more mature foliage characteristic angular lesions form at high humidity. These extend along the veins and gradually spread over the entire leaf. On the undersurface of infected leaves bacterial slime droplets develop in the early morning. In dry conditions these form into a white crust. The whole lesion becomes white to tawny-yellow or brown and may drop out to give the leaves a tattered appearance. Affected petioles and stems develop a water-soaked symptom with the production of copious bacterial slime. On infected fruits small, circular, soft lesions form and in transit these may dry out and crack, again with a whitish crust. Usually fruit lesions remain superficial but permit the ingress of secondary rotting organisms. Bacterial cells are found in the xylem elements of the fruit mesocarp speed leading to seed transmission of this pathogen. Growth of infected plants is retarded and the loss of the foliage reduces fruit yield.

Pseudomonas lachrymans is an aerobic, Gram-negative, non-spore-forming, rod-shaped bacterium, $0.8-1.2$ μm in length which is motile, possessing between one and five polar flagella. On beef peptone agar the colonies are circular, slightly raised, smooth, glistening, transparent, whitish with entire margins. This organism can liquify gelatin, does not reduce nitrate, produces slight ammonia, but does not evolve hydrogen sulphide; litmus milk becomes alkaline and is cleared without coagulation. Acid, but not gas, is produced from glucose, galactose, fructose, mannose, arabinose, xylose, sucrose, and mannitol, but not from maltose, rhamnose, lactose, raffinose, glycerol, salicin or arbutin. Optimal growth occurs at $25-27$ °C. Little physiological specialisation between isolates has been reported, but some isolates of *Ps. lachrymans* have been differentiated into two groups on the basis of inoculation on a standard range of cucurbit hosts. Those isolates from damper, cooler regions were the most virulent.

The main avenue of transmission is via infected seed, leading to invasion of the cotyledons at germination. Overwintering occurs on diseased plant residues and spread within crops is by water- and rain-splash of the bacterial slime. Invasion takes place through stomata, hydathodes or wounds. Geographical distribution is world-wide wherever the environment is sufficiently warm and wet to permit pathogen growth. Spread is very rapid within the host vascular system. Both young and mature leaves reach maximal bacterial concentrations $3-4$ days after inoculation, but young leaves contain $20-40$-fold more bacterial cells. Concentrations of cells are greatest in susceptible cultivars and least in resistant ones, with intermediate levels in hybrids derived from crossing resistant and susceptible lines.

In the USA control has been achieved by use of polygenically inherited resistance. The greatest level of resistance was identified in PI 197087 from southern India, with somewhat less resistance in PI 169400. Susceptibility has been related to the amino-nitrogen status of host foliage since older leaves are more resistant than young leaves. The former contained 100 μg of nitrogen per gram fresh weight whereas young leaves contained twice that amount (van Gundy and Walker, 1957). Seed treatments with 1:100 mercuric chloride or by steeping for 18 h in zinc or manganese sulphate have given effective means of obtaining disease-free seed. Because the organism can perennate in infected crop, debris rotation is essential; at least 2 years' freedom from cucurbit crops is required. The organism cannot survive in soil alone once the infected vines have disintegrated. Under glass it is essential to control temperature and humidity so that free water is not allowed to accumulate on the foliage. In protected environments copper sprays and Bordeaux mixtures may be of value for controlling this disease.

11.1.2 *Erwinia tracheiphila* (bacterial wilt)

This is one of the most destructive pathogens of field-grown cucumber (*C. sativus*) and muskmelon (*C. melo*) crops, but most cucurbits are also susceptible.

Initially the foliage of infected plants takes on a dull green appearance. This is followed by symptoms which are typical of those caused by other vascular wilt organisms. The leaves and eventually entire branches lose turgor, wilt irreversibly and become desiccated. Sticky bacterial slime is exuded from fruits developed on infected vines. When wilted stems are cut, a viscid, sticky bacterial matrix exudes from the bundles and can be drawn out in strands 2 cm or more in length. This character provides a useful diagnostic feature.

Erwinia tracheiphila is a Gram-negative, non-spore-forming bacterium with capsulate rods 0.5–0.7 μm × 1.2–2.5 μm in size which are motile by virtue of peritrichous flagella. Under certain conditions it may grow as a facultative anaerobe. On agar the colonies are greyish-white to cream in colour, circular, smooth and glistening. It is unable to liquify gelatin, produces thin spreading growth; starch, cellulose, pectin, casein, egg albumen and blood serum are not hydrolysed; nitrate is not reduced but ammonia is formed from peptone; hydrogen sulphide is evolved from cysteine but litmus milk is unaffected. Acid, but no gas, is produced from glucose, fructose, galactose, sucrose, and β-methyl-D-glucoside but not from xylose, arabinose, rhamnose, sorbose, lactose, raffinose, cellobiose, melezitose, dulcitol, adonitol, α-methyl-D-glucoside, salicin, aesculin, inulin, dextrin or starch. Optimum growth occurs at 25–30 °C. No physiological variation has been reported. The organism is widespread in Canada and the USA and is sporadically reported from Africa, the Far East, the USSR and parts of Europe.

In distinction to *Ps. lachrymans* it is not seed-borne. Various insects are thought to act as vectors of *E. tracheiphila* of which the best documented are the cucumber beetles, *Diabrotica* spp. The bacterium overwinters in the intestinal tract; it can survive only for short periods on infected debris. Invasion takes place only through the wounds caused by the beetle. Attempts have been made to produce resistant cultivars; a source of resistance has been identified in material from Burma which carries a single dominant resistance gene, but modifying genes interfere with inheritance. Copper compounds such as Bordeaux mixture or low soluble copper dust have been used as bactericides but these can have phytotoxic side effects causing the stunting of young plants. The beetle vector can be controlled by insecticides.

11.2 FUNGAL PATHOGENS

11.2.1 *Pseudoperonospora cubensis* (downy mildew)

This pathogen is confined to cucurbit crops in warm temperate and tropical regions with abundant moisture. It is unable to survive temperatures below 0 °C. Symptoms first become evident on the upper leaf surface as bright yellow lesions and are accompanied on the lower surface by purplish to grey-black zones of sporulation. Lesions on the upper leaf surface turn necrotic brown from the centre outwards. On cucumber (*C. sativus*) foliar death leads to stunting and possibly the death of the entire plant. Primary lesions on cucumber are angular due to their limitation by the leaf veins but on melon (*C. melo*) and other cucurbits no such limitation of lesion growth is seen. Where the host is not killed by *P. cubensis* the effects of infection are to prevent fruit maturation and reduce flavour quality. Although the cotyledons may be invaded it is more usual for foliage 5–15 days old to be infected.

Pseudoperonospora cubensis is a Phycomycete (class Oomycetes). The mycelium is hyaline, coenocytic and intercellular, developing abundantly within the leaf mesophyll layer but also penetrating to the palisade layer. Individual hyphae have an oval shape, with intracellular haustoria formed as finger-like branches; hyphal size is 5.4–7.2 μm in diameter. Sporangiophores develop in groups of between one and five, produced through individual stoma; they are 180–400 μm long and 5–7 μm wide with a bulbous base and are dichotomously branched in the upper third of their growth. Sporangia form singly on subacutely shaped sporuliferous tips; the sporangia are pale grey to purple in colour, ovoid to elliptical in shape, possess a thin wall with a papilla at the distal end and measure 20–40 μm x 14–25 μm. They germinate to produce biflagellate zoospores 10–13 μm in diameter; only rarely do sporangia of *P. cubensis* germinate directly by formation of a germ tube. Each zoospore forms an infection hypha which grows through the host stoma. Oospores may be formed in parts of Asia (northern China, Japan and the USSR) but their existence in the USA is doubtful. When formed they are hyaline, globular and 22–42 μm in diameter. Physiological specialisation is reported, with host-specific races having been identified on cucumber (*C. sativus*) and on cushaw and winter cookneck

squash (*Cucurbita moschata*) in Japan, and on cucumber (*Cucumis sativus*) and
water melon (*Citrullis vulgaris*) in the USA.

Sporulation is rapid and profuse on hosts producing ample photosynthates;
the optimal temperature required is 15 °C, with 6 h moisture on the leaf. Unlike
some other downy mildew pathogens *P. cubensis* thrives in warm as well as cool
temperatures provided fogs or dews are frequent and persistent. Sporangial
dispersal is largely by air currents but can also occur with the aid of an insect
vector, the cucumber beetle. Zoospores germinate only in the presence of free
water, invading through the stomata in less than 5 h at optimal temperatures of
16–22 °C. Incubation within the host takes 4–12 days and is most rapid with
temperatures of 15 °C at night and 25 °C by day and photoperiods of 18 h
light and 6 h dark.

Since no overwintering oospores have been found in the USA it is thought
that fresh inoculum is blown northwards each year from southern frost-free
states such as Florida. By using disease development surveys it is possible to
forecast the rate of epidemic formation and warn growers to spray their crops
in advance of infection. In China and Japan oospores are thought to overwinter,
thereby providing an indigenous source of inoculum.

Polygenic factors for resistance to *P. cubensis* have been identified in some
commercial cucumber (*C. sativus*) cultivars, Chinese Long and Puerto Rico 37.
A further resistance source has been found in PI 197087, which is controlled
by one or two major genes plus one or more minor ones (Sitterley, 1972).
P. H. Williams (personal communication) suggests that resistance in cucumber
(*C. sativus*) is controlled by a single recessive gene. In cantaloupe (*C. melo* var.
cantalupensis) there are levels of tolerance which may be partially dominant and
can be increased by pedigree selection. Cultural control can be achieved by
separating mature and newly sown crops, avoiding high crop population
densities so preventing the build up of moist microclimates within the leaf
canopy, and use of irrigation from overhead which leads to moisture being
retained on the leaves. Chemicals active against *P. cubensis* are dithiocarbamates
and copper, but care must be taken with the latter since some cultivars exhibit
copper phytotoxicity. Sprays must be applied every 4–10 days depending on
the environment.

11.2.2 *Sphaerotheca fuliginea* (powdery mildew)

Several species of powdery mildew fungi have been identified as pathogens
of cucurbits. The nomenclature of these fungi is confused since several species
have been added together or divided up and given different names by various
authorities; also, usually only the asexual *Oidium* stage is seen in the field,
making precise identification of the causal organism difficult. It is thought that
the two major powdery mildews are *Erysiphe cichoracearum* and *Sphaerotheca
fuliginea*. These fungi are closely related and indeed some authorities hold that

they are synonymous. So far as this book is concerned *E. cichoracearum* is dealt with under pathogens of the Compositae (*see* section 7.1.2).

Symptoms caused by *S. fuliginea* on cucurbits are similar to those of powdery mildews on other hosts. Discrete mealy white colonies develop on the upper leaf surface which gradually coalesce and expand on the petioles and stems. Severe foliar colonisation leads to accelerated senescence with the leaves becoming yellow then brown and papery in texture. Fruits are not usually infected but may ripen prematurely and lack flavour. The chief effect of the pathogen is to reduce fruit quality rather than weight or fruit numbers. Loss of quality is particularly severe in the cantaloupe melon (*C. melo* var. *cantalupensis*).

Sphaerotheca fuliginea is an Ascomycete (order Plectomycetes); the mycelium is hyaline, turning brown with age. Asexual conidia, the oidial stage, develop in long chains and they contain distinct fibrosin bodies, which helps to distinguish them from those formed by *E. cichoracearum*. They are ellipsoidal to barrel-shaped and 25–37 μm x 14–25 μm in size. Sexual cleistothecia are only rarely seen but when they are formed they may be scattered or concentrated in clumps, and are usually less than 85 μm in diameter. The number of appendages formed on the cleistothecia is variable; they are usually longer than the cleistothecium diameter, brown in colour and interwoven with the mycelium, alternatively they may be nearly straight and dark brown. The asci are elliptical to nearly globular, measure 50–80 μm x 30–60 μm and containing eight ascospores which are elliptical to spherical and are 17–22 μm x 12–20 μm in size. The pathogen is favoured by dry atmospheric and soil conditions, moderate temperatures, reduced light intensity, fertile soil and succulent plant growth. Optimal conidial germination is at 28 °C with a range of 22–31 °C; conidia can germinate in the absence of free water and in RHs as low as 20 per cent. Germination takes less than 2 h: a penetration tube grows into the centre of the cell lumen to form a haustorium while further germ tubes develop from the same spore; hyphae grow out from the primary appressorium along the leaf surface to produce a superficial mycelium which is dependent on nutrients derived from the host via the haustoria formed within the epidermal cells. Conidiophores are produced within 4 days of initial infection and the conidia abstricted thereafter are disseminated by wind. If cleistothecia develop at all they do so several weeks after infection, their formation depending on the nutritive status of the host.

Uninucleate antheridia and ascogonia develop in the middle of the pustule, coiling around each other. The antheridium withers and disappears when the secondary cleistothecial cell wall develops. Appendages form when the wall has four or five cell layers; conjugation of male and female nuclei in the ascogonium takes place when the outer layers of the wall are formed, followed by division to form asci and division of the ascus nucleus to form ascospores. Heterothallism is thought to be common in *S. fuliginea*. Other hosts of *S. fuliginea* are aubergine (*Solanum melongena*), bean (*Phaseolus* spp.), okra (*Hibiscus esculentus*), soybean (*Glycine max*) and *Vigna* spp. Large numbers of physiological variants have been reported.

Control techniques are largely directed at the use of resistant cultivars or chemicals. Very considerable effort has been put into breeding resistant cantaloupe melons (*C. melo* var. *cantalupensis*) using dominant major genes which in turn has led to the evolution of compatible pathogen races. Host genes for resistance have been designated as follows: Pm^1, single dominant; Pm^1 Pm^2, partially dominant with several modifiers; Pm^3, single dominant; Pm^4, partially dominant; Pm^5, complete dominance (Harwood and Markarian, 1968). Resistance in cucumber (*C. sativus*) is controlled by a major recessive gene, *s*, which determines hypocotyl resistance (intermediate) and is also essential for leaf resistance (complete). Leaf resistance is further controlled by a dominant gene, *R*, which only expresses itself in the presence of *s*. Gene *l* is an inhibitory gene which prevents the expression of complete resistance but does not affect gene *s* (Shanmugasundarum *et al.*, 1971).

A range of eradicant fungicides has been used to control powdery mildew fungi; sulphur and dinocap are the most widely used at present. Development of systemic materials such as dimethirimol and benomyl has given a greater degree of control for longer periods of time but has led to the evolution of chemically resistant pathogen races (*see* section 4.3.3).

A novel suggestion for cultural control is to utilise irrigation water to increase RH, thereby adversely affecting the growth of *S. fuliginea*. Such a technique could give rise to unwanted side effects in that the moist environment would be conducive to development of downy mildew and other pathogens.

11.2.3 *Cladosporium cucumerinum* (scab)

This pathogen is of particular importance on cucumber (*Cucumis sativus*) but also affects musk melon (*C. melo*), cantaloupe (*C. melo* var. *cantalupensis*), pumpkin (*Cucurbita pepo*), squash (*C. maxima*) and marrow (*C. pepo* var. *medullosa*).

Symptoms are superficially similar to those caused by angular leaf spot (*Ps. lachrymans; see* section 11.1.1) with the development of foliar lesions which are roughly circular to angular in shape with a brownish water-soaked appearance. When young plants are infected the leaves and stem rapidly become rotten. Under highly humid conditions an olive-coloured mycelial stroma develops over each lesion. The most severe destruction is caused to fruit on which water-soaked lesions up to 1 cm long and 0.5 cm deep develop. Initially such lesions contain a gummy brown exudate but this gradually dries out, sinks below the surface of the fruit and cracks open. Where semi-mature fruit are infected a corky wound reaction may form around the lesion, with subsequent development of a shallow tan scab. On melon (*C. melo*) the pathogen usually attacks the stem, causing a shallow, soft, spongy decay of the tissues, while on the cantaloupe type (*C. melo* var. *cantalupensis*) decay typically extends deeply into the fruit tissues.

Cladosporium cucumerinum is a Fungus Imperfectus (order Moniliales) producing asexual conidiophores from twisted hyphae which are up to 400 μm long and 3–5 μm thick, often with a basal swelling 8 μm in size. Two forms of conidia develop, these are either aseptate to biseptate up to 30 μm long possessing a coat 3–5 μm thick or they are long branched chains of aseptate or monoseptate conidia which vary in shape from cylindrical to almost spherical with either a smooth or minutely spiny surface having a pale oliveraceous brown colour and measuring 4–25 μm x 2–6 μm. No physiological specialisation has been reported. The fungus is widespread in North America, southern and eastern Asia and Europe, but has not been found in Australasia or South America.

Growth of this fungus occurs at 5–30 °C with an optimum of 20–22 °C and disease develops most severely when the host is exposed to alternating low and high temperatures within the range 15–25 °C, and a RH of 86–100 per cent (Dorozhkin *et al.*, 1976). Conidial germination is encouraged by glucose at 0.01–1 per cent or cucumber sap at 1–10 per cent; germination is inhibited in water alone. During the invasion process conidia adhere to the host surface by secreted material, the germ tube dissolves the cuticle and hyphae grow alongside the host cell wall to become intercellular. In the early stages of pathogenesis *C. cucumerinum* is restricted to the middle lamellae, but later it degrades the host cell walls. Host protoplasm appears unharmed until a late stage in disease development. In resistant tissue the initial pattern of infection is similar to that in susceptible plants, but growth of the fungus is arrested following death of host cells in the vicinity of invading hyphae (Paus and Raa, 1973). It is likely that cell wall degradation is brought about by pathogen-produced pectinases and polygalacturonases (Skare *et al.*, 1975). Fungal cellulases have also been implicated in the disintegration of host tissue (Hussain and Rich, 1958; Strider and Winstead, 1961) while Kuć (1962) suggests that a proteolytic enzyme is also involved which enhances separation and disorganisation of the cells. The cell wall constituents are modified and made available as a carbon source to the pathogen. Translocation pathways are blocked by early necrosis of infected tissue which prevents movement or availability of ammonium ions in the leaf tissue for the manufacture of amides such as asparagine and glutamine. Initial pathogenesis was studied at an ultrastructural level by Laborda and Maxwell (1976) who divide the process into three parts:

(1) Development of fungal penetration structures, conidia and germ tubes which contain numerous lipid bodies. Microbodies are abundant at this stage and often are associated with the lipid bodies, but mitochondria are absent.

(2) The invasion stage, during which no lipid bodies and relatively few microbodies are observed. Mitochondria are abundant but differ markedly in morphology from those observed in the penetration structures.

(3) The colonisation phase, during which hyphal microbodies are the most

abundant organelles, lipid bodies were seldom found, and the mitochondria were similar to those seen during invasion.

Overwintering is probably achieved by *C. cucumerinum* on infected soil-borne debris while transmission within and between growing crops is via the aerially dispersed conidia. Yields of susceptible cucumber cultivars are reduced by 57 per cent following infection (Emmaby *et al.*, 1975). Control of the pathogen has been sought through the use of resistant cultivars. In cucumber (*C. sativus*) resistance is controlled by a single dominant gene (Walker, 1950). In very young seedlings resistance is incompletely dominant and this may be used to separate homozygous and heterozygous resistant progeny. Work by Mahadevan *et al.* (1965) suggests that in resistant plants the pathogen triggers synthesis of an inhibitor which inactivates the pecteolytic enzymes secreted by the pathogen and thus inhibits growth of the pathogen, this process being fully complete 24 h after infection. Some *Cucurbita pepo* accessions have been found to possess tolerance to *C. cucumerinum*: PIs 164957, 167136, 171622, 174183, 174184, 177376 and 227237.

Considerable investigations have been made, particularly in the Netherlands, into chemical control of this pathogen. Benomyl foliar sprays inhibit 98 per cent spore germination at a concentration of 2–5 p.p.m. and produce total control if absorbed by the root system at concentrations of 10–20 p.p.m. Use may also be made of regular applications of dithiocarbamate materials, but these must be applied prior to fruit formation. Substituted indole compounds have antifungal activity against *Botrytis allii* (*see* section 10.2.5) and *C. cucumerinum* especially 3-phenylindole and 3-(2-methylphenyl)-indole (Dekker *et al.*, 1975). Mixtures of mercuric chloride and methionine are also active against *C. cucumerinum* due to the formation of CH_3SHg^+ and $(CH_3S)_2Hg$ ions (Vonk and Sijpesteijn, 1974). Triforine and triamimol, although not preventing conidial germination, inhibit subsequent mycelial growth by action against ergosterol biosynthesis (Sherald *et al.*, 1973). For this host–parasite complex control by cultural rotation is of doubtful value. Crossan and Sasser (1969) found that when cantaloupe (*C. melo* var. *cantalupensis*) and cucumber (*C. sativus*) were rotated with maize (*Z. mays*) on land heavily infected with *C. cucumerinum* the fungus survived for 3 years in the absence of cucurbits and disease was subsequently as severe on rotation plots as those in which cucurbitis had been grown continuously over the 4 year period. Cross-protection of susceptible cucumbers against *C. cucumerinum* has been achieved by prior inoculation with the *Phaseolus* bean pathogen *Colletotrichum lindemuthianum* (*see* section 6.4.4) and may eventually lead to a means of biological control (Hammerschmidt *et al.*, 1976).

11.2.4 *Corynespora casiicola* (blotch or target spot)

Although *C. casiicola* affects a wide host range and has world-wide distribution, its major importance on cucurbits is on those crops grown under protected cultivation in Europe. A range of synonyms is attributed to the fungus but the most widely used is *Cercospora melonis*.

Symptoms are largely restricted to mature foliage but can be found on stems, roots and flowers. These consist of lesions with pale centres having concentric outer rings of olive-green tissue and chlorotic margins. Usually they are water-soaked and appear on the upper leaf surface, increase rapidly in size, turn grey and then brownish and are up to 2 cm in diameter. The lesions are well defined and irregular in shape and affected leaves quickly decay; alternatively, shot holing takes place with subsequent defoliation. Infection severely reduces the dry matter production in leaves even before symptoms become visible (Kazda and Hervest, 1972).

Corynespora casiicola is a Fungus Imperfectus of the order Moniliales. The mycelium is largely intercellular with little found on the host surface. Erect conidiophores develop from the mycelium, which may be branched, pale to mid-brown in colour, septate and composed of up to nine successive cylindrical proliferations; they are 110–850 μm long and 4–11 μm thick. Asexual conidia are usually solitary, of very variable shape from club-shaped to cylindrical, straight or curved, and pale olivaceous brown to brown in colour with a wide size range from 40–220 μm long and 9–22 μm wide at the broadest dimension and 4–8 μm wide at the base.

They often possess a dark hilum having a slight rim. There are over 50 hosts of *C. casiicola* and these are not restricted to Cucurbitaceae but include aubergine (*Solanum melongena*), castor oil (*Ricinis communis*), cowpea (*Vigna sinensis*), sesame (*Sesamum indicum*), soybean (*Glycine max*) and tomato (*Lycopersicon esculentum*). Forms of physiological specialisation have been suggested; isolates from one host will, however, infect botanically unrelated hosts, but two races were erected for isolates from cowpea (*V. sinensis*) and soybean (*G. max*) which cause more severe symptoms on their original host.

Perennation takes place on host debris with the pathogen remaining viable for up to 2 years; the fungus can also be seed-borne. Conidia are transmitted by air currents with the greatest release being before midday. Infection is optimal at temperatures of *c*. 20 °C.

Resistance has been used very successfully to control *C. casiicola*. The production of the cucumber (*C. sativus*) cultivar Butcher's Disease Resister in the 1930s did much to prevent this disease having a catastrophic effect on UK cucumber production. It may be surprising in view of the variability of the organism that this resistance is still operable. More recently, Abul-Hayja *et al*. (1978) showed that resistance derived from the Dutch glasshouse cucumber hybrid 72502 is expressed as an absence of symptoms on the cotyledons and is controlled by a single dominant gene. Resistance is thought to be absent in pickling cucumbers, but Strandberg (1971) found that PIs 255936 and 277741 were highly resistant to *C. casiicola*.

Chemical control can be achieved by use of benomyl, daconil, dithane

or thiabendazole sprays. Under protected cultivation hygiene is especially
important to combat this pathogen. All vines should be disposed of or burnt
at the end of a crop and the house washed with formalin or cresylic acid.
Any infected leaves on growing plants should be removed and destroyed.

11.2.5 Didymella and Phomopsis spp. (black rot)

(a) Didymella bryoniae

The disease syndrome caused by *D. bryoniae* is known as gummy stem blight
as well as black rot. A range of synonyms are applied to the perfect state;
that most frequently found in the literature is *Mycosphaerella melonis*, while
the imperfect conidial state has been classed as *Ascochyta*, *Phyllosticta* or
Diplodina.

Symptoms are initiated on the cotyledons and stems of young plants as
circular black or tan-coloured lesions. If these lead to stem girdling the host
is killed, but where early damage is mild the host will grow slowly,
eventually succumbing to leaf blight. A gummy brown fluid is exuded from
stem cankers and vines affected by such cankers usually wilt when in full
production. Small water-soaked lesions develop on infected fruit, expanding
and exuding gummy material and containing conspicuous black fruiting
bodies. Inoculation of cut cucumber (*C. sativus*) stems, petioles and laterals
with *D. bryoniae* leads to reduced growth by adjacent but symptomless
lateral shoots, indicating systemic effects of this pathogen (Spencer, 1972).

Didymella bryoniae is an Ascomycete of the order Dothideales. Globular
sexual perithecia are formed on most host organs; initially they are immersed
below the surface of the host tissue but eventually ripen and erupt as black
structures 140–200 μm in diameter opening via an apical papillate ostiole.
Within the perithecium are club-shaped asci which may or not be borne on a
short basal stalk, they are 60–90 μm x 10–15 μm in size and possess a bitunicate
wall. Usually eight ascospores are found per ascus; these ascopores are hyaline,
monoseptate, elliptical with rounded ends and constrictions at the septum,
and 14–18 μm x 4–7 μm in size. Pseudoparaphyses produced between the
asci are septate, hyaline and may be branched. Asexual pycnidia may also
form on most parts of the host; as with the perithecia, these are initially
immersed in the host tissue but eventually erupt as dark structures, 120–180
μm in diameter, possessing a wall between two and four yellow-brown cell
layers wide with the outer cells having slightly thicker walls. The conidia are
hyaline, cylindrical with rounded ends, and mostly monoseptate, but with
some being unicellular; they are 6–13 μm x 3–5 μm in size. No physiological
specialisation has been reported. Distribution of this fungus is world-wide.

Optimum growth of *D. bryoniae* occurs at 20–24 °C with the latter being
most favourable to infection in water melon (*Citrullus vulgaris*) although
musk melon (*Cucumis pepo*) is infected at 16–20 °C. Seedling tissue is

penetrated directly through the cuticle, whereas older tissue is invaded through areas of damaged tissue, especially the intercellular spaces around the basal cell of damaged hairs. Infection may also take place through stomata, and pruning and picking wounds provide ideal portals for entry by *D. bryoniae*. Conidia are spread by water-splash and the ascospores in air currents, but still air and lowered temperatures favour dispersal of both spore forms with greatest numbers being found at between soil level and 50 cm (Upenskaya *et al.*, 1974). Peak spore dispersal is between the hours of 18.00 and 20.00 or during darkness. Most ascospores were trapped by Cardaso *et al.* (1974) after rainfall, at average temperatures of 18–25 °C and RH > 85 per cent. Fruit rot begins to develop 2–3 days after ascospore release. Perennation of *D. bryoniae* takes place in the soil as chlamydospores (Uspenskaya *et al.*, 1976). The effect on host plants is loss of photosynthetic activity due to decreased total chlorophyll (Govindarajalui, 1977).

Resistance to *D. bryoniae* is found in cantaloupe melon (*C. melo* var. *cantalupensis*) PI 140471 controlled by a single dominant gene, *Rm Rm*, with moderate resistance controlled by the single gene *Mm Mm*. Plant breeders are producing cultivars containing both genes. An inedible form of water melon (*Citrullus vulgaris*) PI 189225 also possesses resistance, and more recently Sowell (1975) reported resistance in PI 271778.

Field rotation is essential to avoid a build-up of soil-borne inoculum, while under glass soil sterilisation (*see* section 4.3.4) is important. Crop nutrition will influence the severity of infection; increased applications of nitrogen up to 56 mg/1000 g dry soil and added feeding with 0.5 per cent sodium favours disease development but applications of potassium at fruiting at 100 mg/1000 g dry soil reduces disease levels (Prokhorova, 1976).

Control of seed-borne infection is achieved with 0.3 per cent benomyl or 0.2 per cent thiram treatments; on the growing crop sprays of 1 per cent thiram or applications of thiram paste to infected stems have been recommended.

(b) *Phomopsis cucurbitae*

This pathogen causes symptoms similar to those of *D. bryoniae*. Infections are found on mature and senescent tissues as water-soaked lesions producing amber-coloured gummy exudations. Stems may be girdled and the regions above die. Affected tissue becomes pale and separates into strips. Infections on fruit take place through the inflorescence with lesions on the skin, together with softening and water-soaking of underlying material. The whole fruit may become mummified or decay with a typical lemon odour.

The imperfect stage is placed in the order Sphaeropsidales; asexual pycnidia are dark brown to black and of variable shape up to 1 mm wide. The conidiophores are hyaline and either simple or branched, producing two spore forms: A-conidia, which are hyaline, unicellular, needle-shaped to elliptical, 8–12 μm × 2.5–3 μm in size, and B-conidia, which are similar but longer, slimmer, curved, and 18–26 μm × 1 μm in size. No physiological specialisation is reported and so far the pathogen is restricted to Canada, India and the UK. Transmission may be by seed, but other channels seem likely since mature plants which have not previously shown symptoms can become diseased (McKeen, 1957). *Phomopsis cucurbitae* is thought to be capable of both saprophytic and parasitic growth in a manner similar to *Botrytis cinerea* (*see* section 6.4.3).

11.2.6 *Colletotrichum lagenarium* (anthracnose)

Anthracnose was recognised as a disease of cucurbits in the 1860s. It is of greatest importance on the foliage and fruits of cucumber (*Cucumis sativus*), musk melon (*C. melo*) and water melon (*Citrullus vulgaris*) grown in humid conditions.

Symptoms vary from host to host. Lesions on cucumber leaves usually start near a vein, developing into angular or roughly circular spots up to several centimetres in diameter. Infected leaves are usually distorted, while coalescence of foliar lesions can cause total blighting. Lesions on petioles and stems are generally shallow, elongate and tan-coloured; fruit lesions do not become visible until the fruit matures when they are approximately circular, sunken, water-soaked and of considerable size, with mycelium and conidia developing in humid conditions. Symptoms on musk melon foliage resemble those on cucumbers but are more severe on stems and petioles, becoming extensive and darker and causing girdling and general blighting of the foliage. Gummy exudates are excreted from the lesions, which on fruits may attain considerable size. Foliar lesions on water melons are black and accompanied by severe blighting, giving the crop a scorched appearance. Sunken lesions develop on the fruit and there may be floral abortion or fruit malformation. On maturing fruits the lesions are circular and flattened with a water-soaked appearance, and having a central mass of mycelium and conidia.

The imperfect conidial state of *C. lagenarium* is placed in the order Melanconiales. There is confused nomenclature of this organism such that in some literature, especially from the USA, it is referred to as *C. orbiculare*. It closely resembles the causal agent of anthracnose in *Phaseolus* bean, *Colletotrichum lindemuthianum* (*see* section 6.4.4). Mycelium is septate, hyaline when young but darkens with age. Asexual acervuli contain thick walled setae which are bi- or triseptate, variable in number and 90–120 μm long. Conidia are produced singly, from the apex of conidiophores, often aggregating into a slimy pinkish mass; they are hyaline, oblong to almost oval and 4–6 μm x 13–19 μm in size. The sexual perfect stages of this fungus are Ascomycetes of the order Diaporthales and genus *Glomerella*. Some literature even goes so far as to name *G. cingulata* as the perfect state (McLean, 1966), but in view of the variability of *Glomerella* spp. this is doubtful. *Glomerella* spp. produce perithecia on various parts of the host which are globular to pear-shaped, dark brown to black and varying in size up to 300 μm. Within the asci are eight ascospores, and the asci are interspersed with paraphyses forming a group at the base of the perithecium. The ascospores vary from oval to needle-shaped, possibly slightly curved, non-septate hyaline, but may change to faintly brown with a single septum prior to germination.

Physiological specialisation has been identified in the USA and races 1–7 differentiated. This differentiation is based on the ability of individual races to infect a range of cucurbit species and genera as well as individual cultivars of a single species, which gives rise to a complex picture. Attempts to clarify this have been made by distinguishing races using inherent differences in the utilisation of growth factors such as amino acids, sugars and indoleacetic acid (Hadwiger and Hall, 1963). Races of *C. lagenarium* are also reported from Russia where the most widespread race is only mildly virulent to melon (*C. pepo*) and American cultivars of the Charleston type are resistant.

Conidia of *C. lagenarium* germinate to form germ tubes leading to the development of dark, thick walled appresoria. The temperature range for conidial germination is 20–32 °C and for appressoria. The temperature range for Penetration occurs during the first period of leaf wetness following deposition of the conidium on the leaf surface (Leben and Daft, 1968). Epiphytotics of *C. lagenarium* develop when the temperature is 24–26 °C and the RH 70–76 per cent (Senyurek *et al.*, 1977). Protein synthesis in the first 40 min of incubation has been show to be essential to further conidial growth, but subsequent synthesis does not affect germination directly (Furusawa *et al.*, 1977). Invasion takes place up to 72 h after conidial deposition, when the host cells show intracellular localisation of the pathogen with alteration of the host cell wall in contact with the hyphal apex, capsulation of the hyphae by host cell plasmalemma and swelling of the chloroplasts, nuclei and mitochondria. By the time symptoms appear, at about 96 h after infection, there is advanced host cell degradation (Dargent and Touze, 1974).

Several studies have been made of the enzymes produced by *C. lagenarium* which lead to degeneration of the host tissues. The host itself contains xylose-rich polysaccharide fractions. Cell walls of cantaloupe melon (*C. pepo* var. *cantalupensis*) contain xylans with a 1–4-linked backbone. Two xylanases which are able to degrade this substrate are secreted by *C. lagenarium* (Doux-Gayat *et al.*, 1978). Furthermore, in melons (*C. pepo*) infected by *C. lagenarium* there is a sharp increase in hydroxyproline content and peroxidase activity. In the diseased stem, however, increased hydroxyproline concentrations are unrelated to peroxidase activity (Mazau and Esquerre-Tuguye, 1976). In culture *C. lagenarium* produces endoglucanase, exoglucanase and protease. There is strong stimulation of β-1,4-glucanase activity in infected tissues during invasion by *C. lagenarium*. Virulent isolates of the pathogen synthesise and excrete larger quantities of glucanases than avirulent isolates (Rabenantoandro and Auriol, 1975). Similarly, virulent isolates secrete xylanases earlier than avirulent ones and the quantities of enzyme increase as the disease intensifies (Tatareau and Auriol, 1974). In both the conidia and mycelium of *C. lagenarium* glucans are abundant but pentosans are absent. A reduction in mannose and galactose and disappearance of rhamnose is observed in the mycelium as growth progresses (Auriol, 1974). Conidial walls of *C. lagenarium* contain polysaccharides with high proportions of rhamnose, hemicelluloses (probably galactglucomannans), chitin, a cellulosic fraction and proteins rich in proline (Esquerre-Tugaye and Touze, 1971). An attempt has been made to use information of this type to determine quantitatively the amount of fungus present in the host (Toppan *et al.*, 1976). To obtain reliable results four analytical steps were necessary: isolation of the chitin-containing fraction of the infected plant, that is the cell wall fraction; selection of a suitable hydrolysis method; purification of the resultant hydrolysates; and glucosamine determination. By these techniques a reliable estimation of fungal glucosamine in various parts of the host is obtained.

Perennation of *C. lagenarium* takes place on diseased crop debris; also there are indications that the fungus may be carried with seed. During the growing season transmission is by rain-splash and irrigation water.

Resistant cultivars of some cucurbit crops have been bred to control this pathogen. Resistance to race 1 is expressed in cucumber cotyledons as small non-spreading necrotic lesions and is controlled by a single recessive gene (Abul-Hayja *et al.*, 1978). Resistance to race 2 is found in PIs 163217 and 196289. Other accessions possess different forms of resistance: PI 197087 has polygenic resistance while that of PI 175111 is controlled by a single dominant gene. African water melons (*Citrullus vulgaris*) have resistance due to a single dominant gene (Layton, 1937), which results in only slight symptom development and greatly retarded fungal growth rate. Chemical control is available by use of benomyl, carbendazim, mancozeb or thiophanate-methyl. Experiments in Russia have resulted in yield increase where cucurbit seed was treated with zinc sulphate or boric acid. Some work has also been done on biological control. In Russia dipping melon seed in culture filtrates of *Pseudomonas* spp. reduced the numbers of infected plants and increased yields by 35 per cent. Kuć and co-workers in the USA have made several investigations into the use of cross-protection; inoculation of the cotyledon or first true leaf with *C. lagenarium* provided protection against subsequent infection (Kuć and Richmond, 1977) and inoculation with *C. lindemuthianum* gave protection against *C. lagenarium* (Hammerschmidt *et al.*, 1976). These techniques have been extended to field trials of cucumber, water melon and musk melon. Lesions produced on protected plants were reduced in number and size compared with those on unprotected plants (Caruso and Kuć, 1977).

11.2.7 *Fusarium* spp. (wilt and root rot)

At least four forms of *Fusarium* are pathogenic to cucurbits. Of these, three are vascular wilts classified as *forma speciales* of *F. oxysporum* and the fourth is a *forma speciales* of *F. solani* causing root rot. They are differentiated solely on the basis of host range and specificity. Mycological data on both *F. oxysporum* and *F. solani* are given in section 6.1.5.

(a) *Fusarium oxysporum* f. sp. *cucumerinum*
This soil-borne organism is responsible for pre- and post-emergence damping-off of cucumber (*C. sativus*) seedlings and wilt of more mature plants. Infection of young plants is accompanied by cortical decay. Wilt symptoms develop first on single laterals followed later by total collapse of the plant. The syndrome is typical of a vascular pathogen with necrosis of the xylem vessels extending between six and eight nodes up the plant with the lower leaves showing first flaccidity and then irreversible wilting. The vessels become prominent as bleached white lines.

There is world-wide distribution of *F. oxysporum* f. sp. *cucumerinum* affecting protected crops in sub-tropical areas. No physiological specialisation into races has been reported, but there is very marked host specificity. Isolates of *F. oxysporum* f. sp. *cucumerinum*, although pathogenic to cucumber (*Cucumis sativus*), are non-pathogenic to melon (*C. melo*), marrow (*Cucurbita pepo* var. *medullosa*), pumpkin (*C. maxima*) and squash (*C. mixta*). Mature cucumber plants are unaffected by *forma speciales* isolated from other cucurbits.

There is only limited knowledge of the physiology of this pathogen, but it is known to be favoured by temperatures below 20 °C. It is probably only weakly competitive within the soil environment since Endo *et al.*, (1973) found that if *Thanetophorus cucumeris* (*see* section 5.1.6) was mixed with soil infected with *F. oxysporum* f. sp. *cucumerinum* the incidence of wilting plants was reduced and in the damping-off process *T. cucumeris* preceded and prevailed over *Fusarium* wilt.

Until recently no sources of host resistance to *F. oxysporum* f. sp. *cucumerinum* have been available, but Netzer *et al.* (1977) found an inbred line of *C. sativus*, WIS248, which possessed a single dominant resistance gene, F_{oc}. Use has been made of *Cucurbita ficifolia*, which is highly resistant to *F. oxysporum* f. sp. *cucumerinum* as a rootstock on which highly susceptible cucumber cultivars could be grafted (*see* section 4.2.1). Chemical control has been achieved with benomyl and carbendazim and infected soil may be sterilised by use of chloropicrin.

(b) *F. oxysporum* f. sp. *melonis*
This fungus is a destructive cause of wilt of musk and cantaloupe melons (*C. melo* and *C. melo* var. *cantalupensis*) and can invade either seedlings or more mature plants. In the former this leads to pre- or post-emergence damping-off, and in the latter to typical wilting accompanied by foliar chlorosis and stunting. Infected host stems develop necrotic streaks up to 0.5 m long from which typical fusarial salmon-pink sporulations develop; in addition there may be a brownish gummy exudation. The xylem vessels turn orange-red following

colonisation by *F. oxysporum* f. sp. *melonis*. If fruit are produced by infected plants they are greatly reduced in size. Seedlings of water melon (*Citrullus vulgaris*) are susceptible to *F. oxysporum* f. sp. *melonis* but resistant at the adult stage. The pathogen is generally distributed in the melon-growing areas of North America, Australia and Europe and is also reported from Formosa, Iraq, Japan and the Phillipines. It is reputedly seed-borne.

Optimal fungal growth is at 26 °C while maximal symptom expression is observed at 18–22 °C. Survival between hosts takes place in the soil and is dependent on soil moisture level, greatest survival taking place at 60–75 per cent soil moisture content and at pH 5–7.

Several physiological races of *F. oxysporum* f. sp. *melonis* have been identified. Resistance in musk melon to races 1 and 2 is controlled by a single dominant gene $F_{om\ 1.2}$ which acts independently of gene $F_{om\ 1}$ which gives resistance to race 1 (Risser, 1973). A race nomenclature based on Black's system for *P. infestans* is suggested by Risser *et al.* (1976) giving races 0, 1, 2, 1.2 and so on. Expression of resistance is related to host nutrition; high nitrogen levels increase infection whereas high potassium levels reduce it. Potassium fertilisation results in increased total phenols and *o*-dihydroxyphenols in susceptible melons, reducing wilt levels in plants inoculated with *F. oxysporum* f. sp. *melonis*. Caffeic and ferulic acids form in melons which received 150–200 kg K_2O/ha (Ramasamy and Prasad, 1975). Analysis of resistant musk melons showed them to contain more cucurbitacin than susceptible ones, indeed there was a negative correlation between cucurbitacin content and wilt incidence (Kesavan and Prasad, 1974). Resistance does not, however, prevent penetration, since microconidia have been observed for up to 3 months in the hypoctyls of resistant plants but did not spread above the first leaves, suggesting some mechanism in the vascular system for preventing their spread. Resistance to *F. oxysporum* f. sp. *melonis* in other cucurbits may be utilised by using them as rootstocks for melon plants, for example *Cucurbita ficifolia* in the Netherlands, *Benincasa cerifera* in Italy and vegetable marrow (*Cucurbita pepo* var *medullosa*) in Belgium (Benoit, 1974). Resistance from *Cucumis melo* var. *inodorus* has been transferred satisfactorily to musk and cantaloupe melons in the USA.

The fungicide benomyl will control *F. oxysporum* f. sp. *melonis* causing lysis of germinating conidia and reduction of germ tube length. This leads to cell wall thickening and anomalous morphology. Lysosome-like vesicles appear in the cytoplasm, suggesting that the fungicide acts on membrane integrity (Bourgois *et al.*, 1977). It is likely that benomyl-resistant races will develop fairly quickly since Meyer *et al.* (1977) found that tolerance to 2 µg/ml of benomyl arose through spontaneous mutation while tolerance to 1000 µg/ml could be built up by a stepwise selection process. Chemicals such as chloropicrin or methyl bromide may be used to sterilise infected soil. Perennation takes place on infected debris in the soil. Pathogen populations in soil are largely unaffected by low winter temperatures but tend to decline in spring. The fungus can also colonise the roots of non-host plants such as soybean (*Glycine max*) and maize (*Zea mays*) (Banihashemi and de Zeeuw, 1975).

Potential avenues for the biological control of this pathogen are beginning to emerge. For instance, it is possible to use non-compatible races to give cross-protection against compatible ones (Mas and Molot, 1977). The higher the ratio of race 1 (incompatible) to race 4 (compatible) in these experiments the greater was the level of protection. A minimum dose of 10^6 microconidia/ml of race 1 was required.

Certain French soils appear to inhibit the growth of *F. oxysporum* f. sp. *melonis*. This effect is found in the alluvial soils of Chateau-Renard. Even where such soils are inoculated with the pathogen, no infection of susceptible melons takes place. The inhibitory effect persists under different climatic and cultural conditions. It can be transmitted to non-inhibitory soils which have first been heat treated. Fungal inoculum placed in the soil persists but shows no pathogenicity *in situ* (Louvet *et al.*, 1976). The inhibitory properties of the soil persist after treatment with steam/air mixtures at 50 ° C for 30 min but disappear after treatment at 55 °C (Rouxel *et al.*, 1977).

(c) *Fusarium oxysporum* f. sp. *niveum*
The host range of this pathogen is restricted to water melon (*Citrullus vulgaris*) and the citron or preserving melon (*C. vulgaris* var. *citroides*). On young plants it causes damping-off, cortical rot and stunting; the cotyledons and juvenile leaves turn chlorotic and wither while the hypocotyl may be girdled by a soft watery rot. In more mature plants the leaves become flaccid and eventually wilt irreversibly and begin to shrivel. Initially only part of the vine may show symptoms, but eventually the whole plant is affected. The pathogen is also responsible for necrotic lesions on the root system and development of vascular browning, gummosis and tyloses in the host xylem vessels. Once the host is dead cottony sporulating mycelium grows on the surface of the moribund tissue, especially during damp weather. Invasion takes place through the root tip, meristematic zone and the epidermis of the zones of root elongation and maturation and through ruptures caused by growth of new lateral roots.

Fusarium oxysporum f. sp. *niveum* is common in most tropical and sub-tropical areas where water melons are grown. The optimal temperature for symptom development in seedlings and adult plants is 27 °C, but severe wilt will develop within the range 20–30 °C. Perennation takes place in the soil. Soil moisture levels of 70 per cent moisture holding capacity (MHC) favour the survival of this pathogen in loamy soils but not in fine sand or clay. At 40 per cent MHC there were no significant differences in the survival rates betwen different soil types. When weathered water melon stem segments were buried and incubated in soil at 70 per cent MHC containing 8.33×10^3 propagules/g, nearly 50 per cent were colonised within 6 days at 32–35 °C. The fungus was isolated from several weeds and from rice (*O. sativa*) plants (Huang and Sun, 1978). In glasshouse tests the pathogen colonised roots of groundnut (*Arachis hypogea*) and tomato

(*Lycoperiscon esculentum*) and stems of sorghum (*Sorghum vulgare*), and groundnut. Rotations which included maize (*Zea mays*) and sweet potato (*Ipomoea batatas*) reduced the level of *F. oxysporum* f. sp. *niveum* in soils.

Several physiological races of *F. oxysporum* f. sp. *niveum* exist which have been studied largely in the USA (Sitterley, 1972), and a highly virulent race has been identified by Netzer (1976) in Israel. Resistance to *F. oxysporum* f. sp. *niveum* is thought to be polygenically inherited. Some control has been achieved by use of fungicides such as benomyl, thiabendazole, thiophanate-methyl and maneb, but soil sterilisation reduces the efficacy of thiophanate-methyl and maneb while results with benomyl and thiabendazole are variable. Only sodium azide gave consistently good control (Hopkins and Elmstrom, 1975).

Yields are raised and wilt levels reduced by increasing soil alkalinity by applications of hydrated lime. Nitrogen source also affects wilt severity, ammonium nitrogen increases disease whereas nitrate nitrogen does not (Jones *et al.*, 1975). Dipping water melon seeds in 50 per cent culture liquid of *F. oxysporum* f. sp. *niveum* before sowing reduces infection by 10–15 per cent. This effect is attributed to increased resistance due to increased activity of oxidising enzymes (Timchenko and Beider, 1977).

(d) Fusarium solani f. sp. cucurbitae

Squashes (*Cucuribita pepo, C. moschata* and *C. maxima*) and a range of other cucurbits are hosts to *F. solani* f. sp. *cucurbitae*. Symptoms on adult plants are similar to wilt caused by *F. oxysporum* consisting of sudden mid-season wilting of the whole vine, but they can be differentiated from true vascular wilt by the presence at the stem base of extensive dark brown cortical decay and soft mushy tissue maceration. This is due to production of endopectate lyase by the fungus. Damping-off is a typical response where young seedlings are attacked. Abundant sporulation takes place on infected surfaces during humid weather.

Apart from the imperfect conidial stage, which is similar to that of *F. solani* f. sp. *pisi* , there is a perfect Ascomycete stage, *Hypomyces solani*, which produces a subspherical perithecium measuring 150–400 µm x 200–600 µm and containing hyaline, needle-shaped, bicellular ascospores, 3–8.5 µm x 8–16 µm in size. It is heterothallic, but the two mating types are rarely found together in nature. After mating the resultant perithecia are red or white depending on their genetic constitution. Physiological races distinguished by host response are not interfertile. Mutation of the hermaphrodite form can give rise to male, female and neuter forms (Snyder *et al.*, 1975).

The pathogen is seed-borne, soil-borne and probably the conidia are disseminated by air currents. In a survey of cucurbit seed, Sumner (1976) found that 2 per cent were infected. Natural infection in soil survived for 20 months while infectivity of artificially infested soil remained for 40 months. Disease severity was dependent on the inoculum concentration in the soil. Survival in soil is probably in the form of chlamydospores which develop from macroconidia. There is gradual breakdown of the original macroconidial cell wall with simultaneous synthesis of new cell wall material. Cell wall lysing enzymes originate within the fungal propagule and are not the result of activities by external micro-organisms (Eck and Schippers, 1976). The process is favoured by absence of glucose and low pH, but addition of ammonium chloride reduces lysis and inhibits chlamydospore formation (Schippers and Old, 1974). The outer wall is sloughed away and replaced by an accretion of microfibrillar elements adjacent to the plasmalemma.

Control is chiefly achieved by use of crop rotations. Infected seed may be hot water treated (15 min at 55 °C) or soaked in 0.1 per cent mercuric chloride for 10–15 min. Some small differences in host susceptibility have been noted, for instance *C. pepo* is more susceptible than *C. moschata*.

11.3 VIRUSES

11.3.1 Cucumber Green Mottle Mosaic Virus (CGMMV)

No animal vector has been identified for CGMMV; invasion appears to take place via the roots from diseased debris and transmission to develop through foliar contact when handling takes place during cultivation. Virus may also pass from diseased rootstocks such as those used for cucumber (*Cucumis sativus*), and water melon (*Citrullis vulgaris*); in the latter the bottlegourd (*Lagenaria siceraria*) rootstock is a particular source of virus. Seed is also a principle means of infection, but the viability of the virus particles quickly declines with age. Infection is mostly external and can be destroyed by dry heat treatment for 3 days at 70 °C without affecting seed germination. Low concentrations of virus are also found in pollen. Vegetable marrow (*Cucurbita pepo* var. *medullosa*) appears to be the only cucurbit unaffected by CGMMV, at least six strains of which have been identified.

The *type strain* causes slight vein clearing symptoms to develop on cucumber (*C. sativus*) 7–14 days after infection, followed by crumpling of the younger leaves and formation of a light and dark green mottle with blistering and distortion of the foliage and general stunting. Often the younger leaves exhibit symptoms but there is little or no effect on more mature foliage. Where plants are growing slowly in winter, distortion symptoms are more severe, but mottling occurs at any season, often accompanied by leaf flecking, which may become the dominant symptom. Fruits rarely show any symptoms but yield losses of up to 15 per cent have been reported; some Asian cultivars fail to show even foliage symptoms, but their yield is still reduced. Infected melon (*Cucumis melo*) and gherkin (*C. sativus*) show mottling symptoms accompanied by leaf distortion and stunting. Young plants of water melon (*C. vulgaris*) are easily infected, exhibiting mottling but rarely stunting symptoms.

All tissues of infected plants are invaded by the virus, in some cases leading to cytological abnormalities such as mitochondrial vesiculation.

The incubation period in cucumber (*C. sativus*) of the *Cucumber Aucuba*

Mosaic strain is 2—3 days longer than that of the type strain. Affected young leaves exhibit slight vein clearing with some crumpling of the apical foliage, followed by a bright green mottle but with limited leaf distortion. Mottling consists of few to many star-shaped areas which may cover the whole leaf or produce only a vein-banded effect. Their colour varies from a pale yellow to greenish-cream or nearly white on more mature foliage. In poor growing conditions mottling may be a less conspicuous yellow-green. The Aucuba strain causes symptoms on fruits which are chlorotic or silver spots and streaks which become most apparent at high temperatures.

Both the type and Aucuba strains have been found only in the UK. Three further strains, Watermelon, Japanese Cucumber and Yodo are found only in Japan, the latter two causing severe fruit distortion. An Indian strain has been identified on bottlegourd (*L. siceraria*), causing blister mottle, stunting and yield loss.

Symptom expressions on host and indicator plants are not a reliable guide for the identification of CGMMV, serological techniques must be used to obtain positive proof.

11.3.2 Cucumber Mosaic Virus (CMV)

Cucumber Mosaic Virus is transmitted by more than 60 species of aphid, principally *Aphis gossypii, Aulacorthum circumflexum, A. solani, Myzus persicae, Macrosiphum euphorbiae, Phorodon humuli* and *P. cannabis.* All instars can transmit the virus, which is acquired in less than 1 min and inoculated with equal rapidity. There is no latent period; it is retained for less than 4 h and not transmitted to offspring. Some isolates can lose their transmissibility by one aphid species but retain it via another.

Distribution of CMV is world-wide and it is a particularly important crop pathogen in temperate regions. The particle is isometric, 30 nm in diameter. Host range is vast, with representatives of more than 40 Angiosperm families known to be susceptible. All host tissues are invaded, including the meristematic regions, with virus-like particles present in the cytoplasm but no inclusion bodies having been found. Symptoms on vegetable crop hosts only will be described here.

(a) Cucumber (*C. sativus*)
Symptoms become apparent on infected seedlings after 6 weeks when growth is rapid and there are about six to eight leaves. The younger leaves show greenish-yellow zones 1—2 mm in size which are confined by the veins. This is followed by chlorotic mottling of all leaves accompanied by distortion and stunting. Occasionally the yellowing is confined to the leaf tip. There is a general downbending of the leaf which becomes finely blistered, especially between the smaller veins. Growth is stunted, with reductions of internode length, lamina size and petiole length; fewer flowers form and those which do fail to set fruit.

Fruits show mottling and greenish-yellow discoloration at the stem end which spreads, with the spots being distributed amongst darker green areas. The latter are raised in a wart-like appearance. As the syndrome becomes more severe the fruits become whitish-green and misshapen.

(b) Melon and musk melon (*C. melo*)

Initially the youngest leaves become light yellow and bend downwards at a sharp angle. Later symptoms develop into a typical mottled mosaic with irregularly shaped chlorotic areas. The darker leaf areas are very prominent on these hosts with leaf curling an important symptom. Although the foliage becomes yellow death does not take place as quickly in melons as with cucumbers. Fruits are mottled with limited numbers of darker warted areas.

(c) Vegetable marrow (*C. pepo* var. *medullosa*)

On this host extreme mottling is a characteristic symptom of CMV infection. The older foliage rapidly becomes yellow and wilts. A few fruit develop which are mottled and deformed, the foliage becomes puckered and internode length is reduced. Fruits are covered in circular wart-like areas. Younger foliage exhibits some symptoms but the more nature foliage may remain symptomless.

(d) Pumpkin (*C. maxima*) and squash (*C. pepo* var. *condensa*)

Extreme savoying of the younger foliage with conspicuously raised darker areas is typical of infection on these hosts. Light regions show up as a pale yellowish-green, often coalescing into blotches.

(e) Water melon (*C. vulgaris*)

Tips of infected laterals of water melon stand above the general level of the leaf canopy giving a 'petunia-like' appearance. Internode length is reduced, with young leaves being crowded and rolled. Foliar mottling is evident with irregular yellow areas which are somewhat lighter yellow than the surrounding normal green tissue. Extreme malformations develop on the young foliage which may be reduced solely to the mid rib. Flowers are crowded together with distortion of the floral organs; the blossoms usually abort, resulting in few fruit being set.

(f) Carrot (*Daucus carota*)

Carrots infected with CMV show foliar mottling with yellowing and some necrosis.

(g) Celery (*Apium graveolens*)

Cucumber Mosaic Virus causes a syndrome on celery known as 'Southern Celery Mosaic'. Symptoms are mosaicing with outward and downward curling of the young petioles giving the plant a flattened appearance. Along the veins a greenish-yellow discoloration develops which may become blanched. Interveinal regions show up as an intense green which on mature foliage may be thicker than the chlorotic areas. There may be slight savoying and crinkling. As the disease develops, creamy-brown sunken lesions of irregular shape form on the petioles with the vascular system becoming discoloured and eventually the petioles are brown and shrivelled.

(h) Spinach (*Spinacia oleracea*)

Disease development by CMV in spinach was summarised by McClintock and Smith (1918) as follows: (1) a very slight yellowing of the younger leaves of infected plants and occasionally of one or more older leaves; (2) a progressive yellowing of the younger leaves; (3) malformation of the younger leaves which become much wrinkled, narrowed and mottled, yellowing of the older leaves and some stunting of the plant; (4) distinct stunting of the plant with cessation of growth, yellowing of the entire foliage, mottling of the older leaves and extreme malformation of the younger ones which are finely savoyed and feathery in appearance; (5) browning and death of parts of the older leaves usually progressing from the outer tips inwards; (6) total disintegration of the older leaves and some browning of the central ones; (7) browning of the younger leaves; (8) death of the plant, which has become reduced to a very small central whorl of leaves.

(i) Tomato (*Lycopersicon esculentum*)

Cucumber Mosaic Virus causes the 'fern leaf' syndrome in tomato, but this is not a diagnostic feature since similar symptoms may be induced by strains of Tomato Mosaic Virus (*see* section 12.3.6). Symptoms begin to develop 10 days after infection; the leaves twist in a helical manner, fail to unfold and may curl upwards or downwards. Chlorosis is apparent parallel to the veins and when the leaves do unfold they are distorted and filiform, being reduced often only to the mid rib. About 45 days after infection large numbers of lateral leaflets form.

(j) Pepper (*Capsicum annuum*)

The youngest leaves of infected pepper plants curl downwards with the mid rib and proximal ends of the leaves becoming a lighter green than the tip. The leaves rapidly become mottled with leaf size reduced, together with internode and petiole length. Plants take on a rosette-like form with the foliage becoming yellow-green and thickened in texture. Fruits are a normal green colour but their surface is distorted by dark green warty regions.

(k) Onion (*Allium cepa*)

Infected onions show light chlorotic streaks on the youngest leaves while yellow irregular ring shapes develop on the older ones. Eventually the plants become stiff, brittle and stunted.

(l) Maize (*Zea mays*)

Incubation of CMV in maize varies from 3 to 20 days; initial lesions are up to 1 mm diameter and spread along the veins of seedling leaves. After about 8 days systemic symptoms develop with the formation of numerous light elliptical lesions of varying dimensions. The plants become stunted and the leaves tend to split and crinkle at their tips.

At least four strains of CMV have been identified:

(1) *Cucumber Virus Strain 5*   Symptoms caused by this strain differ from those of the type strain, with the formation of necrotic primary lesions on tomato and spinach and yellow necrotic primary lesions on cucumber. Necrosis develops as large lesions or zonate areas which may follow the veins.

(2) *Yellow Cucumber Mosaic Virus*   This strain causes brilliant yellow primary lesions on cucumber, spinach and tomato which become systemic to give a mottling of yellow and dark green areas. Infected spinach leaves may turn wholly yellow.

(3) *Y Strain Cucumber Mosaic Virus*   Systemic disease is caused by this strain in cowpea (*V. sinensis*) with yellow primary lesions and possibly necrotic rings around part or all of the lesion and a severe systemic mosaic of yellow and green.

(4) *Spinach strain*   The spinach strain is highly virulent and will affect several other vegetable hosts. In cucumber, symptoms consist of circular chlorotic local lesions accompanied by reduced leaf size and general mosaicing; young plants usually die after infection but older ones may produce a reduced yield of mottled and deformed fruit. In tomato, the foliage exhibits local necrotic lesions with faint systemic mottle and curling and reduction of the lamina size. In beet, symptoms range from chlorotic or necrotic local lesions to a systemic mosaic with stunting and reduced leaf size.

11.3.3 Cucumber Necrosis Virus (CNV)

The vector of CNV is a soil-borne fungus, *Olpidium cucurbitacearum*. Transmission of virus particles takes place through the fungal zoospores. The virus is adsorbed on the exterior of the zoopores after 5—15 min contact and enters the root with them. The particles are isometric, 31 nm in diameter, with an angular outline. Cucumber is the only host of CNV and distribution is limited to Canada.

Symptoms develop as necrotic lesions leading to severely malformed leaves and stunting. Death of the host occurs 6—8 weeks after systemic lesions appear. A virus serologically related to Tobacco Necrosis Virus (TNV) was identified in the Netherlands, Sweden and the USSR which caused similar symptoms and was named Cucumber Necrosis Virus. This was not, however, the same as the Canadian virus, which is not related TNV.

11.3.4 Cucumber Vein Yellowing Virus (CVYV)

The whitefly, *Bemisia tabaci*, is the vector of CVYV. Symptoms on cucumber

(*C. sativus*) are conspicuous vein clearing and chlorosis terminating in general necrosis.

11.3.5 Cucumber Wild Mosaic Virus (CWMV)

Transmitted by the striped cucumber beetle (*Acalymma trivitata*), particles of this virus are isometric, 30 nm in diameter, and it is serologically related to Turnip Yellow Mosaic Virus (*see* section 5.2.7). Symptoms consist of a general mosaic, but this pathogen is unique in causing systemic infection of water melon (*C. vulgaris*).

11.3.6 Cucurbit Latent Virus (CLV)

The vector of CLV is the aphid *Myzus persicae*. The virus is stylet-borne and non-persistent. Distribution is restricted to California, USA, causing latent infections of cantaloupe (*C. melo* var. *cantalupensis*), water melon (*C. vulgaris*), cucumber (*C. sativus*) and squash (*C. pepo* var. *condensa*).

11.3.7 Cucumber Stunt Mottle Virus (CSMV)

This virus is accepted as a strain of Arabis Mosaic Virus (AMV) which is described here and which affects a wide host range with serious economic consequences. Vectors of AMV are nematodes, *Xiphinema diversicaudatum* and *X. coxi.* Both larvae and adults can transmit the virus but the adult does not pass on AMV to its progeny nor is the virus retained after moulting.

Acquisition takes 1 day and transmission can occur after a further 3 days, infectivity being retained for 31 days in fallow soil. Virus-like particles are found in the cuticular linings of the lumina of the odontophore (stylet extension) and oesophagus of the vectors. Arabis Mosaic Virus is also seed-borne; 15 species of 12 Angiosperm families were shown to have 10–100 per cent seed infection, but in many hosts no symptoms were manifested. The virus is also reported as present in roots of the Gymnosperm *Chamaecyparis lawsoniana.*

Natural distribution is restricted to Europe. Some slight differences in the virulence of various strains have been noted but otherwise strain differentiation in AMV is of limited significance.

Symptoms on various vegetable hosts may be described as follows: In cucumber (*C. sativus*), the true CSMV causes a similar mottle to that attributed to CMV (*see* section 11.3.2). In bean (*Phaseolus vulgaris*), first signs of infection by AMV are systemic symptoms starting as small yellow flecks on the young leaves and raised blisters. The interveinal areas turn pale and the yellow flecks enlarge to produce a bright mosaic-mottle followed ultimately by severe necrosis and death of the meristematic region. In Lettuce (*Lactuca sativa*), the syndrome caused by AMV is known as Lettuce Chlorotic Stunt; symptoms include stunting, chlorosis, necrosis and a failure to heart up.

Control of AMV has been achieved by soil sterilisation to eradicate its vectors. Dichloropropane + dichloropropene (DD) or methyl bromide will reduce the vector populations by 99 per cent.

REFERENCES

Sections 11.1.1 and 11.1.2
Gundy, S. D. van and Walker, J. C. (1957). *Phytopathology* **47**, 35.

Section 11.2.1
Sitterley, W. R. (1972). *A. Rev. Phytopath.* **10**, 471–90.

Section 11.2.2
Harwood, R. R. and Markarian, D. (1968). *J. Hered.* **59**, 126–30.
Shanmugasundrum, S., Williams, P. H. and Peterson, C. E. (1971). *Phytopathology* **61**, 1218–21.

Section 11.2.3
Crossan, D. F. and Sasser, J. M. (1969). *Pl. Dis. Reptr* **53**, 452–3.
Dekker, W. H., Selling, H. A. and Overeem, J. C. (1975). *J. agric. Fd Chem.* **23**, 785–91.
Dorozhkin, N. A., Remneva, Z. I. and Nalobova, V. L. (1976). *Mikologiya i Fitopatologiya* **10**, 497–503.
Emmaby, D. A., Groenewegen, C. and George, B. F. (1975). *Hort. Sci.* **10**, 619.
Hammerschmidt, R., Acres, S. and Kuć, J. (1976). *Phytopathology* **66**, 790–3.
Hussain, A. and Rich, S. (1958). *Phytopathology* **48**, 316–20.
Kuć, J. (1962). *Phytopathology* **52**, 961.
Laborda, F. and Maxwell, D. P. (1976). *Can. J. Microbiol.* **22**, 394–403.
Mahadevan, A., Kuć, J. and Williams, E. B. (1965). *Phytopathology* **55**, 1000–4.
Paus, F. and Raa, J. (1973). *Physiol. Pl. Path.* **3**, 461–4.
Sherald, J. L., Ragsdale, N. N. and Sisler, H. D. (1973). *Pestic. Sci.* **4**, 719–27.
Skare, N. H., Paus, F. and Raa, J. (1975). *Physiologia Pl.* **33**, 229–33.
Strider, D. L. and Winstead, N. N. (1961). *Phytopathology* **51**, 765–8.
Vonk, J. W. and Sijpesteijn, A. K. (1974). *Antonie van Leeuwenhoek* **40**, 393–400.
Walker, J. C. (1950). *Phytopathology* **40**, 1094–102.

Section 11.2.4

Abul-Hayja, Z., Williams, P. H. and Peterson, C. E. (1978). *Pl. Dis. Reptr* **62**, 43–5.

Kazda, V. and Hervest, V. (1972). *Biologia Pl.* **14**, 231–3.

Strandberg, J. O. (1971). *Pl. Dis. Reptr* **55**, 142–4.

Section 11.2.5

Cardaso, R. M. G., Figuerido, M. B., Palazzo, D. and Martinez, J. A. (1974). *Arquivos do Instituto Biologica* **41**, 35–7.

Govindarajalui, T. (1977). *Indian J. exp. Bot.* **15**, 332–4.

McKeen, C. D. (1957). *Can. J. Bot.* **35**, 43–50.

Prokhorova, G. S. (1976). *Dokl. Mosk. S-Kh. Akad. Im. K.A. Timiryazeva* no. 221, 70–5.

Spencer, D. M. (1972). *A. Rep. Glasshouse Crops Res. Inst.* **1971**, 108–17.

Sowell, G. (1975). *Pl. Dis. Reptr* **59**, 413–5.

Uspenskaya, G. D., Lebl, D. O. and Rulova, N. V. (1974). *Mikologiya i Fitopatologiya* **8**, 241–5.

Uspenskaya, G. D., Plukarova, G. A. and Orlova, G. I. (1976). *Biologisheskia Nauki* **19**, 76–89.

Section 11.2.6

Abul-Hayja, Z., Williams, P. H. and Peterson, C. E. (1978). *Pl. Dis. Reptr* **62**, 43–5.

Auriol, P. (1974). *C. r. hebd. Séanc. Acad. Sci. Paris, D* **279**, 1867–9.

Caruso, F. L. and Kuć, J. (1977). *Phytopathology* **67**, 1290–2.

Dargent, R. and Touze, A. (1974). *Can. J. Bot.* **52**, 1319–23.

Doux-Gayat, A., Auriol, P., Joseleau, J. P. and Touze, A. (1978). *Physiologia Pl.* **42**, 301–6.

Esquerre-Tugaye, M. T. and Touze, A. (1971). *Phytochemistry* **10**, 821–7.

Furasawa, I., Nishiguchi, M., Tani, M. and Ishida, N. (1977). *J. gen. Microbiol.* **101**, 307–10.

Hadwiger, L. A. and Hall, C. V. (1963). *Proc. Am. Soc. hort. Sci.* **82**, 378–87.

Hammerschmidt, R., Acres, S. and Kuć, J. (1976). *Phytopathology* **66**, 790–3.

Kuć, J. and Richmond, S. (1977). *Phytopathology* **67**, 533–6.

Layton, D. V. (1937). *The Parasitism of* Colletotrichum lagenarium *(Pass). Ell and Holst.* Research Bulletin no. 233. Agricultural Experiment Station, Iowa, pp. 39–67.

Leben, C. and Daft, G. C. (1968). *Phytopathology* **58**, 264–5.

McLean, D. M. (1966). *Pl. Dis. Reptr* **50**, 871–3.

Mazau, D. and Esquerre-Tugaye, M. T. (1976). *Pl. Sci. Letters* **7**, 119–25.

Rabenantoandro, Y. and Auriol, P. (1975). *C. r. hebd. Séanc. Acad. Sci., Paris, D* **281**, 395–8.

Senyurek, M., Zowrak, Y. and Olcum, S. K. (1977). *Bitki Koruma Bulleti* **17**, 151–6.

Tatareau, J. C. and Auriol, P. (1974). *Phytopath. Z.* **80**, 163–70.
Toppan, A., Esquerre-Tugaye, M. T. and Touze, A. (1976). *Physiol. Pl. Path.* **9**, 241–51.

Section 11.2.7
Banihashemi, Z. and Zeeuw, D. J. van (1975). *Phytopathology* **65**, 1212–7.
Benoit, F. (1974). *Tuinboirberschten Belgium* **38**, 16–20.
Bourgois, J. J., Bronchart, R., Deltour, R. and Barsy, T. de (1977). *Pesticide Biochem. Physiol.* **7**, 97–106.
Eck, W. H. van and Schippers, B. (1976). *Soil Biol. Biochem.* **8**, 1–6.
Endo, S., Strinohara, K., Kikuchi, J. and Hirabayashi, Y. (1973). *Studies on the Soil-borne Pathogens Parasitic to the Same Host. 1. Antagonistic Action of* Rhizoctonia solani *Kuhn to* Fusarium oxysporum *Schlechtendal f.* cucumerinum *Owen and its Effects on the Occurrence of* Fusarium *Wilt of Cucumber Plant.* Bulletin no. 30. College of Agriculture and Veterinary Medicine, Nihon University, pp. 85–95.
Hopkins, D. L. and Elmstrom, G. W. (1975). *Proc. State hort. Soc. Fla* **88**, 196–200.
Huang, J. W. and Sun, S. K. (1978). *Pl. Protect. Bull. Taiwan* **20**, 56–60.
Jones, J. P., Woltz, S. S. and Everett, P. H. (1975). *Proc. State hort. Soc. Fla* **88**, 200–3.
Kesavan, R. and Prasad, N. N. (1974). *Indian J. exp. Biol.* **12**, 476–7.
Louvet, J., Rouxel, F. and Alabouvette, C. (1976). *Ann. Phytopath.* **8**, 425–36.
Mas, P. M. and Molot, P. M. (1977). *Ann. Phytopath.* **9**, 71–5.
Meyer, T. A., Pourtois, A., Luinande, K. and Maraite, H. (1977). *Neth. J. Pl. Path.* **83**, 491.
Netzer, D. (1976). *Phytoparasitica* **4**, 131–6.
Netzer, D., Niego, S. and Galun, D. (1977). *Phytopathology* **67**, 525–7.
Ramasamy, K. and Prasad, N. N. (1975). *Agric. J. Madras* **62**, 313–7.
Risser, G. (1973). *Annls Amerlior. Pl.* **23**, 259–63.
Risser, G., Banihashemi, Z. and Davis, D. W. (1976). *Phytopathology* **66**, 1105–6.
Rouxel, F., Alabouvette, C. and Louvet, J. (1977). *Ann. Phytopath.* **9**, 183–92.
Schippers, B. and Old, K. M. (1974). *Soil Biol. Biochem.* **6**, 153–60.
Sitterley, W. R. (1972). *A. Rev. Phytopath.* **10**, 471–90.
Snyder, W. C., Georgopoulos, S. G., Webster, R. K. and Smith, S. N. (1975). *Hilgardia* **43**, 161–85.
Sumner, D. R. (1976). *Pl. Dis. Reptr* **60**, 923–7.
Timchenko, V. I. and Beider, O. M. (1977). *Ovochivnitstvo i Bashtannitstvo* **22**, 80–83.

Section 11.3.2
McClintock, J. A. and Smith, L. B. (1918). *J. agric. Res.* **14**, 1–59.

FURTHER READING

Sections 11.1.1 and 11.1.2

Bradbury, J. F. (1967). Pseudomonas lachrymans. Commonwealth Mycological Institute Descriptions of Pathogenic Fungi and Bacteria no. 124. Commonwealth Mycological Institute, Kew.

Bradbury, J. F. (1970). Erwinia tracheiphila. Commonwealth Mycological Institute Descriptions of Pathogenic Fungi and Bacteria no. 233. Commonwealth Mycological Institute, Kew.

Sitterley, W. R. (1972). *A. Rev. Phytopath.* **10**, 471–90.

Stapp, C. (1961). *Bacterial Plant Pathogens.* Oxford University Press, London.

Section 11.2.1

Palti, J. (1975). Pseudoperonospora cubensis. Commonwealth Mycological Institute Descriptions of Pathogenic Fungi and Bacteria no. 457. Commonwealth Mycological Institute, Kew.

Section 11.2.2

Kapoor, J. N. (1967). Sphaerotheca fuliginea. Commonwealth Mycological Institute Descriptions of Pathogenic Fungi and Bacteria no. 159. Commonwealth Mycological Institute, Kew.

Sitterley, W. R. (1978). Powdery mildew of cucurbits. In *The Powdery Mildews* (D. M. Spencer, ed.). Academic Press, London.

Section 11.2.3

Ellis, M. B. and Holliday, P. (1972). Cladosporium cucumerinum. Commonwealth Mycological Institute Descriptions of Pathogenic Fungi and Bacteria no. 348. Commonwealth Mycological Institute, Kew.

Section 11.2.4

Ellis, M. B. and Holliday, P. (1971). Corynespora casiicola. Commonwealth Mycological Institute Descriptions of Pathogenic Fungi and Bacteria no. 303. Commonwealth Mycological Institute, Kew.

Section 11.2.5

Punithalingam, E. and Holliday, P. (1972). Didymella bryoniae. Commonwealth Mycological Institute Descriptions of Pathogenic Fungi and Bacteria no. 332. Commonwealth Mycological Institute, Kew.

Punithalingam, E. and Holliday, P. (1975). Phomopsis cucurbitae. Commonwealth Mycological Institute Descriptions of Pathogenic Fungi and Bacteria no. 469. Commonwealth Mycological Institute, Kew.

Section 11.2.6

Chu, S. B. and Alexander, M. (1972). *Trans. Br. mycol. Soc.* **58**, 489–97.

Mordue, J. E. M. (1971). Glomerella cingulata. Commonwealth Mycological
    Institute Descriptions of Pathogenic Fungi and Bacteria no. 315.
    Commonwealth Mycological Institute, Kew.

Section 11.2.7

Holliday, P. (1970). Fusarium oxysporum *f. sp.* cucumerinum. Commonwealth
    Mycological Institute Descriptions of Pathogenic Fungi and Bacteria no. 215.
    Commonwealth Mycological Institute, Kew.
Holliday, P. (1970). Fusarium oxysporum *f. sp.* melonis. Commonwealth
    Mycological Institute Descriptions of Pathogenic Fungi and Bacteria no. 218.
    Commonwealth Mycological Institute, Kew.
Holliday, P. (1970). Fusarium oxysporum *f. sp.* niveum. Commonwealth
    Mycological Institute Descriptions of Pathogenic Fungi and Bacteria no. 219.
    Commonwealth Mycological Institute, Kew.

Sections 11.3.1–11.3.7

Dias, H. F. and McKeen, C. D. (1972). *Cucumber Necrosis Virus.*
    Commonwealth Mycological Institute/Association of Applied Biologists
    Descriptions of Plant Viruses no. 82. Commonwealth Mycological Institute
    Kew.
Gibbs, A. J. and Harrison, B. D. (1970). *Cucumber Mosaic Virus.* Commonwealth
    Mycological Institute/Association of Applied Biologists Descriptions of Plant
    Viruses no. 1. Commonwealth Mycological Institute, Kew.
Hollings, M., Komuro, Y. and Tochihara, H. (1975). *Cucumber Green Mottle
    Mosaic Virus.* Commonwealth Mycological Institute/Assocation of Applied
    Biologists Descriptions of Plant Viruses no. 154. Commonwealth Mycological
    Institute, Kew.
Murant, A. F. (1970). *Arabis Mosaic Virus.* Commonwealth Mycological Institute/
    Association of Applied Biologists Descriptions of Plant Viruses no. 16.
    Commonwealth Mycological Institute, Kew.
Smith, K. M. (1972). *A Textbook of Plant Virus Diseases.* Longmans, London.

12
Pathogens of Solanaceous Crops

In both tropical and temperate areas solanaceous crops are economically important. In the former they are an essential addition to the diet, providing much needed vitamins and minerals as well as flavouring for otherwise monotonous farinaceous foods. Tomatoes (*Lycopersicon esculentum*) are often second only to bananas (*Musa* spp.) in value for these countries. In temperate European countries the tomato crop is the mainstay of the glasshouse industry while the USA and Canada large areas are devoted to field production directed principally at the processing industry as preserved fruit and soups. Other and often equally important solanaceous crops include peppers (*Capsicum annuum*) and aubergines (*Solanum melongena*). Detailed studies of the pathogens which affect this crop family reflect its economic significance. Bacterial pathogens such as *Pseudomonas solanacearum* and *Corynebacterium michiganense* can be controlled only by husbandry techniques, although studies of potential resistance mechanisms are developing. Semi-tropical crops are affected by an endoparasitic powdery mildew (*Leveillula taurica*), which is not only of intrinsic interest but of increasing commercial significance in areas such as Israel where these crops are grown for an expanding export trade. A complex physiological race pattern is revealed for *Fulvia fulva* (leaf mould) attendant on the widespread use of monogenic resistance. Resistance to *Alternaria solani* (early blight) has been related to formation of a phytoalexin, rishitin, and this may eventually point to a means of control. Studies of *Phytophthora infestans* causing late blight to potatoes yield useful information in relation to its effects on the tomato crop. Gradually the complex of pathogens causing damping-off, root, foot and fruit rot is being unravelled. For instance studies of *Pyrenochaeta lycopersici* (corky root rot), which was originally considered to be a Mycelium Sterilium, now show it to be a Fungus Imperfectus. Similar detailed studies in the Netherlands are providing an understanding of a number of *Phytophthora* spp. which cause the buckeye rot syndrome. Wilt-causing fungi (*Fusarium* and *Verticillium* spp.) are dealt with in depth since studies of physiological pathology here have extended our knowledge of how vascular parasites can have such a catastrophic effect on host growth. Virus pathogens of solanaceous vegetable crops are numerous and widespread, especially as many also affect potato (*Solanum tuberosum*) and tobacco (*Nicotiana tabaccum*) crops while others have host ranges extending well beyond this single Angiosperm family.

Their vectors are similarly diverse, including aphids, thrips, white fly and soil-borne nematodes. Resistance mechanisms have been developed to combat Tomato Mosaic Virus (TMV) — a complex pathogen with very considerable numbers of strains. Cross-protection has been utilized to control this pathogen commercially using attenuated strains of a TMV mutant form.

12.1 BACTERIAL PATHOGENS

12.1.1 *Pseudomonas solanacearum* (bacterial wilt)

Over 200 host species have been identified as susceptible to this pathogen, including most important dicotyledonous crops. It represents, therefore, one of the most serious obstacles to crop production in the tropics and sub-tropics.

The most characteristic symptom on tomato (*Lycopersicon esculentum*) is very rapid wilting, especially where the plants are young and succulent. Other primary indications of infection are stunting, downcurling of leaflets and petioles and, where pathogenesis is slow, excessive production of adventitious roots along the stem. Usually infected plants collapse quickly, but where this fails to happen there is the development of blackening of the vascular system at the junction between stem and leaf. Further down the stem the whole vascular system may be completely blackened and when cut oozes creamy bacterial slime. The general syndrome incited by *Ps. solanacearum* is summarised in table 12.1.

Pseudomonas solanacearum is an aerobic, Gram-negative rod, 0.5–1.5 μm in length, with one to several polar flagella. With the exception of those strains infecting Musaceae, it is characterised by the production of a dark brown diffusable pigment on various agar media containing tyrosinase. Glucose, sucrose, fructose and glycerol are oxidised by all strains. Nitrate and/or gas are produced from nitrates; gelatin is not liquified and starch is not hydrolysed. The optimum temperature for growth varies with strain but is within the ranges 25–28, 27–32 and 30–35 °C.

Vast numbers of *Ps. solanacearum* cells are released into the surrounding soil from infected roots and from there invade subsequent crops. The widespread distribution of this pathogen has yet to be explained satisfactorily; seed transmission is possible but has not been proved conclusively. High soil moisture levels affect disease intensity in at least four ways: (1) increasing survival of the pathogen in soil; (2) increasing infection; (3) increasing disease development after infection; and (4) increasing the release of bacterial cells from the host and their spread through the soil. Unlike maize wilt (*Erysiphe stewartii*; *see* section 10.1.2) and cucumber wilt (*E. tracheiphila*; *see* section 11.1.2) this pathogen can survive in soil in the absence of a host.

Two groups of workers have identified resistance in tomato (*L. esculentum*) to

Table 12.1   Disease syndrome incited by *Ps. solanacearum* in relation to mechanisms of pathogenesis (after Buddenhagen and Kelman, 1964).

Symptoms	Cause
External symptoms	
Foliage wilting	Interference with water movement by formation of extracellular polysaccharides in the vessels and tracheids plus bacterial cells plus tyloses
Foliage yellowing	Breakdown of chlorophyll resulting from decreased supply of mineral nutrients and water plus unknown effects of host and pathogen metabolites
Marginal leaf necrosis	Decreased supply of water plus unknown factors
Leaf epinasty	Increased levels of indoleacetic acid (IAA) plus ethylene (formed by pathogen or host)
Stem adventitious roots	Increase in IAA; interference with downward movement in phloem resulting from effects of pathogen
Stunting	Complex of above
Internal symptoms	
Vascular discoloration	Tyrosinase of pathogen
Tyloses	
Vessel collapse	Increase in IAA levels
Parenchyma proliferation	
Dissolution of pectic substances in middle lamella	Pectin methyl esterase and polygalacturonase
Degradation of cellulose on cell walls	Cellulase.

Ps. solanacearum. Those in North Carolina, USA, are using a polygenic and largely recessive system while others in Hawaii have found *L. pimpinellifolium* PI 127805A to be resistant; so far no resistant cultivars have resulted from either programme. No bactericides are available to control *Ps. solanacearum* and soil sterilants produce only variable results. Control must, therefore, rely on husbandry techniques to maintain soil free of the pathogen.

12.1.2 *Corynebacterium michiganense* (bacterial canker)

This organism is more widespread geographically than *Ps. solanacearum*, sometimes affecting crops grown in temperate zones such as Europe, in addition to those in the tropics and sub-tropics. Its host range is restricted to *Lycopersicon* spp. and some *Solanum* spp. but not the potato (*S. tuberosum*). Seed transmission is well authenticated.

Symptoms begin with single leaflets curling at the edges followed by whole leaves shrinking, drying and turning brown; often only one side of a plant may exhibit symptoms. Elongated brown stripes develop on stems, shoots and petioles. The vascular bundles are destroyed leaving cavities within the stem; cracks appear in the epidermis of stems, mid ribs and small veins which under humid conditions break open to vent slimy bacterial masses. There is a characteristic brown discoloration of vessels with yellow to light brown stripes forming on the interior of ripening fruit. From there invasion of the seed coat and of the zone between the testa and endosperm takes place. In tropical environments infected fruit develops small circular white spots which later form lenticular or round light brown roughened centres surrounded by a white halo. These may coalesce to form irregular patches.

Corynebacterium michiganense is an aerobic, Gram-positive, coryneform rod, $0.6-0.7$ μm x $0.7-1.2$ μm in size with cells growing either singly or in pairs. Pigmented mutants develop due to possession of a range of carotenoid compounds. The organism is characterised by oxidation of carbohydrates; being non-lipolytic, it can only liquify gelatin slowly; the ability to hydrolyse starch is weak or absent; optimum growth takes place at $24-27$ °C and amino acids, biotin, nicotinic acid and thiamine are required for growth.

Local dissemination is from open cankers via rain-splash; more widespread distribution is by infected seed and transplants. Once invasion has taken place systemic distribution within the host occurs through the phloem. In this *C. michiganense* is unique, being the only bacterial organism which migrates primarily in the phloem. Perennation takes place on infected debris in the soil. Disease development can occur within the temperature range $16-28$ °C and is most favoured by pH 7. Seed contamination may reach 1 per cent and this level can rapidly give rise to epiphytotics in which 50 per cent of plants are infected.

Breeding programmes aimed at producing resistant cultivars are reported from Denmark, Italy, the USA and the USSR. The wild species *Lycopersicon raciforme* is highly resistant and *L. pimpinelifolium* less so. Cultural controls include dipping pruning knives in 0.1 per cent copper sulphate to prevent passage of the pathogen from one plant to the next, seed treatment with acid or hot water (up to 60 min at 54 °C) to eradicate the main avenue of infection, burning crop residues and extended rotations.

12.2 FUNGAL PATHOGENS

12.2.1 *Fulvia fulva* (leaf mould)

Until recently this fungus was referred to as *Cladosporium fulvum*. It is the most severe foliar pathogen of glasshouse tomato (*L. esculentum*) crops, but its widespread distribution has occasionally led to destructive outbreaks on field crops in moist tropical and sub-tropical areas.

Symptoms first develop on the lowermost leaves then proceed upwards to affect all the foliage. Indefinite chlorotic spots are first seen on the upper leaf surface and spread rapidly under conditions of high humidity. A characteristic velvety, olive-green, downy fructification is found on the leaf undersurface. As the lesions enlarge the leaflets wilt and die. Fruit and flowers may also become infected. Black leathery areas form on the fruit generally originating from the stem end; these may be interspersed with white zones which result from subepidermal air pockets. As infected fruit mature black pin-point stromata appear within the flesh which either decay or become mummified masses.

Fulvia fulva is a Fungus Imperfectus (order Moniliales), the mycelium of which penetrates into the host tissue without the formation of appressoria. An intercellular, pale brown stroma forms composed of cells 2–5 μm in diameter. From this loosely packed groups of septate conidiophores develop. These are usually unbranched, flexuous and narrower at the base then the apex. Nodular swellings form along one side of each conidiophore which develop into conspicuous thickened lateral branches. Conidia of *F. fulva* are pale to dark brown, cylindrical to elliptical, usually straight but possibly slightly curved, produced in branched chains and up to triseptate; they are 16–40 μm x 5–7 μm in size, possessing a conspicuous thickened hilum. There is extensive physiological specialisation of this pathogen.

Disease development is optimal between 22 and 24 °C, but severity of disease is greatly influenced by relative humidity. Incidence of *F. fulva* on tomatoes grown at a constant 20 °C was reduced from 25 per cent leaf area infected at 100 per cent RH to 2.8 per cent and 0 per cent when RH was reduced to 90 and 72 per cent respectively (Winspear *et al.*, 1970). Penetration by *F. fulva* is usually through the stomata. Outside the host no differences in the germination and growth of conidia were found between compatible and incompatible host–parasite combinations and there was no orientation of runner hyphae from the conidia towards the stomata. Penetration took place on the third and fourth days after deposition on conidia on the leaf. In compatible combinations the mycelium grew intercellularly, often in close contact with spongy mesophyll cells. Under optimal growth conditions there was no visible damage to host cells during the initial phases of invasion. Under sub-optimal conditions, however, the host cells often reacted by production of callose, but this did not inhibit growth of the pathogen. Ten to 12 days after infection conidiophores emerged through the stomata and formed conidia (de Wit, 1977). In Canadian studies using the cultivar V121 and Canadian race 1 of *F. fulva*, a combination where moderate resistance is expressed, pathogen growth in the leaf tissue is slower but ultimately colonisation was still extensive. Host cell damage became prominent just prior to formation of aerial mycelium. Cells in the lesion area became necrotic or showed changes such as reduced starch content in the chloroplasts and the association of extracellular material in the cell walls with polyphenols present within the lesions. Mycelia within the tissue of the cultivar V121 became highly vacuolated and sporulation was absent or greatly reduced (Lazarovits and Higgins, 1976*a*). Cytological changes occurred within the lesion just prior to mycelium formation and included cytoplasmic disorganisation, increased electron density of cytoplasm, limited callose formation, and association of extracellular material with the cell walls (Lazarovits and Higgins, 1976*b*). In the highly resistant host–parasite combination of the cultivar Vinequeen and race 1 of *F. fulva* fungal development was restricted to a few cells in the mesophyll region.

Host cells adjacent to and some distance from the fungus showed extensive deposition of material which was at least partially composed of callose (Lazarovits and Higgins, 1976*a*). Cells of resistant cultivars show higher oxidase content and total proteins when invaded compared to susceptible ones. Other studies of incompatible combinations have shown that fungal growth was arrested 1 or 2 days after penetration and confined to stomata and surrounding cells. Host cells in contact with the pathogen rapidly deposited extensive amounts of callose and later these cells turned brown and collapsed (de Wit, 1977).

Nomenclature of *F. fulva* races was initially based on a simple numerical system of race 1 to race *n* (Day, 1954). As breeding for resistance progressed this system became inadequate. In 1953 Butler proposed that genes for resistance in tomato to *F. fulva* should be named Cf_1 to Cf_5. Apart from resistance genes from *L. esculentum*, resistance to *F. fulva* has been derived from *L. chilense, L. hirsutum, L. peruvianum* and *L. pimpinellifolium*. This scheme for resistance gene classification enabled Day (1956) to propose a renaming of virulence factors in the pathogen based on the scheme used by Black for *Phytophthora infestans* and to indicate that there was a gene-for-gene relationship between resistance in the tomato and virulence in *F. fulva*. The various resistance genes manifest themselves by different effects. The resistance reaction of Cf_1 is shown as a large chlorotic spot without a sharp boundary which becomes necrotic. Gene Cf_3 leads to similar effects, but the chlorotic and later necrotic areas are somewhat less extended. The genes Cf_2 and Cf_4 lead to pin-point necrosis. Chlorotic spots extend several cell layers beyond the intercellular cavities occupied by the pathogen, and in incompatible combinations chlorosis starts much earlier than in compatible ones. Necrosis is delayed in susceptible cultivars until the fungus has spread over the whole leaf and sporulation has become abundant.

More recently breeders have simplified the race classification of *F. fulva*, bringing together races into groupings A, B, C, D and E (*see* table 12.2).

Recently a further race group D has been suggested (Boukema, 1977).

Table 12.2   Classification of races of *Fulvia fulva* on tomato cultivars (after N. Hubbeling)

Differential tomato cultivars	Genes for resistance	Group A							Group B					Group C				Group D	Group E
		1	2	5	9	8	7	6	10	·	·	·	11	·	·	·	12		
		0	1	2	3	1.2	2.3	1.2.3	4	(1.4)	(3.4)	(1.3.4)	?	(2.4)	1.2.4	2.3.4	(1.2.3.4)	5	2.3.4.5
Potentate / Moneymaker / Ailsa Craig	*cf*	S	S	S	S	S	S	S	S	S	S	S	S	S	S	S	S	S	S
Leaf Mould Resister No. 1 / Stirling Castle	Cf_1	R	S	R	R	S	R	S	R	S	R	S	S	R	S	R	S	R	R
Vetomold	Cf_2	I	I	S	I	S	S	S	I	I	I	I	S	S	S	S	S	I	S
V121	Cf_3	R	R	R	S	R	S	S	R	R	S	S	S	R	R	S	S	R	S
V473	Cf_1Cf_2	I	I	I	I	S	I	S	I	I	I	I	—	I	S	I	S	I	I
59R	Cf_1Cf_3	I	I	I	I	I	I	S	I	I	I	S	—	I	I	I	S	I	I
L. pimpinellifolium Vineland	Cf_2Cf_3	I	I	I	I	I	S	S	I	I	I	I	—	I	I	S	S	I	S
F 101	Cf_1Cf_3	R	I	R	I	R	I	S	R	I	I	S	—	I	I	I	S	I	I
Purdue 135	Cf_4	I	I	I	I	I	I	I	S	S	S	S	R	S	S	S	S	I	S
L. pimpinellifolium (PI 187002/1)	Cf_5	I	I	I	I	I	I	I	I	I	I	I	I?	I	I	I	I	S	S
Vagabond / Vantage / Vinequeen / V501	Cf_2Cf_4	I	I	I	I	I	I	I	I	I	I	I	S	S	S	S	S	I	S
Eurovite / Lito / Nemavite / Resistase / Sonatine / Virovite	$Cf...?$	I	—	I	—	—	—	—	I	—	—	—	—	—	—	—	—	I	I

* Race classification is given in three forms. Groups A–E are race groupings introduced by breeders; the next classification, immediately below, is the primary numerical classification; the third classification is the gene-for-gene system.

Abbreviations: S, susceptible; R, resistant; I, immune; —, not determined; ?, indistinct reaction

Resistance is largely inherited in an additive manner and depends on more than one gene. Mean percentage infection is a better criterion of selection for resistance than rate of spread of infection (Boukema and Garretsen, 1975). Studies of the mechanism of the gene-for-gene relationship suggest there is an interaction of specific fungal products with specific receptors in the host plasma membrane. This leads to an hypersensitive response. Production of these fungal compounds is postulated as controlled by four avirulence genes (A_1, A_2, A_3 and A_4) and the host receptors are controlled by the genes for resistance Cf_1, Cf_2, Cf_3 and Cf_4 (Dijkman and Sijpesteijn, 1971; Sijpesteijn and Dijkman, 1973).

Since *F. fulva* is capable of rapidly evolving new pathogen races in response to new resistance genes this method of disease control has proved less than satisfactory. Fortunately a range of fungicides are available to reinforce genetic control. Systemic fungicides such as benomyl, thiophanate, thiophanate-methyl and thiabendazole and eradicants such as mancozeb, captafol and zineb are active against *F. fulva*. It may be possible to employ biological control in the future since *Penicillium brevicompactum*, *Trichoderma viride* and *Acremonium* spp. strongly inhibit growth of *F. fulvum* (Kashyap and Levkina, 1977).

12.2.2 *Leveillula taurica* (powdery mildew)

This is the only truly endophytic member of the Erysiphaceae. It is a very important pathogen of such solanaceous crops as tomato (*L. esculentum*), capsicum (*C. annuum*) and eggplant (*S. melongena*) and a wide range of other crops, principally in dry areas around the Mediterranean, central Europe and the Near East. Usually only the imperfect state, *Oidiopsis taurica*, is seen.

Symptoms consist chiefly of the development of extensive yellow lesions on the upper surface of leaves with a white powdery sporulation covering the lower surface. Foliar shedding is a prominent symptom, especially on peppers (*C. annuum*).

Leveillula taurica is an Ascomycete fungus (order Plectomycetes), its mycelium permeates the host tissues and often covers the whole plant in a white or pale buff membraneous or crustaceous stroma. Sexual cleistothecia form within the stroma, but only rarely, embedded in the mycelium and are 135–250 µm in diameter. Numerous hyphae-like appendages are attached to the cleistothecia; these are short, indistinctly branched and colourless to oliveraceous brown. Usually there are 20–35 asci, 70–110 µm x 25–40 µm in size, within each cleistothecium. Each ascus contains two ascospores. The ascospores are large cylindrical to pear-shaped, possibly slightly curved, and measure 25–40 µm x 12–22 µm. Asexual conidia are borne singly on short hyphal branches and vary greatly in size over the range 25–95 µm x 14–20 µm. Information concerning physiological specialisation is conflicting, but it appears that a single isolate is able to infect a range of host genera.

Infection is favoured by temperatures of 18–24 °C and RH values of 70–100 per cent (Alexandri and Lemeni, 1969). Defoliation takes place when RH is low and temperatures are between 15 and 25 °C (Reuveni and Rotem, 1973). On tomato (*L. esculentum*) the optimum temperature for pathogenesis is 25 °C and on pepper (*C. annuum*) 20 °C. Leaf shedding is induced during the initial stages of infection and may be due to an effect on host hormone metabolism. Spraying infected plants with indoleacetic acid or indolebutyric acid retarded shedding (Reuveni *et al.*, 1976). Invasion takes place through the stomata in tomato (*L. esculentum*) and not through the cuticle (Reuveni *et al.*, 1977), but this may vary with host since Tafradjiiski *et al.* (1975) report cuticular invasion of eggplant (*S. melongena*). Spread is by wind-borne conidia.

Sulphur-based fungicides have offered the most effective means of control in dust, water-dispersable or lime sulphur formulations. Additionally 0.1 per cent karathane or 0.05 per cent morestan (Palti, 1971) have been effective. Recently benomyl and thiophanate-methyl have given considerable control. In attempts to breed for resistance heterozygotic peppers (*C. annuum*) developed less sporulation with lower percentage maturing conidia than their homozygotic parents (Beleva *et al.*, 1977). As a means of cultural control Rotem and Cohen (1966) found that disease was 30–40 per cent more severe on furrow irrigated tomatoes (*L. esculentum*) compared to sprinkle irrigated crops since the latter increased RH and lowered air temperature. Use is made of early planting to avoid infection by *L. taurica* and new crops are sown well separated from existing infected ones.

12.2.3 *Alternaria* and *Phytophthora* spp. (early and late blight)

(a) *Alternaria solani* (early blight)
Synonyms of *A. solani* are *Macrosporium solani*, which is often used in eastern European literature, and *A. porri* f. sp. *solani*, which is used in Canada and the USA. In addition to early blight the disease syndrome is referred to as target spot in Australasia. Host range includes many Solanaceous plants such as tomato (*L. esculentum*), potato (*S. tuberosum*) and eggplant (*S. melongena*) and crucifers such as cabbage (*B. oleracea* var. *capitata*) and cauliflower (*B. oleracea* var. *botrytis*).

Symptoms develop first on the foliage as round to angular, brown to black lesions varying in size from tiny dots to lesions 0.5 cm in diameter. These target spots have concentric raised rings of necrotic tissue surrounded by a halo of chlorotic cells. Severe infection leads to premature leaf senescence, withering, drooping and eventually abscission. Such infection reduces leaf dry weight and the rate of leaf expansion but does not affect the number of leaves initiated. The photosynthetically effective leaf area is reduced by expanding necrotic lesions and to a lesser extent by premature leaf fall (Coffey *et al.*, 1975). Stem lesions frequently form in the axis of the main and lateral branches which tend to break as fruit trusses mature. A form of collar rot develops subsequent to lesion development at the stem base, especially on young plants. Lesions form at the soil line, extending above and below the surface and leading to plant death. Flowers and fruits of tomato (*L. esculentum*) are commonly infected, leading to truss abortion and a black rot of semi-mature fruit. Black to brown lesions usually form from the stem end of the fruit, which takes on a leathery appearance and becomes covered in a black felt of sporulating mycelium. Estimates of yield loss on fruiting plants vary from 25 to 100 per cent. A study of disease development on a range of tomato cultivars (Basu, 1974) suggests that 60 per cent of foliage would need to be infected to lead to 10 per cent fruit infection. However, 10–40 per cent of fruit would also be lost due to blemishes causing a reduction in quality.

Alternaria solani is a Fungus Imperfectus (order Moniliales). The mycelium is greyish-brown to black, producing conidiophores either singly or in small groups which are straight or slightly curved, 110 μm long and 6–10 μm thick. Conidia develop singly or in short chains, typically with between nine and 11 lateral septa but few longitudinal septa. The conidia are oblong to elliptical in shape tapering to a whip-like beak which is as long or longer than the main body of the conidium; the main conidial body is pale to mid-pale golden or oliveraceous brown with an overall length of 150–300 μm and 15–19 μm thick at the broadest part. The beak is 2.5–5 μm thick and tapers gradually. Physiological specialisation has not been reported, but there are considerable variations in the aggressiveness of isolates. This is reflected in the differential ability of isolates to grow more quickly on different host organs such as leaves, petioles, stems and fruits. There are considerable differences in the morphological and cultural characters of isolates with a wide tolerance of environmental conditions, for example growth will take place at temperatures of 1–40 °C, RH 30–100 per cent and pH 1–10 (Dorozhkin *et al.*, 1975; 1977).

Conidia are disseminated by air currents and penetration takes place directly through the cuticle, taking 12 h at 10 °C and 8 h at 15–20 °C and 96 per cent RH (Hodosy, 1969). The conidium itself takes 1–2 h to germinate and form a germ tube. Lesions form within 2–3 days of penetration and sporulation begins when the lesions reach 3 mm in diameter. The disease syndrome has been correlated with the production of alternaric acid which inhibits host growth and fruit formation.

The destruction of host tissues by *A. solani* results from production of the enzymes polygalacturonase and pectin methyl esterase (Melita *et al.*, 1974).

Alternaria solani perennates as conidia and mycelium on dead, dry leaves on which viability is maintained for 18 months. Within infected stems and leaves chlamydospores form which are more or less spherical, occurring singly or in clusters. They will also form from condia either alone or in soil at temperatures from −31 to 27 °C, remaining viable for 7 months and thereby providing a bridge between old infected crops and newly planted ones (Basu, 1971). Seed from diseased fruits will carry the pathogen, providing an efficient means for widespread dissemination.

Efforts are being made, particularly in the USA and the USSR to develop resistant cultivars. Resistance in tomato (*L. esculentum*) to *A. solani* appears to be complexly inherited, requiring different genetic factors to prevent the various phases of the syndrome. Resistance to the collar rot stage is thought to be controlled by a single incompletely dominant gene (Walter, 1967), while two or more recessive factors control resistance to leaf spotting and defoliation phases. Single tomato plants with moderate levels of resistance to foliar lesions and higher levels of resistance to stem cankering can be selected from segregating populations at the F_2 stage (Berkdale and Stoner, 1973, 1977). Studies of the mechanism of resistance revealed that there were higher total tannins and phenols in resistant as compared to susceptible cultivars while flavonel compounds were at greater concentrations in young fruit from susceptible compared to resistant fruit (Bhatia *et al.*, 1972). Resistance has also been correlated with production of the phytoalexin rishitin (Dorozhkin and Ivanyuk, 1976). At present, however, resistant cultivars do not present a practical method for controlling this pathogen.

Control may be achieved by foliar sprays with materials such as metallic dithiocarbamates (maneb, mancozeb, zineb), captafol, chlorothalonil and the systemic materials benomyl and carbendazim. Soil-borne infection can be controlled by soil sterilisation using methyl bromide, which has the bonus effect of increasing plant vigour. Seed-borne infection may be controlled by organomercurial dressings.

The epidemic stages of this disease tend to coincide with fruit formation and Walker (1952) states that high soil fertility reduces disease severity. Provision of adequate nutrients at this stage, when the host is under considerable physiological stress due to translocation of nutrients to the developing fruit, is an important aspect of husbandry control. Stringent field sanitation to remove all infected debris, thereby preventing the build up of soil-borne infection, is essential.

(b) *Phytophthora infestans* (late blight)

While *P. infestans* is best known for the extensive damage which it causes to potato (*S. tuberosum*) crops, the same organism is also an important pathogen of field-grown tomatoes (*L. esculentum*). Other hosts include wild *Solanum* spp. and infrequently it is found on eggplant (*S. melongena*), but has not been recorded on pepper (*C. annuum*). Distribution is world-wide. In Australasia the disease on tomatoes is known as Irish blight.

Symptoms on tomato foliage are generally less severe than those found on potatoes. Lesions form on any part of the lamina which are brown to black-purple in colour. In moist conditions the leaf is quickly destroyed, but periods of low humidity will check the progress of the disease. Outer zones of these lesions are yellow, merging into healthy green uninvaded tissue. On the leaf undersurface white mycelial sporulation develops. Brownish streaks form along the stems, while tomato fruits are particularly vulnerable to infection. Invasion will take place at any stage in fruit development, usually beginning at the stem end. Large shapeless grey to green water-soaked lesions form on semi-mature and ripe fruit. Infection of green fruit leads to lesions which are dark brown with a firm corrugated texture possessing a definite border of green uninfected tissue around them. Under conditions of high RH sporulation may be seen on the fruit.

Phytophthora infestans is a Phycomycete fungus (class Oomycetes). As with other fungi of this type the coenocytic mycelium is intercellular and from it haustoria are produced into the host cells. Hyaline, branched, indeterminate asexual sporangiophores develop from the mycelium through the stomata. These bear thin walled, oval, hyaline sporangia (21–38 μm x 12–23 μm). Sporangia may germinate directly by means of a germ tube; this may in turn give rise to a terminal, secondary sporangium, but more commonly the sporangial contents cleave to form up to eight biciliate zoospores. On release these move away from the parent sporangium and germinate to produce a germ tube which can penetrate directly through the host epidermis or invade via a stoma. Sexual reproduction in the field is rare and would play no role in the life cycle or perennation of *P. infestans* in Europe or North America. Oospores are frequently found in potato tissue in Mexico and South America. The fungus is heterothallic, oogonia and antheridia being formed from the mycelia of complementary mating types. Oogonia are 30–50 μm in size, while the resultant oospores are 25–35 μm. They germinate directly by means of a germ tube which may either form a mycelium or produce a sporangium.

The dispersal spores of *P. infestans* are sporangia which are readily detached from the sporangiophore and disseminated by air currents. Optimal conditions for their formation are RH 100 per cent and temperature from 18 to 22 °C; the optimal temperature for zoospore formation is 12 °C and for formation of germ tubes from sporangia 25 °C; zoospores germinate most rapidly at 12–15 °C; and germ tubes develop best at 21–24 °C. The meteorological criteria for *P. infestans* epidemics are given in section 3.2.1. It is likely that RH rather than temperature is the determining factor for epidemic development on tomatoes. Antonelli (1974) found that a minimum mean daily RH of 65 per cent and mean RH greater than 90 per cent for 6 h on 3–4 days with temperatures of 10–12.5 °C was necessary for epiphytotics in Italy.

The most likely source of infection of tomato crops is neighbouring potatoes. Perennation of *P. infestans* takes place on potato ground keepers and in clamps, whereas the tomato provides relatively little debris for overwintering of the fungus. When transmission of infection took place from potato crops in the USSR, a period of 2 weeks elapsed before sporulation was seen on tomatoes (Tsupkova, 1977).

Compared to the voluminous literature on the potato–*P. infestans* combination, there have been relatively few studies using tomato as a host. Penetration was investigated by Pristou and Gallegly (1954), who found that the process was preceded by zoospore encystment, germination and appressoria formation. Appressoria were smaller than the encysted zoospores; protoplasm from a zoospore flowed through the germ tube into the appressorium which was then cut off from the empty spore and germ tube by the wall of the spherical appressorium. Empty spores and germ tubes were usually sloughed off, leaving the appressoria. A minute infection peg developed on the undersurface of the appressorium which entered the host epidermal cell to establish a primary mycelium. Protoplasm passed from the appressorium via the infection peg to form the primary mycelium. Finger-like secondary mycelia then developed and spread throughout the host leaves.

Studies of resistance to *P. infestans* in potato revealed the presence of considerable numbers of major resistance genes (R-genes) and correspondingly numbers of pathogen physiological races compatible with specific R-genes. Use of major gene resistance has been generally discarded by potato breeders, who now attempt to find and use field or non-specific resistance. Resistance to *P. infestans* in tomato was described by Gallegly and Marvel (1955) and Gallegly and Niederhauser (1959), as being of two types: (1) single dominant gene Ph_1 which conveys resistance to the unspecialised physiological race 0; (2) multigenic resistance dependent upon several factors which are considered to be quantitative in effect.

Two races of *P. infestans* have been differentiated on tomato and designated T0 and T1 to distinguish them from potato infecting races. Race T1 is more aggressive than T0 and will displace it in tomato crops. Spore production by T0 was less than 50 per cent of that of T1 on tomato foliage (D'yakov *et al.*, 1975). By crossing and back-crossing with wild and semi-cultivated lines, several field resistant forms have been developed (Kravchenko, 1977). Similar horizontal resistance has been found in *L. pimpinellifolium* line WVa 63 (Laterrot, 1975). At least one further resistance gene has been identified and named Ph_2 (Turkensteen, 1973). Resistance may be related to growth stage in tomatoes since Dowley *et al.* (1975) found greater resistance in more mature plants, but older leaves at the plant base tend to be more susceptible. Hosts possessing major gene resistance inoculated with incompatible isolates react in an hypersensitive manner similar to potato–*P. infestans* combinations. Cell death takes place within 10 min of invasion and there is migration of the host nucleus to the infection site (Matthewson, 1977). In incompatible combinations of tomato–*P. infestans* a proteinase inhibitor develops immediately after penetration, which may indicate that resistance operates by blocking the action of proteolytic enzymes formed by the pathogen (Peng and Black, 1976).

Control of *P. infestans* on tomato largely rests with the use of fungicides. Studies with prothiocarb using potted plants given 100–200 mg a.i. per plant prevented infection of the apical leaves (Beyries and Molot, 1976). In Europe, however, this material is thought to have undesirable side effects and has not been cleared for use on edible crops. A range of metallic dithiocarbamates (mancozeb, maneb and zineb) together with captafol and propineb give effective control when applied at 10–14 day intervals. Systemic materials of the acylalanine type are likely to give considerable control at a lower frequency of application. The use of epidemiological prediction has not reached the level of sophistication with tomatoes which has been achieved for potato crops; work on this aspect would also reduce the need for frequent fungicide sprays. Haulm destruction with desiccant materials such as paraquat will reduce carry-over of infection from one season to the next on crop debris. Biological control may become available by use of capsidol, a phytoalexin formed from pepper (*C. annuum*). Capsidol applied to tomatoes at 5×10^{-4} M controlled *P. infestans* for 8 days (Ward *et al.*, 1975; El-Wazeri and El-Sayed, 1977). Injection of 1 per cent copper sulphate into capsicum fruits will induce capsidol formation.

12.2.4 *Didymella lycopersici* (canker)

Although this pathogen has a widespread distribution, severe outbreaks occur only sporadically. Considerable losses have been caused to glasshouse tomato (*L. esculentum*) crops in Europe and New Zealand.

Symptoms begin as stem lesions at or near to soil level which develop into dark brown sunken girdling cankers. Secondary cankers may form further up the stem. These culminate in a sudden wilting death of the host. Within the softened tissue of each canker are numerous pycnidia which under humid conditions exude conidia as slimy pink masses. Foliage may also be affected with the development of leaf spots, while the fruits of infected plants develop circular black zones at the stem and beneath the caylx leading to total blackening and rotting of the fruit. Damage often occurs to mature tomato plants in full production. The cause is often confused with *Botrytis cinerea* (*see* section 6.4.3), which is distinguished by the typical grey fluffy sporuliferous mycelium of *Botrytis* and the zonate lesions which do not contain pycnidia.

Didymella lycopersici is an Ascomycete fungus, the perfect stage producing light brown, sub-globose pseudothecia which possess papillate ostioles and are 120–200 μm in diameter. These contain cylindrical to club-shaped asci which may have a short stalk and bitunicate wall and measure 50–70 μm x 8–9 μm. Each ascus contains eight ascospores which are elliptical in shape with blunt ends, hyaline and with a single septum and are 12–15 μm x 5 μm in size. Between the asci are long thin hyaline septate pseudoparaphyses. Asexual pycnidia develop either singly or in groups, initially immersed below the host surface but at maturity erupting above; they are dark brown and 180–250 μm in size; the wall is formed of pseudoparenchymatous cells with the outer ones being slightly thicker walled than the inner. Unicellular or monospetate hyaline conidia develop inside each pycnidium; these conidia are elliptical to oval in shape and 6–10 μm x 2–3 μm in size. No physiological specialization has been reported; isolates from tomato (*L. esculentum*) and eggplant (*S. melongena*) cross-inoculate freely.

Penetration can take place directly through the stem epidermis, but the only likely avenue of invasion is via stem wounds. Optimal growth and conidial production takes place at 19–20 °C while symptoms are most severe at 10–15 °C.

Perennation occurs on soil-borne crop debris from which conidia are released leading to primary infections. Seed transmission can take place by hyphae and pycnidia attached to the hairs on tomato seed testas. Conidia remain viable on seed for up to 9 months. Ascospores are not an important means of spread for this pathogen.

Control is largely achieved by husbandry techniques. Hygienic removal of all crop debris is the main means of combating *D. lycopersici*. Soil sterilisation by steam has little effect and may even allow the conidia to survive for longer periods compared to unsteamed soil. Chemical sterilants such as formalin are more effective. Fungicides such as thiophanate-methyl and carbendazim will control this pathogen, particularly if applied as soil drenches. Soil type influences their efficacy since better control is achieved with infected plants grown in loam compared to peat. Chemicals which may help to control *D. lycopersici* when applied as sprays include maneb, captan and nabam. *Lycopersicon esculentum* shows no resistance to *D. lycopersici* but some resistance is found in *L. hirsutum*. Resistance has been studied by Martinson and Hogenboom (1968), who found that watering spores and mycelium around the base of seedlings and maintaining a soil temperature of 10–15 °C for 10 days would cause severe infection of susceptible plants.

12.2.5 Damping-off, root, foot and fruit rot

Several soil-borne fungal pathogens belonging to various genera induce a range of similar symptoms in solanaceous crops. Tomatoes (*L. esculentum*) are extensively affected by these organisms, causing either death of young plants or yield loss on more mature ones. Control of these pathogens, other than by the development of resistant cultivars, is considered collectively at the end of this section.

(a) *Colletotrichum coccodes* (anthracnose)

A widely used synonym for this pathogen is *C. atramentianum*. Symptoms include black dot of tomato (*L. esculentum*) and potato (*S. tuberosum*), fruit anthracnose of tomato and chilli pepper (*C. annuum*) and a brown cortical rot of stems and roots of potato, tomato, chilli and eggplant (*S. melongena*). Root damage caused by *C. coccodes* is found on white mustard (*B. hirta*), cress (*Lepidium sativum*), cabbage (*B. oleracea* var. *capitata*) and lettuce (*L. sativa*). Black dot syndrome derives its name from the formation of large numbers of small sclerotia within the host cortical tissue. This decays and is disrupted leading to foliar wilting which is often the first visual symptom that the root system is affected. Symptoms on fruit consist of blotchiness and development of an amethyst colour in the xylem close to the stem base.

Colletotrichum coccodes is a Fungus Imperfectus (order Melancoliales), the perfect state may be related to *Glomerella cingulata* (*see* sections 6.4.4 and 11.2.6). Asexual acervuli, which are rounded to elongate and up to 300 μm in diameter, form on roots and stems. Initially they develop beneath the host epidermis but eventually erupt above it. Brown septate setae may be attached to each acervulus which are slightly swollen at the base and taper towards the tip. Hyaline, cylindrical, aseptate conidia form from unicellular hyaline conidiophores within the acervulus and are 16—24 μm x 2.5—4.5 μm in size. Sclerotia develop abundantly both in nature and in culture, forming from the intertwining of adjacent hyphae which secrete mucilage into which melanising particles are deposited (Griffiths and Campbell, 1972). Conidiophores develop from the sclerotia; the inner wall of the conidiophore gives rise to each conidial cell wall. Germination of conidia occurs within the range 15—37 °C to form germ tubes, but only at 15 °C do appressoria form. Each is characterised by possession of a thick secondary wall and external deposit of electron-dense granules (Griffiths and Campbell, 1973; Campbell and Griffiths, 1974). *Colletotrichum coccodes* is an unspecialised pathogen with wide host range, for which no physiological specialisation has been reported, but isolates differ in aggressiveness to other hosts. Geographical distribution is world-wide.

The organism can exist as a moderately competitive saprophyte on decaying host roots and weed hosts (Davet, 1976*a*). It is generally accepted as a secondary invader but can cause severe losses to tomato crops if rotation or soil sterilisation controls are not used. Sclerotia can survive in soil for at least 1 year (Farley, 1976). Infection usually develops from sclerotia present on soil-borne debris, but water-borne conidia are an additional source of infection (Davet, 1971). A considerable range of enzymes have been identified in culture filtrates of *C. coccodes* (Davet, 1976*b*), including pectin methyl esterase, endopolygalacturonase, endopectin transeliminase, endopectate transeliminase, α-amylase, β-amylase, cellulase, β-glucosidase, indicating a significant ability to destroy host tissues. Colonisation and penetration of young roots is rapid, with the percentage adherance of conidial appressoria increasing from the tip to the base of roots, but colonisation of roots increases with age. The ratio of diseased root weight to total root weight rose sharply at the beginning of fruit set (Davet, 1972).

Some attempts have been made to develop host resistance to *C. coccodes.* Davet and Ravise (1976) report *L. esculentum* var. *cerasiforme* as weakly resistant, *L. hirsutum* x tomato cultivars as moderately resistant and *L. hirsutum* var. *glabrastum* as resistant. In the USA, Barksdale and Stoner (1975) found resistance in small fruited tomatoes which is probably polygenic in nature. Six genes are involved in the resistance reaction with resistance being dominant and non-additive (Robbins and Angel, 1970).

(b) *Thielaviopsis basicola* (root rot)
Thielaviopsis basicola has a comparably wide host range to *C. coccodes*, invading the roots of solanaceous and cucurbit crops together with *Phaseolus* bean, carrot (*Daucus carota*) and mint (*Mentha* spp.). Symptoms are characterised by rotting of the rootlets, which initially develop purple lesions turning black with age and

leading to stunting of the host. Cortex and periderm tissues of roots are invaded, entry being via ruptures of the cortex due to the emergence of secondary root primordia. The organism is extensively distributed geographically.

Thielaviopsis basicola is a Fungus Imperfectus (order Moniliales). Two types of one-celled asexual conidia are formed:

(1) *Macroconidia* or chlamydospores which are brown with rounded tips are formed in short chains from hyaline basal cells and are 14—16 μm in length. At maturity these turn black and break apart.

(2) *Microconidia* are formed within endoconidiophores; they are cylindrical and produced in series from an endogenous mother cell by growth and septation from a wall layer (Hawes and Beckett, 1977). Microconidia are rectilinear in shape, 6 μm x 4 μm in size and liberated successively through the apex.

The nucleus in the end cell of the conidiophore divides mitotically and successively to produce a chain of uninucleate endoconidia. During chlamydospore formation a daughter nucleus migrates from a mycelial cell into the chlamydospore primordium, which later becomes a one-celled chlamydospore. In multicelled chlamydospores all the nuclei are derivatives of the one in the primordium. Nuclei migrate from one cell to another by anastomosis or through septal pores. Anastomosis occurs between endoconidia and between mycelium and endoconidia. Mitosis takes place within the nuclear envelope, within which four chromosomes have been recorded (Huang and Patrick, 1972).

Isolates of *T. basicola* differ in aggressiveness but no physiological specialisation has been noted. As a soil inhabitant this organism is capable of prolonged saprophytic survival.

(c) *Pyrenochaeta lycopersici* (brown root rot or corky root rot)
Until a causal link was established between *P. lycopersici* and the brown root rot syndrome various organisms, but especially *C. coccodes* (*see* section 12.2.5(a)), were implicated in this syndrome, which is largely restricted to the tomato (*L. esculentum*) host. *Pyrenochaeta lycopersici* had for a long time been regarded as 'grey sterile fungus' which produced neither sexual or asexual states, associated with tomato roots.

Symptoms of *P. lycopersici* infection are usually first noted as a lack of plant vigour, foliar chlorosis, stunting and loss of yield, which are associated with cortical rotting of fine and medium sized roots, the larger roots becoming corky, swollen, cracked with a corrugated surface and eventually rotting at the stem base. Three lesion types have been distinguished:

(1) brown lesions, visible within a month after planting, on the young feeder roots and as darker lesions with cortical splitting on older larger roots;
(2) lengths of corky root often extending for several centimetres;
(3) dark brown cortical basal stem lesions (Ebben, 1974).

Yield losses of 8—20 per cent have been associated with 10—15 per cent root infection by *P. lycopersici* 8 weeks after planting.

Tissue discoloration attendant on infection may be due to the high levels of polyphenoloxidase and peroxidase found in diseased root tissue (Delon, 1974). The pathogen is capable of synthesising a range of cell-degrading enzymes such as pectic hydrolases and transeliminases, α- and β-amylases and a β-glucosidase. The amylases are inducible but the pectic transeliminases are constitutive, although their activity is strongly stimulated in the presence of an inducer (Goodenough and Maw, 1974, 1975; Davet, 1975). Enzyme activities are greatest within lesion tissue or in tissue around the periphery of a lesion and at a comparatively low concentration in the apparently healthy portions of infected roots (Goodenough and Kempton, 1976).

Pyrenochaeta lycopersici is found in nature as the grey sterile mycelial state. But in culture it is a Fungus Imperfectus (order Sphaeropsidales) forming globular to sub-globose pycnidia 150—300 μm in diameter which are brown to black bearing between three and 12 light brown septate setae up to 120 μm x 7 μm in size. The outer wall cells of the pycnidium are sclerotised and heavily pigmented while the inner ones are hyaline and pseudoparenchymatous. Conidiophores develop from the hyaline cells lining the interior of the pycnidial cavity. Unicellular, hyaline, conidia form within the conidiophores as phialospores; they are cylindrical in shape and 4.5—8 μm x 1.5—2 μm in size. A structurally unspecialised microsclerotium is formed by *P. lycopersici* which has cell walls of similar thickness throughout. Sclerotia can survive for at least 2 years in a viable state (White and Scott, 1973). No physiological specialisation is reported. Isolates of *P. lycopersici* from *Capsicum* spp. have been found to be capable of infecting tomato, but there is considerable variation in aggressiveness between isolates. Distribution of this pathogen appears to be restricted to areas of glasshouse tomato production; field-grown crops are seldom affected.

Growth of *P. lycopersici* occurs over a wide temperature range, 8—32 °C, but rate of growth is slow and its lack of saprophytic ability is reflected in the localisation of lesions on roots and the slow rate of lesion spread. In axenic culture growth averaged 1 mm/day and infected roots exhibited reduced xylem, formation of cell wall bodies and lignituber development with changes in mitochondrial and endoplasmic reticulum structure. Eventually the invaded cell died and was invaded by hyphae with simultaneous accumulation of dark bodies with thickening of the cell wall and the appearance of crystalline microbodies in neighbouring tissues (Delon *et al.*, 1973).

Control by resistance initially rested on the use of wild resistant *Lycopersicon* spp. as rootstocks on which susceptible commercial cultivars could be grafted as scions (*see* section 4.2.1). Subsequently, resistance genes from *Lycopersicon* spp. have been transferred to *L. esculentum* to produce a range of resistant cultivars. *Lycopersicon glandulosum* contains one major gene for resistance but this has a low degree of dominance and when in the heterozygous state its expression is influenced by environment (Hogenboom, 1970). Partially dominant genes for resistance are found in *L. esculentum* var. *cerasiforme* and *L. chilense* (Laterrot, 1972; Yordanov *et al.*, 1974). PIs 260397, 262906 and 203231 possess resistance to *P. lycopersici* but heritability is as low as 25–43 per cent and the minimum number of genes involved is between four and eight (Violin and McMillan, 1978).

Husbandry control of *P. lycopersici* by application of potassium and phosphorus, but not nitrogen, to infected plants is advocated by Goodenough and Maw (1973), since there are losses of these elements in the tops of plants infected by *P. lycopersici* due to an inability to accumulate potassium in the roots and transport adequate amounts to the aerial plant parts.

Indications of potential biological control come from observations that non-pathogenic strains of soil-borne *F. oxysporum* inhibited invasion of tomato roots by *P. lycopersici*. In natural soil the balance between these organisms was temperature-dependent (Ebben, 1974; Davet, 1976c).

(d) *Phytophthora* spp. (damping-off, stem rot, foliar blight and buckeye rot)
A variety of disease syndromes occur in pepper (*C. annuum*), eggplant (*S. melongena*) and tomato (*L. esculentum*) caused by several soil-borne *Phytophthora* spp. Nomenclature of the latter is complex and the system adopted here is that of Waterhouse (1963).

Some or all of the following symptoms may develop:

(1) *Damping-off, foot and root rot*   Brown discoloration begins in the lateral roots or at the tip of the taproot. Infection progresses upwards on seedlings along the vascular bundles and into the developing pith tissue. Growth is stunted and the foliage becomes a dull dark green colour. Where seedlings have not developed a complete cylinder of lignified xylem, tissue desiccation ensues, causing the stem base to shrivel and the plants to collapse and die quickly. Infection of more mature plants moves slowly upwards, leading to a range of foliar symptoms such as darkly discoloured apical leaves and chlorotic basal ones. Considerable proliferation of lateral roots may also take place.

(2) *Leaf blight*   Infection may spread directly from the soil to leaves which are in contact with the ground, or water-splash can transfer the pathogen in soil particles. In either case wilting and foliar discoloration result.

(3) *Petiole and stem infection*   Blackish-green lesions develop on infected petioles and stems leading to their collapse. Petiole infection generally originates from infected leaf blades and may eventually lead to invasion of the stem, but can develop from fruit stalks or pruning wounds. That part of the host above a stem lesion wilts and usually dies quickly.

(4) *Fruit rot*   This part of the syndrome is usually referred to as 'buckeye rot', being a wet soft fruit rot. Fruits exhibit greyish-green, partially water-soaked lesions with usually dark brown concentric rings. Mucilage inside the fruit turns dark brown to black and decomposes to a watery consistency. Infected fruits maintain

their original shape and may even be somewhat enlarged, but they detach from the truss easily. Fruit in the first two trusses are most prone to infection.

Differences between this syndrome and that caused by *P. infestans* (late blight; *see* section 12.2.3(b)) are shown in table 12.3. These syndromes may be referred

Table 12.3   Comparison of symptoms on tomato fruit caused by *Phytophthora* spp. (buckeye rot) and *P. infestans* (late blight) (after Weststeijn, 1973)

Host tissue	Buckeye rot	Late blight
Infected tissue	Soft and turgescent	Hard and dry
Wounded fruit	Large brown lesions	Small brown lesions
Unwounded fruit	Endocarp and seeds discoloured	Exocarp only brown
Around the caylx	Usually infected	Not usually infected
Vascular bundles near hilum	Discoloured at an early stage	Discoloured only when tissue around caylx infected
Reddening of fruit	Slow	Very quick
Appearance of epidermis	Green, water-soaked	Bronzing

to as 'wet (*Phytophthora*) fruit rot', that is buckeye rot and associated symptoms, and 'dry (*Phytophthora*) fruit rot', that is late blight. This emphasises the major difference in the consistency of infected fruit. Wet fruit rot is usually restricted to the lower trusses while dry fruit rot may be found on any truss.

The principle *Phytophthora* spp. implicated in these syndromes vary in different geographical areas but include *P. capsici, P. cryptogae, P. drechsleri, P. erythroseptica* var. *erythroseptica, P. mexicana, P. nicotianae* var. *nicotianae, P. nicotianae* var. *parasitica* and *P. palmivora*. As with other *Phytophthora* spp. they are Phycomycetes (class Oomycetes); their general mycological characters have been discussed in sections 10.2.3 (*Phytophthora porri*, white tip) and 12.2.3(b) (*P. infestans*, late blight). Specific distinguishing characters are shown in table 12.4.

Information on most of these species as pathogens of pepper (*C. annuum*), eggplant (*S. melongena*) and tomato (*L. esculentum*) is limited, but the more recent data are summarised in the following paragraphs.

Table 12.4   Specific mycological characters of *Phytophthora* spp. (All values are in micrometres.)

Character	P. capsici	P. cryptogae	P. drechsleri	P. erythroseptica var. erythroseptica	P. mexicana	P. nicotianae var. nicotianae	P. nicotianae var. parasitica	P. palmivora
Hyphal diameter	5–7	8	5	7	6	5	9	5
Sporangiophore width	1.5–2	2–3.5	1–2	1–2	8–10	2	>9	1
Sporansial size								
Average	30–60 x 25–35	37–40 x 23	36–50 x 26–30	43–26	46 x 24	45 x 36	38 x 30	50–60 x 31–35
Limits	Up to 100	55–30	70 x 40	69–47	77 x 33	60–70	50 x 40	93 x 43
Oogonial size	30–39	30–38	36–53	30–35	30–37.5	28–32	24–31	Rare, 30–42
Antheridial size	17 x 15	10–16	14–15 x 13	14–16 x 13	15.5 x 14	10–16 x 10	10–16	15 x 14
Oospore size	Similar to oogonia	Similar to oogonia	Similar to oogonia	Similar to oogonia	Similar to oogonia	24	18–20	Similar to oogonia
Oospore wall thickness	1	3.5	3	2.5	2	1.5–3	2	2
Chlamydospore size	Rare	Rare	Rare	Rare	Rare	20–40, no brown pigment	60, yellowish brown pigment	30–55
Chlamydospore wall thickness	—	—	—	—	—	1.5	3–4	1–2

Phytophthora capsici is an important seedling and foliar pathogen of pepper (*C. annuum*) and tomato (*L. esculentum*). Pepper seedlings infected with *P. capsici* decay completely within 5 days of infection. The main symptom exhibited by infected tomatoes is stem rotting (Elenkov, 1976). Epiphytotics are encouraged by rain and warm conditions. Crop nutrition is also important in determining the severity of symptoms; excess applications of nitrogen exacerbate the disease whereas potassium retards it (Elenkov and Bakharieva, 1975). The fungus remains viable in soil for up to 5 months. An alternative source of infection is via diseased seed, but this can be controlled by use of captan seed dressings. In studies of the invasion process, Jones *et al.* (1975) found *P. capsici* hyphae with dense cytoplasm and functional organelles in the outer walls of cells lining the cavity of sweet pepper (*C. fructescens*) fruit within 3 h or infection. The second layer of cells was invaded in 5–7 h. Pepper cells reacted to invasion by formation of lipid bodies, vacuolation of the cytoplasm, invagination and disruption of the tonoplast membrane, formation of vesicles, and their dispersion throughout the cell cavity.

Extracts of fresh bulb tissue from *Urgina ultissima* have considerable activity against *P. capsici* and this might indicate a means of biological control. Activity is located in the water-soluble extract containing the alkaloid lycorine, which when sprayed at 500 μg/ml on tomato leaves gave protection against invasion by *P. capsici* (Miyakado *et al.*, 1975).

Phytophthora erythroseptica is of great significance as the causal agent of pink rot of potato (*S. tuberosum*), but can cause severe stem rotting of young tomato (*L. esculentum*) plants when the two hosts are grown in the field in close proximity.

Phytophthora palmivora is probably the most common pathogen of tropical and sub-tropical flowering plants, affecting more than 50 genera of 29 families. Its greatest importance is as a cause of seedling wilt, leaf necrosis, stem canker and fruit rot (black pod syndrome) of cacao (*Theobroma cacao*). On tomato (*L. esculentum*) and eggplant (*S. melongena*) lesion maturation could be divided into three stages:

(1) the young lesion stage, where the lesion was grey to greenish-grey resulting from the destruction of pigments but the fruit texture remained firm;

(2) an intermediary stage, when the grey colour began to turn brown initiated at the point of invasion;

(3) browning of the whole lesion.

Different hydrolytic enzyme activities of undialysed extracts could be associated with each of these phases. In the young lesion stage there was a preponderance of phenolase activity followed in the intermediary phase by arabinofuranosidase, and finally when the lesion turned brown polygalacturonase became important (Akinrefon, 1969).

Phytophthora nicotianae var. *nicotianae* is generally a major pathogen of tobacco (*Nicotiana tabaccum*), causing the black shank disease. Detailed studies by Weststeijn (1973) identify this fungus as an important soil-borne pathogen of glasshouse tomato (*L. esculentum*) crops in the Netherlands and to a lesser extent the UK. It is able to persist for up to 9 months in soil, producing abundant chlamydospores. Optimal fungal growth occurs between 22 and 23 °C but severe root infection takes place between 17 and 27 °C. In contrast to *P. capsici*, increased host nitrogen content tends to retard stem infection. No resistance to root invasion could be found in *L. hirsutum*, *L. pimpinellifolium* or *L. peruvianum*, but moderate resistance to the buckeye rot fruit syndrome is present in *L. pimpinellifolium* and some commercial cultivars of *L. esculentum*.

Phytophthora nicotianae var. parasitica is associated with damping-off, root rot, crown rot, stem canker, tip blight, leaf blight and fruit rot in over 58 families. Solanaceous crops affected include tomato (*L. esculentum*) with damping-off and fruit rot and eggplant (*S. melongena*) with fruit rot. Usually isolates from one host are pathogenic to other hosts, but this is not always the case; isolates from parsley (*Petroselinum crispum*) were unable to infect carrot (*Daucus carota*), celery (*Apium graveolens*) and tomato (*L. esculentum*). Differentiation into physiological races is suggested by McIntyre and Hawkins (1977) who found that race 3 could be distinguished from races 0 and 1 by its inability to produce the kestose fructosylsucrose. Temperatures above 28 °C favour this pathogen; it is killed at temperatures of less than 10 °C or above 35 °C; at 0 °C survival is reduced to a few minutes. In contrast to *P. nicotianae* var. *nicotianae* survival in soil may be as oospores rather than as chlamydospores. Oospores are formed in abundance in tomato tissue suffering from damping-off (Sharma *et al.*, 1976). The fungus may also be seed-transmitted, incidence of diseased plants developing from seed harvested from infected fruits was 38 per cent using unsterilised seed and 20 per cent where the seed was surface sterilised. This indicates that the fungus is carried both internally and externally (Sharma and Soli, 1976).

Cultural control may be achieved by stripping leaves and fruit trusses from the basal 30 cm of stem of field-grown tomatoes, thereby preventing splash transmission of infected soil (Sharma *et al.*, 1977). Similarly, the use of taller-growing cultivars will circumvent this invasion pathway. It may be possible to exploit phytoalexin production as a means of control. Trique (1975) found that phytoalexins produced by tomatoes infected by *P. palmivora* and *P. parasitica* (*P. nicotianae* var. *parasitica*) were in inverse proportion to the 'virulences' of the isolate used, opening up the possibility of cross-protection by non-aggressive isolates. Antifungal compounds were restricted to the leaves and stems but production in root tissue was stimulated by applications of glucose.

Control of *C. coccodes*, *T. basicola*, *P. lycopersici* and *Phytophthora* spp. in practice must rest with either techniques of disease avoidance or use of chemicals. So far only limited sources of resistance to these pathogens have been identified and in the main these would appear to be of a polygenic nature. The exception

to this is *P. lycopersici*, where resistant commercial tomato cultivars have been
developed and marketed.

Until recently a useful technique for disease avoidance was the use of
resistant rootstocks for glasshouse tomato crops, particular use being made of an
interspecific F$_1$ hybrid rootstock, *L. esculentum* x *L. hirsutum*. This is now
largely superseded by soil-less growing methods where there is less risk of infection
from soil-borne pathogens.

Field-grown crops of eggplant (*S. melongena*), capsicum (*C. annuum*) and
tomato (*L. esculentum*) can only be protected by chemical means or crop
rotation. The latter should extend to give at least 2–3 years break between
susceptible crops. Soil sterilisation can be used to reduce this requirement with
materials such as chloropicrin, dazomet, methylisothiocyanate, and metham-
sodium. Chemical drenches can be applied to infected soil using maneb, fentin
acetate, fentin hydroxide, captafol or chlorothalonil and will give an effective
control for up to 6 weeks; however, they require the use of high volumes of water.
Sprays of these materials applied to foliage and fruits will control the leaf blight,
stem blight and buckeye rot syndromes.

12.2.6 *Verticillium* and *Fusarium* spp. (wilts)

'Sleepy disease' of tomato (*L. esculentum*) was initially thought to be caused by
Fusarium lycopercici. Bewley (1922) showed that two separate genera, *Verticillium*
and *Fusarium*, were involved. These soil-borne pathogens cause similar syndromes.
Both host–parasite complexes have been studied extensively in an attempt to
elucidate the physiology and biochemistry of wilting which will be considered
collectively at the end of this section.

(a) *Fusarium oxysporum* f. sp. *lycopersici*

Earliest symptoms are clearing of the veinlets and drooping of the petioles. These
are followed by yellowing of the lower leaves, often affecting one side of the host
only. As leaves wilt and die there is a progression of symptoms towards the top
of the plant. The vascular system turns brown, the plant is stunted and foliage
wilts irreversibly. Changes caused by *F. oxysporum* f. sp. *lycopersici* in the leaves
of susceptible tomato cultivars include degeneration of the chloroplasts which
may become elongated and club-shaped. Mitochondria also tend to lengthen and
break up into numerous shorter elements. Polyphenol compounds accumulate in
the upper epidermal cells of infected foliage. In the interveinal areas necrosis of
parenchyma cells begins as agglutination of mitochondria and plastids and is
completed with coagulation of the cytoplasm and nucleus, often accompanied
by plasmolysis. Wall thickening is sometimes found in necrotic areas of the vein
parenchyma (Marte *et al.*, 1975).

Mycological details of *F. oxysporum* f. sp. *lycopersici* are similar to other
formae speciales of *F. oxysporum* (*see* section 6.1.5(a)).

A survey of the extensive literature on *Fusarium* wilt of tomato was produced by Walker (1971). Principle factors favouring disease development are soil temperature of 28 °C and over, low soil moisture, short day-length, low light intensity, nutrition of the host high in nitrogen and low in potassium, and low pH.

Two physiological races of *F. oxysporum* f. sp. *lycopersici*, initially termed races 1 and 2, have been identified. Resistance to race 1 was found in *L. pimpinellifolium* Missouri Accession 160 (PI 79532) and designated the *I* (immunity) gene. Resistance to race 2 was found in several PI accessions, notably PI 126915, a hybrid between *L. pimpinellifolium* x *L. esculentum* and named I_2 (Hubbeling *et al.*, 1971). It would be more logical to rename gene *I* as I_1 and Gabe (1975) suggests that the pathogen virulences should be reclassified as race 0 and race 1 to bring them into line with gene-for-gene terminology. This is because race 0 is virulent only to those cultivars which carry no resistance genes. Those possessing gene *I* are unaffected by race 0 of *F. oxysporum* f. sp. *lycopersici* but are parasitised by race 1; the resistance gene I_2 prevents infection by races 0 and 1 as shown in table 12.5.

Table 12.5   The relationship between physiological races of *Fusarium oxysporum* f. sp. *lycopersici* and genes for resistance in the tomato (*Lycopersicon esculentum*) (after Gabe, 1975).

Resistance gene in host	Physiological races of the pathogen	
	1	2*
	0	1†
None	S	S
I_1	R	S
I_2	R	R
I_1, I_2	R	R

* Original nomenclature.
† Gene-for-gene terminology.

Resistance gene *L* is suggested by Harries (1965) to be a single dominant, simply inherited gene because the first generation (F_1) of a cross between Accession 160 and a cultivar showed resistance as high as that of the wild parent and the second generation (F_2) and back-cross generation (B_1) segregated for resistance in the classic Mendelian ratios, 3:1 and 1:1, respectively. This was questioned by Kedar *et al.* (1967) who obtained significant deviations from these ratios when crosses were made involving susceptible and resistant tomato lines. These they interpreted as suggesting that there was preferential fertilization of ovules by pollen grains carrying the dominant I_1 allele. The location of alleles I_1 and I_2 has been shown to be on chromosome 11 of *L. esculentum* (Laterrot, 1976).

(b) *Verticillium albo-atrum* and *V. dahliae*

Symptoms induced by these two fungi are similar to those described in Section 12.2.6(a) for *F. oxysporum* f. sp. *lycopersici* but develop more slowly, generally causing stunting and yield reduction rather than death of the host (figure 12.1). In the field *V. dahliae* has been found to reduce tomato yields by 23 per cent (Visser, 1977) without obvious differences in the growth between inoculated and uninoculated plants being detected. Inoculum concentrations of less than 10^6 conidia/ml were insufficient to affect yields, but numbers of plants per plot were markedly reduced by inoculum levels of 10^8 conidia/ml. The upper leaves of infected tomatoes become a dull green, the leaflet margins curl upwards and roll inwards while the petioles bend downwards. These are typical symptoms of epinasty which is attributed to hormonal disturbance within the host. Yellow blotches form on the leaf laminae which become crisp and eventually wither and

Figure 12.1   Effect of infection by *Verticillium albo-atrum* (wilt) on the growth of tomato plants; rear three plants are healthy controls, front four plants infected. (Reproduced by permission of National Institute of Agricultural Botany, Cambridge.)

desiccate. The foliage generally wilts, initially recovering during the night but eventually the wilt becomes irreversible. Vascular discoloration is found within the stems, petioles and roots, generally of a lighter brown than that associated with *Fusarium* wilt. Adventitious roots develop in profusion from the stem base of infected plants. The term hadromycosis was used by Ludwig (1952) for the *Verticillium* syndrome to distinguish it from the rapid wilting associated with *Fusarium*. The two species of *V. albo-atrum* and *V. dahliae* differ slightly in their optimal temperature requirements, *V. albo-atrum* growing at 20–25 °C while *V. dahliae* thrives at temperatures of 25–28 °C. In practice this means that *V. albo-atrum* is more predominant in cool temperate climates such as those of northern Europe while *V. dahliae* predominants in warm temperature regions such as those of southern Europe and eastern Mediterranean areas. In culture these species are distinguished principally by the ability of *V. dahliae* to form microsclerotial resting structures and their absence in *V. albo-atrum* (Isaac, 1967). This differentiation has been challenged by workers in California, USA, in particular, where it is reported that intermediate forms between *V. albo-atrum* and *V. dahliae* occur. Thus microsclerotial forms of '*V. albo-atrum*' are described in American literature. Mycological characters of these pathogens are given in table 12.6.

Verticillium has a wide host range and apparently little physiological specialisation. Isolates from one host frequently cause disease in a wide range of species and genera while they may invade others without causing visible symptoms. Some host specificity has been demonstrated however, for isolates of *V. albo-atrum* from lucerne (*Medicago sativa*) and *V. dahliae* from Brussels sprout (*Brassica oleracea* var. *gemmifera*), mint (*Mentha* spp.) and pepper (*C. annuum*).

Two sources of resistance to *Verticillium* have been found in tomato (*L. esculentum*). A multigenic, complexly inherited system present in *L. esculentum* cvs Manx Marvel and Bides' Recruit and a single dominant gene, *Ve*, obtained from wild South American material and used to breed the cultivars Loran Blood and VR Moscow. This single gene is currently used in most American and European breeding programmes for *Verticillium* resistance. Use of multigenic resistance may become necessary since *V. albo-atrum* isolates virulent to the *Ve* gene are reported by Walter (1967).

Other techniques for control of *Verticillium* and *Fusarium* are as follows:

(1) soil sterilisation by steam, steam/air mixtures or methyl bromide;

(2) disease avoidance whereby the crop is produced in peat bolsters or by nutrient film;

(3) use of benomyl soil drenches, although the useful life of this method may be limited since Locke and Thorpe (1976) found an isolate of *V. dahliae* from a commercial crop of the tomato cultivar Sonato which was tolerant to 500 p.p.m. benomyl in culture.

It is essential that seed should be produced in a disease-free environment since *F. oxysporum* f. sp. *lycopersici* at least may be transmitted with the seed.

Table 12.6   Mycological characters of *Verticillium albo-atrum* and *V. dahliae*

Character	*V. albo-atrum*	*V. dahliae*
Conidiophores	Abundant, erect, hyaline with verticillate branching	
Phiallides	2–4 per node, 20–50 μm x 1.4–3.2 μm	3–4 per node 16–35 μm x 1–2.5 μm
Conidia	Arise singly at the apices of the phiallide, elliptical to sub-cylindrical, hyaline, generally single celled, occasionally bicellular	
	3.5–12.5 μm x 2–4 μm	2.5–8 μm x 1.4–3.2 μm
Resting mycelium	Appears after 10–15 days	
	Dark brown to black, tends to develop swellings between the septa giving torulose appearance hyphae 3–7 μm in diameter. No microsclerotia	Dark brown resting mycelium formed only in association with microsclerotia which arise from single hyphae by repeated budding. Microsclerotia variable in shape and size, 15–100 μm in diameter

Work by Besri (1977) in Morocco showed that viable fungal material could be carried with small dried pulp fragments derived from the tomato fruit which cling to the seed surface.

It may be possible to develop forms of biological control in the future since the severity of wilt symptoms caused by *F. oxysporum* f. sp. *lycopersici* were suppressed in glasshouse-grown tomato seedlings by prior inoculation with a range of formae speciales of *F. oxysporum* (Homma and Ohata, 1977). Those which were particularly effective included *F. oxysporum* f. sp. *melongenae, cucumerinum, batatas, F. solani* f. sp. *pisi* and *phaseoli*. Where inoculation preceded the pathogen by 1–3 days, wilt severity was considerably reduced, and many plants remained symptomless 3 weeks after inoculation; the magnitude of symptom reduction depended on the concentration of the protective inoculum and of the pathogen inoculum.

(c) The wilt syndrome
A voluminous literature exists describing studies of host–parasite relations between *Fusarium* and *Verticillium* and their hosts, especially the tomato.

Similar studies have been made for other vascular pathogens such as the bacteria
E. tracheiphila (*see* section 11.1.2) and *Ps. solanacearum* (*see* section 12.1.1).
The following represents a brief résumé particularly of the more recent literature
and is by no means comprehensive. A focal point of interest in physiological
studies of vascular pathogens is in an attempt to understand how pathogens
which inhabit dead lignified xylem vessels are responsible for the host wilt
syndrome and concomitant catastrophic effects on host growth. *Fusarium* and
Verticillium invade through the host root cortex and xylem vessels. The phase
of invasion prior to entry into the vessels has been termed determinative,
particularly as early investigators felt this was the period when host resistance
was expressed in preventing the establishment of infection in the xylem vessels
of resistant plants. Host responses to invasion by cortical and xylem parenchyma
cells in terms of lignituber and suberin production are described in section 2.2.1.
Thereafter colonisation has been termed expressive since mycelial growth within
the xylem correlates with the beginnings of symptom expression. Colonisation is
rapid and complete (Dixon and Pegg, 1969; Pollock and Drysdale, 1976*a*).
Following, or parallel with colonisation, various events take place either as a host
response to colonisation or as direct pathogen effects which contribute to the
wilt syndrome.

Tylose production
Tyloses result from distention of the pit closing membranes between vessels and
adjacent xylem parenchyma or ray cells. The nucleus of the original cell
apparently migrates into one of the several tyloses which may arise from it.
Formation of tyloses involves considerable synthesis of cell wall and cytoplasmic
material. They may fill the vessels so completely as to present the appearance of
a parenchymatous tissue (Talboys, 1972). The role of tyloses is disputed; one
school of thought contends they are a resistance mechanism whereby sections of
invaded xylem are sealed off, thereby preventing further spread of the pathogen
(for example, Tjamos and Smith, 1975), while others (Dixon and Pegg, 1969)
suggest that the very occlusion of xylem vessels when colonised by vascular fungi
exacerbates the wilt syndrome by inhibiting water movement within the vessels.
    Studies with the electron microscope have revealed a further phenomenon
relating to the physical occlusion of xylem vessels when colonised by vascular
fungi. The surface of many vessels were found by Cooper and Wood (1974) to
be blistered. It is possible that these blisters are related to the position of fungal
hyphae within the vessel since outgrowths of some hyphae ended near to the
larger blisters. These observations could not be repeated by Pegg *et al.* (1976)
but they did find that pit membranes in colonised vessels were swollen and
bordered pits occluded by deposits of a similar nature to the electron-dense
material found sheathing the hyphae

Gums and gels
Only limited studies of the effects of gum or gel formation in xylem vessels

invaded by *Fusarium* or *Verticillium* are available. But Beckman (1969*a, b*), working with banana (*Musa nana* var. *sapientum*) and *F. oxysporum* f. sp. *cubense*, proposed that they result from solution of calcium from cell membranes caused by organic acids, which in turn result from the accumulation of fungal respiratory carbon dioxide.

Hormonal effects

Several symptoms of the wilt syndrome such as stunting, epinasty and leaflet curling are similar to those accompanying the application of hormones to healthy plants. It is argued, therefore, that if vascular pathogens produce exogenous hormones this may be the means by which such effects occur in the host. Auxin-like substances have been detected in several vascular pathogens; for example Pegg and Selman (1959) found that indoleacetic acid was produced in tomatoes infected by *V. albo-atrum*. More recently interest has centred on the production of ethylene within diseased plants, the formation of which may be triggered by auxin-like substances and which itself may stimulate defence reactions at a rate dependent on the amount of ethylene formed. Alternatively, ethylene may have a synergistic toxic role with the enzymes released during vascular pathogenesis (Pegg, 1976; Cronshaw and Pegg, 1976). Similar studies of the tomato—*F. oxysporum* f. sp. *lycopersici* host—parasite complex (Gentile and Matta, 1975) showed that in susceptible plants infection induced increased ethylene production which reached a maximum at 9—10 days after inoculation. This corresponded with marked foliar wilting and basal leaf abscission.

Consistently lower cytokinin levels are found in susceptible tomatoes infected with *V. albo-atrum* after the onset of symptoms (Patrick *et al.*, 1977). It is postulated that this may contribute to the rapid loss of chlorophyll in older leaves and progressive development of visible chlorosis in younger leaves.

Enzyme effects

These have been summarised by Cooper and Wood (1974):

(1) The pathogens secrete *in vitro* enzymes which degrade various components of the host cell wall. In particular, *V. albo-atrum* produces enzymes active to each of the main wall components. Synthesis is highly and specifically inducible and subject to catabolite repression.

(2) Chain-splitting pectic enzymes have been isolated from stems of tomato plants infected by *V. albo-atrum*.

(3) The role of pectic enzymes in the wilt syndrome is unclear but it is claimed that cotton plants (*Gossypium* spp.), which take up endopolygalacturonase, exhibit symptoms similar to infection by *F. oxysporum* f. sp. *vasinfectum*, and similar results have been obtained with tomato cuttings and endopolygalacturonase and endopectate *trans*-eliminase.

Host responses include production of peroxidase and chitinase, both of which have been related to host resistance. Chitinase has been shown to cause lysis of

V. albo-atrum mycelium within tomato plants (Pegg and Vessey, 1973); phenols and their oxidising enzymes have also generally been related to resistance in the tomato to *Fusarium* and *Verticillium* infection. There may, however, be exceptions to this since Pollock and Drysdale (1976*b*) found that in the tomato cultivar Red Top, which is susceptible to *V. albo-atrum*, both phenolic compounds and polyphenol oxidases and peroxidases increased during pathogenesis. It is suggested that the amount of these enzymes is related to the quantity of mycelium present in the host since the resistant cultivar Red Top No. 9 contained little mycelium and concentration of these enzymes was less. Furthermore, Montalbini and Raggi (1974) suggest that stimulation of aromatic biosynthesis by increased shikimate dehydrogenase activity in tomatoes infected with *F. oxysporum* f. sp. *lycopersici* is evidence to explain the decrease in lignification found in tomato stems infected by this pathogen. Studies of enzyme activities may shed some light on the mechanism of cross-protection afforded by prior inoculation with non-pathogenic strains. Inoculation of tomato plants with various non-pathogenic formae speciales of *Fusarium* led to discoloration of xylem tissues and induced peroxidase activity within 48 h, in a further 24 h there was enhanced polyphenoloxidase and β-D-glucosidase activity (Homma *et al.*, 1978). It is concluded that growth of the non-pathogenic fungus within the xylem and subsequent host responses result in a reduction of wilt symptoms when pathogenic isolates enter the host.

Water relations

The relationship between physiological and pathological wilting has provoked considerable interest as a means of explaining the wilt syndrome. Studies of the reduction of water flow in xylem vessels occluded by mycelium (Dimond, 1966) and relating this to water flow in tubes in terms of Poiseiulle's and Ohm's laws showed that the effects of vascular occlusion were greatest in small independent xylem bundles. In large interconnected vessels the effects of mycelium on water flow and pressure were small.

Nitrogen metabolism

In resistant cultivars there may be a slight but detectable increase in amino and protein nitrogen after inoculation, but this quickly falls back to the normal levels. Conversely, in susceptible cultivars considerable increases in both types of compound follow infection, although the increases may initially lag slightly behind that in resistant cultivars. But by the time symptoms are apparent host nitrogen metabolism is considerably deranged (Dixon and Pegg, 1972; Raggi *et al.*, 1974). Such increases may be related to increased aromatic biosynthesis which, as Pegg and Sequira (1968) suggest from studies of *Ps. solanacearum* on tobacco (*Nicotiana tabaccum*), lead to production of melanin and subsequent hyperauxiny, which are typical symptoms of wilt diseases. Although stimulation of some phenolic materials may enhance resistance, increased quinic acid production has been correlated with symptom suppression (Carrasco *et al.*, 1978).

Toxins

Studies by Gaumann and co-workers (summarised by Wood, 1967) implicated lycomarasmin and fusaric acid as pathogen-produced toxins responsible for the greater part of the *Fusarium* wilt syndrome. It later became apparent that these compounds were formed too late in pathogenesis to influence the course of wilt development. In the *Verticillium* wilt Talboys (1957) and Stoddart and Carr (1966) implicated toxins as causal agents of the syndrome, but again it is likely that they are only effective in the later stages leading to plant death. Host-produced toxins, phytoalexins, are now being advocated as a means by which conidial germination is retarded within resistant stems. In particular compounds tomatine and rishitin have been implicated (McCance and Drysdale, 1975).

12.3 VIRUSES

12.3.1 Tomato Aspermy Virus (TAV)

At least 10 aphid species are vectors of TAV but their transmission efficiency varies; the most important are *Aulacorthum solani, Myzus persicae, Macrosiphoniella sanborni* and *Rhopalosiphum rufomaculatum*. The virus can be acquired in 15 s and inoculated in less than 1 min; there is no latent period; feeding vectors retain the virus for 30—60 min. An isolate from *Campanula rapunculoides* was shown to be seed-borne, but those from tomato (*L. esculentum*) are not. Under experimental conditions the host range is very wide, 100 species from 27 Angiosperm families have been infected. Virus particles are isometric, 25—30 nm in diameter. Distribution is related to the other major crop host, the florists' chrysanthemum (*C. morifolium*), and the virus is found in Australia, Canada, India, Japan, New Zealand, the USA, the USSR and western Europe.

Symptoms are related to the ability of TAV to inhibit growth of the tomato (*L. esculentum*) growing-point, leading to proliferation of axillary buds giving the plant a bushy character. Foliar distortion and dark green mottling of the axillary buds occurs with stimulation of enations on the upper surface of the leaflet axis. Fruit number and size are reduced and they are frequently devoid of seeds. All tissues are infected; virus particles are found in plasmodesmata and between the cisternae of dictyosomes but no inclusion bodies have been reported nor is there interference with mitotic division. Other vegetable hosts include celery (*Apium graveolens*), lettuce (*Lactuca sativa*), soybean (*Glycine max*) and spinach (*Spinacia oleracea*).

Tomato Aspermy Virus and Cucumber Mosaic Virus (*see* section 11.3.2) are closely related, TAV can be distinguished from CMV since it (1) infects only the cotyledons of cucumber (*C. sativus*), (2) induces seedless fruit in tomato, (3) causes enations on the undersurface of leaves of several *Nicotiana* spp., (4) infects *C. morifolium.*

12.3.2 Tomato Black Ring Virus (TBRV)

Vectors of TBRV are two species of free-living soil-borne nematodes, *Longidorus elongatus* in Scotland and Northern Ireland and *L. attenuatus* in England and Germany. There are serological differences in the strains of virus transmitted by the two vectors, the type strain being most efficiently transmitted by *L. attenuatus* and those more closely related to Beet Ring Spot strain by *L. elongatus*. Both larvae and adults of the latter are vectors, but the adult does not pass on the virus to its progeny nor is the virus retained when the nematode moults. In fallow soil *L. elongatus* retains infectivity for up to 9 weeks. The virus appears to be adsorbed on the stylet guiding sheath of the vectors. In various weed species TBRV is seed-transmitted, being brought to the gynaecium by pollen. Besides aiding dissemination of TBRV, seed infection provides a means of survival in soil. Virus particles are isometric, 30 nm in diameter, with a five- or six-sided angular outline. Distribution is restricted to Europe.

This was the first virus to be isolated from tomato (*L. esculentum*), but has since been found to have a wide host range on cultivated plants. Severe streak symptoms develop on young plants, starting 7–12 days after infection as large numbers of black necrotic rings and followed by streaks underneath the petioles and on stems. Gradually the foliar rings coalesce causing the growing apex to shrivel. Symptoms on spinach (*Spinacia oleracea*) begin as vein clearing of the younger leaves with subsequent chlorotic rings and line patterns giving a mosaic effect. A chlorotic blotchy mottle is characteristic of beet (*Beta vulgaris*) plants infected with TBRV which is often restricted to one or two leaves. Due to death of the primary root a 'fangy' root system may develop. Infected celery (*Apium graveolens*) exhibits intense chrome-yellow vein banding termed Celery Yellow Vein. This may affect leaf morphology, giving rise to an asymmetric shape and smooth texture. Other vegetables recorded as hosts of TBRV are onion (*Allium cepa*) and leek (*Allium porrum*).

Several strains of TBRV have been identified including Bean Ring Spot Virus, Beet Ring Spot Virus, Celery Ring Spot Virus and Lettuce Ring Spot Virus. Distribution of virus-infected plants within a crop tends to be patchy due to the slow migration of the vectors.

12.3.3 Tomato Bunchy-top Virus (TBTV)

No biological vector has been identified for TBTV but it has been identified in the seed of *Solanum incanum* and *Physalis peruviana*. In addition to the tomato (*L. esculentum*) crop hosts include the pepper (*C. annuum*). Distribution is limited to South Africa.

Symptoms on tomato (*L. esculentum*) starts as a cessation of growth and crowding of apical leaves with reduction in size of the leaflets and shortening of the leaf axis. Leaves curl inwards and the tips are twisted downwards with puckering of the lamina. Flower production is unaffected but fruit size is reduced generally with consequent loss of seed production. Streak necrosis is a characteristic symptom.

12.3.4 Tomato Bushy Stunt Virus (TBSV)

Although no vector of TBSV has been identified it is thought to be soil-borne. No seed transmission is reported but it can be present in pollen. The particle is an icosahedron, 30 nm in diameter. It is found in Argentina, Canada and Europe.

Symptoms on tomato (*L. esculentum*) begin as circular necrotic local lesions 5 days after infection. Affected leaves become chlorotic and fall off. This is followed by general chlorosis and necrosis with the lower leaves in particular showing purple discoloration and possibly wilting. Plants given excess nitrogen fertiliser, and which in consequence are soft, may develop necrotic lesions at soil level leading to their collapse. Systemic symptoms include twisting of the youngest leaves whereby the position of the leaf surface becomes reversed; apical necrosis with subsequent proliferation of lateral shoots leads to a 'bushy' appearance. Fruit symptoms include mottling, blotching and ring marking.

There are at least six strains of TBSV but the only one, apart from the type strain, to affect vegetables is Artichoke Mottled Crinkle, which causes mottle, severe leaf deformation, reduced growth and sterility of artichoke (*C. scolymus*). Virus-like particles are found in conducting and parenchyma tissues of infected plants. Within the cytoplasm scattered or arranged crystals with a cubic close-packed structure may be found. Sometimes these are extruded into the vacuoles of vesicles.

Control may be achieved by keeping plants at 36 °C; at this temperature pathogenic activity of the virus is lost although its physical and chemical properties are retained.

12.3.5 Tomato Double Streak

This disease is caused by the interaction of two viruses Tomato Mosaic Virus (TMV) and Potato Virus X (PVX). The former is considered in section 12.3.6. Potato Virus X is transmitted by the grasshoppers *Melanaphis differentialis* and *Tettigonia viridissima* and possibly by the soil-borne fungus *Synchitrium endobioticum*, but in tomatoes (*L. esculentum*) as with TMV mechanical transmission is the most likely mode of infection. The virus has world-wide distribution. The particles are flexuous filaments 515 nm long and 13 nm wide.

In tomatoes (*L. esculentum*) the Double Streak syndrome gives rise to destructive necrosis of stems, petioles, leaves and fruits caused by any

combination of strains of TMV and PVX. Tomato fruits are disfigured by
irregular raised necrotic lesions which later become sunken. In the absence of
TMV the severity of symptoms induced by PVX depends on the virulence of
the infecting strain. Strain S is most virulent, causing local necrosis followed
by systemic mosaic-mottle, necrosis and infrequently necrotic rings. Less
virulent strains of PVX cause dark and light green mottle which may fluctuate
in intensity.

Particles of PVX and spherical inclusion bodies are found near the host
nucleus containing cellular components such as ribosome-like particles either
free or in linear groups from 500—1600 nm in length. Mitochondria, dictyosomes
and areas of endoplasmic reticulum are also present.

12.3.6 Tomato Mosaic Virus (TMV)

Tomato Mosaic and Tobacco Mosaic are caused by closely related strains of
one virus, but in the field these strains tend to be restricted to the respective
crops. No biological vector of TMV has been detected, but since it is one of the
most infectious of plant viruses, transmitted for example in sap from a broken
leaf hair, probably mechanical transmission by man or animals occurs easily.
The virus is seed-borne, carried in the external mucilage, testa and sometimes
endosperm of tomato seeds, but has not been proved to be within the embryo.
Host range is immense; 200 species from 30 Angiosperm families have been
infected experimentally. The virus has world-wide distribution. Particles are
rod-shaped, 15 nm in diameter and 300 nm long, with a central hole running
through the rod. Chemical analysis has shown the rods to consist of 158
amino acids.

Symptoms caused by the type strain of TMV on tomato (*L. esculentum*)
usually consist of a 'mild' mosaic, leaves being mottled with raised dark green
zones possibly with distortion of younger foliage. The reaction, however,
varies, depending upon cultivar, virus strain, time of infection, soil nutrient and
water status, day-length, light intensity and temperature. At high temperatures
and high light intensity mottling is severe with limited stunting; at low
temperatures and low light intensity stunting is a prominent symptom with
very little mottling. Under these latter conditions 'fern leaf' symptoms may be
expressed and anthrocyanins are seen in the stem tissue. Where mature fruit
at the green or pink stage are infected 'internal browning' will develop. Most
types of cell are infected with virus particles which are especially prevalent
in the cytoplasm and associated with all major organelles including cell walls.
Virus-related inclusions visible by both light and electron microscopy range
from hexagonal crystalline plates of virus particles to lateral aggregates of
closely packed particles to linear aggregates of needles, spindles and fibres with
very large unbounded amorphous and vacuolated X bodies of undetermined
function. Another vegetable host of TMV is spinach (*Spinacia oleracea*), in

which infection causes yellowing and mottling, possibly with stunting, but
this is less severe than 'Spinach Blight' caused by Cucumber Mosaic Virus
(*see* section 11.3.2). Beet (*Beta vulgaris*) may also be infected but only localised
chlorosis and necrosis of the foliage develops, which may eventually abscise.

There are large numbers of strains of TMV. One method of classification is
by their ability to cause symptoms in certain *Lycopersicon* spp. or isogenic lines
carrying genes for resistance. This is known as the 'Pelham Grouping', strains
are classified as follows:

0	unable to overcome any resistance genes
1	able to overcome resistance gene *Tm-1*
2	able to overcome resistance gene *Tm-2*
1.2	able to overcome resistance genes *Tm-1* and *Tm-2*
2^2	able to overcome resistance gene *Tm-2^2*

A more conventional classification is by host symptoms:

(1) *Tomato Aucuba Mosaic strain*   Symptoms caused by this strain are seen
first in the apex with downbending of the whole leaf including leaflet margins
with roughened texture due to corrugations. There may be areas of white to
yellow and zones of intense green on the foliage and the fruits are mottled. This
strain is generally associated with the presence of cell inclusions and can be
Pelham types 0, 1 or 2.

(2) *Tomato Streak strain*   This causes severe symptoms with lesions on
leaves, stems and fruits. Stem lesions are long, dark, elongated streaks and the
stem tissue becomes brittle, breaking easily to reveal browned pith and cortex.
Necrotic spots and patches form on leaves which eventually shrivel. Circular or
irregular sunken blotches form on the fruit. Mottling may develop without
necrosis.

(3) *Tomato Enation Mosaic strain*   This strain causes leaf distortions and
enations.

(4) *Dahlemense strain*   This produces yellow mosaic mottling and is Pelham
type 1.

(5) *Yellow Ring Spot strain*   This induces yellow ringspots and is of Pelham
type 0.

(6) *Winter Necrosis strain*   This strain is of Pelham type 2.

(7) *Summer Necrosis strain*   This strain may be synonymous with Tomato
Streak strain and is of Pelham type 1.

(8) *Tomato Crusty Fruit strain*   This strain causes corky crusts on fruit and
is of Pelham type 0.

(9) *Tomato Rosette strain*   This strain causes severe distortion and stunting
similar to hormone herbicide damage.

(10) *Tomato Black Fleck strain*   This strain induces black necrotic foliar
flecks and is of Pelham type 0.

(11) *M11–16 strain*   This strain is a nitrous acid mutant of low patho-

genicity, used for protective inoculation of tomato seedlings and is of Pelham type 1.

Crop losses of about 20 per cent of world tomato production have been attributed to TMV. Control measures have been based on the following methods:

(1) The production of virus-free, heat-treated, seed.
(2) The application of milk or other sprays to foliage to inhibit mechanical transmission of the virus.
(3) Soil sterilisation to prevent root infection.
(4) Inoculation of tomato seedlings with selected or induced mild strains of TMV. Mild strains may, however, recover their virulence or may change the relative prevalence of strain types in subsequent tomato crops.
(5) The use of genetically resistant tomato cultivars using the three major gene factors Tm-1, Tm-2 and Tm-2^2. Cultivars carrying only a single gene for resistance were soon overcome by the evolution of pathogen strains compatible with the resistance gene, but cultivars with all three resistant genes appear to offer a longer period of effectiveness. It is felt that such cultivars should not be grown with others which are either totally susceptible or contain lesser numbers of resistance genes.

12.3.7 Tomato Ring Spot Virus (TRSV)

Transmission of TRSV is by the adult and three larval stages of the soil-borne nematode *Xiphinema americana*. Acquisition occurs within 1 h and infection can take place within a further hour. Seed transmission has been reported in various crops. Distribution is restricted to temperate areas of North America, particulary the Californian coast, although it may have been distributed elsewhere in ornamental crops. Particles of TRSV are isometric, 28 nm in diameter. The name Tomato Ring Spot has been used for two unrelated viruses, one isolated from tobacco seedlings and the other from tomato plants. The former is the type strain while the latter is more nearly related to Tomato Top Necrosis Virus.

Symptoms of TRSV are extensive curling and necrosis of the apical shoot. The lower parts of young leaves turn brown, with definite necrotic rings and wavy markings. Necrotic streaks develop at the junction between petiole and stem. On fruit, symptoms vary from indistinct to conspicuous grey or brown corky markings, developing only on fruit which are immature at the time of· infection.

12.3.8 Tomato Shoe-string Virus (TSSV)

Limited information is available about TSSV. Symptoms appear to develop on glasshouse-grown crops during cool weather and consist of mild mottling and undercurling of the foliage.

12.3.9 Tomato Spotted Wilt Virus (TSWV)

Several species of thrips, *Thrips tabaci, Frankliniella schultzei, F. fusca* and *F. occidentalis* are vectors of TSWV. The virus can be acquired only at the larval stage and is then retained into the adult. Successful infection of the vector increases with feeding time and there is an incubation period of 4–18 days before TSWV can be passed on. Some evidence of a low level of transmission through tomato (*L. esculentum*) seed is available, the virus being carried on the testa. Distribution is common in temperate and sub-tropical regions throughout the world. The particles are isometric, 70–90 nm in diameter, and bounded by a membrane, the outer layer of which consists of a nearly continuous layer of projections 5 nm thick; some particles have a tail-like extrusion. Variant strains which cause differing levels of symptom severity have been identified. The most stable of these, according to different workers, are TB (tip blight), N (necrotic), R (ringspot), M (mild), VM (very mild); strains A, B. C1, C2, D and E; *Vira-cabeca* and the Tomato Tip Blight strain.

Symptoms of the type strain on tomato (*L. esculentum*) commence as a thickening of the veins on younger foliage with the leaves curling inwards and downwards. This is succeeded by the most characteristic symptom, which is a bronzing either of the complete lamina or development of bronze-coloured rings. Later a bold yellow mosaic mottling develops. Fruit which are mature at the time of infection show no symptoms, but immature fruit fails to ripen fully, the flesh remaining pale red or yellow with occasional white zones which vary in shape from irregular mottling to distinct concentric rings. Particles of TSWV are found as clusters in cytoplasmic vacuoles which are possible cisternae of the endoplasmic reticulum and in the dilated lumen of the nuclear membrane. These are distributed throughout root, stem, leaf and petal tissue. The host range is wide, covering 163 species of 34 Angiosperm families of which 60 species belong to the Solanaceae.

Symptoms caused by the Tomato Tip Blight strain are characterised by blighting and blackening of the apical shoots, which stand out above the healthy foliage. Within the stem the medullary tissue is disrupted into scattered patches surrounded by air pockets. On the leaves either a large number of small or small number of large black necrotic areas appear with brown streaks which may later have a silvered appearance. Fruit size is reduced with irregular brown lesions; often the fruit softens with yellow to red blotches and rings.

12.3.10 Tomato Yellow Leaf Curl Virus (TYLCV)

Recently found in Israeli tomato (*L. esculentum*) crops, the vector of TYLCV is the white fly, *Bemisia tabaci*. The virus is acquired by the larval stages but not passed through the egg to subsequent generations. Symptoms include chlorosis and curling of the foliage.

12.3.11 Tomato Yellow Net Virus (TYNV)

The aphid, *Myzus persicae*, is the vector of TYNV which is retained for several days following a 1 day acquisition period. Distribution is limited to California, USA. Symptoms are vivid yellow chlorosis of the tomato (*L. esculentum*) leaf veins, particularly of new growth, but these become less evident with age. Apparently there is no stunting and normal fruit set is retained.

12.3.12 Tomato Yellow Top Virus (TYTV)

The vector of TYTV is the aphid *Macrosiphum euphorbiae*, which retains the virus after moulting in a circulative (persistent) manner. Distribution is restricted to New South Wales, Australia. Symptoms on tomato (*L. esculentum*) develop at least 15 days after infection, with the shoots becoming erect and losing some of their chlorophyll. Leaf morphology changes such that the leaflets are rounded, slightly folded and the veins are sunken into the lamina; stunting and flower abortion result in loss of yield.

12.3.13 Tobacco Broad Ring Spot Virus (TBRSV)

No biological vector is known for TBRSV, which may be a strain of Cucumber Mosaic Virus (*see* section 11.3.2). Symptoms on tomato (*L. esculentum*) are characterised by the development of chlorotic and necrotic ringspots and the foliage is misshapen.

12.3.14 Tobacco Mottle Virus (TMoV)

Although the aphid *Myzus persicae* is the vector of TMoV it can acquire the virus only if the plant is also infected with a 'helper' virus, Tobacco Vein Distorting Virus. Distribution is restricted to Zambia and Zimbabwe. Symptoms on tomato (*L. esculentum*) are an indistinct vein clearing and subsequent fluctuating foliar mottle.

12.3.15 Tobacco Streak Virus (TSV)

No biological vector of TSV has been identified, the particles are isometric,

28 nm in diameter, and it is distributed throughout Europe, North and South America and New Zealand. Seed transmission is reported in bean (*Phaseolus vulgaris*), which is affected by a strain of TSV called Bean Red Node Virus. Distribution of the latter is restricted to Brazil, Canada, the UK and the USA.

Symptoms on tomato (*L. esculentum*) are a necrosis which may consist of a few lesions to severe scorch. Most characteristic symptoms are the appearance on fruit of necrotic sunken lesions which penetrate into the mesocarp tissue. Germination of seed from such fruits is poor, but plants which do develop exhibit no symptoms. The Red Node strain causes a reddish discoloration at the stem nodes and leaf pulvini of *Phaseolus vulgaris*. At the same time similar coloured rings develop on the pods, but these do not affect seed formation.

12.3.16 Potato Leaf Roll Virus (PLRV)

Numerous aphid species are vectors of PLRV; most important is *Myzus persicae* but others include *M. ascalonicus, M. ornatus, M. convulvuli, Macrosiphum euphorbiae, Aulacorthum circumflexum, Aphis nasturtii* and *Hyadaphis foeniculi*. The virus is found to multiply within the vector and is retained throughout their lives, the particles are isometric, 24 nm in diameter, with world-wide distribution.

The virus transfers easily between potato (*S. tuberosum*) and tomato (*L. esculentum*). Symptoms on tomato are indistinct with slight rolling of foliage which is rigid having a leathery texture. Virus particles are restricted to the phloem.

12.3.17 Potato Virus Y (PVY)

Various aphids are non-persistent vectors of PVY, of which *Myzus persicae* is the most efficient, others include *M. certus, M. ornatus, Macrosiphum euphorbiae, Aulacorthum circumflexus, Aphis rhamni* and *A. nasturtii*. The mite *Tetranychus telarius* has also been implicated in transmission of PVY. The particles are flexible rods 730 nm long and 10.5 nm wide. Distribution of PVY is world-wide and it is an important cause of disease in solanceous crops, but will also infect members of the Chenopodiaceae and Leguminosae. At least three strains have been identified, Common strain, Necrotic or Tobacco Veinal Necrosis strain and Potato Virus C.

Symptoms on tomato (*L. esculentum*) begin with vein clearing and mottling followed by green banding. Infected plants may often be symptomless. Pinwheel inclusions develop in systemically infected tissue, these are composed of pinwheel plates having striations every 5 nm.

12.3.18 Potato Yellow Dwarf Virus (PYDV)

The leaf hoppers *Aceratogallia sanguinolenta* and *Agallia quadripunctata* are persistent vectors of PYDV. Recovery of particles from the insect haemolymph and internal organs has shown that the virus does not invade the vector systemically. Particles of PYDV are bacilliform, 380 nm long and 75 nm wide. Distribution is restricted to south-eastern Canada and the north-eastern USA.

Symptoms on tomato (*L. esculentum*) start as chlorotic spots which increase in size and intensity with age. At high temperatures necrosis may develop followed by systemic vein clearing of juvenile foliage. Another vegetable host is broad bean (*Vicia faba*).

REFERENCES

Sections 12.1.1 and 12.1.2
Buddenhagen, I. and Kelman, A. (1964). *A. Rev. Phytopath.* 2, 203–30.

Section 12.2.1
Boukema, I. W. (1977). *Zaadbelangen* 31, 17–18.
Boukema, I. W. and Garretsen, F. (1975). *Euphytica* 24, 99–104.
Butler, L. (1953). *Tomato Genet. Co-op. Rep.* no. 3, 7–8.
Day, P. R. (1954). *Pl. Path.* 3, 35–9.
Day, P. R. (1956). *Tomato Genet. Co-op. Rep.* no. 6, 13–14.
Dijkman, A. van and Sijpesteijn, A. K. (1971). *Neth. J. Pl. Path.* 77, 14–24.
Kashyap, V. and Levkina, I. (1977). *Kestnik. Moskovskogo Universiteta Biologiya* no. 1, 65–9.
Lazarovits, G. and Higgins, V. J. (1976*a*). *Can. J. Bot.* 54, 224–34.
Lazarovits, G. and Higgins, V. J. (1976*b*). *Can. J. Bot.* 54, 235–49.
Sijpesteijn, A. K. and Dijkman, A. van (1973). The host–parasite interactions in resistance of tomatoes to *Cladosporium fulvum*. In *Fungal Pathogenicity and the Plant's Response* (R. J. W.Byrde and C. V. Cutting, eds). Academic Press, London.
Winspear, K. W., Postlethwaite, J. D. and Cotton, R. F. (1970). *Ann. appl. Biol.* 65, 75–83.
Wit, P. J. G. M. de (1977). *Neth. J. Pl. Path.* 83, 109–22.

Section 12.2.2
Alexandri, A. V. and Lemini, V. (1969). *Revta Hort. Vitic.* 18, 66–70.
Beleva, L., Sotirova, V. and Popova, D. (1977). *Gradinarska i Lozarska Nanka* 14, 99–104.
Palti, J. (1971). *Phytopath. Med.* 10, 139–53.

Reuveni, R. and Rotem, J. (1973). *Phytopath. Z.* **76**, 153–7.
Reuveni, R., Perl, M. and Rotem, J. (1976). *Phytoparasitica* **4**, 197–9.
Reuveni, R., Perl, M. and Rotem, J. (1977). *Phytopath. Z.* **80**, 79–84.
Rotem, J. and Cohen, Y. (1966). *Pl. Dis. Reptr* **50**, 635–9.
Tafradjiiski, I., Elenkov, E. and Neshev, G. (1975). *C. r. Acad. agric. George Dimitrov*, **8**, 65–7.

Section 12.2.3
Antonelli, E. (1974). *Informatore Fitopatologica* **24**, 11–20.
Basu, P. K. (1971). *Phytopathology* **61**, 1347–50.
Basu, P. K. (1974). *Can. Pl. Dis. Survey* **54**, 45–51.
Berkdale, T. H. and Stonor, A. K. (1973). *Pl. Dis. Reptr* **57**, 964–5.
Berkdale, T. H. and Stonor, A. K. (1977). *Pl. Dis. Reptr* **61**, 63–5.
Beyries, A. and Molot, P. M. (1976). *Phytiatrie-Phytopharmacie* **25**, 201–7.
Bhatia, I. S., Uppal, D. S. and Bahal, K. L. (1972). *Indian Phytopath.* **25**, 231–5.
Coffey, M. D., Whitbread, R. and Marshall, C. (1975). *Ann. appl. Biol.* **80**, 17–26.
Dorozhkin, M. A. and Ivanyuk, U. R. (1976). *Vesti Akademii Navuk BSSR Biyalagichnykh Navuk* **4**, 60–3.
Dorozhkin, M. A., Remneva, Z. I. and Ivanyuk, I. G. (1975). *Biologicheskie Nauki* **18**, 100–4.
Dorozhkin, N. A., Remneva, Z. I. and Ivanyuk, I. G. (1977). *Sel'shokhozyai-stvennaya Biologya* **12**, 58–61.
Dowley, L. J., Routley, D. G. and Pierce, L. C. (1975). *Phytopathology* **65**, 1422–4.
D'yakov, Yu. T., Aschaie, A. and Vainshtein, V. M. (1975). *Mikologiya i Fitopatologiya* **9**, 277–82.
El-Wazeri, S. M. and El-Sayed, S. A. (1977). *Egypt J. Hort.* **4**, 151–6.
Gallegly, M. E. and Marvel, M. E. (1955). *Phytopathology* **45**, 103–9.
Gallegly, M. E. and Niederhauser, J. S. (1959). Genetic control of host–parasite interactions in the Phytophthora late blight disease. In *Plant Pathology Problems and Progress 1908–1958* (C. S. Holton, G. W. Fischer, R. W. Fulton, H. Hart and S. E. A. McCallan, eds). Wisconsin University Press, Madison, Wisc.
Hodosy, S. I. (1969). *Duna Tisza Koz. Mezog Kiser Int. Bull.* **4**, 83–93.
Kravchenko, V. A. (1977). *Zakhist Roslin* **24**, 70–7.
Laterrot, H. (1975). *Annls. Amelior. Pl.* **25**, 129–49.
Matthewson, D. K. (1977). *New Phytol.* **78**, 643–7.
Melita, P., Vyas, K. M. and Saksena, S. B. (1974). *Hindustan Antibiotics Bull.* **16**, 210–4.
Peng, J. H. and Black, L. L. (1976). *Phytopathology* **66**, 958–63.
Pristou, R. and Gallegly, M. E. (1954). *Phytopathology* **44**, 81–6.
Tsupkova, N. A. (1977). *Zashchita Rastenii* **7**, 62–3.

Turkensteen, L. J. (1973). *Partial Resistance of Tomatoes against* Phytophthora infestans, *the Late Blight Fungus*. Mededelingen van der Instituut voor Plantenziektenkundig Onderzoek no. 633, p. 88.
Walker, J. C. (1952). *Diseases of Vegetable Crops*. McGraw-Hill, New York.
Walter, J. M. (1967). *A. Rev. Phytopath.* 5, 131–62.
Ward, E. W. B., Unwin, C. H. and Stoessl, A. (1975). *Phytopathology* 65, 168–9.

Section 12.2.4
Martinson, V. A. and Hogenboom, N. G. (1968). *Euphytica* 17, 173–82.

Section 12.2.5
Akinrefon, O. A. (1969). *Ann. appl. Biol.* 63, 303–13.
Barksdale, T. H. and Stoner, A. K. (1975). *Pl. Dis. Reptr* 59, 648–52.
Campbell, W. P. and Griffiths, D. A. (1974). *Trans. Br. mycol. Soc.* 63, 19–25.
Davet, P. (1971). *Phytopath. Medit.* 10, 159–63.
Davet, P. (1972). *Phytopath. Medit.* 11, 103–108.
Davet, P. (1975). *C. r. hebd. Séanc. Acad. Sci. Paris, D* 281, 143–6.
Davet, P. (1976*a*). *Ann. Phytopath.* 8, 159–69.
Davet, P. (1976*b*). *Ann. Phytopath.* 8, 79–82.
Davet, P. (1976*c*). *Ann. Phytopath.* 8, 191–202.
Davet, P. and Ravise, A. (1976). *C. r. hebd. Séanc. Acad. Sci. Paris, D* 282, 1351–4.
Delon, R. (1974). *Phytopath. Z.* 80, 199–208.
Delon, R. , Reisinger, O. and Mangenot, F. (1973). *Ann. Phytopath.* 5, 151–62.
Ebben, M. H. (1974). *A. Rep. Glasshouse Crops Res. Inst.* 1973, 127–35.
Elenkov, E. (1976). *Rastitelna Zashchita* 24, 40–3.
Elenkov, E. and Bakharieva, V. (1975). *Rastitelna Zashchita* 23, 31–5.
Farley, J. D. (1976). *Phytopathology* 66, 640–1.
Goodenough, P. W. and Kempton, R. J. (1976). *Physiol. Pl. Path.* 9, 313–20.
Goodenough, P. W. and Maw, G. A. (1973). *Ann. appl. Biol.* 73, 339–47.
Goodenough, P. W. and Maw, G. A. (1974). *Physiol. Pl. Path.* 4, 51–62.
Goodenough, P. W. and Maw, G. A. (1975). *Physiol. Pl. Path.* 6, 145–57.
Griffiths, D. A. and Campbell, W. P. (1972). *Trans. Br. mycol. Soc.* 59, 483–9.
Griffiths, D. A. and Campbell, W. P. (1973). *Trans. Br. mycol. Soc.* 61, 529–36.
Hawes, C. R. and Beckett, A. (1977). *Trans. Br. mycol. Soc.* 68, 304–7.
Hogenboom, N. G. (1970). *Euphytica* 19, 413–25.
Huang, H. C. and Patrick, Z. A. (1972). *Can. J. Bot.* 50, 2423–9.
Jones, D. R., Graham, W. G. and Ward, E. W. B. (1975). *Phytopathology* 65, 1409–16.
Laterrot, H. (1972). *Annls Amelior. Pl.* 22, 109–113.
McIntyre, J. L. and Hawkins, L. (1977). *Mycologia* 69, 756–60.
Miyakado, M., Kato, T., Ohno, N. and Koshimizuk, K. (1975). *Phytochemistry* 14, 2717.
Robbins, M. and Angel, F. F. (1970). *J. Am. Soc. hort. Sci.* 95, 469–71.

Sharma, S. L. and Soli, H. S. (1976). *Indian Phytopath.* **28**, 130.

Sharma, S. L., Chowfla, S. C. and Soli, H. S. (1976). *Kavaka* **4**, 61–63.

Sharma, S. L., Chowfla, S. C. and Soli, H. S. (1977). *Indian J. Mycol. Pl. Path.* **6**, 51–4.

Trique, B. (1975). *Phytopath. Z.* **83**, 1–9.

Violin, R. B. and McMillan, R. T. (1978). *Euphytica* **27**, 75–9.

Waterhouse, G. M. (1963). *Key to the Species of* Phytophthora *de Bary*. Mycological Paper no. 92. Commonwealth Mycological Institute, Kew.

Weststeijn, G. (1973). *Neth. J. Pl. Path.* **79**, Suppl. 1, 86.

White, J. G. and Scott, A. C. (1973). *Ann. appl. Biol.* **73**, 163–6.

Yordanov, M., Mamelyan, H. and Stoyana, Z. (1974). *C r. Acad. agric. Georgie Dimitrov* **7**, 49–50.

Section 12.2.6

Beckman, C. H. (1969*a*). *Phytopathology* **59**, 837–43.

Beckman, C. H. (1969*b*). *Phytopathology* **59**, 1477–83.

Besri, M. (1977). The seed stage of *Fusarium oxysporum* f. *lycopersici*. In *Travaux dédiés à George Viennot-Bourgin*. Sociétié Française de Phytopathologie, Paris, pp. 19–25.

Bewley, W. F. (1922). *Ann. appl. Biol.* **9**, 116–34.

Carrasco, A., Boudet, A. M. and Marigo, G. (1978). *Physiol. Pl. Path.* **12**, 225–32.

Cooper, R. M. and Wood, R. K. S. (1974). *Physiol. Pl. Path.* **4**, 443–6.

Cronshaw, D. K. and Pegg, G. F. (1976). *Physiol. Pl. Path.* **9**, 33–44.

Dimond, A. E. (1966). *Pl. Physiol., Lancaster* **41**, 119–31.

Dixon, G. R. and Pegg, G. F. (1969). *Trans. Br. mycol. Soc.* **53**, 109–18.

Dixon, G. R. and Pegg, G. F. (1972). *Ann. appl. Biol.* **36**, 147–54.

Gabe, H. L. (1975). *Trans. Br. mycol. Soc.* **64**, 156–9.

Gentille, I. A. and Matta, A. (1975). *Physiol. Pl. Path.* **5**, 27–35.

Harries, H. C. (1965). *A. Rep. Glasshouse Crops Res. Inst.* **1964**, 115–24.

Homma, Y. and Ohata, K. (1977). Bulletin no. 30. Agricultural Experiment Station, Shikoku, pp. 103–114.

Homma, Y., Ishii, M. and Ohata, K. (1978). Bulletin no. 31. Agricultural Experiment Station, Shikoku, pp. 71–85.

Hubbeling, N., Alexander, L. J. and Cirulli, M. (1971). *Meded. Fakulteit Landbouwwetenschappen Gent* **36**, 1006–16.

Isaac, I. (1967). *A. Rev. Phytopath.* **5**, 201–22.

Kedar, N., Retig, N. and Katan, J. (1967). *Euphytica* **16**, 258–66.

Laterrot, H. (1976). *Annls Amelior. Pl.* **26**, 485–91.

Locke, T. and Thorpe, I. G. (1976). *Pl. Path.* **25**, 59.

Ludwig, R. A. (1952). *Studies on the Physiology of Hadromycotic Wilting in the Tomato Plant*. Technical Bulletin no. 20. Macdonald College, Canada.

Marte, M., Zazzerini, A. and Tamburi, F. (1975). *Phytopath. Z.* **84**, 47–56.

McCance, D. J. and Drysdale, R. B. (1975). *Physiol. Pl. Path.* **7**, 221–30.

Montalbini, P. and Raggi, V. (1974). *Phytopath. Medit*. **13**, 124–7.

Patrick, T. W., Hall, R. and Fletcher, R. A. (1977). *Can. J. Bot*. **55**, 377–82.

Pegg, G. F. (1976). *Physiol. Pl. Path*. **9**, 215–26.

Pegg, G. F. and Selman, I. W. (1959). *Ann. appl. Biol*. **47**, 222–31.

Pegg, G. F. and Sequeira, L. (1968). *Phytopathology* **58**, 476–83.

Pegg, G. F. and Vessey, J. C. (1973). *Physiol. Pl. Path*. **3**, 207–22.

Pegg, G. F., Gull, K. and Newsam, R. J. (1976). *Physiol. Pl. Path*. **8**, 221–4.

Pollock, C. J. and Drysdale, R. B. (1976 *a*). *Phytopath. Z*. **86**, 353–6.

Pollock, C. J. and Drysdale, R. B. (1976 *b*). *Phytopath. Z*. **86**, 56–66.

Raggi, V., Zazzerini, A., Barberini, B., Ferranti, F. and Draoli, R. (1974).
    Phytopath. Z. **79**, 258–80.

Stoddart, J. L. and Carr, A. H. J. (1966). *Ann. appl. Biol*. **58**, 81–92.

Talboys, P. W. (1957). *Trans. Br. mycol. Soc*. **40**, 415–27.

Talboys, P. W. (1972). *Proc. R. Soc. B* **181**, 319–32.

Tjamos, E. C. and Smith, I. M. (1975). *Physiol. Pl. Path*. **6**, 215–25.

Visser, S. (1977). *Phytophylactica* **9**, 65–70.

Walker, J. C. (1971). Fusarium *Wilt of Tomato*. Monograph no. 6. American
    Phytopathological Society, St. Paul, Minn.

Walter, J. M. (1967). *A. Rev. Phytopath*. **5**, 131–62.

Wood, R. K. S. (1967). *Physiological Plant Pathology*. Blackwell Scientific
    Publications, Oxford.

FURTHER READING

Sections 12.1.1 and 12.1.2

Hayward, A. C. and Waterston, J. M. (1964). Pseudomonas solanacearum.
    Commonwealth Mycological Institute Descriptions of Pathogenic Fungi and
    Bacteria no. 15. Commonwealth Mycological Institute, Kew.

Hayward, A. C. and Waterston, J. M. (1964). Corynebacterium michiganense.
    Commonwealth Mycological Institute Descriptions of Pathogenic and Fungi
    and Bacteria no. 19. Commonwealth Mycological Institute, Kew.

Stapp, C. (1961). *Bacterial Plant Pathogens*. Oxford University Press, London.

Walter, J. M. (1967). *A. Rev. Phytopathol*. **5**, 131–62.

Section 12.2.1

Holliday, P. and Mulder, J. L. (1976). Fulvia fulva. Commonwealth Mycological
    Institute Descriptions of Pathogenic Fungi and Bacteria no. 487. Common-
    wealth Mycological Institute, Kew.

Section 12.2.2

Dixon, G. R. (1978). Powdery mildews of vegetables and allied crops. In *The
    Powdery Mildews* (D. M. Spencer, ed.). Academic Press, London.

Mukerji, K. G. (1968). Leveillula taurica. Commonwealth Mycological Institute Descriptions of Pathogenic Fungi and Bacteria no. 182. Commonwealth Mycological Institute, Kew.

Section 12.2.3
Ellis, M. B. and Gibson, I. A. S. (1975). Alternaria solani. Commonwealth Mycological Institute Descriptions of Pathogenic Fungi and Bacteria no. 475. Commonwealth Mycological Institute, Kew.

Section 12.2.4
Holliday, P. and Punithalingam, E. (1970). Didymella lycopersici. Commonwealth Mycological Institute Descriptions of Pathogenic Fungi and Bacteria no. 272. Commonwealth Mycological Institute, Kew.

Section 12.2.5
Aberdeen, J. E. C. (1976). *Queensland J. Agric.* **102**, 355–81.
Mordue, J. E. M. (1967). Colletotrichum coccodes. Commonwealth Mycological Institute Descriptions of Pathogenic Fungi and Bacterial no. 131. Commonwealth Mycological Institute, Kew.
Punithalingam, E. and Holliday, P. (1969). Pyrenochaeta lycopersici. Commonwealth Institute Descriptions of Pathogenic Fungi and Bacteria no. 398. Commonwealth Mycological Institute, Kew.
Subramanian, C. V. (1968). Thielaviopsis basicola. Commonwealth Mycological Institute Descriptions of Pathogenic Fungi and Bacteria no. 170. Commonwealth Mycological Institute, Kew.
Waterhouse, G. M. and Waterston, J. M. (1964). Phytophthora nicotianae *var.* nicotianae. Commonwealth Mycological Institute of Pathogenic Fungi and Bacteria no. 34. Commonwealth Mycological Institute, Kew.
Waterhouse, G. M. and Waterston, J. M. (1964). Phytophthora nicotianae *var.* parasitica. Commonwealth Mycological Institute Descriptions of Pathogenic Fungi and Bacteria no. 35. Commonwealth Mycological Institute, Kew.

Section 12.2.6
Hawkesworth, D. L. and Talboys, P. W. (1970). Verticillium albo-atrum. Commonwealth Mycological Institute Descriptions of Pathogenic Fungi and Bacteria no. 255. Commonwealth Mycological Institute, Kew.
Hawkesworth, D. L. and Talboys, P. W. (1970). Verticillium dahliae. Commonwealth Mycological Institute Descriptions of Pathogenic Fungi and Bacteria no. 256. Commonwealth Mycological Institute, Kew.
Subramanian, C. V. (1970). Fusarium oxysporum *f. sp.* lycopersici. Commonwealth Institute Descriptions of Pathogenic Fungi and Bacteria no. 255. Commonwealth Mycological Institute, Kew.

Sections 12.3.1–12.3.18

Bercks, R. (1970). *Potato Virus X*. Commonwealth Mycological Institute/ Association of Applied Biologists Descriptions of Plant Viruses no. 4. Commonwealth Mycological Institute, Kew.

Black, L. M. (1970). *Potato Yellow Dwarf Virus*. Commonwealth Mycological Institute/Association of Applied Biologists Descriptions of Plant Viruses no. 35. Commonwealth Mycological Institute, Kew.

Broadbent, L. (1976). *A. Rev. Phytopath*. **14**, 75–96.

Delgado-Sanchez, S. and Grogan, R. G. (1970). *Potato Virus Y*. Commonwealth Mycological Institute/Association of Applied Biologists Descriptions of Plant Viruses no. 37. Commonwealth Mycological Institute, Kew.

Fulton, R. W. (1971). *Tobacco Streak Virus*. Commonwealth Mycological Institute/Association of Applied Biologists Descriptions of Plant Viruses no. 44. Commonwealth Mycological Institute, Kew.

Hollings, M. and Stone, O. M. (1971). *Tomato Aspermy Virus*. Commonwealth Mycological Institute/Association of Applied Biologists Descriptions of Plant Viruses no. 79. Commonwealth Mycological Institute, Kew.

Hollings, M. and Huttinga, H. (1976). *Tomato Mosaic Virus*. Commonwealth Mycological Institute/Association of Applied Biologists Descriptions of Plant Viruses no. 156. Commonwealth Mycological Institute, Kew.

Le, T. S. (1970). *Tomato Spotted Wilt Virus*. Commonwealth Mycological Institute/Association of Applied Biologists Descriptions of Plant Viruses no. 39. Commonwealth Mycological Institute, Kew.

Martelli, G. P., Quacquarelli, A. and Russo, M. (1971). *Tomato Bushy Stunt Virus*. Commonwealth Mycological Institute/Association of Applied Biologists Descriptions of Plant Viruses no. 69. Commonwealth Mycological Institute, Kew.

Murant, A. F. (1970). *Tomato Black Ring Virus*. Commonwealth Mycological Institute/Association of Applied Biologists Descriptions of Plant Viruses no. 38. Commonwealth Mycological Institute, Kew.

Peters, D. (1970). *Potato Leaf Roll Virus*. Commonwealth Mycological Institute/ Association of Applied Biologists Descriptions of Plant Viruses no. 36. Commonwealth Mycological Institute, Kew.

Smith, K. M. (1972). *A Textbook of Plant Virus Diseases*. Longman, London.

Stace-Smith, R. (1970). *Tomato Ring Spot Virus*. Commonwealth Mycological Institute/Association of Applied Biologists Descriptions of Plant Viruses no. 18. Commonwealth Mycological Institute, Kew.

Zaitlin, M. (1975). *Tobacco Mosaic Virus (Type Strain)*. Commonwealth Mycological Institute/Association of Applied Biologists Descriptions of Plant Viruses no. 151. Commonwealth Mycological Institute, Kew.

Host Index

Brassica napus, 15, 72, 112, 113, 117, 119,
122, 123, 125, 126, 128, 135, 137, 139,
140, 141, 144, 145, 147, 148
Brassica nigra, 89, 126
Brassica oleracea, 81, 89, 115, 117, 119,
124, 126, 134, 137, 141, 284
Brassica oleracea var. acephala, 122, 126,
141, 144
Brassica oleracea var. acephala subvar.
lacinata, 72
Brassica oleracea var. botrytis, 12, 64, 65,
87, 89, 105, 112, 113, 114, 115, 116,
117, 120, 122, 126, 128, 135, 141, 143,
145, 146, 147, 148, 185, 345
Brassica oleracea var. capitata, 15, 20, 25,
40, 72, 74, 82, 87, 89, 112, 115, 116,
117, 118, 120, 121, 123, 126, 127, 130,
133, 134, 135, 136, 137, 139, 140, 141,
143, 145, 146, 148, 185, 345, 351
Brassica oleracea var. capitata Langedijk
type, 14, 119, 148, 277, 284
Brassica oleracea var. gemmifera, 13, 22, 58,
62, 64, 65, 82, 89, 112, 113, 115, 116,
117, 118, 119, 120, 122, 126, 127, 128,
135, 138, 141, 143, 148, 149, 185, 363
Brassica oleracea var. italica, 113, 115, 126,
135, 141
Brassica parachinensis, 126
Brassica perviridis, 145, 146
Brassica tournefortii, 125
Broad bean, see Vicia faba
Brussels sprout, see Brassica oleracea var.
gemmifera
Bunching onion, see Allium fistulosum
Buttercup (creeping), see Ranunculus
repens

Cabbage, see Brassica oleracea var. capitata
Cacao, see Theobroma cacao
Cajanus cajan, 159
Calabrese, see Brassica oleracea var. italica
Campanula rapunculoides, 368
Cantaloupe melon, see Cucumis melo var.
cantalupensis
Capsella bursa pastoris, 34, 126, 143
Capsicum spp., 354
Capsicum annuum, 15, 103, 129, 131, 329,
337, 344, 345, 347, 350, 351, 355, 356,
358, 360, 363, 369
Capsicum fructescens, 31, 358
Carrot, see Daucus carota
Castor oil, see Ricinis communis
Caraway, see Carum carvi
Carum carvi, 238
Caucalis tenella, 236
Cauliflower, see Brassica oleracea var.
botrytis
Celeriac, see Apium graveolens var. rapaceum

Celery, see Apium graveolens
Cereal, 41, 88, 240, 265
Chamaecyparis lawsoniana, 331
Chard, see Beta vulgaris var. cicla
Charlock (jointed), see Raphanus
raphanistrum
Cheiranthus spp., 115
Chenopodium spp., 269
Chenopodium capitatum, 271
Chenopodium quinoa, 225
Chervil, see Anthriscus cerefolium
Chichory, see Cichorum intybus
Chinese cabbage, see Brassica campestris var.
pekinensis and Brassica campestris var.
chinensis
Chive, see Allium schoenoprasum
Chrysanthemum (florists'), see Chrysanthe-
mum morifolium
Chrysanthemum morifolium, 368
Cicer arietum, 159
Cichorum endivia, 222, 224
Cichorum intybus, 222
Circium arvense, 35, 239
Citron (melon), see Citrullis vulgaris var.
citroides
Citrullis vulgaris, 307, 311, 317, 318, 319,
321, 323, 324, 325, 326, 328, 331
Citrullis vulgaris var. citroides, 324
Claytonia perfoliata, 271
Citrus, 24
Clover (red and white), see Trifolium spp.
Cole, see Brassica oleracea
Compositae, 27
Conium maculatum, 246, 247
Convolvulaceae, 27
Coriander, see Coriandrum sativa
Coriandrum sativa, 233, 234, 244, 246,
247, 248
Cotton, see Gossypium spp.
Couch grass, see Agropyron repens
Cowpea, see Vigna sinensis
Crambe spp., 135
Cress, see Lepidium sativum
Crotalaria juncea, 14
Crow garlic, see Allium vineale
Cruciferae, 4, 15, 17, 36, 196
Crucifers, see Cruciferae
Cucumber, see Cucumis sativus
Cucumis melo, 309, 310, 313, 319, 321,
322, 323, 324, 326, 328
Cucumis melo var. cantalupensis, 311, 312,
313, 314, 315, 318, 320, 322, 323, 331
Cucumis melo var. inodorus, 323
Cucumis sativus, 14, 35, 65, 74, 82, 84, 93,
98, 105, 131, 145, 173, 188, 248, 269,
307, 308, 309, 310, 313, 315, 316, 317,
319, 321, 322, 326, 327, 330, 331, 368
Cucurbit, 11, 12, 99, 105, 196, 222, 325

Main authorities

Bailey, L. H. (1961). *Manual of Cultivated Plants*. Macmillan, New York.

Clapham, A. R., Tutin, T. G. and Warburg, E. F. (1959). *Excursion Flora of the British Isles*. Cambridge University Press, London.

Micro-organism and Disease Index

*Italicised page numbers refer to the main discussion

Vector Index

General Index